Understanding Children's Development

Fourth Edition

KT-174-080

Basic Psychology

This series offers those new to the study of psychology comprehensive, systematic and accessible introductions to the core areas of the subject. Written by specialists in their fields, they are designed to convey something of the flavour and excitement of psychological research today.

Understanding Children's Development
Fourth Edition
PETER K. SMITH, HELEN COWIE AND MARK BLADES

Understanding Cognition
PETER J. HAMPSON AND PETER E. MORRIS

Understanding Abnormal Psychology
NEIL FRUDE

Online support material, including multiple choice questions, to accompany this text is available at

http://www.blackwellpublishing.com/ucd

Understanding Children's Development

Fourth Edition

Peter K. Smith
Helen Cowie
Mark Blades

PERTH COLLEGE
Learning Resource Centre

ACCN No: 007 05125	SUPPLIER: Dawson
CLASS MARK: Blackwell Publishing 155.4 SMI	COST: 20.09
LOCATION: LOAN	DATE RECEIVED: March 2003

© 1988, 1991 by Peter K. Smith and Helen Cowie; © 1998, 2003 by Peter K. Smith, Helen Cowie and Mark Blades

350 Main Street, Malden, MA 02148-5018, USA
108 Cowley Road, Oxford OX4 1JF, UK
550 Swanston Street, Carlton, Victoria 3053, Australia
Kurfürstendamm 57, 10707 Berlin, Germany

The right of Peter K. Smith, Helen Cowie and Mark Blades to be identified as the Authors of this work has been asserted in accordance with the Copyright, Designs and Patents Act 1988.

All rights reserved. No part of this publication may be reproduced, stored in a retrieval system, or transmitted, in any form or by any means, electronic, mechanical, photocopying, recording or otherwise, except as permitted by the UK Copyright, Designs, and Patents Act 1988, without the prior permission of the publisher.

First edition published 1988
Reprinted 1988, 1989
Second edition 1991
Reprinted 1991, 1992, 1993, 1994, 1995, 1996
Third edition 1998
Reprinted 1999, 2001 (twice), 2002
Fourth edition 2003

Library of Congress Cataloging-in-Publication Data

Smith, Peter K.
  Understanding children's development/Peter K. Smith, Helen Cowie,
Mark Blades. – 4th ed.
    p. cm. – (Basic psychology)
Includes bibliographical references and index.
  ISBN 0-631-22823-3 (pbk. : alk. paper)
  1. Child psychology.   2. Child development.   I. Cowie, Helen.   II. Blades, Mark.
III. Title.   IV. Basic psychology (Oxford, England)

BF721 S57325 2003
155.4 – dc21

                                                              2002012889

A catalogue record for this book is available from the British Library.

Typeset in 10 on 12 pt Palatino
by SNP Best-set Typesetter Ltd., Hong Kong
Printed in Italy, by G. Canale and C. SpA

For further information on
Blackwell Publishing, visit our website:
http://www.blackwellpublishing.com

Contents

Plates and Box Plates

Plates

Box Plates

Figures and Box Figures

Figures

Box Figures

Tables and Box Tables

Box Tables

Series Preface

Psychology is a relatively new science that has already made notable achievements; yet its methods are constantly being questioned and redefined. This book is one of a series of introductory psychology texts, designed to convey the fast-moving and relevant nature of contemporary research while at the same time encouraging the reader to develop a critical perspective on the methodology and data presented. The format of the book is intended to aid such independent inquiry, as is shown in particular by the boxes at the end of each chapter that concentrate on individual studies as 'worked examples'.

The books in the Basic Psychology series should be accessible to those who have no previous knowledge of the discipline. *Understanding Children's Development* can profitably be used by students on their own without a teacher, but resources aimed at group work, for example as part of social work or teacher training courses, are also included: a further reading section and discussion points follow each chapter.

Peter K. Smith

Preface to the Fourth Edition

This fourth edition of the book is mainly marked by an updating of content, as our discipline continues to develop rapidly; and some discarding of older material. There is an additional chapter.

In Part One, changes to chapter 1 have again been modest; this chapter describes core principles and methodologies in studying development. We have added sections on using children as researchers, qualitative methods, and the rights of children. Chapter 2 has been expanded; it now follows a trajectory from the genetic and evolutionary perspectives on development, through to cultural-ecological perspectives and social constructionism, with a new box illustrating the sociocultural approach.

In Part Two, there is a new chapter 3 that includes material on prenatal development, and on birth and the first few months of life; with a new section (and box) on premature babies. Chapter 4 (was 3) has been expanded again to take account of recent developments in attachment theory, including disorganized attachment, and a new box on attachment in an African society; there is a new section on harsh physical punishment. Chapter 5 (was 4), now renamed 'The Peer Group', has been restructured especially in the later sections, with new material on delinquency; and on Harris' group socialization theory. Chapter 6 (was 5) has been updated, including Maccoby's recent writings on sex differences, and a recent longitudinal study of effects of television viewing. Chapter 7 (was 6) has been updated, with a new box on cross-cultural study of pretend play. Chapter 8 (was 7) has a new section on prosocial behaviour in the school and the peer group, with recent findings on peer support systems, and a new box on the impact of peer-mediated conflict resolution on playground aggression. Chapter 9 (was 8) has been restructured considerably in the latter sections, with new material on gay and lesbian sexual development.

In Part Three, chapter 10 (was 9) has been substantially reorganized to reflect current thinking about very young children's abilities, with older material taken out, and with two new boxes. Chapter 11 (was 10) contains new material on explanatory models of language development, including Tomasello's Construction Grammar approach. Chapter 12 (was 11) on Piaget has had minor updating. Chapter 13 (was 12) has been much expanded, with new material on recent theories about cognitive development and research into children's memory and eyewitness testimony, with one new box. Chapter 14 (was 13) on theory of mind, has also been updated throughout. Chapter 15 (was 14) now includes research based on social cultural theory, including guided participation, collective argumentation and communities of learners, and includes a new box on children's constructions of the Earth. Chapter 16 (was 15) has had older material dropped, but has more on attainment tests and a new box on savants. Finally, chapter 17 (was 16) has been updated to include a section on risk and protective factors, recent debates on resilience in the face of adversity and a new section on the Romanian adoptees.

As before, each chapter (after the first) has two boxes featuring a study in detail, and also further reading and discussion points. We hope that this new edition will continue to keep abreast of the exciting new developments in our discipline, while retaining coverage of the core components of knowledge from previous research.

Online support material to accompany this text, including multiple choice questions, is available at http://www. blackwellpublishing.com/ucd

Peter K. Smith, Helen Cowie and Mark Blades

Preface to the Third Edition

Substantial changes have been made in the third edition, to keep pace with changes in the discipline, and in response to user feedback.

The most substantial change is the addition of a third author, Mark Blades. The first two authors were aware of shortcomings in the second edition in the areas of information processing and memory development in children; also, the area of children's understanding of mind has grown tremendously in the years since the second edition. Mark Blades is expert in both these areas, and his joining us gives a welcoming strengthening and expansion to Part Three of the book.

In Part One, only small changes have been made to chapter 1. Chapter 2 has changed considerably, however; the material on animal behaviour has been considerably reduced, while keeping sufficient to make clear the evolutionary background to child development. Material on prenatal development, previously absent, has been added to this chapter.

In Part Two, chapter 3 has been expanded to take more account of recent developments in attachment theory, and includes more on parenting styles. Material on siblings has been moved into chapter 4, which now focuses mainly on peer relationships and friendships, with some deletion of older material on teachers and pupils. Chapter 5 has lost its theory of mind material to a new chapter 13, but is updated in other areas. Chapters 6 and 7 have also been brought up to date without major changes; as has chapter 8, with two new boxes.

In Part Three, chapter 9 has been substantially revised. Chapter 10 incorporates some new material. Chapter 11 has been updated, and chapter 12 on the information processing approach is entirely new. Chapter 13, on children's understanding of mind, is also new, although it does take some material from the second edition's old chapter 5. Chapter 14 is an updated version of the old chapter 12, and chapter 15 is a more substantially revised version of the old chapter 13. Finally, chapter 16 (old chapter 14) contains more material on cultural context and a new box on political violence as it affects children.

Each chapter continues to have two boxes featuring a study in detail (with the exception of chapter 1), and also further reading and discussion points. However, the practical exercises have been removed; they will be assimilated into an Instructor's Manual to accompany the text.

We hope that this new and enlarged coverage of important developmental issues will continue to provide a useful source for readers.

Peter K. Smith, Helen Cowie and Mark Blades

Preface to the Second Edition

For this second edition we have sought feedback from users of the book, to expand the coverage as well as bring material fully up to date. As a result the book has increased from 12 chapters to 14.

Part One has remained largely unchanged; but the opportunity has been taken in chapter 2 to review the recent work on 'mindreading' in primates, which links to similar work on 'theory of mind' in children and strengthens the relevance of this chapter to the rest of the book.

In Part Two, some reorganization has taken place. Chapter 3 has a number of additional sections, to cover topics such as: the role of fathers; siblings; grandparents; divorce and step-parenting; and child abuse. The material on attachment, and day care, also includes more recent research. Chapter 4 is expanded to include material on aggression in childhood, and bully/victim problems in schools.

There is a completely new chapter 5. Much of this is devoted to recent work on emotional development in children, 'theory of mind', and hypothesized deficits in autistic children. This is supplemented by material from the previous chapter 3 on gender identity, together with new material on ethnic identity, and material from the previous chapter 4 on television/mass media, to make a new chapter which seems still most appropriately titled 'Becoming Socially Aware'. Chapters 6, 7 (retitled) and 8 are not changed substantially.

In Part Three, the major change is the introduction of a new chapter 12, 'Learning in a Social Context', which considers alternative approaches to Piaget's theory in some detail. It reviews the work of the Russian psychologist Lev Vygotsky, and the American psychologist Jerome Bruner, emphasizing their views on the social and cultural context of learning and thinking. The remaining changes in Part Three are, again, general updating of material, including some more material on preverbal communication in chapter 10.

We have kept to the original plan of having practical exercises, discussion points, and boxes at the end of each chapter, which readers generally seem to find helpful. In particular, the boxes highlight the advantages and disadvantages of different research designs. There are four new boxes; two reflect experimental design, one is a questionnaire study featuring cohort-sequential design and one features a pioneering study of Vygotsky from the 1930s.

Appendix A has been changed to provide the revised Ethical Principles for Conducting Research with Human Participants, approved by the British Psychological Society in February 1990. In line with BPS guidelines, we have largely removed the term 'subjects' from our text and replaced it by the term 'participants'.

We hope that this new edition will not only broaden the coverage beyond the first edition, but also reflect some of the exciting new developments occurring in child development research over the last few years.

Peter K. Smith and Helen Cowie

Preface to the First Edition

We are bombarded by opinions on child development. Everyone has a view of how children should be brought up, and explanations for why people have turned out the way they have.

Even if you have not studied psychology before, you no doubt already have views on how children develop. You may agree or disagree with the following statements, but you will probably have heard them or opinions very much like them:

1 'Animal behaviour is instinctive; human behaviour is learned. That's the difference.'
2 'She gave me a lovely smile. I'm sure she recognized me even though she's only two months old.'
3 'I wouldn't leave my child at a nursery. If you have a baby you should look after it yourself.'
4 'A good smack never did a child any harm. That's how they learn what is right and what is wrong.'
5 'If things go wrong in the early years of a child's life there's not much you can do about it.'
6 'Parents shouldn't try to teach their children to read. That's best left to the school.'
7 'They don't do any work at Paul's school. They just play all day.'
8 'You can't understand how a child's mind works. They just think differently from us, and that's all there is to it.'
9 'Children see far too much violence on television these days.'
10 'Just wait until they are teenagers. That's when the trouble starts.'
11 'IQ tests don't tell us anything about real intelligence. They're a means of social control.'

12 'Psychologists can't teach us much. What they say is just common sense.'

In this book we don't aim to provide absolute answers to the many questions which arise in the course of rearing children. But we do aim to provide up-to-date accounts of research in this area. We hope to present controversies and to outline the various ways in which child psychologists' research findings enhance our understanding of the developmental process.

The material is arranged in three major sections. In Part One an introductory chapter describes to the reader the ways in which psychologists study developmental processes. It also raises issues about the specific status of psychology, its methods of inquiry and ethical questions in research. This chapter, or parts of it, could profitably be re-read after the rest of the book or taught course has been completed. Chapter 2 surveys the biological and evolutionary background of behavioural development. It introduces conceptual terms such as 'instinct', 'learning' and 'canalization', which are used later in the book.

Part Two deals with social and moral development in childhood, up to and including adolescence. Topics include parent–child attachment, sex differences, peer relationships, the influence of television on social behaviour, play and prosocial behaviour. Part Three covers perceptual, linguistic and cognitive development in children. The contribution of Jean Piaget is given particular attention, as are psychometric and other more recent approaches to assessing intelligence and attainment. Part Three concludes with a consideration of how disadvantage and deprivation affect children from different social classes and ethnic minority groups. Appendices give details of ethical guidelines in carrying out research, resources for teachers and careers in psychology.

We have tried to emphasize the variety, strengths and weaknesses of different kinds of psychological investigation. To bring this out more vividly, each chapter (after the first) concludes with two 'boxes'. Each box consists of a detailed description of one particular study, discussing its aims, design, results, analysis, and strengths and limitations. Study of these boxes should be useful not only in terms of the content of the studies themselves, but also in helping the reader get a feel for how psychological research is carried out. More advanced students may wish to pursue the references to original work given throughout the text, while beginners should read the book without being distracted by them. The references are provided primarily for use by teachers, and also because we feel that acknowledgement should be made to those psychologists who have put forward certain theories or carried out particular studies.

Each chapter offers suggestions for further reading, giving indications of level and content. There are also ideas for discussion points which might be taken up as essay titles or topics for debate in class; and examples are given of practical exercises that might be carried out by students on the basis of the material in the foregoing chapter.

Peter K. Smith and Helen Cowie

Acknowledgements

For the fourth edition, we wish to thank Martyn Barrett, Paul Dickerson, Wendy Haight, Eilis Hennessy, Judy Kegl, Jarmila Koluchova, Patrick Leman, Edward Melhuish, Jacqueline Nadel, Ian Rivers, Alice Sluckin, Mary True, and Dieter Wolke, for providing useful materials or helpful comments on drafts of various sections. John Eade, Lisa Pisani, Stella Vosniadou and Dieter Wolke kindly provided photographs that have been used in this edition.

The editors and publisher wish to thank the following for permission to use copyright material:

Fig. 1.1 Baltes et al., Life span developmental psychology, *Annual Review of Psychology*, 31, 1980. Fig. 1.3 Bronfenbrenner, *The Ecology of Human Development* (Harvard University Press, 1979).

Fig. 2.2 Arey, *Developmental Anatomy: A Textbook and Laboratory Manual of Embryology* (7th edn) (W. B. Saunders, 1965). Fig. 2.3 Reprinted with permission from Plomin, Owen and McGuffin, 'The genetic basis of complex human behaviours', *Science*, 264, fig. 3 (copyright © 1994 American Association for the Advancement of Science). Fig. 2.5 Fishbein, H., *Education, Development and Children's Learning* (Goodyear Publishing Company, Pacific Palisades, California, 1976). Fig. 2.6 Lorenz, K. 'Results of an experiment showing that ducklings follow a model more readily 9–17 hours after hatching than at any other time', *On Aggression* (Methuen, London, 1966). Fig. 2.8 Sternglanz et al., 'Facial stimuli in adult preference for infantile facial features: an ethological approach and the stimulus noted as most effective', *Animal Behaviour*, 25 (Academic Press, 1977).

Fig. 3.1 Seifert, K. and Hoffning, R., *Child and Adolescent Development* (3rd edn) (copyright © 1994 by Houghton Mifflin Company. Used with permission). Fig. 3.2 Bronson, *Human Birth: An Evolutionary Perspective* (Aldine de Grutyer, 1987, copyright © Appleton-Century-Crofts). Fig. 3.3 Watson, John S. and Ramey, Craig T., 'Apparatus used as a contingency mobile', in 'Reactions to response-contingent stimulation in early infancy', *Merrill-Palmer Quarterly*, 18, 3, pp. 219–27 (Wayne State University Press, 1972).

Fig. 4.1 Belsky, 'Belsky's process model of the determinants in parenting', in 'The determinants of parenting: a process model', *Child Development*, 55 (copyright © Society for Research in Child Development, University of Michigan, 1984).

Fig. 5.1 Lewis et al., 'The beginning of friendship', *Friendship and Peer Relations* (John Wiley & Sons, Inc., New York, 1975, copyright © Professors Michael Lewis and Leonard Rosenblum). Fig. 5.2 Clark et al., 'Sociograms of association networks in two classes of preschool children', *Journal of Child Psychology and Psychiatry*, 10 (Cambridge University Press, 1969). Fig. 5.3 Dodge et al., 'A model of social skills and social exchange in peer interaction', in 'Social competence in children', *Monographs of the Society for Research in Child Development*, 51, 2 (Society for Research in Child Development, University of Michigan, 1986). Fig. 5.4 Parker and Asher, 'Two models of the role of peer acceptance in leading to maladjusted outcomes', in 'Peer relations and later personal adjustment: are low accepted children at risk?', *Psychological Bulletin*, 102 (American Psychological Association, Washington, DC, 1987). Fig. 5.5 Patterson et al., 'A developmental progression for antisocial behaviour', in 'A developmental perspective on antisocial behaviour', *American Psychologist*, 44 (American Psychological Association, Washington, DC, 1989). Box fig. 5.1.1 Coie, Dodge and Coppotelli, 'Five types of sociometric status', *Developmental Psychology*, 18 (American Psychological Association, Washington, DC, 1982). Box fig. 5.2.1 Olweus et al. (eds) *The Development and Treatment of Childhood Aggression* (Erlbaum, 1989). Box table 4.1.1 Coie and Dodge, 'Five types of sociometric status', *Developmental Psychology*, 18 (American Psychological Association, Washington, DC, 1982). Box table 5.1.2 Coie and Dodge, 'Five types of sociometric status', *Developmental Psychology*, 18 (American Psychological Association, Washington, DC, 1982).

Fig. 6.1 Emmerich et al., 'Development of gender constancy in disadvantaged children', unpublished report (copyright © Educational Testing Service. All rights reserved. Adapted and reproduced under licence). Fig. 6.3 Lefkowitz et al., *Growing Up to be Violent*, with kind permission from Elsevier Science – NL, Sara Burgerhartstraat 25, 1055 KV Amsterdam, The Netherlands (Pergamon, 1977). Table 6.1 Lewis and Brooks-Gunn, *Social Cognition and the Acquisition of Self* (Plenum Publishing Corporation, New York, 1979). Table 6.2 Kuhn et al., 'Sex role concepts of 2 and 3 year olds', *Child Development*, 49 (Society for Research in Child Development, University of Michigan, 1978). Table 6.3 Barry et al., 'A cross cultural survey of same sex differences in socialization', *Journal of Abnormal and Social Psychology*, 55 (American Psychological Association, Washington, DC, 1957). Table 6.4 Boulton and Smith, 'Ethnic and gender partner and activity preferences in mixed race schools in the UK; playground observations', in Hart, C. H. (ed.), *Children in Playgrounds* (State University of New York Press, 1991). Table 6.6 Friedrich and Stein, 'Aggressive and prosocial television programs and the natural behaviour of pre-school children', *Monographs of the Society for Research in Child Development* 38, 4 (Society for Research in Child Development, University of Michigan,

1986). Table 6.8 Himmelweit et al., *Television and the Child: An Empirical Study of the Effect of Television and the Young*.

Fig. 7.1(a) Hooff, 'A comparative approach to the phylogeny of laughter and smiling', in Hinde (ed.), *Non-Verbal Communication* (Cambridge University Press, 1972). Fig. 7.1(b) Smith, 'Ethological methods', in Foss (ed.), *New Perspectives in Child Development* (Penguin, Harmondsworth, 1974). Fig. 7.2 Krasnor and Pepler, 'The study of children's play – some suggested future directions', in Rubin (ed.), *Children's Play* (Jossey Bass, San Francisco, 1980). Fig. 7.3 Hutt, 'Exploration and play in children', *Symposia of the Zoological Society of London*, 18 (The Royal Zoological Society, London, 1966). Box fig. 7.1.1 Hutt, 'Exploration and play in children', *Symposia of the Zoological Society of London*, 18 (The Royal Zoological Society, London, 1966).

Fig. 8.1 Colby et al., 'A longitundinal study of moral judgement', Monographs of the Society for Research in Child Development (Society for Research in Child Development, University of Michigan, 1983). Table 8.1 Grusec, 'The socialisation of altruism', in Eisenberg, W. (ed.), *The Development of Prosocial Behaviour* (Academic Press, New York, 1982). Table 8.2 Piaget, 1932, *The Moral Judgement of the Child* (Penguin, Harmondsworth, 1977). Table 8.3 Colby et al., 'A longitudinal study of moral judgement', *Monographs of the Society for Research in Child Development* (Society for Research in Child Development, University of Michigan, 1983).

Fig. 9.1 Katchadourian, *The Biology of Adolescence* (W. H. Freeman and Co., 1977). Fig. 9.3 Tanner, J. M., 'Growing up', *Scientific American*, 229, September 1973 (copyright © 1973 by Scientific American, Inc. All rights reserved). Fig. 9.4 Tanner, J. M., 'Growing up', *Scientific American*, 229, September 1973 (copyright © 1973 by Scientific American, Inc. All rights reserved). Fig. 9.6 Meilman, 'Cross sectional age changes in ego identity status during adolescence', *Developmental Psychology*, 15 (American Psychological Association, Washington, DC, 1979). Fig. 9.7 Schofield, *The Sexual Behaviour of Young People* (Longman, 1965). Table 9.1 Katchadourian, *The Biology of Adolescence* (W. H. Freeman and Co., 1977). Table 9.2 Erikson, E., *Identity, Youth and Crisis* (Faber and Faber Ltd, 1968). Table 9.4 Goldman and Goldman, *Children's Understanding of Sexual Terms* (Routledge, 1982). Table 9.5 Reiss, I., *The Social Context of Premarital Sexual Permissiveness* (Holt, Rinehart & Winston Inc., Orlando, 1967, copyright © Dr Ira Reiss). Table 9.8 Rutter et al., 'Adolescent turmoil: fact or fiction?', *Journal of Child Psychology and Psychiatry*, 17 (Cambridge University Press, 1976).

Fig. 10.1 Shaffer, *Developmental Psychology: Theory, Research and Applications* (copyright © 1985 by permission of Brooks/Cole Publishing Company, Pacific Grove, CA 93950). Fig. 10.3 Fantz and Miranda, 'Newborn infant attention to form of contour', *Child Development*, 46 (Society for Research in Child Development, University of Michigan, 1975). Fig. 10.4 Maurer and Barrera, 'Infants' perceptions of natural and distorted arrangements of a schematic face', *Child Development*, 52 (Society for Research in Child Development, University of Michigan, 1981). Fig. 10.6 From: *Development in Infancy* (2nd edn) by Bower (copyright © 1982 by W. H. Freeman and Company. Used with permission) Fig. 10.8 Blakemore and Cooper, 'A kitten in a cylinder with vertical black and white stripes', *Nature*, 228 (reprinted with permission from *Nature*, copyright © 1970 Macmillan Magazines Limited). Fig. 10.9 Eimas, Peter D., 'The perception of speech in early infancy', *Scientific American* (copyright © 1985 by Scientific American, Inc. All rights reserved).

Fig. 11.1 Ferreiro, 'Literacy development: a psychogenic perspective', in Olsen, D. et al. (eds), *Literacy, Learning and Language* (Cambridge University Press, 1985). Table 11.3 Scarlet and Woolf, 'When it's only make believe – the construction of a boundary between fantasy and reality in story-telling', in Winner, E. and Gardner, H. (eds), *Fact, Fiction and Fantasy in Childhood* (Jossey Bass, San Francisco, 1979). Table 11.4 McNeill, *The Acquisition of Language* (Harper & Row, New York, 1970). Table 11.5 Cazden, C. B., *Child Language and Education* (Holt, Rinehart & Winston Inc., New York, copyright © 1972 Dr Courtney B. Cazden). Box table 11.1.1 Bradley and Bryan, in *Nature*, 301 (reprinted with permission from *Nature*, copyright © 1983 Macmillan Magazines Limited).

Fig. 12.5 Inhelder and Piaget, *The Growth of Logical Thinking from Childhood to Adolescence* (Routledge & Kegan Paul, London, 1955/1958). Fig. 12.6 Shayer and Wylam, 'The distribution of Piagetian stages of thinking in British middle and secondary school children: II', *British Journal of Educational Psychology*, 48 (copyright © 1978 Dr M. Shayer). Fig. 12.7 Danner and Day, 'Eliciting formal operations', *Child Development*, 48 (Society for Research in Child Development, University of Michigan, 1977). Box fig. 12.1.1 Borke, in *Developmental Psychology*, 11 (American Psychological Association, Washington, DC, 1975). Box fig. 12.2.1 McGarrigle and Donaldson, in *Cognition*, 3 (reprinted copyright © 1974 with kind permission of Elsevier Science – NL, Sara Burgerhartstraat 25, 1055 KV Amsterdam, The Netherlands).

Fig. 13.1 Atkinson and Shiffrin, 'Human memory: a proposed system and its control processes', in Spence, K. W. and Spence, J. T. (eds), *Advances in the Psychology of Learning and Motivation*, vol. 2 (Academic Press, New York, 1968). Fig. 13.5 Vurpillot, 'The development of scanning strategies and their relation to visual differentiation', *Journal of Experimental Child Psychology*, 6, 1968. Box fig. 13.1.1 Siegler, 'Three aspects of cognitive development', *Cognitive Psychology*, 8 (Academic Press, 1976). Box fig. 13.1.2 Siegler, 'Three aspects of cognitive development', *Cognitive Psychology*, 8 (Academic Press, 1976). Box fig. 13.1.3 Siegler, 'Three aspects of cognitive development', *Cognitive Psychology*, 8 (Academic Press, 1976).

Fig. 15.1 Haste, 'Growing into rules', in Bruner, J. S. and Haste, H. (eds), *Making Sense* (Methuen, London, 1987).

Fig. 16.1 Raven, *Standard Progressive Matrices* (H. K. Lewis & Co., London, 1958). Fig. 16.2 Sternberg, R. J. and Rifian, B., 'The development of analogical reasoning processes', *Journal of Experimental Psychology*, 27, 1978. Table 16.1 Gregory, *Psychological Testing: History, Principles and Applications* (copyright © 1992 by Allyn and Bacon. Reprinted by permission).

Fig. 17.4 Wedge and Essen, *Children in Adversity* (Pan Books, London, 1982). Fig. 17.5 Wedge and Essen, *Children in Adversity* (Pan Books, London, 1982). Table 17.1 Rampton Report (copyright © HMSO). Box table 17.2.1 Lazar and Darlington, 'Lasting effects of early education', *Monographs of the Society for Research in Child Development*, 47 (Society for Research in Child Development, University of Michigan, 1982). Box table 17.2.2 Lazar and Darlington, 'Lasting effects of early education', *Monographs of the Society for Research in Child Development*, 47 (Society for Research in Child Development, University of Michigan, 1982).

Every effort has been made to trace the copyright holders but if any have been inadvertently overlooked the publishers will be pleased to make the necessary arrangement at the first opportunity.

PART ONE Theories and Methods

1 Studying Development

The study of how behaviour develops forms part of the science of psychology. But what do we mean by terms such as 'science', 'psychology' and 'development'? This chapter aims to supply the answer, but although it comes first in the book, it may not necessarily be best to read it thoroughly at the outset. Especially if you have not studied psychology before, it might be useful to read it through quickly at this stage, and return to it later, even after finishing the rest of the book, for a more thorough understanding. The issues raised in this chapter are important, but understanding them fully will be easier if you already know something of psychological theories and methods of investigation.

In an important sense, we are all psychologists. We are all interested in understanding behaviour, both our own and that of our parents, children, family and friends. We try to understand why we feel the way we do about other people, why we find certain tasks easy or difficult, or how certain situations affect us; and we try to understand and predict how other people behave, or how their present behaviour and situation may affect their future development. Will a child settle well with a childminder, or do well at school? Will watching violent films on television be harmful? Will a child be bullied at school? Can we teach children to cooperate? What level of moral reasoning can we expect a child to understand?

Nicholas Humphrey (1984) described us as 'nature's psychologists', or *homo psychologicus*. By this he means that, as intelligent social beings, we use our knowledge of our own thoughts and feelings – 'introspection' – as a guide for understanding how others are likely to think, feel and therefore behave. Indeed, Humphrey went further and argued that we are conscious, that is, we have self-awareness, precisely because this is so useful to us in this process of understanding others and thus having a successful social existence. He argued that consciousness is a biological adaptation to enable us to perform this introspective psychology. Whether this is right or not (and you might like to think about this again after you have read chapter 2), we do know that the process of understanding others' thoughts, feelings and behaviour is something that develops through childhood and probably throughout our lives (see chapter 14). According to one of the greatest child psychologists, Jean Piaget, a crucial phase of this process occurs in middle childhood, though more recent research has revealed how much has developed before this.

If we are already nature's psychologists, then why do we need an organized study of the science of psychology? A professional psychologist would probably answer that it is to try and arrive at greater insight, and greater agreement on contentious issues. Sometimes, common-sense beliefs are divided. For example, attitudes to physical punishment of young children as a form of discipline are sharply divided and polarized in many countries (see chapter 4). Sometimes, common beliefs are wrong. In the course of researching the lives of children of mixed parentage, Tizard and Phoenix (1993, p. 1) reported to a group of journalists that many of the young people in their sample saw advantages in their family situation through the meeting of two distinctive cultures. The journalists responded with incredulity since the findings ran contrary to the popular belief that these children inevitably suffered from identity problems, low self-esteem and problem behaviour!

By systematically gathering knowledge and by carrying out controlled experiments, we can develop a greater understanding and awareness of ourselves than would otherwise be possible. There is still much progress to be made in psychology and in the psychological study of development. We are still struggling to understand areas such as the role of play in development, the causes of delinquency, the nature of stages in cognitive development. Most psychologists would argue, however, that the discipline of child development has made some progress and even in the most difficult areas knowledge has now become more systematic, with theories being put forward. We now know more, for example, about the importance of social attachments in infancy (chapter 4), or the process by which a child learns its native language (chapter 11), or how our understanding of others' minds develops (chapter 14), than previous generations ever did or could have done without organized study.

So, how can we go about this?

Development Observed

The biologist Charles Darwin, famous for his theory of evolution, made one of the earliest contributions to child psychology in his article 'A biographical sketch of an infant' (1877), which was based on observations of his own son's development. By the early twentieth century, however, most of our understanding of psychological development could still not have been described as 'scientific' knowledge; much was still at the level of anecdote and opinion. Nevertheless, knowledge was soon being organized through both observation and experiment and during the 1920s and 1930s the study of child development got seriously under way in the USA with the founding of Institutes of Child Study or Child Welfare in university centres such as Iowa and Minnesota. Careful observations were made of development in young children and of normal and abnormal behaviour and adjustment. In the 1920s Jean Piaget started out on his long career as a child psychologist, blending observation and experiment in his studies of children's thinking (see chapter 12).

Observation of behaviour in natural settings fell out of favour with psychologists in the 1940s and 1950s (though it continued in the study of animal behaviour by zoologists, chapter 2). Perhaps as a reaction against the absence of experimental rigour in philosophy and early psychology, and the reliance on introspection (that is, trying to understand behaviour by thinking about one's own mental processes), many psychologists moved to doing experiments under laboratory conditions. As we will discuss later, such experiments do have advantages, but they also have drawbacks. Much of the laboratory work carried out in child development in the 1950s and 1960s has been described by Urie Bronfenbrenner (1979) as 'the science of the behaviour of children in strange situations with strange adults'.

Durkin (1995, chapter 1) challenged the idea that the best way to understand how a child develops is to remove him or her from his or her usual environment and conduct experiments in laboratory conditions. He argued that development is intimately related to the social context provided by other people and by the wider social structure within which the child grows. Furthermore, individuals themselves also affect their social environment. There is now much more value attached to the study of children in real-life settings despite the methodological challenges that such contexts place on the social scientist.

Schaffer (1996, pp. xiv–xvii) notes other changes in the ways in which psychologists now approach child development. These include the need to understand the *processes* of how children grow and develop rather than simply the *outcomes*, and to integrate findings from a range of sources and at different levels of analysis – for example, family, community, culture.

We hope that in the course of reading this text you begin the process of integrating perspectives – for example, by reflecting on the links to be made by psychologists between the concept of the child's 'internal working model of relationships' (chapter 4) and discoveries about 'theory of mind' (chapter 14). We hope too that you find the opportunity to recognize the complementary virtues of various different methods of investigation and gain a sense that the child's developmental processes and the social context in which they exist are closely intertwined, each having an influence on the other.

What Is 'Development'?

The term 'development' refers to the process by which an organism (human or animal) grows and changes through its life-span. In humans the most dramatic developmental changes occur in prenatal development, infancy and childhood, as the newborn develops into a young adult capable of becoming a parent himself or herself. From its origins much of developmental psychology has thus been concerned with child psychology, and with the changes from conception and infancy through to adolescence. These are the primary areas covered in this book.

Generally, developmental processes have been related to age. A typical 3-year-old has, for example, a particular mastery of spoken language (see chapter 11), and a 4-year-old has typically progressed further. A developmental psychologist may then wish to find out, and theorize about, the processes involved in this progression. What experiences, rewards, interactions, feedback, have helped the child develop in this way? Two important but different research strategies have commonly been used in this endeavour. These are 'cross-sectional' and 'longitudinal' designs. Each method has advantages and disadvantages.

Cross-sectional design: In a cross-sectional design an investigator might look at several age groups simultaneously. For example, she might record language ability in 3-year-olds and 4-year-olds, at the same point in time. The cross-sectional design is quick to do, and is appropriate if the main interest is in what abilities or behaviours are typical at certain ages. Because of the convenience of the method, the majority of developmental studies have been cross-sectional.

Longitudinal design: In a longitudinal design, the investigator follows certain individuals over a given time period, measuring change. For example, our investigator might have recorded the language ability for a sample of 3-year-olds and a year later visited the same children to get a sample of what they can do as 4-year-olds. Longitudinal designs are generally preferable if the focus of interest is the process of change, and the relationship between earlier and later behaviour. In our example, it is longitudinal data which give us the most ready access to information on what kinds of experience foster language development, and whether individual differences at 3 years of age predict anything about individual differences a year later, at age 4.

Although longitudinal studies are more powerful in this way they have a number of drawbacks. One is simply the possibility of subject attrition – some participants may move away, lose contact, or refuse or be unable to participate by the next time of testing. This could influence the generality of conclusions, especially if the reason for participant loss may be related to the dependent variables of the study.

Another problem with longitudinal designs is that they are time-consuming! In our example a wait of one year may not be too off-putting. But, if you wanted to see whether friendships in childhood related to happiness as an adult (see chapter 4), you might find yourself having to wait 20 years! Some longitudinal studies have now in fact proceeded for this length of time and longer.

A few major studies, which originated in the USA in the 1930s, as well as some nation-wide surveys starting in Britain since the 1950s, have provided or are providing longitudinal data spanning 20, 30 or 40 years (see box 9.1 for an example in New Zealand). Such long-term studies give us some of our most powerful evidence on the nature of development, so far available. However, when a study goes on for so long, another problem may arise. When the study was initially designed decades ago, it may not have asked the sort of questions that we now find most interesting. Any long-term longitudinal study will be dated in its conception. It

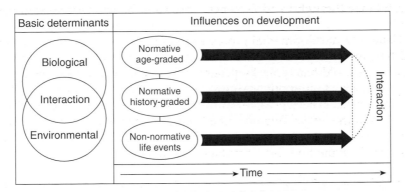

Figure 1.1 Three major influence systems on life-span development: normative age-graded, normative history-graded and non-normative life events. These influence systems interact and differ in their combinational profile for different individuals and for different behaviours (adapted from Baltes et al., 1980).

will also be dated in its conclusions, which will refer to developmental outcomes for people born decades ago. Such conclusions may not always be applicable to today's children. For example, the effects of parental divorce on a child's later adjustment may be different now, when divorce is more frequent and socially acceptable, than 50 years ago when the social stigma attached to divorce in Western societies was much greater (see pp. 121–3).

Baltes's conceptualization of life-span development

Paul Baltes, a German psychologist, has been influential in emphasizing the life-span nature of development and the importance of historical influences (see Baltes et al., 1980). Baltes points out that age-related trends, the traditional staple of developmental psychology, constitute only one of three important influences on development throughout the life-span (figure 1.1). Each of these influences is determined by an interaction of biological and environmental factors (cf. chapter 2), though one or the other may predominate in particular cases.

Of the three kinds of influence, 'normative age-graded' is one that has a fairly strong relationship with chronological age. The advent of puberty at adolescence (see chapter 9) would be an example of a normative age-graded influence with a strong biological component, while entering school at 5 years (in Britain) would be a normative age-graded influence with little biological determination.

'Normative history-graded' influences are those associated with historical time for most members of a given generation (or 'cohort', see below). A famine, for example the Ethiopian famine of the 1980s, would be an example of strong biological determinants on development. The advent of television (see box 6.2), or historical changes in family size (for example the 'one-child' policy in China since the early 1980s) are examples with little biological determination. The attack on the World Trade Center in New York in 2001 was a historical event with world-wide implications, but especially on people growing up in Afghanistan and the middle East, and in the USA.

Finally, 'non-normative life events' are those that do not occur in any normative age-graded or history-graded manner for most individuals. The effects of brain damage in an accident would be an example with strong biological determinants; the effects of job loss, or moving house, or divorce, examples with less strong biological determinants. All are significant events that can occur in the life-span of an individual at many age points and at many historical times.

Many developmental studies examine the effects of a particular kind of non-normative life event when it happens, perhaps irrespective of age, or with age as another factor. The effects of divorce on children, mentioned earlier, is one example. Investigators of this topic typically record the adjustment of children, often of a range of ages, over a period of time from when the parental separation occurred. Another example would be the study of the effects of a traumatic event, such as exposure to warfare, or being in an accident such as the sinking of a cruise ship (see chapter 17).

The consideration of history-graded influences leads to further designs for studying development, apart from the cross-sectional and longitudinal ones already mentioned. One of these is cohort design.

Cohort design: in cohort design, different cohorts (i.e. samples of children born in different years) are compared at the same ages. This design will inform us of the impact of historical change. For example, if we compare leisure activities of 8-year-old children born in a western society in 1930, 1960, and 1990, we will see changes influenced by (among other factors) the advent of television in the 1950s, and the advent of computer culture and games in the 1980s.

The characteristics of the three designs mentioned so far are as follows:

Cross-sectional design
Different participants	Different ages	Same historical time

Longitudinal design
Same participants	Different ages	Different historical times

Cohort design
Different participants	Same ages	Different historical times

Yet another design is a combination called cohort-sequential design.

Cohort-sequential design: This combines aspects of all the above three designs to create a very powerful analytic tool in studying developmental processes. As an example of this, we might look at the effects of compensatory preschool programmes (see chapter 17) on children born in 1970, 1975 and 1980, following each cohort longitudinally through from age 3 years to, say, age 18 years. As well as several sets of cross-sectional and longitudinal data, this hypothetical design (figure 1.2) would let us see whether historical change over the last decade or so (for example in educational policy, or the relative position of minority groups in society) had an impact on whatever long-term effects of the programmes might

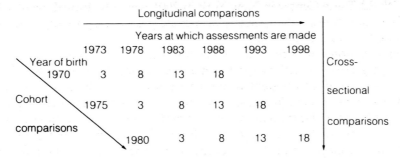

Figure 1.2 A hypothetical study design, combining cross-sectional, longitudinal and cohort comparisons, to examine the effects of compensatory preschool programmes at different ages and different historical periods. If started in 1973, the study would continue until 1998. The ages of each sample of children from each cohort and at each year of study are shown in years.

be detected. Obviously, this would be immensely time-consuming, and indeed such a study has not been carried out! Even one set of actual longitudinal studies originating in the 1970s has proved a major research undertaking (see chapter 17). So far, cohort sequential designs have been rarely used, and only on a smaller scale. An example is given in box 5.2.

Bronfenbrenner's ecological model of human development

The American psychologist Urie Bronfenbrenner has proposed another influential conceptualization of development (Bronfenbrenner, 1979). He emphasizes the importance of studying 'development-in-context', or the ecology of development. 'Ecology' refers here to the environmental settings which the person or organism is experiencing, or is linked to directly or indirectly. Bronfenbrenner conceives of this ecological environment as a set of four nested systems (see figure 1.3) and as an interaction among the processes of person, context and time.

Most familiar to the psychologist is the 'microsystem' – what an individual experiences in a given setting. For a young child, one microsystem may comprise the home environment with parents and siblings. Another microsystem may be the school environment, with teachers and peers. Most psychological research is carried out at the level of one microsystem, for example looking at mother's talk and child's speech in the home (chapter 11), or peer popularity and aggression at school (chapter 5).

At the next level is the 'mesosystem'. This refers to links among settings in which the individual directly participates. For example, the quality of the child's home environment might affect his or her school performance or confidence with peers.

The third level is the 'exosystem'. This refers to links to settings in which the individual does not participate directly, but which do affect the individual. For example, the mother's or father's work environment may affect their behaviour

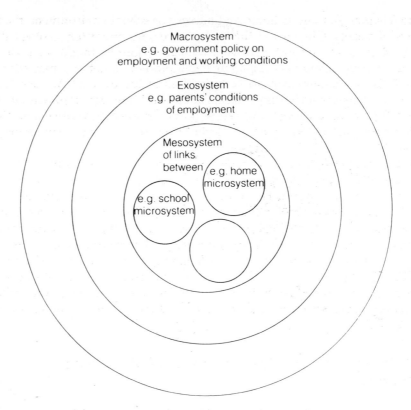

Figure 1.3 The nested circles of macro-, exo-, meso- and microsystems proposed by Bronfenbrenner (1979), with examples relevant to a school-age child.

at home, and hence the quality of parental care. The child does not directly experience the parent's work environment, but he or she experiences the effects indirectly.

The fourth level is the 'macrosystem'. This refers to the general pattern of ideology and organization of social institutions in the society or subculture the individual is in. Thus, the effects of parental stress at work, or unemployment, will be affected by such factors as working hours in that society, rates of pay, holiday and leave entitlement, occupational status, or the degree of social stigma attached to unemployment.

Bronfenbrenner's model illustrates how a decision or change in the macrosystem (e.g. change in employment conditions) may affect the exosystem (parent's work experience) and hence a child's mesosystem and microsystem. This is not controversial in itself. However, recognizing these links does suggest the importance of trying to conceptualize and design psychological investigations extending beyond just the microsystem level.

Bronfenbrenner proposes that we view human development as the process of understanding and restructuring our ecological environment at successively greater levels of complexity. The child first comes to understand its primary caregivers (chapter 3), then its home and nursery or school environment, then wider aspects of society. Changes in the ecological environment (or 'ecological transitions') are especially important in development. Examples might be: having a new sibling; entering school; getting a job; being promoted; getting married; taking a holiday. (Note the similarity to Baltes's ideas of life events.) At such times the person is faced with a challenge, has to adapt, and thus development takes place. Indeed, Bronfenbrenner feels that seeing how a person copes with change is essential to understanding that person: 'If you want to understand something, try to change it.'

More recently, Bronfenbrenner and Ceci (1994) propose empirically testable basic mechanisms called *proximal processes* through which the genetic potential for effective psychological functioning are realized. These proximal processes lead to particular developmental outcomes, including controlling one's own behaviour, coping successfully under stress, acquiring knowledge and skill, establishing mutually satisfying relationships and modifying one's own physical, social and symbolic environment. Bronfenbrenner's model predicts systematic variation in the extent of such outcomes as a result of the interplay among proximal processes, their stability over time, the contexts in which they take place, the characteristics of the persons involved and the nature of the outcome under consideration.

Obtaining Information about Behaviour and Development

As you read through this book, you will see that psychologists have used a wide variety of means to obtain useful information, whatever their theoretical or conceptual orientation has been. Some form of experimental study is perhaps the most common form of investigation reported in psychological books and journals. Nevertheless, non-experimental methods, such as naturalistic observation or field surveys, are also respectable procedures provided there is a clear aim to the research. The crucial variable here is the degree of control the investigator has over what is happening. We shall discuss this in some detail, together with two other aspects of obtaining data – the way behaviour is recorded and the selection of participants. These aspects are also highlighted in the boxes that follow all the subsequent chapters.

What degree of control?

A great deal can be learned from recording behaviour in natural situations or settings. Suppose we were interested in what kinds of help are shown by preschool children to others in distress (chapter 8). Perhaps the most suitable approach here is for the investigator simply to observe children in natural settings such as the home, or ask parents or adults to keep diary records of events. Or, we might try to save time simply by interviewing parents, or giving a questionnaire. The investigator interferes as little as possible, only to the extent of making sure he or she gets reliable data. This kind of approach is most suitable when we do not yet have much systematic knowledge about the phenomenon, and need to gather this descriptive data. As an example, Judy Dunn and Carol Kendrick (1982) gathered observational records of interactions between siblings, in the first few years of life (see chapter 5). Even though some experimental work had been done on sibling relationships, this study produced a richness of detail and uncovered a wide variety of phenomena that fully justified such a naturalistic approach.

From this kind of study we can learn what kinds of behaviour occur, and how frequently. But do we advance our understanding of the processes involved? To some extent, the answer is yes. For instance, we can carry out 'correlational analyses' of various kinds. In a correlation we examine whether a certain behaviour occurs systematically or more frequently together with some other particular behaviour or in some particular situation. For example, we may find that helpful behaviour by children is correlated with clear communications by the mother (p. 249). Such findings certainly suggest explanations as to the processes involved. Parents who communicate clearly may have children who are more helpful because the communications bring this about. However, can we be confident that this explanation is better than some other, different explanation? Not really. The relation between cause and effect might be reversed: for example, children who are for other reasons helpful may have better relationships with parents, who are thus more willing to take time to explain things to them. Or, some other factor may account for both aspects separately. Perhaps parents who are less stressed and more happy have both more time to communicate to children and less stressed children who are therefore more helpful. In that case, stress would be the crucial factor and not parental communication.

This weakness of correlational evidence is a most important concept to grasp. If you find it difficult, think of this example. Suppose you correlated, from day to day through the year, the number of people wearing shorts and the number of people eating ice cream. You would probably get a positive association or correlation. This does not mean that wearing shorts causes people to eat ice cream, or vice versa; we know that in this case the daily variation in temperature, a third variable, is the likely cause of both.

At several points in this book we will draw out these limitations of correlational methods. The way psychologists have tried to proceed further is to use some form of experiment. In an experiment we focus on one or a small number of variables of interest that we think are important: then we try to exclude other variables from our possible explanations. Three kinds of experiment will be described.

The weakest form of experiment is the 'quasi-experiment' (see Cook and Campbell, 1979, for extended discussion). In a quasi-experiment the variable that the investigator thinks is important is changed naturally, and the investigator watches what happens. For example, in box 6.2 we refer to a before-and-after study in 1955 of the effects on children's behaviour of introducing a new television transmitter in Norwich. The investigators felt that the introduction of the opportunity to watch TV was an important variable and they took the opportunity to measure its effects.

Unfortunately quasi-experiments are not much more powerful than correlational studies at excluding alternative explanations. Usually, we know too little about (i.e. have too little control over) the characteristics of our participants and the circumstances of the variable that is changing. For example, in the situation just described, which parents first acquired television sets when they were available? They would almost certainly be different in various ways from those who did not acquire television sets (and indeed the study identified some such differences). Also, children might differentially view programmes of certain types, depending on personality and interest. How can we tell whether changes in behaviour are due to watching the programmes, or whether the programme-watching is just a by-product of differences in behaviour due to other factors?

The most powerful way to answer such cause–effect questions is to carry out a 'true' or 'controlled' experiment. We can distinguish field experiments and laboratory experiments, but both share two important features. The first is that there are two or more well-specified 'conditions' that participants can experience. The second is that participants are assigned to conditions in a systematic fashion. In these ways the experimenter seeks to ascribe an outcome definitely to differences between certain conditions. Alternative explanations in terms of other uncontrolled differences between conditions, or between the participants in different conditions, can be excluded.

Let us take further the idea that television viewing may affect children's social behaviour. Suppose we invite children in small groups to a laboratory, where we randomly assign them to one of three conditions. In one condition they see several violent cartoon programmes; in another they see several non-violent cartoons; in the third (called a control condition) they do not watch television at all but do something else, like drawing. Afterwards they go to a playroom and are filmed by the experimenter, who records their social behaviour.

Suppose the experimenter finds a significant difference. Children who watched the violent cartoons are more aggressive to each other in the playroom than those who watched non-violent cartoons, or did drawing. This difference in aggressiveness can confidently be ascribed to watching the violent cartoons. It cannot be explained by systematic differences in the participants (we assigned them randomly) and it cannot be explained by unknown variations in the children's experiences (we chose the cartoons, and made the children sit through all of them).

Sometimes the investigator compares the effects of two or more conditions he or she is interested in (for example, violent and non-violent cartoon films). Sometimes it is appropriate to include a 'control group', which is a condition including all the same experiences except that which the investigator is particularly interested in. The children who experienced drawing, above, were a control group for the general experience of coming to the laboratory and meeting the experimenters. Any differences between the control group and the two experimental groups showed the effects of watching cartoons. Any difference between the two experimental groups further showed the effects of whether the cartoons were violent, or non-violent.

In all experiments we can identify 'independent variables' and 'dependent variables'. Independent variables are those controlled or manipulated by the experimenter: in our example, the experience of watching cartoons, and whether the cartoons were violent or not. The dependent variables are those we choose to examine for possible effects: in our example, social behaviour in the playroom.

The laboratory experiment allows tight control of assignment of participants and of the independent variables; but is it rather artificial? What do the participants feel about coming to the laboratory? Would they normally choose to watch such cartoons? Can we expect a reasonable range of normal behaviour in this environment? Perhaps not. To some extent we can try to overcome these objections in a 'field experiment'. For example, we might try showing different kinds of television cartoons to different groups of children at a school, or at a summer camp. The children would normally be at the school, or camp, and watching some television might be part of their expected programme.

In general in a field experiment the investigator attempts to combine the rigorous control of experimental design with the advantages of a naturalistic setting (see p. 202 and box 8.2 for examples). This can, at its best, be a very powerful method. However, it is difficult to maintain both experimental control and naturalness, and the field experiment may slip either into becoming a quasi-experiment, or into becoming more constrained and unnatural, like the laboratory experiment.

Thus, in all investigations the naturalness of the setting needs to be balanced against the degree of knowledge and control we have over the setting. Where the balance is best struck depends very much on the kind of behaviour or skill we are interested in. We do want to be reasonably sure that the conclusions we draw from our study apply to the 'real world'. This concern has been labelled as the need for 'ecological validity'. Bronfenbrenner (1979) has defined ecological validity as 'the extent to which the environment experienced by the participants in a scientific investigation has the properties it is supposed or assumed to have by the investigator'. In other words, is it reasonably representative as regards the conclusions we wish to draw from the study? If we felt that the results of a laboratory experiment on cartoon watching were not representative of the effects of real-life television watching, then we would say this experiment lacked ecological validity.

Recording data

Whatever design of investigation we are using, we also have to decide how to record the data. A variety of methods are available. Sometimes several types of data may be gathered in one study.

One method is to make observational records of behaviour (e.g. box 2.1) whereby the investigator watches the participant(s) and makes systematic records of whether certain behaviours occur. Usually the investigator defines certain 'behaviour categories' in advance, and then scores when they occur. Some method of 'time sampling' is often employed to assist in quantifying the scoring (see Martin and Bateson, 1991, for extended discussion). Sometimes the investigator asks the participant(s) to keep his or her own records, perhaps a diary of occurrences (e.g. box 8.1). Again, the participants will probably need some training in what and what not to record in this way.

The method just referred to would be 'non-participant observation' – the observer watches the behaviour from 'outside'. In 'participant observation', the observer is also one of the actors in the situation. For example, in a study of a Chicago gang of adolescent delinquents, Whyte (1943) acted as a gang member in order to get insight into what was really going on. Patrick (1973) described a similar study of a gang in Glasgow, from the insider perspective. This kind of study is more difficult in terms of recording data, but will give unique insights as well.

Another set of methods involves interviews and questionnaires. In an interview, the investigator asks participants about a topic and explores their thoughts, feelings or attitudes with them. Often some degree of structure is imposed on the kinds of questions asked in the interview (e.g. box 15.2). A still more structured approach is to give participants a questionnaire in which they fill in replies to preset questions (e.g. box 9.2). A questionnaire is often given individually, but can be given in groups. A questionnaire sent to large numbers of people is called a 'survey' (e.g. pp. 301–4).

Tests can also be given individually or (in some cases) in groups. In a test the participant may be asked certain questions and also perhaps be asked to carry out certain actions, e.g. solve certain puzzles. The test differs from the interview in that it is designed to measure a particular ability or trait, and it is scored in a strictly defined way that can be compared with normative values obtained earlier in the process of test design (see chapter 16).

Children/young people as researchers

Some studies have gone beyond observing or interviewing children or young people, and have moved to involving them as researchers themselves. So far, this has not generally meant involving them in the research questions to be asked, but it has included involving them in the design of the study, and gathering data. For example the Triumph and Success Project (France, 2000) recruited eight young people aged 15 to 21 years from varying social and economic backgrounds to help undertake research on youth transitions in Sheffield, in northern England. They were involved in designing questionnaires and undertaking surveys and interviews with other young people of their age. This was especially helpful in getting data from ethnic minorities and 'hard-to-reach' groups. However, some young researchers found difficulty in disentangling themselves from the project when it 'finished'.

In a review of over 20 such projects, Kirby (1999) argues that involving young researchers in various aspects of a research project can be an ethical and democratic way of conducting research; has benefits for the young researchers themselves in developing skills, confidence and awareness of issues; and may result in getting more valid data, especially from some young people not easily reached by adult researchers. Some difficulties are that some young researchers may be reluctant to discuss 'sensitive' issues with peers; plus, there may be a tension between their 'inside knowledge' and keeping some 'outside perspective' or objectivity. While there can be some special advantages in involving young researchers, careful thought and planning is essential in making it work.

Reliability and validity

Whatever measuring instrument or method we use, we need to be sure of its 'reliability'. Basically, a reliable method is one that would give the same answer if you, or another investigator, were to repeat the measurement in the same conditions. A straight, firm ruler is reliable, a crooked or floppy one is not. Similarly, if we recorded 'aggressive behaviour' in children, but did not define our behaviour categories or method of time sampling, this would be unreliable; someone else might have a different idea of what is aggressive, and get different results even if watching the same behaviour. Methods need to be carefully specified and tried out if they are to be reliable.

The term 'reliability' is often confused with 'validity': both are very important in any investigation. We have just seen that reliability refers to the recording of data. Validity, in contrast, refers to whether the data we obtain are actually meaningful. Remember the concept of 'ecological validity' we discussed above. Our measurements in a laboratory experiment might be very reliable (well specified and repeatable) but this does not guarantee that they are valid in the sense of meaningful in the 'real world'.

Problems of validity actually arise in all kinds of investigation. If we are making records in a natural setting, we have to beware that the presence of an observer does not change the behaviour being observed. If you stand in a playground recording aggressive behaviour, will less aggression occur than usual because you are there? This is a problem of 'observer effects'. Similarly, in experiments there are 'experimenter effects'. The experimenter may unwittingly help some participants more than others, or score some participants more leniently. One type of experimenter effect is known as the 'Clever Hans' effect. Clever Hans was a horse that apparently could count. If his trainer asked 'what is three and four' Hans would tap with his front foot seven times. However, the German psychologist Oskar Pfungst (1911) discovered that Hans actually relied on subtle non-verbal (and unintentional) cues from his trainer, who inclined his head slightly forward after Hans had tapped the correct number of times. Hans was clever, but not in the way originally thought. The demonstration was a reliable one, but the conclusions drawn initially were not valid.

Participant characteristics

One aspect of validity concerns the representativeness of the participants investigated. If we do a survey of young men's attitudes to sexual relationships, they may not be representative of the views of young women (chapter 9). Or, we may not have enough participants to give us even a reliable source of data.

A data set obtained from one person is called a 'case study'. Normally a case study tells us little about the general population but, if we can obtain very extensive records (for example, the records Piaget obtained of his own children described in chapter 12) or if the person is especially interesting (for example, the case studies of extreme deprivation described in chapter 17) then this method may be very valuable. A case study may often serve as a source of ideas or hypotheses for later study (e.g. p. 293; fig. 11.1).

Many psychological investigations are done on small samples of some 10 to 50 individuals, who can be brought to a laboratory or observed in a single setting. Sometimes a survey or other investigation is carried out on a large sample of hundreds of participants. Such a sample may be regarded as normative, or representative, of some section of the population. For example, one longitudinal study in Britain included all the children born in one week of March 1946. These could reasonably be taken as representative of children born in Britain in the later 1940s.

■ Working with the Data: Quantitative and Qualitative Methods

Once we have got our data, what do we do with it? There is a continuing debate here about the advantages and disadvantages of qualitative methods, and quantitative methods.

Qualitative methods: here, the emphasis is on the meaning of the behaviour or experience for the person concerned. The data recording methods usually used are unstructured or semi-structured interviews, or participant observation. Often, qualitative researchers obtain transcripts of interviews, and then use specialized methods such as grounded theory, and discourse analysis, to extract dimensions of meaning and experience from these. While clearly not suitable for young children, such methods can be used with older children. An example is a study of girls' bullying by Owens et al. (2000). Qualitative methods can also be illuminating in studies of how parents think about child-rearing (Phoenix et al., 1991).

Quantitative methods: here, the emphasis is on predetermined categories, and the researcher has often already decided what he or she is interested in – they are not 'searching the data' but 'looking for the answer to certain questions'. Often, quantitative researchers use experiments, or data from non-participant observation. Usually statistical tests are carried out to look at correlations, or at differences between subgroups in the sample, and to see whether the results are sufficiently stable or characteristic that it is likely they would be true of larger samples. The means of carrying out simple statistical tests (such as correlation, t test, and chi-square) are described in introductory texts such as Robson (1999), together with the meaning of probability or p values. Examples of the results of such tests are given in many of the boxes in this book.

It is possible to combine both approaches; or, to move from an initial, exploratory qualitative study to a more focused quantitative study as an investigation progresses. Unfortunately, ideological and professional biases often lead to unproductive disputes about these approaches, rather than productive selection of methods that best suit the aims of the study.

Objectivity and bias

Scientific investigation is supposed to be objective, not biased by the personal beliefs or values of the individual investigator or the wider society. In practice, this is not entirely the case. The kinds of problems chosen for study, and the way they are tackled, are inevitably affected by personal or societal ideas of what is important. Some qualitative researchers believe that this is quite intrinsic to research, as the investigator is part of society too; the best the researcher can do is to describe their own orientation and background so that others are aware of it. Quantitative researchers tend to believe that by defining units of measurement closely, and training observers or interviewers, a degree of objectivity can be obtained.

Some areas of psychology may be especially susceptible to decreased objectivity, when personal beliefs are closely involved. Stephen Gould (1996) argued this in the instance of the study of intelligence testing and the view held by some psychologists that there were innate racial differences in intelligence. The kinds of study carried out earlier in the century, and the way those studies were interpreted, clearly reflected bias (for example, racial prejudice) in some investigators. At times this involved misconceived inferences from results, or observer bias in scoring or testing. At extremes it bordered on fraudulence (see next section). Gould in turn has been accused of misrepresenting aspects of his case (Rushton, 1997). Even though objectivity is far from perfect, it is possible to recognize and expose biases, at least after the event. Much more sophisticated studies of the issues involved in race and intelligence have now been carried out, bearing these past errors in mind.

Ethical issues

Whenever an investigation is made with human or animal participants, investigators should have due respect for their rights and welfare. Investigations with animals kept for experimental purposes are usually controlled by strict guidelines, for example by the Home Office in the UK. For human investigations, general principles are of informed consent (by children and/or by parents on their behalf), confidentiality of information obtained, and lack of harm to participants. Societies such as the British Psychological Society have issued ethical guidelines for the planning of investigations. Some investigations may involve some disturbance of privacy, inconvenience to participants, or temporary deception concerning the purpose of the study. Even when legally permissible, any such outcomes should be balanced carefully against the likely benefits from carrying out the investigations. Needless to say, any negative outcomes to participants must be very carefully justified and only accepted under the most unusual circumstances; they should never be a feature of student experiments or investigations. The ethical principles approved by the British Psychological Society are reprinted in appendix A and should be consulted in case of any uncertainty on this issue.

Another ethical issue relates to the accurate reporting of results. It is clearly the duty of investigators to report their results in as accurate and unbiased a way as possible, but there have been occasions when this principle is known to have been violated. The British psychologist Sir Cyril Burt reported data on twins, which he claimed to have gathered for many years, in order to prove that intelligence was largely inherited. His results were published in numerous articles as his sample of twins accumulated. However, it has now been shown beyond reasonable doubt that in the latter part of his life Burt did not gather more data, but invented it (Hearnshaw, 1979). Thus a great deal of his twin data set is believed by most psychologists to be fraudulent, and the conclusions drawn from it unwarranted. Much attention has been drawn to this deception, partly because of the social implications of the theory of hereditary intelligence, and partly because fraud on this scale is believed to be rare. Drawing attention to such misdemeanours hopefully serves to make future occurrences less probable.

What Implications does Psychological Knowledge have for Society?

Bronfenbrenner has argued that many people have potential for development that goes far beyond the capacities that they currently display and has proposed that this untapped potential might be realized through appropriate public policies and through programmes of intervention that could provide the resources and the stability over time that enable these processes to become most effective. He argued that this conclusion is extremely salient in today's society where social changes in both developed and developing countries have 'undermined conditions necessary for healthy psychological development' (Bronfenbrenner and Ceci, 1994, p. 583).

Bronfenbrenner was concerned about what he calls the growing chaos in America's children, youth and families that he saw as being caused by disruptive trends in society over the past four decades and by the continuation of public policies that threaten the ability of the family to perform its role effectively. In fact, alarmist writings about the state of youth and families are not new. Pearson (1983) has shown how worries about the unruliness of adolescents and increase in rates of delinquency and adolescent crime and violence, appear to resurface in each generation. Looking at newspapers, books and journals over a period of some 150 years, he found that each generation was bemoaning rising crime and harking back to a golden age of a generation ago! We can go a long way back with such thoughts – Sommerville (1982) cited a tablet from Mesopotamia which stated 'Our Earth is degenerate in these latter days . . . Children no longer obey their parents'; this was dated to 2800 BC!

However, whether new or not, there are clearly important social problems that developmental and child psychologists have a responsibility to address. As a society we have knowledge of ways in which we can foster competence in the young and on interventions that can act as buffers against dysfunction in the family. Bronfenbrenner was one of the founders of Project Head Start, an intervention that had positive and long-lasting effects on disadvantaged children (Project Head Start is described in chapter 17). He is convinced that the belief systems of parents, peers, teachers and mentors can change as a function of education, intervention programmes and the mass media; the Internet is also a growing source of influence. We need to ensure that new knowledge, and new technologies, are used effectively for human betterment.

The rights of children

Are we agreed on what human betterment is, and what is best for children? The United Nations Convention on the Rights of the Child (United Nations, 1989) advocates rights on behalf of all children and places emphasis on non-discrimination, acting in the best interests of the child, and listening to the views of the child. The Convention built on earlier legislation by specifying children's rights not only to protection and provision, but also to participation – so giving some political rights to children (we look at the impact of political violence on children's development in box 17.1). In the context of participation, it addressed such contentious issues as child labour and children's rights to freedom of thought and speech. Its recommendations are binding to those countries that ratified it (including the UK, which signed it in 1991; the USA is one country which did not sign).

Lopatka (1992), the chairman of the United Nations working group that drafted the Convention, argued that the rights of the child are universal, yet he also asserted the need to take into account the cultural values of the child's community. However, as Burman (1996) indicates, a major criticism of the Convention concerns difficulties in implementing it in societies where families are very poor, civil liberties are severely constrained or a country is at war. The tension between a child's universal developmental needs and the realities of his or her social situation may be nearly impossible to resolve.

There are similar controversies with the England and Wales Children Act that came into effect in the UK in 1991. The Children Act states that the child's welfare must be paramount and that adults must ascertain what the wishes and feelings of the child are; in legal cases, courts should take into account the emotional needs of the child. The Children Act requires all local authority agencies to work together in the best interests of protecting the child. This means, among other things, that teachers are legally obliged to share their knowledge of abuse or significant harm to the child with other agencies, most frequently social services.

The Children Act appears to be enlightened in shifting the emphasis from parents' rights over their children to their responsibilities towards the young people in their care. When parents divorce, the local authorities have a duty to protect and promote the welfare of the children involved, and the courts must now pay due attention to the wishes of the child. A process of conciliation is now more common because of the Children Act, in line with its intention to benefit children in this situation. At the same time, in practice, courts have the right to judge the child's competence to make autonomous decisions, and may as a result disregard children's wishes in the wider context of 'the best interests of the child'. You can see that it is extremely difficult to achieve the balance between what the child thinks he or she wants at the time against what in the view of adults may be in the longer-term best for the child. And who is right – the adult or the child?

As one step towards the education of young people in the complexities of rights, roles and responsibilities, citizenship education has developed in many European countries in the past decade, with the broad aim of developing in young Europeans a sense of both national and regional identity. Since 2002, schools in the UK, in line with many other European countries, are required to demonstrate that they are providing citizenship education, to be mandatory in secondary schools and recommended in primary schools. The new curriculum teaches young people about social and moral education through emphasis on current issues, rules and laws, rights and responsibilities, democratic processes and the resolution of differences. The development of such a curriculum has arisen from extensive debates about the skills, values and attitudes that will be required of the global citizen in the twenty-first century. The increasingly global environment that we inhabit calls for citizens who, whether they are consumers or employees, should be able to evaluate the developments in science and technology that have transformed our lives in recent years. There are also growing concerns about the need for global citizens to be aware of human rights and social responsibilities in a culturally diverse world. Against a background of widespread racism and xenophobia in societies where substantial minority groups (including asylum seekers) come from other cultures, the Council of Europe (1993) has called for education in human rights to be offered to children from preschool onwards, and for young people to be educated in democratic processes and values, so heightening awareness of social responsibility and a concern for social justice.

The Scientific Status of Psychology

This chapter began by briefly considering the nature of psychology as a scientific discipline. We shall conclude by discussing briefly what is meant by the term 'science', and whether this is what psychologists practice. The nature of scientific inquiry has been written about by philosophers of science: we shall summarize the views of two – Popper and Kuhn.

For a long time it was generally held that science proceeded by gathering factual data, by observation and experiment, and by deriving general laws from these facts. This has been called the 'traditional' or 'inductivist' view. However, throughout the twentieth century, scientists and philosophers of science have put more emphasis on the role of hypotheses or theories in science. A hypothesis, or theory, is a proposition that some relationship holds among certain phenomena. For example, some psychological hypotheses discussed in this book include: that the fetus can learn characteristics of the mother's voice (pp. 86–8); that the first hours of birth are critically important for mother–infant bonding (pp. 82–3); that viewing violent television programmes makes children behave more aggressively (pp. 202–7); that children's development of moral reasoning is similar in different cultures (pp. 265–7); that children cannot understand another's point of view until about 7 years of age (pp. 399–401); that preschool 'Head start' programmes can benefit a child educationally throughout the school years (pp. 573–6).

The 'traditional' view would be that hypotheses such as these are derived from facts we have gathered, and that if we get enough factual support then the theory will have been 'proved' correct. However, this view is not now generally held. Instead, most scientists and philosophers believe that the role of theory is a primary one, and that theories cannot be proved, only disproved. A most articulate proponent of this viewpoint was Sir Karl Popper (1902–94), who argued that our ideas about the world, or 'common-sense beliefs', serve as the starting point for organizing knowledge from which scientific investigation proceeds. Thus, theory serves a primary role and indeed structures what and how we observe or categorize 'facts', or observations about the world. Psychologists are in a good position to appreciate this argument, as part of their discipline (and part of this book, e.g. chapters 10, 11 and 12) is concerned with how children construct hypotheses about perceptual data and how they gain greater knowledge about the world through forming hypotheses to test against experience. Indeed, we started this chapter by considering how people are 'nature's psychologists' in this sense (see also chapter 14).

Popper considered that science and knowledge progress by advancing hypotheses, making deductions from them, and continuing to do so until some deductions are proved wrong or 'falsified'. The hypothesis is then changed to cope with this. A hypothesis can thus never be finally proved correct, as there is always the possibility that some further observation or experiment might discredit it. A hypothesis can, however, be falsified and it is through this process that science progresses.

You can think about this by examining the hypotheses we have just listed. Have any been falsified (some have)? Did the falsifying lead to better hypotheses (sometimes)? Could any be 'proved' beyond question?

Popper's notion of falsification has been a powerful one, and he used it to distinguish 'science' from 'non-science'. If propositions, hypotheses or theories cannot actually be falsified, then according to Popper, this is not science. It may be interesting and enlightening, like a novel, but it is not science. Not all philosophers of science agree with Popper's approach. At least, not many believe that scientists spend most of their time trying to disprove their theories. A different view was put by Thomas Kuhn (1922–96), who saw a mature branch of any science as having an accepted 'paradigm'. A paradigm is a basic set of assumptions, or way of trying to solve problems. Atomic theory provided a paradigm in the natural sciences, for example.

In psychology, 'psychoanalysis', 'behaviourism', 'sociobiology' (see chapter 2) and the 'information processing' approach (viewing the brain as a computer) could be taken as paradigms in this sense. However, the most influential paradigm informing the present book is the 'cognitive-developmental' paradigm. This links behaviour to the kind of cognitive development or thinking ability expected at the age or level of development the individual is at. Piaget's theory of cognitive development is often taken as a reference point here (chapter 12), though the approach is not necessarily tied to Piaget's ideas.

Kuhn described how a branch of science might develop; it starts in a 'pre-paradigmatic stage' where it would be characterized by rather random fact-gathering, and many schools of thought, which quarrel about fundamental issues. With maturity, one paradigm is accepted and directs the way observations and experiments are made. Kuhn called this phase 'normal science'. Scientists work within the paradigm, extending and defending it. The paradigm is not rejected unless many difficulties or falsifications accumulate, and in addition a superior paradigm appears. A period of 'revolutionary science' with competing paradigms then emerges, with eventually one proving superior, when 'normal science' resumes.

Kuhn characterized science as having a fruitful paradigm that can unify the efforts and direction of study of many scientists. Falsification has a relatively minor role to play, he argued, since all theories have some anomalies (phenomena which cannot yet be well explained). Only the appearance of another paradigm can really upset things.

Kuhn's ideas have been criticized, and modified, but his idea of a paradigm, while rather vague in practice, has had considerable impact. Psychologists in particular often seem to be claiming that a particular approach or theory is setting up a 'new paradigm'! Kuhn himself seems to have thought that psychology and other social sciences may well still be at a pre-paradigmatic stage. It is indeed true that no single paradigm as yet unites the whole of psychology. Still, certain paradigms (e.g., the cognitive-developmental approach) do seem to be fruitful and capable of bringing together several areas of psychology. Perhaps, after working through this book, the reader may decide for himself or herself what kind of scientific status the study of psychological development has, what it has achieved, and what it may reasonably hope to achieve in the foreseeable future.

■ Further Reading

A readable introductory text on methods of studying behaviour is Martin, P. and Bateson, P. 1991: *Measuring Behaviour: An Introductory Guide*, (2nd edn). Cambridge: Cambridge University Press; it has most detail on observational methods, and on studying animals. A more advanced sourcebook for research methodology and experimental design in psychology is provided by Robson, C. 2002: *Real World Research*, (2nd edn). Blackwell Publishers, while Breakwell, G. M., Hammond, S. and Fife-Schaw, C. 2000: *Research Methods in Psychology*. London: Sage, have a wide-ranging collection of chapters on different issues.

For introductions to qualitative methods see Banister, P. et al. 1994: *Qualitative Methods in Psychology*. Buckingham: Open University Press, or Richardson, J. T. E. (ed.) 1996: *Handbook of Qualitative Research Methods for Psychology and the Social Sciences*. Leicester: BPS Books. There are many good statistics texts available for psychology and the social/behavioural sciences. An excellent basic text is Robson, C. 1999: *Experiment, Design and Statistics in Psychology*, (3rd edn). Harmondsworth: Penguin; while a thoughtful, slightly more advanced text is Dunbar, G. 1998: *Data Analysis for Psychology*. London: Arnold. A useful, thorough and broader text is Coolican, H. 1999: *Research Methods and Statistics in Psychology*, (2nd edn). London: Hodder & Stoughton Educational.

The way in which psychologists can be affected by the social climate of the time, and the ethical issues involved in doing research with social policy implications, is exemplified in Gould, S. J. 1996: *The Mismeasure of Man*, (2nd edn). New York: Norton, and by Tizard, B. and Phoenix, A. 1993: *Black, White or Mixed Race?*

Race and Racism in the Lives of Young People of Mixed Parentage. London: Routledge. The journal *Childhood* gives up-to-date debates on the construction of childhood and the family, children's rights and cross-cultural perspectives on society's responsibilities towards children.

Schaffer, H. R. 1996: *Social Development*. Oxford: Blackwell Publishers, explores the ways in which current models of child socialization have implications for policies in such areas as day care, dealing with antisocial behaviour in young people, and addressing family conflict and breakdown. Durkin, K. 1995: *Developmental Social Psychology*, also published by Blackwell, gives thorough coverage on gender issues, the influence of culture and the impact of research in the social sciences on policy-making around families and young people.

An accessible general overview to ideas in the philosophy of science is in Chalmers, A. F. 1999: *What is this Thing called Science?* (3rd edn), Milton Keynes: Open University Press.

Discussion Points

1 Has our knowledge of psychological development advanced beyond 'common sense'?
2 What is meant by 'development' and how can we study it?
3 What are the advantages and disadvantages of carrying out experiments in psychology?
4 What impact has psychological knowledge had on society?
5 In what ways can psychology be considered to be, or not to be, a science?

2 Biological and Cultural Theories of Development

In this chapter we look at the way behaviour develops. We start with our genetic inheritance and how the genetic blueprint interacts with our environment to channel growth and development along a particular pathway. We examine these issues in two ways – ontogenetically and phylogenetically. Ontogenesis refers to the development of behaviour in the individual. Most of the book is concerned with this! Phylogenesis refers to the evolution of behaviour; we examine briefly issues of instinct, maturation and learning in birds and mammals – including our closest non-human relatives, the monkeys and apes. This evolutionary perspective continues with an overview of sociobiology and behavioural ecology, which provide the most successful approach to explaining why animals behave as they do, and which some researchers have tried to apply to human behaviour through the disciplines of evolutionary psychology and evolutionary developmental psychology. But in addition to our biological heritage, the environments we have created for ourselves have enormous impact. Cross-cultural psychologists have written about the ways in which different cultural experiences shape development. Social constructionist approaches emphasize the extent to which we construct ourselves and our environments, and tend to de-emphasize biological factors.

Genetics and the Groundplan for Development

Our bodies are made up of cells – brain cells, blood cells, muscle cells, bone cells and so on. But we all started life as just one cell – the 'zygote' formed by the union of mother's egg and father's sperm, which develops through various stages (described in the next chapter). Let's look at the code for this development, the instructions that enable this development to take place.

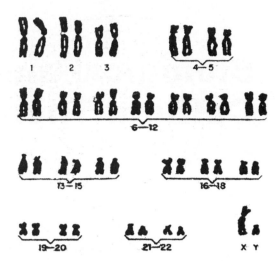

Figure 2.1   Human chromosome complement arranged into a standard karyotype, numbered as shown. The sex chromosomes, labelled X and Y, are at the lower
right. (Original furnished by Dr J. J. Biesele, from H. E. Sutton, *An Introduction to Human Genetics*. New York: Holt, Rinehart & Winston, 1965).

If we look at a cell under powerful microscopes, we find that each cell has a
nucleus containing thread-like structures called chromosomes (see figure 2.1).
These chromosomes are typically arranged in pairs; 4 pairs in fruit flies, 24 pairs
in chimpanzees – and 23 pairs for humans. Each chromosome in turn consists of
a chain of genes; the genes are strung along the chromosomes like beads on a neck-
lace. The genes in turn are composed of DNA (deoxyribonucleic acid), which
are strands of complex molecules twisted around each other in a double spiral
configuration.

The whole collection of genes is called the 'genotype'. It is the genes that
provide instructions for the production of materials in the body for growth and
development. These instructions will lead to an organism having basic body
organs – having wings, or not; legs, or not; and also what kind of wings, legs, etc.
As humans, we owe our basic body plan to our genes. Also, as individuals, such
aspects as the colour of our hair, or of our eyes, whether our hair is curly, depend
on particular genes we may or may not have.

In sexual reproduction, the egg cells (ova) of the mother and the sperm cells of
the father contain only a half-set of chromosomes – one from each pair, following
some reassortment of genes among each pair. After mating and fertilization, the
zygote (fertilized egg) now has a new set of chromosome pairs, with one set of
each pair from the mother and one set from the father. The offspring thus receives
a mixture of the genes of each parent, approximately half from each, reassembled
into new combinations.

The Human Genome Project, started in 1990, is looking in detail at the structure and nature of the human genotype – what genes we have and how they are
laid out along our chromosomes. Since we have some 50,000 to 100,000 genes, this

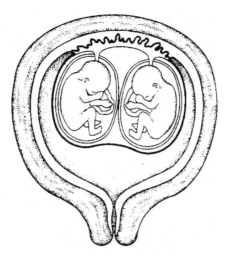

Figure 2.2 Twins in utero. These identical twins have a single placenta but individual amniotic sacs. (Adapted with permission from L. B. Arey, *Developmental Anatomy: A Textbook and Laboratory Manual of Embryology* [7th edn]. Copyright 1965 by W. B. Saunders Company.)

is an ambitious task! Many genes simply ensure the basic groundplan of the species – in our case, that we have two eyes, a nose, a mouth, two arms, two legs, etc. Others vary more between individuals, so that some of us have black hair, some brown, some red. Besides physical development, the genotype also influences behavioural development – a topic known as behaviour genetics (Plomin et al., 1997). There is no doubt that features of the genotype can affect behavioural development in the human species. Some genes affect one particular characteristic strongly, others affect several more weakly or in interactive combination. Effects are probabilistic rather than deterministic. Behaviour geneticists study these influences. Two traditional methods of examining genetic influences are twin studies, and adoption studies.

Twin studies

One source of evidence comes from twin studies. Although mothers usually conceive only one infant at a time, about 1 in every 80 pregnancies involves twins. Twins can be monozygotic (MZ), or dizygotic (DZ):

monozygotic: identical twins, who come from a single fertilized egg cell which has split into two early in development. Usually, the twins share the placenta and surrounding membrane, but have their own umbilical cord to the mother's blood supply, and amniotic sac (see figure 2.2). They are genetically identical and hence of the same sex.

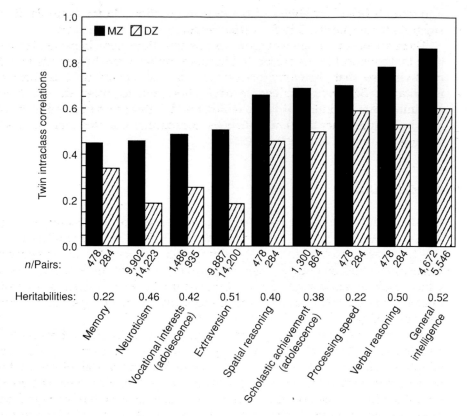

Figure 2.3 MZ and DZ twin intraclass correlations for personality (neuroticism and extraversion), interests in adolescence, scholastic achievement in adolescence, specific cognitive abilities in adolescence (memory, spatial reasoning, processing speed, verbal reasoning), and general intelligence. (Adapted with permission from R. Plomin, M. J. Owen and P. McGuffin 1994: The genetic basis of complex human behaviours. *Science*, 264, 1733–9.)

dizygotic: fraternal twins, who come from two separately fertilized egg cells, each of which develops totally separately in the womb with its own placenta. They may be of the same or different sex. They are siblings, and share 50 per cent of genes in common like other full siblings (although it is possible, and has been documented, for fraternal twins to be half-siblings; Segal, 2000).

Twins can be considered as being reared in very similar environments – normally by the same parents, at the same time and in the same circumstances. But identical and fraternal twins differ in genetic similarity (100 per cent versus 50 per cent). Thus, it can be argued, if identical twins grow up to be more similar in certain respects than fraternal twins, then this should be due to heredity or genetic factors (which differ) rather than environmental factors (which are in common).

In fact, identical twins do often show greater similarity than fraternal twins; see figure 2.3. The extent to which this is so is taken by behaviour geneticists as a measure of the heritability of the trait in question. So for example, figure 2.3 suggests higher heritability for verbal reasoning than for memory.

There are of course some questionable assumptions here; in particular, it is possible that identical twins are treated in more similar ways by parents than fraternal twins, so that their environment is more similar as well as their genetic inheritance. Behaviour geneticists have attempted to avoid this confusion by obtaining data on identical twins reared apart (rather few in number, however); and by using other methods such as comparing adopted and non-adopted siblings (Plomin et al., 1997).

Adoption studies

Children tend to resemble their parents, to some extent – for example in appearance, or temperament. 'He takes after his dad.' Of course, this similarity could be due to genetic and/or environmental influences, as usually the parents are providing their children with both genes, and a rearing environment. 'Family studies', which look at similarities and dissimilarities between relatives according to degrees of relatedness (e.g., are cousins less alike than siblings?) suffer from this confound of genetic with environmental factors.

But, an exception to this occurs with adopted children. Especially when adopted early, these children have the rearing environment provided by their adoptive parents, but a genetic inheritance from their natural, biological parents. So, whom do they resemble most, as they grow up? If environment is more important, it should be the adoptive parents; if genetic factors, the biological parents. There are assumptions in this method too, as adoption is typically non-random; adoptive parents are usually screened; and they may tend to choose, or have assigned to them, infants who resemble them physically or temperamentally, or with whom they feel compatible. Generally twin studies have been used more than adoption studies in recent behaviour genetic work, but the conclusions from the two methods are broadly similar (Pike, 2002).

Genes, and shared and non-shared environment

Using twin and adoption studies, behaviour geneticists usually partition influences on development into three kinds: heritability, shared environmental and non-shared environmental. Heritability refers to variation explained by genetic differences. The shared family environment refers to aspects of the family environment common to all siblings, which makes brothers and sisters similar irrespective of genetics. The non-shared environment refers to other environmental variation, for which siblings differ. For example siblings differ in birth order, and perhaps in the schools they go to and friends they make. Also, parents may treat individual children differently.

The non-shared environment can be influenced by what is called genotype–environment interaction. In other words, to some extent children help create their own rearing environment. A child's temperament for example (which appears to be strongly genetically influenced), influences the ways parents behave towards that child and the expectations they have of them. Also, what are called 'sibling differentiation processes' may operate. Siblings close in age may consciously choose to differentiate themselves in forming their own identity. Feinberg and Hetherington (2000) studied 720 sibling pairs in adolescence and found that generally, siblings closer in age were *less* similar on measures of adjustment than those more distant in age. These kinds of phenomena complicate conclusions from behaviour genetic studies.

The two main findings from much behavioural genetic research in the 1980s and 1990s were that first, heritability was an important factor in many aspects of development (such as personality, intelligence, antisocial behaviour); and second, that most environmental influence was of the non-shared kind. It was argued that shared environment contributed very little to understanding individual differences. For example, children adopted into the same family showed very little similarity as they grew up (Plomin and Daniels, 1987). Harris (1995, 1998; see chapter 4) took the importance of the non-shared environment as a starting point for her 'group socialization' theory of development.

As more evidence and critical analysis has accumulated, this rather strong conclusion has been moderated, and shared environment recognized as an important factor in some cases. As an example, Taylor et al. (2000) used a twin study to examine heritability of delinquency in adolescence. For both boys and girls, they estimated that genetic factors accounted for about 18 per cent of the variance, non-shared environment for 56 per cent, and shared environment for 26 per cent. All three sources were important; the high percentage for non-shared environment here is plausibly related to the importance of peer groups and delinquent gangs in adolescence (see chapter 9), which could vary a lot between siblings from the same family. And although most studies suggest an important role for heritability, this is not always the case. Discussing several twin and family studies of attachment type (see chapter 4), van Ijzendoorn et al. (2000) found that concordance for major mother–infant attachment type was similar for same-sex siblings and monozygotic twins. They concluded that there was 'a relatively small role for a genetic component in attachment security' (p. 1096), and larger roles for both shared environment (e.g., general maternal sensitivity to infants) and non-shared environment (e.g., effects of birth order and maternal experience at child-rearing).

Identifying genes

Recent techniques enable us to examine the structure of DNA (the basis of the genotype), and identify genes and some of their effects more directly than in twin and adoption studies. Genes can be linked to phenotypic outcomes by linkage (inheritance within large family pedigrees) or by association (correlating presence of a gene with a trait, in unrelated individuals). Let's look at two examples of association studies.

Lakatos et al. (2000) examined infant attachment characteristic at 12–13 months, in relation to a gene called DRD4, which is important for a neurotransmitter substance called dopamine. Infant attachment is described in chapter 4; a small per-centage of infants show disorganized attachment (type D), this being a major risk factor in future development. The researchers examined the alleles of the DRD4 gene – the different forms it might take. Most common was a type called the 4-repeat allele. Another form called the 7-repeat allele was more common in disor-ganized attachment (D) infants. We all possess two alleles of each gene (since we get a set from each parent); the chance of having at least one 7-repeat allele was 71 per cent for D infants, and 29 per cent for non-D infants.

Auerbach et al. (2001) report further work on the DRD4 gene, and another gene called 5-HTTLPR, which is associated with transport of the neurotransmit-ter serotonin. Following earlier assessments at 2 weeks and 2 months of age, this study reports on infant behaviour at 12 months, in standard temperament episodes that elicited fear, anger, pleasure, interest and activity. Temperament is described in chapter 3; it refers to characteristic modes of response and emotion that can vary considerably between infants. These researchers found that differ-ences in the DRD4 gene were mainly related to temperament domains of interest and activity; by contrast, differences in the 5-HTTLPR gene were mainly related to temperament domains of fear and pleasure. Lakatos et al. (2003) found evi-dence that these two gene alleles may interact in their behavioural effects: the 7-repeat DRD4 allele appeared to influence wariness of strangers, but to be mod-ulated by the form of the 5-HTTLPR gene to lead to either high anxiety, or low anxiety.

This area of research is likely to expand rapidly. Plomin and Rutter (1998) argue that finding genes can then be used to look at important issues of causation, such as gene–environment interactions and environmental risks associated with certain genes or genotypes.

Chromosomal abnormalities

Another source of evidence for genetic effects on behaviour comes from changes at the level of chromosomes. Of the 23 pairs of chromosomes in humans, 22 pairs (the 'autosomes') are basically matched pairs similar in structure. The twenty-third pair, the 'sex chromosomes', is different. One type called the X chromosome is considerably longer and more complex than the alternative called the Y chro-mosome (see figure 2.1). If you receive two X chromosomes, you will normally develop as a female; if you receive one X and one Y chromosome, you will normally develop as a male. This of course has very definite implications for development, and is discussed further in chapter 5.

Occasionally some mistake is made in genetic transmission, often a change or 'mutation' at the gene level. Sometimes the mistake can take place at a whole chromosome level. The best-known example relates to the twenty-first chromo-some pair; occasionally this pair may fail to separate in forming the egg or sperm, and the offspring may end up having three chromosomes – a trio instead of a pair at this location. This Trisomy 21 condition is usually referred to as Down's syndrome.

Plate 2.1   A child with Down's syndrome.

Down's syndrome

Down's syndrome occurs in approximately 1 in 800 live births. The chromosomal abnormality usually originates in damage to the ovum prior to conception. A woman's ova are present from birth so they are increasingly vulnerable to damage over time; hence, older mothers are more likely than younger mothers to have a baby with Down's syndrome. Mothers aged 20 to 24 have a 1 in 9000 chance of having a baby with Down's syndrome; whereas in mothers aged 45 or more the chances rise to 1 in 30. Paternal age is also associated with increased likelihood of having a baby with Down's syndrome.

A photograph of a person with Down's syndrome is shown in plate 2.1. There are specific physical characteristics in Down's syndrome, including a flat appearance to the face, with a low bridge to the nose and high cheekbones; and upward and outward slanting eyes with a conspicuous upper eye-lid fold. In addition muscles may be floppy, contributing to poor motor coordination.

So far as behavioural development is concerned, persons with Down's syndrome vary greatly but the chromosomal abnormality is a disability. There is likely to be mental retardation, with particular difficulty taking in visual, auditory and other sensory information at speed, and slow reaction times; particularly poor memory for heard speech, leading to poor speech comprehension; poor speech pronunciation; and poor number ability. Young children with Down's syndrome are usually sociable and friendly, though frustration and temper tantrums may occur. The child with Down's syndrome is likely to have better visual skills than hearing and speech skills, so they may find it easier to sign or even to read than to acquire intelligible speech. Their level of spontaneous activity is low, and they need extra encouragement to explore, experiment and learn. Programmes designed to develop play and communication at an early age can be helpful. However, the rate of development of children with Down's syndrome often slows down from infancy onwards; adults commonly show a deterioration of mental abilities and sometimes difficult behaviour. On the positive side, home-rearing can sometimes lead to greater IQ gains than institutional rearing, and some people with Down's syndrome do continue intellectual development beyond adolescence (Rauh et al., 1991).

How Behaviour Develops: Nature and Nurture

The genes regulate the production of amino acids and thus determine the first stages in cell growth and differentiation in the body and in the brain and nervous system. They thus are often thought of as providing a blueprint for growth and also for behaviour. The actual course of growth and of behavioural development, however, depends upon, and is influenced by, the external environment. Not only does the environment provide the 'building materials' such as food and water but the particular environmental experiences of the organism also interact with the genetic instructions to determine in detail which exact course of development is followed.

Figure 2.4 depicts in very simple form the interaction of information from the genotype and information from the environment in determining behaviour. Both genotype and environment are obviously essential for any behaviour. Thus, we cannot say that a particular behaviour is genetic and another behaviour environmental; nor can we sensibly say that a behaviour comprises some percentage of each.

The diagram in figure 2.4 is a simple one, and it is elaborated later when we look at social cultural theory (figure 2.10). However, it helps in conceptualizing terms such as 'instinct', 'maturation' and 'learning', and the issue of the rigidity or flexibility of behavioural development.

Although we cannot say that a behaviour is mostly genetic or environmental, we can say that the difference in behaviour between two individuals is mostly genetic or environmental. In humans, for example, differences in eye colour can usually be ascribed to genetic differences (although both genotype and environment are necessary for the development of eye colour); whereas differences in spoken language can usually be ascribed to environmental differences

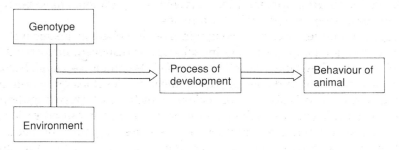

Figure 2.4 Simple model of how both information from the genotype and information from the environment combine and interact to determine the course of behaviour development.

(although both genotype and environment are necessary for the development of language).

Many writers have used the terms 'instinct', 'maturation' and 'learning' in discussing the development of behaviour. There are problems with the definition of these terms, and some psychologists prefer not to use the term 'instinct' at all. However, in order to understand discussion on these matters we need to know what writers who use such terms intend. Representative definitions are given below.

Instinct: Instinctive behaviour is observed in all normal healthy members of a species. Thus, it is little influenced by the environment. The genetic instructions provide detailed information for the development of instinctive behaviour, and only quite general environmental input (such as is necessary for healthy growth) is needed for its expression.

Maturation: Maturation refers to the emergence of instinctive behaviour patterns at a particular point in development. The genetic instructions facilitate the expression of certain behaviour patterns when a certain growth point is reached or a certain time period has elapsed.

Learning: Learning refers to the influence of specific environmental information on behaviour. Within a wide range of variation, the way an animal behaves depends on what it learns from the environment. Thus, individuals of a species may differ considerably in their learnt behaviour patterns.

Issues of instinct, maturation and learning will recur throughout this book. Here, pursuing the evolutionary perspective, we give some examples from animal behaviour.

Bird song: an example of behavioural development

There are many species of songbird, each of which has a characteristic song, or song repertoire, though individuals may differ in the details of their song. We can use the development of bird song in different species to illustrate our discussion of behavioural development. Many ingenious experiments have been performed on this topic (see Thorpe, 1972, for a review).

For some species of bird the song might be described as 'instinctive'. Some birds have been reared experimentally in isolation, or deafened, or fostered by another species, so that they cannot hear the songs of birds of their own kind. In some species, such as doves, hens and song sparrows, the song develops quite normally in such circumstances. This is also true of cuckoos, which are of course regularly reared by foster parents. In such cases there is little environmentally caused variation between healthy individuals and all members of the species sing much the same song.

Even if 'instinctive', however, the song may not appear fully formed. For example, in whitethroats, the male develops its song first as a continuous reiteration of one note, with other notes being added gradually. This occurs whether the bird is isolated, or not. Thus, this is an example of maturation.

The situation is different in chaffinches, whose song was studied intensively by Thorpe (1972). Chaffinches sing a song consisting of three main phrases, followed by a terminal flourish. If a chaffinch is reared in isolation, it will not produce a proper chaffinch song. It will produce a much simpler song, of the right length and frequency but not divided into phrases, and without the terminal flourish. The full song is therefore not instinctive and some more specific environmental input is needed for its development. The song is more complex if chaffinches are reared in groups, but in isolation from adult chaffinches. Presumably, the experience of countersinging with other chaffinches is a helpful environmental input. Even so, the song is not perfect, and only the experience of hearing the adult chaffinch song produces a fully formed song in the young chaffinch. Clearly, learning is important in this species.

However, let us note two constraints on this learning of chaffinch song. One is that the young chaffinch will only learn its song from adult chaffinches. If fostered by another species, it will not learn that species' song. In other words, the type of learning is limited to songs that are within a narrow range characteristic of adult chaffinches. The second point to bear in mind is that this learning can only occur within a certain period. Learning capacity is at its maximum in the first spring, when the bird is 8 months old, and ceases after about 14 months, when the bird's singing behaviour becomes fixed or unalterable.

Chaffinch song provides an excellent example of how genotype and environment interact in constraining development. Some learning occurs in chaffinch song, but it is highly constrained in time and duration. As a result, chaffinch song is stable. Chaffinches introduced into New Zealand in 1862, and South Africa in 1900, still sing very much the same song as European chaffinches.

The situation is different again in other species, where learning of the adult song is much more flexible. In bullfinches, for example, the song is learned and there are few constraints on the type of song; if fostered by canaries, a young bullfinch will adopt canary song and ignore the songs of other bullfinches.

Rigidity and flexibility

As you can see from the bird song example, it can often be rather simplistic to say that a behaviour is either 'instinctive' or 'learned'. Many psychologists now prefer

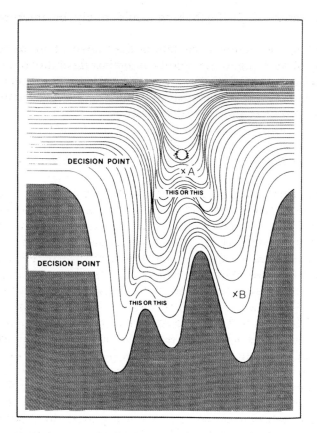

Figure 2.5 Waddington's 'epigenetic landscape' (adapted from Fishbein, 1976).

to talk in terms of the 'rigidity' or 'flexibility' of behaviour, or of how 'modifiable' or 'canalized' behavioural development is. Rigid behaviour is less susceptible to environmental modification, flexible behaviour is more so. In the examples above we can see successive increases in flexibility in the adult song of doves, chaffinches and bullfinches, respectively.

A helpful way of conceptualizing this issue is shown in figure 2.5. This type of figure, produced by Waddington (1957), is called an 'epigenetic landscape'. The ball represents the organism while the landscape represents the possibilities for development constrained by the genotype. The movement of the ball down the slope represents development. The direction of travel (development) is influenced by the shape of the landscape, as it is easier for the ball to roll down the troughs, or canals. However, environmental influences can also influence the direction of travel, pushing the ball in certain directions.

At certain times there are choice or decision points in development, and environmental influences may easily affect the direction of development at such points (for example, the point marked A in figure 2.5). At other times, environmental influence, unless extreme, will have little effect (the point marked B, for instance).

The development of chaffinch song could easily be interpreted within this framework.

Waddington, and others since, talk of the 'canalization' of behaviour. This is another way of referring to the rigidity as against flexibility of behaviour. We talk of canalized behaviour when the troughs or canals in the epigenetic landscape are deep and environmental variations have little effect. If the canals are shallow, the environment produces much greater variation.

Imprinting and the concept of sensitive periods

The concept of imprinting stems from work by the Austrian ethologist Konrad Lorenz. He noted that the young in some species, such as ducks, hens, and deer (called precocial species) learn to follow their mother around very soon after birth. But how do they learn whom to follow? Lorenz discovered that while the following mechanism is highly canalized ('instinctive'), there is some flexibility in learning what (or whom) is to be followed. Generally, the young bird or mammal learns the characteristics of a conspicuous moving object nearby during a period soon after birth or hatching; it then follows this object around. This process of learning which object to follow was described as imprinting. Usually imprinting occurs to the mother, since she is the main figure the offspring encounters during the critical, or sensitive, period after birth. But imprinting to other objects can occur. Lorenz imprinted some ducklings on himself, so that they then followed him everywhere (plate 2.2). This is easy to do with sheep as well (as in the nursery song, where 'everywhere that Mary went, the lamb was sure to go').

Lorenz also introduced the term 'critical period' to describe the restricted period of time in which he believed imprinting took place. In ducklings this period is from about 9 hours to 17 hours after hatching (see figure 2.6). Lorenz also believed that imprinting was irreversible after this period. Subsequent research has suggested that the learning which takes place in imprinting is not quite as rigid as this, but that nevertheless it is the case that such learning occurs most readily within a restricted period. Usually researchers now refer to this as a 'sensitive period'. We have seen another example of a sensitive period already, in the instance of chaffinch song. Another example might be the development of kin recognition in littermates.

Imprinting in which the young learn the characteristics of the parent is known as 'filial imprinting'. It is important in precocial species in order to ensure that the young follow the correct animal (unless an experimenter such as Lorenz intervenes!). Lorenz also believed that at the same time the young learned the characteristics of their species so that they would ultimately choose a member of their own species to mate with. This is called 'sexual imprinting' and the evidence for it is less well established. However, Bateson (1982) has shown that early experience is important for mating preference in Japanese quail. Bateson found that Japanese quail prefer as mating partners other quail that differ in appearance slightly, but not a lot, from quail they were reared with. If quail are reared normally with siblings, then as adults they prefer to mate with cousins, rather than with either siblings or unrelated birds. However, such choices can be altered if

Plate 2.2 Young ducklings 'imprinted' on Konrad Lorenz follow him wherever he goes (from Atkinson, Atkinson and Hilgard, 1981).

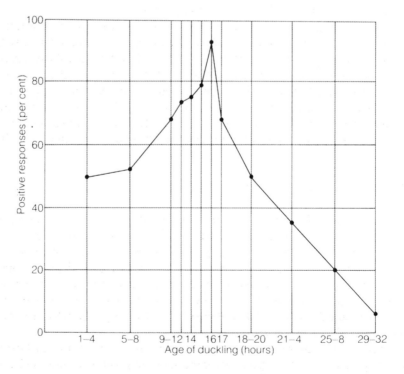

Figure 2.6 Results of an experiment showing that ducklings follow a model more readily 9–17 hours after hatching than at other times.

they are reared with non-sibling quail of different appearance. This species imprinting seems normally to involve learning the appearance of kin, and then later selecting as a mate an individual who would be related, but not too closely, thus achieving a balance between the costs of inbreeding and outbreeding.

Learning processes

Imprinting is often presented as a special form of learning, highly constrained in what is learned and when it is learned. Many forms of learning are more flexible, especially in mammals, though the idea that there are some constraints on learning (some degree of canalization in development, see figure 2.5) seems to apply widely (Hinde and Stevenson-Hinde, 1973). Learning may occur through observation and imitation of others, for example in much bird song acquisition and in the learning of food preferences and tool use in chimpanzees (box 2.1). Some learning occurs through 'trial-and-error'. The degree to which the individual is rewarded or 'reinforced' in its behaviour is also important in learning. For example, rats will learn not to eat food that produces nausea, even if the nausea occurs an hour later (Garcia et al., 1966). In the more advanced mammals, especially the monkeys and apes, it seems as though we are encountering the beginnings of mental activity ('thinking') as we are familiar with it. This involves a kind of internal, symbolic representation of the world in the brain. Thinking consists of the internal manipulation of these symbols.

Some examples of behaviour seen in monkeys certainly suggest this kind of thinking. In species such as macaques and baboons, individuals will sometimes form cliques against a rival (for example, Packer's observations on p. 51); or will give different vocalizations to animals of different social status or relatedness (Seyfarth and Cheney, 1984). It appears as though monkeys are thinking in quite complex ways about their social relationships. This goes along with a relatively larger cerebral cortex in these species. With this sort of brain, behaviour becomes much more flexible, and learning during development much more important.

Communication systems in mammals

Animals often communicate with one another. In communication some sort of signal is sent from one individual to another, which may influence the latter's behaviour. Mammalian calls can be quite complex and sophisticated. A study of ground squirrels in Canada (Davis, 1984) found that they give at least two kinds of alarm call. A short chirp is given in the presence of hawks, and squirrels hearing this immediately run to their burrow. A long whistle is given to weasels, and squirrels then stand erect, watch and flee (they do not go direct to the burrow, as the weasel might follow them in).

Signals used by monkeys and apes seem especially complex (see Seyfarth and Cheney, 1984). For example, vervet monkeys (a ground-living, social species) have three kinds of alarm call, with corresponding responses. 'Leopard alarms' cause other monkeys to run to trees; 'eagle alarms' cause them to look up in the air or

Plate 2.3 Washoe, a young female chimpanzee taught to use sign language, signs 'sweet' for lollipop (left) and 'hat' for woollen cap (on right) (from Atkinson, Atkinson and Hilgard, 1981).

run into bushes; while 'snake alarms' cause monkeys to rise on their hind legs and look into the grass around them. These conclusions, based first on observation, have been confirmed by controlled experiments involving playback of tape-recorded calls. Vervet monkeys also 'grunt' at other monkeys, and the same methods have shown that grunts which sound the same to a human observer, differ in spectrographic analysis according to whether the grunt is directed to a dominant animal, a subordinate animal, or a monkey from another group.

The most dramatic studies of animal communication have been made with captive apes, usually chimpanzees. A husband and wife team, Gardner and Gardner (1969), taught American Sign Language (ASL) to Washoe, a young female chimpanzee who lived with them. Washoe acquired a large number of signs, and could convey messages such as 'please tickle' and 'give drink' (plate 2.3). The Gardners claimed that Washoe could use several signs strung together meaningfully, that she used signs in new situations (e.g., 'water bird' when she first saw a swan), and that altogether Washoe had language competence not dissimilar to that of a 2-year-old human child. Similar methods have been used successfully with other chimpanzees, with a female gorilla called Koko (Patterson, 1978), and with an orang-utan, Princess (Shapiro, 1982).

Other methods have also been used. Premack (1971) taught a female chimpanzee, Sarah, to communicate using plastic shapes, and Savage-Rumbaugh and Rumbaugh (1978) used a computer keyboard to similar effect, teaching Lana (another female chimpanzee) to communicate with the experimenter in verb–object phrases.

Criticisms have been made of these studies, for example that only rote learning is taking place, or that the experimenter, as with 'Clever Hans' (see chapter 1), is giving unintentional cues to the animal as to the right response. Terrace et al. (1979), working with a chimpanzee called Nim, strongly criticized some of the Gardners' more ambitious claims, and the selective way in which they reported their data. The Gardners have defended their position, pointing out that their claims and methods of data reporting are no worse, and often better, than the methods used by those studying child language (Drumm et al., 1986; van Cantfort and Rimpau, 1982).

Human language is much more flexible than any non-human communication system, but it too has a biological underpinning; Steven Pinker's book *The Language Instinct* (1994) strongly expresses this viewpoint. We discuss this perspective, and human language development generally, in chapter 11.

Thinking in primates

Researchers who have studied primates (monkeys and apes) have often been impressed by their thinking abilities; and this is especially true of the great apes, the chimpanzee, the gorilla, and the orang-utan. Studies have been made both in the wild, and in laboratories. An example of a naturalistic study of chimpanzees is provided in box 2.1. Let's look at some examples of advanced intelligence in the great apes:

Tool use and making: Tool use has been observed in a number of species, but tool-making – deliberately altering a natural object to a specific end – was long thought to be uniquely characteristic of humans. However, it has been observed in chimpanzees in natural conditions (see p. 60) and in other great apes in experimental situations. Related to this is an ability to use objects in insightful ways – for example stacking boxes on top of each other to reach an out-of-reach clump of bananas; or using poles as ladders to get over fences.

Pretence: There are some observations of chimpanzees using objects in 'pretend' ways (for a discussion of pretend play in children see chapter 7). A classic example is of a chimpanzee called Viki, home-reared by two psychologists. Viki was observed at times to be acting as if she had an imaginary pull-toy:

> Very slowly and deliberately she was marching around the toilet, trailing the fingertips of one hand on the floor. Now and then she paused, glanced back at the hand, and then resumed her progress . . . she interrupted the sport one day to make a series of tugging motions . . . She moved her hands over and around the plumbing knob in a very mysterious fashion; then placing both fists one above the other in line with the knob, she strained backwards as in tug of war. Eventually there was a little jerk and off she went again, trailing what to my mind could only be an imaginary pull-toy.
>
> (Hayes, 1952)

Self-recognition: Chimpanzees and orang-utans can recognize themselves in a mirror. This has been shown by so-called 'mirror image stimulation' or MIS studies (Gallup, 1982). An animal is first accustomed to a mirror. Then, while anaesthetized, it is marked conspicuously (for example with red dye) on an ear, nose or eyebrow in a way that it cannot see directly. Its reaction on seeing its mirror reflection is noted. Monkeys will reach for the mirror image as if it was another animal. However (after a few days of prior mirror exposure), a chimpanzee or orang-utan will reach for its own body part, strongly suggesting it recognizes itself in the image. Surprisingly, gorillas have not yet been found to have this ability. There has been similar work with children (p. 176).

Learnt symbolic communication: All three species of great ape have been trained to communicate using non-verbal signals (see p. 41); this is at least a rudimentary kind of learnt language. These instances are based on laboratory studies, but there is an example of learnt communication in natural surroundings too. Nishida (1980) has described a 'leaf-clipping display' among wild chimpanzees in Tanzania. A chimpanzee picks several stiff leaves and repeatedly pulls them from side to side between its teeth; this makes a distinctive and conspicuous ripping sound. It is used as possessive behaviour or courtship display by a male to a female, or a female in oestrus to a male. This display has not been seen to be used in this way in other chimpanzee populations, and may be a social custom of this particular group.

Deception: Deception is involved when an individual sends a signal to another individual, who then acts appropriately towards the signal according to its

(a)   (b)

Figure 2.7   Tactical deception in chimpanzees (after Byrne and Whiten, 1987).

obvious meaning, which is, however, untrue. Deception is well-known in many animal species, but is particularly complex in primates. As an example, consider an observation made on chimpanzees by Plooij (in Byrne and Whiten, 1987).

> An adult male (A) was about to eat some bananas that only he knew about, when a second male (T) came into view at the edge of the feeding area. The first quickly walked several metres away from the food, sat down and looked around as though nothing had happened (see figure 2.7a).

Here A is deceiving T by giving signals that 'there is nothing of interest around here' (untrue!). If A looked at the bananas, then T (being more dominant) would take them instead. However, the observation continues:

> The newcomer (T) left the feeding area (see figure 2.7b) but as soon as he was out of sight he hid behind a tree and peered at the male who remained (A). As soon as A approached the food and took it, T returned, displaced the other and ate the bananas.

This is actually counter-deception by the second chimpanzee, who seems to have realized that the first was hiding something!

Deception itself is not necessarily a sign of high intelligence; it depends on what level the deception is at. Mitchell (1986) has described levels of deception:

Level-one deception: describes situations where an animal is programmed to give a deceptive signal, irrespective of circumstances. For example, an insect which is palatable but which mimics in appearance a brightly coloured and inedible wasp.

Level-two deception: is when an animal's signal is still programmed or 'instinc-tive', but is given only in response to certain stimuli. For example, some birds will 'pretend' to be injured when certain predators approach their nest. By feigning a broken wing, for instance, they may distract the predator and lure it away from the eggs or chicks. The display is fairly stereotyped, but only elicited if a predator appears.

Level-three deception: is when the animal's signal can be modified by learn-ing. An example might be a dog, which by limping (even though not injured), gets more petting and attention. This differs from the bird's feigned injury in that it has been learnt in ontogeny as a successful strategy. However, it may be no more than stimulus-response learning of the type 'lifting my paw in a certain way results in my being petted'. Many cases of tactical deception (Whiten and Byrne, 1988) are likely to be of this kind.

Level-four deception: indicates an understanding of deceptive intent, and a flexibility of response, such that the animal deliberately corrects or changes its signals so as to encourage the receiver to act in certain ways. It is as if the animal doing the deceiving knows, and calculates, the effects on the recipient. The chimpanzee examples described above would come at this level.

The evolution of high intelligence

Why has such high intelligence evolved in the primates and especially the great apes? There is a cost to high intelligence – large brains use up more energy for maintenance, and a longer developmental period entails greater risks. So there must be benefits to counterbalance these.

The traditional view has been that high intelligence helps animals cope with the physical environment. Parker and Gibson (1979) suggested that high intelli-gence evolved as a means of better obtaining food. For example, tool use, tool making and imitative learning are all involved in food gathering in chimpanzees (see box 2.1).

An alternative argument is that high intelligence has been selected for because of its advantages in social interaction (Byrne and Whiten, 1988). As we have seen, primates are clever in social contexts – recognizing and deceiving others, forming alliances, achieving dominant status. Being socially clever could have consider-able advantages for an animal's reproductive success. Byrne and Whiten (1987) call this 'Machiavellian intelligence', or tactical deception. The example of the two chimpanzees described above illustrates this high degree of social intelligence.

The evolution of 'mindreading' and of metarepresentations

At these higher levels of intelligence and intentional action, it would seem as though an animal has some idea of what is going on in another animal's mind – it is, as it were, 'mindreading'. Other researchers talk of a 'theory of mind' – implying that an individual can hypothesize about what is going on in another's mind (it might be thinking 'that animal is hungry' or 'that animal is hiding food', for example). Level-four tactical deception is a good indicator of this. Somewhat similar skills can be seen developing in children (see chapters 6 and 14). More generally, mindreading skills, and also the other aspects of high intelligence mentioned previously, can be taken as examples of 'second-order representation', or 'metarepresentation'. A first-order, representation is symbolizing something in your mind – for example an object such as a table, or a banana; or a state such as being hungry. In a second-order or metarepresentation, one or more first-order representations are themselves represented.

For example, in tool-making the first-order representation of the actual action is manipulated relative to the representation of the desired object; this process involves second-order representation. In pretence, the representation of the actual object co-exists with the representation of it as having pretend characteristics (Leslie, 1987). In self-recognition, the representation of the mirror image is related to the representation of one's own self, or body. In symbolic communication, symbols (non-verbal or verbal) stand for or represent other objects or actions. And in level-four deception, the intentionality of deceit implies that the sender can represent both the true and the falsely signalled state of affairs (somewhat analogous to pretence).

Some researchers argue that these abilities all represent a second-order representational capacity which is found in the great apes, and which is also an important aspect of children's development (Suddendorf and Whiten, 2001). Other researchers point out the distinctive differences that remain between the great apes and the human species. Povinelli and Eddy (1996) reported a series of studies on chimpanzees, in which they examined what young chimpanzees (up to 7 years) know about seeing. They trained chimpanzees to gesture for food, and then gave them a choice of two persons to beg from; one could see them, one could not. Could the chimpanzee 'mindread', or at least understand that one person could see their gesture while another was unable to do so?

Plate 2.4 shows one condition in which they succeeded. If one person was facing the chimpanzee and the other had their back to the chimpanzee, the chimpanzee would beg from the person facing them. Not surprising, perhaps! But what was surprising was the failure of the chimpanzees in the other conditions. Here, both persons would face the chimpanzee, but one might be blindfolded; or have a bucket over his/her head. The chimpanzees begged to the blindfolded person, or the person with the bucket over their head, as much as to the other person. In another study, the chimpanzees could not discriminate between two persons with their backs to them, even when one person had his/her head turned round looking over their shoulder at the chimpanzee.

This suggests a lack of mindreading abilities in chimpanzees and pushes us to a more behaviourist interpretation of the anecdotal and naturalistic evidence cited earlier. There are caveats to the work by Povinelli and Eddy. Are the experiments ecologically valid, for example (Smith, 1996)? A chimpanzee persistently begging from someone who is not looking at them might seem stupid, but in the wild it could make sense – another chimpanzee is likely to respond to the grunts or at least see the outstretched hand; who is being stupid, a chimpanzee begging from

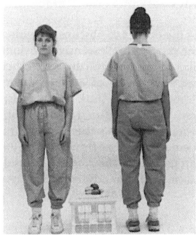

Plate 2.4   (a) The stimulus configuration for bucket probe trials. (b) The stimulus configuration for back-versus-front probe trials.

a person with a bucket over their head, or the person with the bucket over their
head who fails to respond to the begging grunts of the chimpanzee? This general
issue about ecological validity has occurred also with work on children, see
chapter 12. Despite this caveat, other experimental work using non-verbal false
belief tasks have found that apes typically fail them, whereas children typically
pass them by around 4 years of age (Call and Tomasello, 1999).

Suddendorf and Whiten (2001), however, reaffirm the mental achievements
of the great apes, compared to other species. There seems little doubt that
chimpanzees are at least very clever behaviourists – very adept at learning
links between stimulus situations and behaviour, and more so than monkeys. But
maybe they lack the kind of motivation to understand others' mental states that

humans, and even human infants, seem to have. As Tomasello (1996, p. 165) points out, 'in their natural habitats, chimpanzees do not spontaneously point for others to distal entities in their environments, either with or without finger extension. They also do not hold objects up to show them to others, or try to bring others to locations so that they can observe things there, or actively offer objects to other individuals by holding them out to them. Chimpanzees and other apes also do not engage in the intentional teaching of offspring.'

What would happen if chimpanzee infants were raised in a human environment where they *did* receive intentional teaching? There are a number of studies now of such 'human-raised' or 'enculturated' apes – indeed Washoe was an early example. More recent studies have focused more on indices of mindreading and intentionality, such as imitating, and pointing. Tomasello (1999) concludes that enculturated apes do show more human-like skills of social cognition; they are more likely to show deferred imitation of a human action, for example. But there remain differences, and so far it looks as though even human-raised apes lack the motivation for sharing experiences with other intentional beings, which human infants seem to develop in a canalized way.

Tomasello (1999) argues that the crucial difference between apes and humans is that humans understand other individuals as intentional agents like the self. This facilitates joint attention to what others are doing (and intending to do), and imitative learning. This imitative learning is not just at a motor level, but at a representational level, constituting what Tomasello calls cultural learning. This is evident in the way in which children learn words and language, as well as in the way they learn about object use and social conventions, and acquire a theory of mind. All these abilities allow for the accumulation of cultural skills – language, tool use, social conventions – over time, and a true process of cultural evolution to take place in which learnt accomplishments are retained and built upon by future generations.

Evolution and Human Behaviour

Although as humans we are very different from non-human species, we share the basic principles of genetic transmission and the interaction of genes with environment in determining behaviour. We have an evolutionary history, being primates (the taxonomic group including monkeys and the great apes). Our closest animal relatives are the great apes, the chimpanzee, gorilla and orang-utan. We know that early humans, or 'hominids', had become different from the early apes by 5 million years ago. In East Africa scientists such as Richard Leakey and Donald Johanson have unearthed fossil remains of hominids that are 3 to 4 million years old (Johanson and Edey, 1981; Leakey and Lewin, 1977). These very early hominids, called australopithecines, were smaller than us (about 4-foot tall) and had smaller brains, but already walked erect and had moved from the ape habitat of forest to the hominid habitat of open grassland. Over the next few million years fossil remains document the increasing body size and especially brain size of the hominids and their increasing technological and cultural sophistication as evidenced by stone-tool manufacture and later by shelter construction, use of fire and

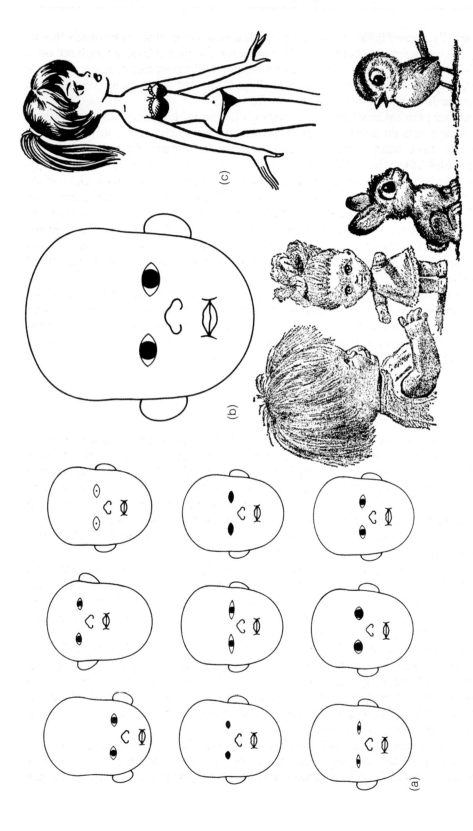

Figure 2.8 (a) Facial stimuli used by Sternglanz et al. (1977); (b) the stimulus noted as most effective; (c) dolls and cartoon animals with similar facial proportions (from Eibl-Eibesfeldt, 1971).

cave art. By some 50,000 years ago early humans were physically much like us today: *Homo sapiens* had arrived. Changes over the past 50,000 years have been largely cultural, not biological, as people learned to domesticate animals, cultivate plants, build cities, pursue the systematic advance of knowledge and develop modern technology.

Does our primate and hominid ancestry tell us anything useful about ourselves now? This has been a very controversial issue. Some scientists studying animal behaviour have tried to make links to human behaviour. Ethologists such as Irenaus Eibl-Eibesfeldt (1971; 1989) developed a field called human ethology, which took ideas such as those of Lorenz and other animal ethologists and applied them to humans. An example of this is an experimental study by Sternglanz et al. (1977) on how the 'cute' facial and bodily appearance of infants elicits caring and parental behaviour. When shown the stimuli in figure 2.8, young adults rated the one shown at (b) as being most attractive. It has quite large eyes and a moderately large forehead. Dolls and 'cute' animals in film cartoons have similar facial proportions (c).

More recently, a deeper understanding of evolutionary theory has led to the development of fields such as human sociobiology, evolutionary psychology, and evolutionary developmental psychology. The last of these is particularly relevant for us. First a brief summary of evolutionary theory, stemming from the work of Charles Darwin in the nineteenth century, will be useful.

Evolutionary theory

Darwin's evolutionary theory was concerned with the ways the characteristics of an animal were selected, over generations, to be especially suited to or 'adapted' for the kind of environment in which it lived. The giraffe's long neck was adapted for feeding on the kinds of leaves and buds found high up on trees and bushes, for example. Although Darwin wrote before modern genetic theory was developed around 1900, the idea of the gene provides a crucial link in modern evolutionary theory. As we saw earlier, the genes code information about development, and they are passed on from parent to offspring.

Giraffes, for example, have genes for long neck growth. In the past, as giraffes were evolving, those individuals which had genes for especially long necks fed better, and thus had more offspring, who themselves were more likely than average to have genes for long necks. Thus, genes for long necks, and actual long necks, came to typify the modern giraffe species.

Behaviour can be selected for during evolution, just as body characteristics can. For example, bird song and communication signals are characteristic of a species and seem to have adaptive value. In considering social behaviour, however, a long-standing controversy has existed about whether we should think of the behaviour as being adaptive for the individual animal, or for the social group it is in, or even for the entire species.

Darwin's approach implied that behaviour should be adaptive for the individual, as the genes that are selected are only passed from parent to offspring. However, it was difficult to explain examples of cooperation and altruism on this

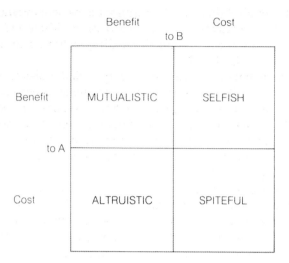

Figure 2.9   Cost and benefit to two animals, A and B, of a social interaction between A and B.

basis. A consideration of figure 2.9 may help explain this. Consider a behaviour by animal A, which affects animal B. The behaviour might have a benefit or a cost to A, and a benefit or cost to B. We measure benefits and costs in terms of how the behaviour increases the chances of surviving and rearing offspring. Animal A's behaviour could be mutualistic, selfish, altruistic or spiteful, according to this framework. Now, if we argue that behaviour is selected for individual benefits, then we should only expect behaviour in the top two cells in figure 2.9. We would not expect altruistic behaviour, and yet this does occur (e.g. communal suckling; communal defence of young).

The predominant response to this, until about 30 years ago, was to argue that behaviour was selected for the good of the whole social group, or species. The difficulty with this approach, appealing as it may seem, is that it predicts only behaviour in the left-hand cells of figure 2.9. No selfish behaviour is expected. Yet, selfish behaviour is also common (e.g., failure to defend others or nurse others' young; aggression over territory and mating rights).

Sociobiological theory provides a solution. It predicts the mixture of mutualistic, altruistic and selfish behaviour that we actually observe in animal societies. The key idea, put forward by Hamilton (1964), is that of 'kin selection'. This is the hypothesis that an animal will behave altruistically towards its kin, especially those closely related. This was always taken for granted for an individual's offspring, as it was only through offspring that genes were directly passed on. Hamilton's insight was that an animal would share a greater than average proportion of genes with relatives too, especially close relatives such as siblings and cousins. Helping relatives is another way in which particular genes get passed on to the next generation, admittedly only an indirect way compared with having offspring oneself.

Kin selection theory then predicts that helpful or altruistic behaviour may be directed towards relatives, provided that it is not too harmful to the animal giving the help, and provided that the other animal is closely enough related to make it worthwhile. Close relatives will be helped more. Much evidence supports this theory. Examples include communal suckling in lions and elephants, and communal defence; see also box 2.1.

Another prediction of kin selection theory is that males will only assist females and offspring if it is likely that they are the genetic father (or close relative). The likelihood that a male is the genetic father is referred to as *paternity certainty*. Paternity certainty will be higher in monogamous species, and it is indeed in such species that males help most in rearing the young (e.g., many nesting birds; a few mammals such as hunting dogs, marmosets). For implications of this for human behaviour, see pp. 74 and 126.

In an interesting extension of kin selection theory, Trivers (1974) postulated that we should expect to see *parent–offspring conflict*. This is because the genetic interests of parent and offspring are not identical. The mother is related to all her offspring equally, and would be selected (other things being equal) to provide each with the same amount of parental investment or help. However, an individual offspring would be selected to favour itself over its siblings, with whom it shares only half its genes; thus, according to Trivers, it should seek more than its fair share of parental investment. This should lead to conflict with the mother, over the amount and duration of parental investment, and also to conflict with siblings, or sibling rivalry. Since Trivers wrote his article, there have been many observations of parent–offspring and sibling conflict in animals. In mammals, suckling is a very important form of parental investment by the mother. In many species, the infant seems to try to continue suckling for longer than the mother wishes; the mother may reject the attempts of older infants to suckle, quite forcefully. Siblings may also compete with each other for access to the mother, in feeding situations.

There is more to sociobiology than just kin selection, however. Another way of explaining altruistic behaviour is through what is called 'reciprocal altruism' (Trivers, 1971). The hypothesis is that one individual will help another, at some smaller cost to itself, if it can expect similar help back from the other animal in the future. This is the old adage 'if you scratch my back, I'll scratch yours.' There is some evidence of reciprocal altruism, the most convincing being in monkeys and apes where it is clear that individuals do recognize each other and could thus stop helping individuals who failed to reciprocate ('cheats'). In a study of baboons, Packer (1977) found that pairs of unrelated males would help each other in challenging a dominant male. Individuals that gave such help to a particular male often received help back from the same male. As the males were unrelated, kin selection could not explain this.

Sociobiology and human behaviour

Sociobiology has become the prevailing theoretical paradigm for explaining why animals behave towards others in the way they do, in terms of the evolutionary advantages of such behaviour. Sociobiologists such as E. O. Wilson (1978) wondered whether human behaviour, like animal behaviour, seems to maximize the survival and reproductive success of individuals. For example, do the predictions of kin selection apply to humans? It does seem to be the case that people are most generous or altruistic to close kin, even when it is not socially sanctioned. In agricultural and tribal societies (i.e., people not yet living in large cities) kinship is a very important organizing framework, affecting expectations about whom you shall marry as well as expectations for help and alliance in warfare. Young children experience a greater risk of abuse or maltreatment with step-parents compared to natural parents, and this has had an explanation based on kin selection theory (Daly and Wilson, 1996; see chapter 4).

There are other parallels to be drawn. For example, almost all human societies are either monogamous or polygynous (though a few tribes are polyandrous, notably in Sri Lanka and Tibet). Sociobiology can explain this, especially when it is also noted that monogamous societies tend to be those where fathers can help directly in child-rearing, whereas in polygynous societies men compete for status, for example by acquiring wealth or cattle, and do little to help their wives directly. As another example, what seem to be characteristic sex differences in men and women, for example in abilities, in aggression and in attitudes to sexual behaviour, have been given a sociobiological explanation (Buss and Schmitt, 1993; Symons, 1979; Wilson, 1978).

The field of evolutionary psychology takes many of the arguments of these sociobiologists, and argues that our present-day psychology – the way we think, feel emotions, and act – can be explained by our evolutionary history. Specifically, these theorists argue that our hominid ancestors evolved for some millions of years in a nomadic hunter-gatherer environment and social organization, and that we have evolved psychological mechanisms that reflect these; as an example, males are better at complex spatial orientation tasks (which might have been useful in tracking and hunting animals), whereas females are better at remembering locations of objects (which might have been useful in remembering where to find and gather plant foods) (Eals and Silverman, 1994). Evolutionary psychologists generally argue that these adaptations are strongly genetically influenced in their development, and represent modularized capacities in the human brain.

Evolutionary developmental psychology

The new discipline of evolutionary developmental psychology applies many of these ideas from evolutionary theory, to studying human development and especially child development. In doing so, it tends to be less dogmatic about the strength of genetic influence and of modular organization of the brain, and to assume that there is a complex interaction of genetic and environmental factors in development (Bjorklund and Pellegrini, 2000; Geary and Bjorklund, 2000).

These theorists argue that many features of childhood prepare the way for adulthood; an example is sex differences in play (see also chapter 7). Boys engage in more vigorous rough-and-tumble play than girls, and this is seen as a preparation for adult hunting and fighting skills, and/or dominance assertion. Girls are described as engaging in more play parenting (e.g., doll play). The sex difference in physical aggression (boys doing more) is also seen as having adaptive value, as males invest less in offspring and more in mating competition.

However some aspects of development are seen as adaptive at that time, rather than a preparation for later. An example is the tendency for young children to over-estimate their competence on a wide range of tasks, which may facilitate their persistence at the task and increase what they learn.

Generally, evolutionary theorists see behaviour as adaptive. However, the reference point for this adaptation is taken as our ancestral environment – what is sometimes called the 'environment of evolutionary adaptedness'. This concept can be a bit nebulous, but is generally taken as being a kind of hunter-gatherer existence. Certainly, settled agricultural and urban life is seen as different from this. As a consequence, some of our developmental adaptations are *not* well adapted to contemporary living.

One example of this is that children love sweets. This is bad for their teeth, and not especially healthy. However in hunter-gatherer environments, taking in energy rich food such as honey when occasionally available, would be adaptive. As another example, formal schooling is a new cultural invention; it may be that attention deficit/hyperactivity disorder (ADHD), to which much attention has been given in recent years, represents a pattern of high motor activity and attention switching which might have been quite adaptive in the environment of evolutionary adaptiveness, but which is not when formal schooling becomes a universal requirement.

Criticisms of the evolutionary approach

Some scientists believe that even to attempt evolutionary explanations is misplaced, because of the dangers of, for example, making sex differences seem natural and inevitable. These scientists believe that the flexibility of human learning is so great that nothing useful is learnt from evolutionary theorizing (e.g., Rose et al., 1984). Evolutionary explanations are criticized as 'just so' stories, made up but not really testable. At times the debate has become more personal than scientific.

A problem for evolutionary thinking is that human behaviour seems to be of an order of magnitude more flexible even than that of other advanced mammals. There are enormous cultural variations in the behaviour of people in different societies: for example in the language spoken, technology used, moral or religious beliefs held, and methods of child-rearing used. These are learned variations. A Chinese baby brought up in China learns Chinese, and Chinese manners; brought up in the USA, it learns American English and American manners. In addition to this flexibility of learning, humans can cumulatively pass on and build up knowledge and beliefs through cultural traditions (e.g., the development of the idea of democracy; the development of electronic and computer technology).

It may, however, be justified to think of some human behaviour development as reasonably canalized. Thus, the development of human language, from babbling to one-word utterances to syntax, may be fairly strongly canalized (see chapter 11), whereas the actual language learned is weakly canalized, if at all.

Probably some sex differences are somewhat canalized, such that they will develop unless positive steps are taken to prevent them, whereas other sex differences may not be canalized at all and could easily be changed. This at least is a language of reasoned debate. The metaphor of canalization, or of the modifiability of behaviour, enables us to consider the possibility of there being some limited links to our evolutionary past, without having to defend the innateness, desirability or complete inevitability of certain human characteristics.

Culture and Development

Anthropologists have long been impressed by the varieties of child-rearing customs, and the variations in human behaviour, between cultures. In the early decades of the nineteenth century, anthropologists such as Margaret Mead and Ruth Benedict emphasized how these different 'patterns of culture' would mould a child: 'from the moment of his birth the customs into which he is born shape his experience and behavior' (Benedict, 1934, p. 2). Mead (who also trained as a child psychologist) did admit some influence of an infant's temperament on development, but generally the view of these authors (and most anthropologists) was that biology had little to say about development within a culture. A particular example in relation to adolescent development is discussed in chapter 9.

The 'culture and personality' school of anthropology followed the work of Benedict, Mead and others in particular societies, by trying to draw more generalized explanations about cultural variability. For example Barry et al. (1959) related the subsistence nature of a society to its childhood socialization practices (see also p. 189). For example, agricultural and peasant societies seemed to put particular value on obedience and conformity in children. The 'Six Cultures Study' (Whiting and Edwards, 1988; and see pp. 189, 255) made very detailed observations in six different societies, with the premise that parents' daily routines would mediate between the organization of a society and its subsistence practices, and the child's socialization environment. Parental practices such as sleeping arrangements, warmth from and control by mothers, extent and nature of father's involvement with infants, extent of caregiving by older siblings, chores given to young children, were all seen as both influenced by the nature of the society, and in turn directing the child's development. As an example, children assigned to take care of younger siblings (as in Kenya) learnt more nurturant behaviour; whereas those who spent more time with peers (as in their USA sample) learnt more competitive and attention-seeking behaviours.

Cultural–ecological models

Several anthropologists have developed more sophisticated models linking culture and ecology to development, building on the earlier decades of work in anthropology and incorporating advances in psychology and other disciplines.

Michael Cole has been influential in promoting the argument that changes in psychological perspectives on *cognition* have led to a more contextualized

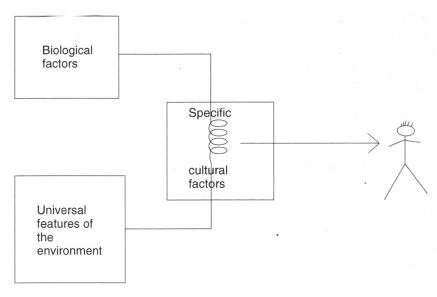

Figure 2.10   Cole's cultural context model of development (adapted from Cole, 1992).

approach to the study of development and a shift of emphasis in the study of socialization away from specific child-rearing practices to the wider context in which children learn about culturally appropriate behaviour. Cole is well known for investigating the cultural–historical claims of Vygotsky about cross-cultural differences in mental makeup (Cole et al., 1971; Cole and Scribner, 1978). On the basis of his research in this field, in particular his research on Vygotsky's concept of the zone of proximal development or ZPD (see chapter 15), he challenged traditional individualistic views in psychology about mental development, arguing instead that cognitive functioning is linked to its *sociocultural* context and that children learn through a form of apprenticeship with adults.

The norms of one culture can differ extensively from those of another and so radically affect the ways in which children learn. For example, one culture may place high value on individual achievement where another may stress the achievements of the group. In one culture it is desirable to be competitive; in another competitiveness may meet with disapproval. Such interaction with adults and more competent peers is, from the Vygotskian perspective, the foundation on which all children's learning occurs. This argument states that children's learning occurs through the particular demands of a task rather than as a general function of the culture. The key to understanding how cognitive development takes place lies in the 'activity settings' in which learners operate; for example, children's experience in an instructional context such as a school setting, results in a particular kind of discourse. A diagram illustrating Cole's view (a variant of figure 2.4) is shown in figure 2.10.

This research was pioneering in leading psychologists to consider more deeply the relationship between culture and learning, and it challenged the widespread view at the time that non-literate peoples in less developed countries were less intelligent than Western people, or that some cultures did not push young people far enough (as, for example, schooling does) so that their cognitive structures operated at a lower level. Cole's view is that children can be viewed as novice participants in their culture and that their induction into the culture is achieved through shared joint activity. As they come to understand objects and relationships they re-create their culture within themselves. In particular, Cole and Scribner's research undermined the view that a psychologist could administer cognitive tests that had been developed in one culture in order to measure the abilities of people in another culture. Within Western societies, this principle has frequently been applied to 'culturally disadvantaged children' (see chapter 17) to explain their relative underachievement in comparison with more privileged groups.

Rogoff and her colleagues (1995) take the perspective that individual development is inseparable from interpersonal and community processes and that individuals' changing roles are mutually defined with those of other people and with dynamic cultural processes. The process is two-way: 'When individuals participate in shared endeavors, not only does individual development occur, but the process transforms (develops) the practices of the community' (Rogoff et al., 1995, pp. 45–6). To illustrate this sociocultural model, Rogoff and her colleagues investigated historical changes in the practice of Girl Scout cookie sales in the USA to demonstrate how generations of Girl Scouts and cookie companies have contributed to the ongoing, developing community processes involved in that practice (see box 2.2).

Looking generally at social and cognitive aspects of child development in different cultures, Super and Harkness (1997) have proposed the concept of a *developmental niche*. The developmental niche 'conceptualizes both the child and the environment as active and interactive systems' (Harkness, 2002). The child is seen as bringing its own temperament, as well as species-specific potentials, to the developmental niche provided by its culture. The niche itself is divided into three major components or subsystems:

1 *The physical and social settings of the child's daily life* [for example, what sort of living space or house is the child in, does she have her own bedroom];
2 *Culturally regulated customs of child care and rearing* [for example, scheduling of activities such as children's clubs or TV programmes]; and
3 *The psychology of the caretakers, especially their belief systems or 'ethnotheories'* [for example, do parents believe that a regular and restful sleep schedule is vital for healthy development].

These three subsystems are seen as homeostatically coordinated; parents tend to feel comfortable if their own developmental theories and belief systems accord with cultural customs; cultural customs conform to physical and social settings; and all are generally functionally embedded in the larger ecology.

These modern anthropological perspectives on child development do strongly emphasize the importance of culture. Examples of cultural differences are taken up in several places in this book, for example relating to attachment security (pp. 96–7) and sex roles (p. 189). Nevertheless researchers such as Cole, and Super and Harkness, do not ignore or disparage genetic or biological factors as having a role to play, both through individual child temperament, and through universal features of our genetic endowment.

Social Constructionist Approaches

Some theorists have chosen to explore childhood itself as a social construction, in effect discounting significant biological or genetic influences. Such an approach is often linked to sociological frames of discourse. Social constructionists argue that, whereas developmental psychologists distinguish between children and adults and have often focused on the child's relative lesser ability in a range of domains, in fact there is nothing 'natural' about childhood; childhood is a social construct that has more to do with how people define it. People's attitudes towards childhood are influenced by the dominant belief systems of the society in which they are located and so will vary across time and culture. We can only begin to understand our views of childhood if we take account of our own position in a particular social, political and cultural context. For example, in some societies it is taken as given that adults have rights over children, whereas in contemporary Western society political debate focuses more on the tensions between the rights of children to protection and their rights to participation and self-determination.

James and Prout (1990) are two sociologists who have argued for a new paradigm in thinking about children's development. They state (1990, pp. 8–9) the following key features of the paradigm:

1   Childhood is understood as a social construction. As such it provides an interpretive frame for contextualizing the early years of human life. Childhood, as distinct from biological immaturity, is neither a natural nor a universal feature of human groups but appears as a specific structural and cultural component of many societies.
2   Childhood is a variable of social analysis. It can never be entirely divorced from other variables such as class, gender and ethnicity. Comparative and cross-cultural analysis reveals a variety of childhoods rather than a single or universal phenomenon.
3   Children's social relationships and cultures are worthy of study in their own right, independent of the perspective and concern of adults.
4   Children are, and must be seen as, active in the construction and determination of their own social lives, the lives of those around them and of the societies in which they live. Children are not just passive subjects of social structures and processes.
5   Ethnography is a particularly useful methodology for the study of childhood. It allows children a more direct voice and participation in the production of sociological data than is possible through experimental or survey styles of research.
6   Childhood is a phenomenon in relation to which the double hermeneutic of the social sciences is acutely present. That is to say, to proclaim a new paradigm of childhood sociology is also to engage in and respond to the process of reconstructing childhood.

Most developmental psychologists would have little problem with features (3) and (4) above, which simply reflect all recent thinking on the topic. Features (1) especially, and (2), emphasize the core social constructionist belief, that childhood is specific to particular social or cultural conditions and does not have natural or universal features – a viewpoint at odds with the interactionist views of most developmental psychologists or, for example, figure 2.10. Feature (5) emphasizes one particular methodological approach. Feature (6) refers to the possibility of reconstructing (and first, deconstructing) childhood.

Deconstructing developmental psychology

Influenced by social constructionism and also feminist theory, some psychologists and sociologists (e.g., Burman, 1994; Singer, 1992) have challenged the ideas that underpin mainstream developmental psychology. Burman claims to 'deconstruct' developmental psychology by scrutinizing the moral and political themes that are dominant in current frameworks in order to look beyond them and explore where they fit into the social practices in which psychology functions. In this sense, she addresses the 'discourses' (that is, the socially organized frameworks of meaning) that define the domains of concern to the developmental psychologist. The social constructionist argues that these discourses do not represent reality – they actually create it.

The kinds of questions posed by these writers include: 'Why is developmental psychology about the child?' and 'Would it be different if developmental psychologists focused on the contexts in which people grow?' In particular they challenge assumptions about parenting. A key theme in this perspective concerns the ideological assumptions inherent in selecting child and mother as a focus for research since this could more accurately be perceived as reflecting 'the widespread and routine subjection of women to the developmental psychological gaze' (Burman, 1994, p. 4). Such a focus, Burman argues, results in 'individualistic' interpretations of socially constructed phenomena, often leading to blame of women for failing to mother their children adequately.

This perspective, in contrast to traditional models of developmental psychology, focuses less on the individual than on the interpersonal, cultural, historical and political contexts in which constructions of childhood are situated. In other words, these writers problematize the very nature of the research carried out by mainstream developmental psychologists by asserting that, since each person is positioned within a discourse of history, politics, gender and culture, it is impossible to take a detached, objective stance.

To illustrate, Singer (1992) points out that Bowlby's (1953) research on maternal deprivation (see chapter 4) was highly influential at a time when men (for example in the UK) were returning from World War II to reclaim the jobs that had effectively been carried out by women. The nurseries that had proliferated in the early 1940s to enable women to work for the war effort largely closed down and mothers were advised that it was in their child's interest to stay at home to provide the nurture that was essential for their children's healthy emotional growth. At a stroke, women were consigned to the home during the early years of their children's development. If the mother failed to provide loving care and support, then she was responsible for any later behavioural or emotional difficulties that might arise. As Burman (1994, p. 80) writes: 'Maternal presence therefore functions as the essential feature in the maintenance of the social-political order.'

Most developmental psychologists see some virtue in taking account of the social context but many would not go as far as the social constructionists in redefining their discipline. Nor would they accept such radical undermining of their capacity to carry out objective studies of, for example, the relationships between children and their parents. Nevertheless, the questions posed by social constructionists about the concept of childhood are challenging and open up critical debates about the position of, for example, children and women in society.

Further Reading

For a readable account of behaviour genetics with special relevance to human behaviour, see Plomin, R., DeFries, J. C., McClearn, G. E. and Rutter, M. 1997: *Behavioral Genetics: A Primer* (3rd edn). New York: W. H. Freeman. Twin studies are described by Wright, L. 1999: *Twins: Genes, Environment and the Mystery of Identity*. London: Wiley; and by Segal, N. 2000: *Entwined Lives: Twins and What They Tell Us About Human Behavior*. New York: Plume.

The work on chimpanzees described in box 2.1 can also be found in van Lawick-Goodall, J. 1971: *In the Shadow of Man*. Glasgow: Collins. A general account of how useful it is to apply animal models to human development is provided by Archer, J. 1992: *Ethology and Human Development*. Hemel Hempstead: Harvester Wheatsheaf. Byrne, R. 1995: *The Thinking Ape: Evolutionary Origins of Intelligence*. Oxford: Oxford University Press, covers many aspects of ape cognition and has two specific chapters on theory of mind research with non-human primates; another good chapter on this topic is in Mitchell, P. 1997: *Introduction to Theory of Mind*. London: Arnold. Bjorklund, D. F. and Pellegrini, A. D. 2002: *The Origins of Human Nature: Evolutionary Developmental Psychology*. Washington: APA Books, describes this new area of theorizing.

For cultural views of childhood see Cole, M. 1996: *Cultural Psychology: A Once and Future Discipline*. Cambridge, MA: Harvard University Press. For sociological/social constructionist perspectives, see James, A. and Prout, A. 1990: *Constructing and Reconstructing Childhood*. Basingstoke: Falmer. A feminist perspective can be found in Burman, E. 1994: *Deconstructing Developmental Psychology*. London: Routledge.

Discussion Points

1 How relevant is behaviour genetics for understanding human behaviour?
2 What is meant by 'canalization' and is it a useful metaphor?
3 Can chimpanzees engage in mindreading?
4 What is meant by evolutionary developmental psychology?
5 Are ideas of social constructionism and social cultural theory, antithetical to those of behaviour genetics and evolutionary psychology?

Box 2.1
The behaviour of free-living chimpanzees in the Gombe Stream Reserve

This study concerns the behaviour of chimpanzees in their natural habitat. Jane Goodall spent 5 years observing chimpanzees in the Gombe Stream area of Tanzania, in Africa. She spent much time approaching and following groups of chimpanzees, and letting them get used to her presence. She then made systematic observations and notes about what she observed. She established a base camp and at later stages in the project put out bananas at a feeding area near the camp to attract the chimpanzees and make observations easier.

She found that chimpanzees moved around singly or in small groups, looking for food such as fruits and leaves within a large home-range area. Group composition varied. Infants (0–3 years) were carried by their mothers or followed them closely, and juveniles (3–7 years) usually travelled with their mothers as well. Subadults (8–12 years) and adults (12 up to around 40 years), however, seemed to join up or disperse quite freely. Chimpanzees live in forested areas and move around both on the ground and in trees. At night, they sleep in nests made from tree branches.

The newborn infant is dependent on its mother for food, transport and protection, but after 6 months or so begins to crawl around on its own while staying in the mother's vicinity. Soon it engages in play, with mother, siblings and peers – tickling, wrestling and chasing play. Infants and juveniles watch and imitate when they see mother obtaining food, or making tree nests, and this is hypothesized to be important for their own acquisition of these skills. When the juvenile becomes a subadult, the frequency of play decreases and mutual grooming increases (box plate 2.1.1). Later observations have established that subadult females often leave their home range and

may join a more distant group. Males, however, usually stay in the home range they were born in. Although older males do not stay with the mother all the time, they may still associate with her frequently. An older sibling may 'adopt' and care for an infant sibling if the mother dies.

There is a dominance hierarchy among the mature chimpanzees within a local group. Though most interactions are peaceful and friendly, long-term observations have shown how, at certain times, the dominance order is challenged and considerable conflict may ensue. Goodall and her co-workers documented how a 20-year-old chimpanzee called Figan came to dominate a 22-year-old, Evered, who was his main rival for being the most dominant, or alpha, male. Figan sought out fights with Evered when circumstances favoured him – especially when he was with his brother, Faben. Faben, a 25-year-old, had a paralysed right arm; he thus was not a serious contender for alpha male himself, but could help his brother. This example illustrates both the importance of dominance for individuals and the way kinship (in this case, a sibling tie) can persist into adulthood. Dominance conflicts are usually between males, and the main benefit of being the alpha male is probably increased opportunity to mate with females.

Goodall's observations also revealed several instances of tool use in chimpanzees, and the first records of actual tool making in a non-human species. Examples of tool use are: leaves for wiping the body; rocks to crack nuts; sticks to prise open the banana boxes; sticks and stones for throwing at baboons or other animals. Two examples of tool making were documented; each involves some deliberate change in a tool to make it more suitable for its purpose. In one

Box Plate 2.1.1 Chimpanzees grooming.

Box Plate 2.1.2 A chimpanzee pokes a twig into a termite nest.

the chimpanzee wishes to drink water out of a crack or hollow. It gets some leaves, chews them in its mouth to make a spongy wad, then uses this to soak up the water and puts it back in its mouth again. In the other, the chimpanzee wishes to eat termites. This is difficult because they are in a termite nest, but it obtains them by poking slender branches or twigs down the entrance holes to the nest, pulling out the twigs with termites attached and licking them off (box plate 2.1.2). Chimpanzees prepare twigs for this by picking suitable small branches and breaking off the accessory stems, which can be inserted readily (this is watched with fascination by younger chimpanzees, who then imitate the process).

Although primarily vegetarian, chimpanzees will eat insects (such as termites), birds' eggs, and will even hunt and kill small mammals such as young bushpigs or baby baboons. Several chimpanzees may co-operate in such a hunt. The kill is divided up rapidly among them, and other chimpanzees may then come up and form 'sharing clusters' around them, requesting a portion of the food.

Goodall's observations provided the first really substantial data on the natural behaviour of chimpanzees. Later research broadly confirmed her findings, with some minor changes. Territorial behaviour between local groups of chimpanzees has now been established, with some violent conflicts between groups and occasional instances of cannibalism. Further instances of tool use and tool-making have been found, with indications of 'cultural' differences among chimpanzees living in different parts of Africa.

This study did not have any prior hypothesis. It is thus not an experiment and there are no dependent or independent variables. It is an observational study, designed to obtain basic data. Studies of a species based on observation in its natural habitat are often called 'ethological studies', and this is an example. Such studies can discover things not expected, such as chimpanzee tool-making. However, they cannot establish cause and effect. The hypothesis that infants watching adults leads to learning, for example, would benefit from some more experimental confirmation. Ethological observation is also difficult and time-consuming – this is why Goodall started putting out bananas, even at the risk of changing the animals' behaviour.

Based on material in Lawick-Goodall, J. Van, 1968: *Animal Behaviour Monographs*, 1(8), 161–311.

Box 2.2
Development through participation in sociocultural activity

This study illustrated how the community practice of Girl Scout cookie sales developed through the contributions of individuals and groups, and how transformations in the practice related to historical changes in other institutions, such as family structure and maternal employment.

In 1990, the time of the study, Girl Scouts of America, a voluntary organization dedicated to girls' moral education, development at home, academic and outdoor skills and career preparation, had an annual fund-raising event centred on the sale of cookies. The average Scout troop raised $420; nationwide revenues were $400 million. Cookie sales were considered to be an educational tool to teach the girls social responsibility, goal setting and business principles.

This highly organized nation-wide annual event had evolved from much simpler, informal sales of home-baked cakes for local fund-raising in the early years of the Girl Scout movement in the 1930s. Many Scouts had mothers or older sisters who had in their time participated in a similar event. Older customers were often eager to buy since it reminded them of their own experience as Girl Scouts years before. (If members of the community were not invited to buy, they were often offended at being left out.) By the 1990s, large baking companies were licensed by Girl Scouts of America to supply the cookies and to deliver orders to a deadline. The administration of the cookie sales had expanded on a regional basis and had developed over time from a simple system of tear-off order stubs to an elaborate system of colour-coded order forms and sales training information. The administrative forms supplied to the participating Scouts were not adapted to be easy for children to use but were retail forms similar to those used by adult sales persons. The layout of the 1990s official form designed by the Girl Scout organization required the girls to calculate amounts of money, present colour-coded information to customers that identified seven different types of cookie, and administer a system for tracking colour-coded deliveries as they arrived at the regional centre for collection by individual Scouts. Understandably, new aspects of the activity that had not been deemed to be necessary in the 1930s had evolved. There was now an elaborate training course for Scouts and the organization was required to send out letters of advice and informed consent to the parents.

The researchers used observational methods and interviews with a small sample consisting of one troop of Girl Scouts, and also researched the history of the movement since its origins by consulting the organization's archives. Their aim was to investigate the processes of guided participation through which the Girl Scouts gained mastery of a complex set of skills. They were also interested to find out how an analysis of individual development requires the researcher to refer to other planes of analysis such as the group and the wider community. The children involved in the activity of cookie sales were learning to solve complex problems that had been defined and organized by their community. At the same time, the changes in the children's roles and understanding extended to their efforts in similar activities in the future,

and so contributed to transformation of the activities in which they participated. For example, the girls in the study began to use and extend cultural tools for calculating and keeping track of customer orders. These cultural tools tied their efforts in to practices in other institutions of their culture, including the number system used in the community and the calculation box used on the order form provided by their organization. Their means of handling the problems of sales and delivery involved using tools borrowed from others, for example using elastic bands to bundle together orders or Post-its to identify customer addresses. In making calculations, the girls would use tools borrowed from teachers or parents, for example, for larger orders, considering that a box of cookies might cost one quarter of $10 rather than multiplying each unit price of $2.50.

Rogoff and her colleagues observed that the girls' roles changed as they became sales persons. There were commonalities among the girls, for example transformations in confidence and a growing identity as cookie sellers. There were also differences that often related to the extent and degree of help that the girls received from others, including parents, troop leaders, customers and siblings. The family circumstances of the girls differed and these differences had an impact on their adoption of the main responsibility for the role of seller. One girl struggled with the primary responsibility herself; others worked in pairs; still others allowed their families to organize the sales for them. Rogoff calls this a process of *guided participation*. Each girl had to coordinate her individual efforts with guidance from other participants; at the group level, she was guided through materials and practices developed over decades by previous Scouts, leaders and customers. There were also links with other systems, such as family structure. Let's look at two case studies to illustrate.

Darlene's parents were divorced, her mother worked long hours and she spent much of her time after school alone by herself. Darlene treated sales as primarily her own responsibility and asked many anxious questions about potential problems at the weekly training meetings. As a result, initially she found it very difficult to work up confidence to approach potential customers, to organize orders and manage deliveries to the deadline. The researchers observed, however, that members of the community played a guiding role in inducting her into the practice of selling cookies. One customer, recognizing Darlene's shyness, invited Darlene to practise her sales skills on her roommates. This encouraged Darlene to practice her sales manner on her mother and stepfather. Another customer helped her to fill out the complex form. With practice, Darlene became a skilled salesperson. She learned to communicate knowledge of her product, used the order form effectively, and adjusted her sales pitch to each customer. However, she found it very difficult to coordinate money collection and product delivery, ended up by collecting too much money, and had to spend time on her own recalculating all her orders in order to track the errors.

By contrast, Carla depended heavily on the leadership of family members. Both her sister and her mother, each of whom had been a Girl Scout, called their friends in advance to let them know that Carla was on her way to sell cookies. Family members also helped her to carry out calculations so that the day's orders tallied correctly, and even did some of the door-to-door selling for her. Carla's mother administered all the names of customers, matched them to the colour-coded boxes as they arrived from the company, and then telephoned customers to tell them that their order was ready for delivery. Not surprisingly, Carla was the first Girl Scout to submit all her money, correctly tallied.

In each case, the girls, new to cookie selling, changed in the process of participating with others to become more expert than they had been before in making sales, planning orders, calculating income and organizing deliveries. They did not simply acquire these skills. Rather, they went through a process of personal transformation. Their experience of shared endeavours varied from person to person, as the two case studies show, but each girl participated in and contributed to, intellectual and economic institutions and traditions of their society with associated cultural values, such as efficiency and honesty. In turn, these individual efforts, along with the thousands of similar individual efforts throughout the USA, would influence the historically changing institution of the Girl Scout movement.

By looking at development from the sociocultural perspective the researchers challenged the idea of a boundary between internal knowledge (such as knowledge of arithmetic) and external phenomena (for example, the availability of order forms listing price information). Rather, the individual develops through participation in an activity and changes in ways that contribute both to the ongoing event (in this case the sale of cookies) and to the person's preparation for involvement in other similar events in the future. Unlike Goodall's research in the Gombe Stream Reserve, this study was based on a prior hypothesis about how individuals learn through guided participation. The researchers used methods similar to those adopted by anthropologists. They were already involved as 'cookie chairs' in their local Girl Scout troop, which gave them easy access to data and gave them a naturalistic role in this particular activity. The study relied on participant observation, interviews and examination of archival records and used these qualitative methods to confirm the prediction. Although the sample was small, involving only selected girls from the troop, it provides an example of real life research grounded in authentic cultural practices.

Based on material in Rogoff, B., Baker-Sennett, J., Lacasa, P. and Goldsmith, D. 1995: In J. J. Goodnow, P. J. Miller and F. Kessel (eds), *Cultural Practices as Contexts for Development. New Directions for Child Development*, 67, Spring. San Francisco: Jossey-Bass Publishers, pp. 45–65.

PART TWO The Social World of the Child

3 Prenatal Development and Birth

In this chapter, we examine the process from conception to birth, a period when genetic determination of development is at its strongest. We look at risk factors in development – prenatal, perinatal and psychosocial. We describe the birth process, and consider the particular situation of babies born prematurely.

The newborn baby has a lot to find out about the social world, and we discuss some of the ways in which the baby, and his or her caregivers, contribute to this during the first months of life.

From Conception to Birth

This period of about nine months (a full-term birth is at about 38 weeks from conception) constitutes the first stage in human development – itself divided into three substages, illustrated in figure 3.1.

Germinal stage

The baby is conceived when a sperm cell from the father unites with an egg cell or ovum from the mother. The fertilized egg is called a *zygote*. The zygote starts dividing, and dividing again, with cells rapidly differentiating. After about a week, it starts to implant onto the wall of the mother's uterus. This is complete after two weeks, at which point it is called an *embryo*.

Embryonic stage

This lasts from about the third to the eighth week after conception. By the end of this time, although only an inch long, the embryo has the basic plan of a human

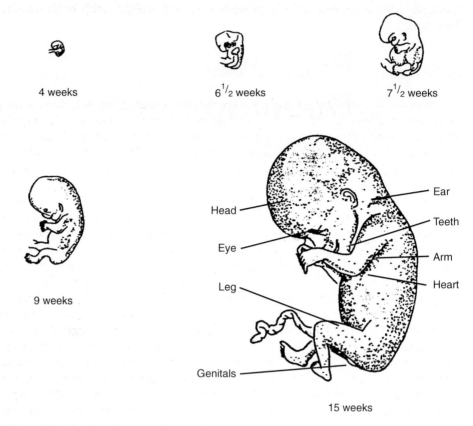

4 weeks   6 ½ weeks   7 ½ weeks

9 weeks

Head

Eye

Leg

Genitals

Ear

Teeth

Arm

Heart

15 weeks

Figure 3.1   Stages of prenatal growth.

body, with head, arms, legs, hands and feet. It connects to the *placenta*, by means of the umbilical cord. The placenta is a special area on the wall of the uterus. Here, the blood supply from the mother meets that of the embryo and they intermingle through thousands of tiny blood vessels. By this means, the mother supplies oxygen and nutrients to the growing embryo. By the eighth week, the embryo is also safely cushioned in a kind of water bed – the amniotic sac – which surrounds it and keeps it at a constant temperature.

Fetal stage

By now, the major structures of the body have differentiated, and bone cells develop, marking the stage of the fetus. Relatively small features develop – fingernails, eyelids, eyebrows; and cartilage in the bones is starting to harden. By the third month, the fetus is starting to move, and its heartbeat can be heard; and the movements become obvious to the mother by the fourth and fifth month. By the seventh month the fetus is able to breathe, cry, swallow, digest and excrete – and has a good chance of surviving premature birth. The last 2 months of normal conception see a considerable increase in size and weight, with birth usually at 9 months.

Prenatal risks

The process of prenatal growth is 'canalized' – that is to say, it is strongly predetermined (see p. 36). There are clear genetic instructions for the zygote to differentiate into the embryo, for the embryo to develop into the fetus, in ways broadly similar for every human being at this period. Prenatal development is an example where nature (i.e. genetic instructions) is very important. But nurture (i.e., the child's environment) is important too.

Things can obviously go wrong in development. Sometimes, the abnormalities are genetic, as with Down's syndrome, a condition arising from a chromosomal abnormality that we discussed earlier (p. 32). Sometimes, they are environmentally caused. One class of environmental hazards are called *teratogens*. Teratogen is an ancient Greek word meaning 'creating a monster' – a reference to the marked abnormalities that can sometimes occur in prenatal development. This is especially so in the embryonic period – this is when the basic ground plan of the body is being formed, with differentiation of major organs including arms and legs. Drugs and other harmful substances can reach the embryo through the mother's blood stream, and if they do so in the embryonic period, some can cause gross body or limb abnormalities. For example, the drug thalidomide, prescribed to prevent morning sickness (pregnancy sickness – see below) in the 1950s, led to babies being born with severe limb deformities – but only when the drug was taken during the first two months of pregnancy. Thalidomide is no longer prescribed in these cases. But other drugs such as cocaine, heavy consumption of alcohol during pregnancy and heavy cigarette smoking are among risk factors for healthy prenatal development.

These are *prenatal risk factors* – ones implicated before birth (we look later at perinatal risk factors, at the time of birth). Other prenatal risk factors include poor maternal nutrition, infectious diseases such as rubella (German measles), exposure to radiation and possibly maternal stress. A risk factor means that later problems are not inevitable, but they are more likely, especially if other risk factors or adverse circumstances are present.

Pregnancy sickness

Many mothers experience pregnancy sickness in the early stages of pregnancy; they may feel nausea at the sight and smell of foods they previously enjoyed, vomit easily, and especially feel 'morning sickness' on rising in the morning. Profet (1992) has argued that pregnancy sickness has been selected for in evolution, as an adaptive mechanism to protect the embryo against teratogens, especially toxic chemicals from foods. She argues that certain foods, including certain plant foods, contain toxins that would not harm the mother but could harm the embryo, notably during the period when major organs are being formed. Her argument is supported by the fact that pregnancy sickness appears to coincide with the period of maximum vulnerability to teratogens, with a peak at around 6 to 8 weeks; that it is found cross-culturally; and that women who experience nausea and vomiting have lower rates of spontaneous abortion than those women who do not.

Fetal learning

Just as the fetus can be affected by toxic environmental stimuli, it is also capable of learning from the environment. This is especially so during the last 3 months in the womb. During this period, the fetus responds to sounds (auditory stimuli), which are filtered through the amniotic fluid. Sounds can reliably affect fetal heart rate and motor responses from as early as 20 weeks of gestational age (indeed, congenital deafness can now be diagnosed during the prenatal period; Shahidullah and Hepper, 1993b). A number of experiments have shown that the fetus actively processes this auditory input, and distinguishes between music, language and other sounds (Karmiloff-Smith, 1995). Box 3.1 describes a study showing how the neonate's discrimination of the mother's voice is linked to auditory experience *in utero*.

■ The Nature of Birth

A full-term pregnancy lasts about 9 months, and then the infant is born. Nine months may seem like a long time to be pregnant. But in fact, from the point of view of our position compared with other primates, including the great apes, 9 months is short. We can compare humans with other primates on the basis of general growth, gestation period and brain size at birth:

- *growth*: complete at age 11 for chimpanzees and gorillas, at age 20 for humans;
- *average gestation period*: 228 days in chimpanzees, 256 days in gorillas, 267 days in humans;
- *brain size at birth as a percentage of adult size*: 41 per cent for chimpanzees, 25 per cent for humans.

On the basis of general growth rates, we might expect the gestation period in humans to be about twice that in the great apes, but it is not – it is quite similar. But it seems as a consequence that human neonates are, in a comparative sense, quite immature, with only one-quarter of brain size achieved at birth compared with about one-half in primates generally. The human infant's brain size only reaches one-half adult size by 1 year (and three-quarters of adult size by 3 years).

The probable explanation for this has its origins in our evolutionary history (see p. 47). A significant development in hominid evolution was bipedalism – being able habitually and easily to walk around on two legs, with an erect posture; the apes can only do this rather awkwardly and for shorter periods, often going on all fours or brachiating – climbing in trees. This shift to bipedalism seems to have gone along with a change in climate and an opportunity for early hominids to gather, scavenge and hunt for food on more open, savanna grasslands (Lovejoy, 1981). Bipedalism also freed up the hands; instead of walking on hands and knuckles, humans could use the hands for carrying, and also for making tools – something incipient in chimpanzees (box 2.1) but a hallmark of human evolution.

But bipedalism seems to have had a price. To be energetically efficient, the pelvic bones and hip joints had to be refashioned; and this in turn meant a restriction on the pelvic opening through which the infant is born – a greater restriction than in the brachiating great apes. According to Leutenegger (1981), there were therefore two competing trends occurring in our evolutionary history – increased efficiency of bipedal locomotion, but also increasing brain size (taking advantage of the manual opportunities of bipedalism and the social opportunities of group living on the savanna). Each was vital; but increased brain size means larger heads, whereas the constraints on size from the birth canal were becoming more restrictive. The inevitable consequence was earlier birth – birth when the neonatal brain was only one-quarter adult size, not one-half. Instead of a gestation period of about 18 months (which one might expect by extrapolation from other primates), gestation period is 9 months. The 'additional' 9 months after birth results in a very helpless infant, and this condition is sometimes referred to as *exterogestation* or *secondary altriciality* (Montagu, 1961; Trevathan, 1987).

This might seem a disadvantage; human infants do indeed need a lot of care and attention for the first year, if they are to survive. But, it has been argued that this actually reinforced the trend to increasing sociality and cooperative group living in early hominids. Basically, mothers needed help with their infants (Lovejoy, 1981; Trevathan, 1987). This help is often needed in parturition (the actual birth process), as well as subsequently. The help can come from the mother's own mother, the father of the infant, other relatives, or friends. In traditional societies, some older women would be experienced in assisting at births; in modern societies, some nurses are trained as midwives for this purpose.

Figure 3.2 shows the usual position in which the infant is born – head first, and with the head facing away from the mother's face. Because of the size of the infant, especially the head, the birth process is not easy; most women find it quite painful. As birth approaches, the mother feels contractions of the uterus (the largest muscle in the human female, it can exert a force of up to 60 pounds during labour). Irregular contractions can occur before, but with the onset of true labour these become regular; there may be difficulties in sleeping, and persistent backache. After some hours these contractions become more forceful and occur around every five minutes. By this time the mother has usually sought out assistance or (in modern societies) gone into hospital. She may be lying on a bed, although the more usual position in traditional societies is to be in a semi-reclining or squatting position.

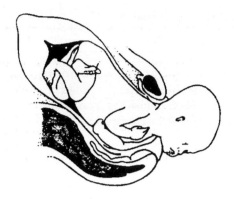

Figure 3.2 Typical birth position.

Contractions become stronger and closer together. The cervix (through which the infant must pass) has softened and dilated. Experiences of pain may actually lessen here, but effort increases – the woman is straining and pushing (hence the term 'labour'). The fetal membranes rupture now, if they have not already done so. The infant's head starts to emerge, often accompanied by a cry from the mother. The midwife, or perhaps the mother herself, helps rotate the head to get the shoulders in the best position to come out. The infant is born, attached still by the umbilical cord. The cord is still pulsating, and for a few minutes the infant is 'cushioned' by the maternal blood supply as its lungs start to fill and it takes its first breaths, and cries. The cord is cut; and within 30 minutes the placenta is also expelled.

This moment of birth is something totally new for the infant, and its cry is a sign of health as it adapts to its new, extrauterine environment. It is often a climactic experience for the mother, and one of joy for the father and other relatives. Here is a transcript of a birth conversation, recorded by Trevathan in Texas, USA, with a bilingual Hispanic mother:

Midwife: Push, Karen. The baby's coming out now. Push hard. Good. Coming down. Grab the baby! Grab the whole thing! There you go.
Mother: Oh, my love. Oh, my baby. Oh, I love you.
Father: It's a boy?
Midwife: Is it really? [laughs] I told you, huh!
Mother: It's a boy?
Father: It's a boy.
Midwife: One minute Apgar? Let's see . . . a little floppy . . . pink feet . . . [suctioning with bulb aspirator].
Mother: What's that?
Midwife: If he gets that down into his lungs he'll end up with pneumonia.
Mother: [Baby crying.] It's alright poor baby, oh, it's alright. Oh my baby, yes, yes. I waited for you so long, now you're here. Oh, my baby, oh, it's OK, it's OK, I love you. It's OK. [To father.] You wanna see it? He's the most beautiful thing [laughs]. Never, never, ever seen a baby so

Table 3.1 The Apgar scoring technique

Score	0	1	2
Colour	Blue-grey, pale all over	Normal, except for extremities	Normal over entire body
Heart rate	Absent	Slow, <100	Over 100
Reflex irritability	No response	Grimace	Cry, pulls away
Muscle tone	Flaccid	Some flexion of extremities	Active motion
Respiratory effort	Absent	Slow, irregular	Good, crying

beautiful. Oh God, oh baby, I love you. [Baby cries.] No, no, no. Oh you do very good, you do very good, good, yes, yes, yes. It's alright. You cry some more? Oh, why you cry? Why you cry, oh yes. Shshshshshshsh. No, noooooo.

Midwife: Give her [mother] some orange juice.

Mother: [To midwife in normal pitch voice.] Can I sit up so I can breastfeed the baby? [Baby cries, mother continues to talk, but hard to hear.] Oh, my baby, don't cry, I'm sorry, I love you. Yes, it's alright.

Midwife: What are you spitting up, fellow?

Father: He's big, huh?

Mother: He's the strongest little thing.

Midwife: Got a good grip, huh?

In the above, the midwife refers to the '1-minute Apgar'. The Apgar score (Apgar, 1953) is a simple and quick way of evaluating an infant's well-being immediately after birth (often, at 1 minute, and 5 minutes). The scoring is shown in table 3.1. A score of 7–10 is healthy, 4–6 somewhat depressed, and below 4 cause for serious concern, especially at 5 minutes. In modern societies women have often been given medication during labour, to relieve pain, this can result in lower Apgar scores and a less immediately responsive infant; hence many women now prefer a more natural labour where possible.

Delivery of the baby is not always straightforward. Some 3 to 4 per cent are 'breech' deliveries; here, the baby is not in the usual, head-first position for coming out, and instead the buttocks, knees or feet may come first with the head last. This prolongs the delivery process, since the buttocks, knees or feet do not dilate the cervix so well as the head. The baby may attempt to breathe before its head is delivered. Even in modern societies mortality is 10 to 20 per cent in breech deliveries. This again suggests that help at birth has a long evolutionary history (Trevathan, 1987).

Interaction after birth

Behaviour after birth is strongly influenced by cultural practices and expectations; and indeed, if the infant is taken away soon after birth in a hospital delivery, mother–infant interaction is obviously curtailed! This is discussed further on pp. 82–3. The usual pattern however is that the mother will stimulate the infant in a variety of ways: touching, stroking and rubbing its body, making eye contact while facing it, and bringing it up to her chest, and talking to it. Usually within the first hour she will breastfeed the infant. Characteristically, mothers will comment on the appearance of the baby, and often on how it resembles the father – perhaps to reassure the father of his paternity (Daly and Wilson, 1982).

Breastfeeding

In traditional societies, breastfeeding was essential for the infant's survival. Breast-feeding is normally done by the mother, but in some societies and in some historical periods (early modern Europe is an example) wet-nursing, or breastfeeding of someone else's infant by a mother who is already breastfeeding, has been quite common. In modern societies, mothers can dispense with breastfeeding and use bottle feeding if they wish. An advantage of this is that fathers can participate equally! However, human milk is particularly well suited to the needs of human infants.

The primary constituents of milk are fat, protein and carbohydrate. Ben Shaul (1962) surveyed the milk composition of a range of mammals, and found that it depends on lifestyle. Mammals that live in cold, wet environments, such as dolphins, produce large amounts of fat in their milk so as to help maintain body warmth. Those mammals that leave their infants in a nest or den site for a long time (such as lions, rabbits, many rodents and carnivores) have relatively large amounts of protein and fat in the milk to sustain the infants between feeding periods. Mammals that carry their young with them (marsupials like kangaroos; species with precocial young such as deer and antelope; and most primates) have milk lower in fat and protein and higher in carbohydrates. Primates have milk especially high in carbohydrates, including lactose, which is a key nutrient for brain growth.

Human milk follows the primate pattern closely. The milk composition is typical for a species where feeding would be on demand (as it would be in traditional societies where mothers carried their infants with them) and where brain growth continues rapidly after birth.

Actually, the very first milk produced by the mother after birth is not typical. It is called the colostrum, and is yellowish or bluish and different from the 'true milk' that appears within about 3 days. The colostrum appears to be useful in providing the infant with a high concentration of a variety of antibodies, providing early immunological protection; it also contains vitamin K, which is essential for blood clotting (and this may prevent blood loss at the site of the umbilical cord). Given these advantages, it is surprising that quite a number of societies, including traditional societies, practise 'colostrum-denial'; the infant is nursed by another mother, or fed a substitute such as sweetened water, for the first 3 days. There appear to be no advantages and some disadvantages to this practice, and the reason why these beliefs are held in some societies is not clear (Barkow, 1989).

Premature and low birthweight babies

A baby born around 38–42 weeks after conception is considered *full-term*. Babies born much earlier than this are considered *premature*, or *preterm*. Being born one or two weeks early is not a major risk, but the more preterm the infant is, the less its chances of survival. Modern medical practices of intensive neonatal care have, however, meant that even infants born as early as 23 weeks gestational age may be able to survive. An infant born before 32 weeks of gestational age is considered as a *very preterm infant* (VPI); see box plate 3.2.1. Premature birth can be a risk for the neonate. They are at greater risk of physical injury and neurological impairment during the birth process, and this can affect their psychological development. Another risk factor is low birthweight – often associated with prematurity, but full term infants can have low birthweight too. A normal birthweight is around 3000–4000 gm. An infant weighing less than 2500 gm at birth is generally considered as *low birthweight*. Those weighing below 1500 gm are usually classed as *very low birthweight* (VLBW), and below 1000 gm as *extremely low birthweight* (ELBW).

This sort of risk factors – prematurity, and low birthweight – are called *perinatal risk factors*, as they refer to difficulties around the time of birth. Other perinatal risk factors are respiratory difficulties, and difficult (e.g., breech) deliveries. By contrast, *psychosocial risk factors* relate to the care of the infant after birth; these will be indexed by the quality of hospital care (when needed), parental care, and the amount of stimulation in the environment.

Generally, research has found that, in the long term, perinatal factors are outweighed by psychosocial factors. In other words, if an infant is at risk because of prematurity or low birthweight, the prognosis will be good if there is high quality care of the infant and a stimulating environment for them to grow up in. A research programme by Emmy Werner and colleagues on the island of Kauai in Hawaii, is a classic statement of this relatively optimistic conclusion.

Werner and Smith (1982) followed all 698 children born during one year in Kauai, from birth to adulthood. They documented both perinatal risk factors, and psychosocial risk factors, and looked at later outcomes such as educational achievement, mental health, and criminality. One finding that emerged was that boys were more susceptible to risk factors generally, than girls were. Another finding was that temperament (see below) was important in predicting later outcomes. Most pertinent to our discussion here, however, was the finding that although perinatal risk factors were important, they could be largely over-ridden by beneficial psychosocial factors. The latter included, for example, a happy and intact family, availability of substitute caregivers, absence of prolonged separation from parents early in life, spacing between siblings, and absence of poverty in the home (Werner, 1993).

Other studies over the past 20 years have also shown that low to moderate perinatal risk factors can often be overcome. Neonatal care practices at the time of birth are important here. If neurological impairment is avoided, then stimulation programmes in the hospital and to help mothers after the infant is discharged from hospital are helpful for a favourable outcome (Rosenblith, 1992).

However, the picture is not so clear when perinatal risk factors are severe. This is the case for example for very preterm infants, and very low birthweight infants (VPIs and VLBWs). One longitudinal study in Germany (Laucht et al., 1997) found that prenatal, perinatal and psychosocial risk factors all contributed to negative outcomes by four and a half years of age. Biological (prenatal and perinatal) risk factors did become relatively less important with age, but were especially associated with poorer motor outcomes. Box 3.2 details another large-scale longitudinal study from Germany, showing that VPIs (who are also usually VLBW) have what may be a specific cognitive impairment in simultaneous information processing at 6 years, which impacts on other cognitive, language and reading skills. A study in Canada (Tessier et al., 1997) reported that both premature and low birthweight children showed greater levels of internalized social problems (shyness, isolation, depression) at 11 years. Another study in the USA (Taylor et al., 2000) found that ELBW children (below 750 gm at birth in this study) performed less well than VLBW who in turn performed less well than full term children, on a range of cognitive, academic and behavioural measures at 11 years – some of these differences remaining significant even after IQ was controlled for.

Recently, investigators have been asking whether genetic factors may play a part in the developmental difficulties often experienced by very premature infants. One report used the Twins Early Development Study to throw light on this (Koeppen-Schomerus et al., 2000); this is a study of all twins born in England and Wales in 1944. Of a sample of 2223 twin pairs for which good information was available, the researchers found 5 per cent to be very preterm (25–31 weeks gestation; mean birthweight 1370 gm), 9 per cent to be preterm (32–33 weeks gestation; mean birthweight 1860 gm), and 86 per cent to be at or near full term (34+ weeks gestation; mean birthweight 2590 gm). They assessed cognitive and language development at 24 months of age, and found the expected gradient of scores according to perinatal risk (degree of prematurity). For the very preterm group, the comparison of monozygotic and dizygotic twins (see pp. 27–8) found no genetic influence, and a very large influence of shared environmental factors – presumably reflecting the environmental experiences associated with prematurity. For the other two groups, there was some genetic contribution and a reduced (although still large) effect of shared environment. This finding suggests that for the very preterm group, the perinatal risk factors are sufficiently severe that any contribution of genetic factors (which might be manifested in temperament, for example) are overwhelmed.

In considering the outcomes of these and other studies, Wolke (1998) argues that larger preterm infants (above 1500 gm) are at only slightly greater risk for long-term psychological deficits. A good psychosocial environment – stimulation and sensitive care – can compensate, in large measure or in most cases, for this degree of perinatal risk. However, it seems that so far, the outlook is less optimistic for VLBW infants (below 1500 gm), born very prematurely. There is much less evidence that a good psychosocial environment after birth can compensate for this more severe degree of perinatal risk. Intensive intervention programmes have had disappointing results. It may be that these children are more likely to suffer some central nervous system damage (as yet not well understood) that affects their later development adversely, even in a very facilitating environment. It is possible that in the future we will find ways to help such children more effectively, but at present these findings present a practical challenge to public health services, and an ethical challenge to our views of very intensive neonatal care to keep alive very preterm infants who are at the limits of survival.

Early Social Behaviour and Social Interactions

The human infant is fairly helpless (or altricial) at birth. He or she depends on parents, or caregivers, for food, warmth, shelter and protection. For these reasons alone it is important for human infants, as for any other young mammal, that an attachment develops between the infant and the mother (or father, or other caregiver; we will use the term caregiver generically). In addition, human infants acquire something from this relationship that is largely absent in other mammals, the beginnings of symbolic communication and cultural meaning. The particular relevance of early caregiver–infant interaction for language development is considered in chapter 11. Although fairly helpless, the human infant does have some reflexive (instinctive or highly canalized) abilities that assist the development of social interactions with caregivers. These are:

1 behaviours that operate primarily in social situations;
2 behaviours to which social responses are given;
3 an enjoyment of contingent responding by others; and
4 an ability to learn, including discriminating social stimuli and attempting to imitate certain observed behaviours.

Let us consider these in turn.

Behaviours that operate primarily in social situations

The types of auditory and visual stimulation that adults provide are especially attractive to infants at or soon after birth (see also chapter 10). For example, infants orientate to (i.e., turn their head towards) patterned sounds rather than mono-tones, and especially to patterned sounds within the frequency range of human speech. They are interested in visual stimuli which move around, and which have a lot of contour information. The human face provides moving stimulation with much contour information, often at just the right distance for the infant to fixate easily. Infant reflexes, such as grasping, and rooting and sucking at the breast, are also used primarily with caregivers. None of these reflexive behaviours is directed only to adults, but all are well designed to operate with adults and to give the infant an initial orientation to social situations.

Behaviour to which social responses are given

Newborn babies will both smile and cry. In both cases this behaviour has no social meaning to the baby at first. She smiles apparently randomly from time to time, and cries if hungry or uncomfortable. However, caregivers respond to these signals as if they were social. They tend to smile and talk back if the infant smiles; and to pick

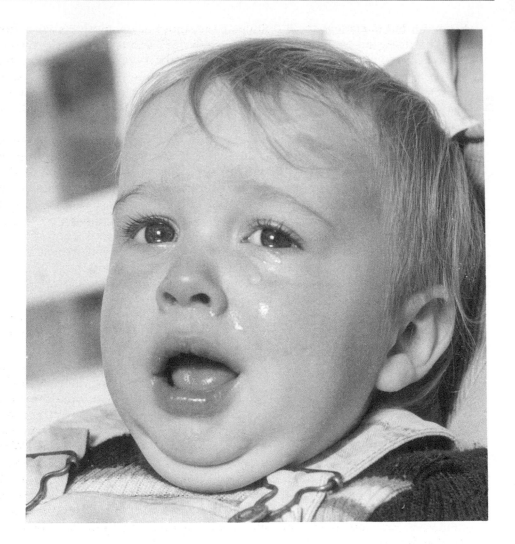

Plate 3.1   Crying is a very powerful message to adults about babies' needs; picking up a crying baby usually reduces the crying.

up an infant and talk to her if she is crying (plate 3.1: one study found that picking up an infant reduced crying on 88 per cent of occasions, which is very rewarding for the adult). Gradually the infant will learn the social consequences of smiling, and crying, because of the social meaning and social responses that caregivers give to them. It is similar with babbling, which begins around 2 months of age.

An ability to learn

The development of perceptual abilities in infancy is discussed in detail in chapter 10. We will see (box 3.1) how some aspects of the mother's voice are learnt even before birth; infants learn to discriminate the sound of the mother's voice from that of a stranger within a few days of birth (p. 335), and learn to prefer pictures of faces to similar but scrambled up pictures by 2 months of age (p. 326; box figure 10.1.2). Throughout the first months of life, infants are discriminating social stimuli and learning the consequences of social actions. By around 6 months of age they quite clearly discriminate between familiar and unfamiliar adults, for example in orienting and in ease of being comforted.

Even a few hours after birth, neonates are also able to perceive temporal relationships between events – that one stimulus event is regularly followed by another. For example, if pressing the infant on the forehead on the left or right side is followed by a drop of water on that side, the infant learns to look to that side after the press on the forehead (Blass et al., 1994). This early capacity to perceive regularities and to anticipate B from A, rapidly includes social events, and forms one aspect of the enjoyment of contingent responses.

An enjoyment of contingent responding by others

From quite early on it seems as though infants like to get 'contingent' stimulation – that is, stimulation which appropriately follows quickly on some action of their own; as it were, a 'reply' to their own action.

An early experiment that demonstrated this was carried out by Watson and Ramey (1972). They used the 'contingency mobile' shown in figure 3.3, with 40 8-week-old infants. The mobile was attached to the infant's cot and hung about 18 inches above the infant's head. There were three conditions: (1) The 'contingency' condition: a pressure-sensing pillow was put in the cot. Small changes in pressure on the pillow activated an electric motor and caused the display to rotate. When the infant was lying with her head on the pillow she could cause the display to rotate by making small head movements. (2) The 'non-contingency' condition: the pressure-sensing pillow was disconnected from the motor. The display rotated once every 3 or 4 seconds, independent of the infant's actions. (3) The 'stable' condition: the pressure-sensing pillow was disconnected from the motor. The display did not rotate at all.

The infants with the contingency mobile significantly increased the number of pillow activations they made per session. For the non-contingency mobile and the stable condition the changes were not significant. This showed that, as early as 8 weeks, infants can learn a simple response to produce contingent stimulation. However, the investigators obtained another interesting result. It turned out that almost all the mothers in the 'contingency' condition reported that their infants smiled and cooed at the mobile, after a few sessions. As one mother said, 'You have to see it, when he's with his mobile, you can't distract him, he loves it.' Almost none of the mothers in the other two conditions reported this kind of strong positive emotional response.

Usually it is caregivers (and not 'contingency' mobiles!) that provide contingent responding in a rapid and appropriate fashion, when they react to the infant's smiling, crying, cooing or babbling; or a bit later on when they engage in games such as peek-a-boo. Enjoyment of contingent responsiveness can develop into

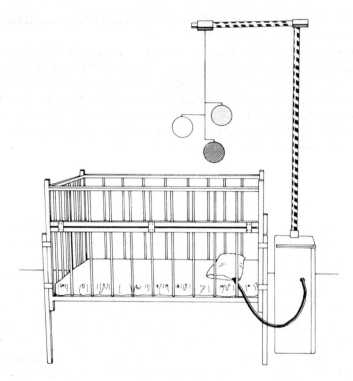

Figure 3.3 Apparatus used as a 'contingency mobile' (adapted from Watson and Ramey, 1972).

turn-taking and into proper interactions such as conversations, or games. A game such as peek-a-boo is initially structured solely by the adult, who takes advantage of the infant's pleasure at the surprise generated by the sudden appearance and disappearance of the adult's face, or a teddy-bear; it becomes a more genuine turn-taking sequence as the infant comes to expect the next repetition of the game and thus take a more active part itself in the exchange (see Bruner and Sherwood, 1976).

A number of studies suggest that infants not only enjoy contingent responsiveness, but they come to expect it from familiar caregivers and to be upset when such expectations are violated. One paradigm used to demonstrate this is called the 'still face' (Tronick et al., 1978). A mother is asked to interact with her infant normally, for say 3 minutes; then adopt a still-face pose; then return to normal interaction. Infants tend to fuss or look away during the still face episode. It could be argued that the still face is artificial, and just less interesting for the infant independent of contingency. Another paradigm, called double video (DV) live-replay, gets around this difficulty. This was first used by Murray and Trevarthen (1985). They set up a video link between mothers and their 6- to 12-week-old infants. First they recorded a section of live mother–infant interaction on video. Then they replayed a previously recorded section to the infant, instead of the live video picture; now, the mother was still giving social and communicative signals to the infant, but not contingently to the infant's responses. Murray and Trevarthen found that the infants (previously happy and attentive) now tended to frown, and look away.

A possible criticism of this work is that over time, the infants were getting more fussy in the experimental conditions. It would be better to have a live-replay-live condition to control for this possibility. This was done by Nadel et al. (1999), with 9-week-old infants; they also avoided a break between the episodes, providing a seamless video transition. They replicated the findings of Murray and Trevarthen, and also found that the infants 'recovered' their normal levels of attention and positive behaviour, once contingency was restored.

Imitation

An important aspect of infant learning is imitation. Research by Kaye and Marcus (1978, 1981) showed that clear imitation of social stimuli occurs between 6 months and 12 months of age. These investigators tried presenting infants with certain actions each time they got their attention. For example, they might open and close their mouth five times, like a goldfish; or clap hands in front of the infant, four times. Each action sequence was contingent on the infant re-establishing eye contact with the experimenter. Besides often establishing eye contact, the infants also tried to imitate the actions themselves, often trying to copy one feature at a time; the imitations improved over trials, and as the infants got older. In fact, there is evidence of imitation at earlier ages. Meltzoff and Moore (1977) studied 12- to 21-day-old babies and found that they showed some imitation of actions such as tongue protrusion, mouth opening and lip-pursing, as performed by an adult. There have since been many studies of imitation by infants (Nadel and Butterworth, 1999). An issue in very early imitation is the extent to which the imitative action by the infant involves an active partnership on their part, or is rather just a 'matching', an automatic and involuntary response by the infant which matches or mirrors the adult action (Papousek and Papousek, 1989).

The respective roles of infant and caregiver

The various abilities of infants, discussed above, assist them in getting into social interaction sequences with adult caregivers. However, the adult has a vital role to play in this, by responding in appropriate ways and at appropriate times. Kaye (1982) calls this 'scaffolding' (see also chapter 15), and likens the infant to an apprentice who is learning the craft of social interaction and communication from an expert. At the beginning the adult has to do most of the work to keep things going: picking the infant up, putting their face at the right distance, responding whenever the infant makes a signal, perhaps having the 'illusion' that the infant is replying when it smiles or grimaces. Things get less one-sided as the infant develops her own social repertoire and begins to learn to take turns in social interaction. Even so, gearing one's behaviour at an appropriate pace and level to the child remains important through infancy and beyond.

Other researchers give a greater role to the infant. Rather than seeing the infant as mainly being paced by the caregiver, Fogel prefers to talk about *co-regulation*, which he defines as 'a social process by which individuals dynamically alter their actions with respect to the ongoing and anticipated actions of their partners' (Fogel, 1993, p. 12). He thus sees these early social interactions as a more negotiated and dynamic process than the 'scaffolding' metaphor would imply.

Trevarthen has consistently argued that infants have much to contribute, from very early. He has made detailed frame-by-frame analysis of video-recordings of mothers and babies, and believes that infants have an innate capacity for intersubjectivity. He refers to *primary intersubjectivity* as being an active and immediate response by an infant to an adult's communicative intentions; and *secondary intersubjectivity* as integrating a person–person–object awareness, with joint attention to and action on objects (Trevarthen and Aitken, 2001; Trevarthen and Hubley, 1978).

Trevarthen describes secondary intersubjectivity as emerging at around 9 months, and primary intersubjectivity much earlier. For example,

> In the gentle, intimate, affectionate, and rhythmically regulated playful exchanges of proto-conversation, 2-month-old infants look at the eyes and mouth of the person addressing them while listening to the voice. In measured and predictable cycles of response to regular time patterns in the adult's behaviour, the infant moves its face, hands and vocal system to modified patterns of adult vocal expression . . . the communicatively active hands of young infants may make expressive movements in rhythmic coordination with a person's speech . . .
>
> (Trevarthen and Aitken, 2001, p. 6)

In fact, these researchers believe that in appropriate conditions – if a newborn is alert, rested, free of stress and with a sensitive caregiver – then primary intersubjectivity is discernible from birth:

> The interactions are calm, enjoyable, and dependent upon sustained mutual attention and rhythmic synchrony of short 'utterances' which include, beside vocalizations, touching and showing the face and hands, all these expressions being performed with regulated reciprocity and turn-taking. Newborn and adult spontaneously display a mutually satisfying intersubjectivity . . .
>
> (Trevarthen and Aitken, 2001, p. 6)

Not everyone accepts these conclusions, which do depend on the way in which one interprets very detailed video records. Research with very young infants is not easy to do! Often they are asleep, and often the requirements of a research project may make it more difficult for them to be 'alert, rested, free of stress and with a sensitive caregiver' for long periods. In many areas of infancy research, debate continues about how early various abilities and behaviours can be found, with confidence and robustness.

Very early bonding: the work of Klaus and Kennell

Although infants learn about their particular parents or caregivers through the first year, it has been claimed that the mother very quickly forms a bond with the infant, in the first hours or days after birth. In its strongest form it is claimed that the first 6–12 hours after birth are a sensitive period for the mother to form a strong emotional bond with her infant through physical contact. If she is absent, the bond is less strong, and later maltreatment or abuse more likely. This 'early bonding' hypothesis, if true, has profound implications for practices in maternity hospitals where, especially a couple of decades ago, mothers were often separated from their infants with little contact for the first day or so.

The hypothesis was proposed by Klaus and Kennell (1976), on the basis of a study of 28 mothers in an American maternity hospital. Fourteen had the traditional treatment – 5 minutes' contact at delivery, then separation for some 6–12 hours followed by half-hour feeding sessions every 4 hours. The other 14 had extra contact – an hour of cuddling after birth, and then an extra 5 hours each day. One month later, and also one year later, there appeared to be some differences favouring the extra contact group. For example, the mothers were more likely to soothe the baby if it cried. This suggests that the extra contact in the first day or so makes a difference.

During the 1980s however, a number of similar studies were carried out by other investigators, some with larger samples. Some have observed small effects, some none at all. Reviews of this evidence (Goldberg, 1983; Myers, 1984) suggest that while early contact is pleasurable for the mother and may have some short-term effects, the long-term effects are very small or non-existent. The positive results of the early studies are flawed by methodological drawbacks, small samples and focusing attention on a small number of significant results out of a very large number of measurements. Thus, the existence of this sensitive period is now thought to be very questionable; many other influences are important in the mother's relationship to the infant, and over a longer time period. The changes in hospital practice are probably beneficial; but parents who miss the first few hours or so of contact (some mothers, most fathers, and all adoptive parents) need not feel that they have lost out on a period crucial for later relationships with the baby.

Temperament

So far, we have considered infants in rather general terms. But, infants vary considerably in their behavioural characteristics. Some will cry a lot, others will be equable; some will be active, others less so; and so on. In a longitudinal study in New York, Thomas and Chess (1977) interviewed mothers about this at regular 3-month intervals, and found considerable consistency in what they call characteristics of infant temperament. Based largely on questionnaires, they identified nine main dimensions of temperament, shown in table 3.2. On the basis of these dimensions, the researchers distinguished *difficult* babies (negative, irregular, and unadaptable), and *easy* babies (positive, regular and adaptable). Subsequent work has tended to group infants according to three major aspects (Sanson et al., 2002):

1   *Reactive or negative emotionality*: irritability, negative mood, inflexibility and high-intensity negative reactions;
2   *Self-regulation*: persistence, non-distractability and emotional control; and

Table 3.2   Temperament dimensions from the work of Thomas and Chess

Activity level – the amount of physical activity during sleep, feeding, play, dressing, etc.
Regularity – of bodily functioning in sleep, hunger, bowel movements, etc.
Adaptability to change in routine – the ease or difficulty with which initial response can be modified in socially desirable ways.
Response to new situations – initial reaction to new stimuli, to food, people, places, toys, or procedures.
Level of sensory threshold – the amount of external stimulation, such as sounds or changes in food or people, necessary to produce a response in the child.
Intensity of response – the energy content of responses regardless of their quality.
Positive or negative mood – amount of pleasant or unpleasant behaviour throughout the day.
Distractability – the effectiveness of external stimuli (sounds, toys, people, etc.) in interfering with ongoing behaviour.
Persistence and attention span – duration of maintaining specific activities with or without external obstacles.

3   *Approach/withdrawal, inhibition or sociality*: tendency to approach, or withdraw from and be wary of, novel situations and people.

Temperamental characteristics seem evident in very young babies, and probably have some biological basis. There is evidence from behaviour genetic studies (chapter 2) of considerable heritability in temperament (Sanson et al., 2002). In addition, some signs can be detected during fetal growth. DiPietro et al. (1996) monitored fetal heart rate and movement in 31 fetuses from gestational age 20 weeks to 36 weeks, and gathered maternal reports at 3 and 6 months. In general, more active fetuses were described later by mothers as more difficult, unpredictable, unadaptable and active infants. By 36 weeks gestation, fetal behaviour was found to be quite strongly predictive of infant temperament.

Thomas and Chess tended to see temperamental characteristics as inherent in the child; an alternative view is that since temperament is usually based on mother (or caregiver) ratings, it is a dyadic characteristic which much more reflects the mother's own psychological state and how she understands her child's behaviour (St James-Roberts and Wolke, 1984). Bornstein et al., (1991) have devised an *Infant Temperament Measure* (ITM) that looks at ten infant behaviours (such as: smiles and laughs to a stranger; fusses/cries) and combines mothers' global ratings, and both mothers' and observers' ratings during a 30-minute session. This multi-method assessment is intentionally designed to assess different perspectives on the infant's temperament.

Temperament may be an important aspect to consider in child development and parenting outcomes. A number of studies have looked at how the approach/withdrawal dimension in infancy may be predictive of shyness and social isolation in the preschool years. Kagan (1997) argues that four-month-old infants who are easily aroused and distressed by unfamiliar stimuli are more likely to be fearful and subdued in early childhood, while those with a high arousal threshold are more likely to become bold and sociable.

Most investigators consider that a transactional model of development is useful in this context. The infant may bring some temperamental characteristics with them, but how caregiver(s) respond are an important part of a developing process. Temperamentally difficult babies are more of a challenge for parents to cope with, and seem to be more at risk for later behaviour problems. The best outcome is if parents are able to respond over time in a way suited to the baby or toddler – providing extra motor opportunities for active babies, for example, or specially encouraging approach in shy babies (see p. 149 and fig. 4.1). The cultural environment is also important. For example Chen et al. (1998) found that behavioural inhibition is a temperamental trait that is more accepted in Chinese infants, than in North American infants.

Caspi (2000) reported long-term correlates of temperament, based on the Dunedin study, a longitudinal study of some 1000 children born between April 1972 and March 1973 in New Zealand's fourth largest city. At age 3, about 40 per cent of the sample could be categorized as temperamentally easy, or well-adjusted; about 10 per cent as undercontrolled (impulsive and negativistic); and about 8 per cent as inhibited (slow to warm up, fearful). Some relations to aggression in childhood are mentioned in chapter 5. Caspi has now followed the sample up to ages 18 and 21, and there continue to be significant differences in these three main groups of persons (as assigned by temperament at age 3) on measures such as mental health, employment, and quality of relationships in adult life. Although the actual size of effects are generally small, this is impressive evidence for some degree of continuity in temperamentally based characteristics.

Further Reading

The development of the fetus, and of the young infant, are covered in greater detail in Rosenblith, J. F. 1992: *In the Beginning: Development from Conception to Age Two*. Newbury Park and London: Sage. The birth process and comparisons of humans with other species are discussed by Trevathan, W. R. 1987: *Human Birth: An Evolutionary Perspective*. New York: Aldine de Gruyter.

For early infancy, useful general texts are Bremner, J. G. 1994: *Infancy*, (2nd edn). Oxford: Blackwell Publishers; Fogel, A. 1994: *Infancy*, (2nd edn). St Paul: West Publishing Co., and Rosenblith, J. F. 1992: *In the Beginning: Development from Conception to Age Two*, (2nd edn). Newbury Park and London: Sage. Nadel, J. and Butterworth, G. (eds) 1999: *Imitation in infancy*. Cambridge: Cambridge University Press, provides a good source for the large literature on this topic.

Discussion Points

1   To what extent is the birth process affected by cultural practices?
2   What practical and moral issues are posed by modern means of intensive neonatal care?
3   How do infants become social?
4   What is the relative contribution of infant and caregiver, to social interaction in the first year?
5   Is research on temperament likely to be strongly affected by how we measure temperament?

Box 3.1
Newborn and fetal response to the human voice

Research in the 1980s had shown that newborn infants could distinguish between the voice of their own mother, and that of an unfamiliar female. DeCasper and Fifer (1980) established this for infants only 1 to 3 days old; and Querleu et al. (1984) found a similar result for infants only 2 hours after birth, largely ruling out the possibility of rapid learning of the mother's voice postnatally. Studies had also found that the fetus could respond to auditory stimuli, with head and body movements. For example, Shahidullah and Hepper (1993a) demonstrated this using an ultrasound scanner, which produces a visual picture of the fetus, in this case showing the head, upper body and arms (see box plate 3.1.1). A headphone for the auditory signals was placed on the mother's abdomen. As early as 20 weeks of gestational age the fetus would show a slow, diffuse bodily response to auditory stimuli presented in this way; and by 25 weeks gestational age, an immediate startle-type response was seen.

It thus seemed likely that learning of the mother's voice occurred *in utero*; however, the fetus would not hear the mother's voice in the same way as the newborn infant, since the sound would be transmitted internally, through the body, as well as externally. Interestingly, a study by Fifer and Moon (1989) had found that 2-day-old newborns preferred the sound of their mother's voice filtered to sound as it would have done in the womb, to the mother's natural voice!

The aim of this series of three studies was to examine further the origins of learning the mother's voice, in the fetus. Two of the three studies were carried out with fetuses in the mother's womb, and using the ultrasound equipment described earlier. In each of the two studies, ten fetuses of gestational age 36 weeks participated. All of the fetuses were subsequently born at 39–40 weeks,

without complications, and with healthy Apgar scores (over 8, at 1 and 5 minutes; see table 3.1).

In one study, two conditions were compared: the mother speaking normally, and a tape recording of the mother's voice (played through the speaker on the mother's abdomen). This was the independent variable; each fetus experienced both conditions, with order being counterbalanced. The dependent variable was the mean number of movements elicited in the fetus (recorded on video). This averaged 5.2 for the mother speaking normally, and 6.7 for the tape of the mother's voice, the difference being just significant at $p < .05$ on a matched pairs t test. The fetuses responded more to the tape of the mother's voice, which the researchers argued would be a more novel stimulus, lacking some components of the mother's voice that would come internally through the body to the fetus when the mother spoke normally. The researchers reported no obvious differences in mother's heartrate or general physical activity between the two conditions, which if present would confound the results.

In the second study of ten fetuses, two tapes were presented to each; of the mother's voice speaking normally, and of a strange female (in fact, another fetus's mother) speaking normally. Again, order was counterbalanced. The mean number of movements elicited in the fetus was 7.2 for the mother's voice, and 6.0 for the strange female's voice. This difference did not approach statistical significance on a matched pairs t test. The researchers concluded that the fetus could not distinguish the mother's voice from a strange female's voice when both were heard externally.

In a third study, the same researchers worked with 35 newborn infants aged 2 to 4 days. They compared the movement responses of the newborns to tape

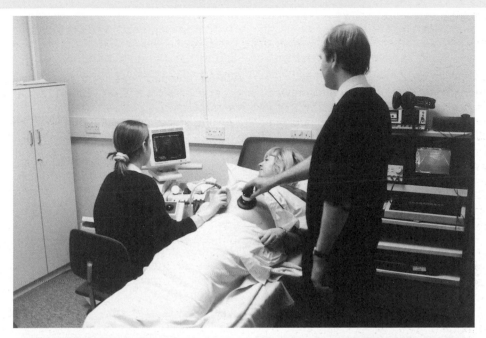

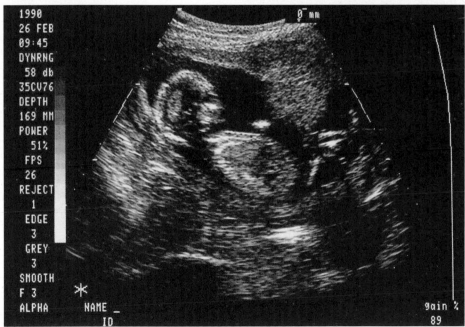

Box Plate 3.1.1 An ultrasound scanner on the mother (above) produces an image of the fetus.

recordings of the mother's voice, and that of a strange female. For half the infants, the voices were normal; for the other half, the voices were in 'motherese' (see chapter 11). An analysis of variance found a significant interaction ($p < .01$); basically, the mother's normal voice elicited fewer movements than did the mother's motherese voice, or either version of the strange female's voice.

In looking at these studies, it seems as though the fetus and newborn infant are going through stages in familiarizing themselves with the auditory stimulus they are most often encountering, the mother's voice. First, the fetus is familiar with the mother's voice as experienced *in utero*; all other voices, even a tape of the mother's voice, appear different. A few hours and days after birth, newborns still prefer the mother's voice as they heard it in the womb (Fifer and Moon, 1989), but they can now discriminate the mother's normal voice from that of other females. However, the mother's 'motherese' voice still seems as strange as an adult female's voice, and recognition of this will come later.

These experiments are ingenious, and carried out in difficult circumstances. Careful precautions were followed in having standard testing conditions and presenta-tion of stimuli. It would be reassuring to have the experiments with the fetuses repli-cated, since the sample sizes were small and a crucial finding in the first study only just reached statistical significance. Also, no direct statistical comparison was made for fetal response to the mother's actual speech and a tape of a strange female, even though the mean movement scores were closer than for the comparison with the tape of the mother's voice. Finally, it would be impor-tant that the videotapes of fetal movements were scored blind to condition, to avoid experimenter effects (see chapter 1).

As Karmiloff-Smith (1995) puts it, 'prior to any *ex utero* experience, newborns show that they have already extracted informa-tion about some of the invariant, abstract features of mother's voice during their period in the womb.' Research such as this forms part of a variety of studies indicating that human development is strongly canalized in the early stages, and that the newborn infant is far from being the 'blank slate' postulated by some earlier theorists.

Based on material in Hepper, P. G., Scott, D. and Shahidullah, S. 1993: *Journal of Repro-ductive and Infant Psychology*, 11, 147–53.

Box 3.2
Cognitive status, language attainment, and prereading skills of 6-year-old very preterm children and their peers: the Bavarian longitudinal study

The Bavarian longitudinal study followed children born between 1 February 1985 and 31 March 1986 in southern Bavaria, in south Germany. It focused on 7505 infants (out of 70,600 total births) who required admission to hospital within the first 10 days of birth; these infants ranged from very ill preterm infants, to those just requiring brief in-patient observation. A control group of 916 healthy infants receiving normal postnatal care, were also included.

The aim of the study reported here was to examine whether prematurity had any implications for cognitive and language development just before the children had started school, at 6 years 3 months of age.

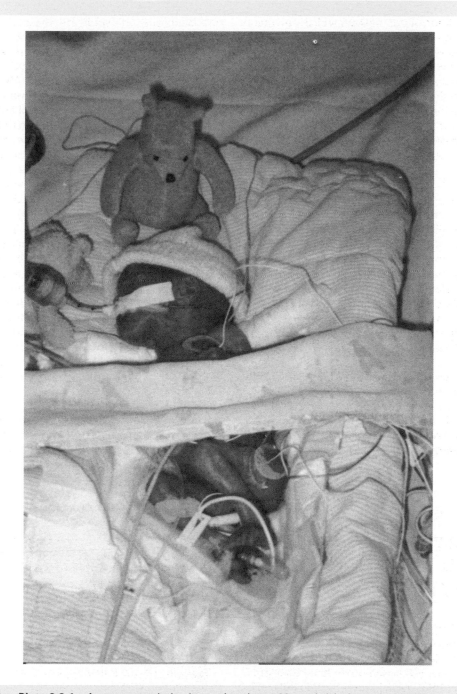

Box Plate 3.2.1   A premature baby (gestational age 28 weeks) in intensive care.

Of the 7505 infants followed up, 560 were VPIs – very preterm infants with a gestation age of less than 32 weeks. Of these 560, 158 died during the initial hospitalization, and another 7 died before they reached 6 years 3 months. Consent to participate was refused for 4; and the investigators did not continue to study the infants of 42 non-

German speaking families. Of the remaining 349 VPIs, 85 could not be traced, leaving 264 who provided data for the study. These VPIs had a mean gestation period of 29.5 weeks, and a mean birthweight of 1288 gm.

These 264 VPIs were compared with a control group drawn from the 916 healthy infants. Of these 916, 718 had continued with assessments, and 689 of these were full term (gestational age greater than 36 weeks). From these, a sample of 264 was drawn, matched with the VPIs for sex, family socioeconomic status, parental marital status, and mother's age. The control group infants had a mean gestation period of 39.6 weeks, and a mean birthweight of 3407 gm.

These groups provided the independent variable of the study. The dependent variables were the assessments made at 6 years 3 months. These were:

- *Cognitive status*: a German version of the Kaufman Assessment Battery for Children (K-ABC), which is a test of intellectual functioning (especially, simultaneous and sequential information processing) and of knowledge.
- *Language development*: subtests of grammatical understanding and production; an articulation test; and quality of speech and grammatical correctness as rated by the research team.
- *Prereading skills*: a measure of phonological awareness based on rhyming and sound-to-word matching tasks (p. 382), and naming of letters and numbers.

In comparing these outcome measures, the obvious step was to compare the VPIs with the control group children. However, the researchers took two other steps in reporting results. First, they noted that 33 of the 264 VPIs had severe medical impairments and disabilities, including severe cerebral palsy and congenital abnormalities; they therefore reported findings when these 33 children were excluded from the VPI sample. In addition, data was available from a normative sample of 311 infants born in Bavaria, drawn from the total 70,600 born in the period, and representative of this total sample on a range of characteristics.

Box table 3.2.1 shows the main findings. Both the normative sample and the control group have near-average scores on cognitive status, and a relatively small proportion (around 7 to 11 per cent) score in the lowest 10th centile for language and prereading skills (since the 10th centile refers to the lowest 10 per cent in the distribution, this is as expected!). By contrast, the VPI group score less well on all of the assessments. These differences are all appreciable, and statistically significant. Excluding the 33 VPIs with very severe disabilities reduces these differences, but only to a modest extent.

Further analyses were carried out in order to deepen the understanding of these results. First, the researchers checked on the 85 children who had dropped out of the VPI sample by 6 years. The medical and biological background data from the birth period showed that (in almost all respects) these children did not differ significantly from the remaining 264; thus, differential dropout was not likely to contribute much to the findings.

Next, they examined effects of socioeconomic status (SES), comparing children from families of upper, middle and lower SES. SES did have an expected, and significant, effect on cognitive status, with differences of 6 to 11 points on the K-ABC scales. These were less than the differences associated with being very preterm however; no overlap of scores between the very preterm infants and controls was found.

Finally, the researchers examined whether differences in intellectual ability could account for the other deficits. They took the two information processing scores from the K-ABC as a measure of intellectual ability, and then used this as a *covariate*; that is, they looked to see if the other differences – in language and prereading skills – would still be found if the differences in

Box Table 3.2.1 Measures of cognitive status, language development and prereading skills in full term and preterm infants, when 6 years 3 months of age

Measure	Normative sample N = 311	Control group N = 264	Very preterm infants without severe impairment N = 231	Very preterm infants (total sample) N = 264
K-ABC: Simultaneous information processing	103.0	103.2	87.0	83.7
K-ABC: Sequential information processing	96.1	96.0	89.0	86.9
K-ABC: Knowledge achievement scale	100.5	100.9	87.2	84.6
Grammatical understanding and production	51.1	51.3	47.8	47.0
Articulation Test below 10th centile	8.7	4.8	23.5	26.2
Poor quality of speech and grammatical correctness	7–8%	about 7%	22–23%	25–26%
Poor phonological awareness	9–11%	9%	25–30%	30–34%
Poor naming of letters and numbers	9–10%	8–11%	28–31%	32–35%

intellectual ability were partialled out. In other words, at a given level of intellectual ability, would VPIs and control infants differ on these other measures? By and large, the answer was in the negative; these differences seemed mostly attributable to the differences in intellectual development.

This study found that the very preterm children scored, on average, about one standard deviation below the norm on cognitive tests; and with an especial impairment in simultaneous information processing. This was a more severe finding than the 0.5 standard deviation reported by many previous studies. However, this study had the advantages of being very representative of all children born in the study area, of having good control of dropouts, and of having a control group closely matched to the VPI sample. The authors stress the importance of further follow-up of these children, and of further research to identify the process that tends to associate early prematurity with cognitive deficits.

Based on material in Wolke, D. and Meyer, R. 1999: *Developmental Medicine and Child Neurology*, 41, 94–109.

4 Parents and Families

If you pick up a newborn baby, she will respond no differently to you than to anyone else. Yet some 9 months later the infant will discriminate familiar and unfamiliar persons, and will probably have developed one or more selective attachments. If you pick her up now she may well look anxious or cry; whereas if her mother or father picks her up, she will be reassured and pacified.

In this chapter we look first at the development of attachment relationships between infants, parents, and other family members. The importance of such attachments for later development is considered, with its implications for policy issues such as institutional rearing, day care and childminding for young children. We also look at research on parenting styles. The effects of growing up in different types of family, are considered. Finally, we examine some of the factors affecting successful and less successful parenting.

The Development of Attachment Relationships

Suppose you are watching a 1- or 2-year-old infant with his mother in a park. This is what you might observe. The mother sits down on a bench, and the infant runs off. Every now and then he will stop to look around, point to objects or events, and examine things on the ground such as leaves, stones, bits of paper, or crawl or jump over grass verges. The infant periodically stops and looks back at the mother, and now and then may return close to her, or make physical contact, staying close for a while before venturing off again. Usually the infant does not go further than about 200 feet from the mother, who may however have to retrieve him if the distance gets too great or if she wants to move off herself.

The infant seems to be exploring the environment, using the mother as a secure base to which to return periodically for reassurance. This is one of the hallmarks of an 'attachment relationship'. The development of attachment has been described in detail by John Bowlby (1969). The observations of children in parks were made in London by Anderson (1972), a student of Bowlby.

Bowlby (1969, p. 79) described four phases in the development of attachment, subsequently extended to a fifth:

1   The infant orientates and signals without discriminating different people. We have already described this as characteristic of the infant in the first few months of life (excepting unusual laboratory situations).
2   The infant preferentially orientates to and signals at one or more discriminated persons. This marks the beginning of attachment. The infant is more likely to smile at the mother or important caregivers, for example, or to be comforted by them if distressed. Exactly when this occurs depends on the measures used, but it is commonly observed at around 5 to 7 months of age.
3   The infant maintains proximity preferentially to a discriminated person by means of locomotion and signals. For example, the infant crawls after the person, or returns periodically for contact, or cries or protests if the person leaves ('separation protest'). This is often taken as the definition of attachment to a caregiver. From 7 to 9 months usually brings the onset of attachment, in this sense. An important related criterion is that the infant becomes wary or even fearful of unfamiliar persons ('fear of strangers').
4   The formation of a goal-corrected partnership occurs between child and caregiver. Until now the mother has served as a resource for the child, being available when needed. The goal-corrected partnership refers to the idea that the child also begins to accommodate to the mother's needs, for example being prepared to wait alone if requested until mother returns. Bowlby saw this as characterizing the child from 3 years of age, though there is evidence that 2-year-olds can partly accommodate to verbal requests by the mother to await her return (Weinraub and Lewis, 1977).
5   Lessening of attachment as measured by the child maintaining proximity. Characteristic of the school-age child, and older, is the idea of a relationship based more on abstract considerations such as affection, trust and approval, exemplified by an internal working model of the relationship.

Bowlby saw attachment as a canalized developmental process. As we saw in chapter 3, both the largely instinctive repertoire of the newborn and certain forms of learning are important in early social interactions. Some aspects of cognitive sensori-motor development (chapters 10, 12) are also essential for attachment. Until the infant has some idea of cause–effect relations, and of the continued existence of objects or persons when out of sight, she or he cannot consistently protest at separation and attempt to maintain proximity. Sensori-motor development is also a canalized process, and an ethological and a cognitive-learning approach to attachment development need not be in opposition.

Many of the characteristic behaviours in attachment were described by Mary Ainsworth (1967, 1973). She observed babies both in the Ganda people of Uganda, and in Baltimore in the USA. She described babies smiling and vocalizing preferentially to the mother, and being comforted; crying when the mother leaves, following her and greeting her by smiling, lifting arms, hugging or scrambling over her and burying the face in her lap; using the mother as a secure base for exploration, and as a haven of safety if frightened.

With whom are attachments made?

Some articles and textbooks have defined the attachment relationship as being to the mother (e.g., Sylva and Lunt, 1981). How true is this? Some studies suggest that early attachments are usually multiple, and although the strongest attachment is often to the mother, this need not always be so.

In a study in Scotland, mothers were interviewed and asked to whom their babies showed separation protest (Schaffer and Emerson, 1964). The proportion of babies having more than one attachment figure increased from 29 per cent when separation protest first appeared, to 87 per cent at 18 months. Furthermore, for about one-third of the babies the strongest attachment seemed to be to someone other than the mother, such as father, grandparent or an older sibling. Generally attachments were formed to responsive persons who interacted and played a lot with the infant; simple caregiving such as nappy changing was not in itself such an important factor. Cohen and Campos (1974) obtained similar results in a study in the USA.

Studies in other cultures bear out these conclusions. In the Israeli kibbutzim, for example, young children spend the majority of their waking hours in small communal nurseries, in the charge of a nurse or *metapelet*. A study of 1- and 2-year-olds reared in this way found that the infants were strongly attached to both the mother, and the *metapelet*; either could serve as a base for exploration, and provide reassurance when the infant felt insecure (Fox, 1977). In many agricultural societies mothers work in the fields, and often leave young infants in the village, in the care of grandparents, or older siblings, returning periodically to breastfeed. In a survey of data on 186 non-industrial societies, it was found that the mother was rated as the 'almost exclusive' caretaker in infancy in only five of them. Other persons had important caregiving roles in 40 per cent of societies during the infancy period, and in 80 per cent of societies during early childhood (Weisner and Gallimore, 1977).

The security of attachment

Ainsworth and her colleagues developed a method for assessing how well attached an individual infant is to her mother or caregiver (Ainsworth et al., 1978). This method is known as the *Strange Situation*, and has been used extensively with 12–24-month-old infants in many countries. Essentially it is a method of checking out, in a standardized way, how well the infant uses the caregiver as a secure base for exploration, and is comforted by the caregiver after a mildly stressful experience.

The Strange Situation   involves seven short episodes, which take place in a comfortably equipped room, usually at a research centre where the episodes can be filmed. Besides caregiver or mother (M) and infant (I), there is a stranger (S) whom the infant has not seen before. The episodes are: (1) M and I in room, I explores for 3 minutes; (2) S enters, sits for 1 minute, talks to M for 1 minute, and gets down on the floor to play with I, 1 minute; (3) M leaves, S plays with I then withdraws if possible, up to 3 minutes; (4) M returns, S leaves unobtrusively, M settles I and then sits down for 3 minutes; (5) M leaves, I is alone for up to 3 minutes; (6) S comes in, attempts to settle I then withdraws if possible, up to 3 minutes; (7) M returns, S leaves unobtrusively, M settles I and sits down (session ends, after about 20 minutes).

In a well-functioning attachment relationship, it is postulated that the infant will use the mother as a base to explore (episodes 1, 2 and end of episode 4), but be stressed by the mother's absence (episodes 3, 5 and 6; these episodes are curtailed if the infant is very upset or the mother wants to return sooner). Special attention is given to the infant's behaviour in the reunion episodes (4 and 7), to see if he or she is effectively comforted by the mother. On the basis of such measures, Ainsworth and others distinguished a number of different attachment types. The primary ones are type A (Avoidant), type B (Secure) and type C (Ambivalent); later, type D (Disorganized) was added.

Type A   babies are characterized by conspicuous avoidance of proximity to or interaction with the mother in the reunion episodes. Either the baby ignores the mother on her return, greeting her casually if at all, or he mingles his welcome with avoidance responses such as turning away, moving past or averting gaze. During separation, the baby is not distressed, or distress seems due to being left alone rather than to mother's absence.

Type B   babies are characterized by actively seeking and maintaining proximity, contact or interaction with the mother, especially in the reunion episodes. He may or may not be distressed during the separation episodes, but any distress is related to mother's absence.

Type C   babies are characterized by conspicuous contact- and interaction-resisting behaviour in the reunion episodes. Rather than ignoring the mother, this is combined with some seeking of proximity and contact, thus giving the impression of being ambivalent or resistant.

Type D   babies show very disorganized or disoriented behaviour in the Strange Situation; there is no one clear pattern, but inconsistent and often bizarre responses to separation/reunion. Main and her colleagues (1985) believe this type to be a useful extension of the original Ainsworth classification.

There are subtypes of these main types, but many studies do not refer to them. In older studies type D babies, who are often difficult to classify as they do not show a clear pattern, were 'forced' into the 3-way scheme; and some contemporary analyses carry out analyses of both 3-way and 4-way classifications.

Often, type B babies (secure) are contrasted with types A and C (insecure), and secure attachment tends to be seen as developmentally more normative, or advantageous. Criticisms have been made of the attachment typing resulting from the

Strange Situation procedure (Lamb et al., 1984), especially of earlier work that was based on small samples, and of the normative assumption that 'B is best'. It was also pointed out that the procedure measures the relationship between mother and infant, not characteristics of the infant. Since attachment security is a dyadic measure, infant–mother attachment type is not necessarily the same as infant–father attachment type. In fact, some studies have found that the attachment type to father is not related to that with the mother; meta-analyses (Fox et al., 1991; van IJzendoorn and De Wolff, 1997) find a very modest association between the two.

However, the strange situation procedure has become a commonly and internationally used technique. An important test of the utility of attachment types is that they should predict to other aspects of development. There is now considerable evidence for this (see Bretherton and Waters, 1985, and Waters et al., 1995, for reviews).

For example Kochanska (2001) followed infants longitudinally from 9 to 33 months and observed their emotions in standard laboratory episodes designed to elicit fear, anger or joy. Over time, type A (avoidant) infants became more fearful, type C (resistant) infants became less joyful, type D (disorganized) became more angry; whereas type B (secure) infants showed less fear, anger or distress. Using the strange situation procedure, secure attachment to mother at 12 months has been found to predict curiosity and problem-solving at age 2, social confidence at nursery school at age 3, and empathy and independence at age 5 (Oppenheim et al., 1988) and lack of behaviour problems (in boys) at age 6 (Lewis et al., 1984).

Is the strange situation valid cross-culturally?

Van IJzendoorn and Kroonenberg (1988) provided a cross-cultural comparison of strange situation studies in a variety of different countries. In American studies, some 70 per cent of babies were classified as securely attached to their mothers (type B), some 20 per cent as type A and some 10 per cent as type C. However, some German investigators found that some 40–50 per cent of infants were type A (Grossman et al., 1981), while a Japanese study found 35 per cent type C (Miyake et al., 1985). Such percentages must raise a question about the nature of 'insecure attachment'. Is it a less satisfactory mode of development, or are these just different styles of interaction?

Takahashi (1990) argued that the Strange Situation must be interpreted carefully when used across cultures. He found that Japanese infants were excessively distressed by the infant alone episode (episode 5), because normally in Japanese culture they are never left alone at 12 months. Hence, fewer Japanese infants scored B. Also, there was no chance for them to show avoidance (and score as A), since mothers characteristically went straight and without hesitation to pick up the baby. This may explain why so many Japanese babies were type C at 12 months (yet they are not at 24 months, nor are adverse consequences apparent). This distortion might be avoided by virtually omitting episode 5 for such babies. Rothbaum et al. (2000) do take a more radical stance, in comparing the assessment of attachment security in the USA and Japan. They argue that these two

cultures put different cultural values on constructs such as independence, autonomy, social competence and sensitivity; such that some fundamental tenets of
attachment theory are called into question as cross-cultural universals.

Cole (1998) suggested that we really need detailed knowledge of the cultures
under study if we are to understand the nature of the everyday interactions that
shape the development of young children in relation to their caregivers. The
strange situation may be a valid indicator but we at least need to re-define
the meaning of the categories of avoidant, secure and ambivalent according to the
local culture. He argued that although it is a standardized test, the strange
situation is really a different situation in different cultural circumstances. However
for successful use of the strange situation in a non-Western culture, the Dogon
people of Mali, see box 4.1.

Why do infants develop certain attachment types?

Are infants born predisposed to develop a certain kind of attachment, as they may
be predisposed to have a certain kind of temperament? Probably not. As mentioned in chapter 2, van IJzendoorn et al. (2000) argued that genetics has only a
modest influence on attachment type. This is shown by twin studies; for example,
O'Connor and Croft (2001) assessed 110 twin pairs in the strange situation, and
found concordance of 70 per cent in monozygotic twins and 64 per cent in dizygotic twins – not significantly different. Their model suggested estimates of only
14 per cent of variance in attachment type due to genetics, 32 per cent to shared
environment, and 53 per cent to non-shared environment. A study of attachments
formed by babies to foster mothers (Dozier et al., 2001) found as good a concordance between mothers' attachment state of mind (from the Adult Attachment
Interview, see below) and infant attachment type from the strange situation, as
for biological mother–infant pairs, again suggesting little genetic influence on
attachment type.

So, what are the environmental influences that lead to different attachment
types? An early candidate was the Maternal Sensitivity Hypothesis. This had been
suggested by Ainsworth's original research (Ainsworth et al., 1978) that had established the nature of attachment types. This, and a number of later studies, reported
that the quality and sensitivity of mother–infant face-to-face interaction from as
early as a few months and through the first year or so, predicted secure or insecure attachment (see also box 4.1). A meta-analysis of relevant studies by De Wolff
and van IJzendoorn (1997) found an average effect size of .24 (an effect size is a
measure of the influence of one variable on another in terms of standard deviations; an effect size of 1 would mean a shift of one standard deviation, obviously
substantial; an effect size of .24 is seen as moderate). For fathers – who often get
left out in such research! – a similar meta-analysis of a much smaller number of
studies (van IJzendoorn and De Wolff, 1997) found a mean effect size of .13, less
than for mothers.

As these effects sizes are small, other environmental influences must be at work.
Meins et al. (2001) suggest that mothers' *mind-mindedness* is an important construct. This is defined as the mother treating her infant as an individual with a

mind, rather than just a creature with needs to be satisfied. The emphasis is on responding to an infant's inferred state of mind, rather than simply their behaviour. In a longitudinal study of 71 mother–infant pairs, they found that maternal sensitivity (responding to infant cues) and some aspects of mind-mindedness, especially *appropriate mind-related comments* by the mother, measured at 6 months, both independently predicted security of attachment at 12 months. True et al. (2001) found evidence that mother's frightened or frightening behaviour may also contribute independently to attachment security, see box 4.1.

We must also remember that a lot of the variance in attachment type appears to be related to non-shared environment, and this cannot be explained by generalized maternal sensitivity. Probably, mothers are more sensitive and behave differently to some infants than others, depending on birth order, gender, and infant characteristics, suggesting the need for a family systems perspective on these issues (van IJzendoorn et al., 2000).

Attachment beyond infancy and internal working models

The strange situation measures security of attachment in terms of behaviours; especially, how the infant behaves at reunion after a separation. It is typically used in the 12–24 months age range. For 3- up to 6-year-olds, variants of the strange situation, such as reunion episodes after separation, have been used with some success (Main and Cassidy, 1988).

Research in the past decade has seen attachment become a life-span construct, with corresponding attempts to measure it at different developmental stages (see Melhuish, 1993, for a review). We have seen how as the infant becomes older, in Bowlby's fourth and fifth stages, attachment relationships become less dependent on physical proximity and overt behaviour, and more dependent on abstract qualities of the relationship such as affection, trust, approval, internalized in the child and also of course in the adult. Researchers have found it useful to think of internal representations of the relationship in the child's mind; the child is thought of as having an *internal working model* of his or her relationship with the mother, and with other attachment figures (Bowlby, 1988; Main et al., 1985). These are described as cognitive structures embodying the memories of day-to-day interactions with the attachment figure. They may be 'schemas' or 'event scripts' that guide the child's actions with the attachment figure, based on their previous interactions and the expectations and affective experiences associated with them.

Dyads of differing attachment type would be expected to have differing working models of the relationship. Secure attachment would be based on models of trust and affection, and a type B child would communicate openly and directly about attachment-related circumstances (such as how they felt if left alone for a while). By contrast, a boy (or girl) with a type A avoidant relationship with his mother may have an internal working model of her that leads him not to expect secure comforting from her when he is distressed. She may in fact reject his approaches. His action rules then become focused on avoiding her, thus inhibiting approaches to her that could be ineffective and lead to further distress. This

Plate 4.1   Boy by Land Rover; a picture from the Separation Anxiety Test.

in turn can be problematic, as there is less open communication between mother and son, and their respective internal working models of each other are not being accurately updated. Type C infants with an ambivalent relationship might not know what to expect from their mother, and they in turn would be inconsistent in their communication with her and often unable to convey their intent.

Over the past 15 years researchers have attempted to measure attachment quality in older children, by trying to tap in to their internal working models (Stevenson-Hinde and Verschueren, 2002). One approach is by narrative tasks, often using doll-play; children use a doll family and some props and complete a set of standardized attachment related story beginnings. Another method has been the *Separation Anxiety Test*, in which children or adolescents respond to photographs showing separation experiences; an example is shown in plate 4.1. The child is asked how the child in the picture would feel and act, and then how he/she would feel and act if in that situation (Main et al., 1985). Wright et al. (1995) found this test to have good rater reliability and consistency for 8- to 12-year-olds. They found large differences in responses between children having clinical treatment for behaviour disturbance and a normal control group (see table 4.1). Securely attached children generally acknowledge the anxiety due to the separation but come up with feasible coping responses; insecurely attached children generally either deny the anxiety, or give inappropriate or bizarre coping responses.

Table 4.1 Two protocols from the Separation Anxiety Test

From control sample:
Child: Mum is going shopping and the boy is staying at home alone.
Interviewer: How would you feel?
Child: A bit scared and try to have some fun.
Interviewer: Why?
Child: Because someone can break in and kidnap me.
Interviewer: What would you do?
Child: Try and have fun and think mum and dad are in the house and no-one can kidnap
  me.

From clinical sample:
Child: Mum is going shopping and the boy is staying at home alone.
Interviewer: How would he feel?
Child: Bad.
Interviewer: Why?
Child: 'Cause he's often seen the video Home Alone and get burglars.
Interviewer: What would he do?
Child: So he sets booby traps and ends up hitting mum in the face with iron bars and
  blow torches. So he sits and watches TV but he gets burnt by the fire and goes to
  hospital, his mum visits him and he's dead.

The Adult Attachment Interview

Internal working models of relationships can normally be updated, or modified, as new interactions develop. It may be that for younger children, such change must be based on actual physical encounters. However, Main et al. (1985) suggest that in adolescents or adults who have achieved formal operational thinking (chapter 12), it is possible to alter internal working models without having such direct interaction. To measure attachment in older adolescents and adults, they developed the *Adult Attachment Interview*. This is a semi-structured interview that probes memories of one's own early childhood experiences. The transcripts are coded, not on the basis of the experiences themselves, so much as on how the person reflects on and evaluates them, and how coherent the total account is.

Main et al. (1985) reported that the Adult Attachment Interview (AAI) yielded four main patterns:

1 *Autonomous*: persons who can recall their own earlier attachment-related experiences objectively and openly, even if these were not favourable.
2 *Dismissive*: persons who dismiss attachment relationships as of little concern, value or influence.
3 *Enmeshed*: persons who seem preoccupied with dependency on their own parents and still actively struggle to please them.
4 *Unresolved*: persons who have experienced a trauma, or the early death of an attachment figure, and have not come to terms with this or worked through the mourning process.

Table 4.2 Normative data on AAI codings (percentages)

33 studies	Dismissing	Autonomous	Enmeshed
Mothers	24	58	18
Fathers	22	62	16
Adolescents	27	56	17
Lower SES	33	48	18
Clinical patients	41	13	46

Van IJzendoorn (1995) summarized work using the AAI, which he argues has satisfactory coding reliability. Van IJzendoorn and Bakermans-Kranenburg (1996) have looked at the distribution of AAI codings across different groups of people, from 33 separate studies, as summarized in table 4.2. Mothers, fathers and older adolescents do not differ significantly in their distribution across the three main categories. People from lower socioeconomic groups are slightly more likely to score as Dismissing. However, the large difference is in persons having clinical treatment, the great majority of whom do not score as Autonomous on the AAI.

Are attachment types stable over time?

Does security of attachment change through life, or does infant–parent attachment set the pattern not only for later attachment in childhood, but even for one's own future parenting? As attachment has become a life-span construct, these questions have generated considerable research and debate.

Several studies have found some continuity of attachment classification over the first few years, but also some discontinuities that can partly be explained by taking account of life events that affect the family system. Vaughn et al. (1979) examined strange situation security at 12 and at 18 months in a sample of US infants from families living in stressful situations. There was significant continuity, but also a lawful pattern of change. Infants who changed from secure to insecure usually had mothers who reported negative changes – loss of partner, worse financial circumstances. Conversely, infants who changed from insecure to secure usually had mothers who reported positive changes.

Bar-Heim et al. (2000) assessed infants at 14 and 24 months using the strange situation, and at 58 months using a Reunion measure (behavioural measure) and the Separation Anxiety Test (representational measure). There was significant continuity from 14 to 24 months (64 per cent of children remained in the same A, B or C category), but not from either 14 or 24 months to 58 months. At 58 months, there was some significant agreement between the behavioural and representational measures of attachment. Again, some of the discontinuity with age could be explained by life events affecting the families; for infants who changed category between infancy and childhood, mothers reported fewer positive and more negative life events over the past year.

Several studies have now spanned a period of some 20 years to examine whether strange situation classification in infancy predicts adult attachment inter-

Table 4.3 Hypothesized relationships between maternal stage of mind (AAI), maternal behaviour, and child attachment type

Mother's state of mind	Maternal behaviour with infant	Infant strange situation type
Mother is open to and freely accesses attachment related experiences: Autonomous on AAI	Mother is sensitive to child's cues	Secure (B)
Mother cuts off or minimizes past attachment memories and feelings: Dismissive on AAI	Mother is unresponsive to child's cues	Avoidant (A)
Mother is angry about or enmeshed in past attachment experiences: Enmeshed on AAI	Mother is inconsistent; sometimes responsive, sometimes not	Ambivalent (C)
Mother has unresolved state of mind about past attachment-related trauma or loss: Unresolved on AAI	Mother exhibits frightened or frightening behaviour to child	Disorganized (D)

view classification as young adults (Lewis et al., 2000; Waters et al., 2000). The outcome is varied, but some of these studies do find significant continuity of the three main attachment types; that is, from Secure to Autonomous, Avoidant to Dismissive, and Resistant to Enmeshed. Also, several studies found relationships between discontinuities in attachment classification, and negative life events such as experience of parental divorce.

Are attachment types stable over generations?

Besides some degree of continuity over time for an individual's attachment typing, there is also evidence for the transmission of attachment type across generations; specifically, from the parent's AAI coding and their infant's strange situation coding. Main et al. (1985) had reported some evidence for such a link, and indeed the AAI coding system is premissed on it; it was argued that Autonomous adults would have Secure infants; Dismissing adults would have Avoidant infants; Enmeshed adults would have Ambivalent infants; and Unresolved adults would have Disorganized infants (see table 4.3).

Van IJzendoorn (1995) looked at a large number of available studies in the decade since Main's work; the results for parent–infant concordance are shown in table 4.4. There is considerable linkage between adult AAI and infant Strange Situation coding; Van IJzendoorn argued that this 'intergenerational transmission' of attachment may be via parental responsiveness and sensitivity. We discussed above how this is only a partial explanation, and other aspects of maternal behaviour and of family systems may also be involved.

Table 4.4 Concordance between infant strange situation coding and parental AAI coding

3-way; 18 studies	Dismissing	Autonomous	Enmeshed	
Avoidant	116	46	27	
Secure	53	304	46	
Ambivalent	10	19	40	
4-way; 9 studies	Dismissing	Autonomous	Enmeshed	Unresolved
Avoidant	62	29	14	11
Secure	24	210	14	39
Ambivalent	3	9	10	6
Disorganized	19	26	10	62

There appears to be considerable evidence for some degree of continuity of attachment security through life, and on to the next generation; but considerable evidence that this can be affected by life events. An adult's attachment security might also be influenced by counseling, clinical treatment, or simply by reflection.

Some insight into this comes from a study reported by Fonagy et al. (1994). They carried out a longitudinal study with 100 mothers and 100 fathers, in London, who were given the AAI and other measures shortly before their child was born. The strange situation was used subsequently to measure security of attachment, to mother at 12 months and to father at 18 months. As other studies have found (table 4.4), the parent's AAI scores predicted the infant's strange situation scores. The researchers also obtained estimates of the amount of deprivation and disrupted parenting which the parents had themselves experienced. They looked to see if this too influenced infant attachment. Interestingly, it did, but it interacted strongly with the way in which the parents had dealt with their own representations of their experiences of being parented. Coding the AAI, the researchers developed a *reflective self-function* scale to assess the ability parents had to reflect on conscious and unconscious psychological states, and conflicting beliefs and desires. Of 17 mothers with deprived parenting and low reflective self-function scores, 16 had insecurely attached infants, as might be expected. By contrast, of 10 mothers who had experienced deprived parenting but had high reflective self-function scores, all had securely attached infants. The researchers argued that reflective self-function may be a way to change internal working models, and demonstrate resilience to adversity and a way of breaking the intergenerational transmission of insecure attachment.

Adults who experienced difficult childhoods but have overcome early adversity and insecure attachment by a process of reflection, counselling or clinical help, are called *earned-secures*. They could be contrasted with *continuous secures*, who had a positive upbringing. Phelps et al. (1998) made home observations of mothers and their 27-month-old children. They found that earned-secures, like continuous secures, showed positive parenting; under conditions of stress, both these groups showed more positive parenting than insecure mothers.

Another fascinating perspective on the issue of inter-generational transmission comes from the Holocaust study (Bar-On et al., 1998; van IJzendoorn et al., 1999). The Holocaust refers to the experiences of Jews and other persecuted minorities in the concentration camps of World War II (1939–45). Besides mistreatment and torture, many people were killed in the camps, leaving children as orphans in traumatic circumstances. Did such experiences impact on attachment, and was this transmitted inter-generationally to children? The study encompasses three generations; those, now grandparents, who came through the Holocaust typically as children who had lost their parents; their children, now parents; and their grandchildren. These generations are compared with comparable three-generation families who had not suffered from the Holocaust.

The effects of the Holocaust were evident in the grandparent generation. The Holocaust grandparents showed distinctive patterns on the AAI, scoring high on Unresolved, as would be predicted, and high on unusual beliefs – another predicted effect of trauma and unresolved attachment issues. They displayed avoidance of the Holocaust topic; a common finding was that the experiences had been so horrific that they were unable to talk about their experiences even with their own children. However inter-generational transmission of attachment type was quite low for this group. The Holocaust parents ('children of the Holocaust') showed rather small differences from controls, scoring just slightly higher on Unresolved on the AAI. This normalization process continued to the next generation ('grandchildren of the holocaust'), for whom no significant differences in attachment security were found, from controls.

Disorganized attachment and unresolved attachment representations

The disorganized pattern of infant attachment from the strange situation, came to be recognized later than the other main attachment types, and appears to have rather distinctive correlates. Disorganized infants may show stereotypic behaviours such as freezing, or hair-pulling; contradictory behaviour such as avoiding the mother despite being very distressed on separation; and misdirected behaviour such as seeking proximity to the stranger instead of the parent. These are seen as signs of unresolved stress and anxiety. It seems that for these infants the parent is a source of fright rather than of safety (table 4.3) (see Vondra and Barnett, 1999, for a collection of recent research).

Van IJzendoorn, Schuengel and Bakermans-Kranenburg (1999) reviewed a number of studies on disorganized attachment. They argue for mainly environmental causation, as for security of attachment generally; although, as we saw in chapter 2, there is some evidence for genetic factors in disorganized infant attachment, and it is also higher in infants with severe neurological abnormalities (cerebral palsy, autism, Down's syndrome) – around 35 per cent, compared with around 15 per cent in normal samples. However D is also especially high for mothers with alcohol or drug abuse problems (43 per cent) or who have maltreated or abused their infants (48 per cent). D is not higher in infants with physical disabilities; and it is not strongly related to maternal sensitivity as such; but there is evidence relating it to maternal unresolved loss or trauma.

Whereas the Maternal Sensitivity Hypothesis suggests that maternal (in)sensitivity predicts secure (B) or insecure (A,C) attachment, a different hypothesis has been proposed to explain disorganized attachment (table 4.3). This is that it results from frightened or frightening behaviour by the mother to the infant, resulting from the mother's own unresolved mental state related to attachment issues (for example, abuse by her own parent; violent death of a parent; sudden loss of a child).

A study by Hughes et al. (2001) in London compared Unresolved scores on the AAI for 53 mothers who had infants born next after a stillbirth, with 53 controls. Of the mothers who had previously had stillborn infants, 58 per cent scored as Unresolved, compared to 8 per cent of Controls; furthermore, 36 per cent had disorganized (D) infants, compared to 13 per cent of controls. A statistical path analysis (looking at relationships among all the variables) showed that the stillbirth experience predicted Unresolved maternal state of mind, and that this latter variable then predicted infant disorganization.

The hypothesized behavioural aspects of maternal unresolved state of mind were supported by the study in Mali reported in box 4.1. A study in Germany by Jacobsen et al. (2000) provided further support. They examined 33 children and their mothers at 6 years of age. Disorganized attachment (assessed from a Reunion episode) was significantly related to high levels of maternal expressed emotion, defined as speech to the child that was highly critical of them or over-involved with them.

In their review, van IJzendoorn et al. (1999) also found that infant disorganized attachment predicted to later aggressive behaviour, and child psychopathology. Carlson (1998) found significant prediction from attachment disorganization at 24 and 42 months, to child behaviour problems in preschool, elementary school and high school. Given the prior links to parental maltreatment and abuse, it may be that the disorganized attachment pattern will be found to be the most relevant aspect of attachment in understanding severely maladaptive or antisocial behaviours in later life.

Attachment theory as a paradigm

Attachment theory is an important and vigorous approach to early social development (see Ainsworth and Bowlby, 1991, or Bretherton, 1992, for accounts of its development) that constitutes something of a paradigm in the sense of Kuhn (see chapter 1). It is developing rapidly. There are some internal challenges. For example Crittenden (2000) believes that the 3-fold AAI classification homologous to the strange situation classification is too simple, and has proposed a much more complex circumplex model. Other criticisms have been made from outside the field. Some feminist psychologists have objected to implications they see coming from attachment theory, for example, that women's identity is expected to be tied to child-rearing; they see a high price being paid for maternal sensitivity, in other areas such as careers and self-esteem (Singer, 1992; Woollett and Phoenix, 1991).

Some of these criticisms may be misplaced however, being reactions to Bowlby's earlier maternal deprivation hypothesis (see below).

Bowlby's 'Maternal Deprivation' Hypothesis

The 'maternal deprivation' hypothesis is that children should not be 'deprived' of contact with the mother during a critical period when the primary attachment relationship is being formed. It was proposed by Bowlby (1953, 1969), in an early stage of his development of attachment theory, and while most attachment theorists later dissociated themselves from it, Bowlby did not. The hypothesis carried strong practical policy implications. Many aspects of it have been strongly criticized, however (Rutter, 1981; Clarke and Clarke, 1998).

Bowlby first put forward his views publicly in a 1951 report to the World Health Organization, published in 1953 as *Child Care and the Growth of Love*. The report was inspired by the needs of refugee or homeless children, separated from or without parents in the aftermath of World War II. At that time, institutional care focused on the physical needs of the child, good food and a clean environment – but little on the child's emotional needs, which were poorly recognized. On the basis of his emerging views on attachment, Bowlby proposed that 'mother love in infancy and childhood is as important for mental health as are vitamins and proteins for physical health.' This viewpoint provided an important corrective to the prevailing current of opinion. Bowlby went further, however. In a now notorious passage, he stated:

> What is believed to be essential for mental health is that the infant and young child should experience a warm, intimate and continuous relationship with his mother (or permanent mother-substitute – one person who steadily 'mothers' him) in which both find satisfaction and enjoyment.
>
> (Bowlby, 1953, p. 11)

This statement was backed up elsewhere in Bowlby's writings by assertions that mothers should not be separated from their young children, for example by work (even part-time), or hospitalization, and that if such separations do occur, there is a poor prognosis for social and cognitive development. The period from about 6 months to 3 years was regarded as especially crucial. Even if not universally believed, this statement had a profound effect on a generation of mothers.

Bowlby held this belief for a number of reasons, which at the present time seem much less convincing than in the 1960s. Much further evidence has accumulated, and the maternal deprivation hypothesis, at least in its strong form, has become largely discredited.

1   Bowlby's idea of a critical period for attachment formation came from ethological work on imprinting and the following response. However, the 'imprint-

ing' characteristic of precocial birds and some mammals is not characteristic of primates (see chapter 2). The 9-month 'fear of strangers' was supposed to prevent subsequent attachment bonds being formed, but more recent evidence suggests that 1- and 2-year-olds can form new social relationships with adults and characteristically form several strong attachment relationships. The crux of the issue here is whether infants only get attached to one person (which Bowlby called 'monotropism') or whether shared care by several attachment figures is normal and satisfactory. In fact as we saw earlier (p. 94), moderate shared care of young children seems to be very common, harmless and even perhaps beneficial.

2   Observations of young children separated from parents and placed in an institution while the mother had a second baby and was to be in hospital for about a week, showed that the children went through a characteristic sequence: first protesting, but able to be comforted; secondly despair, and being inconsolable; thirdly denial and detachment, with the child superficially unconcerned at the separation, but denying any affection or response to the mother on eventual reunion. These stages were vividly shown in a series of films made by J. and J. Robertson (1967–73), entitled *Young Children in Brief Separation*.

However, separation from the mother could be compensated for by the presence of another attachment figure. The Robertsons' work found just this. They found that institutional care led to the phases of protest, despair and denial, but that short-term foster care in a family, especially if the foster-mother got to know the child beforehand, very greatly alleviated the child's distress. Similarly, if a young child is in hospital, regular visits or stays by mother, father and/or other attachment figures can prevent obvious distress.

3   Bowlby quoted much research evidence that suggested that children in long-term institutional care, in orphanages and foundling homes, were severely retarded in social, language and cognitive development; presumably as a result of the effects of maternal separation.

However, the research on the effects of institutional rearing has been re-evaluated (see also chapter 17). No one denies the terrible effects of the pre-war orphanages, which were poorly equipped and staffed by persons with little understanding of the psychological needs of the child. However, any effects of separation from the mother were confounded with the generally unstimulating environment provided. It is not surprising that children become linguistically and cognitively retarded if they are hardly spoken to and given few toys and little sensory stimulation. It is not surprising that they are socially immature, if they receive little social contact and few socially contingent responses. Such was often the case, but these are not necessary concomitants of institutional care. More recent research has found that improved institutional care has fewer dramatically harmful effects (see box 4.2).

4   The adverse effects of long-term maternal separation were apparently further confirmed by research carried out with rhesus monkeys in the USA. Harry and Margaret Harlow (1958, 1969) reported a series of studies in which young rhesus

monkeys were separated from their mothers and raised in isolation. Either they were placed in total isolation, in steel cages with diffused light and filtered sound, or they were placed in partial isolation, in wire cages where they could see and hear, but could not contact other monkeys. Either way, when such an isolation-reared monkey was released and placed with other monkeys, it showed complete social maladjustment, usually being terrified of other monkeys, crouching, rocking and biting itself, and occasionally being hyper-aggressive even to a play invitation. If isolated for only the first 3 months, a young monkey could recover, but isolation for 6 or 12 months seemed to produce irreversible effects. At adolescence these animals were unable to mate satisfactorily, and if a female did have a baby, she abused it rather than cared for it.

This research apparently gave experimental backing for the long-term and irreversible effects of maternal deprivation, in another primate species. Yet these studies also confounded maternal deprivation with general social and sensory deprivation. Moreover, later research in this programme showed how severe deficits can be ameliorated (Novak, 1979; Suomi and Harlow, 1972). The break-through came when the isolation-reared monkeys, instead of being released directly into a peer group, were first placed individually with a younger monkey. For example, 6-month isolates were paired with 3-month-old 'therapist' monkeys. The younger monkey approaches and clings to the older one, rather than attacking it, and seems to help it catch up on the sort of physical contact experiences it has missed. Even 12-month isolates can be helped by this method. This research showed that deprivation effects may not be irreversible, if the right corrective treatment is used. It also suggests that peers can be as effective as mothers in reducing the effects of social isolation.

5   Bowlby cited evidence, from retrospective studies, that linked delinquency or behaviour problems in adolescence to some form of separation experience in childhood, such as hospitalization, or a 'broken home' brought about by parental separation or divorce. Bowlby's interpretation was that the separation experience caused the later behaviour problems.

However this evidence is open to various interpretations. No clear causal link can be inferred. For example, suppose a correlational link has been found between delinquency, and a 'broken home' in early childhood. Parental separation may mean that there was increased discord at the time, or later, or perhaps less supervision of the child given by a single parent. These might be the real causes of the delinquency, not the separation itself. Rutter (1981) argued that it is the discord often present in separating or divorcing families that led to later behaviour problems. It is not separation as such, since death of a parent, while obviously affecting the child, does not usually lead to the negative outcomes that were ascribed to maternal deprivation.

In the long term Bowlby's work in the 1960s had some beneficial effects. Together with other research it led to a marked improvement in the standard of institutional care (see box 4.2) and in many areas the phasing out of institutional care in favour of fostering arrangements. It also led to much easier access of parents to a child in hospital care. A greater awareness of the child's emotional needs was stimulated. However, there were some effects which many people now see as detrimental, particularly a feeling of guilt among mothers who, often out of necessity, went out to work while their children were young.

It appears that Bowlby was wrong to put such a strong emphasis on mothers, and on 'monotropism'. However, it does seem that extreme shared care, with tens of adults involved, can lead to some problems. Perhaps in such situations children cannot form *any* strong attachment relationship. We have two different sources of evidence for this.

One source is institutional rearing. Children reared in homes can experience many short-term caregivers, and find it difficult to form a strong relationship. Studies by Tizard and colleagues in London (see box 4.2) document this, and the kind of clinginess, attention seeking and hyperactivity that may be a consequence. A possible critique of this conclusion is that the adverse effects might be due to genetic factors, or prior adverse experiences, since the children tend to come from very troubled families with multiple psychosocial adversities. Another study by Roy et al. (2000) compared outcomes at around 6 years for 19 children who had been in institutional care, with 19 children who had been in continuous foster care, but who came from similar troubled birth families. Both groups had worse outcome at school than classmates; but the institutional children scored significantly worse on inattention, hyperactivity and emotional disturbance. The likely hypothesis here is that this difference was due to the high levels of multiple caregiving they experienced.

A different source of evidence comes from the Israeli kibbutzim. These communities have had a strong egalitarian philosophy which led to children being raised communally, sleeping in large dormitories away from their parents, and being educated by nurses or *metaplot* (Sing: *metapelet*); children would see their parents for an hour or two each day, but were otherwise raised in a group environment. A comprehensive review of the effects of this system was made by Aviezer et al. (1994). They concluded that collective sleeping arrangements were a problematic aspect of the kibbutz system; in fact, many kibbutzim have now reverted to children sleeping with their parents. Collective sleeping arrangements were associated with a greater incidence of insecure (ambivalent) attachment, as assessed by the strange situation; the authors conclude that in this respect, the traditional kibbutzim deviated too far from what is natural for human infants and their parents. Scharf (2001) reported that adolescents who had experienced prolonged communal sleeping arrangements in kibbutzim, had less autonomous attachment representations on the AAI. In other respects however research suggests that the communal child-rearing environment did foster group-oriented skills and close peer relationships.

An overall assessment is that many of Bowlby's ideas on maternal deprivation are discredited. Nevertheless, it is a normal process for 1- and 2-year-olds to form strong attachments to a few persons, characterized by proximity seeking and separation protest. Bonds can be formed later, as studies of late adoption show, and many of the apparent adverse effects of maternal deprivation are now seen as due to other factors, perhaps not specific to the first 2 or 3 years of life. But, in certain more limited senses than Bowlby first proposed, it may be that this early period is more crucial for social adjustment than are later years.

■ Care Outside the Family: Day Care and Childminding

In many Western societies the standard expectation, at least until recently, has been that mothers of young children should stay at home to look after them until they are old enough to go to nursery or infant school, that is 3–5 years of age. Nevertheless, it has always been the case that many mothers of young children have gone out to work, either through preference or through financial necessity. Some parents manage to share care in their own home with grandparents, older siblings or neighbours. The alternatives are to place the child in a day nursery or crèche, or with a childminder. Day nursery places have long been inadequate to meet demand, and it is difficult to know the numbers of children placed with childminders, as many childminders do not register.

There has been considerable controversy over both nursery-based day care and childminding (which Americans call 'home-based day care' or family day care). Some research in the 1950s and 1960s (including the writings of Bowlby reviewed above) led to cautions about day care. Subsequently, a large body of research (much of it carried out in the USA) suggested that day care does not have adverse effects provided that it is of high quality; that is, there are good staff–child ratios, low staff turnover and a stimulating, well-provided environment. In such circumstances, it was concluded that day care had no overall effects on intellectual development, and did not disrupt the child's attachment relationship with the mother (Belsky and Steinberg, 1978; Clarke-Stewart, 1982); it did increase the degree to which the child interacts, both positively and negatively, with peers.

The controversy over day care was reopened in the late 1980s. Belsky (1988) pointed out that about one-half of US mothers with 1-year-olds were in employment. However, an analysis he made of some recent studies led him to conclude that 'a rather robust association emerges between extensive non-maternal care experience initiated in the first year of life and insecure infant–mother attachment assessed in the Strange Situation' (Belsky, 1988, p. 401). Belsky concluded that initiating day care of more than 20 hours per week before the child is one year of age may be a risk factor for mother–infant relationships. Combining data from five studies, the risk of having insecure attachment to the mother was 43 per cent for infants experiencing high day care, but only 26 per cent for infants experiencing low (or no) day care.

Not everyone agreed with Belsky's conclusion. Clarke-Stewart (1989) queried whether the strange situation is a valid procedure for infants of working mothers (who experience many more routine separations); whether insecure attachment to mothers can be generalized to general emotional security; and whether the differences may be due to other factors (e.g., differences between mothers who choose to work and those who do not). Clarke-Stewart (1991) assessed 150 children aged 2 to 4 years who had experienced different child-care arrangements, in the USA. She found that children in day-care centres had *better* social and intellectual development than those in home care (with either mother or childminder).

However, a survey by Baydar and Brooks-Gunn (1991) of 1181 children in the USA, based on longitudinal data, gave findings more in support of Belsky's views.

They reported that maternal employment starting in the first year of the infant's life had 'significant negative effects on cognitive and behavioral outcomes', but not if maternal employment was deferred to the child's second or third year. (Of alternative arrangements to mother care, grandmother care had the best outcome.)

Another study, of 1100 Bermudan children by Scarr and Thompson (1994), gave yet another result. They compared infants placed in non-maternal care either before, or after, one year of age, and for more, or less, than 20 hours per week; and made assessments when the children were 2 years, and 4 years old. This was a very definite test of Belsky's hypothesis, but the researchers found no differences in cognitive or socio-emotional measures.

The National Institute of Child Health and Development (NICHD) has been pursuing a longitudinal study of some 1200 children with various child care experiences, at 10 sites in the USA. A report on attachment outcomes (NICHD, 1997) did not find any main effects of day care amount or quality on attachment security; there was a main effect of maternal sensitivity/responsiveness, and when low maternal sensitivity/responsiveness was combined with long or poor quality day care, and also especially for boys, there was more insecure attachment. A report on peer interaction (NICHD, 2001) found that children with more hours in day care were rated by caregivers as more negative in peer play, but this was not supported by observational data.

Belsky (2001, p. 845) argues on the basis of the NICHD data and other research that 'concerns raised about early and extensive child care 15 years ago remain valid.' Issues of day care are clearly complex, and influenced by many variables (Melhuish, 2001). Also, the NICHD data clearly suggest that mother/family effects usually outweigh day care effects. In any event, the controversy and evidence do not greatly affect the previous conclusions about day care starting after the first year. Interestingly, in Sweden either parent can take the first 12 months off on full pay, to look after a new baby (on average, fathers take one and a half months of this). Thus, the concern about day care starting in the first year need not worry the Swedes (Hwang et al., 1990).

Childminding (home-based day care) could provide an economic form of day care with high adult to child ratios; it can be provided by professional minders, or by relatives such as grandparents (see below). There has been relatively little research, but studies in the UK of (non-relative) childminding have been very critical of the effects; Mayall and Petrie (1983) in London and Bryant et al. (1980) in Oxfordshire found that children often appeared insecure in the minder's home, and scored below expectations on tests of language or cognitive ability. However these studies did not have proper control groups for comparison, so it is not clear that the children's problems were due to the minding, rather than home circumstances (Melhuish and Moss, 1992; Raven, 1981).

There can certainly be problems with some unregistered minders. Jackson and Jackson (1979) carried out a 'dawn watch' in Huddersfield, England, tracking down where mothers took their children to be minded before the early morning shifts in the factories. They found that some of the unregistered childminders provided a very poor emotional and material environment. American research has also found that much family childcare is unregulated, poorly paid and with high staff turnover (Golbeck and Harlan, 1997). Much can be done here by improving facilities for childminders, providing training courses and encouraging registration and resource back-up (Moss, 1987), and tightening legislation (as with the 1989 Children Act in the UK).

Melhuish and his colleagues (1990a, b) compared the progress of children in London, who (starting before 9 months of age) experienced either care with relatives, childminding or private nursery care. The adult–child ratio was best for care by a relative, next for childminders and lowest for nursery care. At 18 months, communication to children, and also some aspects of the children's language development, were highest for children cared for by relatives and lowest in the nursery group. (Contrary to Belsky's worries there were no apparent differences in attachment to mothers; although the study did not use the standard 'strange situation' procedure, and this methodological difference may account for the discrepancy). By 3 years of age the children in nurseries continued to receive less language stimulation; their naming vocabulary was the least developed, though they did not differ on other language measures. There were no significant differences in cognitive development, however, and the nursery children did show more prosocial behaviour such as sharing, cooperation and empathy with others. These differences held even after controlling for measures of social class (such as mothers' education) that discriminated between the three groups.

Research in this area moves fast and may be overtaken by historical changes. In the UK, the 1989 Children Act helped bring about an expansion of interest in nursery care, and quality of care may have improved in the decade since the Melhuish study. A broad perspective is also useful. Besides looking at effects on children, we need to bear in mind that help with childcare can be liberating for mothers. A mother who stays at home to look after young children full time can feel frustrated or isolated, particularly if she has little support from her husband or relatives. Research on the causes of depression in women has identified a number of contributory factors, one of which is being at home full time with two or more children under five if other stresses are present (Brown and Harris, 1978).

Relationships with Other Family Members

Although many attachment theorists tend to focus on the mother when discussing the child's early social relationships, the child has important relationships with other family members: father and grandparents (we discuss siblings in chapter 5).

Fathers

How important is the other parent – the father? And has the role of the father changed in recent years, as is often suggested? Research in a number of societies has shown that fathers can fulfil a parenting role just as much as mothers, for example in single-parent father families; but that typically, fathers do not have such a large part in child-rearing and domestic tasks as do mothers, especially when children are young (Lamb, 1987).

So far, the highest degree of father involvement in any human society seems to be among the Aka pygmies, a hunter-gatherer people in the Central African Republic. Fathers were found to be present with an infant or child for 88 per cent of the time, and to be holding an infant for 22 per cent of the time. This high degree of physical intimacy by fathers seems to be encouraged by the overlapping subsistence activities of men and women. Men don't just leave women in the campsite to look after children, while they go hunting with nets; women often assist in hunting, and men often carry infants back after the hunt. Nevertheless, even in this society mothers still engage in more childcare than fathers (Hewlett, 1987).

Another society where paternal care is encouraged is Sweden. Equality between the sexes has been encouraged since the 1960s, including legislation about work opportunities and parental leave, and an advertising campaign (see plate 4.2) to encourage fathers to take childcare responsibilities seriously. While this has had some impact, it is still true that Swedish mothers do most of the housework and provide most childcare, even when both parents are working (Hwang, 1987).

In *Becoming a Father* (1986), Charlie Lewis carried out an interview study of 100 fathers of 1-year-old children in Nottingham, UK. One aspect that Lewis documented was that the majority of fathers (65 per cent) now attended all stages of the birth of their child. Many fathers were anxious about it, and had been encouraged to attend by their wives; but most found it a positive experience. As one father put it:

> I found it hard work and much more traumatic than I thought it would be . . . I felt by the end of the experience that I had done a full day's work and was absolutely washed out, but nevertheless I wouldn't miss being there a second time.
>
> (Lewis, 1986, p. 70)

This was undoubtedly a change since in the 1950s fathers were discouraged from attending hospital deliveries (up to the 1960s many more deliveries took place at home anyway). Lewis was able to compare his data, obtained in 1980, with similar data obtained by the Newsons in interviews in 1960. The most significant changes are in the husband helping in the period after birth, and getting up for the baby at night; the changes for nappy changing are not significant (see table 4.5).

It was not the case that fathers who were present at the birth were also much more involved with childcare after the baby was home; Lewis found no correlation between these two. Mothers predominantly did the childcare, feeding and nappy changing. At least two factors seem to contribute to this. First, the father will more often be in longer hours of employment. Lewis did find that fathers contributed more when the mother was also working. Second, it is easy for fathers to feel marginalized in baby care; mothers are seen as the 'experts' at this. Indeed it is only mothers who can breastfeed! However, mothers may contribute to keeping their own areas of expertise, as the following interview demonstrates:

Plate 4.2 A Swedish father cradles his young son. Photographs such as this were used in campaigns directed to increasing paternal involvement in childcare (from the Department of Information, Stockholm).

Table 4.5 Changes in father involvement in childcare, 1960 to 1980

	1960 (N = 100)	1980 (N = 100)
Husband helps in the period after birth? (Yes)	30	77 $p < 0.001$
Husband gets up to baby at night? (Yes)	49	87 $p < 0.001$
Husband involved in nappy changing?		
little/never	37	40
occasional	43	32 n.s.
often	20	28

Source: Lewis, 1986

Interviewer:	How about changing him? Do you often change his nappies?
Father (to wife):	Don't think I've done that, have I?
Wife:	In the first week when I weren't well.
Interviewer:	Is there any reason why you haven't?
Wife:	Only 'cos I've always been there. They don't bother me in the slightest, you know.
Father:	Nappies don't bother me, you know. If Jan [wife] turned round to me and said, 'Could you do it for me, then?' . . . Like I say, she's a very competent mother.

(Lewis, 1986, p. 100)

Differences in mother's and father's behaviour with children may lessen after infancy, especially when mothers are also working outside the home. In the USA, Cabrera et al. (2000) suggest that a dramatic increase in mothers working over the past 40 years, has led to an appreciable increase in the time fathers spend with their children. Russell and Saebel (1997), in a review of studies examining mother and father relationships with sons and daughters, believe that differences in mothers and fathers later in childhood may be exaggerated; out of 116 studies reviewed, only 16 found significant mother–father differences. However, there is some evidence that while mothers continue to spend more time in caregiving tasks, and remain closer to children, fathers do spend more time in play and recreational activities.

Another increase noted by Cabrera et al. (2000) is in the number of single-parent families – usually mother-headed families. In the USA, these constituted 6 per cent of families in 1960 but 24 per cent by 2000. This could be seen as a worrying trend, in that supportive father involvement with children is generally related to positive outcomes in the school and peer group (Lamb, 1997). However mother-headed families could cover a wide range – including families still suffering from stress of separation and divorce (see below); families where fathers retain active involvement through joint custody or frequent visits; and families where fathers are effectively absent. A longitudinal study in New Zealand (also featured in box 9.1) found that of young men aged 26, 19 per cent had become fathers; but that those who had experienced a stressful rearing environment and had a history of conduct problems were more likely to become fathers at an early age, and to spend less time living with their child (Jaffee et al., 2001). The authors conclude that these absent fathers might have difficulty providing positive parenting without effective support to help them deal with poor social-psychological adjustment.

Grandparents

About 70 per cent of middle-aged and older people become grandparents. Since the average age of becoming a grandparent, in Western societies, is about 50 years for women, and a couple of years older for men, they are likely to remain grandparents for some 25 years or more; about a third of their life-span. Grandparenthood is thus an important part of the life cycle for most people. Many grandparents live fairly close to grandchildren, while those who are more distant characteristically keep contact via letters, phone calls, emails and visits.

Grandparents can have considerable influence on their grandchildren's behaviour. Tinsley and Parke (1984) described both indirect and direct influences. Indirect influence has an effect without there necessarily being any direct interaction. For example, the parent–child interaction will be influenced by the way the parent has been brought up and the experiences of child-rearing which the parent has had modelled by his or her parent, i.e. the grandparent (see discussion of intergenerational transmission of attachment, pp. 102–3). Grandparents can also provide emotional and financial support for parents, which will be especially valuable at times of emotional or financial stress.

Direct influences can also take many forms. The strongest is when a grandparent acts as a surrogate parent; either in a grandparent-maintained household, or being co-resident in the household (for example in a single-parent family, or with a teenage pregnancy); or as a temporary caregiver while both parents are working – although statistics are hard to come by, it is believed that grandparents are the primary source of non-parental care of young children. It is most often the maternal grandmother who fills these roles (plate 4.3). However, grandfathers can be important too; Radin et al. (1991) found that grandfathers can have a direct positive influence on young grandchildren of teen mothers, especially for grandsons.

While only a small proportion of grandparents live in the same house as grandchildren in western societies, in the Pacific Rim countries of China, Japan and Korea, family ties including grandparental bonds tend to be especially close. In China, many grandparents still live in three-generation households, and family ties are perceived as very close (Shu and Smith, 2001). A survey of Chinese children by Falbo (1991) found that grandparental preschool care was associated with somewhat better school performance than parental care; there are possible confounds in this finding (such as socioeconomic status), but frequency of grandparental contact, plus grandparental educational attainment, did predict language and mathematics scores in first and fifth grade children. Similarly, Korean grandmothers from a sample of 1326 extended families were accredited with increasing their grandchildren's resiliency by providing sources of attachment, affection, and knowledge, as well as having indirect effects through their support of parents (Hwang and St James-Roberts, 1998).

Plate 4.3 A grandmother looks after her grand-daughter aged 1.

Even if not acting as a surrogate parent, grandparents can pass on information and values directly to grandchildren. They are particularly well placed to pass on the family history, and knowledge of times past. A grandparent who has contact with a grandchild can act as a companion and be an important part of the child's social network. Many grandparents enjoy conversations with grandchildren, asking them to run errands, and giving them small gifts.

Grandparents can also act directly as a source of emotional support, acting as a 'buffer' in cases where a grandchild is in conflict with parents, or where the parents are in conflict with each other. For example, Johnson (1983) analysed the responses of 58 US grandmothers to the divorce of one of their children. These grandmothers generally maintained their level of contact with the grandchildren, and the younger ones especially (below 65 years of age) often increased their level of contact. One grandmother described how she filled a gap in the custody arrangements:

> I pick them up on Friday after work. We go to the Pizza Hut for dinner – then home to watch TV. I keep lots of goodies around for them. They fight, I shush them. Then they zonk out. The next morning, I fix breakfast – they watch TV. Then I take them to their dad's and dump them. It's kinda nice.
>
> (Johnson, 1983, pp. 553–4)

However it is not always easy for grandparents to see grandchildren after parental divorce. Some paternal grandparents especially may be prevented from seeing grandchildren after an acrimonious divorce and when the children stay with the mother. The issue of rights of access of grandparents to their grandchildren has been of recent concern in many countries, and grandparents rights groups have sprung up to represent the interest of grandparents. A study in Canada of such grandparents deprived of access to grandchildren, found a strong grief reaction, with nearly half reporting related health problems and emotional difficulties (Kruk, 1995). In a similar UK sample Drew and Smith (1999) found that many grandparents were experiencing chronic grief, mental health problems, symptoms of post traumatic stress (mostly intrusive thoughts) and lowered life satisfaction:

> Since the loss of my grandson it has been a dreadful time mentally and physically, my health has suffered, I don't sleep well, and some days the pain is unbearable. Birthdays and Christmas time are devastating. I just long to give him a big hug and tell him how much I love him. What really worries me, is does my grandson think I've abandoned him and that I don't love him anymore, he is such a special little boy.

Sometimes the values of grandparents may conflict with those of the parental generation; for example, in an interview study of older people in London, Townsend (1957, pp. 106–7) remarked that 'the grandparents were notably lenient towards grandchildren'. As one informant put it, 'the grandmother can be free and easy. She [her daughter] has to be fairly strict with them.' At other times grandmothers have been thought of as being too strict and punitive. Some negative stereotypes of grandparents still persist, related to aging; many children's books portray grandparents as somewhat inactive persons in their eighties or nineties, rather than (as many grandparents are) actively employed and in their fifties or early sixties (Janelli, 1988).

Types of families

The stereotypical family is of a heterosexual married couple with their biological children (usually, two of them!). But in reality there is much variation in types of families. In Great Britain for example, about 80 per cent of children under 16 are with both natural parents (Clarke, 1992). About 10 per cent are in lone-parent families (usually, but not always, the mother), about 9 per cent are with one natural parent and one step-parent, and about 1 per cent are in other arrangements. These figures apply to one moment of time; it is estimated that through their entire childhood, only about one-half of British children (53%) will stay with both married natural parents.

A small number of children are brought up, not by a heterosexual couple, but by gay or lesbian parents of the same sex. What are the effects of this on children? Patterson (1992) reviewed a number of relevant studies. She concluded that gender identity, gender role behaviour and sexual preferences of children of gay and lesbian parents fall within the normal range of variation; peer relationships were found to be satisfactory. This is supported by more recent research. For example, Golombok et al. (1997) compared children aged around 6 years in the UK, in 30 lesbian mother families, 42 single heterosexual mother families and 41

2-parent heterosexual families. They found little difference between lesbian and heterosexual single mother families. In the fatherless families (whether lesbian or heterosexual) there was actually greater mother interaction, and attachment security, although children had lower self-esteem. In the US, Chan et al. (1998) report findings from 80 families with children aged around 7 years, conceived by donor insemination: 55 were lesbian and 25 heterosexual families; 50 were couples, and 30 single parent families. They found that child adjustment was unrelated to number of parents or sexual orientation (but was related to parental stress and conflict, irrespective of family type).

To date, this research does not suggest that children of gay or lesbian parents develop differently in any significant sense. Other aspects of parenting (such as parenting style, and conflict between parents) appear to be more important.

Styles of Parenting

Independent of the body of research on attachment security, studies have been made of how parents may vary in their styles of child-rearing. Some parents believe in strong discipline, others do not, for example. An American psychologist, Diana Baumrind, tried to conceptualize three global styles of child-rearing in the USA (Baumrind, 1967, 1980). Her styles were:

1   *Authoritarian* – parents who have strict ideas about discipline and behaviour that are not open to discussion.
2   *Authoritative* – parents who have ideas about behaviour and discipline, which they are willing to explain and discuss with children and at times adapt.
3   *Permissive* – parents who have relaxed ideas about behaviour and discipline.

Maccoby and Martin (1983) felt that it would be best to separate out two dimensions of parenting style – how demanding or undemanding parents are about their children's behaviour, on the one hand, and how responsive or unresponsive they are to their children on the other. They therefore produced the four-fold classification shown in table 4.6. This approach to parenting styles, typically measured by questionnaires given to parents, has been widely used and does predict to aspects of children's development. Let's look at a couple of examples.

Dekovic and Janssens (1992) had a sample of 112 children aged 6 to 11 years. They ascertained their sociometric status in school (see chapter 5), and their prosocial behaviour from ratings by teachers and classmates (see chapter 8). They estimated parenting style from observations at home in the evenings when both parents were present (time-consuming, but probably more valid than self-report questionnaires). They found that authoritative parents tended to have popular, prosocial children; authoritarian parents tended to have sociometrically rejected children.

Steinberg et al. (1992) carried out a larger, longitudinal study, of 6400 adolescents aged 14 to 18. For this size sample they obviously had to rely on questionnaire measures of parenting style. They also asked the adolescents to report on

Table 4.6 Styles of parenting from Maccoby and Martin (1983)

	Responsive	Unresponsive
Demanding	Authoritative	Authoritarian
Undemanding	Permissive	Uninvolved

parental involvement in their schooling, and obtained their school grades for achievement. They found that authoritative parenting was related to better school performance. Interestingly, there was a mediating effect of parental involvement, usually thought of as helpful in this context. The parent's involvement in the adolescent's school work was especially helpful when it came from authoritative parents, but not so much when it came from authoritarian parents – maybe the latter can be too critical and not so supportive as authoritative parents can be (with *laissez-faire* or undemanding parents not being involved very much with school anyway).

Steinberg et al. characterized authoritative parenting in their study as having three components – parental acceptance and warmth; behavioural supervision and strictness; and psychological autonomy granting or democracy. However, this highlights difficulty with the Maccoby and Martin scheme (table 4.6), which includes the last two components, but does not explicitly include warmth – nor, indeed, other possibly important dimensions such as parental punitiveness. Baumrind's original global approach does include more components (Baumrind identified authoritative parents as being warm and accepting of their children, in contrast to authoritarian parents), but confounds them so that one does not know which aspect is responsible for the effects obtained. These difficulties are discussed in a review by Darling and Steinberg (1993), who also point out the possible cultural specificity of this work. There is evidence, for example, that these parenting-style schemes have greater predictiveness for Euro-American families than they do for African-American families. However, a similar pattern of outcomes for authoritative and authoritarian parenting to that found in western samples, was reported by Chen et al. (1997) for 8-year-old children in Beijing, China.

Conflict between parents

There is considerable research evidence that conflict between parents can in itself be distressing for children – whether it precedes marital separation and divorce, or not. A study by Gottman and Katz (1989) in Illinois, USA, of 56 families with a 4- to 5-year-old child, used both laboratory observations and home interviews. The researchers found that more maritally distressed couples had more stressed children who showed more negative peer interactions, and more illness. A follow-up of the same families was made when the children were 8 years old (Katz and Gottman, 1993). Teacher ratings of the children's internalizing and externalizing behaviour problems were made. Earlier marital mutual hostility predicted later externalizing (antisocial) behaviour in the children, and earlier husband angry-withdrawn behaviour predicted later internalizing (self-blame) behaviour in children. Cummings and Davies (2002) review research in this area; parental conflict clearly has adverse effects on children, and this contributes to the effects found in studies of separation and divorce (though it does not appear to be the only factor involved).

Divorce and Step-parenting

Divorce has become more common in modern Western societies (Clarke, 1992). It can be distressing for children when the apparently secure base of the family is broken in this way. There is likely to be conflict between spouses, uncertainty for the future, effects on family income, possible relocation, and possible loss of contact with one parent and related kin (Richards, 1995). Wallerstein (1985) described three phases in the divorce process. First is the acute phase, typically lasting about 2 years, in which the emotional and physical separation takes place. Second is a transitional phase, in which each parent experiences marked ups and downs while they establish separate lives. Third is a post-divorce phase, in which each parent has established a new lifestyle, either as a single parent or remarried.

What are the consequences of this for the child's development? The effects of divorce have been found to vary considerably with the child's age when the separation occurs (Hetherington and Stanley-Hagan, 1999). Preschool children, although upset, are least able to understand what is going on. By middle childhood the changes are better understood, but there may be persistent wishes or fantasies of the parents reuniting. For early adolescents, the reaction may more often be one of shame or anger, perhaps siding with one parent or the other. The impact on children varies over time as well; clearly longitudinal studies are vital to get any real understanding of the impact of divorce on children. Several such studies have been made.

One influential study commenced with 144 middle-class white families in Virginia, USA (Hetherington et al., 1982). Half the children were from divorced, mother-custody families, and half from non-divorced families; their average age at separation was 4 years. After 1 year, most children from divorced families (and many parents) experienced emotional distress and behaviour problems associated with the disruptions in family functioning. This was much improved after 2 years; the main exception being that some boys had poor relations with their custodial mothers and showed more antisocial and non-compliant behaviour than boys from non-divorced families.

A follow-up was made after 6 years, when the children had an average age of 10 years, of 124 of the original 144 families. By now, 42 out of 60 divorced mothers had remarried (and 2 of these had redivorced); also 11 of 64 originally non-divorced families had divorced. A general finding was that children of divorced parents experienced more independence and power in decision making at an earlier age, and their activities were less closely monitored by parents. They 'grew up faster'. Mother–daughter relationships were generally not much different from those in non-divorced families. However, mother–son relations continued to be rather tense for divorced mothers who had not remarried; even despite warmth in the relationship, sons were often non-compliant and mothers ineffective in their attempts at control.

Another study, starting in 1971, was of 131 children from 60 divorcing families in Northern California (Wallerstein, 1987). The children were between two-and-a-half and 18 years at the time of decisive parental separation. Initially, virtually all the children were very distressed at the separation. Things were not much better after 18 months; some of the younger girls had recovered somewhat, but some of the younger boys showed significantly more disturbance. A follow-up after five years showed a more complex picture. What was most important now was the overall quality of life within the post-divorce or remarried family. About one-third of the children, however, still showed moderate to severe depression.

At a follow-up after 10 years, some 90 per cent of the original sample could still be located. Interviews with children now 16- to 18-years-old, who had perhaps experienced the separation at the most vulnerable time, showed that many still felt sad and wistful about what had happened, while often accepting its inevitability. As one girl said:

> I don't know if divorce is ever a good thing, but if it is going to happen, it is going to happen. If one person wants out, he wants out. It can't be changed. I get depressed when I think about it. I get sad and angry when I think about what happened to me.
> (Wallerstein, 1987, p. 205)

All the children had been in the legal and physical custody of their mothers; about 40 per cent had moved in for a while with their fathers during adolescence, but most had returned; visits to father varied greatly, but were not usually more than weekly due in part to geographical separation. However, the quality of the father–child relationship was an important determinant of adjustment.

Although traditionally custody is given to one parent, usually the mother, joint custody is being increasingly advocated where possible (i.e. where both parents live fairly close and maintain a reasonable relationship). Luepnitz (1986) compared children who were in sole custody with the mother, sole custody with the father, or joint custody, 2 years or more after final separation. In fact, measures of child adjustment were found to be independent of custody type. Joint custody has the advantages of the child being able to develop two independent relationships, and of reducing financial and parenting pressures on a single parent. Luepnitz reported that 'the vast majority of children in joint custody were pleased and comfortable with the arrangement.' Single custody can however protect wives from possible abuse, and give more flexibility to relocation and remarriage.

Interestingly, Luepnitz found that only 11 per cent of her sample of children showed signs of maladjustment. This is less than one-third the level reported in Wallerstein's study, and may be due to sample differences. Wallerstein recruited subjects by promising counselling, and thus may have recruited particularly distressed families; whereas Luepnitz may have recruited rather non-distressed families who were willing to discuss custody arrangements and their outcome. Whatever the extent of maladjustment, however, all the major studies agree that experiencing good relationships with both parents and an absence of continuing conflict are generally conducive to the most positive outcome for the children involved. Hetherington (1989; see also Hetherington and Stanley-Hagan, 1999) describes 'winners, losers, and survivors' of parental divorce. Depending on circumstances, some children may continue to be damaged and insecure through to adulthood; others recover and 'survive'; yet others may develop particularly caring and competent ways of behaving as a result of coping with the experience.

Some of the ill-effects of divorce are probably attributable to conflicts between partners which predate the actual separation of the parents. A longitudinal analysis was made by Cherlin et al. (1991) of 7–11-year-olds in Britain, using the National Child Development Study (a survey of mothers of all 17,000 children born in one week in 1958), and of 7–11 and 11–16-year-olds in the USA, using the National Survey of Children, which began in 1976. These analyses looked at children's school achievement and behaviour problems before, as well as after, divorce. Generally, the apparent effects of divorce (compared with children in non-divorcing families) were considerably reduced when the situation pre-divorce was taken into account. As the authors put it, 'at least as much attention needs to be paid to the processes that occur in troubled, intact families as to the trauma that children suffer after their parents separate.'

This conclusion tends to be supported by results from another longitudinal study in the UK – the ALSPAC study, which recruited over 14,138 children born between April 1991 and December 1992 from the area around Bristol. A report by O'Connor et al. (1999) used retrospective data from up to 13,000 mothers in the sample, and found a link between parental divorce and depression in adulthood (also found in the NCDS study). However this link was mediated by a number of factors, including the quality of parent–child and parent marital relationships (in that person's childhood), as well as by concurrent stress, and social support.

Step-parenting

Divorced parents often remarry. They have chosen a new partner, but their children usually have the choice thrust upon them. How do they adapt to this? Remarriage does generally increase the life satisfaction of the adults, but forming strong relationships in the reconstituted family is often a gradual and difficult process. Step-parents are almost inevitably seen as intruders by stepchildren, and often try to tread an uneasy path between assisting their spouse in discipline problems (which may lead to their rejection by stepchildren), and disengagement. According to the study of divorced families by Hetherington et al. (1982), remarriage and the presence of a stepfather seemed to improve matters for sons, who perhaps responded well to a male figure with whom to identify; however, the stepfamily situation often made matters worse for daughters, with the stepfather–stepdaughter relationship being a particularly difficult one.

The difficulties facing some stepfamilies were also documented by a study in London by Ferri (1984); however many such families had successfully met the challenge. As with divorced families, the problems of stepfamilies may be exaggerated, in the sense that often other associated factors may be responsible for difficulties. This was suggested by a longitudinal study of 907 children in New Zealand, by Nicholson et al. (1999). Following the progress of these children up to age 18, they found that entering a stepfamily between ages 6 to 16 meant a higher risk of drug abuse, juvenile crime, and poor school achievement. But these differences largely disappeared when account was taken of the families' socio-economic status, parent characteristics, any family history of conflict, and pre-existing child problems.

Harsh Physical Punishment, and Child Abuse

Usually, parents love and care for their children. No parent is perfect, but most provide 'good enough' parenting. Some conflict between parents and their off-spring is inevitable (and indeed is predicted from evolutionary theory, see chapter 2), but generally this is kept within reasonable bounds.

Harsh physical punishment

What constitutes 'reasonable bounds' for parental discipline? A very difficult area to reach consensus on here, is the use of physical punishment with children. Is it acceptable for a parent to physically punish a child, for example by smacking and hitting? Is this a form of bullying or abuse, or is it sometimes a necessary form of parental control? Opinions are divided. Several countries – Sweden, Finland, Denmark, Norway, Austria, Cyprus, Latvia, Croatia, Israel and Germany – have legally abolished the use of corporal punishment. In the UK and the USA it is widely accepted, although pressure groups are attempting to change the law. The United Nations Convention on the Rights of the Child (see p. 20) has criticized the UK government for failing to prohibit all corporal punishment in the family.

Surveys in the UK and the USA suggest that a majority of parents practice some physical punishment. Table 4.7 shows some representative data from urban families in England by Nobes et al. (1999). 362 mothers and 103 fathers were interviewed about their punishment of their children (aged 1, 4, 7 or 11 years). The researchers grouped the types of punishment into the four categories shown. Clearly most parents smack their children now and then, and over a third do so monthly. Mothers and fathers report similar levels, except that fathers report using higher levels of physical restraint. The most severe incidents of physical punishment were also reported by fathers. Similar high figures are found in the USA. However in Sweden the percentage of parents who reported hitting their children fell from 27.5 per cent in 1980 (it was made illegal in 1979) to 1.1 per cent in 2000.

Does it matter if parents smack their children? Many studies have found correlations between parental punitiveness, and childhood misbehaviour and aggression. However there could be many explanations for this, other than the smacking causing the aggression (see also p. 12). Well-controlled longitudinal studies give more insight. A review by Larzelere (2000) concluded that smacking could be an effective, unharmful form of discipline provided that: (1) it was not too severe;

Parents and Families   125

Table 4.7   Percentages of mothers and fathers using four types of physical punishment on their children; adapted from Nobes et al. (1999)

		In last year	Monthly or more often
Smacking/hitting	spanking, slapping, beating	Mothers 76.8 Fathers 76.7	39.8 35.9
Physical restraint	pushing, shoving, shaking, throwing, holding	Mothers 25.4 Fathers 42.2	4.7 18.6
Punishment by example	squeezing, hair pulling, biting, pinching	Mothers 12.7 Fathers 14.6	1.1 2.9
Ingestion	washing mouth out with soap/water; forced feeding	Mothers 5.2 Fathers 3.9	0.0 0.0

(2) was kept under control, not in moments of anger; (3) was limited to the 2 to 6 year age range; and (4) used in conjunction with reasoning. However critics point out that these are quite stringent limitations (for example, many parents in Nobes et al.'s 1999 sample were punishing one-year-olds, and 7- and 11-year-olds; and some 15 to 20 per cent used severe physical punishments). If smacking often slides into inappropriate and severe chastisement, this could be seen as becoming abusive behaviour (which has clear negative outcomes, see below); the most powerful argument of the anti-smacking lobby is that it is safer to make all smacking illegal (as many countries have successfully done) than condone behaviour for which the boundary of acceptability is dangerously vague and difficult for parents to follow (Leach, 2002).

Child abuse

Some children suffer clear physical or sexual abuse from parents. Physical abuse has been defined as 'the intentional, non-accidental use of force on the part of the parent or other caretaker interacting with a child in his or her care aimed at hurting, injuring or destroying that child' (Gil, 1970). Sexual abuse has been defined as 'the involvement of dependent, sexually immature children and adolescents in sexual activities that they do not fully comprehend, to which they are unable to give informed consent or that violate the social taboos of family roles' (Kempe, 1980).

The extent of child abuse is difficult to determine, as naturally parents are secretive about it, and children are often too young or too frightened to seek help. In the UK the National Society for Prevention of Cruelty to Children (NSPCC) has reported some 9000 cases of physical abuse and 6000 cases of sexual abuse per year (Creighton and Noyes, 1989). Some 200 children may die each year as a result of direct or indirect maltreatment by their parents; child abuse is in fact the fourth commonest cause of death in preschool children (Browne, 1989). The peak of physical abuse is in early childhood, with boys being more at risk than girls;

the peak for sexual abuse appears to be later in middle childhood, with girls primarily at risk.

Diagnosis of abuse has its own set of problems. Questioning of young children has to be done carefully to maximize the accuracy and usefulness of children's testimony (Fundudis, 1989). In the case of sexual abuse, observation of unstructured play with anatomically correct dolls may be useful. Unlike conventional dolls, these dolls have sexual organs and characteristics. Some studies suggest that most children, while noticing the characteristics of the dolls, do not show sexually explicit play with them; when it is observed, such explicit play (for example, sucking a doll's penis) may well arise from the child's preoccupations based on previous exposure to explicit sexual information or activity (Glaser and Collins, 1989). However, the use of these dolls remains controversial (Westcott et al., 1989).

It can also be very difficult and distressing for victims of child abuse to speak out. At times they may not be believed and interviews by police and judges can seem very intimidating (see chapter 13). In the USA and the UK it is increasingly possible to allow children to give evidence by means of a closed circuit television 'video link', so that they need not directly face their abuser (Davies, 1988). Psychologists are closely involved in this work, and in attempts to help victims of abuse recover from their experiences (British Psychological Society, 1990).

In cases of physical abuse, mothers and fathers are about equally likely to be involved (though there are obvious questions about who is willing to admit abuse – a mother may 'shelter' an abusing father or cohabitee). In cases of sexual abuse, some 95 per cent involve males as the perpetrators. Another risk factor, for young children, is abuse by step-parents. Studies in Canada, the UK and elsewhere indicate that the risk of abuse, including fatal abuse, is much greater for children with stepfathers (Daly and Wilson, 1996).

What leads a parent to abuse a child? For the step-parent data, Daly and Wilson take an evolutionary perspective, arguing that it is not in the stepfather's genetic interest to divert parental investment to children not related to him (cf. p. 52); in terms of proximal mechanisms, a few stepfathers may just not develop any attachment to their new stepchildren. More generally, abusing parents have been found very often to have insecure attachment relationships with their children. In one study, 70 per cent of maltreated infants were found to have insecure attachments to their caregivers, compared with only 26 per cent of infants with no record of maltreatment (Browne, 1989).

Crittenden (1988) has examined the representations of relationships in abusing parents, using the idea of internal working models discussed earlier. She interviewed 124 mothers in Virginia, USA, many of whom had abused or maltreated their children, and gave them the Separation Anxiety Test (p. 99). She reported that adequate mothers generally had warm and secure relationships with both their children and their partner. By contrast, abusing mothers appeared to conceptualize relationships in terms of power struggles. They tended to be controlling and hostile with anxiously attached children, and to have angry and unstable adult relationships. Another group, of neglecting mothers, appeared to conceive of relationships as emotionally empty. They were unresponsive to their anxiously attached children, and were involved in stable but affectless relationships with partners. These findings have implications for working with these families. Crittenden argues that 'the problem for those offering treatment to abused and abusing individuals is to find ways both to change their experience and also to change their conceptualization of it. Without a change in the representational model, the new experience will be encoded in terms of the old model and will be rendered useless' (Crittenden, 1988, p. 197).

The effects of child abuse can be wide-ranging and long-lasting. Malinosky-Rummell and Hansen (1993) reviewed the evidence regarding childhood physical abuse and find links to adolescent criminal behaviour, adult family violence, and non-familial violence. Spaccerelli (1994) reviewed effects of childhood sexual abuse, finding it to be a risk factor for long-term effects on mental health. Both reviews point out that other factors can moderate the effects – for example, the kinds of coping strategies used by the individual, the nature of support that they have, and the way in which they are able to appraise and understand what has happened to them. Stevenson (1999) also reviews long-term consequences of abuse, and the effectiveness of treatment for abused children, and abusive parents.

Models of Parenting

We've looked at aspects of parenting where there are difficulties – where parents separate or divorce, or where there is actual abuse of children. But what about the more normal range of parenting? There is still a lot of variation in how different parents carry out the task. Belsky (1984) advocated a model of parental functioning that distinguishes three main influences on the quality of parental functioning. In order of suggested importance, these are:

1   *personal psychological resources of the parent*: this will include parental mental health, the quality of internal representations of relationships and their development history;
2   *contextual sources of support*: including the social network of support from partner, relatives and friends, and job conditions and financial circumstances; and
3   *characteristics of the child*: in particular easy or difficult temperament (see p. 83).

Belsky's actual process model of factors influencing parenting is illustrated in figure 4.1. The model is also useful for understanding how variations in family functioning, satisfactory as well as unsatisfactory, may come about, and in thinking of ways to help parents with difficult or disruptive children. There has been considerable interest in the area of parenting skills, and ways of helping parents change, improve their coping and child-management skills, or develop a more secure relationship with their child. These approaches have mainly focused on the first area of Belsky's model, that of personal psychological resources of the parent.

Van Ijzendoorn et al. (1995) reviewed 16 studies that involved working with parents to improve parental sensitivity and attachment security. Interventions were varied but covered increased support from home visitors, use of videos,

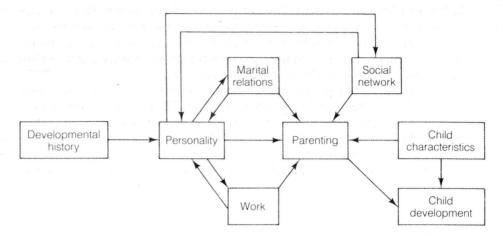

Figure 4.1   Belsky's process model of the determinants of parenting.

parent education, and individual (mother) and joint (mother–child) psychotherapy. Generally, short-term preventive interventions seemed more effective than long-term therapy-based interventions. There were appreciable improvements in many studies in maternal sensitivity to the child, but only small improvements in attachment security.

This review suggests that it is easier to produce changes at the behavioural level, than at the representational level. This need not be surprising; changes at the representational level may be deeper and need more sustained effort to bring about.

It is a continuing challenge to see how parents of difficult or disruptive children can be helped. The studies cited here have used theoretical models based on attachment theory; others have used models based more on social skills and behavioural approaches. Belsky's model also draws attention to the wider social context; the employment status of parents, housing conditions and social support.

The extent to which parents make a difference to childen's development has, however, been disputed. Scarr (1992) argues that by and large, parents need only provide a basically warm, supportive and nurturant environment for their children to develop their innate potential. She supports her argument by reference to studies in behaviour genetics (see chapter 2) which found that what is called the shared family environment – the aspects of the family environment common to all siblings – contributes rather little to understanding individual differences in many areas. To some extent children help create their own rearing environment. A child's temperament for example (which appears to be strongly genetically influenced), influences the ways parents behave towards that child and the expectations they have of them.

Of course, no one denies that extremes of environment can adversely affect development. Studies of children reared in profoundly non-stimulating environments, and studies of environmental enrichment, show that children can be held back if they do not receive a basic minimum of language and intellectual stimulation, and love and affection (see chapter 17). Scarr accepts this, and says that children require this average expectable environment for normal development; but that beyond this, individual variation in development is mainly due to inherited individual potential, finding expression in a reasonably good environment that is partly created by the person for themselves.

Scarr's views give greater prominence to genetic factors than some psychologists think is justified; and they appear to downplay the importance of parenting, beyond the basic minimum or good enough parenting. They also imply that many parent–child similarities are due to genetic rather than environmental factors. These issues are controversial and hotly debated (Baumrind, 1993). The importance of parents (after the preschool years) is also downplayed by Harris (1995) in her group socialization theory; this is discussed further in chapter 5.

Further Reading

For a good overview of attachment theory see Goldberg, S. 2000: *Attachment and Development*. London: Arnold. Holmes, J. 1993: *John Bowlby and Attachment Theory*. London: Routledge, provides a readable biography and assessment of Bowlby's work; his last book was published as Bowlby, J. 1988: *A Secure Base: Clinical Applications of Attachment Theory*. London: Tavistock/Routledge.

Golombok, S. 2000: *Parenting: What Really Counts?*. London: Routledge, is a readable overview of many contemporary topics. Lamb, M. E., Sternberg, K. J., Hwang, P. and Broberg, A. (eds) 1992: *Child Care in Context: Cross-cultural Perspectives*. New York: Erlbaum, is a useful source. Browne, K. Davies, C. and Stratton, P. (eds) 1988: *Early Prediction and Prevention of Child Abuse*. Chichester and New York: John Wiley & Sons, gives a comprehensive review of these topics; and Schaffer, H. R. 1990: *Making Decisions about Children*. Oxford: Blackwell, explores the ways in which our psychological knowledge can influence crucial decisions about children in matters such as custody, adoption and fostering. Pryor, J. and Rodgers, B. 2001: *Children in Changing Families: Life after Parental Separation*. Oxford: Blackwell, is a useful overview of issues around divorce, step-parenting, and family transitions. The ultimate reference for parenting issues is the series of volumes edited by Bornstein, M. 2002: *Handbook of Parenting*, 2nd edn. Mahwah, NJ: Erlbaum.

Discussion Points

1   What is meant by 'secure' and 'insecure' attachment? Are these culturally biased terms?
2   Do mothers, fathers and grandparents have different influences on a child's behaviour?
3   What did Bowlby mean by 'maternal deprivation'? How useful or valid has this concept proved to be?
4   What impact does parental divorce have on children?
5   What are the problems in diagnosing, and treating, child abuse?

Box 4.1
Infant–mother attachment among the Dogon of Mali

Although Ainsworth's pioneering work on attachment had been carried out among the Ganda people of Uganda, rather few subsequent studies in attachment have used non-urban populations. This study is an exception. It took place amongst the Dogon people of Eastern Mali, a primarily agrarian people living by subsistence farming of millet and other crops, as well as cash economy in the towns (box plate 4.1.1). The study was carried out in 2 villages (population around 400) and one town (population 9000), with the researchers attempting to get a complete coverage of infants born between mid-July and mid-September 1989. Not all infants could take part, due to relocation or refusal, and the researchers excluded 2 infants who had birth defects, and 8 suffering from severe malnutrition. In addition, after recruitment 2 infants died before or during the two-month testing period. Finally, 42 mother–infant pairs took part and provided good quality data. The infants were 10–12 months old at the time of testing.

The Dogon are a polygamous society, and mothers typically lived in a compound with an open courtyard, often shared with co-wives. There was some degree of shared care of infants, but about one-half were cared for primarily or exclusively by the mother, and about one-third primarily by the maternal grandmother with the mother however being responsible for breast-feeding (box plate 4.1.2). Breastfeeding is a normative response by the mother to signs of distress in Dogon infants. Three related features of infant care in the Dogon – frequent breastfeeding on demand, quick response to infant distress, and constant proximity to the mother or caregiver – are seen as adaptive when there is high infant mortality (as in some other traditional African cultures).

The researchers had several objectives. They wished to see if the strange situation could be used successfully in Dogon culture; what distribution of attachment types was obtained; whether infant security correlated with maternal sensitivity – a test of the Maternal Sensitivity Hypothesis; whether infant attachment type related to patterns of attachment-related communications in mother-infant interaction – a test of what the authors call the Communication Hypothesis; and to see if frightened or frightening behaviour by the mother predicted disorganized infant attachment.

Three situations were used to obtain relevant data, with behaviour being recorded on videotape in each case. One was rather unusual – the Weigh-In, part of a regular well-infant examination, in which the mother handed over the infant to be weighed on a scale – a mildly stressful separation for the infant, especially in Dogon culture. The other two were more standard – the strange situation, carried out in an area of a courtyard separated off by hanging mats; and two 15 minute observations in the infant's home, when the mother was cooking, and bathing/caring for the infant.

The following data were obtained:

- Infant attachment classification (from the strange situation)
- A rating of infant security on a 9-point scale (from the strange situation)
- Mother and infant communication related to attachment, coded by 5-point Communications Violations Rating scales (from the Weigh-In)
- Maternal sensitivity, rated in terms of promptness, appropriateness and completeness of response to infant signals (from the home observations)
- Frightened or frightening behaviours by the mother, such as aggressive

Box Plate 4.1.1 Dogon mother spinning cotton, with child on her lap.

approach, disorientation, trance state, rough handling as if baby is an object, on a 5-point scale (from the home observations, and the Weigh In).

The strange situation was found to be feasible, following quite standard procedures. The distribution of attachment types was 67 per cent B, 0 per cent A, 8 per cent C, and

Box Plate 4.1.2   Dogon mother breastfeeding her child.

25 per cent D (or on a forced 3-way classification, 87 per cent B, 0 per cent A, 13 per cent C). This is unusual in having no avoidant (A) classifications; D is high but not significantly greater than western norms.

The Maternal Sensitivity Hypothesis only received weak support. The correlation between infant security and maternal sensitivity was r = 0.28, with p < .10; the difference in means between attachment classifications was not statistically significant (B = 5.26, C = 5.00, D = 4.20).

The Communications Hypothesis did get support. Infant security correlated –.54 with Communications Violations (p < .001), and the attachment classifications differed significantly (B = 2.66, C = 3.50, D = 3.89; p < .01).

Finally, frightened or frightening behaviour by the mother correlated r = –.40 (p < .01) with infant security, and was particularly high in children with disorganized attachment (B = 1.23, C = 1.33, D = 2.35; p < .01).

Besides demonstrating the general applicability of the strange situation procedure in a non-Western culture, the findings provide support for the Communications Hypothesis. The case here would have been stronger if the different kinds of communication patterns for each attachment classification had been described in more detail. For example, the authors earlier predicted that ambivalently attached (C) infants would be 'inconsistent and often unable to convey their intent, or to terminate their own or another's arousal', whereas disorganized (D) infants would 'manifest contextually irrational behaviors and dysfluent communication' (p. 1451). As it is, the main finding shows that insecure infants show more communications violations, but do not describe the detailed typology. Indeed, since some of the Communications Violation rating scales were of 'avoidance, resistance, and disorganization' (p. 1456), there is a possible danger of conceptual overlap between this scale and the attachment classifications.

Although support for the Maternal Sensitivity Hypothesis was weak, the correlation of r = .28 is in line with the average of r = .24 found in the meta-analysis by De Wolff and van IJzendoorn (1997) on mainly western samples. The researchers used a multiple regression analysis to examine the contributions of both maternal sensitivity, and mother's frightened/frightening behaviour, to attachment security. They found that the contribution of maternal sensitivity remained modest, whereas the contribution of mother's frightened/frightening behaviour was substantial and significant; ratings of maternal sensitivity do not normally take account of mother's frightened/frightening behaviour, and the researchers suggest that this might explain the modest effects found for maternal sensitivity to date.

The absence of avoidant (A) type infants is interesting. The researchers argue that, given the close contact mothers maintain with Dogon infants, and the normal use of breastfeeding as a comforting activity, it would be very difficult for a Dogon infant to develop an avoidant strategy (this may have some similarity with the low proportion of A type in Japanese infants, see p. 96). If avoidant attachment is rare or absent when infants are nursed on demand (which probably characterized much of human evolution, see p. 76), this might suggest that A type attachment was and is rare except in Western samples in which infants tend to be fed on schedule, and often by bottle rather than breast, so that the attachment and feeding systems are effectively separated.

Most Dogon infants showed secure attachment, but one-quarter scored as disorganized (though mostly with secure as the forced 3-way classification). The researchers comment that the frightened or frightening behaviours were mild to moderate, and did not constitute physical abuse. But why should mothers show these sorts of behaviour at all? An intriguing possibility is that it is related to the high level of infant mortality prevalent in the Dogon. About one-third of infants die before 5 years of age, and most mothers will have experienced an early bereavement. Unresolved loss experienced by a mother is hypothesized to be connected to disorganized attachment; perhaps, frightened behaviours are more rational or expected, when the risks for infants are so much higher.

This study took great efforts to be sensitive to the cultural venue, when using procedures and instruments derived mainly from western samples. A Malian researcher assisted in developing the maternal sensitivity coding, and Dogon women acted as strangers in the strange situation. The Weigh-In and home observations were natural settings. The authors comment, however, that future work might make more effort to tap the perceptions of mothering and attachment held by the Dogon people themselves, in addition to the constructs coming from western psychology.

Based on material in True, M. M., Pisani, L. and Oumar, F. 2001: Infant–mother attachment among the Dogon of Mali, *Child Development*, 72, 1451–66. Photos by Lelia Pisani supplied by ORISS archives, Lari, Italy.

Box 4.2
The effect of early institutional rearing on the behaviour problems and affectional relationships of 4-year-old children

The objective of this study was to see whether institutional rearing in early life resulted in behaviour problems and disturbances in affectional relationships. The research was carried out in London, and focused on 26 children aged 4 years who had been admitted to a residential nursery before 4 months of age and were still there. (In 17 cases the mother or putative father still spoke of reclaiming the child; the remaining 9 had not been adopted, for various other reasons.) There were two comparison groups. One consisted of 39 children who had also been admitted to a residential nursery before 4 months, but had either been adopted (24 children) or restored to their mothers (15 children) before 4 years of age. The other group comprised 30 children from local working-class homes who had not experienced any residential care. All the children were assessed at age 4.

The residential nurseries contained around 15–25 children, in small mixed-age groups. They were well provided with books and toys. Owing to rota systems and high staff turnover, the average number of staff who had worked with each child for at least a week over the previous 2 years was 26 (range 4–45).

Each child was interviewed individually, usually with a familiar nurse or the mother present. An intelligence test was given, ratings made of the child's observed behaviour, and questionnaires given to the parent or nurse about the child's behaviour problems and attachments. Most comparisons of the three groups employed chi-squared tests of significance. On the ratings of the child's behaviour, the main differences were between the adopted/restored children, and the other two groups. The adopted/restored children were more friendly to the interviewer, and more co-operative and talkative during testing.

The institutional children had the highest score for behaviour problems, but only marginally. Their scores were significantly higher for 'poor concentration', 'problems with peers', 'temper tantrums' and 'clinging'. However, the home-reared children scored significantly higher for 'poor appetite or food fads', 'over-activity' and 'disobedience'. In the answers to the attachment questionnaire, the nurses reported that many of the institutional children (18 of the 26) did 'not care deeply about anyone'. While sometimes clinging and following, their attachments seemed shallow. Some of them, and some of the adopted/restored children (who otherwise had good attachments to natural or adoptive parents), were also described as being 'overfriendly' to strangers.

The independent variable in this study is the early rearing experience; the dependent variables are measures of behaviour problems and social behaviour. The encouraging findings of the study are that the children who had experienced institutional rearing did not have very marked or severe behaviour problems (and a related study found quite good linguistic and cognitive development in this group, see chapter 17). Also, the adopted children generally did well and formed good relations with foster parents. However, most of the children still in institutional care had failed to form any strong attachments; this is not surprising as staff turnover was high and staff tended to discourage strong specific relationships from developing.

A real-life study such as this cannot be as neatly designed as a laboratory experiment. The children in the three groups differed in some respects (including sex and racial background), so rearing experience is confounded by these other factors. Ideally, also, the investigator would not know the background of each child interviewed, but this was not possible. Finally, the interview material relies on nurses' or mothers' reports, which may be less objective than actual observations of the child's behaviour.

A follow-up of the same children at 8 years of age was subsequently reported (Tizard and Hodges, 1978). Only 8 of the 26 children now remained in institutions. The late-adopted children generally had good relations with their adoptive parents. The children all had reasonably good scores on IQ tests, and the early adopted children especially had high IQ and reading test scores. However, the long-term effects of institutional-rearing experience did show up in teachers' ratings. Compared with the home-reared controls, the children who had experienced some institutional rearing were rated as more attention-seeking, restless, disobedient and not getting on well with other children. Teachers' ratings, however, could be biased by negative stereotyping (i.e., if the teachers had negative beliefs about the effects of having been brought up in an institution, irrespective of the child's actual behaviour).

A further follow-up of the same children was made when they were 16 years of age (Hodges and Tizard, 1989). The sample available was now only about two-thirds of the original one, and a new comparison group of home-reared children was used, matched for sex, social class and family position. The findings were fairly clear. IQ scores were similar to those at 8 years, and the small variations were with family placement (adoptive/restored) rather than whether the child had or had not experienced early institutional care. However, both parents and teachers rated the ex-institutional children higher on emotional and behavioural problems than the home-reared children. Ex-institutional children had more problems with social relationships, both inside the family (mainly for children restored to natural parents), and outside the family, with peers (for both adopted and restored children). The adopted children tended to score higher on symptoms of anxiety, while those who had been restored to natural families tended to score higher on antisocial behaviour and school problems. These findings were supported by interviews with the young people themselves, suggesting they were not just due to stereotyped judgements by adults.

The careful follow-up of these children is an excellent example of the power of a longitudinal study, even with a relatively small sample size. The findings do indicate that experiencing extreme multiple caretaking in the first few years of life can be a noticeable risk factor for developing satisfactory social relationships, even by adolescence.

Based on material in Tizard, B. and Rees, J. 1975: The effect of early institutional rearing on the behaviour problems and affectional relationships of 4-year-old children. *Journal of Child Psychology and Psychiatry*, 16, 61–73.

5 The Peer Group

In this chapter we look at children's relationships with other children – with siblings, and with peers. A 'peer' is someone who is about the same age as yourself; for children, this is usually someone in the same year, class or age grade. We examine the concept of friendship; what is a friend? How do we measure friendship? We also consider the concept of 'sociometric status'. We then examine the nature of aggression between children, its relationship to friendship and popularity; and the specific topic of school bullying. We conclude by examining the controversy over the relative influence of parents, and of peers, for children's development.

■ Early Peer Relationships

From an early age, peers seem to be especially interesting to children. In one study of 12–18-month-old infants, two mother–infant pairs who had not previously met shared a playroom together. The investigators observed whom the infants touched, and whom they looked at. The results are shown in figure 5.1. The infants touched their mothers a lot (thus remaining in proximity to them, as we would expect from attachment theory, chapter 4). However, they looked most at the peer, who was clearly interesting to them (Lewis et al., 1975).

The interactions between under-2s have been examined using video film. Video is very useful, since at this age range peer interactions are short, subtle and easy to miss. They often consist of just looking at another child and perhaps smiling, or showing a toy, or making a noise. In toddler groups an infant might make such overtures to another child once every minute or so, and each may last only a matter of seconds (Mueller and Brenner, 1977). This rather low level of peer interaction is probably because infants are not yet very accomplished at the skills of

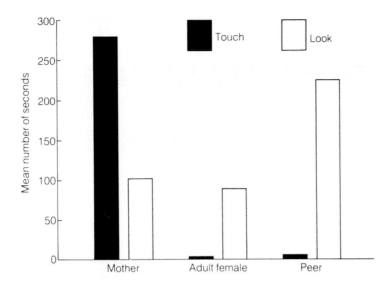

Figure 5.1 Amount of time during a 15-minute period in which children aged 12–18 months touched and looked at mother, an unfamiliar adult female and an unfamiliar peer (from Lewis et al., 1975).

social interaction, such as knowing what are appropriate behaviours in certain situations, what behaviour to expect back, and waiting to take one's turn. As we saw in chapter 3, adults can 'scaffold' social interactions with infants; but it takes young children some 2 or 3 years to become really competent at interacting socially with age-mates.

Early peer experience in toddler groups or day nurseries can assist these peer skills (p. 110), as can being 'securely attached' to the mother or caregiver (p. 96). And under-2s have some abilities that help develop peer interaction. One is imitation, which we also discussed in chapter 3. A study in France by Nadel-Brulfert and Baudonniere (1982) observed 2-year-olds in a laboratory playroom equipped with pairs of identical objects. It was found that when one child picked up or played with an object, the other child was very likely to pick up the corresponding identical object; these imitations had a definite social function, helping to maintain communication and play between the children.

Another study of French children showed evidence of a different range of abilities at 11 months and at 23 months (Tremblay-Leveau and Nadel, 1996). Here, pairs of toddlers from the same day-care centre were observed with a familiar experimenter and some toys; so, this was a 'triadic' situation. Both dyadic and triadic interactions were observed, with some degree of turn-taking even by the younger, 11-month-old children. The particularly interesting feature of the results from this study was the differing reactions of infants when they were 'included' within an ongoing interaction with the adult, or 'excluded'. When temporarily out of the interaction, the other child made many more attempts to interact with the peer; perhaps by 'showing-off' or interposing their body between the adult and peer, or by naming the toy being played with, or another toy, and smiling. At 11 months they were 5 times more likely to attempt interactions with the peer when excluded, and 8 times more likely at 23 months. The researchers conclude that this shows an early awareness of one's social position and an active attempt to overcome loneliness when excluded; and also of attention to others and, perhaps, some awareness of their mental states. If so, this would be a precursor of the kinds of theory of mind abilities that we consider further in chapter 14.

It was probably important in this study that the toddlers knew each other. However, the situation in which young children will know each other best of all is when they are raised in the same family; typically, siblings aged a year or so apart.

Siblings

Eighty per cent of us have siblings – brothers or sisters. Usually, siblings only differ in age by a few years. Thus, while not exactly 'peers', they are generally close enough in age, and similar enough in interests and developmental stages, to be important social partners for each other in the home and family environment. Characteristically, older siblings can show great tolerance for younger ones, and can act as an important model for more competent behaviour. They can also show hostility and ambivalence, and this has been observed in many different societies (Eibl-Eibesfeldt, 1989).

A study by Stewart (1983) in the USA showed that older siblings can act as attachment figures in the strange situation. Stewart used an extended version of the procedure, with 54 family groups. At one point the older sibling (who was aged from 30 to 58 months) was left alone with the infant (who was aged from 10 to 20 months). Every infant responded to the mother's departure with some degree of distress. Within 10 seconds of the mother's departure, 28 of the older siblings had responded by showing some form of caregiving behaviour; for example approaching and hugging the infant, offering verbal reassurance of the mother's return, or carrying the infant to the centre of the room to distract him or her with toys. These actions were quite effective. The other 26 older siblings, however, ignored or moved away from the infant and did not show caregiving responses. This pattern of pronounced variation in the quality of sibling relationships is in fact a recurrent one in studies of siblings.

What is found in actual sibling relationships in the home? Extensive research of this kind has been carried out by Judy Dunn and her colleagues (Dunn, 1984; Dunn and Kendrick, 1982; Dunn et al., 1991). Dunn and Kendrick (1982) started making observations in the homes of 40 firstborn children living with both parents in or near Cambridge, UK. At first visit, a new sibling was due in a month or so, and the first child was in most cases nearing their second birthday. Subsequent visits were made after the birth of the sibling, when the second child was about 1 month old, and again at 8 months and at 14 months. Besides interviewing the parents, the natural behaviour between the siblings and with their parents was observed.

Naturally enough, many firstborns showed some signs of jealousy when the new sibling arrived. Previously they had been the centre of attention from mother, father or grandparents; now, the new brother or sister got the most attention. Parents do of course make some efforts to involve the firstborn in this, for example in feeding sessions, but inevitably rates of interaction with firstborns do decline overall (at times, fathers can play a more important role with the older child while the mother is undertaking primary caregiving responsibilities with the new baby). At this point, much of the jealousy and ambivalence of the firstborn is directed towards parents:

Mother: He keeps having tantrums and misery. Anything sets him off. He's just terrible.

(Dunn and Kendrick, 1982, p. 31)

Not many firstborns show much overt hostility to the infant, but some do; and some behaviour can be ambivalent. In the following example it is difficult to know if the behaviour is friendly, hostile, or more probably a mixture of both:

Mother: He wants to play with her but he's so rough. Lies on top of her. Then she cries. He wants to roll all over her. I have to keep her away from him 'cause I can't let her be bashed about yet.

(p. 36)

Other children may express hostility in conversation, as the following extract shows:

Child: Baby, baby (caressing her). Monster. Monster.
Mother: She's not a monster.
Child: Monster.

(p. 68)

However, such hostility really is ambivalent. The great majority of the firstborns do show much interest and affection towards their new sibling:

Mother: He asks where she is first thing in the morning. He's happy when he can see her.

(p. 34)

They may also show empathy and prosocial behaviour (see also chapter 8):

Mother: When she cries he's very concerned. Gets her dummy [pacifier], then comes and tells me.

(p. 32)

There was considerable variation in the typical response when the infant was upset. Fourteen of the firstborns were themselves upset, like the boy just mentioned. Ten were neutral. Five were sometimes gleeful, while ten children actually increased their younger sibling's upset. Overall, Dunn and Kendrick feel that the sibling relationship is one in which considerable emotions may be aroused –

both of love and of envy. (Incidentally, evolutionary psychologists would not be surprised at finding sibling rivalry – see chapter 2.) However, the title of Dunn and Kendrick's book, *Siblings – Love, Envy, and Understanding*, brings out another important feature; that of the enhanced understanding which this close and emotionally powerful relationship may generate. This may be an optimal situation in which to learn how to understand and hence influence others. Very early on (under 2 years of age) siblings seem to be learning how to frustrate, tease, placate, comfort or get their own way with their brother or sister. This is true not only of the older siblings, but of the younger ones as they grow up; consider the following observation of Callum, now 14 months, with his older sister Laura, aged 3 years:

> Callum repeatedly reaches for and manipulates the magnetic letters Laura is playing with. Laura repeatedly says 'NO' gently. Callum continues trying to reach the letters. Finally, Laura picks up the tray containing the letters and carries it to a high table that Callum cannot reach. Callum is furious and starts to cry. He turns and goes straight to the sofa where Laura's comfort objects, a rag doll and a pacifier, are lying. He takes the doll and holds tight, looking at Laura. Laura for the first time is very upset, starts crying, and runs to take the doll.
>
> (p. 116)

The obvious interpretation here is that Callum has figured out how to annoy Laura so as to get his own back on her. These are interesting observations to consider in the light of ideas about children's 'theory of mind' (see chapter 14), and the critique of Piaget's ideas about egocentrism (chapter 12). Nevertheless it is also worth bearing in mind that children can learn these social cognitive skills with adults and peers, as well as with siblings. Research on children with no siblings (only children) appears to suggest that they show no deficits in sociability or adjustment and do well on achievement and intelligence scores (Falbo and Polit, 1986).

Also important, is the way mothers talk to one sibling about the other sibling, or discuss feelings within the family. This was illustrated by another observational study of 40 pairs of siblings in home settings, in Japan (Kojima, 2000). The younger siblings were aged around 2–3 years, and the older siblings around 5–6 years. Each sibling showed a fair balance of positive, and negative, behaviours to each other. When siblings argued, mothers might try distraction – mainly to the younger sibling, perhaps offering some different toy. Also, they would often explain the actions or emotional states of one sibling, to the other. Mother's use of such explanations to the older sibling correlated quite highly ($r = .50$) with the older sibling's positive behaviour to the younger one. In a follow-up of the Cambridge sample at middle childhood, Dunn et al. (1991) found that mother's talk about siblings' feelings related to later understanding and emotional quality of relationships.

Siblings continue to influence each other, beyond childhood. Dunn et al. (1991) found that in early adolescence, someone who had grown up with an unfriendly or hostile sibling was more likely to be anxious, depressed or aggressive. Siblings may engage in a *sibling comparison* process; one sibling doing well (for example in school achievement) and getting praise from parents might lead the other sibling to have lower academic self-esteem – or, it might spur them to greater efforts, or to redirect their energies into a different area, such as sports. One possibility is a *'sibling barricade'* effect, in which parental treatment results in opposite effects for the siblings – for example, negative treatment of one sibling affects him/her negatively, but the other sibling positively (through a social comparison process). Feinberg et al. (2000) found some evidence for these effects in an adolescent US sample.

Another study in adolescence (Updegraff et al., 2000) found that brother–sister pairs engaged in social comparison processes; for example in older sister–younger brother pairs, sex-typed choices of friends were particularly exaggerated. However sisters (both first- and second-born) learned control tactics from their brothers, that they applied in their friendships.

Peer Relationships in Preschool and School

By 2 or 3 years of age a child is usually thought ready for nursery school. Certainly the period from 2 to 4 years sees a great increase in the skills children have interacting with peers. As we shall see in chapter 7, sociodramatic play and rough-and-tumble play with one or more partners become frequent in this age range. Parallel with this, the child is beginning to develop concrete operational thought and to be able to take the perspective of others in simple ways (chapters 12 and 14).

The increase in social behaviour in preschool children was documented by Mildred Parten at the Institute of Child Development in Minnesota in the late 1920s. She observed 2–4-year-olds and described how they might be 'unoccupied', an 'onlooker' on other's activities, or, if engaged in an activity, they could be 'solitary', in 'parallel' activity with others or in 'associative' or 'co-operative' activity with others. Parallel activity is when children play near each other with the same materials, but do not interact much – playing independently at the same sandpit for example. Associative activity is when children interact together at an activity, doing similar things, perhaps each adding building blocks to the same tower. Co-operative activity is when children interact together in complementary ways; for example, one child gets blocks out of a box and hands them to another child, who builds the tower. Parten (1932) found that the first four categories declined with age, whereas associative and co-operative activity, the only ones involving much interaction with peers, increased with age.

Subsequent researchers have frequently used Parten's categories, though often simplified to 'solitary' (including unoccupied and onlooker), 'parallel' and 'group' (comprising associative and co-operative). Studies in the UK and the USA have found that, very approximately, preschool children in free play divide their time equally among these three categories, with the balance shifting more towards 'group' activity as they get older (Smith, 1978). Most group activity involves just two or three children playing together, though the size of groups does tend to increase in older preschoolers. These trends continue in the early school years.

Plate 5.1 The beginnings of social relations and friendship between peers can be seen in toddler groups and nursery schools; these 3-year-olds are very much aware of each other's behaviour.

According to a study of more than 400 Israeli children, group activity rises to about 57 per cent of the time in outdoor free play, while parallel activity falls to about 6 per cent; the number of groups comprised of more than five children increased from about 12 per cent to 16 per cent between 5 and 6 years of age (Hertz-Lazarowitz et al., 1981). The size of children's groups continues to increase through the middle school years, especially in boys, as team games such as football become more popular (Eifermann, 1970).

By the middle school years, sex segregation of children's groups is becoming very marked. In fact, children tend to choose same-sex partners even in nursery school, but by no means exclusively; typically, some two-thirds of partner choices may be same-sex, though this is influenced by such factors as the class size, toys available and the role of teachers in encouraging (or not) cross-sex play. However, by the time children are getting into team games, from about 6 or 7 years onward, sex segregation in the playground is very much greater (Maccoby, 1998; and see p. 194).

In a study of 10–11-year-old children in American playgrounds, Lever (1978) found that there were distinct differences between boys' and girls' activities and friendships. Boys more often played in larger mixed-age groups, while girls were more often in smaller groups or same-age pairs. Boys tended to play competitive team games that were more complex in their rules and role-structure, and seemed to emphasize 'political' skills of co-operation, competition and leadership in their social relations. Girls seem to put more emphasis on intimacy and exclusiveness in their friendships (Maccoby, 1998).

The nature of children's groups changes again as adolescence is reached. Large same-sex 'cliques' or 'gangs' become common in early adolescence, changing as heterosexual relationships become more important in later adolescence. A study of Australian adolescents aged 13–21 years (Dunphy, 1963) presents a picture of this process. Natural observations were supplemented by questionnaires, diaries and interviews in this study. At the younger end of this age range many teenagers went around in cliques comprising some three to nine individuals of the same sex. They would interact little outside their own clique. A few years later, however, adolescents would be participating in larger groups or 'crowds', made up of several interacting cliques. These would still be same-sex groups, but the more mature or higher-status members of the crowds would start to initiate contacts with members of the opposite sex. Gradually, other members of the crowd would follow their lead. This led to a stage where heterosexual crowds were made up of male and female cliques in loose association. Finally, young people associated most in heterosexual couples, going on dates, and loosely associated with other couples, prior to engagement and marriage.

Measuring peer relationships: sociometry

How can we find out about the structure of children's peer relationships? This has been done in three main ways: by direct observation of behaviour; by asking another person, such as a teacher or parent; or by asking the child (see Pepler and Craig, 1998, for a review).

If you watch a class of children, you can record which children are interacting together. If you do this at regular intervals, it is possible to build up a picture of the social structure in the class. For example, in a study of two classes in a nursery school, Clark et al. (1969) observed a child for 10 seconds to see with whom he was playing, then they observed another child, and so on through the class; this was continued over a 5-week period. From this data the authors constructed a 'sociogram' for each class, as shown in figure 5.2. Each symbol represents a child; the number of lines joining two children represents the percentage of observations on which they were seen playing together. The concentric circles show the number of play partners a child has: if many, that child's symbol is towards the middle, if none, at the periphery. This enables us to see at a glance that in class A, for example, there is one very popular girl who links two large subgroups; one boy and one girl have no clear partners. In class B there are several subgroups, and, unlike class A, there is almost complete segregation by sex; two boys have no clear partners. This is a very neat way of illustrating social structure, provided the class is not very large.

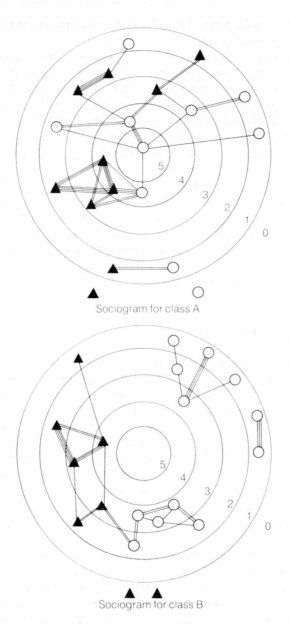

Figure 5.2 Sociograms of association networks in two classes of preschool children; circles represent girls, triangles boys (from Clark et al., 1969).

Observation gives a valid measure of who associates with whom. An alternative procedure is to ask a teacher, for example, 'who are John's best friends in the class?', or to ask John himself, 'who are your best friends?' These nomination methods also give data that can be plotted on a sociogram. If John chooses Richard as a 'best friend', but Richard does not choose John, this can be indicated by an arrow from John to Richard; if the choice is reciprocated, the arrow would point both ways on the sociogram.

A common nomination method is to ask each child to name their three best friends. Other methods are to ask children to rate each child for liking (e.g., asking them to sort names into three piles of 'like', 'neutral' and 'don't like'), or to ask them which they prefer of all possible pairs of children. For younger children who cannot read well, photographs of classmates can be used.

For older children – approaching or in adolescence – Robert Cairns developed a method for examining the more complex cliques or groups that characterize this period. Besides asking for friendship nominations, Cairns and his colleagues got information on social groups and networks by asking questions like 'are there people who hang around together a lot at school? Who are they?' By combining information from different informants, it is possible to develop a 'social-cognitive map' of the peer group structure in adolescents. Besides looking at the position of an individual in the group (as in traditional sociometry, e.g., figure 5.2), it is then also possible to look at the centrality of a group or clique in the wider peer group network of the school (Cairns et al., 1995).

The concept of sociometric status

Some investigators have also asked children to say whom they do not like. Researchers who have obtained both positive and negative nominations have not constructed sociograms (which would then look very complicated), but have rather categorized children into 'sociometric status types': as 'popular', 'controversial', 'rejected', 'neglected' or 'average', according to whether they are high or low on positive and on negative nominations. This procedure was initiated in a seminal study by Coie, Dodge and Coppotelli (1982) described in box 5.1; see especially box figure 5.1.1. Hymel et al. (2002) review different types of sociometric assessment developed since then, and also discuss the ethical issues involved (since questions about 'not liking' someone might bring about increased negative behaviour to unliked peers, although so far there is little evidence for such effects being found).

Sociometric status typologies have attracted researchers into a large number of studies. Newcomb et al. (1993) reviewed these, some 10 years after the initial work of Coie and colleagues. They concluded that rejected peer status was associated with high levels of aggression and withdrawal and low levels of sociability and cognitive abilities, whereas neglected peer status was associated with less sociability and aggression. Controversial children compensated for high aggression with better cognitive and social abilities.

A social information processing model

The sort of findings summarized by Newcomb et al. (1993) can be taken to suggest that children of different sociometric status types vary in some social-cognitive skills, in important ways. This is a widely held view, and was developed by Dodge

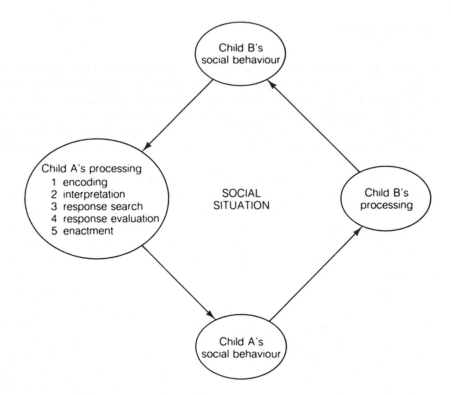

Figure 5.3 A model of social skills and social exchange in peer interaction (adapted from Dodge et al., 1986).

et al. (1986). Dodge and his colleagues suggest that the social skills of peer inter-action can be envisaged as an exchange model of social information processing (see figure 5.3). Suppose child A is interacting with child B. According to this model she has to (1) encode the incoming information to perceive what child B is doing, (2) interpret this information, (3) search for appropriate responses, (4) eval-uate these responses and select the best, and (5) enact that response. For example, suppose child B is running forward with arms raised, shouting and smiling. Child A needs to perceive all these actions, interpret their meaning (is this friendly or aggressive?), search for appropriate responses (run away? ignore? play fight?), select what seems best, and then do it effectively. Child B, of course, will be engaged in a similar process with respect to child A.

Crick and Dodge (1994) summarize evidence relating to this model, together with some reformulation of its details. More recently Lemerise and Arsenio (2000) have suggested that the Crick and Dodge model is primarily cognitive, and present a revised model in which emotion processes are integrated.

Models of this kind are certainly helpful in conceptualizing some reasons why children may be successful, or less successful, in peer relations. However, other factors are involved too. We will look at some evidence for the main status types.

Rejected children

Probably the greatest interest and concern of researchers has focused on rejected children. In a study of 8- and 11-year-olds over a 4-year period, Coie and Dodge (1983) looked at the stability of sociometric status categories on a year-to-year basis, and found that this was highest for 'rejected' children; 30 per cent of those rejected at the start of the investigation were still rejected four years later; another 30 per cent were 'neglected'. By contrast, those merely 'neglected' at the start of the study tended to become 'average'.

Other studies have found that 'rejected' children differ in their behaviour in what seem to be maladaptive ways. Ladd (1983) observed 8- and 9-year-olds in playground breaks. Rejected children, compared with average or popular children, spent less time in co-operative play and social conversation, and more time in arguing and fighting; they tended to play in smaller groups, and with younger or with less popular companions. In another study, Dodge et al. (1983) looked at how 5-year-olds attempted to get into ongoing play between two other peers. They suggested that whereas popular children first waited and watched, then gradually got themselves incorporated by making group-orientated statements, and neglected children tended to stay at the waiting and watching stage, rejected children tended to escalate to disruptive actions such as interrupting the play.

There appear to be several subtypes of rejected children, and different reasons for peer rejection. In particular, there appears to be a major distinction between some children who are rejected because they are aggressive, and others who are rejected because they are submissive – a distinction between externalizing and internalizing problems in behaviour (Asher et al., 1990).

A study in the Netherlands (Cillessen et al., 1992) provided evidence on this. From a sample of 784 boys, aged 5 to 7 years, they found 98 rejected children. The researchers gathered peer nominations, teacher and peer ratings, observations of behaviour, and a measure of skills in problem-solving. They used a statistical procedure called cluster analysis on this range of measures, to see what natural groupings of children with similar characteristics their sample fell into. They found that the largest cluster (48 per cent of their sample) was of the rejected–aggressive children. Besides being aggressive, these boys tended to be dishonest, impulsive and non-cooperative. A smaller cluster (13 per cent) was of the rejected–submissive children; these were shy children, not particularly aggressive (or cooperative). The remaining 39 per cent of their rejected children formed two further clusters, which were not so well defined and seemed more average in their characteristics. The researchers examined the stability of rejected status one year later; this was highest for the rejected–aggressive groups, with 58 per cent of these children still being rejected; it was only true for 34 per cent of the other children.

These two sub-groups may also differ in academic achievement. In a study of 11–13-year-olds, Wentzel and Asher (1995) found that rejected–aggressive children had problematic academic profiles, whereas rejected–submissive children did not have such problems.

Many researchers think that rejected–aggressive children are lacking in components of social skills. For example on the model discussed above, they might misinterpret others' behaviour (stage 2), or too readily select aggressive responses (stage 4); there is some evidence for both of these. However, not all aggressive behaviour may be due to lack of social skills. As we discuss later, some aggressive children may be quite skilled at manipulating others. And some rejected children may be simply reacting to exclusion by the popular cliques and would not necessarily be rejected or lacking in social skills in other situations outside the classroom.

Sandstrom and Coie (1999) looked at factors involved in children escaping from 'rejected' status over a two-year period. Important factors for this were the child's own perception of their social status, participation in extracurricular activities, internal locus of control, and high parental monitoring. Interestingly, aggressive behaviour was *positively* related to status improvement, among initially rejected boys.

Popular and controversial children

Newcomb et al.'s (1993) meta-analysis suggested that popular children have good interpersonal skills, are not high in aggression, and are not withdrawn. Other factors also affect popularity. Popularity may be influenced by the composition of the peer group a child is in. It may be difficult for a child to be popular if he or she differs in salient respects (such as ethnicity, interests, intelligence) from most others in the class. Around puberty, early physical maturation is also a variable affecting popularity and status (chapter 9).

Another factor is physical attractiveness. Children, like adults, differ in how physically attractive they are rated by persons who know them. In one study (Vaughn and Langlois, 1983) ratings of physical attractiveness were obtained for 59 preschool children. The correlation with sociometric preference using a paired-comparison method was 0.42 ($p < 0.01$); the correlation was higher for girls (0.66, $p < 0.01$) than for boys (0.22, n.s). Several other studies have found that ratings of physical attractiveness correlate with sociometric status (e.g., box 5.1).

The relationship between popularity and aggression is complex; it varies with age, and social context. In preschool and early school years, aggressive children tend to be disliked and unpopular as we saw in the summary of 'rejected' sociometric status. Such studies usually make it clear that it is unprovoked aggression that causes such children to be actively disliked – they may push another child, or disrupt a game, with little or no reason or provocation. By adolescence the picture is much more mixed, with several studies finding that aggressive boys especially may appear tough, competent and popular (Pellegrini and Bartini, 2001; Rodkin et al., 2000).

Even before adolescence, some children are quite aggressive but not clearly disliked. These are the 'controversial' children in box figure 5.1.1. Such children can be highly socially skilful and highly aggressive. Peers may describe them as good leaders, but also as starting fights – a pattern of behaviour that appeals to some peers but not to others. In other words, some children may use aggressive behaviour as a means of acquiring status in the peer group.

An illustration of this comes from an intensive study of playground behaviour in an Oxford first school and a middle school by Sluckin (1981). In the first school he describes how a boy called 'Neill' was known by his peers as the 'boss' of the playground. Neill was often observed in conflicts, although usually these were not overt fights (Neill was not particularly strong physically) but verbal conflicts by which Neill sought to enhance his prestige and manipulate social situations. Neill disliked losing, and would try to redefine or reinterpret situations so that it appeared he had won. For example, in a race with Ginny, where they finished at the same time, Neill cried out 'yes yes' (I'm the winner). Ginny called out 'draw', to which Neill replied 'no, it wasn't, you're just trying to make trouble'. In another example, playing football, Neill says 'I'm in goal, bagsee'. Nick replies 'no, I'm in goal'. Neill retorts 'no, John's in goal' and John goes in the goal. Here (perhaps avoiding a fight) Neill has kept the initiative and given the impression of being 'in charge' even though he did not get his own way entirely. Neill was clearly a leader of sorts, but he does not seem to have been especially popular. His leadership was often disruptive, since he always insisted on winning games. However, he had a high dominance status in the playground, and would seem to qualify as 'controversial'.

Neglected children, loneliness and social withdrawal

Neglected children have not been studied so much as rejected children, although as they receive few 'liked most' nominations they may be lonely and lack friends (see below). However, in their US sample of 11–13 year olds, Wentzel and Asher (1995) found that neglected children were quite well-liked by teachers, being prosocial and compliant, and did fairly well academically.

Do neglected (or rejected) status children feel lonely? Asher and Wheeler (1985) developed a Loneliness and Social Dissatisfaction questionnaire, which is a 24-item self-report scale for children. It includes 16 items such as 'It's hard for me to make friends at school', and 'I have nobody to talk to in class', as well as eight 'filler' items about hobbies and interests. This and subsequent work found that neglected children did *not* score particularly highly; in fact it was rejected children, especially the rejected–submissive subgroup, who scored highest on self-reported loneliness (Asher et al., 1990).

Neglected children do seem to be low on sociability (Newcomb et al., 1993). A related construct is *social withdrawal*, defined by Rubin et al. (2002) as the consistent display of all forms of solitary behaviour when encountering familiar and/or unfamiliar peers. Rubin et al. argue that this may develop from the temperamental attribute of behavioural inhibition in childhood (which shows moderate stability), augmented by ambivalent (type C; see p. 95) attachment type, which results in emotional dysregulation in unfamiliar or threatening circumstances. Overprotective or over-solicitous parenting can also contribute to children (especially boys) showing social withdrawal, if they have not developed good interpersonal coping skills. The sociometric status of socially withdrawn children is not well investigated, but they may be sociometrically rejected as much as neglected.

◼ Friendship

Usually we take friendship to mean a close relationship between two particular people, as indicated by their association together or their psychological attachment and trust. Friendship is related to social participation, and to sociometric status, but it is not the same thing. While a solitary child obviously does not have friends, a child who interacts a lot with others may or may not have friends. A rejected child might be generally disliked, but still have a good, close friendship with a peer.

What characterizes friendships?

What actually characterizes friendship? It may seem an obvious question, but it deserves looking at in some detail. Only if we know what friendship involves, can we start seriously examining what a lack of friendships is likely to lead to.

A considerable body of research over the past 20 years has been summarized by Newcomb and Bagwell (1995), and by Hartup (1996). Newcomb and Bagwell conclude that relations between friends, compared with non-friends, exhibit four particular features: reciprocity and intimacy; more intense social activity; more frequent conflict resolution; and more effective task performance. Let's look at three of the many studies that illustrate these characteristics.

One is by Howes et al. (1994). It was carried out with pairs of 4-year-olds, who were videotaped in a room at a child-care centre. Altogether, 24 dyads were observed; 6 had been long-term friends, for about 3 years; 12 had been short-term friends, for about 6 months; and 6 had never been friends (based on observation, and nomination). The levels of communication and play between the dyads were recorded over a 20-minute session.

Two main findings emerged from the analysis. First, friends (whether long- or short-term) engaged in more complex levels of pretend play than did non-friends (for Howes' work on levels of pretend play, see chapter 7). Second, there were differences in the amount of high-level cooperative pretend play, and in the communications which served to extend such play; here, friends did more than non-friends, but in addition long-term friends did more than short-term friends. These differences were substantial, as shown in table 5.1, and statistically significant despite the small sample.

This finding illustrates two of the main characteristics of friendship; there is more intense social activity between friends, and this goes along with more intimacy and reciprocity, as in the cooperative forms of pretend play in this study. A third characteristic was more frequent conflict resolution; an Italian study by Fonzi et al. (1997) illustrates this. Friendship pairs of 8-year old children were compared with pairs of non-friends, in two structured tasks designed to simulate real life situations of potential conflict – games in which equipment had to be shared, or turns had to be taken. Friends were more effective about this: they made more proposals than non-friends, spent more time negotiating sharing arrangements, and were more able to make compromises. Those friend-

Table 5.1 Differences in behaviour in dyads of differing friendship status, adapted from Howes, Droege and Matheson (1994)

	Long-term friends	Short-term friends	Never friends
Parallel play	3.2	4.1	11.5
Simple social play	24.7	24.2	13.0
Complex pretend	11.5	12.8	4.3
Cooperative pretend	2.0	0.7	0.0

ship pairs that had been stable through the school year, showed more sensitivity in negotiations.

As a final example, let's look at a study of older children, by Azmitia and Montgomery (1993), that demonstrates more effective task performance. This study was carried out with 11-year-olds, in schools in California. Same-sex pairs of pupils were given scientific reasoning tasks (these were tasks of formal operational thinking, as is discussed in chapter 12). There were 18 pairs of friends (who had each nominated the other as a friend, so they were mutual friends); and 18 pairs of acquaintances (who had not nominated the other as a friend, but who did not dislike them either). The problem-solving efforts were recorded on videotape and audiotape.

The researchers found that friends achieved higher problem-solving accuracy, especially in the harder problems, than did the non-friends. This seemed to be related to greater transaction between them in evaluating possible solutions. Friends appeared more willing to elaborate and critique each other's reasoning; even if they disagreed, they could handle this constructively to take things further.

In this study, besides the more effective task performance, friends appeared better able to handle disagreements or a conflict of view. More generally, as Newcomb and Bagwell (1995) found over many studies, friends may well have conflicts, but they differ from non-friends in that they are better able to resolve these conflicts. A conflict with a friend is more likely to be made up than a conflict with a non-friend.

Conceptions of friendship

How do children themselves conceive of friendship? In one research programme (Bigelow and La Gaipa, 1980), children aged 6–14 years were asked to write an essay in class about their expectations of best friends. Essays were obtained from 480 Scottish children and also from 480 Canadian children, and analysed for their content. Results were similar in Scotland and Canada. At the earlier ages children mentioned sharing common activities, receiving help and living nearby; later, admiring and being accepted by the partner; and later still, such aspects as loyalty and commitment, genuineness and potential for intimacy. These last were found to be especially important in adolescence. Bigelow and La Gaipa have suggested a three-stage model for friendship expectations (table 5.2).

Table 5.2   Two analyses of stages of understanding friendship

Bigelow and La Gaipa (1980)	Reward–cost stage
	  Common activities, living nearby, similar
	  expectations
		Around 7–8 years

	Normative stage Shared values, rules and sanctions	Around 9–10 years

	Empathic stage
	  Understanding, self-disclosure, shared
	  interests
		Around 11–12 years

Selman and Jaquette (1977)	Momentary physical playmate Playing together, being in proximity	Around 3–7 years

	One-way assistance
	  A friend helps you, but no notion of
	  reciprocation
		Around 4–9 years

	Fairweather cooperation
	  Reciprocity focused on specific incidents
	  rather than the friendship itself; conflicts
	  may sever the relationship
		Around 6–12 years

	Intimate; mutual sharing
	  Awareness of intimacy and mutuality in a
	  relationship which continues despite
	  minor setbacks
		Around 9–15 years

	Autonomous interdependence
	  Awareness that relationships grow and
	  change; reliance on friends but
	  acceptance of their need for other
	  relationships
		Around 12–adult

In similar research, Selman and Jaquette (1977) interviewed 225 persons aged from 4 to 32 years on their understanding and awareness of friendship relations. They documented five stages of understanding, also outlined in table 5.2, linked to stages in perspective-taking abilities (chapter 12). Although different in detail, there are considerable correspondences between the two schemes. There clearly seems to be a shift towards more psychologically complex and mutually recipro-cal ideas of friendship during the middle school years, with intimacy and com-mitment becoming especially important later in adolescence (Berndt, 1982). Older children are obviously aware of characteristics of friendship such as reciprocity and intimacy.

Quality of friendship

In his review, Hartup (1996) suggested that it is not only having a friend that may be important; it is also important to consider who your friends are – are they of high or low status in the peer group, for example; and what the quality of the friendship is.

Bukowski et al. (1994) used some of the suggested characteristics of friendship to develop a Friendship Qualities Scale. This is an instrument in which children

Table 5.3 Sample items from the Friendship Qualities Scale

Companionship	My friend and I spend all our free time together.
Help	My friend helps me when I am having trouble with something.
Security	If I have a problem at school, I can talk to my friend about it.
	If my friend and I have a fight or argument, we can say 'I'm sorry' and everything will be alright.
Closeness	If my friend had to move away, I would miss him.
Conflict	My friend and I disagree about many things.

rate friends and peers on several subscales, as indicated in table 5.3. Bukowski et al. used this Scale with 10–12-year-olds. They found that the subscales of Companionship, Help, Security and Closeness were related – that is, someone rated high on one of these tended to be rated highly on the others. Reciprocated friends rated higher on these subscales than non-reciprocated friends; and in a longitudinal sample, friends who had remained friends after 6 months scored higher than those who had not stayed friends.

The remaining Conflict subscale related negatively to the others. Reciprocated friends scored lower on Conflict than non-reciprocated friends; however, stable friends did not differ on Conflict from non-stable friends. Note that the Conflict items here refer mainly to frequency of conflict. Items to do with resolving conflicts successfully appear in the Security subscale (table 5.3), again illustrating how conflict resolution is an important aspect of friendship, and one that predicts to stability of friendship more than does simple frequency of conflict.

One study suggesting the importance of friendship quality was reported by Ladd et al. (1996). They studied 82 children aged 5 years, all of whom had a reciprocated and stable 'best friend' in their classroom. The quality of this friendship was associated with the children's development and adjustment in school; for example, perceived conflict in friendships was (for boys) associated with more loneliness and less liking of school.

The Importance of Peer Relations and Friendship

We have seen that there are immediate benefits to being sociometrically accepted, and to having friends; you can avoid feelings of loneliness, engage in more intense and reciprocal social activities, and with the help of friends, solve tasks more effectively. So, is having close friends an important developmental milestone? Hartup (1996) suggested that both aspects – sociometric status, and/or having close, trustworthy friends – could be important. However as he also pointed out, these are difficult questions to answer, not easy to test experimentally. However, several sources of evidence support the general idea that sociometric status and friendship have a wider importance, both at the time and for later development (Hartup, 1996).

An interesting small-scale study at the preschool age range was carried out by Field (1984) in a US kindergarten. This class of 28 children had been together from the age of 6–12 months and half the children were now due to leave the kindergarten. Field noted in the 2-week period prior to leaving that these children showed increased rates of fussiness, negative affect, aggressive behaviour, physical contact and fantasy play – possibly signs of anticipation and attempted coping with the separation from peers and their familiar environment. Also, this could be due to anxiety about attending a new school. However, in observing the children who stayed behind, Field found these children showed similarly increased agitated behaviour after the other children had left. This could have been, on a small scale, a 'grief' response to the friends they had lost.

This suggests that friendships are affectively important to a child, even at 3 or 4 years of age. Do they have other consequences? In a study of pre-adolescents, Mannarino (1980) identified those who had 'chums' – close, stable best friendships – and compared them with those who did not, on measures of altruism and self-concept. Pre-adolescents with chums had higher levels of altruism, and higher levels of self-concept, than those who lacked chums. This is further support for the importance of friendship, though being a correlational study, it does not prove that having a chum in itself caused the greater altruism or self-concept (rather than, for example, the other way round).

Are peer relationships in childhood important for later development? In one US study data were gathered on a large number of 8-year-olds in school, including IQ scores, school grades, attendance records, teachers' ratings and peer ratings. Eleven years later, when the participants were nearly adult, the researchers checked mental health registers to see who had needed any psychiatric help during this period. Those who had were two-and-a-half times more likely to have had negative peer ratings at 8 years; indeed, the peer ratings were the best of all the earlier measures at predicting appearance in the mental health registers (Cowen et al., 1973).

A large-scale review of all available studies was undertaken by Parker and Asher (1987); more recently, Deater-Deckard (2001) has reviewed links from childhood peer relationships, to psychopathology in childhood and adolescence. Parker and Asher looked at three measures of peer relationships: peer acceptance/ rejection; aggressiveness to peers; and shyness or withdrawal from peers. They examined the relationship of these to three main kinds of later outcome: dropping out of school early; being involved in juvenile and adult crime; and adult psychopathology (mental health ratings, or needing psychiatric help of any kind).

Parker and Asher found that different studies were very consistent in linking low peer acceptance (or high peer rejection) with dropping out of school; and suggestive but not so consistent in linking it with juvenile/adult crime. Conversely, the studies were very consistent in linking aggressiveness at school with juvenile/adult crime; and suggestive but not so consistent in linking it with dropping out of school. The data on effects of shyness/withdrawal, and on predictors of adult psychopathology, were less consistent; while some studies found significant effects, others did not, and thus any links or effects remain unproven at present.

Most of the studies were 'follow-back' designs; that is, retrospective data on peer relations was sought for people who were currently dropping out of school, getting in trouble with the law or seeking psychiatric help. A smaller number were

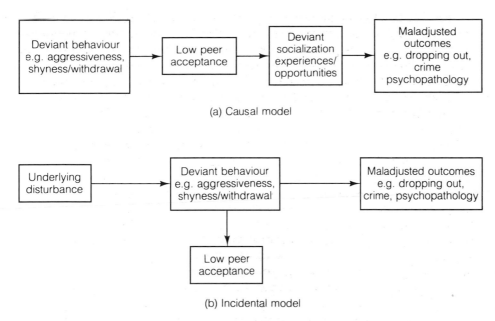

(a) Causal model

(b) Incidental model

Figure 5.4   Two models of the role of peer acceptance in leading to maladjusted outcomes (from Parker and Asher, 1987).

'follow-up' designs – taking a large sample of schoolchildren, obtaining data on peer relations, and seeing what happens later. Whichever design is used, the data is correlational in nature. We cannot be certain that low peer acceptance, for example, is a causal predictor of later problems. However, longitudinal 'follow-up' designs, while more costly to organize, are likely to provide more valid data for establishing predictive links.

Two somewhat different causal models, discussed by Parker and Asher in the context of low peer acceptance, are shown in figure 5.4. In (a) the low peer acceptance has a direct causal role; in (b), it is an outcome of more enduring traits such as aggressiveness, or shyness, rather than a cause in itself. (In both models, the original reasons for the deviant behaviour are not spelt out; you might consider whether some of the factors discussed in chapter 4 would be relevant in making the models more complete). These models could of course apply to other peer relationship or friendship difficulties, as well as peer acceptance.

Woodward and Ferguson (2000), in a longitudinal study of children from 9 to 18 years in New Zealand, argued that both these causal models have some validity. Peer relationship problems at age 9 did predict educational under-achievement and unemployment at age 18. Further analyses suggested that personal characteristics (such as low IQ) and adverse family and socioeconomic circumstances, explained some of this association (effectively, model (b) above); however, the childhood peer relationship problems did appear to lead directly to later relationship difficulties with peers and teachers, and earlier school leaving (effectively, model (a) above).

A study that looked at the separate contributions of sociometric status (specifically, peer rejection) and friendship, to later adjustment, was reported by Bagwell et al. (1998). This was a longitudinal, follow-up study in the mid-West USA, of students in school (at 10 years) to when they were young adults (at 23 years). At school, 334 students were asked to name 3 best friends, and 3 classmates they liked least, of the same sex, twice one month apart. The researchers then formed two subgroups:

- *Friended subgroup* (n = 58): these children had a stable, reciprocated best friend at both times.
- *Chumless subgroup* (n = 55): these children had no reciprocated friendship choice at either time.

In addition they scored *Peer Rejection* from the liked most/least ratings.

At the follow-up, 30 young adults from each subgroup (15 m, 15 f) were given questionnaires to assess life status, self-esteem, psychopathological symptoms, and quality of adult friendships. The main findings were:

- *peer rejection* predicted poorer life status (job aspiration and performance, extent of social activities);
- *friendship* predicted relations with family members; and self-esteem;
- *both lack of friendship, and peer rejection*, predicted psychopathological symptoms; and
- *neither* predicted quality of adult friendships.

This study suggests that both presence/absence of a close friend in preadolescence, and the experience of peer rejection, may be important for later well-being; but with each being stronger predictors of different aspects of later life.

Enemies

While there has been a great deal of research on friends in childhood, there has been very little indeed on enemies. As Hartup and Abecassis (2002) point out, mutual antipathies ('whom do you dislike more than anyone else?') are rare among young children, but become more common in middle childhood. Having enemies overlaps with bully–victim relationships (see below), but applies more widely. Hartup and Abecassis argue that we should analyse the correlates and consequences of having enemies, as we have done for friends, and that it is an additional factor to consider separate from sociometric status or peer rejection.

Social skills training

Many psychologists believe that social skills training may be useful for those children who lack friends; this training is usually directed at changing behaviours that are the correlates of peer rejection (such as high aggression, or high withdrawal).

Attempts have been made to help improve social skills in neglected children and rejected children. In one study (Furman et al., 1979), 4- and 5-year-olds who seldom played with other children were identified by observation. Some were given special play sessions with a younger partner, to see if this might give them more confidence in social interaction. This did seem to help, and more so than play sessions with a same-age peer, or no intervention at all. However, this study only used levels of social interaction as the measure of adjustment, so it does not directly address the issue of friendship and rejection.

Other researchers, working with middle-school children, have used more direct means of encouraging social skills – modelling techniques, for example. A child might watch a film showing an initially withdrawn child engaged in a series of increasingly complex peer interactions. Watching such films has been shown to increase social interaction subsequently (O'Connor, 1972). A more instructional approach was used by Oden and Asher (1977). They coached 8- and 9-year-old children identified as socially isolated (neglected or rejected) on skills such as how to participate in groups, cooperate and communicate with peers; they did this in special play sessions with the target child and one other peer. These children improved in sociometric status more than those who had special play sessions without the coaching. This effect was present a year later at a follow-up assessment, and was also replicated by an independent study (Ladd, 1981). However, another study with 9-year-olds found that academic skill training was even more effective than social skill training (Coie and Krehbiel, 1984). The hypothesis that rejected children are lacking in social skills, while promising, may not be the whole story. Malik and Furman (1993) provide an overview of clinical interventions to help children's social skills in peer relationships; while Ladd et al. (2002) give a wider overview of interventions in school settings (see also pp. 252–3).

Dominance and Aggression in Children

Dominance

The playground observations of Sluckin (1981) and others suggest that school children can rank others for 'dominance' or 'fighting strength' in a consistent way. Several psychologists have confirmed that this can be done reliably from about 4 or 5 years of age onwards. They have used the concept of a 'dominance hierarchy' in children's groups, just as it has been used in the study of animal social groups. Winning fights is one criterion of dominance, but more generally it is taken as getting one's own way or influencing others. Thus, the concept is close to that of 'leadership'.

While some of this research has involved asking children for their rankings of peers, other researchers have used direct observation of which individuals win conflicts. Strayer and Strayer (1976), observing children in a Canadian preschool, separated out three kinds of conflict behaviours: 'threat-gesture', 'physical attack' and 'objection/position struggles'. They then examined the usefulness of a dominance hierarchy for each of these three kinds of behaviour, separately, whenever there was a clear winner or loser. Strayer and Strayer looked at the linearity of the hierarchies (basically, how many reversals of expected position there were) to assess how descriptively useful the concept of a hierarchy was in each case. The values were very high, though slightly lower for 'object/position struggles' than for the other two behaviours.

Savin-Williams made studies of dominance formation in groups of American teenagers (aged 10–16 years), mostly previously unacquainted, who came together in 5-week summer camps. In one report (Savin-Williams, 1976) he studied intensively one cabin group of six boys aged 12 and 13. It took about 3 days for a stable, ordered hierarchy to emerge; it then remained very consistent throughout the duration of the camp. Observational measures of dominance correlated highly ($r = 0.90$) with a sociometric measure from the children themselves. The most frequently observed dominance behaviours were verbal ridicule (seen 235 times), giving a verbal command that was obeyed (seen 190 times) and ignoring or refusing to comply with another's command (seen 158 times). The most dominant boy also was, usually, the leader in hiking and athletics, and was well liked. However, the least dominant boy, quiet, serious, but friendly, was also popular.

Another study (Savin-Williams, 1980) was of four groups of five girls (aged 12–14) at summer camp. Again dominance hierarchies formed, although they did not seem as clear-cut as in boys' groups, perhaps because girls more often formed smaller groups (pairs or threesomes). Verbal ridicule was again the most frequently observed indicator of dominance. The position in the dominance heirarchy correlated significantly with ratings of leadership. However, Savin-Williams distinguished between 'maternal leaders' who were perceived by peers as a source of security and support, and 'antagonists' who imposed themselves on others.

Although dominance, when acknowledged, can reduce aggression (the person lower in dominance gives way), if dominance is challenged or uncertain then aggression may be used to sort out the hierarchy. Pellegrini and Bartini (2001) studied boys in US schools as they made the transition from primary to middle school (11 to 12 years). These boys moved from being the oldest and most dominant, to the youngest and least dominant in their school settings. Aggression increased at the start of the new school, and aggressive behaviour was related positively to dominance status. This changed by the end of the year, when aggression decreased and the more dominant boys were not more aggressive; the payoff to dominant boys was that they were more attractive to girls, at an age when heterosexual relationships were just beginning to be of interest.

Aggressive behaviour

We have mentioned children's aggressive behaviour several times, and its possible links to peer rejection. In this section, we look at the development of aggressive behaviour, and its causes.

As with Parten's study of social participation, some of the early studies on aggressive behaviour in children were based on observational studies in nurseries and child-care centres. For example, Jersild and Markey (1935) observed conflicts in 54 children at three nursery schools. Many kinds of conflict behaviour were defined: for example, *snatches* as 'takes or grabs toys or objects held, used, or occupied by another child; uses, tugs at, or pushes material away with hands or feet; all contacts with material which, if completed, would deprive the other child of the use and possession of material'; and *unfavourable remarks about persons* as comments like 'you're no good at it'; 'you don't do it right'; 'I don't like you'. Jersild and Markey recorded who was the aggressor and who the victim, what the outcome of the struggle was, and the role of the teacher. They found some decline in conflicts with age, and overall boys took part in more conflicts than girls. A follow-up was made of 24 children, after about 9 months. Conflicts had become more verbal, but individual differences between children in types and frequencies of conflict tended to be maintained. Very similar results were found in an observational study by Cummings et al. (1989); they reported that aggressive boys tended to stay aggressive between 2 and 5 years of age, even though the overall level of physical aggression declined over this period.

In another early study, Appel (1942) made observations in 14 different nursery schools. She delineated 15 kinds of adult responses to children's aggression. Five are 'ending techniques': diverting; separating or removing; restraining; arbitrary decision making; enforcing a rule. Ten are 'teaching techniques': explaining property rights; urging self-defence; suggesting a solution; suggesting the child find a solution; interpreting; encouraging friendly acts; making light of troubles or hurts; requiring good manners; disapproval; retaliation. An evaluation of the effectiveness of these different techniques was made, by deciding whether the conflict continued or ended after the adult intervention. Some techniques were much more effective than others at ending the immediate conflict. Least effective was suggesting to the children that they find a solution themselves. Appel concluded that 'teachers should not intervene too readily in children's conflicts. Children will teach each other a great deal. Too much interference prevents self-reliance.'

Through the 1950s and early 1960s direct observation was neglected, and more constrained investigations in laboratories, often experimental in nature, were seen as the preferred method (see p. 5). Aggression was assessed by means of observing children punching inflatable dolls, and pressing buttons to supposedly deliver punishment to another child. These studies have subsequently been criticized as lacking ecological validity (p. 14). By the late 1960s, direct observation had started to make a comeback. For example, Blurton Jones (1967) observed the social behaviour of children in an English nursery school. Most aggressive behaviour occurred in the context of property fights. Blurton Jones drew a clear distinction between aggressive behaviour, evidenced by beating or hitting at another with a frown or angry face, and rough-and-tumble play, where children chased and tackled each other, often smiling or laughing (see also chapter 7). These two kinds of behaviour can be confused because of their superficial similarity.

Types and typologies of aggressive behaviour

As observations of aggressive behaviour accumulated, researchers started distinguishing the main categories. Some long-standing distinctions have been between

Table 5.4   Peer-estimated aggression of different types, at different ages, for boys (B) and girls (G); adapted from Björkqvist et al., 1992

		8 yrs	11 yrs	15 yrs	18 yrs
Physical aggression	B	0.61	0.82	0.50	0.15
e.g. kicking	G	0.15	0.22	0.07	0.07
Verbal aggression	B	0.44	0.96	0.95	0.75
e.g. verbal abuse	G	0.15	1.09	0.98	0.90
Indirect aggression	B	0.32	0.83	0.81	0.60
e.g. gossip	G	0.40	1.30	1.14	1.06

verbal and non-verbal aggression (based on the presence or absence of verbal threats or insults); between instrumental and hostile aggression (based on whether the distress or harm is inferred to be the primary intent of the act); between reactive aggression (done in angry retaliation) and proactive aggression (dominant behaviour employed to achieve a specific goal); and between individual and group aggression (depending on whether more than one child attacks another).

The distinction between reactive and proactive aggression has been used considerably by proponents of the Social Information Processing model. Crick and Dodge (1996) showed that reactively aggressive children tended to differ from others in the stage of attributing intent to another's actions – they showed a *hostile attribution bias*, very readily assuming aggressive intent in a peer; by contrast, proactively aggressive children differed in the stage of evaluation of consequences – they evaluated aggressive acts more positively, in terms of their outcomes.

The distinction between verbal and non-verbal aggression has been elaborated by Björkqvist and colleagues, based primarily on data from nominations and ratings of peers in a study in Finland (Björkqvist et al., 1992); they added a third category of indirect aggression, which is aggression not aimed directly at someone but via a third party. Thus, examples of 'physical aggression' would be: hits, kicks, pushes; of 'direct verbal aggression': insults, calls the other names; and of 'indirect aggression': tells bad or false stories, becomes friends with another as revenge. Physical aggression falls off rapidly in adolescence, but verbal and indirect aggression increase, as can be seen from table 5.4. As is also clear from table 5.4, girls may show less physical aggression, but there is not much difference in verbal aggression, and girls appear to show more indirect aggression. This sex difference has been confirmed by subsequent studies, including Crick and Grotpeter (1995) in the USA, who use the term 'relational aggression'; Galen and Underwood (1997) use the similar term 'social aggression', as aggression intended to damage another's self-esteem or social status.

Causes of high aggression

For most children, while a certain amount of aggressive and assertive behaviour is normal, it is kept within reasonable bounds such that they are not disruptive of peer group activities and hence rejected by peers. However, some children show high levels of aggression, often of a hostile or harassing nature, which can be quite stable over time and for which some adult intervention seems justified. If not dealt with at the time, such children who show persistent high aggressiveness through the school years are at greatly increased risk for later delinquency, antisocial and violent behaviour (Farrington, 1995; Lahey et al., 1999).

Genetic factors have been implicated in high aggressiveness. Mason and Frick (1994) summarized 12 twin studies and 3 adoption studies (see also chapter 2); they found there was a moderate degree of heritability for measures of antisocial behaviour, especially severe (violent or criminal) behaviour. Of course, it is unlikely that a propensity for specific criminal acts is inherited; what may be inherited are certain temperamental characteristics (see p. 83). In a longitudinal study in New Zealand (see also p. 85), Caspi et al. (1995) assessed temperament on a sample of 800 children at ages 3, 5, 7 and 9 years; and behaviour problems at 9, 11, 13 and 15 years. They found that early 'lack of control' (emotional lability, restlessness, short attention span, and negativism) correlated with later externalizing problems (such as aggressiveness).

Low self-esteem (and underlying insecurity) is often thought to be an explanation of aggressive behaviour, but this is not well supported by research. Baumeister et al. (1996) argued that often aggression is associated with *threatened egotism* – that is, highly favourable views of oneself (not necessarily realistic) that are disputed or threatened by someone; aggression serves to buttress the favourable view of oneself, by belittling the other person.

There is considerable evidence that home circumstances can be important influences leading to aggressive and later antisocial behaviour. In a review, Patterson et al. (1989) suggest that certain key aspects of parenting are involved. They argue that children who experience irritable and ineffective discipline at home, and poor parental monitoring of their activities, together with a lack of parental warmth, are particularly likely to become aggressive in peer groups and at school. Such children are experiencing aggressive means of solving disputes at home, and are not being given clear and effective guidance to do otherwise. Antisocial behaviour at middle school is likely to be linked to academic failure and peer rejection, according to this view (cf. box table 5.1.1); and in adolescence, especially if parental monitoring is lax, these young people are likely to be involved in deviant and delinquent peer groups. This hypothesis is shown in figure 5.5. (You may find it interesting to compare figure 5.5 with figure 4.1 and figure 5.4; all relate to different linked aspects of parenting and peer relations. Do you feel they can be linked together, or are some aspects in disagreement?)

Patterson's approach suggests that the social skills of parenting are very important in early prevention of antisocial behaviour; and his interventions focus on helping parents improve their child-management skills, for example, via manuals and videotaped materials (cf. chapter 4). However, another component of this model is the importance of the deviant peer group in adolescence. Although, in early and middle childhood, aggressive behaviour often leads to peer rejection, the picture becomes more complex in adolescence.

Studies by Cairns on social networks of US adolescents confirm that aggressive pupils tend to associate with other aggressive pupils (Cairns et al., 1988). Dishion et al. (1995) also found that in 13–14-year-olds, highly antisocial boys had more antisocial friends; these friendships were more coercive and of shorter duration

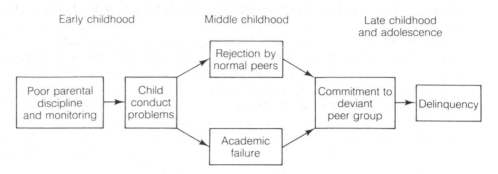

Figure 5.5 A developmental progression for antisocial behaviour (from Patterson et al., 1989).

than those between less antisocial pupils, but were still seen as satisfying by those involved. It seems that at this age, an aggressive child may not necessarily be rejected but may congregate with others of a similar antisocial tendency in ways which they can find rewarding. A longitudinal study of 13–14-year-olds, by Berndt and Keefe (1995), found that pupils with disruptive friends tended to become more disruptive themselves over a half-year period. Although pupils with high-quality friendships (intimate, reciprocal) were generally less likely to be disruptive, those whose friends were both of high quality *and* disruptive were particularly at risk of becoming more disruptive themselves.

These findings support the aspect of Patterson's model that suggests that friendship with antisocial peers can help maintain antisocial behaviour. *Reputation enhancement theory* suggests that 'deviant' adolescents and adolescent peer groups have different values concerning antisocial behaviour; for non-deviant groups antisocial behaviour might be a reason for exclusion, but for deviant groups it is a reason for inclusion (Carroll et al., 1999; Emler et al., 1987).

Another important aspect in the even wider ecological context (cf. p. 10) is the neighbourhood the young person is growing up in. Linares et al. (2001) studied 160 children growing up in high-crime neighbourhoods in the USA. Exposure to community violence (including witnessing violent acts) predicted child behaviour problems in 3- to 5-year-olds, although how mothers coped with community violence was also an important mediating factor. At 10–12 years, Brody et al. (2001) found that community disadvantage predicted deviant peer affiliations, especially when combined with a lack of nurturant or involved parenting. Pettit et al. (1999) found that at 12–13 years, lack of neighbourhood safety, especially combined with low parental monitoring and unsupervised peer contacts, predicted teacher ratings of externalizing behaviour problems.

Delinquency

Delinquency is the legal definition of antisocial behaviour. As such it overlaps greatly with violent and aggressive behaviour, although it also includes crimes such as vandalism and shoplifting which do not cause harm to people directly.

Patterson et al. (1989, 1992), describes 'early starters' and 'late starters' for delinquency. 'Early starters' are those who are aggressive and disruptive in primary and middle school, and often peer rejected at that time; but who associate with others like them in secondary school, and form the core of antisocial peer groups. They commit offences from around 10–12 years, and are more likely to reoffend. 'Late starters' are those who follow a more normal developmental path, but who show some aggressive and antisocial behaviours for a period, as they get drawn into the risk-taking behaviours of antisocial peer groups during adolescence (when these behaviours have more appeal; see chapter 9). They only commit offences from around 15 years; and desist after a few years of involvement with a deviant peer group.

Farrington (1995) describes findings from a longitudinal study of 411 working class boys in London (born c.1953) that support this distinction. Of those convicted of an offence between 10 and 15 years, 23 boys (about one-third of offenders) were chronic offenders, having at least 6 offences by 18 years. These boys were responsible for half of all the convictions from the 411 boys in total. By contrast, none of those first convicted after 15, classified as chronic offenders.

Farrington's work also delineated risk factors for delinquency, quite similar to those often found for aggression. In this sample, the seven most powerful predictors from middle childhood to chronic delinquency in adolescence were: troublesomeness in school (from both teacher and peer ratings); hyperactivity; poor concentration; low intelligence and poor attainment; family criminality; family poverty (low income, large family size, poor housing); and poor parental child rearing. Moving out of London was a protective factor!

Interventions

There are a great many programmes designed to reduce aggression, antisocial behaviour and conduct disorders in school, including social skills interventions (similar to those used for peer rejection, described earlier), and anti-bullying programmes (see next section). Generally, effects have been rather limited; as a result, more comprehensive programmes have started early (well before adolescence, so as to tackle the 'early starters'), and attempted to incorporate parent/family components as well as the child in the school setting.

An ambitious intervention programme in the USA, currently continuing, is the Fast Track project (Conduct Problems Prevention Research Group, 1999). This is based at four sites: Durham, North Carolina; Nashville, Tennessee; Seattle, Washington; and central Pennsylvania, a rural area. A multistage screening procedure was used to identify behaviourally disruptive kindergarten children, who would be at high risk of later problems in school. Entire schools in the sample areas were then assigned to either intervention (445 children in 191 classrooms) or control (446 children in 210 classrooms) conditions. The intervention included a school-based social skills curriculum (the PATHS model, described in detail in chapter 8), and various interventions directed at the target parents and children,

Table 5.5 Some pre- and post-test measures for intervention and control group children in the Fast Track project, at Grade 1

	Intervention		Control		
	Pre-test	Post-test	Pre-test	Post-test	significance
Social problem solving	0.61	0.70	0.63	0.67	p < .002
Hostile attribution	0.67	0.66	0.67	0.67	n.s.
Aggressive retaliation	0.43	0.31	0.42	0.35	p < .04
Parent-rated social competence	2.45	2.41	2.45	2.44	n.s.
Teacher-rated externalizing behaviour	61.64	62.68	61.31	62.76	n.s.

Source: Conduct Problems Prevention Research Group, 1999

including emotional understanding and communication, social problem solving, and home-based tutoring.

A variety of assessment measures were used. Table 5.5 shows a few of a large number of outcomes, for which there were pretest measures before or at the start of Grade 1 (6 years), and post-test at the end. The first three are child measures, based on responses to vignettes; the intervention group did not change on hostile attribution scores, but did improve more than controls on aggressive retaliation scores and on social problem solving skills. The non-significant findings for parent-rated social competence of the child, and teacher-rated externalizing behaviours, indicate the difficulty in having substantial effects, even with such an ambitious programme; however there were some other significant trends on some measures. The project is designed to continue through grade 10, so it is possible that continued intervention will have more cumulative impact.

Bullying in School

Bullying or harassment is usually defined as repeated aggressive actions against a particular victim, in which the child(ren) doing the bullying is generally thought of as being stronger, or perceived as stronger; at least, the victim does not feel him/herself to be in a position to retaliate effectively. Over the last decade, the topic has become a worldwide research area (Smith et al., 1999), and bullying and victimization in schools has become a topic of considerable public concern in many countries.

Research in western Europe suggests that bullying is quite pervasive in schools, and probably to a greater extent than most teachers and parents realize, since many victims keep quiet about it. It is difficult to observe bullying, for obvious reasons. It is often assessed by means of an anonymous questionnaire, which children or young people can fill in confidentially; although teachers ratings, diaries, and direct observations may also be used (Pellegrini and Bartini, 2000). Results from questionnaire surveys show that the most common forms of bullying are verbal – nasty teasing, threatening. Some is physical – hitting, pushing and (more occasionally) taking money; these may seem the more serious forms, but some 'teasing', especially that related to a disability, or which takes the form of racial or sexual harassment, can be very hurtful to the victim. Indirect and relational forms of harassment such as telling stories and social exclusion are also increasingly recognized as being bullying.

The occurrence of bully/victim problems varies considerably in different studies. In the UK, for example, reports by Smith and Shu (2000) and Wolke et al. (2000) present rather different estimates, mainly because of different methodologies and criteria. However a substantial minority of children are clearly involved. It is a fairly common finding that boys report, and are reported as, bullying more than girls; whereas boys and girls report being bullied about equally. Girls' bullying more usually takes the form of behaviours such as social exclusion, or spreading nasty rumours, rather than the physical behaviours used more by boys. Only a minority of victims report that they have talked to a teacher or anyone at home about it, or that a teacher or parent has talked to them about it.

Victims are more likely to report being alone at break time, and to feel less well liked at school; having some good friends can be a strong protective factor against being bullied. Hodges et al. (1999), in a longitudinal study of 10-year-old US children, found that internalizing behaviours (being alone, tearful, anxious) were risk factors in victimization, but that this risk was lessened if the child had a good friend. High status or high quality (strong, trustworthy) friends are likely to be more helpful.

Bullies may or may not be popular (they are often 'controversial', see p. 148). There has been some debate about the social skills of bullying children, with some literature on aggressive children suggesting that they may be deficient in some aspects. However, Sutton et al. (1999, and commentaries) suggested that many bullies may be skilled manipulators, possessing good theory of mind abilities which enable them to organize a gang effectively and hurt a victim while avoiding detection by teachers.

A sub-category of children may self-report or be nominated as both bullies and victims. These aggressive victims (or bully/victims) may have experienced punitive, hostile and abusive treatment at home (Schwartz et al., 1997) (cf. p. 124).

Salmivalli et al. (1996) pointed out the social roles involved in bullying: besides bullies and victims, they described the roles of onlookers (who watch the bullying), defenders (who help the victim) and outsiders (who ignore the bullying completely).

Consequences of being victimized

The more serious forms of bullying, at least, can have very serious consequences. For children being bullied, their lives are made miserable often for some considerable period of time. Kochenderfer and Ladd (1996) found that in 5–6-year-olds, continued victimization led to loneliness and school avoidance. Already probably lacking close friends at school, victims of bullying are likely to lose confidence and self-esteem even further. In a meta-analysis, Hawker and Boulton (2000) found that victimization was most strongly related to depression, moderately associated for social and global self-esteem, and less strongly associated with anxiety. Research using retrospective data suggests that children and young people persistently victimized are at increased risk for relationship difficulties later in life.

Such long-term effects can be brought out by in-depth case-study interviews. The following extract, from a woman aged 28 who experienced being bullied throughout much of her school career, and was now engaged to be married, illustrates this:

> *Do you feel that it's left a residue with you . . . what do you feel the effects are? . . .*
>   I'm quite insecure, even now . . . I won't believe that people like me . . . and also I'm frightened of children . . . and this is a problem. He [fiance] would like a family. I would not and I don't want a family because I'm frightened of children and suppose they don't like me? . . . those are things that have stayed with me. It's a very unreasonable fear but it is there and it's very real.

Those who bully others are learning that power-assertive and sometimes violent behaviour can be used to get their own way. We saw earlier how children who are aggressive at school are more likely to be involved in criminal activity later. A follow-up by Olweus (1991) of Norwegian secondary-school pupils up to age 24, found that former school bullies were nearly four times more likely than non-bullies to have had three or more court convictions.

Interventions against bullying

A lot can be done to reduce bully/victim problems in schools. The most extensive intervention has been carried out in Norway, and is described in box 5.2. In the UK, a large intervention study was carried out in Sheffield, in 16 primary and 7 secondary schools (Smith and Sharp, 1994). Results were generally encouraging; rates of bullying fell in most schools, especially in primary schools; and in secondary schools there was an increase in willingness to seek help from teachers. The main intervention was the development of a school anti-bullying policy, involving consultation between teachers, pupils, parents and other school personnel. This could be backed up by curriculum work, playground improvements, assertiveness training for victims, and peer support services such as peer counselling (Cowie and Sharp, 1996). A pack, *'Don't Suffer in Silence'*, was circulated to many schools as a result of this intervention. Many countries in Europe, the USA, Canada, Australia and Japan are developing programmes about bullying in school, and some countries (including the UK, Sweden and Malta) have specific legal requirements on schools concerning this (Ananiadou and Smith, 2002).

Group Socialization Theory and the Role of the Peer Group: How Important are Families?

As we saw in chapter 4, many developmental psychologists have assumed that parents have a formative and even decisive influence on the development of children. Important theoretical views have buttressed this assumption, including the psychoanalytic tradition of Freud, carried forward into more modern views of attachment theory by Bowlby; as well as the learning theory views of Watson and Skinner. The past three decades have seen very many studies of parenting styles and parenting influences on children's development, which have largely looked at the nature of such effects rather than querying whether such effects exist.

Judith Harris provided a vigorous challenge to this view. Her 'group socialization' theory of development was expounded in 1995, and is taken further in her 1998 book '*The Nurture Assumption*'. There are undoubtedly similarities between parents and children; but Harris suggests two main reasons for this, which do not involve children learning from parents; these are first, genetic effects, and second, community effects mediated by the peer groups children are in.

Parents and children share genes in common. From recent behaviour genetic work (described in chapter 2), Harris argues that some similarities between parent and child in temperament, personality and intelligence can be expected from genetic factors. This behaviour genetic research also leaves plenty of scope for environmental effects; however, much of it suggests that the major environmental effects are due to non-shared rather than shared environment. What this means is that the shared environment of a household, with particular parents, has not made siblings substantially more alike than if they were not in the same household with the same parents. The major environmental effects seem to come from outside the shared home environment. These conclusions come from research on identical and non-identical twins, and on natural and adoptive children (pp. 29–30).

Harris suggests that the major environmental factor in growing up is the child's peer group. She believes that, at least after infancy, the peer group provides the major important reference group for children. They adapt to peer group norms and compare themselves to their peers (for similar views in relation to sex differences, see Maccoby 2000 and p. 194). Harris proposes that (apart from genetic factors), the peer group has the main environmental influence on children, outside the home. In the peer group, children can learn to behave in quite different ways from the home [e.g., speak a different language, in the case of immigrants]. Correlations found between parents and children [e.g., punitive parents have aggressive children] may reflect (a) effects of children on parents, or (b) similarities of peer groups for children within a particular subcultural group.

Of course, there is – at a cultural and subcultural level – some correspondence between peer group values and parental values. Depending on ethnicity and social class, there are likely to be some shared values and assumptions held widely in a community. These will be shared in the peer group of children, and also in the older generation 'peer group' of parents. Thus, some similarity of parents and children will just reflect this general community similarity of values. Harris, however, argues that this similarity comes via the peers rather than directly via the parents.

The situation of immigrant children provided what Harris sees as a compelling argument for her view. She takes as an exemplar a family coming to a country such as the USA from a quite different country – say, Poland. The parents speak Polish, and although they learn English they speak it with a strong accent, and they keep many Polish traditions. Their children, however, once they enter school, very rapidly learn American English and an American way of life; the strong influence of the peer group produces assimilation in a generation or at most two.

Harris argues for the importance of code switching, or the context dependency of learning. Here, code can refer to a language, or to values, ways of behaving. Even if children learn one code for the home context, they learn another code for the peer context. Harris invokes ideas from social psychology and evolutionary psychology to suggest the importance of group processes, especially in the peer group, such as group affiliation, hostility to strangers, improving one's status in the group and forming close dyadic relationships from within the group.

On these bases, Harris argues that what children learn from parents specifically (rather than peers, and others generally) is transient to the infancy period and/or limited to the home context. Empirical data showing parent–child effects – which are often quite low, she claims – are explained by genetic similarities with the parent, and general cultural similarities mediated via the peer group.

Harris' theory has occasioned considerable controversy, and some hostility from those committed to the view that the behaviour of parents can have strong positive or negative effects on their children's development. Rutter (1999) suggests that the challenge of Harris' theory is to be welcomed, but that it is premature to accept all her conclusions. He believes that even if parents have rather little effect within the normal range of parenting, there is good evidence for specific effects at the extremes (for example, in cases of child abuse). He suggests that Harris also neglects the more complex effects of parents on children's development, via their choice of neighbourhoods, schools and peer groups for their children. The issues were debated further by Vandell (2000) and Harris (2000); for a restatement of the importance of both families and peers in development, see Parke et al. (2002).

Further Reading

For sibling relationships see Dunn, J. 1984: *Sisters and Brothers*. Glasgow: Fontana/Open Books; and more generally, Dunn, J. 1993: *Young Children's Close Relationships: Beyond Attachment*. Newbury Park and London: Sage, and Boer, F. and Dunn, J. (eds) 1992: *Children's Relationships with Siblings: Developmental and Clinical Issues*. Hillsdale NJ: Erlbaum.

Two good overviews of peer relations in childhood are Schneider, B. 2000: *Friends and Enemies*. London: Arnold, focusing on the psychological literature, and Pellegrini, A. D. and Blatchford, P. 2000: *The Child at School*. London: Arnold, having a wider coverage of peer relations, friendship, play and aggression in the school setting. For a collection on children's friendships, see Bukowski, W. M., Newcomb, A. F. and Hartup, W. W. (eds) 1996: *The Company They Keep: Friendship in Childhood and Adolescence*. Cambridge and New York: Cambridge University Press.

Asher, S. and Coie, J. D. (eds) (1990): *Peer Rejection in Childhood*. Cambridge: Cambridge University Press, discuss the evidence on peer rejection, loneliness and consequences of lacking friends. A classic ethnographic account of the social life of a school playground is in Sluckin, A. 1981: *Growing Up in the Playground*. London: Routledge & Kegan Paul.

Cairns, R. B. and Cairns, B. D. 1994: *Lifelines and Risks: Pathways of Youth in Our Time*. New York and London: Harvester Wheatsheaf, provide a fascinating longitudinal account of changes in friendship networks and developmental pathways of 695 American children through adolescence. Pepler, D. and Rubin, K. (eds) 1991: *The Development and Treatment of Childhood Aggression*. Hillsdale, NJ: Erlbaum, is a wide-ranging collection.

Rigby, K. 1996: *Bullying in Schools and What to Do About It*. Melbourne: ACER, covers a lot of general material on school bullying. Juvonen, J. and Graham, S. (eds) 2001: *Peer Harassment in School: The Plight of the Vulnerable and Victimized*. New York: Guilford Publications, is a useful collection of recent psychological studies on this topic.

■ Discussion Points

1   How special are sibling relationships compared with peer relationships?
2   Are friendships important for children? How can we find out?
3   Why are some children popular, and others not?
4   Why are some children more aggressive than others?
5   What would be the best ways of tackling bullying in schools?

Box 5.1
Dimensions and types of social status: a cross-age perspective

Two studies were carried out in this investigation of the types of social status in children's groups, and the kinds of behaviours which correlated with them.

In the first study approximately 100 children at each of three age levels (8, 11 and 14 years) were interviewed at two schools in North Carolina, USA. Each child was seen individually, and asked to name the three classmates whom he or she liked most, and the three classmates whom he or she liked least. Then, he or she was asked to name the three children who best fitted each of 24 behavioural descriptions, such as 'disrupts the group' or 'attractive physically'. The interview was repeated 12 weeks later to check that the data were reliable.

The scores used were the total nominations each child received for each of the 26 questions (liked most, liked least, and 24 behavioural descriptions). The correlations between the liked most and liked least scores, and some of the behavioural descriptions, are shown in box table 5.1.1. (The results were similar when each age group was treated separately.) The interesting thing about these results is that different behavioural descriptions correlate significantly with the 'liked most' and 'liked least' ratings. The two measures are not simply opposites of each other. 'Liked most' children tend to be supportive, co-operative leaders and attractive physically; 'liked least' children tend to be disruptive, aggressive and snobbish.

If 'liked most' is not just the opposite of 'liked least', the researchers argued that it made sense to think of them as independ-

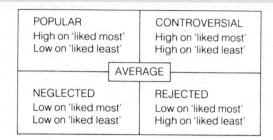

Box Figure 5.1.1   Five types of sociometric status (based on material in J. D. Coie, K. A. Dodge and H. Coppotelli 1982: *Development Psychology*, 18).

Box Table 5.1.1   Correlations between nominations for 'most-liked' and 'least-liked' and behavioural descriptions for 311 children aged 8 to 14

	Liked most	Liked least
Supports peers	−0.63*	−0.24*
Leads peers	−0.51*	−0.08*
Cooperates with peers	−0.51*	−0.31*
Attractive physically	−0.57*	−0.25*
Remains calm	−0.43*	−0.28*
Defends self in arguments	−0.37*	−0.03
Acts shy	−0.12	−0.05
Gets rejected by peers	−0.28*	−0.30*
Acts snobbish	−0.04	−0.66*
Starts fights	−0.02	−0.70*
Gets into trouble with teacher	−0.03	−0.71*
Disrupts the group	−0.07	−0.78*

*$p < 0.001$

ent measures (in fact the correlation between them was 0.21, which is quite a small value). In that case, there are four possible status outcomes shown in box figure 5.1.1 and mentioned in the text above (see p. 145), with a fifth if 'average' children are included.

In the second study the differences between these five status groups were examined more closely. More children of the same ages were interviewed at the same schools over the next 2 years. They were asked to nominate the three peers whom they liked most, liked least and who best fitted the descriptions 'cooperates', 'disrupts', 'shy', 'fights', 'seeks help' and 'leader'. Out of a total of 848 children, 486 were selected who clearly fitted one of the five social status groups. It was then possible to calculate the average 'behavioural profile' for children of each social status in terms of the six behavioural descriptions obtained from peers. Box table 5.1.2 shows the results. Children who lead in a cooperative way are 'popular'. Children who lead but fight and are disruptive are 'controversial', liked by some but disliked by others. Disruptive children who lack any cooperative or leadership skills are 'rejected'. Children who lack cooperative or leadership

Box Table 5.1.2 Behavioural profiles associated with five types of sociometric status in 486 children

	Leads peers	Cooperates	Acts shy	Seeks help	Fights	Disrupts group
Popular	HIGH	HIGH		Low	Low	Low
Controversial	HIGH		Low	High	HIGH	HIGH
Rejected	Low	LOW		HIGH	HIGH	HIGH
Neglected	Low	Low		Low	Low	Low
Average						

Use of upper case denotes a stronger difference than lower case; a blank cell implies the score was near the average for all the children

skills and are not aggressive either are 'neglected'. The pattern of results was similar across the three ages, for both sexes, and for different ethnic groups.

The strengths of this study are the large pool of participants and the attempt to make important distinctions in types of sociometric status. The authors speculate, for example, that 'controversial' children, high on both leadership and aggression, may become leaders of delinquent peer groups in adolescence. A weakness is that no direct observational measures were taken; we do not know that 'rejected' children really fight a lot, for example, only that other children (who do not like them) say they do. Some subsequent work (see p. 147) has linked the status groups to more direct behavioural measures.

Based on material in Coie, J. D., Dodge, K. A. and Coppotelli, H. 1982: Dimensions and types of social status: a cross-age perspective. *Developmental Psychology*, 18, 557–70.

Box 5.2
Bully/victim problems among schoolchildren: basic facts and effects of a school-based intervention programme

Norway has been very active in researching and intervening in problems of school bullying. Local and then nationwide surveys of the extent of the problem revealed that some 9 per cent of the school population were fairly regular victims of bullying, and some 7–8 per cent engaged in bullying others. Often, these children and young people did not tell teachers or parents about their involvement in bullying. In 1982 two young people in Norway took their own lives because of bullying at school. This and the associated media interest and public concern, combined with the previous research findings, led to the Ministry of Education supporting a nationwide Norwegian Campaign Against Bullying. This commenced on 1 October 1983.

The intervention programme, aimed at students, teachers and parents, had a number of components:

• a 32-page booklet for school personnel, giving detailed suggestions about what teachers and school can do to counteract bullying;

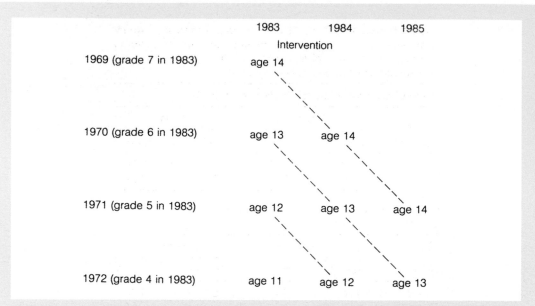

Box Figure 5.2.1 Design of cohort-sequential study of effects of an intervention programme against school bullying. Year of assessment is shown horizontally, and cohort (year of birth/initial grade level) vertically. The approximate ages of each sample of children from each cohort and at each year of study are shown in years.

- a 4-page folder with information and advice for parents;
- a 25-minute video cassette showing episodes from everyday lives of two bullied children, a 10-year-old boy and a 14-year-old girl. Child actors were used in making this video, which could be used as a basis for class discussion; and
- a short inventory or survey given to pupils, to ascertain the level and nature of bully/victim problems in each school.

In an evaluation carried out by Dan Olweus in the Bergen area of Norway, the effects of this intervention programme were assessed in 42 primary and junior high schools, with some 2500 students. Children start school at age 7 years in Norway; these students were aged around 11 and 14 years. A cohort-sequential design was used (cf. pp. 8–9 and figure 1.2), and is illustrated in box figure 5.2.1. The four grade (age) cohorts started at grades 4, 5, 6 and 7 (ages 11, 12, 13 and

14) in May 1983, shortly before the intervention campaign was started. Measurements were taken at this point (time 1), and again in May 1984 (time 2), and May 1985 (time 3).

This cohort-sequential design was important for interpreting any results. Suppose that there was some improvement in bullying problems with time. This could be due to the intervention programme; or it could be due to age or historical changes. Usually in a study of this kind we would control for these by comparing the results for other children who did not experience the intervention, or 'treatment'. However, as the intervention campaign was on a national basis, there could not be any 'no-treatment' control groups. What could be done was to make 'time-lagged contrasts between age-equivalent groups'. For example, the children who were grade 6 at time 2, and had experienced one year of intervention, could be compared with those who were grade 6

Box Table 5.2.1 Effects of intervention programme: questionnaire scores for (a) being bullied, and (b) for bullying others, for boys and girls, for each of the two time 1–time 3 comparisons (at grade 6, and grade 7)

How often have you been bullied in school?

(a)	Boys		Girls	
	Grade 6	Grade 7	Grade 6	Grade 7
Time 1	0.36	0.47	0.46	0.19
Time 3	0.19	0.18	0.11	0.07

How often have you taken part in bullying other students in school?

(b)	Boys		Girls	
	Grade 6	Grade 7	Grade 6	Grade 7
Time 1	0.49	0.47	0.26	0.23
Time 3	0.33	0.31	0.10	0.04

at time 1, before the intervention started. Later, the same comparison could be made with children who were grade 6 at time 3, after 2 years of intervention. Altogether, five such time-lagged comparisons can be made (see box figure 5.2.1).

These comparisons are matched for age, obviously an important factor. The children are different, but in the same schools, and given the large sample size this should not matter. Also, you will be able to see from the design that the same children, starting in grades 5 and 6, serve as both baseline groups and treatment groups in different comparisons.

The measurements made at the three time points were based on anonymously filled-in questionnaires from the students. These indicated the frequency of being bullied and bullying others, and of spending playtime alone; self-ratings of antisocial behaviour; ratings of satisfaction with school life; and ratings of the number of peers in the class being bullied or bullying others.

The results were encouraging. There were substantial reductions in the levels of both being bullied, and bullying others, reported by both boys and girls. Box table 5.2.1 shows the changes for the two time 1–time 3 comparisons (shown in box figure 5.2.1), on the questionnaire scores for 'How often have you been bullied in school?' and 'How often have you taken part in bullying other students in school?' Similar reductions were found for ratings of peers involved in being bullied or bullying. The bullying was not just displaced elsewhere; there were no changes in reports of bullying on the way to and from school. There were some decreases in the self-reports of antisocial behaviour, and some increases in student satisfaction with school life, such as liking playground time.

This research programme provides a convincing account of the application of psychological research to diagnosing a social problem, helping devise an intervention programme, and then assessing the results of such an intervention. The independent variable is time of assessment, while the dependent variables are the questionnaire measures. The data do depend largely on self-reports, which could be open to distortion or to effects of repeated testing; but are supported by ratings of peers.

The cohort-sequential design overcomes the absence of conventional no-treatment control groups. However, the comparisons do not control for historical effects. For example, suppose some other events had happened in 1984, such as severe economic depression, or increased racial tension such as with the Rushdie affair in the UK in 1989; these might influence the comparisons. In effect, the comparisons are measuring the effects of the intervention programme (itself an historical effect!) and any other large-scale effects felt in 1983–5. Nevertheless, there were no other such obviously important effects in Norway in the period concerned.

Another study, carried out on 37 schools in the Rogaland area of Norway around Stavanger, did not obtain such encouraging findings (Roland, 1989). Here follow-up assessments were made in 1986; preliminary results showed that levels of bullying had remained largely stable for girls, but had actually increased for boys. Nevertheless the schools that had implemented the intervention programme most thoroughly did have better results. The discrepancy between this study and the one based in Bergen remains to be fully explained.

Based on material in Olweus, D., Rubin, K. and Pepler, D. (eds) (1991): *The Development and Treatment of Childhood Aggression*. Hillsdale, NJ: Erlbaum.

6 Becoming Socially Aware

So far, we have looked at the child developing in the context of the family, the peer group and the school. In this chapter we shall look at how the child develops an understanding of him- or herself, and of others; and discuss various influences on this process. There is an important body of research that makes links between the child's social world (the focus of part two of this book) and the child's thinking and language abilities (the focus of part three). We will start by considering children's developing sense of self; their understanding of their own emotions; and how the child learns to categorize others and understand their emotional expressions. (This further relates to the developing awareness of others' mental states, beliefs and desires: what has been called a 'theory of mind', or skills in 'mindreading', discussed in chapter 14.)

The second part of the chapter examines the development of gender and ethnic differences – how children understand these, as well as what behavioural differences are found. Finally, we shall look at the effects of television on sex stereotyping and on social behaviour.

How Children Begin to Understand Self and Others

One basic step the infant must take in understanding about others is to realize that he or she is distinct from other people, who have a separate continuing existence. In other words, they must acquire a sense of self as distinct from others.

One early landmark of this is referred to as 'person permanence'. It has been assessed in terms of infants' recognition of particular others, and search for them when that person disappears from view. Person permanence implies an internal representation of a social being, corresponding to that person's continuity in time and space. Closely related to the concept of person permanence is that of 'object permanence', applied to non-social objects, and discussed in chapter 12. Both are achieved during the sensori-motor period (up to about 18 months of age), with major progress in the degree of permanence achieved (measured by the success of the infant's search strategies) towards the end of the first year.

The infant's recognition of self

While person permanence experiments show that an infant can recognize particular others and expect them to continue existing, they do not tell us specifically about the infant's own sense of self. Lewis and Brooks-Gunn (1979) found evidence that infants as young as 9 to 12 months were capable of some differentiation between pictorial representation of themselves, and others; for example, they would smile more and look longer at pictures of themselves than at pictures of other same-age babies. By 15 to 18 months, children are using verbal labels such as 'baby', or their own name, to distinguish pictures of themselves and others. One ingenious technique to assess self-recognition has been the 'Mirror test', also used with primates (chapter 2). In a study of this kind, Lewis and Brooks-Gunn (1979) used 16 infants at each of six age groups – 9, 12, 15, 18, 21 and 24 months. Each infant was first placed by the mother in front of a fairly large mirror, and their behaviour observed for about 90 seconds. Then, the infant's nose was wiped with rouge discreetly, on the pretence of wiping the infant's face (only one of the 96 infants immediately felt for his nose after this). The infant was subsequently placed in front of the mirror again and observed for another 90 seconds. How would the infant react?

At all ages, most of the infants smiled at their image in the mirror (see table 6.1), and many pointed to the mirror or reached out to touch it. However, in the first, 'no rouge' condition, very few touched their own nose, and not many touched their own body at all. When the rouge had been applied, the effect depended markedly on the infant's age. The 9- and 12-month-old infants never touched their own nose, despite being able to see their unusually red nose in the mirror; a minority of 15- and 18-month-olds, and most 21- and 24-month-olds, did reach for their own noses. This suggests that after about 18 months, an infant has a pretty good idea that the reflection in the mirror is a representation of him- or herself.

Lewis and Brooks-Gunn (1979) had also tried experiments with photographs and video presentations of children, and had found that children showed visual interest or verbal labelling of these stimuli by 18–24 months. Povinelli et al. (1996) tried similar tasks, playing delayed videos, and showing Polaroid photographs taken a bit earlier, to 2- to 4-year-old children; for example, they would unobtrusively put a large sticker on a child's head, and play back a video of the child a few minutes later. Older 3-year-olds, and 4-year-olds, reached for the sticker when they saw the video or photograph, but 2-year-olds and younger 3s would not. This suggested to Povinelli and his co-workers that although the younger children might have some immediate sense of self, in terms of recognition, they did

Table 6.1   Percentages of infants smiling, and touching own nose, on viewing their reflection in a mirror

Infants' behaviour	Age (months)	9	12	15	18	21	24
Smiling	No rouge	86	94	88	56	63	60
	Rouge	99	74	88	75	82	60
Touching own nose	No rouge	0	0	0	6	7	7
	Rouge	0	0	19	25	70	73

Source: Lewis and Brooks-Gunn, 1979

not yet have a full temporal sense of self, in terms of recognizing that the stimulus representing them some time ago, was still them at the present time.

How children categorize others

We have seen how infants achieve person permanence through the sensori-motor period, often ahead of object permanence. As concepts of particular persons become more stable, persons can begin to be categorized along social dimensions. Lewis and Brooks-Gunn (1979) argued that the three earliest social dimensions learned are familiarity, age and gender. They argue that these are concurrently developed in relation to oneself and to other persons.

The importance of familiarity is apparent from the research that shows that infants behave differently to familiar and to strange adults by around 7 to 9 months of age (when attachment relationships have usually formed), if not earlier (see chapter 4; and Sroufe, 1977). A bit later, infants respond differently to familiar and unfamiliar peers. Jacobson (1980) found that wariness of an unfamiliar peer (compared with a familiar peer) developed between 10 and 12 months. Greater previous experience with the familiar peer predicted an earlier onset of wariness of the unfamiliar peer.

Age is also used very early on in a categorical way. Infants aged 6 to 9 months discriminate in their behaviour between the approach of a child and of an adult, and infants aged 9 to 12 months can differentiate between photographs of baby and adult faces. Lewis and Brooks-Gunn (1979) suggest that height, movement, voice, and extreme differences in facial and hair characteristics (in baby and adult photographs) are the cues which infants use to categorize by age. Verbal age labels (e.g., baby, mummy, daddy) begin to be used correctly by 18 to 24 months of age. By the preschool years, age can be used as an explicit criterion for classification. Edwards and Lewis (1979) found that 3½ year-olds could successfully sort head-and-shoulders photographs of persons into four categories: little children, big children, parents and grandparents.

Differentiation of people by gender also occurs early. Nine- to 12-month-olds respond differentially both to photographs of female and male strangers (Brooks-Gunn and Lewis, 1981) and to direct approach by male and female strangers (Smith and Sloboda, 1986). Verbal gender labels (e.g., mummy, daddy, boy, girl) begin to be used correctly after 18 months of age. The development of gender identity is considered further, later in this chapter.

Emotional Development

Producing emotions

From birth onwards, babies start signalling their emotional state (see also chapter 3, p. 78; chapter 11, p. 350). Perhaps the earliest distinction one can make for babies is between positive and negative affect – whether they are contented and happy, as indicated by smiling; or discontented and distressed, as indicated by pursing the lips and crying. A study by Ganchrow et al. (1983) showed that at the time of the very first feed, newborns would produce distinct facial expressions to a sweet liquid (slight smile) or bitter liquid (mouth corners down, pursed lips). Observers who watched the babies without knowing which liquid was being given, could judge whether the babies liked or disliked the liquid, and also the intensity of response.

Interviews with mothers suggest that they can distinguish a variety of emotions in their infants in the first few months of life (Campos et al., 1983). Some basic or 'primary' emotions, which may be discernible from the first few weeks onwards, are happiness, interest, surprise, sadness, fear, anger and pain. For example, surprise is indicated by wide-open eyes and mouth, together with a startle response by the trunk and limbs. Fear responses increase considerably after about 7 months of age, when infants become wary and fearful of unfamiliar persons and objects; and sadness can occur in periods of separation from a familiar caregiver. (The balance of different emotional expressions is crucial in scoring the 'strange situation' procedure, see chapter 4, where anger as well as happiness may occur in reunion episodes).

Anger and pain also become increasingly easily distinguished from each other, especially after about 7 months. This was shown in a study by Izard et al. (1987). They looked at babies' facial expressions when they were given routine inoculations. The babies were aged from 2 to 8 months. For younger babies the reaction was one of generalized distress, but for older babies a distinctly angry expression (brows compressed together, eyelids tensed, mouth compressed or squared) became progressively more frequent.

One of the earliest descriptions of emotional development comes from Charles Darwin (1877), who published an article about the early development of one of his own children. Here is his description of the development of anger:

> It was difficult to decide at how early an age anger was felt; on his eighth day he frowned and wrinkled the skin round his eyes before a crying fit, but this may have been due to pain or distress, and not to anger. When about ten weeks old, he was given some rather cold milk and he kept a slight frown on his forehead all the time that he was sucking, so that he looked like a grown-up person made cross from being

compelled to do something which he did not like. When nearly four months old, and perhaps much earlier, there was no doubt, from the manner in which the blood gushed into his whole face and scalp, that he easily got into a violent passion. A small cause sufficed; thus, when a little over seven months old, he screamed with rage because a lemon slipped away and he could not seize it with his hands. When eleven months old, if a wrong plaything was given him, he would push it away and beat it: I presume that the beating was an instinctive sign of anger, like the snapping of the jaws by a young crocodile just out of the egg, and not that he imagined he could hurt the plaything.

Darwin's account is interesting for several reasons. It brings out clearly both his skill as an observer, and also the difficulty in interpreting emotions especially at younger ages. Darwin's account is an example of the diary method (p. 14); though in this case Darwin actually wrote up the article 37 years after keeping the diary on which it is based! Finally, you will see that Darwin suggests that some emotional displays are 'instinctive', in children as well as in animals. The very early development of emotional display in infants does seem to suggest that some of the mechanisms for producing emotion are 'innate', or strongly canalized in development (p. 36). The main alternative view would be that infants learn emotional expression from others, through observation and imitation; this seems less plausible in early infancy, but more plausible later, for example in explaining cultural differences in emotional expression.

Recognizing emotions in others

If infants were to learn aspects of emotional expression from others, they would have to understand something of their meaning. How early does this occur? We will look at two kinds of evidence, both suggesting that during the first year infants can distinguish and react appropriately to different emotional expressions by caregivers.

Some studies have looked at dialogues between mother and baby (cf. pp. 82, 350–2). Usually mother and baby are interacting happily. What would happen if the mother adopted a sad face, or an angry face? Haviland and Lelwica (1987) asked mothers to do this for a short while with their 10-week-old babies, adopting appropriate facial expressions and tone of voice. The babies did react differently. If the mother appeared happy, so did the baby. If the mother appeared angry, so did the baby. If the mother appeared sad, the baby did not particularly look sad, but did engage in chewing, mouthing and sucking.

These studies show that babies can discriminate emotions in others early on. Their reactions seem broadly appropriate, but it could be misleading to say that the baby 'understands' the mother's angry emotion; they might for example simply find the angry tone of voice (loud and harsh) unpleasurable in itself. However, evidence that infants can sensibly interpret the emotional expression of their mother comes from studies of 'social referencing'.

Social referencing

Sometimes, an infant will look carefully at his or her mother (or familiar care-giver), as if to gauge their emotional expression, before as it were deciding how to react to a situation. This kind of behaviour is referred to as 'social referencing', and has been defined as a 'process characterized by the use of one's perception of other persons' interpretation of this situation to form one's own understanding of the situation' (Feinman, 1982, p. 445). Not surprisingly, it is more likely in ambiguous situations, where some extra 'advice' is needed by the infant. Two well-studied examples are: reactions to strangers or to strange toys, and behaviour on the 'visual cliff'.

From about 7 months of age, infants do tend to be wary of strangers. Feiring et al. (1984) observed how 15-month-olds would respond to a stranger. They would often turn to the mother when the stranger entered, as if to ascertain her reaction. The experimenters asked the mother to either interact positively with the stranger, or ignore the stranger. The reaction of the infants to the stranger was less positive when the mother ignored the stranger. Similar results have been obtained with the reactions of 12-month-old infants to toys, depending on the facial expression of the mother (Klinnert, 1984). Mumme et al. (1996) however found rather little effect of mothers' facial emotional signals, but stronger effects of negative vocalizations, on the infants' behaviour with a novel toy.

Another experiment was carried out using the 'visual cliff' (see plate 10.1). In the visual cliff, infants generally refuse to move onto a glass surface when it appears that there is a large drop at the boundary. The situation can be made more ambiguous by making the apparent drop smaller. This was done by Sorce et al. (1985) with a sample of 12-month-olds. The mother was opposite the baby (see the right-hand photo on plate 10.1), so her face was very visible. Some mothers were asked to adopt a happy face, others a fearful face. Of 19 infants whose mother had a happy face, 14 crossed the visual cliff; of 17 whose mother had a fearful face, none crossed. This suggests that the infants interpreted the mother's expression appropriately, as a commentary on the situation. This is well illustrated by this experiment, as a mother's fearful expression would normally cause an infant to approach the mother for safety; but in this experiment, the mother's fearful expression actually prevents approach across the apparent cause of danger, the visual cliff.

Some criticisms have been made of these social referencing experiments; while it is clear that the infants are making use of emotional messages in some sense, are they actually using the mother's emotion to *refer to* the new object, person or situation encountered? Perhaps the mother's emotional signaling simply alters the infant's emotional state, or their regulation of proximity (Baldwin and Moses, 1996). Such criticisms certainly could apply to the experiments with strangers or novel toys cited above, although less obviously to that with the visual cliff. In any event, a study by Moses et al. (2001) provided rather clear evidence for social referencing in the full sense of the term, in 12- to 18-month olds. They found that infants would use vocalizations of an adult (positive, such as 'nice!', 'wow!' or negative such as 'Iiuu!', 'yeech!') to modulate their behaviour with a strange toy, such as a 'bumble ball'; the infants would often look at the adult when they vocalized. However they only modulated their behaviour to the toy that the adult was looking at.

The relationship between sense of self, and understanding others

We saw earlier how a sense of self develops by around 18 months. A sense of self can be used as a reference point for understanding others, and some psychologists regard the two as inextricably linked. The idea goes back to an American child psychologist, J. M. Baldwin (1861–1934). It is supported by Lewis and Brooks-Gunn (1979), who advanced three principles regarding early social awareness:

1 Any knowledge gained about the other also must be gained about the self.
2 What can be demonstrated to be known about the self can be said to be known about the other and what is known about the other can be said to be known about the self.
3 Social dimensions are those attributes of others and self that can be used to describe people. (Related ideas were developed by Paul Harris (1989) in his theory of how children come to understand others, which we shall discuss shortly.)

The link between knowledge of self and of others is also supported by empirical work. Bischof-Kohler (1988) carried out the mirror test (p. 176) on infants aged 16 to 24 months; she also assessed their level of empathy when playing with an experimenter who is 'sad' when the arm of a teddy bear falls off. There was a high correlation between a child's level of self-recognition, and their level of empathic behaviour, irrespective of the child's age. In general, it seems as if the beginnings of a truly empathic understanding of others emerges at around 20 months (see also chapter 8), at the same time as other aspects of understanding others (for example, jealousy and deception) and as self-recognition as assessed by the mirror test emerge.

This awareness of others *vis-à-vis* oneself also seems to be a prerequisite for the 'secondary' emotions such as pride, guilt or shame, which develop after the 'primary' emotions such as happiness, fear, anger and surprise. The secondary emotions depend on some understanding of how others perceive your situation; they are self-conscious emotions. A study of the development of embarrassment in children, a secondary emotion of this kind, is given in box 6.1.

Talking about mental states

From about 18 months, further insight can be obtained into emotional development by looking at how infants talk about emotions – how they use 'emotion words' in natural conversation (Bretherton et al., 1986). Both diaries of child speech and observations in the home show that use of words which label emotions (such as 'have fun', 'surprised', 'scared', 'yucky', 'sad'), while rare at 18 months, are common by 24 months. Interestingly, although these words are used somewhat more frequently by children to refer to themselves than to refer to others, the use of these words for self and others goes very much in parallel; this supports the ideas discussed above of the interdependence of concepts of self and other.

By 28 months, children are using language to comment on and explain their own feelings, for example:

'I see tiger. That too scary.'
'Me fall down. Me cry.'

And the feelings of others, for example:

'Grandma mad. I wrote on wall.'
'You sad Mommy. What Daddy do?'

They can also use them to guide or influence someone else's behaviour, for example:

'No not angry. Not nice.' (age 19 months; parents are quarrelling.)
'Baby crying. Kiss. Make it better.' (age 22 months; to mother, in shop where child noticed other child crying.)
'I hurt your hair. Please don't cry.' (age 24 months; to child victim, after being scolded for hair-pulling.)

(from Bretherton et al., 1986)

Emotional deception

When can children first deliberately manipulate emotions to achieve a certain effect on others? For example, can they deceive others by hiding or changing a facial expression of emotion? It looks as though they can do this by 3 or 4 years of age.

In one study, Cole (1986) looked at how 3- and 4-year-old girls would react when given a disappointing present. The girls were given picture-story tasks to do. Before the tasks, each girl had rated ten possible gifts from best to worst. After the first set of tasks, the children were given their 'best' present; but after the second set of tasks, they were given their 'worst' present (a broken toy, or some raisins). How would they react? Cole found that when the interviewer was not present, the children (filmed by a videocamera) would show disappointment to the 'worst' toy, but that when the interviewer stayed present, many would hide their disappointment with a half-smile. (The children were subsequently given the opportunity to trade in their 'worst' toy for another one.)

Another study (Lewis et al., 1989) was done with children who were just 3 years of age (33–37 months). The child sat at a table with the experimenter (and the mother in the background), and was told that the experimenter was going to put out a surprise toy (actually, a Fisher-Price zoo), but that they must not peek while the experimenter left the room; they could play with the toy when the experimenter returned. The experimenter then left the room, and the children were observed and filmed through a one-way mirror. The experimenter returned and asked 'did you peek?' before playing with the child and reassuring them that it was all right if they did peek.

Of 33 children taking part, 29 did peek at the toy when the experimenter left! Of these, 11 admitted to peeking, 11 denied it and 7 gave no answer to the question. Besides the verbal deception of many children, there was evidence of facial deception. The children who peeked tended to put on a smile when the experimenter re-entered and looked at them (unlike the few children who did not peek, who did not smile), and when questioned, these children continued smiling; those who denied peeking had the most relaxed and positive facial expression!

As we saw in chapter 2 (p. 43–4), there can be different levels of deception. The above examples would seem to indicate level-four deception, that is a deliberate intent to deceive. In the Lewis et al. (1989) study, it could however be argued that the child's response 'no', to 'did you peek?' may have been just an avoidance reaction, or a stereotyped denial strategy; but this does not explain the manipulation of facial expression which occurred as well. The development of deception is discussed more in chapter 14 (see pp. 470–1).

Understanding Others' Emotions, Desires and Beliefs

We have seen that there is considerable evidence that children can understand other people's emotions, desires and beliefs by 3 or 4 years of age, and indeed that the beginnings of this can be seen by 2 years of age. How does this understanding come about? One theory was put forward by Paul Harris in his book *Children and Emotion* (1989). Harris believes that it is a child's awareness of his or her own mental state which allows them to project mental states on to other people using an 'as if' or pretence mechanism; understanding someone else results from imagining yourself in their position. (This is in fact similar to the argument by Humphrey, chapter 1, p. 3.) On this basis, Harris argues that there are three important precursors, or preconditions, for the child to be able to understand another person's mind. These are self-awareness; the capacity for pretence; and being able to distinguish reality from pretence:

- *Self-awareness*: as we saw earlier, children are aware of themselves by about 18–20 months of age and can verbally express their own emotional states by 2 years.
- *The capacity for pretence*: in chapter 7 (pp. 222–4) we see that the ability to pretend that something in the world is something else emerges in pretend play during the second year. Specifically, children start acting out scenes with dolls or stuffed animals, for example feeding teddy 'as if' he were hungry. By 2 and 3 years of age, children are conjuring up animate beings in their pretend play, with emotions and desires of their own.

- *Distinguishing reality from pretence*: when children are in pretend play, they do not usually confuse this with reality. Admittedly this can happen sometimes. When an adult joins in with a 1- or 2-year-old's play, the child can be confused as to whether the adult is in 'pretend' or 'real' mode; for example, if a child knocks an empty cup over in play and mother says 'you spilled your tea, better wipe it up', the child may actually pick up a cloth to wipe it. However, more usually, and especially by 3 or 4 years, the pretence–reality distinction is a stable one. Things would be difficult if it was not! Suppose a child pretends a wooden block is a cake, for a tea party; if they confused pretence and reality, they would actually try to eat the wooden block! This seldom happens. By 3 years, children often signal the pretend mode in their play, for example 'let's pretend to be families. You be daddy . . .'. Direct interviews with 3-year-olds also confirm that they can distinguish real from imaginary situations, and understand the use of the words 'real' and 'pretend'.

How do all these precursors come together in Harris's theory? He supposes that once a child is aware of his or her own emotional state, he or she can use the ability to pretend in order to project this emotional state on to inanimate beings (in pretend play), or on other people; and to realize that the other person's imagined reality may differ from their own reality. Let's take as an example the child who said 'You sad Mommy. What Daddy do?', cited earlier. We can suppose that previously this child has experienced sadness herself; and perhaps has experienced sadness because her Daddy was nasty to her. Her ability to imagine things in an 'as if' or pretend mode enables her to suppose that Mummy too may be sad, because Daddy was nasty to her also. Furthermore, she does not confuse this with her own emotional state; the child does not have to be sad herself, in order to imagine that Mummy is sad, for a certain reason.

There is one obvious alternative interpretation which would dispense with Harris's 'as if' mechanism. That is that young children learn to link common situations with common emotions (compare the discussion of Borke's results in chapter 12, pp. 415–16). Perhaps they just have learnt that mummies are usually sad because daddies have been nasty to them, and it doesn't require any imaginative projection of one's own emotional state.

One way to distinguish this alternative explanation from Harris's theory is to see whether children can understand that someone else's emotion in a given situation depends on what they desire or want. To ascertain this, Harris and his colleagues asked children to listen to stories about animal characters, for example, Ellie the elephant and Mickey the monkey. Ellie the elephant is choosy about what she likes to drink. Some children were told that she likes milk to drink and nothing else; others that she likes coke to drink and nothing else. Mickey the monkey is mischievous and mixes up the drink containers; for example, he might pour all the coke out of a coke can, fill it with milk, and offer it to Ellie. How would she feel when she tastes the drink? Four-year-olds are able to answer correctly that (if she likes milk) she will be pleased, or that (if she likes coke) she will be sad, and explain why in terms of Ellie's desires.

This does tend to suggest that, at least by 4 years, children are taking account of someone's desires in predicting their emotional state; they are not just basing their judgement on a stereotyped situation–emotion link (such as: you are pleased if you are given a drink). In a subsequent study, the experimenters also asked children how Ellie would feel before she tasted the drink. How would she feel if she likes coke, and is given a coke can (which Mickey has secretly filled with milk). By 6 years (though in this study, not at 4 years), children correctly judge that Ellie would be happy when given the can, though sad when she tasted the contents. Here, belief and desire of another are being successfully linked in the prediction of emotion, even when the belief is different from the child's own belief (the child knows the coke can has milk, but Ellie has a 'false belief'), and the desire may be different from the child's desire; not all children like coke (or milk).

From the above account, we might say that children are developing hypotheses about other persons' emotions, desires and beliefs. This could be described as developing a 'theory of mind' or skills in 'mindreading'. As we saw at the end of chapter 2, there are similar ideas about the evolutionary origins of intelligence in the higher primates. Further research on development of 'theory of mind' in children is considered in chapter 14.

By 6 or 7 years children seem able to understand and manipulate emotions in a more complex way. It would appear that, as well as being able to understand that someone else can feel a different emotion (meta-representation), they can begin to operate recursively on such understanding (Harris, 1989). Consider, for example, how children might respond to the following story:

> Diana falls over and hurts herself. She knows that the other children will laugh if she shows how she feels. So she tries to hide how she feels.

What will Diana do, and why? Many 6-year-olds (but not 4-year-olds) are able to say that Diana will look happy, and explain why; for example, 'she didn't want the other children to know that she's sad that she fell over'. This is an embedded sentence with a recursive structure of the form 'I may not want you to know how I feel'. We've seen that 4-year-olds can cope with 'I know how you feel', but only by 6 years does this further recursion seem to become possible (see also discussion of higher-order false belief tasks in chapter 14).

Self-concept and Self-esteem

A general term for how people think about themselves is self-concept, or identity. This can refer to all aspects of the self – appearance, personality, ability, as well as gender, or ethnic group (which we look at next). Some aspects of one's self-concept are evaluative; we all compare ourselves with others and think that we are good at some things and not so good at other things. These evaluations we make are called by psychologists self-esteem.

It is possible to measure self-esteem by means of questionnaires. For example, in the Harter Self-Perception Profile for Children (Harter, 1985), designed for 8–13-year-olds, children read a series of paired items such as:

> some kids find it hard to make friends BUT some kids find it's pretty easy to make friends

They decide which statement is true for them, and whether it is 'sort of true' or 'really true'. There are 36 such statements, and the answers give scores for the child's own perception of their 'global self-worth', as well as for more specific aspects of self-esteem such as scholastic competence, social acceptance, athletic competence, physical appearance, and behavioural conduct.

For a review of measures of self-esteem see Davis-Kean and Sandler (2001).

Early Sex Differences and the Development of Gender Identity

We saw earlier how infants use sex, or gender, as one way of categorizing people. We will now look further at sex differences in behaviour and the development of children's awareness of these differences. Then some hypotheses about why sex differences develop are compared. Some authors prefer to use the term 'gender' rather than 'sex' when referring to differences that may have been produced by upbringing or social convention, reserving 'sex' for purely biological differences. In practice, the distinction is not always that easy. Here we refer to 'sex differences', but to 'gender identity', these being common usages.

Sex differences among children in Western societies

Many studies have been carried out in the UK and the USA on sex differences in infants and young children, most involving observations of behaviour in the home or in nursery classes. Individual studies often have rather small samples, say 20 children or so, and measure a large number of behavioural categories; so even by chance one or two measures may give apparently 'significant' differences. (Remember a result significant at the 0.05 level occurs by chance 1 in 20 times.) Thus, it is important to look for replication of findings over a number of studies. There are many reviews of this subject area in the literature (e.g., Golombok and Hines, 2002; Maccoby, 1998, 2000).

The results of research in the infancy period (up to 2 years) do not reveal many consistent differences between boys and girls. The similarities certainly outweigh the dissimilarities. However, the replicated findings include: girl infants may be more responsive to people, staying closer to adults, whereas boy infants may be more distressed by stressful situations which they cannot control (such as the 'strange situation' separations discussed on pp. 94–6). Girls also seem to talk earlier.

Figure 6.1   Stereotyped female and male figures (adapted from Emmerich et al., 1976).

Among 2-year-olds and in older children some sex differences in toy choice are apparent. Observations of 2-year-olds at home, and of 3- and 4-year-olds in nursery classes, show that boys tend to prefer transportation toys, blocks and activities involving gross motor activity such as throwing or kicking balls, or rough-and-tumbling; girls tend to prefer dolls, and dressing-up or domestic play. Many activities, however, do not show a sex preference at this age.

School-age children tend to select same-sex partners for play, and more so as they get older. Also, boys tend to prefer outdoor play and, later, team games; whereas girls prefer indoor, more sedentary activities, and often play in pairs. Boys more frequently engage both in play-fighting and in actual aggressive behaviour (Maccoby, 1998). Girls tend to be more empathic, and remain more orientated towards adults (parents and teacher) longer into childhood.

Awareness of gender identity and sex differences

If you ask a 2-year-old 'are you a boy or a girl?', quite a few will not know the answer or will be easily confused, although many will answer correctly. The easiest task seems to be to show pictures of a male and female of stereotyped appearance (such as figure 6.1). In one such study, Thompson (1975) found that 24-month-old children gave 76 per cent correct identification of sex; this rose to 83 per cent by 30 months and 90 per cent by 36 months. By 3 years most children can correctly label their own, or another person's sex or gender, and are said to have achieved *gender identity*.

Table 6.2 Beliefs about boys and girls, held by both boys and girls aged 2½ and 3½

Beliefs about girls	play with dolls
	like to help mother
	like to cook dinner
	like to clean house
	talk a lot
	never hit
	say 'I need some help'
Beliefs about boys	like to help father
	say 'I can hit you'

[a] Only results at or approaching statistical significance are recorded.
Source: Kuhn et al., 1978

The next stage, called *gender stability*, is achieved by around 4 years. This is when a child realizes that gender is normally stable; for example, a girl will answer that she will be a mummy when she grows up. A bit later the child reaches '*gender constancy*', a mature awareness that biological sex is unchanging, despite changes in appearance. This is tested by questions such as 'could you be a girl if you want to be?' (to a boy), or 'suppose this child (picture of boy) lets their hair grow very long; is it a boy or a girl?'. This is reported to be achieved around 7 years of age, at or soon after the child can conserve physical quantity (see chapter 12), but may be achieved earlier if children understand the genital difference between the sexes (Bem, 1989).

Sex-role stereotypes are also acquired early; these are beliefs about what is most appropriate for or typical of one sex, or the other. In one study (Kuhn et al., 1978), preschool children were shown a male doll and a female doll, and asked which doll would do each of 72 activities, such as cooking, sewing, playing with trains, talking a lot, giving kisses, fighting or climbing trees. Even 2½ year-olds had some knowledge of sex-role stereotypes (see table 6.2). This sex-stereotyping increases with age and is well established by the middle school years (Serbin et al., 1993, is an excellent summary). In a study of 5- and 8-year-old children in England, Ireland and the USA (Best et al., 1977), the majority of boys and girls, of both ages and in all countries, agreed that females were soft-hearted whereas males were strong, aggressive, cruel and coarse. Many more characteristics were stereotyped in the 8-year-olds.

By 8 years of age children's stereotypes are very similar to those obtained with adults. Several studies have shown that adult stereotypes are quite consistent across a variety of ages and social backgrounds. They are also reflected in the mass media, such as books, comics, films and TV programmes (see later in this chapter). By and large, of course, such stereotypes correspond to actual differences in behaviour. Nevertheless, they can seem to exaggerate such differences, especially in periods when sex roles may be changing quite rapidly. For example, until recently few children's books depicted working mothers, even though a substantial proportion of mothers of young children have been in employment for decades.

Table 6.3   Incidence among different cultures of training girls or boys more strongly for certain characteristics

	Girls trained more (%)	Boys trained more (%)	No difference (%)
Nurturance (n = 33)	82	0	18
Responsibility (n = 84)	61	11	28
Obedience (n = 69)	35	3	62
Self-reliance (n = 82)	0	85	15
Achievement (n = 31)	3	87	10

n = number of cultures rated
Source: Barry et al., 1957

Cross-cultural studies

The sex differences in behaviour and sex-role stereotypes so far discussed apply to Western urban societies such as the UK and the USA. But how widely do they apply in other societies? Much of what we know here comes from the work of anthropologists. One study made a survey of the anthropological literature on child-rearing in 110, mostly non-literate, societies (Barry et al., 1957). They found that in more than 80 per cent of those societies where accurate ratings could be made, girls more than boys were encouraged to be nurturant, whereas boys more than girls were subject to training for self-reliance and achievement. In many societies responsibility and obedience were also encouraged in girls more than boys (table 6.3). The degree of pressure for sex-typing does vary with the type of society, and appears to be especially strong in societies where male strength is important for hunting or herding, and less strong in societies with small family groups, where sharing of tasks is inevitable.

A more detailed study of child-rearing was made in the 'Six Cultures Study' (Whiting and Edwards, 1973; Whiting and Whiting, 1975), in which direct observations were made on samples of children in Kenya, Japan, India, the Philippines, Mexico and the USA. In the majority of these societies girls were more nurturant and made more physical contacts while boys were more aggressive, dominant and engaged in more rough-and-tumble play. Differences among the six cultures could often be related to differences in socialization pressures, e.g. the extent to which older girls were required to do 'nurturant' tasks such as looking after younger siblings.

Theories of Sex-role Identification

Why do boys and girls come to behave in different ways, and to have certain beliefs about sex-appropriate behaviour? There are several theories about this process of acquiring a sex-role, or *sex-role identification*. Here we consider biological factors, social learning theory, the cognitive–developmental approach and gender schemas, social cognitive theory, and Maccoby's attempted synthesis (1998, 2000).

Biological factors

Boys and girls differ in one chromosome pair; girls have two X chromosomes, whereas boys have one X and one Y chromosome. This genetic difference normally leads to differential production of hormones, both in the fetus and later in adolescence (chapter 9). These hormones lead to differentiation of bodily characteristics, such as the genital organs, and may also influence brain growth and hence behaviour patterns.

Much of the evidence linking sex hormones to behaviour comes from animal studies, but there have now been a number of studies on human children who have received unusual amounts of sex hormone early in life, for example while in the uterus. The most common syndrome is called Congenital Adrenal Hyperplasia (CAH), in which due to a lack of certain enzymes, the adrenal glands produce excessive androgens (a male sex hormone).

A pioneering study of this kind was reported by Money and Ehrhardt (1972). They examined girls who had been exposed to unusually high levels of androgen before birth, in this case because of a hormone treatment given to some mothers for problems such as repeated miscarriages (subsequently discontinued). Any malformation of the genitals was corrected surgically and the children were reared as girls. Compared with a matched group of girls who had not been exposed to excess androgen, these girls and their mothers reported themselves as being more tomboyish and less likely to play with other girls and like feminine clothes. In evaluating this study the parents' knowledge of the hormonal abnormalities must be borne in mind; this could have affected their behaviour towards the children. However, it may seem unlikely that the parents actually encouraged these girls to be tomboyish, for example.

In a comprehensive review, Collaer and Hines (1995) examined the evidence for the effects of sex hormone abnormalities on behaviour over a range of outcome variables. They conclude that the evidence is strongest for childhood play behaviour; in normal fetal development male sex hormones seem to predispose boys to become more physically active and interested in rough-and-tumble play. They also argue that the evidence is relatively strong in two other areas: aggression (see chapter 5), and sexual orientation (for an overview of work on development of sexual orientation, see Patterson, 1995). Such effects are consistent with evidence that some sex differences appear early in life, and in most human societies (such as boys' preference for rough-and-tumble).

However, while biological factors are probably important in any comprehensive explanation of sex differences, they do not in themselves explain the process of sex-role identification, and they do not explain the variations in sex roles in different societies.

Social learning theory

An early approach to the learning of sex-role identification was that children are moulded into sex-roles by the behaviour of adults, especially parents and teachers – the social learning theory approach (Bandura, 1969; Mischel, 1970). In its early version (which Maccoby, 2000, calls 'direct socialization') this theory postulates that parents and others reward (or 'reinforce') sex-appropriate behaviour in children. Parents might encourage nurturant behaviour in girls, and discourage it in boys, for example.

Do parents behave differently towards boys and girls? The answer seems often to be yes. Besides the cross-cultural evidence referred to above, observations have been made in homes and nurseries in Western societies. For example, Fagot (1978) studied children aged 20–24 months in American homes. She found that girls were encouraged by their parents to dance, dress up, follow them around, and play with dolls, but were discouraged from jumping and climbing; boys, however, were encouraged to play with blocks and trucks, but discouraged from playing with dolls or seeking help. In a similar study of 3- to 5-year-olds (Langlois and Downs, 1980), mothers, fathers and also same-age peers reinforced sex-appropriate behaviour and discouraged sex-inappropriate behaviour in children.

Nevertheless, many reviews have felt that this evidence has not been very compelling (Golombok and Hines, 2002; Maccoby, 2000). Many differences in behaviour of parents to boys, and girls, are small in magnitude. Also, it might be that any differential behaviour by parents is simply responding to pre-existing differences in boys' and girls' behaviour.

At times, researchers try hard to find effects. In a study of mothers and fathers playing with a feminine-stereotyped toy (food, plates) and a masculine stereotyped toys (track, cars), Leaper (2000) stated that 'one of the most consistent ways parents treat girls and boys differently is through the encouragement of gender-typed activities and the discouragement of cross-gender-typed activities' (p. 389). However Leaper's own findings were that 'the hypothesized child gender effects on parent's behavior were not confirmed' (p. 386), and 'Support for this hypothesis [that parents generally – and fathers especially – would use lower mean levels of affiliation during cross-gender-typed activities] was not found' (p. 387).

Does reinforcement actually affect the child's behaviour? Several studies have found that nursery school teachers tend to reward 'feminine' type behaviours (e.g., quiet, sedentary activities near an adult) in both boys and girls equally, yet this does not prevent boys engaging more in noisy, rough-and-tumble play. Fagot (1985) observed 40 children aged 21–25 months in playgroups, looking at what activities were reinforced (e.g., by praise or joining in) and by whom. She found that the teachers reinforced 'feminine' activities in both boys and girls. She also looked at the effectiveness of the reinforcement (in terms of continuation of the activity). This varied with who was reinforcing, and with what was being reinforced. Girls were influenced by teachers and by other girls, but not much by boys. Boys were influenced by other boys, but not much by girls or teachers. Furthermore, boys were not influenced at all by girls or teachers during 'masculine' activities such as rough-and-tumble or playing with transportation toys.

The limited importance of reinforcement by teachers is also brought out in a study by Serbin et al. (1977). They asked teachers in two preschool classes to praise and encourage cooperative play between boys and girls for a 2-week period. This did increase the level of cooperative cross-sex play, but as soon as the special reinforcement was discontinued, cross-sex play declined to just as low a level as before.

In a slightly later version of social learning theory (which Maccoby calls 'indirect socialization') it is also supposed that children observe the behaviour of same-sex models, and imitate (or 'model') them; for example, boys might observe and imitate the behaviour of male figures in TV films, in their playful and aggressive behaviour. This introduces a more powerful set of influences on behaviour – but at the price of having to acknowledge cognitive factors. Clearly, observation and imitation must be selective. If observation in itself were important, we would expect most young children to acquire a female sex-role identity, as the great majority of caregivers of young children, and of nursery and infant school teachers, are female! If selective modeling is happening, then children must have some sense of gender identity in order to know who to observe and imitate, and perhaps which activities it is appropriate to imitate. In other words, their own cognitions must be playing an important role.

Cognitive-developmental theory and gender schemas

The cognitive-development approach in this area stems from the writings of Kohlberg (1966, 1969). He argued that the child's growing sense of gender identity is crucial to sex-role identification. Children tend to imitate same-sex models and follow sex-appropriate activities, because they realize that this is what a child of their own sex usually does. This process was termed *self-socialization* by Maccoby and Jacklin (1974), since it does not depend directly on external reinforcement. The difference between the cognitive-developmental and social-learning viewpoints is summarized in figure 6.2.

What evidence is there for this cognitive-developmental view? In a number of studies the development of gender identity and constancy has been found to correlate with the degree of sex-typed behaviour. For example, in a study of 2- and 3-year-olds by Weinraub et al. (1984), it was found that the children who had achieved gender identity more securely were also the ones who were observed to make more sex-stereotyped toy preferences. In another study of 4–6-year-olds (Ruble et al., 1981), the level of gender constancy was measured, and each child was shown a film of either same- or opposite-sex children playing with a new toy. Only children high on gender constancy were influenced by the film; if a child high on gender constancy saw opposite-sex children playing with the toy, that child avoided playing with it subsequently.

In the 1980s, ideas of *gender schemas* were introduced (Bem, 1981; Martin and Halverson, 1981). Gender schemas are cognitive structures that organize gender knowledge into a set of expectations about what it is important to observe, and what it is appropriate to imitate. Schemas also help children to form evaluations of and make assumptions about peers, based on their sex. Martin and Halverson (1987) argued that early gender schemas are formed around a basic ingroup/outgroup division; the child then focuses on a further understanding of their own gender identity through a grasp of the characteristics of their ingroup.

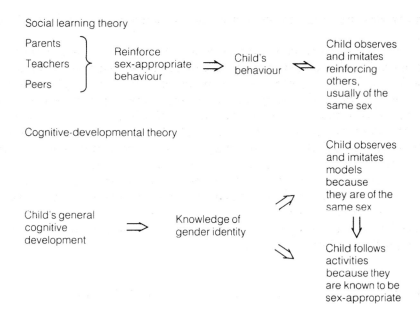

Figure 6.2   Summary of two earlier approaches to sex-role development: social learning theory and cognitive-developmental theory.

Social cognitive theory

Social cognitive theory (Bussey and Bandura, 1999) in effect draws together the ideas of social learning theory, and of the cognitive-developmental and gender schema insights; which after all are complementary rather than antagonistic. Social cognitive theorists stress the variety and complexity of mechanisms that are at work – for example:

- self-regulatory mechanisms – children monitor their own behaviour with reference to a self-accepted standard of what is appropriate;
- identification with a peer group – monitoring their behaviour in relation to how they expect same-sex peers might react; and
- motivational mechanisms – children are most likely to imitate behaviour which they think they can master and which will enhance their self-efficacy and self-esteem.

Gender schema theorists cite evidence that children not only selectively imitate same-sex models, but selectively observe and remember information that is relevant to or consistent with their own gender schema, or ignore and reject information that is not relevant or consistent with their gender schema. For example, Martin et al. (1995), in a study of 4- to 5-year olds, found that if a girl likes a toy, she will assume that girls will like it more than boys (even if it is actually highly attractive to both sexes).

Martin et al. (1999) assessed cognitions or gender schemas that children aged 3 to 6 years held, about playing with same- or opposite-sex playmates. As other studies have found, same-sex preference increased over this age period. They also observed the children playing in the day care or after school care centres they attended. They found that cognitions – assessed by beliefs about what peers would think appropriate, and what partner preferences peers would have – did correlate significantly with the observed same-sex play preference.

Maccoby's attempt at synthesis

We have seen that if reinforcement does have some effects, they are being 'filtered' through other factors. From a number studies it seems that the child's own gender identity, and their gender schemas, are important here. In Fagot's (1985) study, however, the children were so young (21–25 months) that gender identity was unlikely to have been achieved. The effects of reinforcement must have been mediated either by some early, non-verbal awareness of gender not tapped by the usual tests (figure 6.2); perhaps by a basic ingroup/outgroup identification, as Martin and Halverson (1987) proposed.

One aspect pointed to by recent work is the influence of the peer group, and cognitions of the peer group. Preference for same-sex peers seems to be a ubiquitous cross-cultural phenomenon, and one that increases through childhood into adolescence. Maccoby (1998, 2000) has documented this thoroughly, and argues that it is a key factor in integrating not only cognitive and social factors, but also the biological factors affecting sex differences (which are often ignored or at least downplayed by social learning theorists). She argues that there are canalized processes of activity preference and behavioural compatibility between the sexes that lead to primarily same-sex peer groups, and that these have an evolutionary basis (as also believed by evolutionary developmental psychologists, see chapter 2). Furthermore, boys' and girls' peer groups differ; boys' peer groups tend to be larger, more competitive and risk-taking; girls' groups are smaller, more collaborative and based on sharing information.

Maccoby argues that the same-sex peer group has a key role in developing sexual identity; and sees this pivotal role as requiring biological factors for a full understanding, while not denying the insights that the social learning view and the cognitive-developmental view have provided.

Ethnic Awareness, Identity, Preference and Prejudice

Besides differing by gender, people differ in terms of their racial or ethnic group; both are usually obvious from physical characteristics such as hair and skin colour, and facial appearance. There is not universal agreement on how people should be classified by ethnic group. In the UK, for example, some people whose (grand)parents come from the Indian subcontinent might wish to be called by the general term of British Asian, others might wish to be called Indian, Pakistani or

Bangladeshi from the country of origin of their (grand)parents, while yet others might wish to be called Black, in common with Afro-Caribbeans and other ethnic minority groups seen as being in an underprivileged position in a predominantly white society.

The UK government census of 2001 asked people to identify themselves into one of five main ethnic groups: White, Mixed, Asian or Asian British, Black or Black British, and Chinese or other ethnic group. In North America, main ethnic groups would include White, Black, American Indian, Chinese and Hispanic. An inclusive group such as White could be broken down into finer ones, e.g. Anglo-Saxon, Celtic. Other important dimensions are language (e.g., English Canadian and French Canadian) and religion (e.g., Muslim Indian and Hindu Indian). In this section we will look at how children become aware of ethnic differences and identify with an ethnic group; and how this affects their behaviour.

Ethnic awareness

As a child grows up he or she will become aware that people differ by ethnic origin. This ethnic awareness can be assessed by, for example, showing a child photographs of different persons and saying 'show me the Afro-Caribbean person', 'show me the Chinese person', and so on. By the age of 4 or 5 years children seem able to make basic discriminations, for example, between black and white; and during the next few years more difficult ones, such as Anglo-American and Hispanic.

A bit later, at around 8 or 9 years, children understand that ethnic identity remains constant despite changes in age, or superficial attributes such as clothing. For example, in one study children were shown a series of photos of an Italian-Canadian boy, labelled as such, putting on native-Indian clothes (plate 6.1). When asked to identify the boy in the final photo, half the 6-year-olds thought that he was different from the boy in the first photo and that he really was Indian. By 8 years, none made this mistake (Aboud, 1988). This development is similar to that of gender awareness and gender constancy (pp. 187–8), though it seems to occur a year or so later.

Ethnic identity

Ethnic identity can be thought of as awareness of one's own ethnicity. It closely parallels the developing awareness of ethnicity in others. It is usually assessed by using dolls, or photographs, and asking the child to point to one that looks most like them. Generally, children of 4 years and above choose the doll or photograph of someone from their own ethnic group, though there are variations in different studies (Aboud, 1988). Of course, a child might quite well use other (non-ethnic) criteria to decide which is most like them, such as facial expression; so it is best to provide several examples for each ethnic group, for the child to choose from.

Plate 6.1   Part of test for understanding that a child's ethnic identity does not change with superficial attributes such as clothes (from Aboud, 1988). Courtesy Frances Aboud.

Ethnic preference

How do children react to, and evaluate, the ethnic differences that they become aware of from about 4 years? We can look at this in several different ways.

First, we could use similar test situations to those used in assessing ethnic awareness and identity, with dolls or photographs representing different ethnic groups. This time, however, we could ask the child which they would like to be themselves; or which they would like to play with.

A number of studies of this kind have found that most white children choose or prefer the white doll (or photo) from 4 years, whereas black and other ethnic minority children are more divided, with (in some of the earlier studies) most of them choosing the white doll too. These preferences strengthen up to about 7 years. Beyond 7 years, black children tend to choose the black doll or photo more frequently. These studies were mostly carried out in North America or the UK, where whites form the dominant and more privileged social group; and this probably influences the results. Effects of historical period are likely to be very important here. With the rise of ethnic minority group consciousness and pride in their own culture which has characterized more recent decades in North America and the UK, the extent to which minority group children choose their own group has increased, at least among 7- to 11-year-olds (Davey, 1983; Milner, 1983). Spencer (1983) found that African American children whose parents had educated them about the civil rights movement in the US, developed more positive attitudes to their own ethnic group.

Table 6.4   Mean percentage of White and Asian play-mates, by gender, summed for 8- and 9-year-olds in two UK middle schools

	White playmates	Asian playmates
White boys	62.9	19.9
White girls	84.4	7.0
Asian boys	16.2	79.9
Asian girls	9.4	89.6

Source: Boulton and Smith, 1991

Another way of looking at ethnic preference is more naturalistic; we could observe whom children actually choose as play partners, in playgroup or playground situations. We have seen that children tend to segregate by sex; do they segregate by race?

The answer from available studies seems to be a definite 'yes'. For example, Finkelstein and Haskins (1983) observed black and white kindergarten children in the USA. They found that even these 5-year-olds showed marked preferences for playmates from the same ethnic group, and that this increased over the kindergarten year. However, when interacting with a peer neither black nor white children behaved differently to other-race peers than to same-race peers.

In older children too, segregation by ethnic group is noticeable, whether in the US (e.g., Schofield and Francis, 1982), or in the UK (e.g., Boulton and Smith, 1991). However, such segregation seems to be less marked than segregation by sex, at least in the middle-school period. Table 6.4 shows choice of playground partners from two UK middle schools with a mixture of white and British Asian children. Among these 8- to 9-year-old children, segregation is marked by both sex and ethnicity, in that order of priority. It may be noted that ethnic segregation is less marked among boys than among girls, a finding consistent with that of Schofield and Francis (1982). This may be because boys play in larger groups than girls; when playing football, for example, ethnic group may be ignored in order to fill up a team with the requisite number of good players (see also Foster et al., 1996).

Ethnic prejudice

Preference is not in itself the same as prejudice. One might choose to play with same-sex or same-race partners, but still regard other-sex and other-race children as being just as good or able as oneself and one's friends. Indeed, the limited evidence from Finkelstein and Haskins' (1983) study is that their kindergarten children showed preference, but not necessarily prejudice; when a white child played with a black child his or her behaviour did not change (and vice versa).

Prejudice implies a negative evaluation of another person, on the basis of some general attribute (which could be for example sex, race or disability). Thus, racial prejudice means a negative evaluation of someone as a consequence of their being in a certain racial or ethnic group. If a white child dislikes a black child because of some individual attribute, this is not prejudice. But if a white child dislikes a black child (and black children) because of his or her colour, this is racial prejudice. It may not always be easy to be sure whether an action is racial prejudice in individual cases, but the experience of prejudice can be very damaging and at times tragic. The disastrous effects of racial prejudice in the school system was illuminated in a case study of a British school, *Murder in the Playground* (Mac-Donald, 1989; see also chapter 17).

Many children do seem to show racial prejudice from 4 or 5 years of age, as they become aware of ethnic differences. For example, children can be asked to put photos of children from different ethnic groups along a scale of liking (Aboud, 1988). Or, children can be asked to assign positive descriptions such as 'work hard' and 'truthful', or negative adjectives such as 'stupid' or 'dirty', to all, some, one or none of the photos representing different ethnic groups (Davey, 1983). The results are rather similar to those of ethnic identity; prejudice seems to increase from 4 to 7 years, mainly at the expense of minority ethnic groups. During middle childhood, white children tend to remain prejudiced against black or minority-group children, while the latter show a more mixed pattern but often become more positive towards their own group.

Although the causes of racial or ethnic prejudice are not well identified (Aboud and Doyle, 1996), Aboud (1988) argues that there are definite stages in children's development of prejudice. Before about 3 or 4 years of age, ethnic awareness is largely absent and prejudice is not an issue. From 4 to 7 years, she argues, children perceive other ethnic groups as dissimilar to themselves, and because of this tend to have negative evaluations of them. From 8 years onwards, children can think more flexibly about ethnic differences, and in terms of individuals rather than groups. For example, Takriti, Buchanan-Barrow and Barrett (2000), in a study of 5–11-year-old Christian and Muslim children, found a shift away from assigning mainly positive attributes to the ingroup and mainly negative attributes to the outgroup at 5 years of age, to assigning both positive and negative attributes to both the ingroup and the outgroup by 11 years of age.

Thus, the rather natural prejudice of the younger child against dissimilar others could be modified especially from around 7–8 years onwards. (This theory however has some difficulty in explaining why some minority-group children prefer the majority group up to 7 years of age.)

Schools have been a focus for work to reduce racial prejudice in children. This can be assisted by a multi-racial curriculum approach that emphasizes the diversity of racial and cultural beliefs and practices and gives them equal evaluation. Procedures such as Cooperative Group Work (Cowie et al., 1994) may help to bring children of different race (and sex) together in common activities, and thus reduce ethnic preference and prejudice in the classroom.

The rationale for such efforts finds support from Boulton and Smith (1996). A study was made of liking and disliking between white and Asian students aged 8–10 years in racially mixed classes (following procedures similar to those in box 5.1). It was found that generally, 'liked most' nominations were given to own-race classmates; but 'liked-least' nominations were not so strongly biased by race.

Nominations for 'cooperates' also tended to follow same-race lines. However, racial bias in liking was not strongly correlated with general racial prejudice as measured by a traditional photo task. In a follow-up study, it was found that the most common reason given for liking other children was that they cooperated and played together; the most common reason for liking someone least was that they were a bully. Race was hardly ever mentioned as a reason for liking or disliking a classmate.

These results present an apparent paradox; children prefer own-race class-mates, and rate them as more cooperative; but this is not related to general racial prejudice, and is not consciously based on race. Boulton and Smith hypothesize that it stems from a 'developmental legacy' of playing more with same-race class-mates, following the sequence Aboud (1988) proposed. Playing together leads to perceptions of cooperation, and to liking, which will then tend to follow same-race lines unless children are brought into appreciable, close contact with other-race children.

Boulton and Smith also hypothesize that perceptions of bullying are less dependent on actual contact; it is quite possible for peers to see bullying going on, without being involved themselves. Thus, disliking based on perceptions of bullying might be less biased by own-race perception, as indeed was found. On this basis, the authors argue that cooperative group work activities could help improve inter-racial liking, but only if they really do enhance cooperation and are carried out in an environment free from bullying and disruption (Cowie et al., 1994).

Recent developments

Some recent work on prejudice/identity development has focused on applications of intergroup theory to examine the basis of social categorization and its effects, in effect taking insights from the social psychology of intergroup relationships into the developmental domain. See Cameron et al. (2001) for a discussion of this.

Another development has been to look more generally at children's knowledge of other countries and other nationalities. While of interest in its own right, this has had particular significance in Europe as many European countries move towards greater integration in the European Community. The overall picture which emerges in this domain is that there is considerable learning about national groups from 5 years of age onwards, and strong attitudes and affective biases towards the national ingroup and national outgroups are formed. However, even by early adolescence, children still have a great deal more to learn about nations and national groups; see Barrett and Buchanan-Barrow (2002) for a review of this and related areas.

The Influence of Television

The mass media exert an important influence on children's awareness of their world, and their behaviour (Clifford et al., 1995). Patricia Greenfield's *Mind and*

Table 6.5 Estimates of time spent (in hours/day) in various activities by children and adolescents

	Overall mean time estimate	Sex difference	Age difference
TV viewing (including VCR)	2	boys more	less in adolescence
Reading	0.5	girls more	more in adolescence
Music listening	0.25	–	more in adolescence
Sports	0.5	boys more	–
Other active structured leisure activities	0.25	–	more in adolescence

Source: Larson and Verma, 1999

Media (1984) is a useful study that looks at and compares the impact of various media forms.

Historically, printed matter (for children, comics and books) and then radio, have been forms of mass media that have affected children's lives. However, television has been available since the late 1940s, and the television set (often several sets) is now commonplace in the great majority of homes in postindustrial societies. We also know that children watch a great deal of television. Even when it was first introduced, children in Britain watched about 2 hours a day (box 6.2). Larson and Verma (1999) have reviewed the time budgets of young people. A summary of some of their findings is presented in table 6.5.

Table 6.5 paints a broad brush picture, but it confirms that watching television is the largest category of media use among children and adolescents in post-industrial societies, with the time spent considerably exceeding that spent in reading, listening to music, engaging in sports, or time in other active structured leisure activities (such as arts, hobbies, playing music).

The Larson and Verma (1999) review omits radio (although some music listening may fall into this category), probably because it is no longer a very salient category. Also, it omits use of computers and the Internet. The use of the Internet for surfing, games, chat rooms and similar activities has grown and continues to grow enormously in the past few years – a worldwide phenomenon which parallels the equally rapid advent of television in the 1950s (Larson, 2001). Use of the Internet poses very similar problems to those of all other media – they can be used for informative, educational ends; they can be purely recreational; and they can be used in ways that may cause concern, such as incorporating violence and pornography. As yet, research on children's use of the Internet is sparse, but no doubt it will grow rapidly. However the issues raised and methodologies used may not differ too much from the research on effects of television, which now has a history of nearly 50 years. Most research has been done on television, and it is this we will discuss next.

Television viewing has a remarkably similar profile across countries, with in most cases average daily viewing figures being 1.5 to 2.5 hours (Larson and Verma, 1999). A survey in the UK by Cullingford (1984) found that most children (well over 80 per cent at all ages from 7 to 12) reported watching television the previous evening, and typically watching three to six programmes each evening. Many 9-year-olds and almost all older children had watched television after midnight, at some time. Thus, children do not only watch children's programmes. Even from the early surveys (e.g. box 6.2) evidence is that crime thrillers, dramas and comedies have been popular from middle childhood onwards.

Effects of watching television

Children, then, spend a great deal of time watching television. So how does it affect them? An early report by Himmelweit et al. (1958) looked for changes in children's behaviour as television started coming into most people's homes in Britain (see box 6.2). The effect of television probably depends on many factors, such as the child's age, sex and background, and of course the nature of the programmes shown. There has been considerable concern in the USA at the use of children's television advertising to promote 'war toys', linked to corresponding programmes (Carlsson-Paige and Levin, 1987; see chapter 7). There is also concern that violence on television may make children more aggressive, and that many programmes portray stereotyped images of sex roles, or of ethnic minorities. Conversely, some social scientists think that television can be used to encourage prosocial and cooperative behaviour, or reduce stereotyped views (Greenfield, 1984). Other researchers think that television does not have nearly as much effect, either way, as most people fear (Cullingford, 1984).

There are different theoretical perspectives on these issues. Consider the effects on a child of watching violence on television. One point of view is that this might be 'cathartic' – a Greek word referring to the purging of emotions which was supposed to result from watching classical drama. Perhaps children watching James Bond films or any programmes featuring violence have their emotions purged or drained in a similar way. A more prevalent view is that watching television violence may encourage aggression. The child may imitate actions seen on television, especially if they are associated with admired figures, or if aggression seems to have successful outcomes. The issue is certainly an important one: it has been estimated that the average child in the USA, by the age of 16, will have seen 13,000 killings on television!

The 'imitation' theory receives some support from a study looking at how young children respond to actual violence between others (Cummings et al., 1985). Two 2-year-old children and their mothers were brought to an apartment-type room in a research laboratory. After settling in, two actors entered a kitchenette area at the far end of the room. Following a script, they simulated first a friendly exchange, then a period of angry verbal conflict, then a reconciliation of their differences. It was observed that the children typically responded to the conflict episodes with signs of distress, and also increased aggression to the other child. Furthermore, some of the children who experienced the simulation the second time, a month later, showed still higher levels of aggression and distress. The witnessing of anger on the part of others seemed to arouse emotion in these children and release aggression, rather than purge it vicariously.

Table 6.6   Mean changes in rates of behaviour (per minute) in preschool children exposed to television programmes with aggressive, neutral or prosocial content

	Aggressive	Neutral	Prosocial	
Aggression				
initially low	0.039	0.079	0.046	n.s.
initially high	−0.019	−0.123	−0.088	$p < 0.05$
Prosocial				
lower social class	−0.007	−0.026	0.093	$p < 0.05$
higher social class	0.071	0.047	−0.017	$p < 0.05$
Tolerance of delay	−0.016	0.036	0.019	$p < 0.05$
Task persistence	−0.039	−0.068	0.014	n.s.
Rule obedience	−0.039	−0.014	0.014	n.s.

Source: Friedrich and Stein, 1973

The children in Cummings' study were 2 years old. At that age children do not watch much television. But from 3 years of age onwards children will be watching people on television a lot. Do we have any direct evidence that television violence produces aggression?

There have been a number of laboratory studies that have suggested this. Typically, children would be shown aggressive or non-aggressive films, and then placed in situations where they could hit a punch bag or inflatable doll, or push buttons that supposedly 'helped' or 'hurt' another child. Children who watched aggressive films punched the bag or doll, or pushed the 'hurt' button, more. However, these experiments have been criticized as very artificial. Hitting the punch bag might have been playful, not aggressive; and some of the experiments seem so contrived that the main effect being measured may be obedience to the experimenter (Cullingford, 1984). We will look in detail at three more naturalistic studies: one is a 'field experiment', while the other two have a correlational, longitudinal design.

A field experiment on nursery-school children

Friedrich and Stein (1973) studied 4-year-old children enrolled in a 9-week summer nursery-school programme. After 3 weeks of baseline observations, the 100 children were assigned to 'aggressive' ($n = 30$), 'prosocial' ($n = 30$), or 'neutral' ($n = 40$) conditions. For the next 4 weeks, children saw a total of 12 television programmes. The children in the aggressive condition were taken as a group to see 'Batman' or 'Superman' cartoons; those in the prosocial condition saw *Mr Rogers' Neighbourhood*, which prompted themes of cooperation, sympathy and friendship; while those in the neutral condition saw factual films with little aggressive or prosocial content. During the 4-week period, and also the final 2 weeks, the children's behaviour was closely observed.

Some of the results are shown in table 6.6. It seems that the children who watched the prosocial programmes were scored as more patient ('tolerance of delay') than the children who watched the aggressive programmes, and tended to be more persistent at tasks and more spontaneously helpful or obedient ('rule obedience'). However, the findings on aggressive and prosocial behaviour were complicated. Aggressive behaviour decreased among those children who were initially high in aggression, and watched the prosocial or neutral programmes, but there was no significant effect for children initially low in aggression. For prosocial behaviour, it was found that this increased in children from lower-social-class families who watched the prosocial programmes; but it also increased in children from higher-social-class families who watched the aggressive programmes!

The results of this study are rather mixed. They do suggest some positive effects from watching programmes with prosocial rather than aggressive content, but some effects are not statistically significant or even go in the opposite direction. The researchers carried out many analyses and clearly tried to emphasize the 'desired' findings in their report, which is often cited. Nevertheless, the results of these and similar studies leave scope for sceptics. A meta-analysis of 23 experimental studies (including that by Friedrich and Stein) was reported by Wood et al. (1991). Although they state that 'exposure to media violence significantly enhanced viewer's aggressive behavior when the findings were aggregated across studies' (p. 371), in fact this analysis only approached significance ($p < 0.10$), thus hardly justifying such a strong conclusion.

A longitudinal, correlational study on adolescents

Quite a different research strategy is exemplified in a study by Lefkowitz et al. (1977). These researchers interviewed the parents of 8–9-year-old children (184 boys, 175 girls) to find out their favourite television programmes, and hence constructed a measure of exposure to television violence. This score was higher for boys than for girls. The children were also asked to rate the others in their class for aggressiveness. They found that the correlation between the two measures was 0.21 for boys, but only 0.02 for girls. The correlation for boys, while small, was significant ($p < 0.01$); but this correlation could mean either that viewing television violence caused aggression, or that aggressive boys liked watching violent television programmes. Yet another explanation could be that some other factor, parental discord in the home for example, led a child both to watch violent television programmes and also to be aggressive himself.

The same measures were taken 10 years later, when the children were 19 years old. The correlations between the same two measures at this time, and the correlations between the two time periods, are shown for both boys and girls in figure 6.3. The results for the boys are the most interesting and the most quoted. They show that watching a lot of violent television at age 9 is significantly correlated ($r = 0.31$) with peer-rated aggression at age 19; however, peer-rated aggression at age 9 is not correlated ($r = 0.01$) with watching violent television at age 19. This certainly suggests that watching violent television leads to aggression, rather than vice versa. A similar, though less strong, association was found when aggression was measured by self-ratings, or personality questionnaires. Some other factor or factors might still be responsible for the associations, but this technique (known

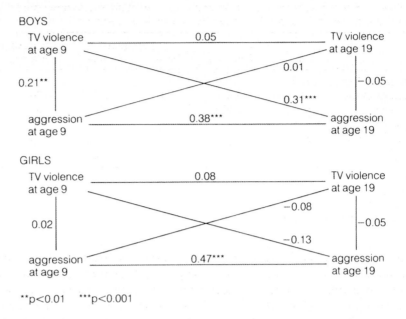

Figure 6.3   Cross-lagged correlations between amount of television violence viewed at ages 9 and 19 and peer-related aggression at ages 9 and 19, for 184 boys and 175 girls (from Lefkowitz et al., 1977).

as 'cross-lagged correlations') does give more weight to the findings than a simple correlation would do. The researchers felt they had identified a small but statistically reliable influence of television violence on aggressive behaviour in boys.

The findings for girls (figure 6.3) are much weaker, and tend to go in the opposite direction. The researchers attempted to explain this by arguing, first that there were few aggressive females portrayed on television (this was in the 1960s), and second, that since female aggression was less socially approved of, then 'for girls, television violence viewing may actually be a positively sanctioned social activity in which aggressive girls may express aggression vicariously since they cannot express aggression directly in social interactions' (Lefkowitz et al., 1977, p. 122). It seems that the researchers have resorted here to a 'cathartic' explanation, despite there being no direct evidence to support it.

This longitudinal study was continued until the participants were 30 years of age (Eron, 1987); throughout, there was significant continuity of aggressive tendencies; aggressive youngsters were more likely to have criminal convictions as adults. However, as we saw in chapter 5, there could be many causal factors producing such continuity, independently of watching violent TV programmes.

A two-site longitudinal study

This longitudinal investigation (Anderson et al., 2001) took advantage of two earlier studies of preschool children in the USA, carried out in Topeka, Kansas,

Table 6.7   Some results of regression analyses predicting adolescent characteristics from preschool and current television viewing; two sites combined

| | Grades | | Creativity | | Aggression | |
	Males	Females	Males	Females	Males	Females
Preschool TV						
informative	.21***	.05	.07	.11	−.20***	−.10
violent	.03	−.19**	.02	.03	.07	.50*
Teen TV						
informative	.04	.08	−.04	−.004	−.03	.14
violent	−.12*	.01	.06	−.08	.00	−.24

* p < .05
** p < .01
*** p < .001
Source: Anderson et al., 2001

and Springfield, Massachusetts. The two studies had been quite independent, but had used sufficiently similar methodologies that the findings could later be combined. In particular, in both studies parents had kept diary records of the television viewing of their children, aged 5 years at the time. Mean viewing times were around 15 hours/week in Massachusetts and 19 hours/week in Kansas.

Of 655 children in the original combined samples, the researchers were able to follow up 570 young people in their later teens (87 per cent); a total of 287 males and 283 females. Those interviewed were now aged around 16 years (Kansas) or 18 years (Massachusetts) at re-interview. According to their own self-reports, they watched about 12 hours (boys) or 10 hours (girls) of television per week. Of this about 1 to 1.5 hours was classified as 'violent' (the researchers included cartoons and action-adventure shows in this category). Some 2.5 to 3 hours per week might be spent watching videos, and a similar amount of time on listening to the radio, and reading books not associated with school or work.

The researchers were mainly interested in seeing whether the kind of television programmes watched when the children were 5 years, was an enduring indicator of their progress at or around school-leaving age. They could also look at concurrent relationships with their viewing as teenagers. They assessed current academic achievement (from self-report of school grades, in most cases validated by transcripts), aggression (from a self-report scale), creativity (from a test of divergent thinking – how many uses can you think of for a [shoe, key, tyre]?), and other aspects of leisure time use. Some results from their study are shown in table 6.7. The figures shown are from regression analyses – similar to correlations, but taking account of various covariates such as site, parental education, and birth order.

The results for school grades (in English, mathematics and science) showed that watching informative programmes as a preschooler correlated positively, for boys only; watching violent programmes as a preschoolers had negative relationships, for girls only. The relationships were much less strong for current viewing (although for boys there was a modest negative relationship with violent television viewing).

The results for the creativity test were all non-significant (though the researchers did report some other findings on leisure use). The results for aggression showed a negative relationship of watching informative programmes as a preschooler, for boys only; and apparently showed a significant positive effect for watching violent programmes as a preschooler, for girls only. Surprisingly, this high correlation of 0.50 is not discussed directly in the report, which however indicates that the statistic is not stable or significant when split by site (Anderson et al., 2001, Table 26 p. 85).

As can be seen, these results are again complex, and mixed in the picture they give. Comparing with the Lefkowitz et al. (1977) study earlier, there is no clear relationship between violent television viewing, either earlier or currently, on aggressive behaviour (if the 0.50 correlation is discounted, which the researchers do). For boys only, watching informative programmes as a preschooler has a 'protective' relationship. Concerning grades, there are different findings for boys and girls; the authors hypothesize that early television viewing has greater effect when it counteracts normative developmental trends and predominant sex-typed socialization influences, than when they reinforce them. In other words, they argue that early viewing of violent television by boys does not influence them much, because it is more normative for boys to be aggressive. The percipient reader may notice that this argument is brought up to justify an opposite pattern of sex-related findings from Lefkowitz et al. (1977), who found that early violent television viewing affected boys but not girls!

A continuing controversy

The influence of violent television continues to be debated, and has expanded to the influence of war toys (chapter 7), and of violent videos and computer games. In the UK, there was particular concern about violent videos following the murder of a 2-year-old child, Jamie Bulger, in February 1993 by two 10-year-old children; according to Elizabeth Newson, in a widely circulated report *Video Violence and the Protection of Children* (1994), there had been an increase in these kinds of crimes; the new factor which she implicated as the cause of this 'has to be recognised as the easy availability to children of gross images of violence on video' (p. 273). Although the studies we have looked at, and others, do tend to give some support to the hypothesis that television can affect social behaviour, the evidence is not clear-cut. Some findings are small, or not significant. Some are present only for certain measures, or for one sex or for children initially high in aggression.

Some reviewers feel the case is not proved (e.g., Freedman, 1984; Gunter and McAleer, 1997). After all, they would argue, much television violence involves fantasy figures (such as the Batman and Superman films in the Friedrich and Stein study), which older children certainly distinguish from real violence. Also children may be 'desensitized' to violence in serials that are viewed basically as entertainment. Cullingford (1984) found that many children could not remember much of what they had viewed the evening before, and that the more programmes they had watched, the fewer details they could remember. He argued that children 'see that television is not to be taken seriously, that the murders are there as stunts, that shooting is a part of entertainment. Thus the violence on television passes them by.' This may seem a bland and complacent view, but the research evidence so far, while suggestive that television does have some effects, is not of sufficient weight for us to be really certain how important this is. We know from case studies of a few abnormal individuals that television violence can on occasion provide a stimulus or model for some violent crime. But it may be that for most children, most of the time, the impact of television is rather small.

If we are considering aggression, then other influences may be much more important. For example, actual aggression in the home between parents might be a more potent influence than fictitious aggression on television. Parental discord has been consistently found to predict later conduct disorders (Rutter, 1981; and chapter 4). We saw the impact of actual (though simulated) aggression on young children in the study by Cummings et al. (1985). The latter state that viewing actual discord in the home could be a powerful influence on aggression in the home, an influence that is not so easily turned off as a television set (cf. pp. 120–1).

Television programmes as a source of social stereotypes

Another major concern in connection with television is that programmes may present a stereotyped picture of real life that may encourage undesirable prejudices. These might be, for example, about female roles (in what is arguably still a male-dominated society), about minority ethnic groups or other nationalities, and about people with disabilities.

Television programmes, like many children's books, do seem to present a one-sided view of sex-roles. Researchers in both the UK and the USA have carried out 'content analyses' of television programmes, seeing how many male and female characters there are, and what sort of roles they have. These studies have found that there are often two or three times as many male as female characters, and that the males are usually portrayed as more powerful, dominant, rational and intelligent. Females are often depicted as weak and passive, watching admiringly while the males have most of the action (Durkin, 1985). There has been increasing awareness of this imbalance, and some attempt to redress it.

We saw earlier how parents, and later peers, can be important in sex-role learning, so how important is television viewing in this process? In *Television, Sex Roles and Children* (1985), Kevin Durkin reviewed the evidence. He concluded that there is little to suggest that the more television children watch, the more sex-stereotyped are their views. The few studies that did report this seem to have been methodologically unsound (as with some of the work on television violence and aggression). Durkin emphasizes that the child or young person is an active agent in interpreting television programmes, not just a passive recipient of a 'dose' of sex-role stereotyping. Thus, it is important to consider the age of the child, his or her understanding of gender, as well as the family and sociocultural context.

Table 6.8 Percentage of heroes/heroines and villains having certain characteristics in 13 television plays (Himmelweit et al., 1958)

	Heroes/heroines (n = 27)	Villains (n = 11)
British nationality	60	37
Upper or upper/middle class	93	55
Glamorous and high-powered occupations	70	55

Source: Himmelweit et al., 1958

A related topic is whether television programmes can be used effectively in 'counter-stereotyping' – presenting sex roles of a deliberately non-traditional kind. This was attempted in a British children's programme *Rainbow*, and in an American programme *Freestyle*. There is some evidence that 9- to 12-year-olds who watched *Freestyle* did have less stereotyped views of sex roles, especially when viewing at school was followed by teacher-led discussion. There are, however, important ethical issues to consider in such attempts to 'manipulate' attitudes, which are discussed in Durkin's book.

Other ethnic groups or nationalities may also be portrayed adversely in the mass media. Table 6.8, taken from Himmelweit et al. (1958) (see box 6.2), shows how 'villains' were much more often foreigners than 'heroes' and 'heroines' were (and also of lower social class, though the upper/middle-class bias of British television programmes in the 1950s may have lessened somewhat and does not now get so much attention). Until the 1990s there were few programmes that showed people from ethnic minorities, such as people of Asian or Afro-Caribbean origin, in ordinary roles, or which presented their cultural background. Programmes for young children such as *You and Me* in Britain, or *Sesame Street* (first made in the USA), were early attempts to remedy this. Some research has indicated that these programmes do have positive effects on interracial attitudes and encourage greater cultural pride and self-confidence among ethnic minority children (Greenfield, 1984). Similar findings have also been made concerning the portrayal of disabled persons in a more realistic and positive light, for example in *Sesame Street* (Clifford et al., 1995; Greenfield, 1984).

Most reviewers agree that parents have an important role to play in the effects television may have on their children. Besides encouraging responsible viewing habits, parents can talk about programmes with their children, discussing information or attitudes that are being transmitted. From the beginning (e.g., box 6.2) research has indicated that children are influenced most by television portrayals that are not counteracted or put in different perspective by anything in their immediate environment. Thus besides influencing the educational value of television programmes, parents and teachers can probably have an appreciable effect on how programmes influence children's social attitudes and behaviour (Greenfield, 1984).

Further Reading

A good introduction to emotional development in children is Harris, P. 1989: *Children and Emotion*. Oxford: Blackwell. Also useful is Dunn, J. 1988: *The Beginnings of Social Understanding*. Oxford: Blackwell.

A review of sex differences in children (and adults) is provided by Golombok, S. and Fivush, R. 1994: *Gender Development*. Cambridge: Cambridge University Press, while Maccoby, E. E. 1998: *The Two Sexes: Growing Up Apart, Coming Together*. Cambridge, MA: Belknap Press, is an excellent review as well as an exposition of her views.

The development of racial awareness in children is considered by Aboud, F. 1988: *Children and Prejudice*. Oxford: Blackwell.

An earlier but readable review of the effects of television and other mass media on behaviour is in Greenfield, P. M. 1984: *Mind and Media: the Effects of Television, Computers and Video Games*. Aylesbury: Fontana; followed by Greenfield, P. M. and Cocking, R. (eds) 1995: *Interacting with Video (Advances in Applied Developmental Psychology, Vol 11)*. New York: Ablex. A recent resource is Singer, D. and Singer, J. (eds) 2001: *Handbook of Children and the Media*. Thousand Oaks, CA, Sage. Sceptical views of the impact of television are in Howitt, D. 1982: *Mass Media and Social Problems*. Oxford: Pergamon; and Cullingford, C. 1984: *Children and Television*. Aldershot: Gower. The impact of television on sex roles is reviewed by Durkin, K. 1985: *Television, Sex Roles and Children*. Milton Keynes: Open University Press. Another good source on this is Gunter, B. and McAleer, J. 1997: *Children and Television*, (2nd edn). London: Routledge.

Discussion Points

1 When does a child develop a sense of self?
2 When can a child understand someone else's emotional state?
3 What causes sex differences in behaviour?
4 How does awareness of ethnicity develop?
5 How good is the evidence relating television violence to aggressive behaviour in children?

Box 6.1
Changes in embarrassment as a function of age, sex and situation

This research aimed to examine the origins of a secondary emotion, embarrassment. Some researchers had treated shame and embarrassment as identical emotions. The present researchers argued that whereas shame results from unfavourable comparison of oneself relative to a standard, embarrassment can have a wider meaning and

Box Table 6.1.1 Percentage of children showing embarrassment in different situations

Age	Dance/M	Mirror	Overpraise	Dance/E
2 yrs/C–S	27.7	25.0	29.5	29.5
2 yrs/LONG	16.7	26.7	30.0	33.3
3 yrs/LONG	20.0	35.3	26.7	56.7

Source: Adapted from Lewis et al., 1991

can result from a simple awareness of being observed. Embarrassment was operationalized as a smiling facial expression, combined with or followed by gaze aversion and nervous touching (hand movements to touch hair, clothing, face or other body parts).

How early does embarrassment appear? The researchers worked with 44 children who were around 22 months old; 30 of these were seen again at 35 months. About half the children were boys, half girls. Visits were made to the child's home, and video recordings made, in the mother's presence, of four standard situations.

The four situations were:

1 dance (mother): the mother took a small tambourine and asked the child to dance;
2 overpraise: the experimenter interacted with the child and praised him/her effusively about clothes, appearance, etc.;
3 mirror: the mother called the child to a mirror to see their reflection (the camera was positioned to see the reflection in the mirror);
4 dance (experimenter): the experimenter asked the child to dance.

Altogether 52 per cent of the children showed embarrassment (using the above definition) in at least one situation at 22 months; and 82 per cent at 35 months (a significant increase). The percentage of children who showed embarrassment in each situation is shown in box table 6.1.1. At 2

years, this shows percentages for the cross-sectional analysis (all children) and for the longitudinal analysis (only the 30 children also seen at 3 years).

At 22 months there was no significant difference, statistically, between the four situations. At 35 months, the most embarrassment was observed in the dance (experimenter) and mirror conditions, with the dance (experimenter) condition showing a significant increase with age.

There was some indication that more girls showed embarrassment at 22 months, with no sex difference at 35 months; however, the sample size may be rather small to establish sex differences. As it is, one can see some appreciable differences at 2 years between the cross-sectional and longitudinal data (especially for dance/mother), which probably reflect sample size variations. Children do vary individually in how much embarrassment they show; and in this study, significant consistency in likelihood of showing embarrassment was obtained from the longitudinal data.

The researchers took their findings to indicate that embarrassment could emerge following self-referential behaviour. Referring to other data on the latter (as in the mirror task, see table 6.1), they reported that the 2-year-olds who did not show self-referential behaviour, did not show embarrassment. However, some 2- and 3-year-olds who did show self-referential behaviour, did not show embarrassment; thus, self-referential behaviour was a necessary but not a sufficient condition for this self-conscious emotion to be displayed.

This study is an attempt to do a naturalistic experiment; the child is in the home with the mother, the mother is asked to act as naturally as possible, but there are standardized procedures to follow, and a video camera is present. The report does not give any details of how intrusive the procedure was, or what familiarization procedures (if any) were followed. Some of the sample variability in responses (box table 6.1.1) might be attributed to these factors. There was a high dropout rate in the longitudinal study (14 out of 44) due to 'family moves and family unwillingness to participate in the follow-up visit' (p. 7), suggesting that intrusiveness was a problem for some families. However, research of this kind is likely to be difficult and have drawbacks, whatever procedures are followed.

Based on material in Lewis, M., Stanger, C., Sullivan, M. W. and Barone, P. (1991): *British Journal of Developmental Psychology*, 9, 485–92.

Box 6.2
Television and the child: an empirical study of the effect of television on the young

The objective of this research study was to assess the impact of television on children and young people. The study was funded at the suggestion of the Audience Research Department of the BBC. Television sets were only just becoming common in households during the 1950s, thus there was considerable interest and concern about what the effects might be. At this time there was also still the opportunity to compare large numbers of children who both did, and did not, have a television set in their home.

The researchers carried out both a 'main survey' and some subsidiary studies, in particular a 'before-and-after study'. The main survey was carried out in London, Portsmouth, Sunderland and Bristol, from May to July 1955. Questionnaires were given to children aged 10–11 and 13–14 years. In addition, children filled in diaries of their activities after school for one week, and measures of personality and teachers' ratings were obtained.

The design compared children who had television at home ('viewers') with those who did not, and were not regular guest viewers ('controls'). Viewers and controls were matched individually for age, sex, intelligence score and social class; altogether 1854 matched viewers and controls were tested. The results of this comparison could give an indication of how television viewing affected children; but a critic might still raise objections. The design is not tightly controlled (for which participants should be assigned randomly to conditions) but is correlational in design, taking advantage of the fact that many homes did not yet have television. Despite the matching on some criteria, viewer children and their families might differ from controls in other respects – as they clearly did in so far as viewers' parents had chosen to acquire a television set while control families had not, despite having similar incomes. In other words, there might be pre-existing differences between children from homes which bought a television set early, and those which did not. These, rather than the effects of television *per se*, might be responsible for any findings from the main study.

As a check on this, the researchers carried out a before-and-after study (a quasi-experiment, p. 12) in Norwich, where a new television transmitter was being introduced. They gave questionnaires to 10–11- and 13–14-year-olds both before the installation (when hardly any family there had a television set) and one year later (when many, but not all, had). At the later point in time they matched viewers and controls as in the main study, with 370 children in all. They could then see whether differences found later were already present in families before a television set had been acquired. In some cases this was so: for example, the main study found that viewers attended Sunday School less regularly. The before-and-after study revealed that this, and a generally lower level of religious interest and observance, was a characteristic of families who bought television sets early and not an effect of television as such.

The main findings were that both age groups watched television for about two hours a day; more than any other single leisure activity. There were no sex or social class differences in this, but more intelligent children did spend less time viewing. Also, more active, outgoing and sociable children spent less time watching. Children settled down to a routine within about 3 months of their family acquiring a set. Many children watched, and preferred, 'adult' programmes, particularly crime thrillers, comedies, variety programmes and family serials. Viewers spent less time than controls listening to the radio, going to the cinema and reading. The findings for reading were complex, however; acquisition of a television caused an initial decline in the time spent reading books and comics, but book-reading tended to recover, especially as some television programmes such as serials encouraged children to read the books on which they were based.

There were small but consistent differences in values and outlook. Viewers were more ambitious about jobs and more 'middle class' in their values. Adolescent girl viewers were more concerned about growing up and marrying than controls. Viewers made fewer value judgements about foreigners, though where stereotypes were given, they tended to reflect those offered by television. In general, television had most impact where the child could not turn for information to parents, friends and the immediate environment. Effects tended to be greatest in older children of least intelligence.

Many children spoke of being frightened by certain programmes, and sometimes of how these caused nightmares or difficulties in falling asleep. Such reactions seemed accentuated by viewing in the dark. Children enjoyed exciting programmes and being a little frightened, but not being really scared. Aggression on television upset them if they could identify themselves with the situation; the sheer amount of physical violence was less important. Viewers were no more aggressive or maladjusted than controls.

There was little difference in general knowledge between viewers and controls, except for less intelligent or younger children unable to read well, where the stimulus of television did give them an advantage. Viewing seemed to have little effect on school performance, or teachers' rating of concentration; teachers did say that they felt television viewing was a cause of tiredness in the morning, but this stereotype was not borne out by the comparison of viewers and controls.

This research has strengths in its scope and its large number of participants. It is in some ways of historical interest, as both the nature of television programmes and children's behaviour will have changed in the 45 intervening years. At the time there were no programme transmissions between 6.00 pm and 7.30 pm; only one or two channels were available; programmes were in black and white; and the content was probably more 'middle class' and certainly contained less for ethnic minorities than at present. Probably levels of violence on television were lower than now, although it was already a cause for concern. It is also possible that 'second and third generation' television-viewing families have adapted to television in a way that affects its impact on their children. However, the study is virtually unrepeatable in that it took advantage of a time when genuine comparisons of viewers and non-viewers in Britain could still be carried out.

Based on material in Himmelweit, H. T., Oppenheim, A. N. and Vince, P. 1958: *Television and the Child: An Empirical Study of the Effect of Television on the Young*, London: Oxford University Press.

7 Play

Three sequences of behaviour are described below. Study them and think what they have in common.

Example 1   A 2-year-old lies in his cot, babbling to himself: 'Big Bob. Big Bob. Big Bob. Big and little. Little Bobby. Little Nancy. Little Nancy. Big Bob and Nancy and Bobby. And Bob. And two three Bobbys. Three Bobbys. Four Bobbys. Six.' (All with giggles and exaggerated pronunciation.)

Example 2   Helen, a 4-year-old, is sitting in a play house, by a table with a plastic cup, saucer and teapot. She calls out 'I'm just getting tea ready! Come on, it's dinner time now!' Charlotte, also 4, answers 'Wait!'; she wraps up a teddy in a cloth in a pram, comes in and sits opposite Helen, who says 'I made it on my own! I want a drink.' (She picks up the teapot.) 'There's only one cup – for me!' (pretends to pour tea into only one cup). Charlotte pretends to pour from the teapot into an imaginary cup, which she then pretends to drink from. Darren, a 3-year-old, approaches. Charlotte goes and closes the door, shutting a pretend bolt and turning a pretend key; but Helen says 'No, he's daddy; you're daddy aren't you?' (to Darren). Charlotte 'unbolts' and 'unlocks' the door, and Darren comes in (see plate 7.1).

Example 3   Some 6- and 7-year olds are in a school playground. A boy runs up to another, laughing, and grabs his shoulders, turns and runs off. The second boy chases the first, catches him by the waist and pulls him round. They tussle and swing around, then fall and roll over on the ground, grappling. They get up and run off, laughing and chasing again (see plate 7.2).

Most observers would agree in saying that, despite their differences, all three are examples of play, or playful behaviour. Respectively they could be described as

Plate 7.1   Preschool children acting out a pretend sequence of preparing a meal.

Plate 7.2   Children play fighting.

language play, fantasy or pretend play and rough-and-tumble play. This chapter first discusses why we consider such behaviour sequences to be playful, what are the defining characteristics of play, and how it differs from the related behaviour of exploration. The next section examines the development of various kinds of play in childhood. The ideas of leading play theorists are then discussed, before the final section examines what empirical studies can tell us about the significance of play in children's development.

The Characteristics of Playful Behaviour

There have been numerous attempts to characterize or define play, but it has not proved an easy task. Fagan (1974) made a distinction between two kinds of definition: the functional approach, and the structural approach.

The functional approach suggests that play does not have an obvious end in itself, or an external goal. Thus, if an external goal is present (such as a need to eat, or to seek comfort, or to overpower another) then the behaviour is not play. This led to a definition of play, that it has no clear immediate benefits or obvious goal. Symons (1978) advanced this sort of definition for monkey social play, but it can equally apply to human play. If you look at examples 1 to 3 above, it is not clear when an episode is completed, or obvious what the purpose of the behaviour is. In fact, many theorists *do* believe the child gets benefits from playing, but they are not clear, immediate ones; and there is continuing disagreement about exactly what the benefits of play are (see pp. 232–7).

The structural approach attempts to describe the sorts of behaviour that only occur in play, or the way in which behaviours are performed playfully. The main examples of behaviours that only occur in play, are play signals. In mammals they often take the form of an open-mouthed play face (as in monkeys grappling), or a bouncy gambol (as in puppies or kittens initiating a chase). In children similarly laughter and the associated 'open mouth play face' (see figure 7.1) usually signals play. Such play signals are especially useful in rough-and-tumble play (example 3 above), where they can indicate that no aggressive intention is implied in a chase or wrestle.

Not all play is indexed by play signals, however. Often play is made up entirely of behaviours familiar in other contexts – such as running, manipulating objects. According to the structural approach, we think of these behaviours as being done playfully if they are 'repeated', 'fragmented', 'exaggerated' or 're-ordered'. For example, a child just running up a slope may not be playing; but if she runs up and slides down several times (repetition), runs just half-way up (fragmentation), takes unusually large or small steps or jumps (exaggeration) or crawls up and then runs down (re-ordering), we would probably agree that it was playful.

This structural approach is not in opposition to the functional one. After all, the child running up and down the slope has no immediate purpose, apart from enjoyment. The two approaches are logically distinct, however.

Another approach, which can encompass both the previous ones, is to say that observers identify play or playfulness by a number of different *play criteria*. No

(a)

(b)

Figure 7.1   Play signals: (a) 'open mouth face' in a chimpanzee (from Hooff, 1972); (b) 'play face' in a human child (from Smith, 1974).

one criterion is sufficient, but the more criteria are present, the more agreement we will have that the behaviour is play. A formal model along these lines, proposed by Krasnor and Pepler (1980), is shown in figure 7.2. 'Flexibility' sums up the structural characteristics of play – variation in form and content. 'Positive affect' refers to the enjoyment of play, especially indexed by signals such as laughter. 'Nonliterality' refers to the 'as if' or pretend element (see example 2 above). 'Intrinsic motivation' refers to the idea that play is not constrained by external rules or social demands, but is done for its own sake.

An empirical test of Krasnor and Pepler's model was made by Smith and Vollstedt (1985). They used the four criteria above, and a fifth – means/ends, i.e., the child is more interested in the performance of the behaviour than in its outcome. They made a video film of nursery-school children playing and designated short, discrete episodes which they asked 70 adults to view. Some scored each episode as to whether it was playful or not, others as to the applicability of the play criteria. Analyses showed that the episodes seen as playful were often seen as nonliteral, flexible and showing positive affect. Furthermore, the more of these that were present, the higher the ratings for playfulness. Means/ends also correlated with play, but did not add anything to the first three criteria. Interestingly, the intrinsic motivation criterion did not correlate with play judgements, despite its common occurrence in definitions of play. Observers often rated non-playful activities (such as watching others, or fighting) as intrinsically motivated; equally some play episodes were externally constrained, e.g., by the demands of others in social play.

The play criterion approach does not attempt a one-sentence definition of play – a seemingly hopeless task. It does acknowledge, however, the continuum from non-playful to playful behaviour, and seeks to identify how observers actually

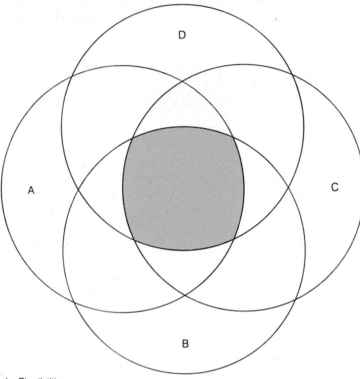

A - Flexibility
B - Positive affect
C - Nonliterality
D - Intrinsic motivation

Figure 7.2   A model of play criteria. The shaded area is that most likely to be considered as playful (from Krasnor and Pepler, 1980).

decide to call a behaviour sequence 'play'. The main criteria so far identified for young children, as we have seen, are enjoyment, flexibility and pretence.

Exploration and play

A behaviour that is sometimes confused with play is exploration. These were often subsumed together in earlier writings, perhaps because of the influence of behaviourism and learning theory. Both exploration and play were awkward for traditional learning theorists, as neither was obviously goal-seeking or under the control of reinforcers. It is also true that with very young children, during sensori-motor development (see chapter 12), the distinction between exploration and play is difficult to make, as for young infants, all objects are novel. By the pre-school years, however, the distinction is clearer. An experiment illustrating this, by Hutt (1966), is detailed in box 7.1. Using a novel toy, Hutt suggested that children typically proceed from specific exploration of the object to more playful behaviour.

The Development of Play

Play types and sequences

Researchers have identified a number of different types of play. These include locomotor or physical activity play (covering exercise play, and rough-and-tumble play), play with objects, fantasy and sociodramatic play, and language play. Exercise play is found in most if not all mammal species (Power, 2000), and over the past decade has been given more attention in human children. Most child developmental research however has focused on object and especially pretend play (see the article title in Box 7.2 as an example, where 'play' is taken as synonymous with 'pretending').

Piaget (1951) was one of the first to describe a developmental sequence in children's play. This went from practice play, through symbolic play (fantasy/pretend play), to games with rules; Piaget saw these as overlapping stages through the childhood years. By 'practice play', Piaget mainly meant early sensori-motor play in infants, and most animal play. However, if practice play means play that is neither symbolic nor rule-governed, then it can occur well beyond the sensori-motor period. Indeed rough-and-tumble would seem to count as practice play, unless it has symbolic elements (as in monster play), or is rule-governed (as in tig).

Smilansky (1968) later postulated a four-fold sequence, from functional play (similar to practice play) to constructive play (making something, e.g., from Lego bricks), then dramatic play (like Piaget's symbolic play) and finally games with rules. She thus suggested that constructive play was intermediate between functional and dramatic play (plates 7.3, 7.4 and 7.5). Some American play researchers have used this scheme as a 'play hierarchy'. Piaget (1951), however, thought that 'constructive games are not a definite stage like the others, but occupy . . . a position halfway between play and intelligent work, or between play and imitation.' The goal-directed nature of much constructive activity, for Piaget, made it more accommodative than purely playful behaviour (see later, and also chapter 12). Either it was work-like, or some symbolic element might be present. The distinct, sequential nature of constructive play in Smilansky's scheme is thus questionable (Takhvar and Smith, 1990).

Physical activity play

As anyone watching a yard or school playground can observe, a lot of play involves physical activity, often without objects. In a review of what they argued was a neglected aspect of play, Pellegrini and Smith (1998) suggested there were

Plate 7.3 Practice' or 'functional' play in a 1-year-old infant; simple actions like mouthing, banging or pushing are performed with one or two objects.

three developmental phases in physical activity play. First were 'rhythmical stereotypies', bodily movements characteristic of babies such as kicking legs, waving arms. Then, during the preschool years there is a lot of 'exercise play' – running around, jumping, climbing – whole body movements which may be done alone or with others. Overlapping with and succeeding this is rough-and-tumble play, most common in the middle school years.

Rough-and-tumble play

The origins of play fighting and chasing may lie in the vigorous physical play that parents often engage in with toddlers – tickling, throwing and crawling after them, for example. Actual play fighting between peers is common from 3 years on through to adolescence. Wrestling generally involves some struggle for superior position, one child trying to get on top of another and pin him or her down; though roles quickly reverse themselves. More fragmentary episodes involve pushing, clasping, leg play and kicking. Chasing play is generally included in rough-and-tumble as well (example 3, p. 214).

The friendly intent in play of this kind is typically signalled by smiling and laughter. Up to adolescence play fighting seems distinct from serious fighting, at least in the majority of cases. The former is carried out with friends, who often stay together after the episode. The latter is often not between friends, involves different facial expressions and the participants usually do not stay together after the encounter. Play fights tend to be shorter, are not watched by others (plate 7.2) and participants do not hit hard.

Plate 7.4   These 3-year-olds are engaged in 'constructive play' – making things from objects.

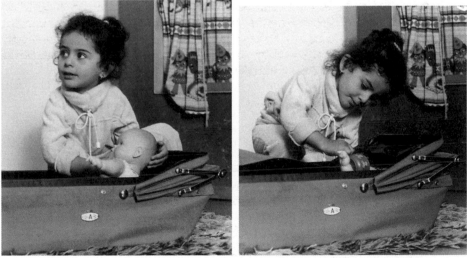

Plate 7.5   This child is engaged in a simple pretend sequence – putting a doll to sleep in a pram.

Young children themselves are aware of these differences. One study (Costabile et al., 1991) used videofilms of play fighting and real fighting made in Italy, and England. The researchers showed the films to children aged 8 and 11 years, and asked them to say whether each episode was playful or real fighting, and why. Children were very good at this, and gave reasons such as:

'It didn't last long enough to be a [real] fight'
'It was only a play fight because he didn't hit him hard'
'It was a real fight because they were both angry'
'That was a play fight as the other boys didn't watch them'.

Interestingly, children from both countries were just as good at recognizing play fighting in the videofilm from the other country, as their own; the evidence to date suggests that the forms of play fighting are very similar across cultures.

Although play fighting and real fighting are usually distinct, they sometimes get confused. Pellegrini (1988, 1994) has shown that in boys, sociometrically rejected children (see p. 147) are much more likely than other children to be involved in play fights which turn into real fights – whether deliberately or through a lack of social skills, these children may respond inappropriately to the usual play signals. Primary school teachers often say that a lot of play fighting becomes real fighting, and it is possible that they are basing this judgement on the minority of children for whom this is true (Schafer and Smith, 1996). For most children, only around 1 per cent of play fights turn into real fights. However, there is evidence that by adolescence, strength and dominance become more important in the choice of partners in play fighting, and deliberate manipulation of play conventions may then become more common (Boulton, 1992; Pellegrini, 2002; Smith, 1997).

Fantasy and sociodramatic play

The beginnings of fantasy play can be seen from about 12–15 months of age. In the course of his extensive observations of his own children, Piaget (1951, p. 69) recorded the following behaviour on the part of his daughter Jacqueline (the numbers refer to Jacqueline's age, in years, months and days):

every appearance of awareness of 'make-believe' first appeared at 1;3(12) in the following circumstances. She saw a cloth whose fringed edges vaguely recalled those of her pillow; she seized it, held a fold of it in her right hand, sucked the thumb of the same hand and lay down on her side, laughing hard. She kept her eyes open, but blinked from time to time as if she were alluding to closed eyes. Finally, laughing more and more she cried 'Nene' [Nono]. The same cloth started the same game on the following days. At 1;3(13) she treated the collar of her mother's coat in the same way. At 1;3(30) it was the tail of her rubber donkey which represented the pillow! And from 1;5 onwards she made her animals, a bear and a plush dog, also do 'nono'.

The earliest pretend play tends to involve the child directing actions towards herself – in Jacqueline's case, pretending to sleep on a cloth. It is clear from Piaget's records that a month or so later Jacqueline directed the same actions to a toy bear and a stuffed dog. This has been called *decentration* – incorporating other participants into pretend activities. The others may be parents (e.g., the child tries to feed a parent with an empty cup), or stuffed animals or dolls. By around 24 months the child can get the doll itself to act as an agent, rather than have things done to it (see above).

Early pretend play also depends heavily on realistic objects – actual cups, combs, spoons, etc., or very realistic substitutes. *Decontextualization* refers to the ability to use less realistic substitute objects – for example, a wooden block as a 'cake', or a stick as a 'gun'. Experiments have shown that the more different the object from its referent, the more difficulty children have in using it in a pretend way. It has also been shown that adults can help the process, by modelling or prompting the pretend use. In one study (Fein, 1975), after modelling by an adult, some 93 per cent of 2-year-olds would imitate making a detailed horse model 'drink' from a plastic cup; however, only 33 per cent would imitate making a horsey shape 'drink' from a clam shell. The less realistic objects made the pretence more difficult, especially as two substitutions were needed (the horsey shape, and the clam shell). If the horse alone, or the cup alone, was realistic, 79 per cent and 61 per cent of the children respectively could imitate successfully.

By 3 years of age this kind of decontextualized pretence occurs much more spontaneously in children's play. Here we also begin to get quite imaginary objects or actions, without any real or substitute object being present (example 2 on p. 214 has several examples). While possible for 3- and 4-year-olds, this is easier still in middle childhood. When asked to pretend to brush their teeth, or comb their hair, one study (Overton and Jackson, 1973) found that 3- and 4-year-olds used a substitute body part, such as a finger, as the brush, or comb; whereas most 6–8-year-olds (and indeed, adults) imagined the brush or comb in their hand.

These studies have usually relied on laboratory situations, where infants have been provided with particular toys. A much more naturalistic study has been reported by Haight and Miller (1993), in a book *Pretending at Home*. They reported a longitudinal study of nine children (four girls and five boys), each observed in the home environment and videofilmed for 3 or 4 hours at 12, 16, 20, 24, 30, 36 and 48 months of age. An interesting finding was that three-quarters of pretend play was social; usually with mothers, though equally often other children by 48 months. Even the earliest pretend play episodes were more likely to be social, than solitary. The authors describe one characteristic of this mother–child social, pretend play as being mutual responsiveness, with neither partner initiating or dominating most episodes. Joint episodes were generally longer than episodes of solo pretend play. Another study of this kind, giving detailed descriptions of naturalistic pretend play in small samples (in this case in two cultural contexts) is described in Box 7.2.

Reviewing both laboratory-based and more naturalistic studies, Howes and Matheson (1992) have developed a scheme for the development of social pretend play, with mothers, older siblings and peers. A slightly simplified version of this is shown in table 7.1. The work of Howes and others shows the change from predominantly adult-oriented to predominantly peer-oriented social pretend. You could look again at example 2 at the start of the chapter; match the role

Table 7.1 Stages in social pretend play with mothers, and with peers; adapted from Howes and Matheson, 1992

Age period	Play with mother	Play with peers
12–15 months	Mother structures child's actions by commenting, suggesting, and demonstrating. Child is corrected when her pretend acts violate the real world	Isolated pretend acts within social play do not elicit a response; but children watch and imitate the partner's pretend
16–20 months	As above; and child imitates, watches and complies with mother	Children engage in similar or identical pretend acts; and attempt to recruit partner to joint pretend
21–24 months	Mother becomes an interested spectator who creates a context and provides support for the child's enactments	Children engage in similar pretend actions while they simultaneously engage in social exchange; join the pretend of the partner, attempt to recruit the partner to joint play, and organize materials for joint pretend.
25–30 months	Child offers storyline or script. Mother requests creation of new elements and prompts child to a more realistic or detailed enactment	Each partner's pretend reflects the same script but their actions show no within-pair integration. Partners inform each other of the script by comments on their own pretend and telling the other how to act
31–36 months	Mother praises and encourages independence; may pretend with child	Joint pretend with enactment of complementary roles. Children discriminate between speech used for enactment and speech about enactment; assign roles, and negotiate pretend themes and plans
37–48 months	As above	Children adopt relational roles, are willing to accept identity transformations and generate or accept instruction for appropriate role performance; they negotiate scripts and dominant roles and use metacommunication to establish the play script and clarify role enactment

assignment and negotiation of the action at the end with the 37–48 months stage in table 7.1.

In table 7.1 the word 'script' appears from the 25–30-month stage onwards. Pretend play sequences become more integrated with age. Initially, one action is involved; then variations on a single theme, such as stirring the spoon in the cup; then drinking; or feeding two dolls in succession. By 2 years of age multischeme combinations are in evidence. Mini-stories begin to be acted out, following 'scripts' such as shopping, or bedtime (plate 7.1). Language plays an increasing role in maintaining the play structure (see also table 11.3). All these developments come together in *sociodramatic play*, prominent in 3- to 6-year-olds. Here, two or more children act out definite roles, such as mummy and daddy, spacemen and monsters, doctors and patients (Singer and Singer, 1991).

The ultimate in imagination in childhood play is perhaps the *imaginary companion*, who may follow the child around, or need to be fed at mealtimes, or tucked up in bed with the child. Some one-quarter to one-half of children have some form of imaginary companion, especially between 3 and 8 years (they are mostly abandoned by age 10). These children tend to engage in a lot of sophisticated pretend play generally (Taylor et al., 1993). Children are not confused about the imaginary status of imaginary companions and are aware they are different from real friends.

Language play

The most well-known examples of language play come from Weir's book *Language in the Crib* (1962). Weir left a tape recorder on under her 2-year-old son's crib at night-time. At this age toddlers often talk to themselves a lot before going to sleep, or waking up. Sample extracts are shown on p. 214 and p. 355 (table 11.2). A similar study (Keenan and Klein, 1975) recorded social play, with syllables and words, between twins aged 21 months. Children appear to use these presleep monologues or dialogues to play with and practise linguistic forms they are in the process of acquiring (Kuczaj II, 1986; and p. 355).

The humorous use of language becomes very prominent in the older preschool child. Chukovsky (1963) reports examples of rhyming poems created by 3- and 4-year-old children:

> I'm a whale
> This is my tail
> I'm a flamingo. Look at my wingo.

Preschool children will spontaneously express a whole range of humorous responses, including interactive 'pre-riddles', conventional riddles and joking behaviours. However, what they find amusing changes with age and cognitive development. By about age 2, incongruous language and labelling of objects and events appear humorous:

> J., aged 3 years, while drawing a picture of her mother, put hair all round the circle face and then called it 'Mommy porcupine' with shouts of glee.

By about age 4 conceptual incongruity appears humorous:

> C., aged 5, said to her mother 'I can play a piano by ear'. Then she banged her ear on the piano keyboard and laughed.

By about age 6, children begin to understand and enjoy humour with multiple meanings (McGhee, 1979); however, they usually cannot do so when younger, and often laugh inappropriately or make up 'pre-riddles':

> L., aged 3 years, after her older sister told the riddle, 'Why does the turtle cross the road? To get to the Shell station', insisted on telling a 'riddle' also. Her riddle was 'Why does the dog cross the road? To get to the station' (she laughed at the 'riddle').
>
> B., aged 5 years, asked 'What's red and white? A newspaper' and laughed at his 'riddle'.
>
> S., aged 6, asked his uncle and father this riddle, 'Why was 6 afraid of 7? Because 7, 8, 9!' Everyone laughed at this joke.
>
> (Examples adapted from Bergen, 1990)

Language is often used playfully in sociodramatic play episodes. Several examples have been given by Garvey (1977): 'Hello, my name is Mr Elephant!'; 'Hello, my name is Mr Donkey!' In school-age children rhymes and word play are common, and have been documented by Opie and Opie (1959). The repetition of well-known verses, with variations, has more in common with the rule-governed games common by the age of 6 or 7 years (see below and also chapter 11).

War toys and war play

Another kind of aggressive play is when children use toy guns or weapons, or combat figures, to engage in pretend fighting or warfare. This kind of play is banned in some nurseries and playgroups. Parents too have mixed views about it. Costabile et al. (1992) surveyed parents in Italy, and England. Some actively discouraged it: 'I do not like it. In fact children who do war play become less sensible and less obedient.' Some were uncertain, or felt it should be allowed within limits: 'Unsure. We don't encourage it, but don't discourage it, either.' Some allowed it unconditionally: 'A natural part of a child's development, just as they act out cooking etc. War/fighting is featured in so many things it would be difficult and unnatural to exclude it from a child's life.'

Researchers too are divided. Nancy Carlsson-Paige and Diane Levin have written two books on the issue, *The War Play Dilemma* (1987) and *Who's Calling the Shots?* (1990), in which they argue that war toys and combat figures encourage stereotyped good-versus-evil aggressive scripts, which impoverish the child's imagination and encourage actual aggressive behaviour. They recognize the difficulties in banning such play entirely (there are plenty of stories of children making toy guns out of Lego, if replica guns are banned in the nursery); but advocate adults intervening to turn such play to more constructive, and less aggressive ends (a policy also favoured by most parents, in the survey by Costabile et al.). However, Brian Sutton-Smith (1988) argues that for children, war play is clearly pretend, and just reflects an aspect of real life. As one boy said when his father asked him not to use toy guns: 'But Dad, I don't want to shoot anybody, I just want to play.'

The developmental issues regarding war play have still to be resolved (see Smith, 1994; Goldstein, 1995; and also p. 206). The issue bears some similarity to the debate about violent videos and television (see chapter 6). On the one hand, for most children such activities are natural, separated from real life, and probably do little if any harm. But it is easy to feel uncomfortable when the activity becomes very prominent; and, although the evidence is uncertain, there is the possibility that for children who are already disturbed or have violent tendencies, sanctioning violent play (or violent videos) can make matters worse. Dunn and Hughes (2001) studied 40 'hard-to-manage' and 40 control children in London, filming them playing alone in a room with a friend when they were 4 years old. They found that the 'hard-to-manage' children showed more violent fantasy; and the extent of violent fantasy (across both groups) was related to poorer language and play skills, more antisocial behaviour, and also to less empathic understanding two years later at age 6.

Video and computer games

'Space Invaders' hit the computer game market in 1979. Since then, there has been a rapid increase in the time children spend with computer games or in video arcades. As with war toys, much of this activity is engaged in by boys, and it is very popular in the 9–15-year age range (Goldstein, 1994). Many such games do have aggressive fantasy themes.

Playing video games may increase hand–eye coordination and skill at that particular game, but what are the other effects? A review by Harris (2001) pointed out that available studies are cross-sectional and often retrospective, and there is a dearth of longitudinal investigations that could yield more reliable conclusions. Some – but not all – studies point to a link to aggressive behaviour. Some games appear quite addictive, and parents sometimes fear that playing video games leads to social isolation. However, a study of 300 French schoolchildren (Bonnafont, 1992, in Goldstein, 1994) found that while parent–child communication might be disrupted (since parents often did not understand the games), there was a lot of social contact with peers in the context of video games. A few studies have also suggested benefits in terms of relaxation, and improvement of reading skills (Harris, 2001).

Games with rules

Games with rules ended the developmental sequences of Piaget, and Smilansky. The play of preschool children often has some rule structure; for example, if someone is role-playing 'doctor' to a 'patient', there are some constraints on what he or she is expected to do, exerted by the other participants. Nevertheless, any rules or constraints are largely private to that particular play episode, and can be changed at any time ('I'm not the doctor now, I'm a policeman'). By the time children are 6 or 7 years old, rule-governed games like hopscotch, tig or football take up much more playground time. These are games with public rules, sometimes codified, with much less latitude for change. The transition from play to games is nevertheless a gradual one (see also chapter 8, and Piaget's study of the game of marbles).

Factors affecting play

We have seen how parents often encourage play when it starts to appear in their young children. Some researchers think this early encouragement is very important. MacDonald (1992) argues that it is a form of parental investment (cf. p. 51) in children, which is of recent historical origin. He contrasts typical high levels of parent–child play in higher socioeconomic groups in urban societies with lower levels in lower socioeconomic groups and in traditional societies, where there is more emphasis on sibling rearing.

Social class differences have been reported in children's sociodramatic play in nurseries and playgroups. Several studies have suggested that children from disadvantaged backgrounds and non-urban societies show less frequent and less complex fantasy and sociodramatic play, starting with a large-scale study by Smilansky (1968) in Israel. McLoyd (1982) criticized these studies for poor methodology. Some failed adequately to define social class, or confounded it with other variables such as race, or school setting. McLoyd claims that the general pattern is one of marginal and conflicting findings. Global statements about social class may be unwarranted, since any such effects will vary with historical time, cultural group and even location within a country.

If children, for whatever reason, do not engage in much fantasy or sociodramatic play in nursery school, it does seem that nursery staff can encourage it by play tutoring. This technique was pioneered by Smilansky (1968). Such intervention at its least intrusive involves verbal guidance or suggestions; alternatively, more direct involvement in the play may be made by acting as a model for roles and actions, or by giving deliberate training in imaginative activities or fantasy themes. Play tutoring can be made even more effective if appropriate toys are provided (e.g., dressing-up clothes, hospital props), and if children are taken on visits (e.g., to a zoo, hospital or factory).

Several investigators have studied sex differences in children's pretend play (Goncu, 2002). Differences in the frequency of pretend play are inconsistent, but there are sex differences in the choice of roles in sociodramatic play. Girls tend to act out domestic scenes – shopping, washing the baby, etc. Boys less often imitate male roles, as they have usually not been able to observe their father at work; rather, they rely on roles familiar from books (e.g., police, fireman), or act out film or television characters.

There does appear to be a reliable sex difference in rough-and-tumble play; this has almost always been found to be preferred by boys. A predisposition for boys to engage more in this activity may be related to the influence of sex hormones during the period of fetal growth, as indicated by Collaer and Hines (1995). However, social factors are likely to be very important too; fathers engage in more rough-and-tumble play with boys, even by 2 years of age, and this kind of play is very much socially stereotyped as a male activity (Goldstein, 1994; see also chapter 6).

Play Theorists

Theoretical perspectives on the nature of play and on its role in development cover a wide range. Several influential ideas can be traced back to the late nineteenth century and early twentieth century. The views of a number of earlier play theorists and educators are summarized here.

Friedrich Froebel   The ideas of Froebel, as expounded in *The Education of Man* (published posthumously in 1906), were influential in the start of the kindergarten and nursery school movement. 'Kindergarten' translates from German as 'child-garden', and this aptly sums up Froebel's ideas about play and development: 'Play, truly recognized and rightly fostered, unites the germinating life of the child attentively with the ripe life of experiences of the adult and thus fosters the one through the other.' On this view play exemplifies development from within the child, but can be nurtured by adult guidance and the provision of appropriate materials. Froebel's influence, following that of Pestalozzi (with whom he studied for two years), encouraged a positive evaluation of the educational significance of play, as compared with the rote-learning approach which nevertheless became characteristic of many infant schools at the end of the nineteenth century (Whitbread, 1972).

Herbert Spencer   In his book *The Principles of Psychology* (1878, final edition 1898), Spencer proposed a less enthusiastic view of play. He believed play is carried out 'for the sake of the immediate gratifications involved, without reference to ulterior benefits'. He suggested that the higher animals are better able to deal with the immediate necessities of life, and that the nervous system, rather than remaining inactive for long periods, stimulates play. 'Thus it happens that in the more evolved creatures, there often recurs an energy somewhat in excess of immediate needs . . . Hence play of all kinds – hence this tendency to superfluous and useless exercise of faculties that have been quiescent.' Spencer's approach has been labelled the 'surplus energy' theory.

Karl Groos   At the turn of the century, Groos published two influential works, *The Play of Animals* (1898), and *The Play of Man* (1901). Groos criticized Spencer's theory on a number of grounds. He thought that surplus energy might provide 'a particularly favourable condition for play', but was not essential. He also thought play had a much more definite function than in Spencer's theory. Groos argued that a main reason for childhood was so that play could occur: 'perhaps the very existence of youth is largely for the sake of play.' This was because play provided exercise and elaboration of skills needed for survival. This has been called the 'exercise' or 'practice' theory of play, and in its modern form it has many adherents.

G. Stanley Hall   In his book *Adolescence* (1908) and elsewhere, Hall argued that Groos's practice theory was 'very partial, superficial, and perverse'. This was because Groos saw play as practice for contemporary activities. By contrast, Hall thought that play was a means for children to work through primitive atavisms, reflecting our evolutionary past. For example, 'the sports of boys chasing one another, wrestling, making prisoners, obviously gratify in a partial way the preda-tory instincts'. The function of play was thus cathartic in nature, and allowed the 'playing out' of those instincts that characterized earlier human history. This became known as the 'recapitulation theory' of play. In the form proposed by Hall, it has had little or no recent support.

Maria Montessori   The work of Montessori has been another major influence in the education of young children (see Kramer, 1976). Like Froebel, Montessori saw the value of self-initiated activity for young children, under adult guidance. She put more emphasis on the importance of learning about real life, however, and hence on constructive play materials, which helped, in sensory discrimination and in colour and shape matching. She did not value pretend or sociodramatic play, seeing pretence as primitive and an escape from reality. She preferred to encour-age children actually to serve meals, for example, and to clear up around the house themselves, rather than play at mealtimes in a 'play house'. However, contempo-rary Montessori schools have largely abandoned this particular aspect of her philosophy.

Jean Piaget   The place of play in Piaget's theory of cognitive development has often been misunderstood (see Piaget, 1966; Sutton-Smith, 1966; and Rubin and Pepler, 1982 for reviews). Piaget saw adaptation as depending on the two processes of accommodation and assimilation (see chapter 12). Play 'manifests the peculiarity of a primacy of assimilation over accommodation'. Children acted out their already established behaviours, or schemata, in play, and adapted reality to fit these. For example, referring to episodes such as his daughter Jacqueline's pretending to sleep (p. 222), Piaget wrote:

> It is clearly impossible to explain this symbolic practice as being pre-exercise; the child certainly does not play like this in order to learn to wash or sleep. All that he is trying to do is to use freely his individual powers, to reproduce his own actions for the pleasure of seeing himself do them and showing them off to others, in a word to express himself, to assimilate without being hampered by the need to accommo-date at the same time.

Here is a criticism both of some aspects of Groos's approach (play as pre-exercise), and of play as being important in learning. For Piaget learning was related more to accommodation to reality. This emphasis may be linked to Montessori's influ-ence, for Piaget carried out his early research at a modified Montessori school, and for many years was president of the Swiss Montessori Society. The functions of play in Piaget's framework are two-fold. Play can consolidate existing skills by repeated execution of known schemas, with minor variations. Also, it can give a child a sense of 'ego continuity', that is, confidence and a sense of mastery. It does this because failure is largely circumvented in fantasy play, where the real properties of the materials are not at issue, and no external goal is aimed for.

Sigmund Freud   Freud himself did not write a great deal about play, but it has come to have an important role within the psychoanalytic movement, and especially in play therapy. Freud thought that play provided children with an avenue for wish fulfilment and mastery of traumatic events. As Peller (1954) put it, 'play . . . is an attempt to compensate for anxieties and depression, to obtain pleasure at a minimum risk of danger and/or irreversible consequences.' Thus play provided a safe context for expressing aggressive or sexual impulses which it would be too dangerous to express in reality. In addition play could, within limits, help achieve mastery of traumatic events: 'Small quantities of anxiety are mastered in play, but anxiety of high intensity inhibits play.' Both aspects are important in play therapy. First, play expresses the child's wishes and anxieties (Peller relates the development of fantasy play themes to Freud's psychosexual stages). Second, play can help overcome such anxieties, by catharsis or by working through them.

Susan Isaacs   The view of play as essential to both emotional and cognitive growth of young children, strong in the British educational tradition, owes much to Susan Isaacs and to her successor at the Institute of Education at London University, Dorothy Gardner. Isaacs combined a belief in the emotional benefits of play (deriving from the psychoanalytic tradition) with a wider view of its benefits for physical, social and cognitive development generally, echoing the evolutionary perspective that animals that learn more, also play more: 'Play is indeed the child's work, and the means whereby he grows and develops. Active play can be looked upon as a sign of mental health; and its absence, either of some inborn defect, or of mental illness' (Isaacs, 1929).

Lev Vygotsky   Another combination of the affective and cognitive aspects of development occurs in Vygotsky's approach to play (1966; from a lecture given in 1933). Like psychoanalysts, Vygotsky saw the affective drive behind play as being 'the imaginary, illusory realization of unrealizable desires'; not with very specific or sexual impulses, but in a much more general sense, to do with the child's confidence and mastery (for example, in attitudes to authority in general): 'Play is essentially wish fulfilment, not, however, isolated wishes but generalized affects.' Furthermore, Vygotsky saw play as being 'the leading source of development in the preschool years'. Essentially, this was because the nature of pretend play meant that the child was liberating itself from the immediate constraints of the situation (e.g., the actual object), and getting into the world of ideas (e.g., what that object might become): 'The child is liberated from situational constraints through his activity in an imaginary situation.'

Recent theorists   In recent decades, theorists have tended to argue the benefits of play for cognitive development and creative thinking. Jerome Bruner (1972) suggested that play in the advanced mammals, and especially in human children, serves both as practice for mastery in skills, and as an opportunity for trying out new combinations of behaviour in a safe context. Sara Smilansky (1968; Smilansky and Shefatya, 1990) and Dorothy and Jerome Singer (1991) have advanced the value of fantasy and sociodramatic play in particular. Brian Sutton-Smith (1967) initially supported the importance of play for creative processes; but more recently (Sutton-Smith, 1986) has come to argue against what he sees as the 'idealization' of play. In sharp contrast to the other theorists we have considered, he now concludes that many theories about play, and even the way we define play, reflect the needs of adults in organizing and controlling children, rather than the actualities of children's behaviour. Stephen Kline (1995) has drawn attention to the 'global toy curriculum', the worldwide promotion and marketing of particular theme toys and play products, which must be taken account of when considering any benefits of play for children's development.

Empirical Studies

Much theorizing about the importance of play was carried out in the absence of any real evidence that play does, or does not, have the effects or benefits postulated. Here we will review the evidence about the importance of play from three different perspectives: the forms of play, or 'design studies' – does the actual nature of play behaviour reveal something of its value?; correlational studies – what tends to go with playfulness in children?; and experimental studies – attempts to compare the value of play experiences in controlled conditions.

The forms of play

If we look closely at what goes on in playful episodes we may form hypotheses as to what uses the behaviour has. Indeed, it is this approach that Piaget used, and which led him to his own theory of play (p. 230).

Byers and Walker (1995) examined the nature of locomotor or physical activity play in mammals generally. Both the form of the play, and its peak time of occurrence in development, led them to conclude that this kind of play has important training functions in affecting brain growth and in training for physical strength and endurance.

Some theorists have speculated on the importance of pretend play for theory of mind development (see pp. 473–4). Leslie (1987) argued that pretend play is an indicator of metarepresentational abilities as early as 18 months, and is important in developing these latter abilities for understanding that someone else may represent things differently (have different knowledge, or beliefs) from yourself. Lillard (1993) and Jarrold et al. (1994) have reviewed the evidence on pretend-play skills and theory of mind, and each conclude that the evidence is not strong. Much early pretend play appears to be largely imitative, as is shown in table 7.1. On the basis of Howes' model, there is little reason to suppose that social pretend implies metarepresentational abilities on the part of the child until 37–48 months, which is when theory of mind abilities emerge by most criteria; so, it is not necessary to postulate that it has a leading role in theory of mind development. However, quite a lot of talk about mental states does take place in pretend play (see chapter 14, p. 468).

Observations of the flexibility present in play with objects led Bruner (1972) to postulate its role in problem-solving and creativity. Working with Bruner, an extensive study of Oxfordshire nursery schools was made by Sylva, Roy and Painter (1980). They documented which activities of nursery-school children resulted in what they considered to be complex or challenging activities. They concluded that activities with some sort of goal, and the means to achieve it, were the most challenging – activities such as building, drawing, doing puzzles. They called these 'high-yield' activities. Depending on one's exact definition, these might be considered less playful (i.e., more constructive, or goal-directed) than what they thought of as 'medium-yield' activities – pretending, play with small-scale toys, manipulating sand or dough. Finally, 'low-yield' activities comprised informal and impromptu games, gross motor play and unstructured social playing and 'horsing around' (i.e., rough-and-tumble play).

The Sylva et al. study actually suggests that the unstructured, free play kinds of activities may be less cognitively useful than more structured activities. It would seem though that the emphasis in Sylva and colleagues' study is on cognitive, rather than social, challenge or complexity. Observations of sociodramatic play suggest there is considerable negotiation about social roles (cf. table 7.1). Observations of rough-and-tumble show that coordination with a large number of partners is often involved, and suggest it may have social functions in terms of making friends, or practising fighting or dominance skills.

Studies on the forms of play are suggestive of functional hypotheses, and may rule out some hypotheses; are these conclusions supported by other forms of evidence?

Correlational studies

If playful behaviour has useful developmental consequences, then we would expect that children who practise a lot of a certain type of play should also be more advanced in other areas of development for which play is supposed to be beneficial.

One study, by Hutt and Bhavnani (1972), used data from the novel toy experiment mentioned earlier (see box 7.1 and pp. 218–19). They traced 48 children who had been observed with the novel toy at around 4 years of age, when they were 4 years older. From the earlier data they had recorded those children who, after investigating the toy, used it in many imaginative ways (15 of the 48). Four years later they gave the children some tests designed to measure creativity (see also p. 205). The imaginative players scored significantly higher on these tests than did the children who at 4 years had not played much with the novel object.

This is consistent with the idea that imaginative play fosters creativity; but no more than that. An alternative explanation would be that another factor (for example, shyness with adults) was responsible for the poor performance both with the novel object, and later in the tests. Or, perhaps the playfulness of the imaginative children is just a by-product of their creativity, not a cause of it. As discussed elsewhere (chapter 1), correlations may be due to extraneous factors, and we cannot infer causal relations from them.

Many other correlational studies have been reported in the literature. In one (Johnson et al., 1982), 34 4-year-olds were observed in play and also given cognitive and intelligence tests. The researchers found that constructive play, but not sociodramatic play, was positively and significantly correlated with intelligence scores. This finding would be congruent with the position of Sylva's group (above). In another study (Connolly and Doyle, 1984), 91 preschoolers were observed in social fantasy play, and measures of social competence were obtained from observation, role-taking tests (see chapter 12) and teacher ratings. It was found that the amount and complexity of fantasy play significantly correlated with several measures of social competence. This would be congruent with the point made above that the benefits of sociodramatic play may be social more than cognitive.

Taylor and Carlson (1997) studied 152 children aged 3 and 4 years, and correlated various measures of pretend and fantasy play with theory of mind tasks. They found no relationship for 3-year-olds, but a significant relationship for 4-year-olds. The correlation for the whole sample (which had 57 3-year-olds and 95 4-year-olds) was modest: $r = .16$ for the correlation of a Principal Fantasy Component with theory of mind – significant, but accounting for only 2.6 per cent of the variance. The authors' conclusion that 'The results of this study provide strong evidence that there is a relation between theory of mind and pretend play development in 4-year-old children' (p. 451) seems a very positive gloss on their findings.

A study by Watson and Peng (1992) has been one of the few to look at effects of war-toy play. They coded for pretend aggression play and real aggression in 36 preschool children (taking care to distinguish these from rough-and-tumble play). Parents completed questionnaires saying how much toy-gun play the children did at home, and how aggressive were the TV programmes that they watched. There was an association for boys (but not for girls) between a history of toy-gun play (based on parents' ratings) and levels of real aggression in the day-care centre. However, this finding could simply reflect that temperamentally aggressive children also like playing with toy guns. Pretend aggression in the day-care centre did not correlate with real aggression. All these studies are subject to the same caveats about drawing conclusions from correlational evidence.

Experimental studies of play

Experimental studies of play take two main forms: deprivation studies, and enrichment studies. If participants are randomly allocated to the various conditions, it should be possible to make better causal inferences than is the case in correlational studies.

The effects of depriving children of play opportunities have largely been limited to studies of physical activity play. Pellegrini et al. (1995) examined the effects of keeping children in primary school classrooms for longer (delaying the recess breaks). The results showed that greater deprivation led to increased levels of play when opportunities became available. Also, the experience of break time increased children's attention to school tasks when they returned to the classroom. These researchers discuss their findings in relation to the *cognitive immaturity hypothesis* proposed by Bjorklund and Green (1992). This argues that nonfocused play activities, such as those found at break time, are adaptive in providing a break from more cognitively demanding activities (such as school work) for younger children.

The more usual form of experiment on play is in the form of enrichment. The benefits of some form of extra play experience are compared with the benefits of non-play experience. Some experiments have been done on object play, usually using short sessions of about 10 minutes' duration. Children, usually of nursery-school age, are given some play experience with objects; others are given an instructional session, or an alternative materials condition (e.g., drawing), or are put in a no-treatment control group. After the session is over, they are then given an assessment, for example, of creativity (e.g., thinking of unusual uses for the objects they have played with), problem-solving (e.g., using the objects to make a long tool to retrieve a marble) or conservation. A number of such studies claimed some form of superiority for the play experience, but subsequent work has not always borne these claims out.

In a review, Smith and Simon (1984) argued that these early studies were methodologically unsound due to the possibility of experimenter effects (see p. 16). When the same experimenter administers the conditions and tests the participants immediately after, some unconscious bias may come in. Some studies were criticized for inadequate control for familiarity with the experimenter. When these factors are properly taken account of, there is little evidence that the play experience helps, or indeed that such sessions have any real impact. Smith and Simon concluded that either the benefits of play in real life occur over a longer time period, or they are not substantial enough to measure by this sort of experimental procedure.

Experiments on the effects of make-believe and imagery on deductive reasoning in 4- to 6-year-olds were reported by Dias and Harris (1988, 1990). The results were suggestive of a role of pretence in theory of mind development; but unfortunately, full protection against experimenter effects was not taken. Leevers and Harris (1999) have done further studies within this paradigm that led them to reinterpret the earlier work. Harris now argues that it is not the fantasy or pretend component, but simply any instruction that prompts an analytic, logical approach to the premises, that helps at these syllogistic tasks.

A more ecologically valid approach is to look at the effects of play over periods of weeks, or perhaps a school term. This has been done in studies examining the effects of play tutoring (see p. 228) in preschool classes. Several studies on disadvantaged preschool children in the USA found that play tutoring, besides increasing children's fantasy play, also had benefits in a variety of areas on cognitive, language and social development. The problem with these studies was that the play-tutored children were compared with children who received little or no extra adult intervention. Thus, general adult involvement and conversation might have caused the gains, rather than fantasy play *per se*. This alternative idea has become known as the 'verbal stimulation' hypothesis. Some play-tutoring studies

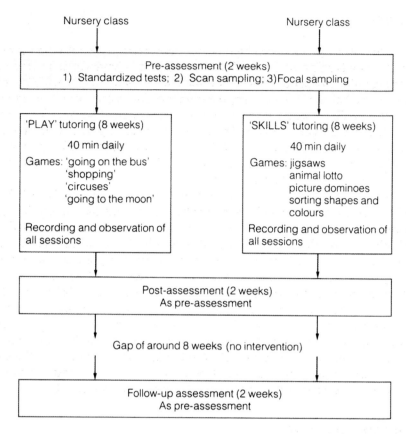

Figure 7.3 Design of experimental study comparing effects of play tutoring and skills tutoring.

since then have embodied controls for 'verbal stimulation', or more generally, adult involvement; see Figure 7.3. These found little superiority for the play-tutoring conditions. This does not mean that play tutoring is not worthwhile, but it does imply that it is of no more value than some other kinds of adult involvement (Smith, 1988).

There has been one experimental study looking at the hypothesis that pretend play assists theory of mind. This was carried out by Dockett (1998) in an Australian preschool. Four-year old children were naturally split into two groups and pre- and post-tested on measures of shared pretence and on theory of mind ability. One group of children received sociodramatic play training for 3 weeks; the other, control group experienced the normal curriculum. The play training group significantly increased in frequency and complexity of group pretence, relative to the control group; and improved significantly more on the theory of mind tests, both at post-test and at follow-up 3 weeks later. This study provides the best evidence yet for a causal link from pretend play to theory of mind; however the groups were small and not well matched; and the testing was not done blind to condition.

Summary

Considerable empirical investigation has now been made into the benefits of play, but 'the jury is still out'. Most of the investigations have concentrated on the supposed cognitive benefits of play, and have been made in an explicitly educational framework. Yet as we have seen, the evidence for strong cognitive benefits, either from theory, observation, correlational or experimental studies, is not convincing. If anything, the evidence is better for the benefits of play for social competence. This has been less thoroughly studied, while the postulated benefits of play for emotional release and catharsis (see p. 201) have scarcely received any well-controlled experimental study at all.

According to a Department of Environment report in the UK in 1973, 'the realisation that play is essential for normal development has slowly but surely permeated our cultural heritage.' This, like the words of Isaacs quoted on p. 231, embodies a prevalent view that Sutton-Smith (1986) called 'the idealization of play'. Yet, in some societies children seem to play little but still develop normally. As we have seen, the empirical evidence is mixed. Another view emerging from studies of both animal and human play is that, while play is likely to have benefits, it is unlikely that they are essential. Rather, these benefits could be achieved in a number of ways, of which play would be one: for example, children can acquire social competence by playing, but by other activities as well. Whatever the final verdict, it will not detract from the enjoyment of play, on the part of both the participant and the observer. This in itself gives an enduring value to play, whatever the extent of its developmental consequences may be.

▐ Further Reading

An excellent overview of play (and exploration!) generally, in nonhuman species as well as in children, is Power, T. 2000: *Play and Exploration in Children and Animals*. Mahwah, NJ: Lawrence Erlbaum. The best text on children's play, especially for those interested in educational relevance, is Johnson, J. E., Christie, J. F. and Yawkey, T. D. *Play and Early Childhood Development* (2nd edn). New York: Longman. A useful collection is Moyles, J. R. (ed.) 1994: *The Excellence of Play*. Buckingham and Philadelphia: Open University Press.

For social, pretend play see Howes, C. 1992: *The Collaborative Construction of Pretend*. Albany, NY: SUNY Press; for make-believe play generally, D. and J. Singer 1991: *The House of Make-Believe: Children's Play and the Developing Imagination*. Cambridge, MA: Harvard University Press; Harris, P. L. 2000: *The Work of the Imagination*. Oxford: Blackwell, takes forward his ideas on pretence, role play, and imagination more generally. For pretence in animals as well as children, see Mitchell, R. W. (ed) 2002: *Pretending and Imagination in Animals and Children*. Cambridge: Cambridge University Press. For work on the nature and benefits of play in school yards, see Pellegrini, A. D. 1995: *School Recess and Playground Behaviour*. Albany, NY: State University of New York Press. Gunter, B. (1999): *The Effects of Video Games on Children*. Sheffield: Sheffield Academic Press, is a useful review of this topic.

Hellendoorn, J., van der Kooij, R. and Sutton-Smith, B. (eds) 1994: *Play and Intervention*. Albany, NY: SUNY Press, considers issues of play therapy, and play for children with special needs. Goldstein, J. H. 1994: *Toys, Play and Child Development*. Cambridge: Cambridge University Press, considers a range of educational and policy issues in relation to research on play. For an anthropological perspective, try Lancy, D. F. 1996: *Playing on the Mother-Ground*. New York: Guilford Press, an account of play in the life of the Kpelle people of Liberia. Sutton-Smith, B. 1997: *The Ambiguity of Play*, Cambridge, Mass: Harvard University Press, is an idiosyncratic and eclectic account of play in a broad, multi-disciplinary perspective.

■ Discussion Points

1   How important is it to define play? Does play at different ages require different definitions?
2   Are exploration and play really distinct?
3   How useful is it to distinguish stages in the development of play?
4   Have theorists been too ready to speculate about the value of play, without sufficient evidence?
5   Are experimental studies of play worthwhile?

Box 7.1
Exploration and play in children

The aim of Hutt's study was to see how a novel object elicited exploratory behaviour in young children, and how this behaviour changed with repeated exposure. The main participants were 30 nursery-school children, aged 3–5 years. Each child had eight 10-minute sessions in a room in the nursery school. The first two sessions were for familiarization, and five toys were provided. For the ensuing six experimental sessions a novel toy was also available – a red metal box with a lever, whose movements could be registered on counters and could result in a buzzer sounding and a bell ringing (see box figure 7.1.1).

There were two independent variables. One was the complexity of the novel object; the other was exposure to the object, measured over the six successive sessions. The object complexity was varied through 'no sound or vision' (bell and buzzer switched off, counters covered up), 'vision only', 'sound only', to 'both sound and vision' available. The dependent variables were taken from counter readings (showing how much lever manipulation had taken place) and observations of the children, especially the amount of time spent exploring (visually or tactually) the novel object.

The results showed that children looked at the object immediately on entering, and often approached it or asked the observer what it was. They would then examine the object visually and manually, holding and manipulating the lever. For the 'no sound or vision' and 'vision only' conditions, this exploration and manipulation declined rapidly over sessions. However, for the 'sound only' and 'both sound and vision' conditions, manipulation of the lever increased over the first five sessions. More detailed analysis of the observations showed that in these conditions, although exploratory behaviour declined, more

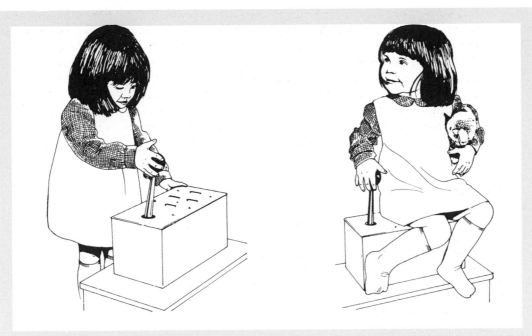

Box Figure 7.1.1 A child exploring and later playing with a novel object (based on material in C. Hutt 1966: *Symposia of the Zoological Society of London*, 18).

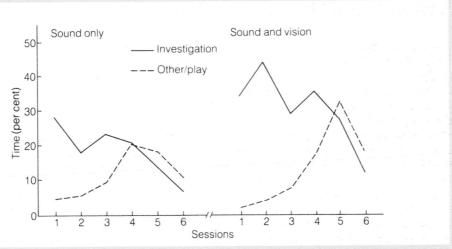

Box Figure 7.1.2 Proportions of time spent in investigating and in other activities, including play with the novel object, when sound, or sound and vision, were available.

playful or game-like behaviours increased (see box figure 7.1.2), for example running around the object with a truck and ringing the bell each time, or using the object as a seat and pretending it was a car.

These observations led Hutt to suggest that exploration could lead on to play, and to characterize the two behaviours distinctly. Exploration was characterized as relatively serious and focused, essentially asking 'what does this object do?' Play was characterized as relaxed, and by a diversity of activities essentially asking 'what can I do with this object?'

This study combined an experimental design with some degree of natural observation of the child's behaviour. Note that the less-structured observations allowed for the distinction between exploration and play to be made; an outcome not expected in the initial aims of the study. The results are shown as graphs of changes over sessions, as in box figure 7.1.2, and the exploration/play distinction is reported qualitatively. No statistical tests are used, though some might have been appropriate. No control group is really necessary for this study, as exploration of the novel object could not occur in its absence.

The exploration/play distinction was considered further by Weisler and McCall (1976) and Wohlwill (1984). It has been noted that the particular novel object used in this study probably makes the distinction clearer than some situations might do. In other reports Hutt (1970) stated that boys were much more exploratory than girls in this setting, but this sex difference has not been well replicated in other studies of exploratory behaviour (McLoyd and Ratner, 1983).

Based on material in Hutt, C. 1966: Exploration and play in children. *Symposia of the Zoological Society of London*, 18, 61–81.

Box 7.2
Universal, developmental, and variable aspects of young children's play: A cross-cultural comparison of pretending at home

This study aimed to provide an in-depth, longitudinal account of pretend play in two different cultural contexts, and thereby suggest not only what were universal trends, but also more culturally specific aspects of this kind of play. All participants were 'relatively well off' intact families with 1 to 3 children, including a target child aged 2.5 years at the start of the study.

The two cultural contexts were:

• Irish-American families in Chicago, USA: these families lived in spacious, single-family homes, and there were many toys available to play with, including 'extensive and elaborate collections of toy miniatures' (realistic toys such as dolls, cups, trucks). The children had extensive contact with other children and adults in the neighbourhood. Five families participated (3 girls, 2 boys).
• Chinese families in Taipei, Taiwan: these families lived in compact single-family apartments, and with a modest number of toys including a few miniatures. Contact with other children and adults in the neighbourhood were few until children attended formal preschool. Nine families participated (5 girls, 4 boys).

The study proceeded in three phases:

1 Ethnographic fieldwork: researchers familiarized themselves with the community, and collected descriptions of the home and play areas; this period also allowed the children to get acclimatized to the researcher's presence.

Box Table 7.2.1 Differences in pretend play observed in young children in Chicago, USA, and Taipei, Taiwan

Proportion of pretend play that:	Chicago, USA	Taipei, Taiwan
is social	89	98
is with mother	64	98
is with other children	64	13
uses toy miniatures	57	28
does not use objects	10	36
uses fantasy themes	21	05
involves caretaking roles	29	07
is initiated by the child	.70 (2.5 yrs) to .94 (4 yrs)	.09 (2.5 yrs) to .34 (4 yrs)
involves routine social interactions with non-kin adults	08	70
used by mother to practise 'proper conduct'	00	38

2 Naturalistic observations: video records were made of the children's behaviour at home, during the day, with mother present (and sometimes siblings), at 2.5, 3 and 4 years of age; at each age point, two separate 2-hour records were obtained. The video records, including transcriptions of speech in pretend play, were coded.

3 Formal interviews: with parents, to obtain basic information including socialization beliefs and practices.

Altogether, 14 hours of pretend play were recorded: 5 (out of 108 hours) in Taipei, and 9 (out of 60 hours) in Chicago. Some features were universal. First, all 14 of the target children showed some spontaneous pretend play. Also, the majority of this play was social, the majority was with the mother, and the majority involved objects of some kind. Some developmental changes were also common to both cultures. The proportion of pretend play episodes initiated by the child increased from 30 to 48 months, as did the proportion of responses to other's initiations which elaborated on the play theme. Also, although the mothers started off primarily treating pretend in a purely playful way, their use of pretend in non-play fashion increased over this period; for example to distract a child from an angry mood, to enliven a tedious task such as clearing up, or to teach the child a new social skill.

There were also some pronounced cultural differences. Those shown in Box Table 7.2.1 were all statistically significant on analysis of variance, despite the small sample size. Related to the conditions described in the ethnographic fieldwork, the pretend play of the Taiwanese children was more often with the mother, less often with other children, compared to the US children. Less use was made of toy miniatures (they had few of these), but more use of pretence without objects. The US children made more use of fantasy themes (for example based on TV or comic strips), and more use of caretaking or home-based themes (such as shopping, feeding, cleaning), and more often initiated these themes themselves. The Taiwanese children's play more often involved routine social interactions with non-kin adults (such as with teachers, shopkeepers).

Based on the ethnography and the observations, the researchers also argued that mothers and caregivers generally may use pretend play for somewhat different purposes, in these two cultures, based on differing views of socialization. They argue that an important priority for the US parents is developing self-esteem in their children; and they may think that this is fostered by providing many play materials and encouraging the spontaneous initiation of play by the child. On the other hand, an important priority for the Taiwanese parents is to encourage moral development. These parents might use pretend play to encourage 'proper conduct' in an interpersonal context, such as bowing to the teacher in class.

The strengths of this study are in the high quality of records obtained, by a combination of methods. In particular, the naturalistic observations in the home provide a wealth of detail that is more ecologically valid than laboratory studies on pretend play. The primary limitation, and a severe one, is the small sample size; this was no doubt dictated by the time and expense of obtaining and coding the video records, even for just 14 families. Clearly, the cultural differences cannot be generalized with confidence to families in the USA and in Taiwan in general (especially as all families were relatively prosperous). However, the magnitude of the differences are often substantial and certainly make the point that – superimposed on a common and probably universal core nature of pretend play – both the physical and social context, and socialization beliefs of parents, can impact on the kinds of pretend play seen in these families.

Based on material in Haight, W. L., Wang, X-L, Fung, H. H-T., Williams, K. and Mintz, J. 1999: Universal, developmental, and variable aspects of young children's play: A cross-cultural comparison of pretending at home. *Child Development*, 70, 1477–88.

8 Helping Others and Moral Development

In a broad sense, prosocial behaviour can be taken to mean helping, comforting and sharing on the part of one person to another. Grusec et al. (2002, p. 2) define prosocial behaviour as:

> any voluntary, intentional action that produces a positive or beneficial outcome for the recipient regardless of whether that action is costly to the donor, neutral in its impact, or beneficial. In this sense, it is distinguished from 'altruism' which clearly implies that assistance to others came at some cost to the donor.

Although most people believe that it is wrong to harm others, there is considerable ambiguity around the concept of acting prosocially to help others. Individuals in need may respond negatively to being helped; on the other hand, an over-caring approach to others can be damaging to the self-concept of the helper. Durkin (1995, p. 433) points out that kindness towards others is not always motivated by selfless concern for others, and it may be useful to distinguish between *prosocial behaviour*, which can occur for both selfish and unselfish reasons, and *altruistic behaviour*, in which there is no intentional benefit to the helper and where in some cases there may even be disadvantage or danger. Some researchers are greatly concerned about such definitional matters, whereas others are happy to label helping and sharing behaviours as prosocial, largely irrespective of context, intent or reward. You may like to compare these definitions of prosocial and altruistic behaviour with the definitions of mutualism and altruism used by ethologists and given in chapter 2: they are similar.

Some psychologists have used the concept of costs and benefits in an attempt to explain why it is that apparently self-sacrificing behaviour – where the helper incurs a 'cost' – persists and is not eliminated through natural selection. McGuire

(1994), for example, points out that helping often occurs between people who are known to one another, so helping has the benefit of enhancing one's reputation in the social group. One study (Eisenberg, 1983) found that children (aged 7–17 years) clearly differentiated among people whom they might help. When faced with hypothetical moral dilemmas, they indicated that they would be more likely to help family than non-family members; friends rather than non-friends; people they knew rather than people they did not know; people more similar to themselves in race or religion; and non-criminals rather than criminals. Despite the costs, McGuire argues, there are also likely to be benefits to those who act prosocially, such as enhanced self-esteem, the development of empathy and the internalization of socially acceptable norms of cooperation and support.

Other researchers, for example, Trevarthen and Logotheti (1989), have considered the *intrinsic* value of prosocial behaviour from the earliest years of life and argue that, as social beings, we have inborn motivation to form cooperative relationships with one another; strategies for reaching out to others in a spirit of mutual trust and giving are established and developed initially in the context of the family, and children learn about how to act towards others by engaging in shared activities and routines with those who are close to them. This human quality is universal, although the ways in which this is expressed will vary from culture to culture. And, as we have seen in chapter 4, when attachments within the family are insecure, the capacity to relate in a trusting, empathic way towards others may be impaired where the child has internalized a working model of relationships rooted in the experience of *not* being helped at times of need.

Foot et al. (1990) point out that our social practice in Western society has emphasized the role of children as recipients of help when the reality is that there is an enormous, often untapped, potential for harnessing children's capacity to respond prosocially towards peers. They argue that we are only at the threshold of realizing the range of ways in which children could be sources of practical help and emotional support towards one another, and so further influence their own and their peers' cognitive and social development. We need to look at prosocial and altruistic behaviour in a wide social context if we are to understand it in all its complexity.

The Development of Prosocial Behaviour

Children are capable of demonstrating prosocial behaviour from a very early age as we can see from the following examples, taken from mothers' reports.

1   Bobby, at 19 months As I was vacuuming I began to feel a little faint and sick . . . I turned off the vacuum cleaner and went to the bathroom kind of coughing and gagging a little. Bobby followed me to the bathroom door, and the whole time that I was in there he was pounding on the bathroom door saying 'OK Mommie?' I finally came out and picked him up and he looked at me with a very concerned, worried look in his eyes, and I said 'Mommie OK'. Then he put his head on my shoulder and began to love me.

(Zahn-Waxler and Radke-Yarrow, 1982, p. 116)

2   Todd, almost 2 years Today there was a little 4-year-old girl here, Susan. Todd and Susan were in the bedroom playing and all of a sudden Susan started to cry . . . I said 'What happened?' and she said 'He hit me'. I said 'Well, tell him not to hit you', and I said, 'Todd!' He didn't seem particularly upset, he was watching her cry. I said 'Did you hit Susan? You don't want to hurt people.' Then they went back in the bedroom and there was a second run-in and she came out. That's when I said sternly 'No, Todd. You musn't hit people'. He just watched her sniffle as she was being stroked by her mum . . . on the table right by us were some fallen petals from a flower and he picked up one little petal and smiled and handed it to her and said 'Here'. She kind of reached out and took it and then he searched for other petals and gave them to her.

(Zahn-Waxler et al., 1979, p. 322)

3   Cynthia, at 4 years We were getting ready to go to friends for the rest of the day and preparations were becoming rather frantic. Cynthia said to Richard (her younger brother) 'Come on, I'll read you a story and we'll stay out of Mum and Dad's way.' They sat together on the couch and Cynthia 'read' (memorized) two books to him. When they were finished I said 'It was great being able to get ready without any interruptions.'

(Grusec, 1982, p. 140)

Comforting occurs in example 1, helping in example 3 and a form of sharing in example 2. These behaviours occurred when the child saw someone else in difficulty or distress, either through some event to which the child was a bystander (e.g., examples 1 and 3), or because the child itself had caused the distress (e.g., example 2). Example 1, of a child only 19 months old, suggests that prosocial behaviour can occur very early on. However, we might question whether the action is intended to aid another person, as our initial definition stipulated. Did Bobby intend to help his mother, or was he just reacting to her behaviour? It is difficult to tell at such an early age, whereas it is clear from what she herself says that Cynthia, aged 4, did intend to help her parents. However, we can also see that Cynthia was rewarded (verbally at least) for her behaviour; did she anticipate this, and therefore was hers not prosocial behaviour after all?

As Grusec et al. (2002) point out, children engage in prosocial behaviours for a variety of reasons. Two motivations in particular have been extensively studied by psychologists. The first concerns vicarious feelings of *empathy* (responding to another's distress with a similar emotion) or *sympathy* (responding to another's distress with feelings of sadness or concern) that are generated in response to another person's distress or need and that may promote attempts to modify that state. The second concerns the motivation to act prosocially through adherence to a social or cultural norm. We explore each of these in the sections that follow where we describe both experimental and naturalistic studies of children's prosocial behaviour, explore the emergence of prosocial action in a range of settings at home and in school, and discuss the effect of social context and culture on its emergence.

Experimental studies

Earlier researchers attempted experimental studies to elucidate more clearly the causes of prosocial behaviour. A technique that many researchers focused on in the 1970s was reinforcement (verbal or material reward). Let us look at a typical experimental study. Gelfand et al. (1975) reported a study with 21 children aged 5–6 years. The children came to a research caravan where they played a marble-drop game to earn pennies. The pennies accumulated could be spent on a prize at the end, but periodically the child was told that he or she could donate a penny earned to help another child in a nearby room win a prize (in fact there was no other child; this was simulated by a tape recording of an adult and child in conversation). Over a series of trials, the effects of both prompts by the experimenter ('maybe it would be nice if you helped the other boy/girl once or twice') and praise for donating ('very good! Think how that boy/girl must feel now') were evaluated in terms of the subsequent rate of donations. It was found that both prompts, and praise, were effective in increasing donation rates – temporarily for some children, more permanently for others. The authors concluded that this was a clear 'demonstration of reinforcement effects on donating' (p. 983). Other studies have suggested that material reinforcement may be more powerful than social reinforcement for young children, and that the nature of the person giving the reinforcement is an important factor.

Early experimental studies attempted to see whether modelling was a useful technique. Here, an adult models a helpful or altruistic act, which the child observes. One study (Grusec et al., 1978) compared this with moral exhortation (preaching) for its effectiveness as a technique. The participants were 96 boys and girls aged 8–10 years. Children came individually to a research caravan in a school yard to play a marble-bowling game in which they could win marbles (the game was fixed so that all the children won the same number of marbles). Nearby was a poster reading 'Help poor children: Marbles buy gifts' over a bowl with some marbles already in it. An adult (of the same sex as the child) played the game first; she then either exhorted the child to give half her marbles, or said nothing (two preaching conditions), and then either gave, or did not give, half her own marbles (two modelling or performance conditions). The child was then left alone to play, but was observed through a one-way mirror to see how many marbles she donated. It was found that most children who saw the adult give marbles did so themselves, irrespective of preaching; whereas few children who saw the adult not giving marbles did so, although preaching did have some effect here. The children were asked to play the game again three weeks later and, irrespective of previous condition, few of them donated any marbles. This, and other studies, suggests that the behaviour children actually observe in others may be more important than moral exhortations from them though both do have some effect.

The experimental design of these studies is such as to enable us to make fairly certain inferences; for example, that modelling (performance) by an adult does increase the likelihood of altruism in a child who is watching. However, one could criticize these experiments for being rather artificial. The experimenters are unfamiliar, the situations are contrived and some deception is involved. Is it really helpfulness and altruism that is being measured in these settings, or is it just some kind of conformity to adult demands? For instance, in the study by Grusec et al. (1978) is it the case that modelling (performance) causes altruism in the child, or is it simply that the child is trying to puzzle out what is going on, and that the more compliant children, or perhaps the more uncertain children, tend to go along with what the adult seems to be suggesting? The fact that there was no effect of modelling at the 3-week follow-up would be consistent with this explanation.

An experimental study on 6–10-year-olds suggests just this sort of interpretation as regards age differences in generosity. Zarbatany et al. (1985) found that older children were only affected by experimenter obtrusiveness, not by other factors such as whether peers would know how generous the child was. The authors concluded that 'the finding that older children were more generous than younger children only under conditions of experimenter obtrusiveness provides some justification for concerns that laboratory analogue investigations of age differences in children's generosity may assess age differences in conformity to adult expectations rather than age differences in altruism' (p. 753). This critique could apply to other inferences made from laboratory studies, too. Of course, it could be argued that such compliance is similar to, or involved in, altruistic behaviour; but if so, it does seem different from the kind of 'genuine' helpfulness envisaged in our original definition, or seen in very young children who have as yet little notion of what is socially expected of them.

Observational studies

Many of the problems inherent in such experimental studies of prosocial behaviour can be overcome by observing children in natural settings. Zahn-Waxler and Radke-Yarrow (1982) have described a study of 24 children that used a combination of cross-sectional and longitudinal design to span the age range from around 12 to 30 months. These researchers relied on mothers' recordings. Mothers were asked to report on their children's response to events in which negative emotions were expressed (a subset of this investigation is highlighted in box 8.1, and examples 1 and 2 above are from their studies). On the basis of these observations, it was possible to identify progressive levels of empathy on the part of the target child towards another's emotion: *personal distress*, where the child was emotionally affected by the incident; *emotional contagion*, where the child displayed an emotion in sympathy with the other person; *egocentric empathy*, where the child offered support to the other person in the form of something that they would find comforting themselves, such as a favourite toy or blanket. Two noticeable changes were found between the younger children (aged up to about 20 months) and the older children (20–30 months). The younger children often orientated to someone's distress, and often cried, fretted or whimpered themselves, but only seldom acted prosocially. Such prosocial behaviour as there was usually took the form of simply touching or patting the victim, or presenting objects. Prosocial behaviour was much more likely in the older children, however, and occurred in about one-third of all incidents reported. It took a variety of forms, such as reassurance ('you'll be all right'), combative altruism (hitting an aggressor), giving objects (e.g., bandages, comfort objects) or getting help from a third party. This developmental pattern was similar whether the child was a bystander to the distress or had caused it. From this study it is clear that children below 3 years of age can show some forms of prosocial behaviour. This is especially so after about 20 months, which is when sensori-motor development is completed (chapter 12), and thus when children understand cause–effect relations and the distinction between themselves and other people (chapter 6). Before this age children often seek comfort as much for themselves as for the other person, but after about 20 months they are increasingly aware that the distress is in the other person (and, somewhat later, of whether they have caused it or not), and act more appropriately.

Other researchers have documented prosocial behaviour by children in nursery school. Eisenberg-Berg and Hand (1979), for example, watched 35 children aged 4 and 5 years in preschool classes. They found that a child showed sharing, helping or comforting behaviour about once every 10–12 minutes, on average. There were few age or sex differences. In an Israeli study, Bar-Tal et al. (1982) observed 156 children aged 18 months to 6 years. Prosocial behaviours made up some 10–20 per cent of all social contacts. Again, there were no sex differences and no very prominent age changes.

Grusec (1982) used the same technique as Zahn-Waxler and Radke-Yarrow (1982), namely mothers' reports, to examine prosocial behaviour in children aged 4 and 7 years (example 3, p. 245, is from her study). She asked mothers to record, over a 4-week period, any act in which their child intended to help another (excluding regular duties). Mothers recorded about one such act every day or so. No difference was found between boys and girls. Some interesting results from this study are shown in table 8.1. The top half of the table shows it was rare for mothers not to respond when they observed an act of helpfulness by their child. The great majority of such acts were 'rewarded' verbally, by thanking or praising, or physically by smiling or hugging. Similarly, the lower half of the table shows that if a child was not helpful when the mother thought that help was appropriate, it was very rare for the mother to accept this. Usually she encouraged the child to be helpful, either directly ('altruism requested') or in general terms ('moral exhortation'), or by expressing disapproval ('scolding', 'frowning'). More rarely, she would explain to the child how his or her lack of helpfulness might affect others ('empathy training'), or directly instruct or coerce the child to behave appropriately.

Grusec et al. (2002) note that the general ability of a child to take the perspective of others affects their capacity to demonstrate emotional responsiveness to the distress of another in a specific context. For example, children who regularly and intensely express negative emotions tend to demonstrate less empathy and more personal upset when faced with the distress of another. By contrast, children who are able to regulate their own emotions effectively show more empathic responsiveness and less personal upset towards another person's distress (Eisenberg et al., 1998). Grusec et al. conclude that the ability to maintain an optimal level of arousal in response to the distress of another is conducive to high empathy and relatively low personal distress, whereas becoming over-aroused leads to high personal distress and low empathy.

Table 8.1 Mothers' reports of reactions to their child's behaviour

	Child spontaneously helpful (% of incidents)	
	4-yr-olds	7-yr-olds
Acknowledge, thank, express personal appreciation	33	37
Smile, thank warmly, hug	17	18
Praise act or child	19	16
No outward response	8	9

	Child fails to be helpful (% of incidents)	
	4-yr-olds	7-yr-olds
Moral exhortation	26	30
Request altruism	22	30
Scold, frown	18	15
Empathy training	6	5
Direct or force behaviour	6	5
Accept lack of altruism	8	5

Source: Grusec, 1982

Factors Influencing Prosocial Behaviour in the Family and in School

Temperament plays an important part in such emotional responsiveness to others' distress but so too do the socialization practices of the family. We have seen that mothers do not stand by idly when their child does, or does not, show helpful or altruistic behaviour; the evidence is that they often intervene. Fathers, teachers and peers are also likely to respond to a child's prosocial behaviour. What effect do such interventions have? We have also seen that interventions may take the form of reinforcement (e.g., praise) or punishment for not being helpful, modelling of altruistic behaviour, or moral exhortation. Are some techniques more effective than others? And what does the child contribute to this process?

One attempt to look at the effectiveness of different parental techniques in a naturalistic way is documented in box 8.1. This study suggests that (for 2-year-olds) affective explanation as to the consequences of their action (moralizing or prohibition with reasons), perhaps combined with some power assertion by the mother, is associated with prosocial behaviour by the child. However, this being an uncontrolled correlational study, cause-and-effect relations cannot be deduced with confidence.

Mothers who are empathic, who score highly on perspective-taking tasks and who respond sensitively to their children's needs are more likely to have children who are high in empathy towards others. There are clear links with secure parent–child attachment (see chapter 4 on attachment theory), with securely attached children demonstrating greater empathy towards their peers. Krevans and Gibbs (1996) also found that when mothers regularly encouraged their children to reflect on the consequences of their behaviour and how it might affect other people there was a greater likelihood that their children would show empathy for others and also demonstrate more prosocial behaviour. Grusec and Goodnow (1994) suggest that this process occurs through the internalization of parental values in two stages:

1   the child's accurate perception of the parent's message through frequent and consistent expression of that value in a form that is appropriate for the child's cognitive level;
2   acceptance of that value by experiencing it as reasonable and appropriate, by being willing to listen to the message and by having some sense of self-generated action.

Punishment for failing to act prosocially behaviour would not be effective since it would be perceived by the child as unfair. However, where parents regularly demonstrated empathy for that child, and where the child was happy to respond to parental reasoning and experienced little threat to their own autonomy by helping another, then the internalization of prosocial values was more likely to occur.

Experiences with siblings are also important in promoting prosocial behaviour because of the differences in age between siblings. This has implications for the emergence of sensitivity and empathy towards others. Some quite striking age consistencies were reported in a longitudinal study on siblings (Dunn and Kendrick, 1982; see also chapter 5): for example, they found that children (aged 1–3 years) who showed friendly interest and concern for a new baby in the first 3 weeks after birth were also likely to respond with concern if their younger sibling was hurt or distressed at a follow-up 6 years later (the correlation was 0.42, significant at the 0.05 level). They also noticed an interplay between helping and rivalry. The help that children offered their siblings was not necessarily appreciated by the recipients! The giving of help by an older child could, for example, elicit anger from a younger sibling.

When Dunn et al. (1991) followed up the siblings who had been observed as preschoolers, they found that there were links between the quality of the relationships between the siblings in the preschool period and the children's behaviour at a later stage. Those who had grown up with a sibling who was unfriendly or aggressive were more likely as adolescents to have emotional difficulties in their relationships with others than were those whose siblings had been warm and affectionate towards them. Children who perceived that their sibling was receiving more attention and affection from the mother were more likely to show aggressive or difficult behaviour in childhood and adolescence. It appeared that relative differences in how loved a young person feels have an influence on how socially adjusted they are. Dunn and her colleagues suggest that the growth of social understanding develops out of the child's experience of balancing her preoccupation with self against responsiveness to the feelings and emotions of others.

Dunn (1995) argues that participation in the moral discourse of the family begins very early on in the child's life and that prosocial behaviour can only be fully understood if we consider it in the context of the dynamic web of family relationships.

Dunn is convinced that current theories of moral and sociocognitive development neglect key aspects of the ways in which children come to understand and relate to one another. It is her belief that the growth of understanding involves more than 'an unfolding of cognitive abilities', and that 'self-concern and affective experience play central roles in the interactions in which moral and social rules are articulated and fostered, and the development of the child's theory of mind' (see chapter 14) (Dunn, 1995, p. 341). In other words, the complexity of a young child's social understanding and awareness of others' mental states is closely linked to the nature of their family interactions and interpersonal relationships. Dunn's research suggests that psychologists should place more emphasis on social understanding as a phenomenon that *emerges from* relationships rather than as an *individual* characteristic of a particular child. The study of siblings in the family context has highlighted the importance of differences in family discourse about the social world in influencing the nature of a child's social development. For example, children who grow up in families where there is a great deal of discussion about feelings and causality perform better than other children on assessments of social understanding 14 months later. Dunn (1992) suggests that the foundations for such qualities as caring, consideration and kindness are well established by the age of 3 years:

> For a young child whose own goals and interests are often at odds with – and frustrated by – others in the family, it is clearly adaptive to begin to understand those other family members and the social rules of the shared family world. The study of siblings has highlighted why it is important that social understanding should be high on the developmental agenda.

Prosocial behaviour in school and the peer group

Boulton et al. (1999) found that young people who have a reciprocated best friend are much more likely to be protected from aggressive acts of social exclusion on the part of the peer group. The implications of this finding are that, in the context of a reciprocated friendship, young people are motivated to help one another against peer relationship difficulties (see chapter 5). This confirms the view that vulnerable young people can be protected by appropriate befriending interventions but that in the absence of such support they cannot rely on their peers to act prosocially. The influence of peer group values on young people is very important (Craig and Pepler, 1995) (see also chapter 5 on bullying and social exclusion).

These are not surprising findings, but they do put helping behaviour in a social context. Rogers and Tisak (1996) found that 2nd, 4th and 6th grade children, when asked to reason about peers' responses to aggression, reasoned out of a concern for the well-being of all peers involved in a conflict and showed awareness of the relationship between victim and perpetrator. The findings indicated that children were able to consider the logic of different responses to aggression. It may well be that some ways of promoting prosocial and altruistic behaviour are those which both provide some social reward or praise for the child, and also appeal to the child's developing sense of reasoning or justice.

One arena in which these ideas about training young people to act prosocially can be put to the test is in the school. There is a great deal of evidence giving support to the idea that, in order to foster prosocial behaviour in educational settings, teachers must incorporate values of trust and cooperation into the whole school community and not simply 'teach' prosocial behaviour as a series of separate lessons, for example a once-a-week discussion of social and moral issues (Cowie et al., 1994; Foot et al., 1990; Hertz-Lazarowitz and Miller, 1992).

Peer support systems in schools

In order to create a structure in which prosocial behaviour can be enhanced, many schools are developing systems of peer support to supplement the work of pastoral care staff (Cowie et al., 2002; Cowie and Wallace, 1999). Peer support systems take many forms but there are three broad types:

1 *Befriending* approaches: schemes in which specially trained pupils support peers who are, for example, new to a school or have particular learning difficulties. In some cases, (as in buddying or peer tutoring) pupils are paired with another pupil. In others, befrienders look out for pupils who may be socially excluded or bullied during break times, offer companionship and try to integrate them into appropriate friendship groups.

2 *Mediation/conflict resolution* approaches: these schemes offer a structured method for empowering young people to defuse interpersonal disagreements among their peers, including bullying, racist name-calling, fighting and quarrelling. These methods are reported to result in a substantial reduction in the incidence of aggressive behaviour. During the mediation the peer supporters are responsible for facilitating a resolution of the conflict and for working out a joint solution. For a more detailed description see box 8.2.

3 *Counselling* approaches: these schemes extend befriending and mediation approaches into interventions based more overtly on counselling models. Training is often carried out by a qualified counsellor or psychotherapist who will offer supporters a wider range of counselling skills. Supervision is modelled on professional counselling supervision, usually facilitated by a person with knowledge of experiential work. These approaches are usually implemented through a system of formal referral soon after the request for help has been received and can include telephone helplines, individual meetings or small group sessions.

Given the appropriate training and supervision, peer helpers demonstrate that they are able to offer themselves as a resource to peers troubled by experiences of victimization, rejection, isolation, relationship difficulties and other problems common during childhood and adolescence. Other studies have confirmed that this prosocial behaviour has benefits for the helpers as well as for those who seek help, and for the school as a whole (Naylor and Cowie, 1999).

Summary

We can summarize the factors in the family and the school that encourage prosocial behaviour in young people. According to Grusec et al. (2002) there are three aspects to the parent–child relationship that are conducive to the internalization of prosocial values:

1   The parents are warm and nurturing, and offer unconditional approval of their children's actions.
2   The child is securely attached and experiences his or her caregivers as empathic and sensitive.
3   The parents are responsive to the reasonable demands of their children.

In addition, research supports the idea that reasoning is a better strategy than punishment or power assertive interventions to control the child; reasoning helps children to consider the outcomes of their actions and is conducive to the emergence of empathy to others' feelings. It is also important for adults to model good practice in the course of everyday interactions with children.

The reciprocal nature of peer and sibling relationships also play a crucial part in the development of prosocial behaviour, both through direct experience of others' responses and through witnessing the distress of others. Interactions among peers and siblings provide many opportunities to help and comfort others and so offer a rich source of influence on prosocial development. We need to take account of the role of the peer group as the social setting in which children and adolescents discover how to deal with their own emotions, how to interact with others in distress, how to deal with relationship difficulties, how to present their emotions publicly and how to hide them, and how to maintain their status within the peer group. In school settings peer support systems have been found to be effective methods for training young people to become prosocial when faced with conflicts or social problems among their peer group.

Sex differences in prosocial behaviour

It is widely believed that girls are more prosocial than boys and indeed many studies seem to confirm this view. Cowie et al. (2002), in their longitudinal study of peer support in 35 secondary schools, found that girls (80 per cent) regularly outnumbered boys (20 per cent) in the ranks of peer supporters. In interviews, 80 peer supporters described threats to boys' sense of masculinity if they participated in caring activities such as peer support:

'It is seen as wimpy . . . Yeah, they (boys) dropped out – peer pressure.'

(13-year-old girl peer supporter)

'We used to get called "queer supporters".'

(15-year-old boy peer supporter)

Only a minority of boys felt strong enough to challenge the stereotype:

When I became a peer supporter, we all thought it unmanly, but now all my friends think it brilliant. There are none of my mates that call me names because they know that you are there and you can help them, and I have helped a lot of my friends.

(15-year-old boy peer supporter)

There was no evidence to suggest that boys were incapable of acting in the role of peer supporter. In fact, in an earlier study (Cowie, 2000) it was found that in single-sex boys' schools teachers who organized peer support schemes were inundated with offers of help. But in the context of coeducational schools, boys appeared to find it difficult to withstand the pressure from peers to maintain a distance from caring activities.

Björkqvist et al. (2000) argue that girls are better at peaceful conflict resolution just as they are more skilled than boys at indirect aggression (see chapter 5). One explanation is that both types of conflict behaviour require a relatively high level of social intelligence, so girls can use their skills either to escalate conflict or to resolve it. At the same time, they found that empathy correlates strongly with peaceful conflict resolution. They argue that indirect aggression requires more intelligence than direct verbal aggression, which, in turn, requires more intelligence than physical aggression. Since empathy mitigates interpersonal aggression, empathy training has a key role to play in reducing aggression in young people. Similarly, Cunningham et al. (1998) (box 8.2) found gender differences in involvement in conflict resolution interventions in junior schools. They conclude that, since boys are less likely to experience or employ relational or verbal aggression, they may be less likely to detect this type of aggressive interaction, especially when it involves girls. In addition, if boys are less disturbed by relational aggression, they may assume that it is not worth intervening to prevent it.

Olweus and Endresen (1998) found significant differences between adolescent boys and girls in the capacity to respond with empathy towards a fellow pupil in distress (as described in a vignette). Girls showed a straightforward pattern of development, with an increase over time in empathic concern towards both boys and girls. Boys, by contrast, showed a similar pattern with regard to girls but a decreasing trend in empathic responsiveness towards peers of their own gender. Olweus and Endresen suggested that the male decrease in empathy for other boys may reflect an increasing identification with a masculine role and a desire to enhance their status in boys' peer groups. Boys' increasing empathic responsiveness towards girls indicates that while it is acceptable to be protective towards girls since this is in harmony with the masculine role, it is much less acceptable to offer this kind of support to another boy.

However, Grusec et al. (2002) overview recent studies that indicate the need to view such results critically. Girls, they suggest, are more likely than boys to be kind or considerate but not more inclined to share, comfort or help. They are more likely to act prosocially when the person in need is an adult rather than another child. They are also more likely to be judged as prosocial when the measure is one of self-report but less so when it is a direct observation or where physiological measures of empathy are used. Grusec et al. consider that these results may be due to differential socialization practices on the part of parents towards their sons and daughters. For example, girls may be praised for altruistic actions while boys are criticized for them (see also pp. 190–4).

Cross-cultural differences in prosocial behaviour

Research into cross-cultural differences in prosocial behaviour provides us with further insights into the process. As Fry and Fry (1997) argue, through socialization within a culture, individuals acquire views on the nature of the social world, develop sets of values and understand the meaning of events within their community. Cross-cultural studies add a new perspective since there are quite wide variations in the values that different cultural groups place on prosocial behaviour and altruism.

Whiting and Whiting (1975) observed children between 3 and 11 years in six different countries (p. 189). They found that children from Kenya, Mexico and the Philippines acted more prosocially than those from Okinawa, India or the USA. One especially important difference among the cultures lay in the assignment of household chores, especially in the case of younger children. The more prosocial cultures were those in which women's contribution to the family economy was highest. As a result, these women delegated more responsibility to their children so giving them opportunities to develop their prosocial behaviour. By contrast, cultures that place high value on individual success are more likely to foster competitiveness than cooperation in their children in order to enhance their chances of personal success in the future.

Robarchek and Robarchek (1992) studied two cultures' different sets of values and consequent behaviour towards one another. The Waorani people of the Amazon are extremely warlike, fight constantly with their neighbours and have a strong philosophy of individualism. If there is a raid from a neighbouring tribe, each person will save themselves regardless of the fate of friends or members of their family. By contrast, the Semai of the Malaysian rainforest are an extremely cooperative society, and place great emphasis on mutual support among family members and the community. The children in these two contrasting societies are exposed to different value systems and, not surprisingly, develop differently with regard to prosocial behaviour. Yet it would be mistaken to assume that these people differ in the extent to which they love their children. In everyday life, both the Waorani and the Semai adults are affectionate and non-punitive towards their children, so there is evidence of the caring, supportive patterns of behaviour which we expect to find in families and communities. How can we explain the contrasting ways in which prosocial behaviour is expressed in different social settings? Eisenberg and Mussen (1989), in a review of cross-cultural studies of cooperation among children, conclude that in societies where cooperation is rewarded, the children show high levels of prosocial behaviour; where it is not rewarded or valued it is less likely to appear. Trevarthen and Logotheti (1989) make a similar point when they contrast children from communities where there is a large amount of violence and conflict. In those circumstances, they argue, children are much more likely to develop relationships that are unsociable and manipulative, in which the emphasis is on individual survival rather than on mutual cooperation (but see box 17.1 for another perspective).

Österman et al. (1997) carried out a study of 2094 boys and girls from four cultures and in three age groups (8, 11 and 15 years). They found that age trends in the different countries were almost identical. However, there were some cultural differences. Finnish and Israeli children used more constructive conflict resolution behaviour than Polish and Italian children. Finnish children withdrew from conflicts more than others. Polish children used less of all types of conflict resolution behaviour than the others. In all cultures, however, the researchers found that girls were consistently more likely than boys to make use of constructive conflict-resolution and third-party intervention; in addition, girls were significantly more likely to recommend socialized tactics in resolving a conflict than were boys. One explanation is that females across cultures are more skilled at interpreting and sending nonverbal signals. Another is that females are generally smaller in size and have less physical strength than males so females learn that overt, aggressive behaviour does not pay. Instead, they learn to use socialized tactics to resolve conflicts (or alternatively indirect strategies to escalate conflicts).

These findings add further confirmation to the view that the development and fostering of prosocial behaviour takes place within a social and cultural framework of moral values. Some psychologists (for a review see Woodhead et al., 1998) argue that there is a collective dimension as opposed to individual functioning in social processes and that shared discourses about conflict resolution and social responsibility are socially constructed within a particular context. Although there is still controversy over the existence of a direct relationship between cultural values and specific manifestations of prosocial behaviour in children, in a broad sense we can be justified in concluding that there are cultural variations in what constitutes desirable prosocial behaviour in any society. For example, as we have seen, qualities of reciprocity and responsiveness to others' needs are judged more positively in a culture that values interdependence and compliance with social roles than in one that values autonomy and feelings of self-generation. This has led a number of researchers in the field to ask whether current Western emphases on autonomy and self-generation may need to be replaced. 'The growing heterogeneity of Western culture challenges researchers to rethink some very basic theoretical issues in the study of socialisation.' (Grusec et al., 2002).

In the next section, we examine in more detail how children and adolescents develop the capacity to act and reason morally.

The Development of Moral Reasoning

Moral reasoning refers to how we reason, or judge, whether an action is right or wrong: it is different from moral behaviour. Often, of course, we do follow our moral reasoning when we decide on a course of behaviour. For example, we might reason that it is right to give some money for overseas aid, and then do so. It is equally clear that we do not always follow our moral reasoning. For example, if we are incorrectly given extra change in a supermarket, we might reason that it is wrong to keep it, but still do so.

We are concerned here with the way in which moral reasoning (often referred to as moral judgement) develops. One important strand in the study of moral reasoning by psychologists is closely linked to cognitive development. Such an approach is called 'cognitive developmental'. Work in this area was pioneered by Piaget, and this tradition has been carried on in the USA by Kohlberg and others.

Piaget's theory

Piaget turned his attention to moral reasoning in children early in his career. He spent time in the suburbs of Geneva watching children at play and also posing them moral dilemmas. The results of his investigations were reported in *The Moral Judgement of the Child* (first English publication in 1932). Piaget describes how he studied the boys' game of marbles. He was interested in how children acquired the rules of the game, where they thought the rules came from, and whether the rules could be altered. Here, the 'rules of the game' are taken as corresponding to the 'rules of society' for adults – you should follow the rules, you can break them, but there are sanctions if you do so. Piaget used four methods here.

1   he asked the children directly ('teach me the rules');
2   he played with a child, pretending to be ignorant so that the child had to explain the rules – though not too ignorant in case the child gave up in frustration!;
3   he watched the child play with others; and
4   he interviewed children about where rules came from and whether they could be changed.

From his results Piaget distinguished three stages in children's awareness of rules. In the first (up to 4 to 5 years), rules were not understood. In the second stage (from 4–5 to 9–10 years) the rules were seen as coming from a higher authority (e.g., adults, God, the town council) and could not be changed. In the third (from 9–10 years onwards) rules were seen as mutually agreed by the players, and thus open to change if all the players agreed. (Piaget also distinguished corresponding stages in how the child's awareness of rules was put into practice. He also examined a girls' game, a version of hide-and-seek, in much less detail and described similar stages occurring somewhat earlier, perhaps as the game was simpler.)

Here are two protocols (slightly edited) from Piaget's book, which illustrate the second two stages, and also Piaget's method of interview (called the 'clinical method', see p. 389).

B. E. N. (10 years, but still at the second stage)

Piaget: Invent a rule.
B. E. N.:   I couldn't invent one straight away like that.
Piaget: Yes you could. I can see that you are cleverer than you make yourself out to be.
B. E. N.:   Well, let's say that you're not caught when you are in the square.
Piaget: Good. Would that come off with the others?
B. E. N.:   Oh, yes, they'd like to do that.
Piaget: Then people could play that way?
B. E. N.:   Oh, no, because it would be cheating.
Piaget: But all your pals would like to, wouldn't they?
B. E. N.:   Yes, they all would.
Piaget: Then why would it be cheating?
B. E. N.:   Because I invented it: it isn't a rule! It's a wrong rule because it's outside of the rules. A fair rule is one that is in the game.

(Piaget, 1932, p. 58)

G. R. O. S. (13 years, and at the third stage)

Piaget: Are you allowed to change the rules at all?
G. R. O. S.:   Oh, yes. Some want to, and some don't. If the boys play that way you have to play like they do.
Piaget: Do you think you could invent a new rule?
G. R. O. S.:   Oh, yes you could play with your feet.
Piaget: Would it be fair?
G. R. O. S.:   I don't know. It's just my idea.
Piaget: And if you showed it to the others would it work?
G. R. O. S.:   It would work all right. Some other boys would want to try. Some wouldn't, by Jove! They would stick to the old rules. They'd think they'd have less of a chance with this new game.
Piaget: And if everyone played your way?
G. R. O. S.:   Then it would be a rule like the others.

(Piaget, 1932, p. 63)

The difference between these two stages was thought of by Piaget as being that between a 'heteronomous' morality of coercion or restraint, and an 'autonomous' morality of cooperation or reciprocity. As the child's conception of rules changes, from their being absolutely fixed to their being mutually agreed, so a unilateral respect for adult or higher authority changes towards an equality with peers. These are cognitive changes, which in Piaget's later theory can be linked to the decline in egocentrism and the growth of operational thought (chapter 12). Important other factors are the growing independence from parents, and especially interaction with same-aged peers. Different children may have acquired slightly different versions of the rules, and through playing together these discrepancies will come to light and have to be resolved. This contact with divergent viewpoints, Piaget thought, was a crucial element in evolving the autonomous morality of reciprocity.

It is surprising that this ingenious, semi-naturalistic study was not followed up for decades. Despite its impact, it was only based on an unspecified but small number of participants. A large-scale follow-up was made some 50 years later by a Spanish psychologist, José Linaza (1984). He interviewed several hundred children, in England and Spain, about a number of games. He confirmed the main aspects of Piaget's sequence, and elaborated it. No difference was found in the sequence between English and Spanish children, or between boys and girls playing the same game, though different games did vary in the age at which certain stages were usually attained.

Piaget also reported the results of another study in his 1932 book. In this he presented children with several pairs of short episodes or stories which posed a problem of moral judgement. An example is given below:

> A little boy who is called John is in his room. He is called to dinner. He goes into the dining room. But behind the door there was a chair, and on the chair there was a tray with fifteen cups on it. John couldn't have known that there was all this behind the door. He goes in, the door knocks against the tray, bang go the fifteen cups and they all get broken!

> Once there was a little boy whose name was Henry. One day when his mother was out he tried to get some jam out of the cupboard. He climbed up on the chair and stretched out his arm. But the jam was too high up and he couldn't reach it and have any. But while he was trying to get it he knocked over a cup. The cup fell down and broke.

Piaget would tell children this pair of stories, and get them to repeat each to make sure that they remembered them. Then he would ask them to make a judgement as to which child in the two stories was the naughtiest. He found that before 9 or 10 years children often judged on the basis of the amount of damage, whereas after this age the child judged by motive or intention. Here are two short extracts from the protocols:

S. C. H. M. A. (aged 6)

Piaget:	Are those children both naughty, or is one not so naughty as the other?
S. C. H. M. A:	Both just as naughty.
Piaget:	Would you punish them the same?
S. C. H. M. A.:	No. The one who broke fifteen plates.
Piaget:	And would you punish the other one more, or less?
S. C. H. M. A.:	The first broke lots of things, the other one fewer.
Piaget:	How would you punish them?
S. C. H. M. A.:	The one who broke the fifteen cups: two slaps. The other one, one slap.

(Piaget, 1932, p. 120)

Table 8.2 Summary of Piaget's stages of moral judgement

Up to 4 or 5 yr	From 4–5 yr to 9–10 yr	After 9–10 yr
Premoral judgement	*Moral realism* (Heteronomous morality of constraint)	*Moral subjectivism* (Autonomous morality of cooperation)
Rules not understood	Rules come from higher authority and cannot be changed	Rules are created by people and can be changed by mutual consent
	Evaluate actions by outcomes	Evaluate actions by intentions
	Punishment as inevitable retribution	Punishment as chosen to fit crime

Source: Based on Piaget, 1932

C. O. R. M. (aged 9)

> *C. O. R. M.*: Well, the one who broke them as he was coming isn't naughty, 'cos he didn't know there was any cups. The other one wanted to take the jam and caught his arm on a cup.
> *Piaget*: Which one is the naughtiest?
> *C. O. R. M.*: The one who wanted to take the jam.
> *Piaget*: How many cups did he break?
> *C. O. R. M.*: One.
> *Piaget*: And the other boy?
> *C. O. R. M.*: Fifteen.
> *Piaget*: Which one would you punish the most?
> *C. O. R. M.*: The boy who wanted to take the jam. He knew, he did it on purpose.
>
> (Piaget, 1932, pp. 123–4)

In the first of these stages, children judge by the objective amount of damage, and also tend to see punishment as inevitable and retributive. Piaget called this stage 'moral realism', as compared with the 'moral subjectivism' of the following stage, in which subjective intent is taken account of, and punishment is seen more as a lesson suited to the offence. Piaget related these stages to his idea of heteronomous and autonomous morality from the marbles study. A summary of his stages is given in table 8.2.

There are problems with Piaget's dilemma method; many are pointed out in a critique by Turiel (1998). Characteristically, Piaget makes it difficult for the child by having unequal consequences in the two stories (15 cups versus one cup broken), thus in effect tempting the child to ignore intention. The stories are badly designed: for example, it is not clear that Henry was being naughty in going to get the jam, and he probably didn't intend to break the cup, he was just careless. So the 'bad intention' in this story has to be inferred. There are also considerable memory demands made on young children (Kail, 1990). Several studies have shown that when methodological improvements are made (e.g., contrasting intent and accident when there is equal damage) children as young as 5 years will judge on the basis of intent.

Further research has shown that young children do not have a monolithic conception of rules as constraints. They distinguish between behaviours that violate purely social conventions (e.g., not putting your belongings in the right place), and those that violate moral conventions (e.g., not sharing a toy, hitting a child). A study by Smetana (1981) of children aged 2–5 in two American nursery schools found that children distinguished between these two kinds of behaviour in terms of whether it was dependent on context (home, or school), and on the amount of punishment it deserved. Children are able to distinguish between different kinds of social rules and acts, and they are able to demonstrate conceptions of autonomy, rights and democracy. Even young children have moral concepts that are independent of authority or existing social rules, and their moral judgements are sensitive both to the context of these rules and the context of their application (Helwig and Turiel, 2002; and p. 287).

Despite limitations, the approach of presenting children and young people verbally with moral dilemmas has been pursued by a number of psychologists in the USA. It was used especially by Kohlberg, over a longer age span than Piaget and on a more ambitious scale.

Kohlberg's theory

Kohlberg researched on the development of moral reasoning for some 30 years, and his theory has proved influential in education and criminology, as well as psychology. The work started with, and extended from, research for his doctoral thesis, in which he commenced in 1955 a longitudinal study of 50 American males initially aged 10–26 years. These participants were re-interviewed every three years. Kohlberg asked them questions, such as 'why shouldn't you steal from a store?', and also posed them story dilemmas. Of a number of dilemmas, the most famous is that of Heinz and the druggist (Kohlberg, 1969, p. 379).

In Europe, a woman was near death from a special kind of cancer. There was one drug that the doctor thought might save her. It was a form of radium that a druggist in the same town had recently discovered. The drug was expensive to make, but the druggist was charging ten times what the drug cost him to make. He paid $200 for the radium and charged $2,000 for a small dose of the drug. The sick woman's husband, Heinz, went to everyone he knew to borrow the money, but he could only get together about $1,000, which is half of what it cost. He told the druggist that his wife was dying, and asked him to sell it cheaper or let him pay later. But the druggist said 'No, I discovered the drug and I'm going to make money from it.' So Heinz got desperate and broke into the man's store to steal the drug for his wife.
Should Heinz have done that? Why or why not?

This might seem an artificial dilemma, but in fact something very similar can occur in real life! (see table 8.4). On the basis of these questions and dilemmas, Kohlberg postulated three levels of moral reasoning, each subdivided to make six stages in

Table 8.3   Kohlberg's stages of moral judgement

Level	Stage	What is right
Preconventional	Stage 1 Heteronomous morality	To avoid breaking rules backed by punishment, obedience for its own sake, avoiding physical damage to persons and property
	Stage 2 Individualism, instrumental purpose, and exchange	Following rules only when it is to someone's immediate interest; acting to meet one's own interests and needs, and letting others do the same. Right is what's fair, an equal exchange, a deal, an agreement
Conventional	Stage 3 Mutual interpersonal expectations, relationships and interpersonal conformity	Living up to what is expected by people close to you or what people generally expect of people in your role. 'Being good' is important and means having good motives, showing concern about others and keeping mutual relationships, such as trust, loyalty, respect, and gratitude
	Stage 4 Social system and conscience	Fulfilling the actual duties to which you have agreed. Laws are to be upheld except in extreme cases where they conflict with other fixed social duties. Right is contributing to society, the group, or institution
Postconventional or principled	Stage 5 Social contract or utility and individual rights	Being aware that people hold a variety of values and opinions, that most values and rules are relative to your group but should usually be upheld in the interest of impartiality and because they are the social contract. Some non-relative values and rights like life and liberty, however, must be upheld in any society and regardless of majority opinion
	Stage 6 (hypothetical) Universal ethical principles	Following self-chosen ethical principles. Particular laws or social agreements are usually valid because they rest on such principles. When laws violate these principles, one acts in accordance with the principle. Principles are universal principles of justice: the equality of human rights and respect for the dignity of human beings as individual persons

Source: Adapted from Colby et al., 1983

all. These levels and stages are defined in table 8.3. We look briefly at each level in turn.

Level one: preconventional morality   This is similar to Piaget's morality of constraint. Kohlberg (1976) thinks of it as 'the level of most children under 9, some adolescents, and many adolescent and adult criminal offenders' (p. 33). On this

Table 8.4 'Man tells police that he robbed bank to pay for wife's cancer treatment' (adapted from *Japan Times*, Friday, 25 November 1994)

A man told police he robbed a bank so he could afford cancer treatment for his terminally ill wife. Larry A., 22, was arrested at a police roadblock after a chase on Tuesday following a holdup at the Mid-South Bank.

Detective Rick E. said that Larry A's account of his wife's illness was true. A woman who answered the telephone at Larry A's home and identified herself as his mother said his wife has ovarian cancer.

Larry A. told police he decided to rob the bank after several banks turned him down for a loan.

In the hold-up, a man handed a teller a note demanding $10,000 and threatened to 'blow you up', Detective E. said. The robber had no weapons.

Larry A. was given $4,000, police said. He was jailed on charges of robbery. Bail was set at $200,000.

level the individual reasons in relation to himself and has not yet come fully to understand and uphold conventional or societal rules and expectations. Here is a level-one response from Joe, aged 10 years, one of Kohlberg's original longitudinal sample:

Kohlberg: Why shouldn't you steal from a store?
Joe: It's not good to steal from a store. It's against the law. Someone could see you and call the police.

(Kohlberg, 1976, p. 36)

Level two: conventional morality This is 'the level of most adolescents and adults in our society and in other societies' (p. 33). At this level the individual thinks of what is right as conforming to and upholding the rules, expectations and conventions of society. Here is a level-two response from Joe, now aged 17 years:

Kohlberg: Why shouldn't you steal from a store?
Joe: It's a matter of law. It's one of our rules that we're trying to help protect everyone, protect property, not just to protect a store. It's something that's needed in our society. If we didn't have these laws, people would steal, they wouldn't have to work for a living, and our whole society would get out of kilter.

(Kohlberg, 1976, p. 36)

Level three: postconventional morality This level 'is reached by a minority of adults and is usually reached after the age of 20' (p. 33). Someone at this level broadly understands and accepts the rules of society, but only because they accept some general moral principles underlying these rules. If such a principle comes in conflict with society's rules, then the individual judges by principle rather than by convention. Here is a level-three response from Joe, now aged 24 years:

Kohlberg: Why shouldn't you steal from a store?
Joe: It's violating another person's rights, in this case to property.
Kohlberg: Does the law enter in?

Joe:	Well, the law in most cases is based on what is morally right so it's not a separate subject, it's a consideration.
Kohlberg:	What does 'morality' or 'morally right' mean to you?
Joe:	Recognising the rights of other individuals, first to life and then to do as he pleases as long as it doesn't interfere with somebody else's rights.

(Kohlberg, 1976, pp. 36–7)

As a cognitive-developmental theorist, Kohlberg supposed that the level of moral reasoning was dependent on having achieved a level of cognitive development, and also of social perspective or role-taking (chapter 12). He thought that someone still at the concrete operational stage would be limited to preconventional moral judgement (stages 1 and 2). Someone at early formal operations would be limited to conventional morality (stages 3 and 4). Postconventional morality would be dependent on late formal operations being achieved.

Kohlberg hypothesized that in all societies, individuals would progress upwards through these stages, in sequence (stages would not be skipped, and subjects would not regress). He also hypothesized that an individual would be attracted by reasoning just above their own on the scale, but would not understand reasoning more than one stage above; if true, this would have obvious implications for moral education.

Early criticisms

Kurtines and Greif (1974) made a substantial number of criticisms of Kohlberg's methodology. They pointed out that the moral judgement score of an individual was assessed from his or her scores on a number of dilemmas, yet the different dilemmas were derived intuitively and did not intercorrelate very highly. The scale was criticized as being unreliable, and the 'clinical method' of interview (similar to Piaget's) as being subjective. The validity of the scale was also called into question, since the invariance of sequence could not be properly proved from Kohlberg's sample if that was the sample from which he derived the sequence in the first place.

Damon (1977) elaborated the criticism that the original dilemmas were intuitive, and in many ways unrealistic. How does the 'Heinz' problem appear to a 10- or 17-year-old? Damon listened to actual moral debates among children, and made up a number of interview items, such as:

All of these boys and girls are in the same class together. One day their teacher lets them spend the whole afternoon making paintings and crayon drawings. The teacher thought that these pictures were so good that the class could sell them at the fair. They sold the pictures to their parents, and together the whole class made a lot of money.

Now all the children gathered the next day and tried to decide how to split up the money.

What do you think they should do with it? Why?

Kathy said that the kids in the class who made the most pictures should get most of the money. What do you think? [More probe questions follow.]

From using these more realistic items, Damon derived a six-step 'positive-justice sequence', which describes children's reasoning about sharing, fairness and distributive justice. Other scales and sequences have also been published.

Another criticism has been that Kohlberg's original participants were all male, and that the consequent sequence of stages reflects the development of male morality and is male-biased. This viewpoint has been put most strongly by Carol Gilligan in her book *In a Different Voice: Psychological Theory and Women's Development* (1982). In fact, Gilligan argues quite widely for a 'female psychology' to complement the predominantly 'male psychology' so far developed. So far as moral reasoning is concerned, Gilligan described a short-term longitudinal study in which she interviewed 29 women, aged 15–33, who were attending abortion- and pregnancy-counselling services. These women were faced with a very real moral dilemma – whether to have an abortion or go through with the pregnancy. Gilligan found that these women considered their dilemma in somewhat different terms from what she calls the 'justice' orientation of Kohlberg; rather they focused more on 'responsibility'. Instead of abstract, principled judgements that are universally applicable, as in Kohlberg's stages 5 and 6, these women made rational, context-dependent judgements that were more concerned about the impact of behaviour on people's actual feelings. Put simply, it is a question of whether you put principles before people (a 'male' characteristic), or people before principles (a 'female' characteristic). On this basis, Gilligan suggested an alternative ethic of care and responsibility as being more representative of women's moral-reasoning development.

Later revisions

Kohlberg and his co-workers, especially Anne Colby, revised some aspects of the theory. This, and independent replications, go some way to answering earlier criticisms. A new scoring system, called Standard Issue Scoring, was published in 1978. This scores, separately and with clear referents, the responses to the issue chosen by the respondent for each dilemma; in the Heinz dilemma, for example, this would be the law issue if the respondent says Heinz should not steal, the life issue if Heinz should save his wife. High reliabilities are reported for this scoring method. A rescoring of the original American longitudinal sample produced the results shown in figure 8.1. The stage sequence model is well supported for the first four stages. The low incidence of stage 5 is noticeable. Stage 6 is absent. Kohlberg therefore considered this to be a hypothetical stage, which has not been established empirically (Colby et al., 1983).

This sequence of stages has now been broadly confirmed in many other societies. A review by Snarey (1985) lists studies in 27 different cultural areas; most are cross-sectional, but there have been longitudinal studies in the Bahamas, Canada, India, Indonesia, Israel, Turkey and the USA. Naturally the dilemmas are adapted slightly for different cultures; the Turkish version of the Heinz dilemma, for example, involves a man and his wife who have migrated from the mountains, and are running out of food so that the wife becomes sick; there is only one food store in the village, and the storekeeper charges so much that the man cannot pay. Here is an example of a level-one (stage two) response from Turkey (Snarey, 1985, p. 221):

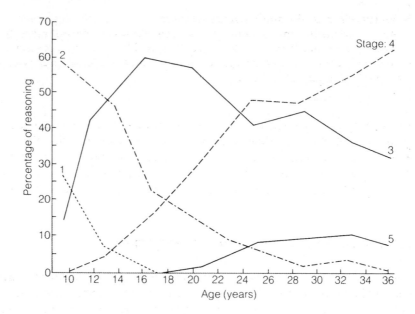

Figure 8.1   Mean percentage of moral reasoning at each stage for each age group (from Colby et al., 1983).

Should the husband have stolen the food?
    Yes. Because his wife was hungry . . . otherwise she will die.
    Suppose it wasn't his wife who was starving but his best friend; should he steal for his friend?
    Yes, because one day when he is hungry his friend would help.
    What if he doesn't love his friend?
    No, [then he should not steal] because when he doesn't love him it means that his friend will not help him later.

In his review Snarey found that almost all the studies in different societies agreed in finding a progression from stages 1 through to 4, at reasonably appropriate ages. There was some discordance about stage 5, however. Very few studies found true stage 5 reasoning, and even transitional stage 5 reasoning was only found in urban societies. It was not found at all in rural or village societies (e.g., Alaskan Eskimos, Guatemala, rural Kenya, New Guinea, rural Turkey). Rather than argue that individuals in these societies are in some sense inferior in moral reasoning, Snarey and other psychologists argue that Kohlberg's level three (stage 5) is significantly culturally biased. It reflects the individualistic, capitalistic orientation of middle-class Western, urban society. Other religions, such as Hinduism, may put less value on individual human life than does the Christian religion. Other societies, socialist or rural, may put more emphasis on collectivist values based on reciprocity and on conflict resolution by interpersonal means. This is illustrated by an extract from an interview with an Israeli kibbutz male (Snarey, 1985, p. 222):

Should Moshe steal the drug? Why or why not?

Yes. . . . I think that the community should be responsible for controlling this kind of situation. The medicine should be made available to all in need: the druggist should not have the right to decide on his own . . . the whole community or society should have the control of the drug.

In this example the person interviewed is somewhat at cross-purposes with the assumptions of the interviewer. Such responses may be difficult to score on Kohlberg's scheme, but (Snarey and others argue) should not therefore be devalued. Oser (1996) criticizes Kohlberg for orienting his theory of moral development too far towards cognitive development and ignoring social contextual influences.

The domain approach to moral development

Turiel, in contrast to Piaget and Kohlberg, proposes that children's thinking is organized from an early age into the domains of *morality* and *social convention*. The moral domain refers to issues of fairness, harm and rights, while the social conventional domain consists of behavioural uniformities that serve to coordinate social interactions in social systems, for example, through dress codes, rules of classrooms, etiquette at meals, etc. Turiel assessed children's moral development in two ways. The first concerns *criterion judgements*. These include judgements about generalizability, university, rule contingency and alterability of prohibitions about the act. For example, judgements about hitting and stealing are found to be generalizable, that is wrong across contexts, and non-rule-contingent, that is wrong even if there were no rule against them. Rules that pertain to moral acts are viewed as unalterable. By contrast, social conventional transgressions, such as calling a teacher by his or her first name, or eating with your fingers, are seen as relative to the social context, or contingent on a specific rule. Such rules that are to do with social conventions are seen to be alterable by authority.

Secondly, Turiel measured the judgements that children use to *justify* their own opinions or actions. He found that children can distinguish between the two domains (morality and social convention) and reason about them in different ways (Turiel, 1998). For example, children judge it acceptable to call a teacher by his or her first name in a school where there is no rule to prohibit it. By contrast, hitting is judged to be wrong, even if a teacher permitted it, and children do not consider that rules about hitting can be altered by the commands of those in authority. Children's judgements of acts are independent of social conventional aspects of the social system and many studies have shown that they distinguish between morality and social convention from quite an early age. Turiel criticized Kohlberg's theory for failing to acknowledge the different ways in which children learn to distinguish between social rules and conventions on the one hand (for example, 'You shall not undress in public' is a social convention) and moral rules which apply to principles of justice, truth and right (for example, 'It is wrong to kill' is a moral rule). Social conventions can be negotiated and changed but moral rules have an intrinsic quality.

Turiel observed that children as young as 4 years could understand the difference between these two domains and found that they saw moral rules as more binding than conventions. From an early age, children are aware of the consequences of moral actions, and understand the emotions felt by other children when they experience pain or injury. Most observational studies have shown that young children do not respond as frequently to conventional violations as to moral transgressions. By contrast, adults more frequently focus on children's violations of social conventions, such as untidiness, rule-keeping and obedience. In the view of Helwig and Turiel (2002), these findings confirm the view that children's domain distinctions are based on early social experiences. Their findings are certainly consistent with the research of Dunn on siblings in the family and the much greater social understanding that young children demonstrated in naturalistic surroundings than they did in the laboratory (p. 140). Turiel's research similarly challenges Kohlberg's view that the principles only outweigh the conventions at a later stage of development, that is during adolescence. However, we need to consider carefully the implications of such research for establishing in law the age at which a young person may be deemed to be morally culpable for their actions.

The age of moral responsibility

The issues that we have been discussing are not only of theoretical interest. They have important applications in real life. A key question concerns the age at which a child may be considered to be morally responsible. This issue has been especially salient in recent years with public moral debate (often highly emotional) over the culpability of children who commit violent crimes. Focusing on cases where children have been killed by other children (for example, the killings in the UK of the toddler James Bulger by two 10-year-old boys and in Norway of 5-year-old Silje Marie Redergard by three boys, one aged 6 and the others aged 5), Asquith (1996) points out the radically different ways in which these tragic deaths were treated in the two countries. In the UK, the 10-year-olds were characterized as 'evil' and there were strong and vociferous public demands for them to receive severe punishments, including life sentences. By contrast, in Norway, no-one, not even Silje's mother, seemed to blame the boys. Silje's mother stated publicly that it was impossible for her to hate small children, despite what they had done to her own daughter.

These reactions illustrate wide differences in the social construction of childhood in these two countries and have implications for the ways in which we begin to consider the development of moral reasoning in children and adolescents. The age of criminal responsibility in the UK is currently one of the lowest in Europe. Asquith argues that these disturbing cases challenge a society to consider and reconsider its concept of moral development and moral reasoning in children. Any system of justice for children must, he claims, be viewed in the wider context of the social, political and economic climate in which it takes place. In the judgment of the European Court of Human Rights, child offenders should be treated differently from adults since such children are still going through the process of development and there is some chance that they can change. Account should be taken not only of their maturity of reasoning and grasp of moral issues but also of their capacity for impulse control.

As Wolff and McCall Smith (2000, p. 136) urge, 'the only purpose of detaining juveniles should be the protection of society and rehabilitation, the second of course promoting the first.' The moral development of children must also be viewed in the context of the family and the community. The harsh treatment of children who commit crimes may be inappropriate if these are children who have been raised in homes that are poverty-stricken and by parents who are themselves inadequate or under severe stress. In this instance, the reason for the child's offending behaviour may clearly lie in the adverse circumstances in which he or she was brought up (see also chapter 17). This leads to another critical question. Can we teach children to act and judge morally?

Can we teach moral values?

Kohlberg's research has encouraged psychologists and some educators to consider the social constructivist principles at the heart of moral reasoning. Although Piaget emphasized the role of peer interaction in the formation of moral judgements, he did not sufficiently explore the ways in which these kinds of social interaction promote further changes in the child's thinking. Doise (1990, p. 61) argues that 'in order to promote ethical behaviour, social representations of ideal relationships have to govern interaction patterns. Normative meta-systems such as the democratic conception of freedom and equality are necessary to further moral development in the Piagetian and Kohlbergian sense.' He proposes that:

- By coordinating their own actions with others, children are led to construct new cognitive coordinations which they are not capable of individually.
- Children who have participated in various social coordinations often become capable of executing these coordinations alone.
- Cognitive operations can be transposed from one setting to another.
- Social interaction becomes a source of cognitive progress through the sociocognitive conflict that it generates.
- Initial competencies are necessary for individuals to benefit from a specific interaction situation.

(adapted from Doise, 1990, p. 62)

The cognitive-developmental approach to moral reasoning has been very influential with definite implications for moral education. In becoming self-aware, children and young people are engaging in a process of learning about significant relationships and social roles. By cooperating with others in a social group that is significant to them, they can gain direct experience of learning about what is morally right for that group as well as the opportunity to learn that reciprocity is of greater value than the maximization of individual benefits.

Schools are in a position to create this kind of context by actively promoting participative involvement in responsible action (involvement in school council; being a class representative; taking part in a peer-support service would all be examples of this in practice) and by teaching democratic procedures and social responsibility through such curriculum initiatives as citizenship education. The Council of Europe (1993) has particularly recommended that education in human rights should be offered to children from pre-school onwards, so heightening awareness of social responsibility and a concern for social justice. A key aim is to produce future citizens who are informed about topical issues and who engage actively in the issues of their community and society at large.

We give one example from UK education policy. The Department for Education and Skills (DfES) recommends that pupils should be taught:

- to research and debate topical issues and problems;
- to understand why and how rules and laws are made and enforced;
- to recognize that there are different kinds of responsibilities, duties and rights at home, at school and in the community;
- to reflect on spiritual, social, moral and cultural issues;
- to resolve differences by looking at alternatives, making decisions and explaining choices;
- to learn about democracy and the institutions that support it;
- to recognize the role of voluntary organizations and pressure groups; and
- to appreciate the range of national, regional, religious and ethnic identities within the UK.

(adapted from QCA/DfEE, 1999, p. 139)

This curriculum is grounded in existing models of social and moral education but teachers are expected to go beyond the immediate family and school to explore democratic processes and national institutions, and to become familiar with topical national and international issues. Where children have been asked about these curricular developments, the results have been encouraging. Holden (2000) interviewed Year 4 and Year 6 (aged 8 and 10 years) primary school children about citizenship lessons that they had recently experienced. She found that children were interested in discussing social relationships and right and wrong. They were able to talk at length about the behaviour expected of them by different people and had a strong sense of some moral values, especially when they were grounded in actual experience, such as the practice of cooperation and respect in the everyday life of the classroom. In this study, peer mediation was stated by the children to be central to their learning of prosocial behaviour (see also box 8.2).

At the same time, the citizenship curriculum by its nature is likely to be controversial in its implementation, and will require teachers to reflect deeply on their own values, with particular reference to social and cultural practices in the home and the community. Parents too will make their voices heard and may not always be in accord with the values being promoted in school. As Walkington and Wilkins (2000) indicate in their commentary on education for critical citizenship, the citizenship curriculum may provide encouragement for teachers already inclined towards a discursive stance in their approach to education. But for those who prefer a didactic style of teaching, it will be difficult to address controversial issues around which inevitably there will be a range of opinions and perceptions. Valsiner (2000) makes the point that adolescents may often develop an anti-establishment stance despite efforts on the part of the state to inculcate them into dominant social values. In fact, by their participation in a number of social groups, not all of which are likely to be mainstream, adolescents may reject the political system by, for example, becoming apathetic or by embracing anti-establishment ideologies.

Oser (1996) argues that the ethos of a community depends as much on its moral heart or emotional conviction, and frequently the 'heart' and the 'head' are not in agreement. In many everyday situations, teachers may find themselves mediating among conflicting parties. This situation is likely to involve discussing the moral values at stake and considering the options that meet criteria of truth, justice and care. Oser suggests that, from an educational point of view, no dilemma discussion leading to a higher developmental stage should occur without relation to action and context. For example, in the case of the Heinz Dilemma, there should be discussion around 'What would I really do in this situation?' A more concrete form would exist in real-life dilemmas where, for example, helping behaviour would be the required outcome of the discussion (for example, through peer support). Most concrete of all would be the decision of a community that was voted upon and enforced by this whole community, and where the outcomes of the decision-making processes were evaluated collectively. From this perspective, educators would need to be familiar not only with cognitive stimulation techniques but also be embedded in what Oser calls 'participatory pedagogy'. (See also collective argumentation, pp. 506–8.)

Emotional literacy

A recent development in the educational domain is the emotional literacy movement (Goleman, 1996) which recognizes the need for schools to educate young people in the management of emotions, in settling disputes peacefully and in learning to live cooperatively with one another. Emotional literacy programmes such as the PATHS (Promoting Alternative Thinking Strategies) curriculum are designed to provide school-aged children with education in issues involved in the expression, understanding and regulation of emotions. The components of an emotional literacy curriculum include:

- *Self-awareness*: self-monitoring and recognition of feelings; building a vocabulary of feelings, making links between thoughts, feelings and behaviour.
- *Personal decision making*: self-monitoring of actions and recognition of their consequences; distinguishing between thought-led and feeling-led decisions.
- *Managing feelings*; self-monitoring of 'self-talk'; challenging negative self-messages; recognizing triggers for strong feelings; finding ways of handling fears, anxieties, anger and sadness.
- *Handling stress*: self-monitoring for signs of stress, recognition of sources of stress, learning to use relaxation methods.
- *Empathy*: understanding others' feelings and concerns; recognizing that different people have different perspectives.

- *Personal responsibility*: taking responsibility for self-management; recognizing consequences of actions and decisions; accepting feelings and moods; persisting to achieve goals and commitments.
- *Conflict resolution*: understanding the difference between need and want; using a 'win-win' model for negotiating solutions.

The PATHS intervention

Here we describe one attempt to teach children about their own and others' emotions and about the ways in which emotions can be managed and regulated in social settings. We have selected this particular intervention because it has been evaluated by a research team (Greenberg et al., 1995), and has been used in the Fast Track project described in chapter 5. PATHS is a preventive intervention that places importance on the developmental integration of affect (emotion), behaviour and cognitive understanding as they relate to social and emotional competence. As we have seen, by the end of the pre-school years, most children are able to interpret the emotional states of themselves and others (see chapter 6), but the development of more complex social cognitions about the emotions has a major impact on children's social behaviour, for example in thinking through the implications of acting pro- or anti-socially. They need to cope with unpleasant emotions and learn to regulate emotions with positive outcomes for self-awareness, self-esteem, self-control, awareness of others' emotions and the capacity to act prosocially. 'Cold' cognitive processes (see chapter 14 on theory of mind) are most effective if the child has also processed the emotional aspects of a particular situation. The peer group plays a key role in developing these social cognitions and the school curriculum provides an influential arena for the facilitation of change.

PATHS is a 60-lesson intervention composed of units on self-control, emotions and problem solving. Lessons involve didactic instruction, role play, class discussions, modelling by teachers and peers, social and self-reinforcement and worksheets. A critical aspect of PATHS focuses on the relationship between cognitive-affective understanding and real-life situations. The evaluation by Greenberg and his colleagues involved 286 children attending first and second grade at pretest, and second and third grade at post-test. Ages ranged from 6 years 5 months to 10 years 6 months at pretest (mean age 8 years) and from 7 years to 11 years 2 months (mean 8 years 10 months) at post-test. 130 received the intervention (83 in mainstream education, 47 in special education) and 156 were in control classrooms (109 in mainstream education and 47 in special education). Special education children received a modified version that placed more emphasis on self-control and less emphasis on the more advanced steps of problem solving.

Children were individually interviewed in the autumn or spring prior to the intervention year; during the following spring, around one month after the end of the intervention they were interviewed again using the same measure, the Kusche Affective Interview Revised (KAI-R) to assess their emotional understanding and to probe a wide range of affective situations and emotional states. Five domains of emotional understanding were assessed: ability to discuss one's

Table 8.5 Affective interview summary variables using the Kusche Affective Interview Revised, KAI-R

1. *Ability to discuss one's own emotional experience*
    a) *Feelings vocabulary*
        Total number of positive feeling words
        Total number of negative feeling words
        Total definitions score: proud, guilty, jealous, nervous, lonely.

    b) *General questions about feelings*
        'Are all feelings okay to have?' ('How do you know that?')

    c) *Discussion of own emotional experiences*
        Proportion of appropriate responses for self:
        Happy, sad, mad, scared, love
        Proud, guilty, jealous, nervous, lonely

2. *Cues used to recognize emotions*
    self: happy, mad, jealous
    other: happy, mad, jealous

3. *Understanding simultaneous feelings*
    sad/mad; sad/happy; love/anger

4. *Display rule for emotions*
    'Can you hide your feelings?' 'How can you do that?'
    'Can other people hide their feelings from you?' 'How can they do that?'

5. *Changing emotions*
    'Can feelings change?'
    'If you felt upset, could your feelings change?' 'Tell me what would happen'
    Sum of developmental level for pictures: happy/sad, jealous/happy.

Source: Adapted from Greenberg, Kusche, Cook and Quamma, 1995

own emotional experiences, cues used to recognize emotions, issues regarding the simultaneity of emotions, display rules for emotions, and whether and how emotions can change. A list of the summary variables is given in table 8.5.

Results of the PATHS intervention

Overall, the evaluation indicated the effectiveness of the one-year PATHS curriculum in improving children's range of feelings vocabulary, their ability to provide appropriate personal examples of the experience of basic feelings, their beliefs that they can hide, manage and change their feelings, and their understanding of cues for recognizing emotions in others. In special-education classes the intervention also significantly improved their understanding of how others manage and hide their feelings and how feelings can be changed. In some instances, there was greater improvement in children whose teachers had rated them as having behavioural difficulties. Among mainstream education children only, the intervention improved their comprehension of complex feeling states. On the other hand, there were no effects with the meta-cognitive recognition of one's own feelings, or in understanding that feelings can happen simultaneously. PATHS' most influential impact was on the children's fluency in discussing basic feelings as well as their beliefs in their own efficacy about managing and changing feelings.

This research gives support to the idea that cognitive knowledge about emotion may affect how we respond to others and how we reflect about ourselves. Thinking ahead about one's actions and their effects on others may therefore lead to greater empathy towards others and a more reflective, responsible stance. More advanced knowledge of emotions may also lead to more advanced strategies for regulating emotions, so to less impulsivity in action. Greenberg and his colleagues acknowledge that there was a wide variation among the teachers in the extent to which they modelled emotional awareness, shared their own emotions and created an ethos of respect for others in the classroom. In this sense, progress is likely to be slow in the early stages as educators become used to working more directly with emotions in schools. It could be argued, therefore, that the potential for interventions such as PATHS is much greater than the present results indicate. It is also interesting to note that this type of intervention is part of a wider movement on the promotion of emotional literacy in children and young people (Kusche and Greenberg, 2001). This study illustrates that it is possible to teach aspects of emotional fluency and understanding in school settings in both mainstream and special education with positive outcomes.

■ Further Reading

For a clear account of the domain approach to moral development see Turiel, E. 1998: The development of morality. In W. Damon and N. Eisenberg (eds), *Handbook of Child Psychology: Vol 3 Social, Emotional, and Personality Development* (5th edn, pp. 863–932). New York: Wiley. Durkin, K. 1995: *Developmental Social Psychology*. Oxford: Blackwell Publishers, has two useful chapters on the topic of prosocial behaviour and moral development.

For a cross-cultural perspective you may find it helpful to read Fry, D. and Björkqvist, K. (eds) 1997: *Cultural Variation in Conflict Resolution: Alternatives to Violence*. Mahwah, NJ: Lawrence Erlbaum Associates.

Piaget, J. 1977 [1932]: *The Moral Judgement of the Child*. Harmondsworth: Penguin, is worth reading for an insight into Piaget's style and methods; the theoretical excerpts are, however, rather dated and heavy going. Unfortunately, there is not a good, simple primer on Piaget's and Kohlberg's theories. For a useful critique of Kohlberg's ideas in practice, read Oser, F. K.1996: Kohlberg's dormant ghosts: the case of education. *Journal of Moral Education*, 25, 253–75.

A useful collection is Foot, H., Morgan, M. and Shute, R. (eds) 1990: *Children Helping Children*. Chichester: John Wiley.

Discussion Points

1 How should we define prosocial behaviour? What implications does the definition have for the way in which prosocial behaviour is studied?
2 Contrast the use of naturalistic and experimental designs for studying what influences prosocial behaviour and altruism.
3 Compare Piaget's two methods of studying moral reasoning.
4 Is Kohlberg's way of obtaining levels of moral reasoning biased towards male, upper/middle-class, urban, Western-educated respondents?
5 How can either moral reasoning, or moral behaviour, be encouraged?

Box 8.1
Child-rearing and children's prosocial initiations towards victims of distress

The objective of this study was to examine the relationship between a mother's behaviour and her child's willingness to help others in distress. Particular attention was paid to mothers' reactions when their child observed or caused distress in another child. An intensive study of a small sample was used. Sixteen mothers of children aged between 18 and 30 months volunteered to take part. For a 9-month period they kept diary records of all incidents of distress in which someone in the child's presence expressed painful feelings, whether due to the child's own actions or not. The child's responses, and the mother's own behaviour, were recorded as soon as possible after the event, on a tape recorder. Mothers received initial training and an investigator visited the home every third week to check on the observations. At these visits the investigator also rated the mother on empathic caregiving (defined as anticipating difficulties, or responding promptly to the child's needs).

The analysis distinguished between those distress incidents that the child did not cause ('bystander incidents'), and those which the child did cause ('child-caused distress'). The children's prosocial behaviour took the form of physical or verbal sympathy ('All better now?'; hugs victim); providing objects such as food, toys or bandages; finding someone else to help; protecting the victim; or giving physical assistance. In bystander incidents children were altruistic on 34 per cent of occasions (range 5–70 per cent), and in child-caused distress they made reparations on 32 per cent of occasions (range 0–60 per cent). There were clearly large individual differences between children, and these are fairly consistent over the two types of incident; the correlation between the two was 0.55, $p < 0.05$.

The mother's behaviour was categorized into various techniques, and the use of each technique calculated (more than one technique could be used in any incident). In bystander incidents, more frequent maternal techniques were:

• no reaction (56 per cent);
• reassurance ('Don't worry, it's OK') (36 per cent); and
• modelling altruism to victim (e.g., picks up and pats crying child) (21 per cent).

In child-caused distress the most frequent maternal techniques were:

• no reaction (31 per cent);
• affective explanation often involving moralizing ('You made Doug cry. It's not

Box Table 8.1.1 Average percentage of incidents in which child shows altruism in bystander incidents and reparation for child-caused distress incidents when mothers are high or low in use of different techniques

Mother's technique	Altruism			Reparation		
	High use	Low use	t test	High use	Low use	t test
No reaction	29	40	n.s.	28	33	n.s.
Affective explanation	42	21	2.60 $p < 0.05$	44	13	4.77 $p < 0.01$
Neutral explanation	37	31	n.s.	37	23	n.s.
Unexplained verbal prohibition	24	42	2.41 $p < 0.05$	18	40	3.37 $p < 0.01$
Suggestion of positive action	32	37	n.s.	30	31	n.s.
Physical restraint	41	27	n.s.	31	29	n.s.
Physical punishment	29	28	n.s.	27	42	n.s.

nice to bite') or verbal prohibition ('Can't you see Al's hurt? Don't push him') (22 per cent);

- neutral explanation ('Tom's crying because you pushed him') (18 per cent);
- unexplained verbal prohibition ('Stop that!') (15 per cent);
- suggestion of positive action ('Why don't you give Jeffy your ball') (13 per cent);
- physical restraint ('I just moved him away from the baby') (13 per cent); and
- physical punishment ('I swatted her a good one') (9 per cent).

Was the way in which mothers reacted to child-caused distress related to the likelihood that a child behaved in a prosocial way in distress incidents? The investigators took the mothers scores for each technique, found the median and grouped mothers into those above or below the median (high or low on that technique). Then, the child's likelihood of prosocial behaviour was compared for 'high' and 'low' mothers on each technique, using independent groups t tests. The results are shown in box table 8.1.1, giving the analysis for the likelihood of children showing altruism in bystander incidents, and the corresponding analysis

for the child showing reparation in child-caused distress incidents.

It can be seen that mothers who gave affective explanations to their children when they caused distress are likely to have children who spontaneously show altruism to others, and also make reparation for distress they have caused themselves. On the other hand, mothers who gave more unexplained verbal prohibitions were likely to have children who showed less prosocial behaviour in both situations. Other techniques gave non-significant correlations. Physical methods (restraint, or punishment) were neither strongly effective nor ineffective, but they were positively correlated with some aspects of affective explanation; that is, many mothers combined affective explanation with some physical action.

The mothers' empathic caregiving ratings were also split into 'high' and 'low' groups. Mothers high in empathic caregiving had more prosocial children than did mothers low in empathic caregiving. For altruism in bystander incidents, the respective percentages were 46 per cent and 24 per cent; for reparation, the figures were 47 per cent and 17 per cent; both comparisons are significant at the 0.01 level on the t test.

The investigators conclude that 'the prototype of the mother whose child is reparative and altruistic is one whose communications when her child transgresses are of high intensity and clarity both cognitively and affectively ... [it] is not calmly dispensed reasoning, carefully designed to enlighten the child, it is emotionally imposed, sometimes harshly and often forcefully. These techniques exist side by side with empathic caregiving.'

This study has noticeable strengths and weaknesses. The strengths are that it examines prosocial behaviour in real-life situations, and over some considerable time. One weakness is the small sample, composed only of volunteer mothers. It would certainly be problematic to generalize very widely, without a replicative study on a different sample. Another weakness might be the use of the mother's records: how objective were they? The training procedures, and investigators' recordings, went some way to alleviate this concern. Finally, the authors are tempted to infer causation from the correlations they discovered. They suggest that maternal techniques are influencing the child's behaviour. However, it could be that child characteristics influence the mother's behaviour. All we can be sure about is that, in this sample, empathic and affectively explaining mothers have prosocial children. We cannot be sure whether one causes the other, although we can generate plausible hypotheses from the data of this study.

Based on material in Zahn-Waxler, C., Radke-Yarrow, M. and King. R. A. 1979: Child-rearing and children's prosocial initiations towards victims of distress. *Child Development*, 50, 319–30.

Box 8.2
The effects of primary division, student-mediated conflict resolution programmes on playground aggression

In this Canadian study, the researchers sought to discover the effects of a student-mediated conflict resolution programme on levels of playground aggression in primary schools. Mediation teams of grade 5 students (approximately age 10 years) participated in 15 hours of training in mediation skills.

The study employed a multiple-baseline design with weekly observations of aggressive behaviour in three schools serving as baselines. The researchers used observational methods at three time-points – before the intervention, during the intervention and at a follow-up – to evaluate the effect of introducing the mediation service into three primary schools on a staggered basis. Following 7 weekly baseline observations, mediators began intervening in conflicts on the playground of School 1. Mediators began intervening in conflicts in School 2 following 11 weekly baseline observations. Mediation was introduced onto the playground of School 3 following 14 weekly baseline observations. Weekly observations were continued throughout the school year, with follow-up observations the following year.

A team of three coders conducted the observations once weekly during two 20-minute break times, with one observer assigned to each of three schools. In general, observations were conducted at the same time, from the same location, by the same observer. The coders did not attend the mediation training programme, were not told the identity of the mediators, and were not told when the programme began in each of the schools. Before the study began, the coders engaged in 2 months of coder training. Interrated reliability averaged .90 for coder 1, .72 for coder 2 and .90 for coder 3.

The following behaviours were recorded at regular intervals:

- *Physical aggression*: this category included instances of physical aggression, such as taking equipment from peers, pushing another pupil, or hitting.
- *Adult intervention*: instances in which adults intervened to prevent or resolve conflicts.

The multiple baseline design of this study was selected as a controlled design and provided immediate and continuous feedback about the impact of the programme on children's behaviour in the playground in three different contexts, variability across time and longer-term stability.

Peer mediators carried a clipboard with a prompt sheet (called a mediator monitoring form) for examples of behaviours that warranted or did not require intervention. For each conflict in which they intervened, mediators noted the gender and grade of the disputants, the nature of the conflict (*physical* versus *verbal/relational*), and whether the conflict was resolved successfully. Mediators coded *physical conflict* when disputants engaged in aggressive behaviour with physical contact, for example pushing, kicking or hitting. *Verbal/relational conflict* referred to aggressive behaviours such as nasty teasing or another person or social exclusion.

Mediation was judged to be successful if:

- both disputants agreed to mediate in the conflict;

- a solution was agreed on; and
- the mediator felt that the solution solved the problem.

Probe inter-observer reliability checks were conducted for 51 mediators from the 3 schools. Overall agreement on the outcome of mediation was .86. Agreement on the grade of disputants, the gender of disputants and the type of dispute (physical versus verbal/relational) was 1.00.

The results were analysed in terms of both the mediator monitoring forms and the direct observations. The mediator monitoring forms showed that the three mediation teams recorded 1010 mediations during year 1. Box table 8.2.1 shows the number of disputes between boys, girls and boys versus girls at grades 1–5 in which mediators intervened. (Data for kindergarten pupils are not included here.) Mediations involving conflicts between boys, and between boys and girls, declined from Grade 1 to Grade 5. The number of mediations involving only girls, by contrast, remained relatively stable from Grade 1 to Grade 5.

There were significant gender differences in the types of conflict that required mediation. Conflict involving boys was more likely to be physical whether it was boys vs. boys (61.5 per cent of disputes) or boys vs. girls (56.7 per cent); for girls vs. girls, only a minority of disputes were physically aggressive (29.1per cent).

Box table 8.2.2 shows that for both verbal/relational and physical aggression, mediators showed a significant gender preference. The percentage of disputes mediated by boys and girls did not differ significantly from the proportions predicted on the basis of their membership in the team. However, boys were more likely to intervene in disputes involving boys: 77.6 per cent of the verbal/relational and 90.4 per cent of the physical conflicts that boys mediated involved either boys or boys versus girls. Girls showed a similar (though less pronounced) preference to mediate in dis-

Box Table 8.2.1   Number of mediations at grades 1–5

	Grade 1	Grade 2	Grade 3	Grade 4	Grade 5
Two boys	117	95	76	58	49
Two girls	59	47	45	28	48
Boy vs girl	67	71	46	38	26
Total	243	213	167	124	123

Box Table 8.2.2   Percentage of the disputes, mediated by boys and girls, which involved disputants who were both boys, both girls, or boys and girls

	Gender of disputants				
	Boys v Boys	Boys v Girls	Girls v Girls	χ^2	p
Verbal/Relational conflicts					
Boy mediator	55.1	22.5	22.5	33.74	<.001
Girl mediator	26.5	26.9	46.5		
Physical conflicts					
Boy mediator	63.1	27.3	9.6	17.16	<.001
Girl mediator	45.1	22.3	32.6		

The figure of 32.6 on the bottom row is a correction for what appears to be a mistake in the original article

putes involving girls: 73.4 per cent of the verbal/relational and 54.8 per cent of the physical disputes mediated by girls involved girls or girls versus boys.

The results from the direct observations of physically aggressive playground behaviour in School 1 are shown in box figure 8.2.1 (playground observation during baseline, mediation and follow-up). Aggressive behaviour remained stable for 5 weeks; rates dropped after the winter break then increased over the next 4 weeks. After the introduction of mediation, rates dropped abruptly from an average of 57 per cent during baseline observations to an average of 28 per cent during mediation. These effects were still evident during the follow-up period.

On the basis of the observations, the authors concluded that the introduction of the mediation scheme resulted in a sustained drop in aggressive behaviour in the playground in each of the three schools. The multiple baseline design of the study suggested that the decline in physically aggressive behaviour was not due to the passage of time but specifically to the introduction of the mediation programme. The authors found that mediators successfully resolved 90 per cent of the playground conflicts in which they intervened. The mediator monitoring records confirmed that pupils cooperated with the mediation team. Staff were unanimous in recommending that the programme should be maintained in each of the schools after the experiment was over. In fact, all of the schools in the study selected and trained a second generation of mediators in the following year. The mediators detected conflict early and were able to intervene quickly before it escalated. Although boys and girls contributed equally to the mediation teams' efforts, they displayed distinct preferences:

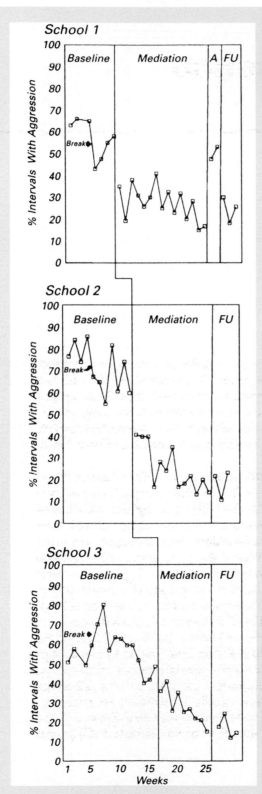

Box Figure 8.2.1 Percentage of 120 intervals in which physically aggressive behaviour was observed each week during baseline, mediation, and follow-up (FU) conditions at three primary division schools. "A" indicates a reversal when the mediation team was reduced from eight to two members.

boys intervened more in disputes involving boys and girls intervened more in disputes involving girls. The authors conclude that, as a relatively low-cost intervention, it merits wider use and further study as part of an anti-violence school programme.

Based on material in Cunningham, C. E., Cunningham, L. J., Martorelli, V., Tran, A., Young, J. and Zacharias, R. 1998: The effects of primary division, student-mediated conflict resolution programmes on playground aggression. *Journal of Child Psychology & Psychiatry*, 39, 653–668.

9 Adolescence

Adolescence is the period of transition between childhood, and life as an adult; covering basically the teenage years. Biologically, it is marked by the onset of puberty. After puberty, a person is sexually mature and could potentially become a mother or father of a child. Socially, adolescence is marked by an increasing independence from parents as the young person prepares to leave home, to complete his or her education, to form sexual partnerships and to seek some vocation or employment.

Adolescence has been thought of as a difficult period, as indeed times of transition often are. The historian Philippe Aries (1962) actually argued that adolescence was a modern invention, and that in the Middle Ages 'children were mixed with adults as soon as they were considered capable of doing without their mothers or nannies' (p. 411). However, historians since then have criticized Aries' views as 'simplistic and inaccurate' (Hanawalt, 1992, p. 343); in medieval literature, adolescence was characterized in not unfamiliar ways, and potential conflict with the adult world was recognized. This conflict was perhaps overemphasized, by writers from both psychoanalytic and sociological traditions, during the 1950s and 1960s. Phrases, such as 'the identity crisis of adolescence', and the turmoil or 'storm and stress' of the adolescent period, have become familiar. In this chapter we will look at the nature of adolescence and examine how well the evidence supports these views. In doing so we shall note again the importance of the social and historical context in considering development. We need to keep a balance between the real cultural and historical variations, and the relatively invariant features that characterize adolescence. The most obvious universal feature is the onset of puberty, and we will start with an overview of the biological and physical changes that this involves.

Table 9.1   Approximate age and sequence of appearance of sexual characteristics during puberty

Age (yr)	Boys	Girls
9–10		Growth of bony pelvis
		Budding of nipples
10–11	First growth of testes and penis	Budding of breasts
		Pubic hair
11–12	Activity of prostate gland producing semen	Changes in lining of vagina
		Growth of external and internal genitalia
12–13	Pubic hair	Pigmentation of nipples
		Breasts fill out
13–14	Rapid growth of testes and penis	Axillary hair (under armpits)
		Menarche (average: 13.5 years; range 9–17 years). Menstruation may be anovulatory for first few years
14–15	Axillary hair (under armpits)	Earliest normal pregnancies
	Down on upper lip	
	Voice change	
15–16	Mature spermatozoa (average: 15 years; range: 11.25–17 years)	Acne
		Deepening of voice
16–17	Facial and body hair	Skeletal growth stops
	Acne	
21	Skeletal growth stops	

Source: Adapted from Katchadourian, 1977

The Biological and Physical Changes of Puberty

The precise timing of puberty depends on the measure taken, but in girls the onset of menstruation (menarche) provides a fairly definite marker, and in boys the time of first ejaculation (spermache). Puberty comes later for boys. The typical age sequence of physical changes is shown in table 9.1.

The physical differences between boys and girls become much more obvious at puberty, due to hormonal changes. The reproductive organs become fully functional. In girls both the external genitalia (the vulva, including the clitoris) and the internal genitalia (the ovaries, fallopian tubes, uterus and vagina) become enlarged. The clitoris becomes more sensitive to stimulation, and the lining of the uterus and the vagina are strengthened. Menarche follows these changes. In boys, the testes and penis become larger, and so does the prostate gland, which is important for the production of semen. This is followed by the first ejaculation.

Other changes are linked to these, but are not directly part of the reproductive system. In both sexes there is a growth of body hair, especially under the armpits and in the pubic areas. In boys there is more coarse body and facial hair, and the beginnings of beard growth. There are skin changes, and the sweat glands become more active, often leading to acne. The voice deepens, especially in boys. In girls, breast development occurs.

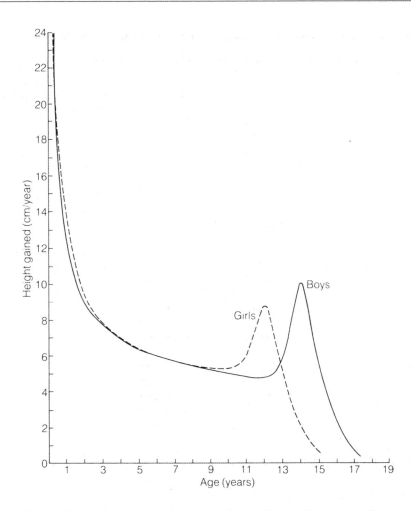

Figure 9.1 Typical individual curves showing velocity of growth in height for boys and girls (from Katchadourian, 1977).

Another feature of the pubertal period is the adolescent growth spurt. Through-out the school years growth is fairly steady, averaging about 5 or 6 cm per year. This increases early on in puberty reaching about 9 cm per year in girls and 10 cm per year in boys before falling off sharply at adulthood (figure 9.1 shows these changes in growth velocity for an average boy and girl). The extent of this growth spurt is largely independent of the child's previous height and some 35 per cent of the variation in adult height is due to these rapid changes in adolescence.

All of the physical changes at puberty are linked to biological changes in the body. These are summarized in figure 9.2. The key role is played by the hypo-thalamus, as it controls the action of the pituitary gland that produces the neces-sary hormones. The action of the hypothalamus resembles that of a thermostat regulating temperature – it 'shuts down' when high enough levels of sex hor-mones are circulating in the body. These sex hormones (especially androgen,

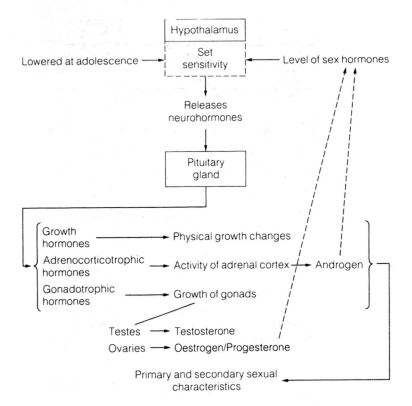

Figure 9.2   Summary of hormonal changes at puberty.

testosterone, oestrogen and progesterone) are produced by the adrenal cortex, and by the gonads (the testes and ovaries). The growth of the latter is in turn stimulated by hormones released by the pituitary gland. At puberty there is a change in the 'setting' or sensitivity of the hypothalamus. As a result, the pituitary gland works harder, and sex-hormone levels are raised.

Variations in physical maturation rates

The age of pubertal development can vary a great deal between individuals. This is dramatically illustrated in figure 9.3, which shows the growth and sexual development of three boys, each aged 14 years and 9 months, and of three girls, each aged 12 years 9 months. To some extent this variation may be genetic. For example, two randomly chosen girls will differ in age of menarche by, on average, 19 months; for two sisters, however, the average difference is only 13 months, and for identical twins, less than 3 months (Tanner, 1962). The variation is also linked to general body build. Children who are short and stocky tend to mature earlier than children who are slimmer and more linear in body shape (Katchadourian, 1977).

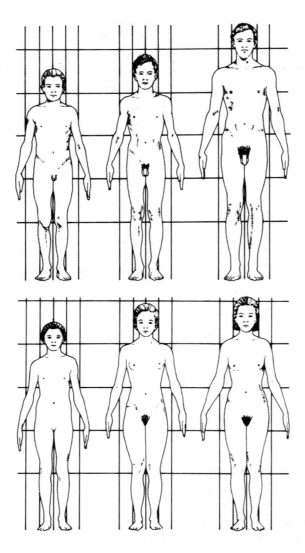

Figure 9.3   Individual variation in pubertal development: each of the 3 boys is 14¾ years old, and each of the 3 girls is 12¾ years old (from Tanner, 1973).

Environmental factors can also have very pronounced effects on maturation. Undernourishment or malnutrition can slow down growth and retard the onset of puberty. This is not surprising, as caloric requirements increase with puberty. Although it is difficult to prove, it is highly likely that nutritional differences are largely responsible for social-class and cultural differences in the timing of puberty. In less wealthy countries especially, social classes may differ by about a year in the age of menarche; the difference is less marked or absent in richer countries, where perhaps almost all young people get adequate nourishment (Katchadourian, 1977).

In a provocative analysis, Belsky et al. (1991) proposed that stressful early family circumstances – such as parental conflict and divorce – may bring forward the onset of puberty. They based this on an evolutionary psychology argument – that stressful early family circumstances may 'signal' a difficult environment and thus the advantage of reproducing early rather than waiting. A review suggested that there was some, although mixed, support for this hypothesis (Kim et al., 1997). A longitudinal study of 87 adolescent girls in the USA has found that both stressful relationships with their mothers, and presence of a stepfather, contributed independently to earlier pubertal maturation (Ellis and Garber, 2000).

The secular trend in age of puberty

A fascinating phenomenon in western Europe and North America has been the secular trend in the age of menarche, illustrated in figure 9.4. This is based on records from the Scandinavian countries, going back to the mid-nineteenth century, and more recent records, including those in the UK and the USA. Figure 9.4 indicates that the age of menarche in girls declined over a hundred-year period from an average of around 16 or 17 in the 1860s to around 13 in the 1960s. The change averaged about 0.3 years per decade. There have been similar secular trends in height. Over the same period the average height of 12-year-olds increased by about 1.5 cm per decade; the trend for adult height was less – about 0.4 cm per decade – since some 'catching up' occurs in later maturers in early adulthood. Since the 1960s these changes in height and in age of menarche seem to have slowed down, as must happen eventually (Roche, 1979)! Neverthe-less, a study in West Germany reported a continuing decrease in menarcheal age, from 13.3 years in 1979/80 (as in figure 9.4) to 13.0 years in 1989 (Ostersehlt and Danker-Hopfe, 1991). Another study in north America found only a very small decline, from 12.9 years in 1948 to 12.8 years in 1992; but possibly with other aspects of puberty such as breast development, coming earlier (Hermann-Giddens et al., 1997).

Figure 9.4 has been extensively reproduced in textbooks, but in fact it seems that some of the earlier data are in error. Bullough (1981) re-examined available data from the nineteenth century, which suggests that menarche occurred between 14 and 16 years of age. The data for the nineteenth century in figure 9.4 suggest-ing an age of 17 years are based on very small samples from Scandinavia that are not representative. Nevertheless no-one denies that there has been a secular trend. The historian Herbert Møller (1985, 1987) has looked at available evidence for still earlier periods, and for males. One source of evidence was records of Bach's choir-boys in Leipzig for 1727–47. Their voices broke distinctly later, at around 17 years, than would be the case nowadays (14–15 years, table 9.1). An analysis of beard growth in males, from writings and portraits, suggests that before the nineteenth century many young men did not grow a beard until their twenties; for example, the series of Rembrandt self-portraits only show him with a beard by age 24. Nowadays beard growth happens at around 17 years (table 9.1).

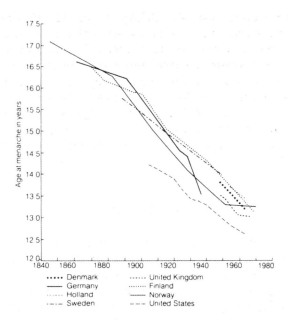

Figure 9.4   Changes is age of menarche over the past 120 years (from Tanner, 1973).

The secular trend is believed to have been due to improving nutritional and health standards. Decreases in mean family size may have been a contributing factor (see Malina, 1979, and Frisch, 1988, for a discussion).

Psychological Effects of Puberty

Through this chapter we will discuss a number of psychological changes associated with puberty – including a decrease in parent–child closeness and an increase in risk-taking behaviours (Alsaker, 1996; Arnett, 1999). But how does puberty actually bring about such changes? Paikoff and Brooks-Gunn (1991) discuss a range of possible models; these cover direct and indirect effects of the physical changes themselves, of the increased level of sex hormones, and of the cognitive and self-definitional changes characteristic of this period.

Effects of physical changes

We have seen how the onset of puberty produces marked physical changes. These in their turn have psychological effects on the young person. The adolescent is becoming aware of his or her sexual development, and of associated changes in body size and shape, depth of voice, skin texture, and facial and body hair. Many writers on adolescence have ascribed the awkwardness or self-consciousness that is often thought to characterize this period to awareness of these changes.

A number of studies have examined the psychological impact of menarche on girls (Greif and Ulman, 1982). Retrospective studies, in which women are asked to recall their menarcheal experience, suggest that it remains a clear and vivid event in the memory; it is recalled in rather negative terms, as an unpleasant experience for which social support was lacking. These conclusions are limited by the samples (mainly middle-class American) and historical period studied (occurrence of menarche in the first half of the twentieth century).

A few studies have looked at attitudes in pre- and post-menarcheal girls. After menarche girls tend to report more negative emotions or experiences than they had expected, despite some educational preparation and support, usually from mothers. In a longitudinal study of 120 girls through menarche, Ruble and Brooks-Gunn (1982) found that menarche did initially create some inconvenience, ambivalence and confusion, but that typically it did not seem to be a traumatic experience. The negative feelings were greater for early maturers, and also for girls who thought themselves poorly prepared for the experience. There can be positive features to menarche as well. Some studies have found that menarche can serve as a focal reference point, bringing a girl closer to her mother and heightening an awareness of and interest in her femininity. Menarche, or at least general changes associated with menarche, may be correlated with greater maturity on some personality characteristics (Greif and Ulman, 1982).

Some authors believe that the experience of menarche was better handled in traditional cultures, in which there were or are well-defined rituals surrounding menstruation which give it a symbolic meaning and importance (Greif and Ulman, 1982; Mead, 1949). In the village of Lesu in Melanesia, for example, the focus of a classic anthropological study by Powdermaker (1933), the onset of menstruation was an important ritual event for the women in the community. The girl was washed in the sea before sunrise by an old woman, who dipped the leaves of a branch in the water and over the girl, saying:

> Leaf, leaf I wash her
> Soon her breasts will develop
> I take away sickness of blood.

The leaves were then mixed with white lime and rubbed over the girl's body. This ritual was thought necessary if the girl's breasts were to develop, and full womanhood achieved. A feast was held later the same day.

In many traditional societies boys also go through initiation ceremonies, often grouped together into an 'age set' spanning some 5 years. For example, in the Karimojong, a cattle-herding people of Uganda, boys to be initiated first have to spear an ox. Semi-digested food from the stomach sack of the slaughtered animal is smeared over the initiate's body, while the elders call out 'Be well. Become wealthy in stock. Grow old. Become an elder.' After further rituals, the boy has become a man and is allowed to grow his hair long in the fashion of men in the tribe (Dyson-Hudson, 1963).

These rituals are important in signalling the transition point from child to adult. Some anthropologists believe that they also reinforce the authority of the elders of the tribe, who perform the ceremonies. Another idea is that male initiation rites serve to break the close link children have with the mother; elaborate initiation rites were especially likely in societies where mothers nursed infants and shared the same bed with their child for a long period (Whiting et al., 1958). However, other explanations are possible for this finding. It may simply be that in male-dominated societies men may have several wives (so prolonged nursing and post-partum sex taboos are tolerated) and, independently, male initiation rites are important in forging male solidarity (Young, 1965).

Effects of hormones

Some researchers have argued that hormones may have a fairly direct effect on psychological functioning in adolescence, as well as any indirect effect through response to physical changes. Steinberg (1987) reported that pubertal maturation was associated with increased emotional distance from parents, in a US sample. Of course, this could just reflect an effect of chronological age; older adolescents being more mature, and less close to parents. However, utilizing individual variations in age of puberty, Steinberg showed that the effect of pubertal maturation was independent of chronological age. This was a cross-sectional study; further evidence that it is the pubertal maturation that causes the changes in parent–child relationships (rather than vice versa) came from a similar, longitudinal study (Steinberg, 1988; in fact Steinberg found influences in both directions). Puberty was associated with adolescent autonomy and parent–child conflict, and decreased closeness.

To what extent these and other studies can actually show that hormonal changes are in some way responsible is discussed by Buchanan et al. (1992). They also review a small number of studies that have actually measured hormone levels in relation to behavioural measures. They argue that there is some evidence to suppose that hormone levels affect such outcomes as moodiness and aggression, but that these effects interact in a complex way with the cognitive and self-evaluation changes occurring simultaneously. They conclude cautiously, quoting from a review 20 years earlier, that 'we have only begun to comprehend the many ways in which hormones affect and are affected by human emotions and behaviors' (p. 101).

Effects of cognitive changes

Entering the period of formal operational thought, adolescents are increasingly able to think about abstract issues and hypothetical situations (chapter 12). Thus, they may well reflect on how they are perceived by hypothetical others, and have problems adjusting to their changing physical appearance. A study in the USA found that girls (but not boys) experienced increased dissatisfaction with their bodies over the period 13 to 18 years; furthermore this dissatisfaction was only weakly related to how other adolescents rated their physical attractiveness (Rosenblum and Lewis, 1999).

David Elkind (1967) suggested that adolescents often imagine how their appearance or behaviour would seem to an 'imaginary audience' of others, hence their own self-consciousness. Elkind also argued that adolescents often thought that their own actions were very important in the eyes of others, and that they became bound up or obsessed with their own feelings, constructing a 'personal fable', an imaginary story of their own life, perhaps containing fantasies of omnipotence or immortality. These concepts of the 'imaginary audience' and the 'personal fable' led Elkind to postulate that a new kind of egocentrism appeared in adolescence (cf. chapter 12). In this 'adolescent egocentrism' young people are unable to differentiate their own feelings about themselves from what others might be feeling. Elkind was writing at a time when the 'storm and stress' view of adolescence was popular and empirical work on his concepts has yielded rather mixed results (Buis and Thompson, 1989).

Effects of early and late maturation

At 11 years a girl would be early in experiencing menarche; at 14 she would be late. Similarly a 12-year-old boy would be early, a 16-year-old late, in reaching puberty. Do these differences have important psychological consequences?

Early maturing boys tend to be at an advantage socially, as their growth spurt favours strength and sporting achievement, usually highly valued in boys' groups (chapter 5). A boy who is late in reaching puberty may feel less confident socially and be rated as less mature, attractive or popular (Mussen and Jones, 1957).

A study in Sweden found a more complex picture for girls (Magnusson et al., 1985). Data on 466 girls were obtained before puberty, after puberty at 14 years, and in a follow-up at 25 years. At 14 years it was clear that girls who had reached puberty early (before 11 years) were much more likely to be involved in drinking alcohol, smoking hashish, playing truant and generally breaking social norms more than girls who matured on time or late. However, this was found to be the case because these girls were more likely to mix with an older peer group who were more likely to engage in these activities. In other words, early maturation often led to associating with older peers, and if and when this happened the norm-breaking followed. This was a temporary effect; by age 25 the differences between early and late maturers in drinking alcohol had vanished. Nevertheless there was a more permanent effect of early maturation on education. Early maturing girls tended to engage in sexual activity earlier, get married and have children earlier, and were less likely to be in tertiary education than late maturers (2 per cent compared with 15 per cent). A study in New Zealand focusing on how early maturation relates to delinquency in girls, is featured in box 9.1; this also points to the influence of older peers on early maturing girls. A longitudinal study in the USA also found that early maturing girls were more vulnerable to deviant peer pressure (Ge et al., 1996).

Maturational timing may impact on academic achievement. A longitudinal study in the UK by Douglas and Ross (1964) was based on the National Survey of Health and Development, which followed 5000 boys and girls born in one week in March, 1946. At secondary school, it emerged that both boys and girls who were early maturers scored higher than late maturers on tests of mental ability and performance while at school. Some other studies have reported similar results. However, the superior performance of early maturers might not be due to the physical changes of puberty and greater physical maturity. First, the effect seems to interact with social class, being larger in lower social class groups. Also, family size may explain much of the effect. Puberty tends to be later in large families, and being a member of a large family also tends to depress intelligence and school achievement in a slight but consistent fashion. When children of similar family size are compared, the differences between early and late maturers are small (Douglas and Ross, 1964).

A similar study in Sweden used a sample of 740 children followed from 9 to 14 years (Westin-Lindgren, 1982). In relation to achievement in Swedish, English and mathematics, the effects of social class were generally much greater than effects of early or late maturation. Thirteen- to 14-year-old early maturers did score better in Swedish and English if they came from families of manual workers, but there was little effect for children from families of salaried workers or employers. There were no effects of early or late maturation on mathematics scores. The possibly confounding effects of family size were not looked at in this study.

Adolescence as a Period of Turmoil, or 'Storm and Stress'

In the earlier half of the twentieth century many theorists thought of adolescence as a time of acute identity crisis and turmoil. One influence here was that of psychoanalysis. Freud, at the turn of the century, was elaborating his views on human psychosexual development. On this view much of an individual's psychic energy was hypothesized as being taken up with trying to cope with unacceptable sexual impulses early in childhood. In the 'oral', 'anal' and 'oedipal' stages the very young child experiences frustration and anxiety at his or her developing sexual impulses, resulting in psychological defences and repression of these impulses during a 'latency period' from about 5 years of age to puberty. However, at puberty there was a renewed upsurge of sexual 'instincts' that reawakened old conflicts. The psychoanalytic approach was developed by Peter Blos (1962) in his book *On Adolescence*. Blos likened the adolescent transition to independence, to the earlier transition that the infant went through to become a self-reliant toddler; in both, ambivalence and regression were likely. Blos called adolescence a 'second individuation process', because of this parallel.

Freud's and Blos's theories have received much criticism. The 'instinct' model is outdated (chapter 2), and the emphasis on sexual concerns is generally felt to be exaggerated. However, a revision of the psychoanalytic approach made by Erik Erikson (1902–94) attracted a lot of support. Erikson realized that Freud emphasized innate impulses too strongly; he gave a much larger role to cultural influences in personality formation. He accepted Freud's insight into the importance of sexual desires, but regarded other concerns as equally, or more, strong at various stages of the life cycle; he therefore described 'psychosocial' rather than 'sexual' stages of development. Finally, he thought that adolescence (rather than

Table 9.2 The eight developmental stages proposed by Erikson (1968)

Normative crisis	Age (yr)	Major characteristics
Trust vs. mistrust	0–1	Primary social interaction with mothering caretaker; oral concerns; trust in life-sustaining care, including feeding
Autonomy vs. shame and doubt	1–2	Primary social interaction with parents; toilet training; 'holding on' and 'letting go' and the beginnings of autonomous will
Initiative vs. guilt	3–5	Primary social interaction with nuclear family; beginnings of 'oedipal' feelings; development of language and locomotion; development of conscience as governor of initiative
Industry vs. inferiority	6–puberty	Primary social interaction outside home among peers and teachers; school age assessment of task ability
Identity vs. role confusion	Adolescence	Primary social interaction with peers, culminating in heterosexual friendship; psychological moratorium from adult commitments; identity crisis; consolidation of resolutions of previous four stages into coherent sense of self
Intimacy vs. isolation	Early adulthood	Primary social interaction in intimate relationship with member of opposite sex; adult role commitments accepted, including commitment to another person
Generativity vs. stagnation	Middle age	Primary social concern in establishing and guiding future generation; productivity and creativity
Integrity vs. despair	Old age	Primary social concern is a reflective one: coming to terms with one's place in the (now nearly complete) life cycle, and with one's relationship with others; 'I am what survives of me'

early childhood) was the most decisive period in the formation of adult personality. A summary of Erikson's eight stages in the life cycle is shown in table 9.2. In each stage there is a 'normative crisis' – the area in which Erikson considered conflict to be most characteristic.

The idea of adolescence as a turbulent, rebellious period was popular in the 1960s and 1970s – a period of considerable social and attitudinal change (for example, in sexual permissiveness, see p. 300), of increased use of drugs, and of social protest (for example, against the Vietnam war in the USA). In the later 1970s and 1980s however, more researchers stressed the view that the conflicts in adolescence were by no means universal, and were often about mundane matters such as mode of dress or getting home times. These may have over-stressed the 'normality' of the adolescent period; recent reviews tend to point out that there are indeed stresses particular to the adolescent period. Arnett (1999), in a review of the 'storm-and-stress' view, contends that it is 'a real part of life for many adolescents and their parents' (p. 324). He reviews three main areas: conflict with parents; mood disruption; and risk behaviour (see box 9.2). He also remarks on cultural variations in these. We will look at some evidence regarding all these areas – but first, review work on identity, another area in which adolescents are faced with challenges in their development.

Identity development and the 'identity crisis'

Erikson elaborated his ideas about role confusion and identity in adolescence in an influential book *Identity: Youth and Crisis* (1968). He argued that while identity was important throughout the life cycle, it was in adolescence that the most turmoil in this area could normally be expected (table 9.2). He thought that adolescents typically went through a psychological or psychosocial 'moratorium', in which they could try out different aspects of identity without finally committing themselves. For example, a young person might temporarily adopt different religious beliefs, or changed views about their vocation, without adults expecting this necessarily to be a final choice. After this period of crisis, a more stable, consolidated sense of identity would be achieved.

There are good reasons why one's sense of identity might change considerably through adolescence. We have seen how marked physical changes occur, which will affect one's body image or sense of physical self. At this time also a pattern of sexual relationships needs to be decided upon. Society expects a young person to make some choice of vocation by around 18 years, and in many countries they also get the vote at this age and have to decide on their political preferences. Nevertheless, Erikson's ideas were not obtained from any large-scale survey; they were based on his own observations, and on his clinical practice. They certainly needed to be tested against empirical findings.

Espin et al. (1990) reported an interesting longitudinal case study that tested Erikson's ideas. They carried out a content analysis of 71 letters written by a Latin-American girl to her former teacher, over a 9-year period, between the ages of 13 and 22. Besides her adolescence, this was a traumatic period for her, since she and her parents were imprisoned for political reasons. According to the content analysis, themes to do with Identity predominated in the earlier letters. These increased from 13 to 18 years, then declined. Themes to do with Intimacy increased steadily through the period and became predominant after age 19. Themes to do with Generativity were very low at first, but did start to increase after age 19. This single case study does support the notion of three successive overlapping stages from Erikson's model (table 9.2), but clearly more normative studies were needed.

The most thorough attempt to do this has been made by James Marcia (1966, 1980). Marcia developed an interview technique to assess 'identity status' in certain areas, notably those of occupation, religion, political belief and attitudes to sexual behaviour. He would ask questions such as 'Have you ever had any

Figure 9.5 Most likely predicted changes in identity status.

doubts about your religious beliefs?' Depending on the answer to these and other questions, a subject would be characterized as in 'diffusion' (or 'confusion'), 'foreclosure', 'moratorium', or 'achievement of identity' (Marcia, 1966).

Someone in diffusion (confusion) status has not really started thinking about the issues seriously, let alone made any commitment. Thus in answer to the above question, they might answer 'Oh, I don't know. I guess so. Everyone goes through some sort of stage like that. But it really doesn't bother me much. I figure one's about as good as the other!' By contrast, someone in foreclosure status has formed a commitment, but without ever having gone through a crisis or seriously considered alternatives. They probably accept unquestioningly parental or conventional beliefs. They might answer 'No, not really, our family is pretty much in agreement on these things' to the question about religious doubts.

Someone in moratorium status is going through the crisis predicted by Erikson. They are going to form a commitment, but at present are still considering various alternatives. They might answer 'Yes, I guess I'm going through that now. I just don't see how there can be a god and yet so much evil in the world or . . .' Finally, someone in achievement status has been through the crisis and has reached a resolution. They have consolidated their identity in this respect. Thus, they might answer 'Yeah, I even started wondering whether or not there was a god. I've pretty much resolved that now, though. The way it seems to me is . . .'

In this scheme diffusion is seen as the least mature status, and achievement as the most mature. The most likely transitions in identity status are shown in figure 9.5. The results of a cross-sectional study (Meilman, 1979) on 12- to 24-year-old males are shown in figure 9.6. It can be seen that only just over half the persons interviewed had reached identity achievement at 24 years. Thus, identity achievement may go on well into adulthood. This is borne out by a study by O'Connell (1976), who carried out retrospective interviews with married women who had school-aged children. Most of the women said that they had experienced an increasingly strong sense of identity as they moved from adolescence through to when they married, then had their first child, then when their children went to school. Such findings suggest that identity development is not so strongly focused in adolescence as Erikson suggested.

Another study (Waterman and Waterman, 1975) compared identity status in a number of male college students and their fathers. The students were mainly of diffusion or moratorium status, while the fathers (aged 40–65) were mainly in the foreclosure status and had not reached identity achievement. These men had grown up in the 1930s to 1950s, and it could be that social expectations favoured a more conforming, 'foreclosure' kind of identity development at that time.

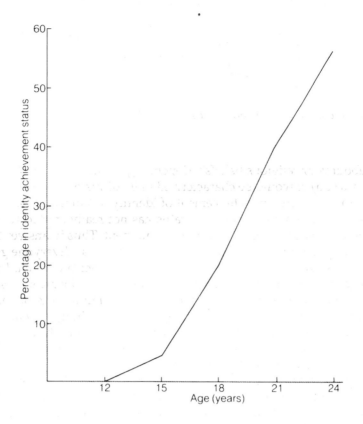

Figure 9.6   Percentage of males who were in identity achievement status at five age levels (from Meilman, 1979).

The best evidence on identity development would come from longitudinal studies, following the same participants. One, by Waterman et al. (1974), used American college students (as with the great majority of the studies in this area). Over a 3-year period, there was a decrease in foreclosure and an increase in achievement, although many students remained in diffusion status. However, college students are not typical of the whole population.

We can have more confidence in identity status measures if they correlate with, or predict, other variables. Persons in moratorium for vocation are indeed more likely to change their academic plans. Students in identity achievement have a wider range of cultural interests and express more interest in expressive writing and poetry (Waterman, 1982). Sex differences in identity status are not very marked (Archer, 1982), except in the area of sexual attitudes (which we shall discuss shortly). Identity status has been related to family background. Those in foreclosure report close relationships to parents, those in moratorium and achievement more distant or critical ones.

The work on identity status is an interesting attempt to try to pin down Erikson's ideas, but criticism has been made of how useful the status categories are and how adequately they assess identity (Cote and Levine, 1988). Also, the idea of an *'identity crisis'* seems suspect on at least three counts. First, adolescents do not experience the moratorium status in different topic areas at the same time; at one particular time one content area may be stable while another area of life decisions is in crisis. A second point is that crisis can occur throughout adult life, and identity development can be quite prominent in the early adult years. Finally, changes in identity and self-esteem may be gradual. Savin-Williams and Demo (1984) examined changes in self-esteem in a longitudinal sample of about 40 young people from 12 to 15 years of age. They found that changes were gradual, both on a daily and on a yearly basis. Feelings of self-esteem increased slowly but gradually through the early adolescent years. There were a few exceptions – a small number of young people who did experience very fluctuating feelings. The authors' general conclusion however is that there is 'a gradual process whereby adolescents' developing cognitive abilities permit greater self-awareness . . . adolescence appears more to be a stage of development, in the true sense, than of disruption'.

Occupational identity: the transition to work, and leisure pursuits

For adolescent school leavers one of the main areas of identity achievement has traditionally been through the normal transition from school to work. But in the wake of widespread economic recession in many developed countries the majority of early school leavers experience unemployment at some stage in the 16- to 19-year age period. In the UK, whereas 52 percent of 16-year-olds entered the labour market in 1988, this fell to 42 per cent in 1990 and 34 per cent in 1991 (Payne, 1995). This is partly explained by a growth in numbers in further and higher education. To some extent, the impact of youth unemployment is 'buffered' by short-term training schemes, further education opportunities, as well as leisure opportunities. Nevertheless, studies have pointed to the personal consequences of youth unemployment in terms of psychological distress, anxiety, unhappiness, dissatisfaction, stigma and lowered self-esteem (Banks and Ullah, 1986). However such distress is probably less than that experienced by unemployed older people, who are not 'buffered' in the ways described (Winefield, 1997).

Both before and after school, adolescents spend a great deal of time in leisure pursuits, often with media products – watching TV and videos, playing computer games, surfing the Internet, playing music; these can take up about half of a young person's waking hours (Larson and Verma, 1999; and p. 200). They also spend a lot of time 'hanging out' with friends. Arnett (1995) considers that these activities are not just recreational but have an important role in identity formation and in becoming a part of 'youth culture'.

Some of these leisure activities – such as watching TV – may be rather passive activities. However, Larson (2000) points to the positive aspects of leisure activities such as sports, arts, hobbies and clubs. He argues that modern Western societies lack such clear roles and responsibilities for adolescents as are found in most traditional societies, and that as a result many adolescents lack a context for developing initiative in a context that can build identity and self-esteem. He thinks that such activities require both *intrinsic motivation* – the young person must want to

Table 9.3 High-school adolescents' ratings of their psychological state, in four contexts; adapted from Larson, 2000

	Intrinsic motivation	Concentration
In class	−0.46	+0.20
With friends	+0.34	−0.12
During sports	+0.48	+0.37
Arts and hobbies	+0.53	+0.60

take part – and *concerted engagement* – a concentration in order to meet some challenge in the activity. In work on high-school adolescents in the USA (aged about 15 years) he assessed these in four major contexts: see table 9.3. School and class-work experiences are moderately challenging, but are not self-chosen and score low on intrinsic motivation (for most pupils); time with friends is enjoyable, but does not usually evoke much concentration. However both sports activities, and arts and hobbies, score high on both counts. The activities of girl guides selling cookies, described in box 2.1, would be just such an activity.

Larson argues that such activities provide a context for 'positive youth development' and that outcome studies show benefits for higher aspirations and self-esteem, and lower rates of delinquency. A difficulty with many such outcome studies is that they are prone to self-selection: adolescents who are already more able may preferentially choose such activities. Certainly the context is important. One study in Sweden of youth recreation centres (Mahoney et al., 2001) found that these were often attended by youths with problem behaviour, and that attendance at the youth centres actually correlated with increased criminal offending! This finding may relate to the influence of deviant peer groups in adolescence, discussed earlier (pp. 161–3).

Sex-role identity

We examined the development of gender identity in children in chapter 6, where we saw that this referred primarily to the awareness of oneself as a boy or girl. Many writers use the term 'sex-role identity' to refer to the acquisition of a set of standards for appropriate masculine or feminine behaviour, in a particular culture. This develops through middle childhood, but many aspects are likely to become much more significant at adolescence.

It could be argued that young men have less choice of different routes to establish sex-role identity. Female roles may at present be more changeable and varied (i.e., a young woman can readily choose to be either career-orientated, or a mother). Also, research has generally found that cross-sex interests or behaviour (e.g., boys doing needlework; girls doing metalwork) are tolerated in girls more than in boys (Golombok and Fivush, 1994). Overall, it is difficult to draw conclusions about whether boys or girls find sex-role identity a more difficult process.

Many young men and women develop attitudes and behaviours conforming to conventional stereotypes of masculine and feminine behaviour. For example, the majority of caring for young children is still done by women (see chapter 4); the majority of car repair tasks are done by men. Using questionnaires it is easy to obtain measures of sex-role orientation in terms of tasks such as these. In the USA, especially, there has been interest in the concept of 'androgyny' – an androgynous person is someone, male or female, who scores fairly equally on both masculine and feminine items of sex-role orientation. For example, an androgynous person might enjoy both baby-minding and car-repairing. Some researchers have argued that androgyny is more psychologically healthy, and leads to higher levels of self-esteem (Bem, 1975; Spence and Helmreich, 1978). In part such arguments and findings may reflect questioning of conventional sex roles, and the restrictions of choice and inequality of opportunity which they may embody.

Sex-role conventions, besides changing with time, also vary between different societies (see also chapter 6). Margaret Mead documented many instances of such cultural variations. For example, from studies of three tribes living close to each other in New Guinea (Mead, 1935), she reported that among the Arapesh, both men and women were sensitive and non-aggressive and had 'feminine' personalities; among the Mundugamor, both men and women were ruthless, unpleasant and 'masculine'; among the Tchambuli, women were dominant and men more emotional and concerned about personal appearance, an apparent reversal of our own conventions. The pattern seems almost too neat to be believed, and indeed Mead has been criticized for being selective in her presentation of results (Blurton Jones and Konner, 1973; Harris, 1968). For example, in all three tribes men seem to have shown the most violent behaviour, and in all three societies men did the hunting. In her later writing Mead did recognize a possibly greater importance of biological factors in sex roles (Mead, 1949). However, her demonstration of cultural differences, while perhaps exaggerated, is in many respects a valid indication of how society can powerfully influence sex-role development, which has been borne out by many other studies (Archer and Lloyd, 1986).

Lesbian and gay adolescents

Recent prospective research on lesbian and gay adolescent development suggests that their process of sexual identity formation begins around the ages of 10–11 years when young women and men first become aware of their attraction to members of the same sex. Data collected by D'Augelli et al. (1998) from 260 lesbian and gay youth in the US indicate that boys become aware of their same-sex orientation at around 10 years of age and girls a little later (10.4 years). Self-labelling as lesbian or gay tends to occur around 15 years of age for boys and 15.5 years for girls, with first disclosure at around 16.5 years for both sexes. The process of identity formation is complex as it often requires young people to review and, in some cases, renew their relationships with others as they take on an outwardly different identity to that perceived by their family, friends, school and local community. D'Augelli (1994) has suggested that lesbian and gay identity formation occurs after the individual has considered the implications of disclosure – popularly known as 'coming out'. Young lesbians and gay men have to consider questions such as: What does it mean to be lesbian or gay? How do I behave and how should I behave? How will my parents react? How will my family react? How will my peers/friends react? Can I be openly lesbian or gay? What does the law, religion, family or social custom say about homosexuality?

It is only after considering the personal, family and sociocultural ramifications of being lesbian and gay that a person can decide upon whether or not to disclose and develop a public lesbian or gay identity. Reactions to 'coming out' are varied. Mothers may show the strongest reactions – sometimes the most rejecting compared to fathers, brothers or sisters, sometimes the most accepting of their lesbian or gay child. D'Augelli et al. (1998) found that gay men tend to tell their mothers first rather than their fathers, while lesbians tend to tell both parents at the same time. Parental reactions are often intensified by the reactions of other adults and family members to a young person's disclosure, and the way in which a young person is received by their own peers.

Currently, estimates suggest that between 3 and 8 per cent of the secondary school population in the UK will identify as lesbian or gay, or will at least go through a process of questioning their sexual orientation by 16 years of age (Rivers and Duncan, 2002). In the United States, demographic data collected from the Youth Risk Behavior Surveys in Minnesota (N = 35,000) suggests that while only 1.1 per cent of junior-high and high school students identify as lesbian or gay, almost 11 per cent questioned their sexual orientation at some point (Remafedi et al., 1992).

Sexual knowledge and attitudes

Adolescence is a time when knowledge of the processes of reproduction and of sexual intercourse assumes great importance. We have seen earlier how an understanding of menarche, for example, can ease the pubertal transition in adolescent girls. But how much do adolescents know about these matters? A large-scale study of children's sexual thinking was carried out, in four different countries, by Goldman and Goldman (1982), and their results showed that knowledge of sexual matters did increase greatly in early adolescence, but that surprising areas of ignorance remained.

The Goldmans interviewed children aged 5 to 15 in schools in Australia, England, North America (Canadian/US border area) and Sweden. About 30–40 children were interviewed in each country, at each age. Among many other items, the children were asked to explain the meaning of certain words such as 'pregnancy' and 'puberty'. Some of the results, for the three older age bands, are shown in table 9.4. This shows the percentage of participants who gave 'fully appropriate' answers (for example for 'puberty', some understanding that having children became possible).

It can be seen that early adolescence saw a rapid increase in understanding of terms such as 'rape' and 'virgin'. Some terms remained poorly understood at 15, however, notably 'venereal disease' and 'puberty' itself. This is taken by the Goldmans to point to the importance of increased sex education in schools. They consider this argument strengthened by the greater understanding shown by the

Table 9.4   Children's understanding of sexual terms: percentages of 'fully appropriate' responses at 11, 13 and 15 years of age in four different countries

	Age	Australia	England	N. America	Sweden
Rape	11	25	38	10	47
	13	73	65	64	87
	15	100	87	87	86
Virgin	11	8	15	0	13
	13	48	38	39	70
	15	83	63	61	93
Pregnancy	11	20	18	13	50
	13	27	45	30	77
	15	38	50	52	87
Venereal disease	11	0	0	0	0
	13	3	0	0	3
	15	20	10	20	20
Puberty	11	0	0	0	17
	13	3	3	9	20
	15	5	3	3	43

Source: Goldman and Goldman, 1982

Swedish children (e.g., for 'pregnancy', and 'puberty'). Sweden does have compulsory courses in sex education and personal relationships for 7–16-year-olds; in the other countries studied, sex education is largely confined to late in the secondary school. In all countries most children said they would have liked more sex education in school, and at an earlier age. The home remained the most cited source of information on sexual matters.

An interesting feature of the Goldmans' study is that they had difficulty gaining access to many North American schools, simply because they wanted to ask questions with a sexual content. For many people sex is still a 'taboo' area. However, the Goldmans might have encountered even more difficulties if they had been doing their research 30 years earlier. Attitudes to sexual matters generally seem to have been much more restrictive then, and to have changed markedly since the 1960s and 1970s.

This shift in attitudes can be gauged from such sources as parents' manuals on how children should be brought up and educated; teachings of the churches on sexual matters; articles in the mass media; and direct attitudinal surveys by social scientists. As an example from parents' manuals, consider the following extract on masturbation from *What a Boy Should Know*, published in 1909:

> The results on the mind are the more severe and more easily recognised . . . A boy who practises this habit can never be the best that Nature intended him to be. His wits are not so sharp. His memory is not so good. His power of fixing his attention on whatever he is doing is lessened . . . The effect of self-abuse on a boy's character always tends to weaken it, and in fact, to make him untrustworthy, unreliable, untruthful, and probably even dishonest.

These stern warnings had scarcely lessened in the *Mothercraft Manual* of 1928 (Liddiard, 1928):

> This is a bad habit . . . The habit, if left unchecked, may develop into a serious vice. The child's moral nature becomes perverted; one such child has been known to upset a whole school.

Current medical opinion, however, is that masturbation is normally harmless, and we also know that it is the usual way in which young males first reach orgasm following puberty. Masturbation became much more socially acceptable, especially in adolescents, by the 1970s, when. Dr Spock's (1976, p. 413) manual stated that:

> Some conscientious adolescents feel excessively guilty and worried about masturbation . . . If a child seems to be generally happy and successful, doing well in school, getting along with his friends, he can be told that all normal young people have these desires and that a great majority do masturbate. This won't take away all his feeling of guilt, but it will help.

Attitudes to premarital sexual intercourse also changed. Over the 1960s and 1970s surveys showed that older generations had less permissive attitudes on such matters than younger people. This is not just a matter of age – it is not the case that everyone gets less permissive as they get older. Rather, it seems to reflect a genuine historical trend which has been working its way through the population as people socialized in earlier decades get older and eventually die. For example, in a general survey in the USA in 1969, only 21 per cent of Americans judged premarital sex to be 'not wrong'; yet by 1979, this had risen to 55 per cent (Reinhold, 1979). Similar changes occurred in the UK and other Western societies.

Attitudes to sex vary with the nature of the relationship with one's partner. Most people, including adolescents, regard intercourse as more acceptable if there is affection for and emotional commitment to one's partner – if it is a 'steady' relationship. Reiss (1967) identified four standards of sexual behaviour in the USA, shown in table 9.5. Some form of the 'single standard' or 'double standard' seems to have been most common up to the 1950s, but the 'permissiveness with affection' standard seems most common among a majority of American college students since the late 1960s, while 'permissiveness without affection', although more tolerated recently, remains less approved of. However, there is still a lot of cultural variation in such matters. Ma (1989) reported a comparison of attitudes to premarital sex in university students in the USA, and in Taiwan. This study confirmed that 'permissiveness with affection' was the most common standard for students in the USA; but that the 'single standard' of no sexual intercourse before marriage was most common among the Chinese students in Taiwan – but with some indication of a 'double standard', as women were less permissive than men.

Table 9.5 Four standards concerning premarital sexual intercourse, according to Reiss (1967)

Single standard:	no sexual intercourse before marriage
Double standard:	no sexual intercourse before marriage, for women; permitted for men
Permissiveness with affection:	premarital sexual intercourse allowed if partners have some emotional commitment to each other
Permissiveness without affection:	premarital sexual intercourse allowed or encouraged even without emotional commitment

Sexual behaviour

How have these general changes in attitudes affected the sexual behaviour of adolescents? What we know of sexual behaviour in young people, and adults also, comes from questionnaire and interview studies. The first modern large-scale survey was by Kinsey and his co-workers in the USA (Kinsey et al., 1948, 1953). There have been a number of other studies in the USA, and three notable studies in the UK by Schofield (1965), Farrell (1978), and Breakwell and Fife-Schaw (1992). A lot of this work was done in the late 1960s and early 1970s; the interest shown by social scientists in sexual attitudes and behaviour at this time probably reflects the considerable change attitudes and behaviour were undergoing. There was then less interest up to the mid-1980s but this has changed again as the spread of AIDS has its impact on sexual attitudes and behaviour (Cowan and Johnson, 1993).

Obviously there are problems with interview or questionnaire studies in which adolescents are asked questions about their attitudes to sexual behaviour, whether they have had sexual intercourse, if so how many partners they have had, and so forth. These are usually considered very personal matters only to be revealed to a close confidant, if at all. Problems of truthful responding, which will always qualify interview studies, are likely to be particularly strong for sexual matters. There may also be problems in understanding terms (see table 9.4), as illustrated by the question and answer 'Are you a virgin?' 'Not yet' obtained in one study! The interviewer must obviously try to obtain rapport with the person being interviewed, stress the confidentiality with which the answers will be treated, make sure questions are properly understood, and make clear the reasons for carrying out the survey. Some assurance that replies are reasonably truthful can be obtained when systematic trends are found in the results, for example an increase in sexual experience with age. Finally, if results are to be generalized, a representative or random sample must be obtained, and not too many participants should refuse to answer or drop out of the survey.

In the UK, the Schofield report of 1965 was based on a sample of 2000 adolescents aged 15–19; about 15 per cent of teenagers approached refused to take part. Young people reported going through successive stages of sexual experience. Dating was usually the first form of independent contact with a member of the opposite sex, often leading to kissing. This was usually lip kissing; deep kissing

Table 9.6 Percentage of participants reporting having had sexual intercourse in three UK studies of adolescents

	at 17 years		at 19 years	
	males	females	males	females
Schofield 1965	25	11	37	23
Farrell 1978	50	39	74	67
Breakwell and Fife-Schaw 1992	60	60	77	80

Figures from Breakwell and Fife-Schaw (1992) are an average of their 16–17/17–18 and 18–19/19–20 percentages

or 'French kissing' (where one partner's tongue enters the mouth of the other) was less common at this stage, and was usually preceded by breast stimulation over clothes. Further forms of petting included breast stimulation under clothes, and direct touching or stimulation of the partner's genitals. These heavier forms of 'petting' usually preceded full sexual intercourse, which only a minority of the sample reported having had (table 9.6).

A similar survey in the UK was reported by Farrell in 1978. This showed that the increased permissiveness in sexual attitudes had been reflected by an increased incidence of sexual behaviour in young people. Table 9.6 shows how the proportion of teenagers reporting having had sexual intercourse at 17 and 19 years of age approximately doubled in males and tripled in females over the period between the two studies.

Breakwell and Fife-Schaw (1992) surveyed sexual behaviour in 16–20-year-olds, but using questionnaires rather than interviews. They obtained 2171 replies, a response rate of 37 per cent. While these response rates are quite good for surveys of this kind, they are much lower than in the Schofield study and this puts some limits on the reliability of the figures obtained. Nevertheless, the pattern of results for sexual intercourse, shown in table 9.6, suggests a continuing trend to earlier sexual activity; and, a disappearance of the 'double standard' of greater permissiveness for males than females.

A similar change over historical time has been found in American studies, as figure 9.7 shows, for incidence of premarital intercourse. Again, the increase in sexual experience has been more marked in females.

Another approach to documenting these historical trends has been to send short questionnaires to people of differing ages, asking at what age they first had sexual intercourse; this is something one might usually remember quite accurately. In a study of this kind in Norway, by Sundet et al. (1992), short anonymous questionnaires were sent to 10,000 people aged 18 to 60, in 1987. The response rate was 63 per cent. Answers to the question 'How old were you (in years) when you had your first intercourse' are shown in table 9.7. Younger persons report an earlier age than do older persons. Note that the main drop occurs between persons born in the 1940s and 1950s, that is, those who would be 18 in the 1960s and 1970s. Note also the change from a later age for females, to an earlier age in more recent samples. In a similar study in Sweden in 1967, people in their 50s recalled an

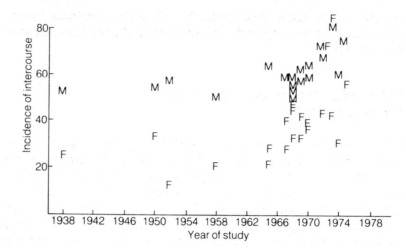

Figure 9.7 Incidence of premarital intercourse in American college men (M) and women (F) from 1938 to 1975 (from Hopkins, 1983).

Table 9.7 Age of first intercourse in different cohorts of Norwegian adults (adapted from Sundet et al., 1992)

Birth years	Age in 1987	Males	Females
1963–9	18–24	18.3	17.2
1956–62	25–31	18.0	17.2
1949–55	32–38	18.2	17.9
1942–8	39–45	18.6	18.9
1935–41	46–52	18.8	18.8
1927–34	53–60	19.3	19.6

average age of 18.6 years; this fell to an average of 17.0 years in people in their early 20s. A study ten years later found that this had fallen further, to 16.0 years.

No doubt many factors contributed to these changes in attitudes and behaviour, which were especially marked in the 1960s and 1970s. Probably increased affluence and also a greater availability of effective contraceptives played a part. Sexual attitudes and behaviour will continue to change. The possibility of contracting venereal disease has always been some deterrent to more permissive or promiscuous sexual behaviour, and considerable publicity has been given to the risks of new strains of sexually transmitted diseases, especially the AIDS virus, in the 1990s. Nevertheless, many young people continue with sexual practices that are risky. Breakwell and Fife-Schaw (1992) found that between 16 to 20 years, rates of reported heterosexual anal penetration increased from around 4 per cent to 14 per cent; and homosexual anal penetration to about 1 per cent of male respondents. This tends to be a high-risk activity for infection. This research and other surveys (Meyrick and Harris, 1994) also suggest that only a minority of young people use effective contraception. Research such as this continues to feed in to public debates about necessary and desirable levels of sex education and availability of contraception.

Relations with Parents: Conflicts, and Mood Disruption

Some studies have suggested that parents and their younger adolescent children actually agree on many things, and that areas of disagreement can be exaggerated. In a longitudinal study of 112 young adolescents, from 11 to 13 years of age, Galambos and Almeida (1992) measured parent–adolescent conflict in five domains: chores, appearance, politeness, finance and substance use. Generally, parents and adolescents agreed that there was a decrease with age in conflicts over chores, appearance and politeness, though there was an increase in conflicts over finance.

Yau and Smetana (1996) reported a study of parent–adolescent conflicts in families in Hong Kong. Hong Kong is a very densely populated urban community, but the Chinese population there presents a somewhat different picture of socialization to western norms, with more emphasis on family obligations and responsibility to elders. Nevertheless, Yau and Smetana found a range of typical conflicts reported by their 13–17-year-old informants, often (37 per cent) about choice or regulation of activities (using the phone, watching TV, bedtimes), doing household chores (16 per cent) or doing homework for school (16 per cent). A similar study of African-American adolescents in the USA (Smetana and Gaines, 1999), this time of 11–14-year-olds, found a fairly similar profile, the most frequent conflicts being about choice of activities (24 per cent), chores (21 per cent) or issues of interpersonal relationships such as choice of friends (17 per cent). In these studies, the researchers found that parents seemed to see the conflicts primarily as being matters of 'social convention' (see also chapter 8); for example one African-American mother stated: 'I want her to share the load in the household. This is a team effort, and she knows she has two working parents'.

However the adolescents themselves seemed to view these conflicts as being about issues of personal autonomy. They were seeking to develop their own rights in decision-making, rather than automatically give way to parent's wishes. Thus, even though many conflicts are about mundane matters, they may contribute to a decrease in parent–child closeness if parents resist this bid for autonomy. A study of Asian-American adolescents in the USA (Juang et al., 1999) found that in families where parents did allow an earlier timetable of autonomy, adolescents reported greater closeness to parents, and higher self-esteem. This might suggest that parents should 'give in' to adolescent demands, but clearly there are arguments both ways. One area of conflict is about adolescent bedtimes. Wolfson and Carskadon (1998) have documented how, in a US sample of over 3000 young people aged 13–19 years in Rhode Island schools, sleep patterns changed through the adolescent period. Late bedtimes became more frequent, together with much later rising at weekends (a pattern called *delayed phase preference*). Despite the late weekend rising, these students got less sleep overall than they wanted, or needed;

and those getting less sleep reported greater negative or depressed moods, and also did less well at school. This is one area where some parent–adolescent conflict may be difficult to avoid.

Mood disruption – feeling depressed or having fluctuating moods – was identified by Arnett (1999) as another factor contributing to adolescent difficulties. Larson and Ham (1993) carried out an ingenious study with 483 10–14-year-olds in the USA. Students carried an electronic pager for 1 week, and recorded their emotional affect in response to randomized signals. They also filled in a life-events questionnaire. The 12–14-year-olds experienced significantly more negative affect than the 10–11-year-olds, and this was related to negative life events connected with family, as well as school and peers.

Laursen et al. (1998) review a number of studies (such as Steinberg's, p. 238) that suggest that while the actual frequency of conflicts is high in early adolescence, their intensity is highest in the mid-adolescent years. Another example, relating to affective closeness, is drawn from a large-scale study by Rossi and Rossi (1991) in the USA. Figure 9.8 shows ratings for closeness to parents, at ages 10, 16 and 25; for different parent–child dyads; and for two birth cohorts, those born in 1925–39 who were adolescents in the 1940s–50s, and those born during 1950–9 who were adolescents in the 1960s–70s. What is apparent is that in every case, rated closeness is lower at 16 than at 10 years, though it recovers by 25. It is also clear that this dip in closeness is more pronounced (and rates of closeness generally are lower) in the later cohort, probably reflecting the turbulence and social protest of the 1960s (see p. 292).

The 'Isle of Wight' study

The 'Isle of Wight' study carried out by Michael Rutter and his colleagues made an important contribution to examining the 'storm and stress' hypothesis of adolescence. This study attempted to avoid problems of selective sampling. The Isle of Wight, in the English Channel off the coast of Hampshire, provided a bounded area of population living in small towns and villages. Behavioural questionnaires were completed by parents and teachers for all the 14- to 15-year-olds on the island, numbering 2303. The most detailed results, however, were obtained from two subsamples. One, of 200 teenagers, was a random sample of the total population; the other, of 304 teenagers, was of those with extreme scores from the parent and teacher questionnaires, which pointed to 'deviant' behaviour. The adolescents in both these subgroups were given further questionnaires and tests, and were interviewed individually by psychiatrists. Their parents and teachers were also interviewed. Two main areas are explored in the report (Rutter et al., 1976): one is the extent of conflict between adolescents and their parents (the 'generation gap'); the other, the extent of inner turmoil and of observed behavioural or psychiatric disorder ('storm and stress'). Some of the results are shown in tables 9.8 and 9.9, based on the random sample of 200.

Regarding the extent of conflicts, only about one parent in six reported any altercations or arguments with their children about when and where they went out, or about their choice of activities (table 9.8). About one parent in three

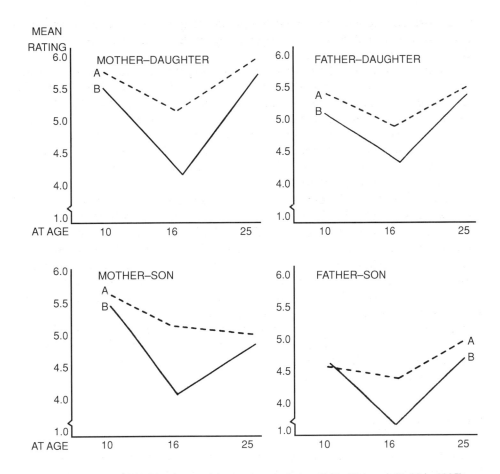

A Birth cohort 1925–39, whose adolescence was during 1941–55 (aged 46–60 in 1985).
B Birth cohort 1950–59, whose adolescence was during 1966–75 (aged 26–35 in 1985).

Figure 9.8 Affective closeness of children and their parents: cohorts whose adolescence was in 1941–55 (dotted lines) vs. 1966–75 (full lines). (Mean rating on 1–7 closeness scale).

however said they disapproved of their youngster's clothing or hairstyles. The great majority of parents approved of their children's friends, and nearly all had discussed with them their plans after leaving school. Rather more of the teenagers themselves reported having altercations with parents. However, only about one-third made any criticism of their mother or father during the interview, and only a small percentage expressed outright rejection of either parent.

By and large these results confirmed that the average adolescent is not in a state of crisis and severe conflict with parents. Nevertheless, such conflict did characterize a minority (for example 9 per cent of girls expressed outright rejection of their father, table 9.8). These difficulties were much greater in the children with some behavioural or psychiatric disorder (the second subgroup). Altercations with

Table 9.8 Percentages of parents and 14-year-old children in the Isle of Wight study reporting conflicts and feelings of inner turmoil (Rutter et al., 1976: based on the random sample of 200)

	Boys	Girls
Parental interview		
any altercation with parents	18	19
physical withdrawal	12	7
communication difficulties	24	9
Adolescent interview		
any altercation with parents	42	30
any criticism of mother	27	37
any criticism of father	32	31
any rejection of mother	3	2
any rejection of father	5	9
Often feel miserable or depressed (questionnaire)	21	23
Reported misery (psychiatric interview)	42	48
Observed sadness (psychiatric interview)	12	15

Source: Rutter et al., 1976: based on the random sample of 200

Table 9.9 Percentages of those interviewed in the Isle of Wight study having any psychiatric disorder, at different ages

	10 yr	14–15 yr	Adult (parent)
Males	12.7	13.2	7.6
Females	10.9	12.5	11.9

Source: Rutter et al., 1976

parents, physical withdrawal of children from the rest of the family, and communication difficulties or problems parents had in 'getting through' to adolescents, were all some three times more common in this sample.

What about mood disruption? Only about one-fifth of the adolescents reported on the questionnaire that they often felt miserable or depressed; from the psychiatric interview, nearly a half were diagnosed as reporting miserable feelings, though a much smaller proportion actually looked sad in the interview (table 9.8). It would seem that severe clinical depression is rare, but that some degree of inner turmoil may well characterize many adolescents.

In making judgements about adolescence as a stage, it is obviously necessary to compare with other ages and stages of development. In the Isle of Wight study such comparisons were made for the prevalence of psychiatric disorder, as based on parental interview. Table 9.9 shows the rates of disorder for the teenagers at 14–15 years, for the same children at the age of 10, from a previous survey of psychiatric disorder, and for adults (the parents of the teenage sample). There was a rather modest peak in adolescence (though the adolescent interview data gave a slightly higher figure for disorder of 16.3 per cent at this age). Again, this suggested that adolescent turmoil is not a myth, but that it should not be over-exaggerated. As Rutter et al. (1976) conclude, 'adolescent turmoil is a fact, not a fiction, but its psychiatric importance has probably been over-estimated in the past.'

Relations with Peers and Risk Taking Behaviours

As adolescents become independent from their parents, they may spend more time with peers and turn to peers more for social support and identity. We saw in chapter 5 how researchers such as J. S. Coleman in the USA and David Hargreaves in the UK documented the importance of peer groups or cliques in secondary schools, and how the values of such peer groups might diverge greatly from those of teachers and parents. Also, some evidence suggests that conformity with peers, especially in antisocial situations, does increase up to early adolescence before declining again. Anxieties about friendships with peers also peak at about this age, according to a study by J. C. Coleman (1980). Coleman asked adolescents to complete unfinished sentences about friendships in a small group, and analysed the results for their emotional content. Themes of anxiety and fear of rejection by friends increased from 11 to 13 and then to 15 years, but declined by 17 years (the effect being stronger for girls than boys).

The nature of an adolescent's social relationships with peers may be substantially different from that with his or her parents. Through childhood the parental relationship is often characterized as one of 'unilateral authority', in which parents strive to impart an already constructed set of knowledge and attitudes to their children. Friendship, however, is a form of mutually reciprocal relationship in which divergent opinions may be expressed and new ideas discussed. We have come across these conceptions previously, in discussing the development of friendship (chapter 5) and Piaget's views of the development of moral reasoning (chapter 8). While parent–child relations may become more mutual during adolescence, it is thought that they do not become as truly mutual or reciprocal as peer relationships (Youniss, 1980).

In one study in the USA, 180 adolescents aged 12–20 years were asked to check on a questionnaire how father, mother or friend might react when a disagreement arose, or when they were being consulted about an important decision (Hunter, 1984). Responses such as 'he points out where I'm wrong for my own good', or 'he tells me that I would realize his ideas are right when I get more experience', were considered representative of unilateral influence, while responses such as 'he tries to figure out with me whether or not I'm right', or 'he tells me he wonders about the same thing' were considered representative of mutual influence. It was confirmed that parents were seen as more unilateral, and friends as more mutual, in their influence. This difference was greater for females than for males. There was not much effect of age, although parents were at their most unilateral with the 14–15-year age group.

Peers and friends clearly have a distinctive and valuable role to play in development (see chapter 5). However, in adolescence it seems as though peer groups may reinforce risk-taking behaviour. Some degree of deviant or risk-taking behaviour (such as substance use, minor delinquencies such as shoplifting) are quite common in adolescence. We saw in chapter 5 how association with deviant peers may encourage delinquent behaviour; and earlier in this chapter, how early maturing girls may be influenced in this way by an older peer group (see also box 9.1). Studies of sexual behaviour in adolescents, such as that by Breakwell and Fife-Schaw (1992) (p. 304) also show risk-taking behaviour in unprotected sexual intercourse. A study of risk taking in Danish adolescents is described in box 9.2.

■ Adolescence in Different Cultures

So far we have looked mainly at adolescents in Western societies. We have seen that the view of adolescence as a difficult period does have some validity, even if it has probably been exaggerated by some writers (perhaps especially by psychoanalytic or clinical authors, such as Blos or Erikson, who would have come into most contact with the minority of adolescents who are particularly disturbed). But are such difficulties an inevitable part of puberty, sexual maturity and gaining independence from parents, or merely a product of our particular kind of society, and the way we treat adolescents? Different cultures vary widely in the treatment of adolescents, as we have noted earlier in connection with puberty rites. However although the extent of parent–child conflict may be less in some traditional societies, it has been argued to be a common feature (Schlegel and Barry, 1991).

Margaret Mead and Samoa

One study has often been quoted to support the view that adolescence can be a tranquil and conflict-free period. This is Margaret Mead's book *Coming of Age in Samoa* (1928). In this, Mead described adolescence as 'the age of maximum ease', with 'an absence of psychological maladjustment'. Indeed, Samoan society as a whole was described as 'replete with easy solutions for all conflicts'. This picture of an island paradise was supported by drawing attention to two important differences between Samoan and American society at the time. The first related to the context of child rearing. Compared with what, at its extreme at least, can be the oppressive and confining atmosphere of the Western nuclear family, the Samoans had a more open and extended family-rearing system, in which 'the child is given no sense of belonging to a small intimate biological family'. As a result, an adolescent who might be in disagreement with parents could easily go and stay with another relative. Human relationships were thus warm, but diffuse.

The second point related to methods of child rearing. There was little physical punishment of children by parents, and little repression or sense of guilt. Therefore, there was little for teenagers to rebel against. Mead stated that Samoan society 'never exerts sufficient repression to call forth a significant rebellion from the individual'. There was 'no room for guilt'. In particular, there was no guilt about sexual behaviour and experimentation before marriage. According to Mead, adolescents had 'the sunniest and easiest attitudes towards sex', and promiscuity and free love were the norm in the adolescent period.

Samoan society would thus seem to be about as different from the 'storm and stress' model of adolescence as one could imagine. Mead's work, and that of other anthropologists such as Ruth Benedict, suggested that the adolescent experience was entirely a matter of social structure and cultural pressures. The biological impact of puberty was of little consequence. As Franz Boas, the eminent anthropologist who supervised Mead's work in Samoa, put it: 'much of what we ascribe to human nature is no more than a reaction to the restraints put upon us by our civilisation'.

Mead's work was influential for a long time, but not all writers on Samoa agreed with her interpretations. Australian anthropologist Derek Freeman (1996) publicized these disagreements; he argued that Mead's methodology was poor and that she had simply found what she was looking for. The study was Mead's first (in a long and distinguished career) and at the age of 23 (as Mead herself said) she did not 'really know much about fieldwork'. Although Mead reported that she had spent 9 months in Samoa, 'speaking the language and living in the conditions in which they lived', she only spent six weeks learning Samoan, and only three months on her study of adolescence. She did not live in the native way, but stayed with the only white family on Ta'u, the island where her interviews were carried out. Thus, it is not clear how much trust or rapport she had with the adolescents whom she interviewed (often about very personal matters such as sexual experience). Mead interviewed 50 girls and young women, but only half of these (aged 14–20) were past puberty. In fact only 11 of these reported having heterosexual experience. Thus, Freeman suggested that Mead was selective in the way she interpreted her results, and was also misled by some female adolescents who, taking advantage of her naïvety and poor understanding of the language, fooled her about the extent of their sexual adventures. One elderly Samoan lady, Fa'apua'a Fa'amu, who had known Mead well, testified to Freeman of just such hoaxing in a 1987 interview.

Freeman states that both earlier and later studies of Samoa give a different overall picture from Mead's. Recent studies (and reports by older Samoans of their society in the 1920s) suggest that family bonds are strong, that physical punishment is used, that brides are expected to be virgins (in one survey Freeman found that about three-quarters are), and that strong emotions including sexual jealousy and competitiveness are common.

Not all researchers agree with all Freeman's conclusions. He bases many of his contentions on his own work in Samoa in the 1940s and the 1960s; yet, due to the influence of Christian missionaries and American military bases, Samoan society may have changed greatly even since the 1920s. But further analysis of Mead's writings and of how she obtained her evidence (Freeman, 2000, plus commentaries) do strongly suggest that the picture of an adolescent paradise may have been more a wish-fulfilment dream, than a reality.

Broad and narrow socialization

Arnett (1992) has drawn attention to the trend in Western societies for adolescents to be over-represented in categories of what he calls 'reckless behaviour'; primary components of which are having sex without contraception; delinquency and crime; illegal drug use; and driving at high speeds and while drunk. While reviewing evidence that these may be influenced by hormonal changes, cognitive factors such as adolescent egocentrism, and peer influences, he also draws attention to marked cultural differences. He summarizes this in terms of a distinction between narrow and broad socialization patterns.

Arnett argues that narrow socialization is characterized by firm expectations of, and restrictions on, personal (including adolescent) behaviour. He argues that this will be typical of smaller societies, usually pre-industrial, in which neighbours know each other. Family, peers and community (and the mass media, if present) will all tend to act to reduce reckless behaviour, though at the expense of producing conformity and reducing independence and creativity.

By contrast, broad socialization is characterized by few personal restrictions. There are more expectations of self-expression and autonomy. Arnett argues that this will be typical of modern Western societies, with large diverse communities. There is less conformity and more creativity, but also more reckless behaviour. An example of a study in this framework, carried out in Denmark, is given in box 9.2.

Arnett does not make judgements about which system is better. Each has costs and benefits. Some societies are clearly in transition; Russia, the Eastern European countries and to some extent China, for example, are relaxing personal restrictions but with consequent increases in delinquency and sexual experimentation, often in adolescents.

▪ **Further Reading**

A good general overview is Coleman, J. C. and Hendry, L. B. 1999: *The Nature of Adolescence*, 3rd edn. London: Routledge.

Tanner, M. 1973: Growing up. *Scientific American*, gives a succinct overview of the physical aspects of adolescence. More detail is available in Tanner's books (e.g., 1978: *Fetus into Man*. Cambridge, MA: Harvard University Press; 1981: *A History of the Study of Human Growth*. Cambridge: Cambridge University Press).

For work on identity, see Kroger, J. 1996: *Identity in Adolescence*, 2nd edn. London: Routledge. For a collection of work on parent and peer relations, see Montemayor, R., Adams, G. R. and Gullota, T. P. (eds) 1994: *Personal Relationships during Adolescence*. Thousand Oaks and London: Sage.

Rutter, M. and Smith, D. J. (eds) 1995: *Psychosocial Disorders in Young People: Time Trends and Their Causes*. London: Wiley, looks further at why psychosocial disorders such as crime, drug abuse and depression may be higher in adolescence.

■ Discussion Points

1   Does the biological phenomenon of puberty have any direct psychological effects?
2   Is there an 'identity crisis' at adolescence?
3   How have attitudes to sexual behaviour changed over the past 50 years? Why might this have happened?
4   Why might parent–child closeness change during adolescence?
5   Is adolescence inevitably a period of 'storm and stress'?

Box 9.1
Unravelling girls' delinquency: biological, dispositional and contextual contributions to adolescent misbehaviour

This study in New Zealand aimed to examine whether early maturation in girls was related to delinquency, as in the Swedish study of Magnusson et al. (1985); and whether such a link was related to dispositional factors (childhood history of externalizing problems), and contextual factors (single- or mixed-sex secondary school).

This kind of study aims at delineating developmental pathways; and for this, a longitudinal design is essential. The researchers drew on data from the Dunedin Multidisciplinary Health and Development Study, which sampled all children born in Dunedin, NZ, between 1 April 1972 and 31 March 1973; the children were followed up at 3, 5, 7, 9, 11, 13 and 15 years of age. Of 1139 eligible children, 1037 were assessed at 3 years, of whom 501 were girls; 415 girls were re-assessed at age 13 and 474 at age 15. Of these, 279 lived in the city of Otago and their data were used in this study, which also took account of schooling. Single-sex schools are still common in New Zealand, unlike many other industrial countries, and 165 girls entered all-girl secondary schools at age 13, while 132 entered mixed-sex schools.

Three pupil self-report questionnaires provided data relevant to this study. At 13, girls filled in an Early Delinquency scale, which measured whether they had engaged in activities such as breaking windows, getting drunk, making prank telephone calls, stealing from pupils at school. They also filled in a Familiarity with Delinquent Peers scale, which measured whether their friends, or other kids they knew, did these behaviours. At 15, the girls filled in a Delinquency scale, which measured whether they had engaged in activities such as shoplifting, car theft, smoking marijuana, using weapons.

To examine effects of maturational timing, the researchers used self-reports of menarche to divide their sample into: early maturers (those reaching menarche before 12 years 6 months; 30 per cent of sample), on-time (12 years 6 months to 13 years 6 months; 40 per cent of sample) and late maturers (after 13 years 6 months; 30 per cent of sample).

The results are shown in box table 9.1.1. Considering the aims of the study, it does confirm that early maturing girls are more at risk. Effects of maturational timing are significant for all three of the measures used.

Box Table 9.1.1 Rates for early delinquency, familiarity with delinquent peers, and delinquency, at ages 13 and 15, by onset of physical maturation

		Early maturers	On-time maturers	Late maturers
Age 13	All girl	2.0	2.5	1.3
Early delinquency	Mixed sex	4.3	2.4	1.2
Age 13	All girl	14.1	13.7	12.1
Delinquent peers	Mixed sex	19.3	17.0	13.6
Age 15	All girl	1.8	2.5	1.5
Delinquency	Mixed sex	3.2	3.5	1.3

Source: Adapted from Caspi et al., 1993

However, this effect is a complex one. For one thing, it interacts with context, in the sense of type of school. For the Familiarity with Delinquent Peers measure, there is a statistically significant effect, with more evidence of familiarity with other girls' delinquency in the mixed-sex schools than in the same-sex schools; and this effect is largest for early-maturing girls. This interaction effect is statistically significant for the Early Delinquency measure, which confirms that early maturing girls are more at risk of being delinquent themselves, but only in mixed-sex schools. The effect is not significant for the Delinquency at age 15 measure, where it seems that both early and on-time maturers are scoring higher than late maturers. The authors suggest that by this time, the on-time maturers have 'caught up' with the early maturers so far as delinquency is concerned.

In addition, the researchers examined what they called dispositional factors, measured here as parent and teacher ratings of externalizing (e.g., aggressive) behaviour problems at age 9. They found that familiarity with peers was especially important in predicting delinquency, for early-maturing girls without an earlier history of externalizing problems.

In interpreting these results, the authors argue that (as Magnusson et al., 1985, found), early-maturing girls are likely to associate with older peers, who are more into norm-breaking activities. Also, such peer pressures may be particularly strong in mixed-sex schools, with higher delinquency rates among boys, and possibly greater opportunities for observing or engaging in delinquent activities. These effects of peers were particularly strong for early-maturing girls with no earlier history of externalizing problems. Probably, those who did have an earlier history of externalizing problems were already familiar with delinquent acts by age 13 and did not need peer familiarity to get into such activities.

The New Zealand context provided an unusual opportunity to show the effects of single-sex versus mixed-sex secondary schooling. The researchers were aware that school differences might reflect differences in families due to parental choice of school; however, they found no differences between the school samples in parental values, or in behaviour problems at age 9. There was a trend for higher-social-class parents to choose all-girl schools, so social class was taken account of in the statistical analyses.

The study shows the power of a longitudinal design with a large, representative sample. Dropout rates were not large. There is a reliance on self-report measures, which characterizes much work on antisocial behaviour (see also box 5.2), due to the difficulties of getting valid alternative measures on a large scale. This is a sophisticated quantitative study; the use of more qualitative methods (for example, in-depth interviews with some early and late maturers) might throw even more light onto the processes involved.

Based on material from Caspi, A., Lynam, D., Moffitt, T. E. and Silva, P. A. 1993: Unravelling girls' delinquency: biological, dispositional and contextual contributions to adolescent misbehaviour. *Developmental Psychology*, 29, 19–30.

Box 9.2
Cultural bases of risk behaviour: Danish adolescents

In this study, risk behaviour (similar to, but wider than, reckless behaviour or delinquency) was assessed in 1053 Danish adolescents. The authors wished to assess absolute levels of types of risk behaviour, and also see how these varied by community size and family type. In addition, they made comparisons with similar behaviours in the USA.

Like most Western societies, Denmark tends to what Arnett calls 'broad socialization', with few restrictions on adolescent behaviour; however, car driving is not permitted until 18 (and per capita, car ownership is about one-half of US levels). There is much better provision for cyclists than in many countries such as the USA or even the UK. Sex education including knowledge of contraception is provided in schools before adolescence.

Denmark has a rather homogeneous population of about 5 million. One million live in Copenhagen; there are three cities of 100,000–150,000, including Odense; and about four-fifths of the population live in small cities (population less than 50,000). The researchers chose three schools/colleges each, in Copenhagen, Odense and Varde, a small town. Risk behaviours were measured by a short self-report questionnaire on the frequency of engaging in a variety of risk activities over the past year; participation rates were 99 per cent. Family measures were taken using a Family Relationships questionnaire.

A sample of the results, broken down by age and sex, is given in box table 9.2.1. There are low rates of driving a car while drunk, but much higher rates of riding a bicycle while drunk. Rates of sex without contraception are quite considerable in older adolescence, although less than rates with contraception (included not as a risk behaviour, but for comparison); in fact, those who engaged in sex with contraception were also more likely to do so without contraception. Marijuana use and cigarette dependency were fairly frequent, but use of cocaine or other drugs was very rare. All these risk behaviours increased with age; but shoplifting and vandalism peaked in the 16–17-year-old period. Generally, risk-taking behaviours were less frequent in girls, with the exception of sexual behaviours, and cigarette dependence.

Family influences did not appear to be very strong in this study. There were few differences between intact and divorced or lone-parent families, for example; and no effects of parental strictness. However, lower parental monitoring did predict to increased drink/cycling and marijuana use and cigarette dependency; and poorer family relationships generally did predict to greater risk of shoplifting and vandalism.

Many types of risk behaviour were greatest in Copenhagen (large city) compared with the smaller communities; for example, sex without contraception, cigarette dependency and marijuana use, and shop-

Box Table 9.2.1   Prevalence (at least once during last year) of risk behaviours, in male (M) and female (F) Danish adolescents

		12–13 yrs	14–15 yrs	16–17 yrs	18–20 yrs
Drink/cycling	M	18	56	77	76
	F	13	52	61	63
Drink/car driving	M	0	0	7	15
	F	0	0	2	8
Sex without contraception	M	4	4	25	42
	F	2	12	20	34
Sex with contraception	M	2	14	53	65
	F	3	15	43	75
Marijuana use	M	12	22	33	32
	F	10	13	22	24
Cigarette dependency (20 days in last month)	M	6	18	23	19
	F	5	18	18	33
Cocaine use	M	2	0	0	1
	F	0	0	1	2
Shoplifting	M	14	21	25	17
	F	5	16	14	11
Vandalism	M	18	38	33	34
	F	5	12	14	10

Source: Adapted from Arnett and Balle-Jensen, 1993

lifting; however, vandalism was more frequent in Odense (mid-size city).

Drawing comparison with US studies, the authors conclude that rates of sex without contraception are somewhat similar; but since teenage pregnancy rates are much lower in Denmark, this may reflect occasional lapses in the Danish adolescents rather than a consistent pattern. The low rates of drink/driving (but high rates of drink/cycling) can be related to legal restrictions and cultural opportunities. Surprisingly, the authors do not comment on the very low rates of hard drug use; they do comment that cigarette dependency is higher than in US studies, perhaps because of more intensive media anti-smoking campaigns in the USA.

This study, cross-sectional in design, does potentially confound historical factors with what are apparently age changes (in box table 9.2.1, for example); but it could be argued that historical changes might not be very large over the eight-year period which represents the total age range in the study, at least compared with the size of age changes obtained. The data on risk behaviour and on family factors are all obtained from adolescent self-report, as is quite common in research of this kind; but other sources of data could help validate the conclusions. A strength of the study is the way it takes account of the social and legal context of the country of study, Denmark, and contrasts it with much more widely studied adolescent populations in the USA.

Based on material in Arnett, J. and Balle-Jensen, L. 1993: Cultural bases of risk behaviour: Danish adolescents. *Child Development*, 64, 1842–59.

PART THREE Children's Developing Minds

10 Perception

Psychologists make a distinction between sensation and perception. 'Sensation' refers to the process through which information about the environment is picked up by sensory receptors and transmitted to the brain. It is known that infants have certain sensory abilities at birth because they respond to light, sound, smell, touch and taste. 'Perception' refers to the interpretation by the brain of this sensory input. It is through perception that we gain an understanding about the events, objects and people who surround us.

As adults we can discriminate speech from birdsong, or a distant tree from a nearby flower. But can infants, with their limited experience, understand the variety of stimuli that their sensory receptors detect? Are they born with certain perceptual capacities or must these be acquired through learning and experience?

The debate about the relative influence of heredity and environment in perception has a long history. Empiricists, following the tradition of the philosopher John Locke (1690/1939), argued that the newborn infant is a 'tabula rasa' (blank slate), on which experiences are imprinted. For example, the psychologist William James (1890) asserted that, to the infant, sensory inputs become fused into 'one blooming, buzzing confusion' and that it is only later, through experience, that children can discriminate among them. In other words, children's ability to perceive develops as the result of a long learning process.

A contrasting view was proposed by nativists, who claimed that many perceptual abilities are present at birth. Philosophers such as Descartes (1638/1965) and Kant (1781/1958) argued that infants' capacity to perceive space, for example, is innate. Later, psychologists of the Gestalt school (in the early twentieth century) lent support to the idea that certain perceptual abilities were present at birth because of the structural characteristics of the nervous system. Furthermore, they argued that the infant, far from being a tabula rasa, actively tries to create order and organization in her perceptual world.

In recent years experimental psychologists have been able to make an important contribution to our knowledge of perceptual development in the infant. Researchers have found that infants are born with a wider range of perceptual capabilities than empiricists suggest, and that infants' capacity to learn rapidly from experience is greater than the nativists propose (Gordon and Slater, 1998). The newborn infant possesses many abilities for exploring events and objects in her world, and this is enough to form the basis for rapid learning and development (Mehler and Dupoux, 1994). In this chapter we will give some examples of infants' perceptual abilities, and in doing so we will concentrate on the research that has been carried out with newborn and very young infants.

Methods for Studying Infants' Perception

It is not easy to work with young infants, because they cannot tell you what they are thinking, and therefore what they know has to be inferred from their behaviour. But infants' repertoire of behaviours is limited and researchers have had to invent ingenious techniques for measuring their perceptual abilities.

Preference technique: In this procedure a researcher presents two stimuli to an infant at the same time – for example these might be two pictures (A and B). The researcher can then measure how long the infant looks at each picture. If, over a period of time, the infant looks at each picture equally it may be because she does not differentiate between them. If she looks at A more than B it can be inferred that she 'prefers' A and two conclusions follow from this: first, that the infant can in fact distinguish between the two pictures (having a preference is indicative of discriminating between the two stimuli); second, that for some reason, the infant finds A to be the more stimulating picture to look at, and whatever infants find particularly stimulating may give us clues about which aspects of the environment are contributing to their development.

The preference technique is a comparatively easy technique to employ if accurate measures of the infants' looking can be made. The early research was based on an observer watching the infant's face and measuring how long she looked at a stimulus (see box plate 10.1.1). But contemporary research is carried out using video film of the infants' face, and the video can be scored objectively to accurately measure what the child looked at. Infant's eye fixations can also be recorded so that researchers can measure not only how long an infant looks at a stimulus but also on which parts of the stimulus the infant focuses. An example of early research based on the preference technique is given in box 10.1.

Habituation: Another method involves habituation and dishabituation to a stimulus. If an infant is shown an interesting stimulus (A) she may look at it for some time, but eventually she will lose interest in it. If A is presented again and again it is likely that each time it is presented the infant will spend less and less time looking at it (i.e., she habituates to it). Then, if A is changed for a different stimulus (B) she is likely to show a renewed interest in the novel stimulus and start looking at it for some time (i.e., she dishabituates to it).

A researcher can exploit this pattern of habituation and dishabituation. For example, suppose you wanted to know if an infant can distinguish between two very similar pictures. You could show her picture A until she has habituated to it. Then show her picture B. If she does not start looking at B it is as if she treats it as A (which she's already lost interest in). It can then be inferred that she cannot distinguish B from A. If, however, the infant does start looking at B, it can be assumed, from this dishabituation, that she can discriminate between A and B. This technique is effective for finding out just how large or small a difference there needs to be between two stimuli for an infant to detect the difference between them.

Conditioning: Infants will learn to carry out behaviours if those behaviours are reinforced, and this is called conditioning. For example, Bower (1965) conditioned infants to turn their head to one side by 'rewarding' the infant every time she turned her head. The reward in this case was an adult popping up into the infant's line of sight and playing peek-a-boo (something that infants like!). At the start of such an experiment, the adult has to wait until the infant naturally moves her head to one side, and then gives a peek-a-boo response. If the adult does this every time the infant turns her head, the infant will learn to make the head movement each time she wants to get the same response. In Bower's experiment he conditioned infant's head turning as part of an investigation of infants' visual perception (see below).

Other experimenters have used infants' responses in a manner similar to the habituation and dishabituation paradigm described above. For example, suppose an infant is sucking on a teat, if she increases her sucking rate above the usual rate this can be rewarded by presenting a stimulus (e.g., sound A). The infant will learn that every time she increases her sucking rate she is rewarded by hearing the sound. For as long as the sound remains an interesting stimulus the infant is likely to go on sucking to hear it. However, there will come a point when the infant's interest in the sound declines and she no longer sucks so frequently (i.e., she has habituated to it). At that point the experimenter can alter the sound (e.g., to sound B). If the infant does not increase sucking the experimenter can assume that she does not differentiate between A and B, but if she does increase sucking (i.e., dishabituates) when she firsts hears B it can be inferred that she treats B as a different sound from A. In this way researchers can find out how well infants distinguish between different stimuli.

As well as behaviours that can be observed (like looking, sucking or head turning) other less obvious responses can also be measured. In particular, researchers have measured changes in infants' heart rate. If infants are surprised or upset their heart rate increases and if they are focusing or attending to a stimulus their heart rate tends to slow down. To use the example of differentiating sounds again, an infant hearing sound A for the first time may show a decline in heart rate (assuming that A is not such a frightening noise that the infant's heart rate increases rapidly). After having heard sound A several times, she will habituate to it and then the researcher can present sound B. If the infant's heart rate slows down at the sound of B it indicates dishabituation which can be taken as evidence that the infant distinguishes between sounds A and B.

Summary

Infants' preferences, habituation and conditioning are all important in their own right. Preferences indicate those aspects of the environment that the infant finds most stimulating at the time. Habituation is important because it means that an infant will not just concentrate on one object, but after a time will lose interest in that object and therefore seek out new stimuli. Habituation is, in effect, a constant encouragement to explore new things. Conditioning allows an infant to have some control over her environment (e.g., by turning her head an infant can make an adult appear to play peek-a-boo, or by sucking harder on a teat, she can hear an attractive sound). These responses reflect infants' understanding of patterns and relationships within the world and are the first signs of learning.

It should be added that none of the above methods can be used without difficulty. Very young children are hard to work with, they may be easily distracted, they may become upset, or they may even fall asleep during an experiment! Apart from these problems researchers may sometimes find it difficult to measure or interpret the sort of infant behaviours (like head turning, or heart rate change) that are fundamental to the investigation of perceptual abilities. Nonetheless, the application of different experimental techniques permits researchers to approach each question about perceptual development in several ways, and if researchers using different techniques all find similar results it gives us confidence in the reliability of those results.

■ Visual Perception

Investigating infants' perception

The visual abilities of a newborn infant are different from those of an adult (Hainline, 1998). For example, a newborn infant has much poorer visual acuity. Visual acuity is a measure of how well an individual can detect visual detail. People can be asked to look at a visual display made up of vertical black and white lines (of equal width) while the lines are made progressively narrower. There will be a point when people can no longer distinguish the lines as separate, and the display will appear as a grey image. Newborn infants can only detect the separation of the lines if they are about 30 times wider than the minimum width that adults can detect (Atkinson and Braddick, 1981). Children's acuity does improve rapidly, but their limited acuity during the first few months means that young children view a world that is more fuzzy and blurred than an adult's.

The vision of a newborn infant is also limited in other ways. For example, infants younger than two months cannot track a moving object very smoothly, instead they tend to follow a moving object by making a series of jerky eye-movements (Aslin, 1981). To take in the whole of an object it is usually necessary to scan across the object, but infants may have less effective scanning abilities. Salapatek (1975) investigated the eye movements of young infants as they scanned geometric shapes such as triangles, circles, and squares. Salapatek found that at

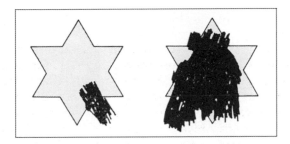

Figure 10.1 Visual scanning of a geometrical figure by one- and two-month-old children. The older infants scanned more of the figure (from Schaffer, 1985).

one month of age infants tended to focus on a single, or limited number of features in the shape (for example, just part of the boundary of the shape – see figure 10.1). By two months of age infants have adopted more comprehensive scanning strategies.

Newborn infants have only a limited ability to detect colours. Adams et al. (1994) found that newborn infants could distinguish between red and white, but not between white and other colours. By the age of two months infants can discriminate several other colours from white, including orange, blue, some greens and some purples (Teller et al., 1978).

In summary, young infants have a functional and effective visual system, but the quality of their vision, at least in the first few weeks and months of life is poorer than adults' vision. Nonetheless, as Hainline (1998) has emphasized what might be classed as 'limitations' when compared to adults' vision, may not be detrimental for very young infants. Although infants' limitations may reduce the range of stimuli they experience this may actually help them to focus on the most important aspects of their environment during the first few months of life (see chapter 3).

Pattern perception

Infants may have very early preferences for particular patterns. For example, Fantz (1961) found that infants as young as two days could discriminate between patterned and unpatterned shapes. For example, they preferred to look at striped, bulls-eye or checkerboard patterns rather than at plain discs or squares. Fantz therefore concluded that infants prefer to look at more complex patterns (see box 10.1).

In another experiment, Fantz and Fagan (1975) showed one- and two-month-old children two stimuli which each had identical amounts of light and dark areas on them, but differed in the complexity of their patterns (see figure 10.2). The one-month-old infants preferred the less complex stimuli (with eight 1-inch squares), and the two-month-old infants preferred the more complex pattern (with 32 smaller squares). It may be that as infants' acuity improves and they can see more

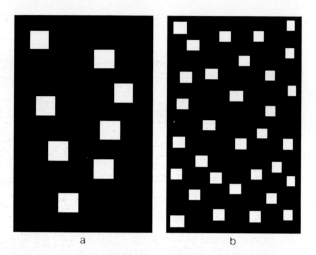

a   b

Figure 10.2 Stimuli similar to those used by Fantz and Fagan (1975).

detail the more complex patterns become more interesting and stimulating (Banks and Ginsburg, 1985).

Infants may also prefer patterns with particular shapes. For example, Fantz and Miranda (1975) showed patterns to infants who were less than one-week-old. These patterns are shown in figure 10.3 and were presented in pairs (e.g., the curved and straight contoured versions of the type 1 pattern would be presented together). Fantz and Miranda found that infants had a preference for patterns that had curved edges rather than straight edges. But this preference disappeared if the patterns were placed in a surround (see lower two rows of figure 10.3). This may be because, as we mentioned above, infants often prefer to look at the edges of figures or shapes. In other words, if there are curves within a pattern they will attract less attention than if the shape itself is curved.

Face perception

Faces are an important aspect of infants' environments (see chapter 3). Not only do infants have frequent experience of faces from immediately after birth, but they also have to learn to interpret the faces they see. Research into the development of face recognition is one of the largest areas of investigation in infant cognition, and many issues have been considered. For example, when do infants first recognize faces? Do infants have a specialized ability to process information about faces? When do infants distinguish between different faces? Can they recognize different facial expressions?

In one of the earliest studies of face recognition Fantz (1961) showed infants three stimuli based on a face. Fantz's study is summarized in box 10.1 and the stimuli are illustrated in box figure 10.1.2. At all ages from a few days old to six months of age the infants spent the longest time looking at a face, slightly less

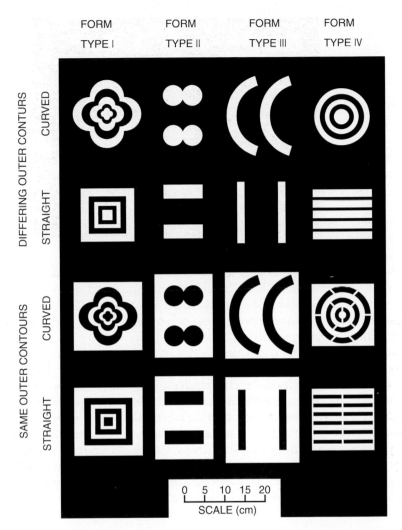

Figure 10.3   Patterns with straight and curved edges used by Fantz and Miranda (1975).

time looking at a scrambled face and much less time at a non-face like pattern. But it was not clear from Fantz's experiment why the infants preferred the face and the scrambled face. As described above, Fantz himself found infants prefer to look at more complex patterns (see box 10.1). Both the face and the scrambled face were more complex than the non-face and the infants may have simply preferred to look more at the two complex patterns.

Maurer and Barrera (1981) overcame the issue of complexity by using the three stimuli illustrated in figure 10.4 with one- and two-month-old infants. One stimulus was a 'natural' face, the second was a symmetrical scrambled face, and the third was an asymmetrical scrambled face. All the stimuli had the same facial features, and thus the same complexity. There was no difference in how long the

Figure 10.4 Face stimuli used by Maurer and Barrera (1981).

one-month-old infants looked at any of the stimuli, but the two-month-olds looked longer at the natural face than either of the other two stimuli. This suggested that any preference for natural faces at two months of age was more than just a preference for more complex stimuli.

However, other researchers have found, using different techniques, that newborn infants can recognize faces. Goren et al. (1975) showed newborn infants a schematic face, a schematic symmetrical scrambled face, or a blank outline. While an infant lay on her back Goren et al. moved the stimuli in an arc from one side of the infant to the other. The infants' eye and head movements were measured to assess how long they tracked each stimulus. The infants tracked the schematic face more than the other two stimuli and this suggests that infants have some ability to detect face-like stimuli from birth.

Johnson et al. (1991) confirmed Goren et al.'s findings with newborn infants, but also found that by the age of about three months infants no longer spent more time tracking the schematic face than the other stimuli. Johnson and Morton (1991) pointed out this contrast in the findings. If children are shown moving faces they show a face preference at birth, but not after about three months. If children are shown a static face (as in Maurer and Barrera, 1981) they do not show a face preference until about two months. To explain these results Johnson and Morton proposed that early face recognition may be based on two different processing systems (Johnson, M. H., 1998). They proposed a very early system that operates during the first few weeks of life to draw infants' attention to moving faces. As faces are one of the most important stimuli in an infant's environment such processing would be advantageous in helping infants select what is relevant in the world around them. By attending to faces, infants can then begin to learn about different faces, and at this time a second processing system takes over and contributes to infant's ability to identify individual faces, including static ones.

Johnson and Morton's (1991) proposal goes some way in explaining the diversity of results found in the earlier studies of face recognition, and it implies a processing system that is dedicated to tracking faces during the first few weeks of life. In other words, children are born with a specialized ability to process faces or some aspect of faces. Other researchers have argued that face processing is no different to processing any other visual stimuli. Simion et al. (2001) pointed out that faces have more elements in their upper part, and it might be the case that infants prefer any stimuli where the upper part is more salient. Simion et al. showed newborn infants pairs of patterns like the ones shown in figure 10.5. In each of the four pairs one pattern had more elements in the upper part and one

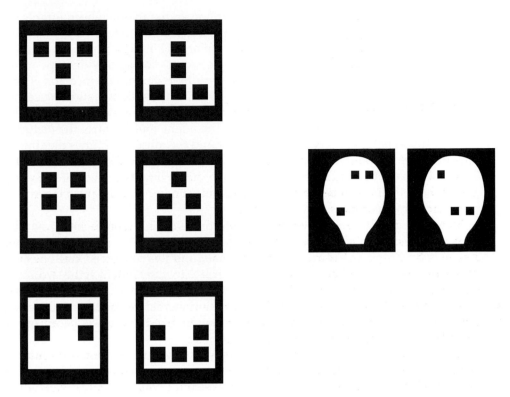

Figure 10.5 Four pairs of stimuli used by Simion et al. (2001). In each pair of stimuli one has more elements in the upper half and one has more elements in the lower half. Redrawn from Simion et al., 2001.

had more elements in the lower part. Simion et al. found that infants looked longer at the stimuli with more elements in the upper part.

Simion et al. also found that the infants looked longer at both the schematic outline faces than at the rectangular stimuli – this may have been because infants prefer patterns with curved rather than straight edges (see box 10.1). Simion et al. (2001, p. 61) therefore concluded that: 'face preference at birth would simply result from the match between the general properties of the stimulus, which are a greater number of elements in the upper portion of the configuration and a curved contour, and some generalized newborn's abilities, such as a preference for stimuli with more elements in the upper part and with curved contours.'

As pointed out above very young infants show preferences for face-like stimuli (Goren et al., 1975; Johnson et al., 1991). This preference may be because infants are born with face-specific processing abilities (e.g., Johnson and Morton, 1991) or may be the outcome of more general processing abilities (e.g., Simion et al., 2001). As yet, this issue has not been resolved (Gauthier and Nelson, 2001; Nelson, 2001).

Nonetheless, over recent years much evidence has accumulated to show that very young infants have good face recognition skills and can learn faces very rapidly. For example, Walton et al. (1992) demonstrated that newborn infants can distinguish their mother's face. Walton et al. showed one- to four-day-old infants a videotape showing their mother and a similar looking but unfamiliar female. All the adults maintained a neutral expression, and the use of videotape meant that there were no olfactory cues. Infants were first shown one face and if they sucked on a teat that face remained on the screen. If they did not suck the second face appeared (and remained on the screen as long as the infants sucked, otherwise the first face re-appeared). In this way the infant could control the picture at which they were looking. Walton et al. measured the number of times that infants sucked while keeping their mother's face visible and how often they sucked to keep the stranger's face in view. All but one of the infants in the study sucked more to see their mother's face, and this result showed that infants start to distinguish individual faces very quickly.

How do newborn infants distinguish their mother's face from another person's? Pascalis et al. (1995) found that four-day-old infants could discriminate between their mother and an unfamiliar female, and this confirmed Walton et al.'s findings. But Pascalis et al. then carried out a further study in which the two adults wore scarves so that only their internal facial features were visible. The infants in this experiment did not distinguish between their mother and another female, and Pascalis et al. concluded that early recognition of familiar faces is based on the external contours of the face.

Pascalis et al.'s finding suggests that very young infants do not process the internal features of a face, and if that is the case we would not expect them to recognize facial expressions (de Haan and Nelson, 1998). Nonetheless, newborn infants do respond to internal features when those features move. For example, newborn infants will imitate an adult's facial expression, like tongue protrusions or mouth opening (Meltzoff and Moore, 1983) – see chapters 3 and 12. And some researchers have argued that very young infants can recognize expressions. For example, Field et al. (1982) showed newborn infants happy, sad and surprised expressions that were posed by an adult. The adult maintained one expression until the infants stopped looking at her (i.e., until they had habituated to the expression) and then the adult changed to one of the other expressions. When the expression changed the infants started to look again (i.e., dishabituated) and Field et al. argued from this result that the infants could discriminate between different facial expressions.

Perceptual constancies

As a person or object moves relative to the viewer, the visual size, shape and colour information it projects on the eye will change. Yet we perceive a given object as the same, even though its apparent size, shape and colour change in this way. This effect is referred to as a perceptual 'constancy'. Size constancy can be illustrated with the following example. If we observe a car driving away from us along a road, the image of the car on the retina becomes smaller but we do not perceive the car as getting smaller. We perceive that the car remains the same size, but is actually getting further away. To perceive this way is to display 'size

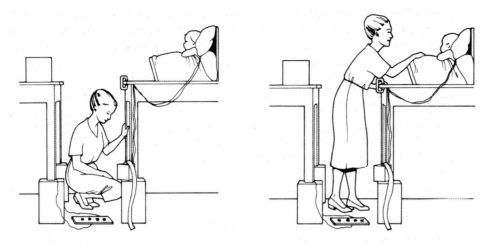

Figure 10.6 The apparatus used in Bower's experiment (from Bower, 1982).

constancy'; in other words, we understand that the size of an object remains constant even though the object may be at a different distance. This is an observation that seems obvious to the adult, but does the infant have the same knowledge at birth or must she learn to respond to the appropriate cues?

Bower (1965) carried out one of the first investigations into size constancy with infants who were six- to eight-weeks-old. The infants were rewarded for turning their heads to the left. An adult, who was hidden from the infant knew when the child had turned her head because the infant's action operated a sensitive pressure switch on a pad behind the infant's head. The adult then stood up and gave a 'peek-a-boo' response, and then disappeared again (see figure 10.6). As we saw in chapter 3 infants enjoy contingent responses like an adult playing peek-a-boo, and therefore they learn to make head turns to get the adult's response.

Once the head-turning response was firmly established, Bower changed the procedure slightly. Sometimes a 30 cm cube was placed at 1 metre distance from the infant. The infant only received the reward (the peek-a-boo response) if she turned her head when the cube was present. In this way infants learnt (or were 'conditioned') to make a head turn only when they saw the cube at that distance.

In a later test phase Bower (1965) presented various stimuli. For example, the original 30 cm cube to which the infant had been conditioned was placed three metres away from the infant. At the greater distance this cube projected a smaller retinal image than at the original distance of one metre. Bower also used a 90 cm cube which was placed three metres away. This larger cube at a greater distance produced the same size retinal image as the original stimulus.

Bower (1965) argued that if infants did have size constancy they would continue to display head turning when they saw the 30 cm cube, even though it was placed further away. If the infants did not have size constancy and were responding on the basis of the size of an object's retinal image, then they would not respond to the 30 cm cube further away. But they would respond to the 90 cm cube at three metres because this projected the same retinal image to which the infants had been conditioned. Bower found that the infants responded three times more often to the 30 cm cube than the 90 cm cube. In other words, the infants responded on the basis of the size of the object rather than the size of its retinal image and Bower concluded that young infants do have size constancy.

The infants in Bower's (1965) experiment were a few weeks old, but other researchers have suggested that even younger children may also have size constancy. Slater et al. (1990) showed newborn infants the same cube six times, and each time the cube was shown at different distances from the infant. In this way the infant was familiarized with the cube. Slater et al. then showed the infant two cubes at the same time. One cube was the original cube that the child had seen six times (but shown at a distance that had not been used previously) and the other cube was a new one of a different size. The two cubes were positioned so that they both formed the same size image on the infant's retina. Slater et al. found that all the infants looked longer at the new cube (presumably because they had habituated to the original which they had already seen six times) and this demonstrated that the children could distinguish between the two cubes even though they both produced the same retinal image. Slater et al. argued that if newborn infants could distinguish between the cubes they must have been doing so on the basis of the actual size of the cubes. In other words, size constancy is present from birth.

Shape constancy refers to the fact that we see the shape of an object as the same even when its orientation changes. Several researchers have shown that young infants have shape constancy. For example, Caron et al. (1979) showed three-month-olds a shape (e.g., a rectangle) several times and each time the rectangle was tilted at a different angle. Then on a test trial Caron et al. showed infants the rectangle (tilted to a new angle) paired with a new shape and measured the infants' preference. Although the infants had never seen the rectangle tilted at the angle used in the test trial the infants still preferred to look at the new shape. The infants' preference for the new shape suggested that they had habituated to the rectangle, and this habituation applied even when the rectangle was presented at a new angle. If the angle of presentation did not make any difference to the children this implies that the infants had achieved shape constancy for the rectangle – i.e., the infants treated the rectangle as the same shape in whatever position they saw it. Slater and Morison (1985) used a similar procedure to Caron et al. (1979) to test newborn infants and they found that newborn infants also had shape constancy.

The research into perceptual constancies shows the same pattern of discoveries. As described above researchers have first found that infants have, for example, size and shape constancy, and then progressively more experimentation has shown that it is possible to demonstrate the same constancies in newborn infants. In areas like this the increase in studies with newborn infants has supported the idea of the competent infant – one that is born with many abilities (Slater, 1998).

If newborn infants have size and shape constancy, it is unlikely that the infant's experience will have much effect on the ability to detect such constancies.

However, other perceptual abilities may be only partially developed or not developed at all at birth and these are ones that will be dependent on learning and experience. In the following sections we give examples of how children's experience contributes to the development of visual abilities.

Object separation

Most studies of infants' object perception involve infants looking at one or two separate objects, but the real world is made up of many objects, with some objects touching or occluding others (S. P. Johnson, 1998). Given the complexity of most real world environments, when can infants perceive distinct objects in the world around them?

Kellman and Spelke (1983) investigated this by showing three- to four-month-old infants a rod moving from side to side behind a box. The rod was never fully visible but both ends of the rod could be seen above and below the box (see figure 10.7a). Even though it would be possible to imagine the two parts of the rods as separate, when adults see this display they assume that the two parts of the rod are part of a common object. Presumably adults see the rod as a single object because the two parts are aligned with each other and the fact that they move in unison strengthens the impression of a single object. Do infants also perceive the scene as a single rod behind a box?

After Kellman and Spelke (1983) had shown infants the rod and box display, the infants were presented with two stimuli. One was a complete rod and one was a broken rod (see figure 10.7b). Kellman and Spelke argued that if the infants had interpreted the rod behind the box as a complete object they would have habituated to it and would therefore prefer to look at the broken rod. Alternatively if the infants had treated the rod behind the box as two separate objects they would have habituated to those and prefer to look at the complete rod. In fact, the infants looked more at the broken rod and this implied that they had seen the rod behind the box as a complete object.

The infants tested by Kellman and Spelke were three-months of age, and other researchers have also found the same result for two-month-old infants (e.g., Johnson and Aslin, 1995). But do newborn children also perceive occluded objects as complete ones? Slater, Morison, Somers, Mattock, Brown and Taylor (1990) used the same procedure as Kellman and Spelke to test newborn infants and found that the infants preferred to look at the complete rod rather than the broken one. This implied that the infants had habituated to the broken rod (that is they had treated the rod behind the box as two separate parts). Therefore newborn infants do not perceive occluded objects as ones that are made up of seen and unseen parts. However, at least for the type of stimuli used by Kellman and Spelke, this understanding is achieved within the first two or three months. Presumably infants need some experience of objects before they realize that the coordinated movement of what appear to be two separate objects may indicate that those two objects are parts of the same item.

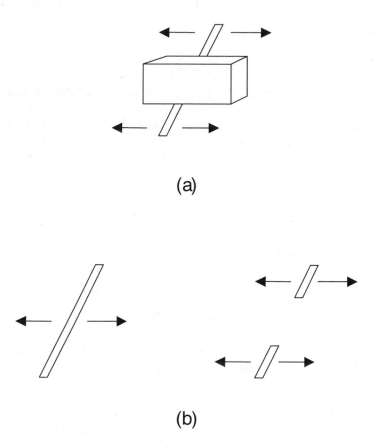

(a)

(b)

Figure 10.7 (a) Rod and box display (b) test stimuli, used by Kellman and Spelke (1983). The arrows on either side of the rods indicate that the rods moved from side to side during the display. Redrawn from Kellman and Spelke (1983).

Several researchers have demonstrated the importance of experience on perceptual development. For example, Needham and Baillargeon (1998) showed four-month-olds a scene that included two objects touching each other. While the infant watched, the objects were sometimes moved individually and sometimes they were moved together. The infants spent as long looking at the objects moving separately as they did looking at the objects moving together. In other words, they did not show surprise when the objects moved together and Needham and Baillargeon suggested that infants of this age were not sure when objects in a visual scene were separate or not. In a second experiment Needham and Baillargeon showed infants one of the objects on its own before showing them the objects moving separately or together. In this experiment the infants looked longer (i.e., showed surprise) when the two objects moved together. These results suggested that when infants had first experienced an object on its own they could later distinguish it when they saw it as part of a complex scene, and demonstrated the importance of experience in the development of perceptual abilities. Needham and Baillargeon's studies are summarized in box 10.2.

Depth perception

Other perceptual abilities may develop more directly as a result of experience. For example, Gibson and Walk (1960) used the ingenious 'visual cliff' to investigate infants' depth perception. The visual cliff was a glass table with a checkerboard pattern underneath the glass. There was a central platform and on the shallow side of this platform the pattern was immediately below the glass. At the other, deep, side the pattern was several feet below the glass (see plate 10.1). Gibson and Walk argued that if infants had no depth perception they would be willing to crawl over the 'deep' side of the table. But if infants did have depth perception, they might be unwilling to go over the edge. The children were six to 14 months old, that is they were old enough to crawl, so Gibson and Walk placed infants on the central platform and observed which way they moved. The infants were willing to crawl on the shallow side of the table, but would not crawl over the 'cliff' even when encouraged to do so by their mothers.

Although Gibson and Walk's (1960) result demonstrated depth perception in infants after six months of age, their experiment depended on the infants crawling (or not crawling) over different sides of the visual cliff. As younger infants are not able to crawl, later researchers considered other measures to find out if they have depth perception. Schwartz et al. (1973) placed five- and nine-month-olds on the shallow and deep sides of the visual cliff, and measured their heart rate. As we pointed out earlier infants' heart rate tends to increase if they are surprised or frightened and slows down during periods of increased attention. Shwartz et al. found that the nine-month-olds' heart rate increased when they were over the deep side of the cliff, but the five-month-olds' heart rate decreased over the deep side. The fact that the younger infants' heart rate changed showed that they noticed a difference between the sides, but as their heart rate did not increase (which would have reflected fear or surprise) there was no evidence that they recognized they were over a drop.

Some researchers have argued that rather than age, experience is an important factor in developing the depth perception needed to recognize the drop on the deep side of the visual cliff. Campos et al. (1992) found that the heart rate of infants who could crawl increased when they were placed over the deep side of the cliff, but the heart rate of similarly aged infants who could not crawl decreased on the deep side. In a similar study infants, who did not crawl on their own, were given several hours of experience of moving in a wheeled walker and then they were placed on the visual cliff. The heart-rate of these infants increased when they were over the deep side. These findings suggest that learning not to move onto the deep side of the cliff is the result of experience that infants have gained from crawling.

The visual cliff has also been used to investigate infants' recognition of facial expressions and emotions, and an example of such studies is given on p. 180.

◼ Auditory Perception

For adults, vision is the most important of the senses. For young infants, this may not be so. Relative to adults, the auditory acuity of newborn infants is much better

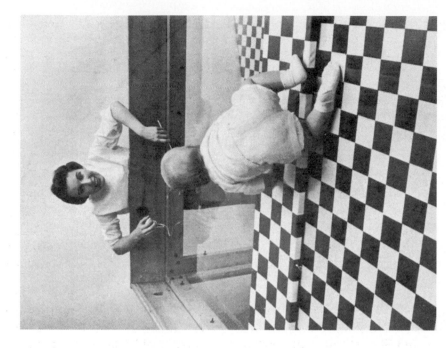

Plate 10.1 A mother encourages a child to venture over the 'visual cliff' (from Gibson and Walk, 1960).

than their visual acuity, for example, newborns will turn their heads towards a sound, which suggests they can locate sounds very soon after birth. In this section we will give examples of young infants' responses to voices and speech sounds, as these are important auditory stimuli both for the early development of attachment relationships (chapter 4) and language (chapter 11).

Auditory perception develops before birth (Lecanuet, 1998). Recordings within the uterus have demonstrated that sounds like voices and in particular the mother's voice (because it is transmitted both externally and internally through bones and body tissue) can, to some extent, be heard in the uterus. Several researchers have shown fetal reactions to sound, and some of these studies are described in chapter 3 (see box 3.1). Typically an external sound is played and the fetal reaction (called a startle response) is measured by asking the mother if she is aware of any fetal movement, by observing that movement by ultrasound scanning, or by measuring changes in fetal heart rate. Reactions to some sounds can be identified from about 20 weeks (Shahidullah and Hepper, 1993a). The discrimination of sounds becomes better over time and near term fetuses can distinguish between male and female voices (Lecanuet et al., 1993).

In studies with newborn infants, researchers have tested their auditory perception by, for example, giving them the opportunity to suck on a teat to hear sounds. Infant preferences are measured by how much they suck on the teat. DeCasper and Fifer (1980) found that when three-day old infants could suck to hear their mother's voice or the voice of a stranger, the infants sucked more to hear their mother's voice. By this age the infants had only had about 12 hours contact with their mothers and their preference would imply either very rapid learning after birth, or some learning before birth. When DeCasper and Prescott (1984) tested two-day-old infants' preference for their father's voice or the voice of another male, the infants showed no preference, even though they had had several hours contact with their father. The preference for mother's voice and the lack of preference for father's voice in the first few days after birth suggests that the preference is less to do with post-natal learning and more to do with prior experience. Fifer and Moon (1989) and Moon and Fifer (1990) showed that infants may recognize their mother's voice from before birth (see box 3.1). They gave infants the choice between listening to their mother's voice that simulated the way they would have heard it in the uterine environment and listening to their mother's voice as they heard it after birth. Moon and Fifer found that the infants preferred the former version of their mother's voice. Taken together these findings suggest that infants have learnt to recognize their mother's voice before they are born.

There is evidence that other learning is also possible before birth. Moon et al. (1993) gave two-day-old infants the opportunity of hearing an unfamiliar adult speaking the native language of the infant's mother or hearing an adult speaking an unfamiliar language. The infants preferred to listen to the mother's language, suggesting that they had become familiar with some aspects of that language before birth. In another study DeCasper and Spence (1986) showed that young infants could even distinguish different passages in the same language. They asked mothers to read a story out loud twice a day for six weeks before they gave birth. At two days old their infants were tested with that story and a new story and DeCasper and Spence found that infants sucked more to hear the story that they had been exposed to before birth, even when the story was read by a stranger. The fact that the infants could recognize the same story in a different voice suggests some aspects of the rhythm or pacing of the story itself were recognized by the infants. All these findings indicate prenatal learning.

Newborn infants can distinguish between different syllables (Moon et al., 1992) and there is evidence that young infants can distinguish speech sounds in the same way as adults (Jusczyk et al., 1998). Speech sounds like 'ba' and 'pa' are part of a continuum in the sense that by a series of gradual changes 'ba' can be changed into 'pa'. On such a continuum there will be a range in the middle of the continuum where it is difficult to distinguish between the two sounds. However, adults do not hear a range of sounds, rather there is a point on the continuum and before that point adults perceive a sound as a 'ba' and after that point they perceive it as a 'pa'. For this reason the perception of such sounds is referred to as 'categorical perception' to reflect the fact that we only hear those sounds in either one or other category.

Several researchers have shown that, like adults, infants also have categorical perception. Eimas et al. (1971) tested one- to four-month-old infants' ability to distinguish sounds that were between category (i.e., 'ba' compared to 'pa') and sounds that were within a category (e.g., different 'ba' sounds). The infants distinguished between the former, but not the latter. Other researchers have also shown that by about six-months of age infants can distinguish between consonants that sound similar but differ in the way they are articulated (e.g., 'b', 'd', and 'g'), and also distinguish between different vowel sounds. For example, Kuhl (1979) trained six-month-old infants to turn their heads towards a loudspeaker whenever contrasting vowel sounds interrupted background noise. The infants were able to identify the vowel 'i' (as in 'peep') against a background noise of 'o' (as in 'pop'), and these vowels were heard in a variety of voices and intonations. The infants were very successful and Kuhl concluded that infants are sensitive to the acoustic dimensions of speech long before they understand language.

Intermodal Perception

So far we have examined visual and auditory perception separately. In everyday life, however, it is unusual to receive perceptual information from one source only. Normally we coordinate information from a number of senses – vision, audition, touch, taste and smell. For example, we see, taste and smell our food as we eat. We see a bus approaching and hear the sound of its engine getting louder. This coordination of information from different sensory modalities is called intermodal perception. Adults use their knowledge of intermodal perception in a number of ways. It can be used to direct a person's attention, so for example, the increasing sound of the engine round the corner from the bus-stop results in a visual search for the approaching bus.

There are several types of intermodal relationships (Bahrick, 2000) and these include *amodal perception* and *arbitrary intermodal perception*. Some events result in two (or more) senses receiving information from the same event. For example, a hammer will be seen and heard hitting an object at the same time, and this is called amodal perception because the sight and sound of a hammer being used always occur together. Other sensory combinations may be specific to a particular event. For example, the sound that a hammer makes when hitting a nail and when hitting glass will be different and could not be specified in advance of hearing those sounds. This is referred to as arbitrary intermodal perception. In the same way, a speaker's voice is always synchronized with the movements of the speaker's mouth, and these aspects of perception are therefore amodal. But Jill's voice and Jo's voice are different and associating Jill's voice with Jill and Jo's voice with Jo means leaning arbitrary relationships.

Amodal perception may be an early achievement. For example, Muir and Field (1979) found that when newborn infants heard a sound they would usually turn their head towards the source of the sound. Bahrick (1992) showed four-week-old infants films of various objects hitting a surface and making a noise as they did so. The infants were shown these events until they habituated to them (i.e., showed little interest in them). Then Bahrick presented the same events again, but this time the sound track of the film was not in synchrony with the event. The infants dishabituated to this change and began looking again. From this result Bahrick argued that very young infants are sensitive to the synchrony involved in events like an object making a sound as it hits a surface, and this implies early amodal perception.

Slater et al. (1997) have also claimed that very young infants can learn arbitrary intermodal relationships. They tested newborn infants with two arbitrary combinations of auditory and visual stimuli. At the same time as hearing the word 'teat' the infants saw a green line, and at the same time as hearing the word 'mum' the infants saw a red line. After the infants had experienced both auditory-visual pairs several times they were tested with two pairs of stimuli. One pair was a familiar one (for example, the word mum and the red line) and one was a novel pair (for example, the word mum and the green line). During the test the infants preferred the novel combination. Their preference for the novel pair implied that the infants had learnt (and habituated to) the original combination. If so this showed that even newborn infants can learn associations between two concurrent stimuli. In other words, they have the ability to learn arbitrary intermodal relationships.

Having intermodal perception means that an object familiar in one sensory mode may be recognized when presented in another mode. For example, we can often recognize an object by touch that previously we have only identified visually and this ability is called *cross-modal* perception. Evidence for cross-modal perception has also been found to be an early achievement. Meltzoff and Borton (1979) gave four-week-old infants a dummy to suck on. Some of the infants were given a dummy with a smooth surface and some infants were given a dummy with a knobbly surface. The dummies were placed directly into the infants' mouths so that they could not see them. After this experience the infants were shown the two dummies visually. Meltzoff and Borton found that infants showed a preference (i.e., looked longer) at the dummy they had experienced orally, and they argued that this showed the infants had cross-modal perception

Given what we said earlier in this chapter about habituation and dishabituation, it might be thought a little surprising that Meltzoff and Borton interpreted infants looking more at the dummy on which they had sucked as evidence for cross-modal transfer. After all, it might be thought that if infants had had experience of (for example) the smooth dummy (from sucking) they would have habituated to it and would have preferred to look at the knobbly one when the two were presented visually because the knobbly one was novel. However, this pattern of behaviour does not apply in cross-modal studies. Rather, infants show a preference for the object that they have experienced previously. In the context of cross-modal perception the greatest interest is generated by experiencing a previously known stimulus, but experiencing it in a novel way.

■ Effects of the Environment on Perceptual Development

The environment in which infants are reared may have an effect on the development of their perceptual abilities, and in this section we will give some examples of experimental studies that have investigated such environmental effects.

Binocularity means that many visual cortical cells will respond to a visual stimulus shown to either eye, and binocular vision develops after about three months of age in humans. But researchers have found that this is not so if one eye is covered early in life. Such experiments cannot be carried out on infants but have been conducted on animals. For example, Weisel and Hubel (1963) investigated the effect of covering one eye in kittens soon after the kittens were born. The eye was covered for up to three months. Weisel and Hubel found that the kittens had defective vision in the deprived eye, and recordings from the visual cortex showed that few cortical cells would respond binocularly and subsequent experience could not reverse the effects of this early deprivation.

In another study Blakemore and Cooper (1970) investigated how the visual environment might affect the development of cells in the visual cortex in kittens. The kittens were housed from birth in a completely dark room. From the age of two weeks each kitten was put into a special apparatus for five hours a day. This was a tall cylinder, without visible corners or edges, covered with high-contrast black-and-white stripes. The kitten was also prevented from seeing its own body by a wide black collar round its neck. Some kittens were put in cylinders with vertical stripes (see figure 10.8) and some were put in cylinders with horizontal stripes.

After five months in these environments, the kittens were put in a small, well-lit room containing tables and chairs. The kittens used clumsy, jerky head movements in following objects, tried to reach out for objects that were well out of reach, and often they bumped into table legs. These deficits applied to all the kittens. In addition, the kittens reared with vertical stripes were effectively blind for the horizontal contours in the room, and those reared with horizontal stripes were effectively blind for the vertical contours. Their limited rearing environment had clearly affected the kittens' visual behaviour.

When the kittens were seven-months-old they were anaesthetized and recordings were made from neurons in the visual cortex. Blakemore and Cooper found that in kittens that had been reared with vertical stripes nearly all the neurons

Figure 10.8   A kitten in a cylinder with vertical black-and-white stripes (from Blakemore and Cooper, 1970).

responded most to stimuli that were at or near vertical, and none responded to horizontal stripes. The reverse was true for kittens reared with the horizontal stripes. The vertically reared kittens may have been effectively blind to horizontal stimuli, because they lacked visual cortical neurons to respond to such stimuli (and vice versa for the horizontally reared kittens). In other words, the nature of the visual cortex was altered by the rearing environment, because the neurons had developed to respond just to the kinds of visual features encountered during the kittens' infancy.

To give an example of environmental effects on auditory perception we can refer to the research into the development of sound discriminations. As we pointed out on p. 336 young infants can distinguish between many sound contrasts long before they understand language. Infants in different cultures (who therefore have exposure to different languages) can make the same sound discriminations. However, some sound contrasts may not actually be used in the infant's native language and adults speaking that language may have difficulty distinguishing those sound contrasts (Werker and Lalonde, 1988). There is a paradox here because within a particular culture adults may not be able to make some sound discriminations, but infants can! For example, Japanese adults find it difficult to distinguish 'r' and 'l' even though Japanese infants are sensitive to differences between these consonants.

When do infants lose the ability to discriminate sounds that are not part of their own language? Werker and Tees (1985) found that six- to eight-month-old infants from an English-speaking community could distinguish consonantal contrasts in Hindi. But by 12-months of age the same infants could no longer detect the differences. By comparison, Hindi infants retained their ability to perceive the consonantal contrasts in Hindi (see figure 10.9). These findings suggest that infants are born with the underpinnings of language, but without the reinforcing

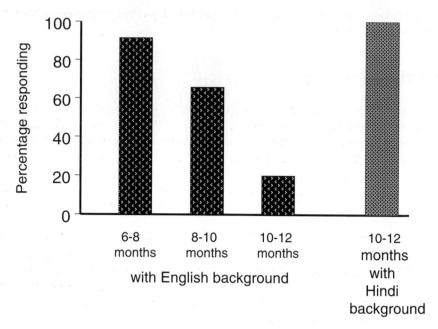

Figure 10.9   The decline in unused perceptual abilities among infants from English back-grounds compared to those from Hindi backgrounds. Between six and twelve months the infants from English backgrounds became less able to make sound discriminations that were not used in their environment. (Adapted from Kuhl, 1979.)

experience of hearing particular sound contrasts, the ability to distinguish certain sounds is lost during the first year of life. In other words, the perceptual abilities with which infants are born are modified by the infants' environment.

Conclusions

Research with very young children can address fascinating questions about early abilities and we are starting to learn more about how infants interpret the world about them and how well they are adapted to that world when they enter it. There has been a rapid increase in research with infants during the past few years. This is not just because of the importance of this period in development, but also because the advent of resources like video filming and computer controlled stimuli that result in much greater objectivity in designing and scoring empirical studies of infants' behaviour. As experimental techniques have improved so has our understanding of early perceptual abilities. The increased focus on infants has shown that they demonstrate some abilities at earlier ages than previously thought. Nonetheless, in several areas of perceptual research there are results that have not been fully replicated or are still ambiguous, and there still many questions about the development of early perception that need to be resolved. Related research with very young children is considered in chapter 3 (on prenatal development and birth) as well as in chapter 11 (on language) and chapter 12 (on cognitive development).

Further Reading

A very clearly written source on perceptual development and all other aspects of early development is Bremner, J. G. 1994: *Infancy*, 2nd edn. Oxford: Blackwell. A more recent collection of papers on most topics related to infant perception is Slater, A. (ed.) 1998: *Perceptual Development. Visual, Auditory and Speech Perception in Infancy*. Hove, East Sussex: Psychology Press, and there is a collection of reprinted journal papers on infant development included in Muir, D. and Slater, A. (eds) 2000: *Infant Development. The Essential Readings*. Oxford: Blackwell.

For encyclopedic coverage of infancy research see Damon, W. (ed.) 1998: *The Handbook of Child Psychology. Volume 2 (Cognition, Perception and Language)*, 5th edn. New York: Wiley. This handbook provides a critical review of research into infants' perception and action, visual and auditory processing, as well as chapters on early cognitive development. But the level of detail in this book makes it less accessible than the ones recommended above.

Discussion Points

1 Discuss some of the difficulties of working with very young children and explain how researchers have attempted to overcome those difficulties.
2 Why do psychologists sometimes refer to the 'competent infant'?
3 How does face recognition develop?
4 Explain how an infant's own experience contributes to their perceptual development.
5 How does an infant's environment influence their perceptual development?

Box 10.1
The origin of form perception

One of the first studies of infants' ability to perceive objects and patterns was carried out by Fantz (1961). Fantz argued that if children were shown shapes and patterns and preferred to look more at one pattern than another they must be able to distinguish between that pattern and the others. Fantz tested infants in a 'looking chamber' (box plate 10.1.1.). Attached to the ceiling of the chamber were pairs of objects. There was a peephole in the ceiling of the chamber so that the experimenter could see the objects mirrored in the infants' eyes. The experimenter recorded the length of time that the infant looked at each object.

In one experiment Fantz tested 30 infants aged one- to 15-weeks in the looking chamber. The infants were tested each week

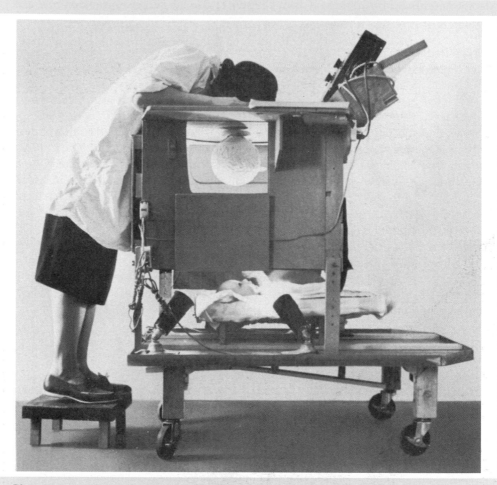

Box Plate 10.1.1   The 'looking chamber' used by Fantz (1961).

for ten weeks. They were shown the following four pairs of patterns: horizontal stripes compared to a bull's-eye; checkerboard compared to plain squares; a cross compared to a circle; and two identical triangles. Fantz found that infants spent more time looking at the more 'complex' patterns and that the comparative attractiveness of each pair depended on the presence of a pattern, so that that the bull's-eye was preferred to the horizontal stripes and the checkerboard was preferred to the plain square. There was no difference between the cross and the circle or between the two triangles (see box figure 10.1.1).

In a second experiment Fantz showed infants three flat objects the size and shape of a head. One was painted with a stylized face in black on a pink background, one had the same features but the features were scrambled, and one was painted with a solid area of black that was equivalent to the area of the features on the first two stimuli.

The three stimuli were presented as pairs (in all possible combinations). Fantz tested infants from four days to six months old and found a similar pattern of preference at all ages. The infants looked most at the 'real' face, slightly less frequently at the scrambled face, and much less at the solid pattern

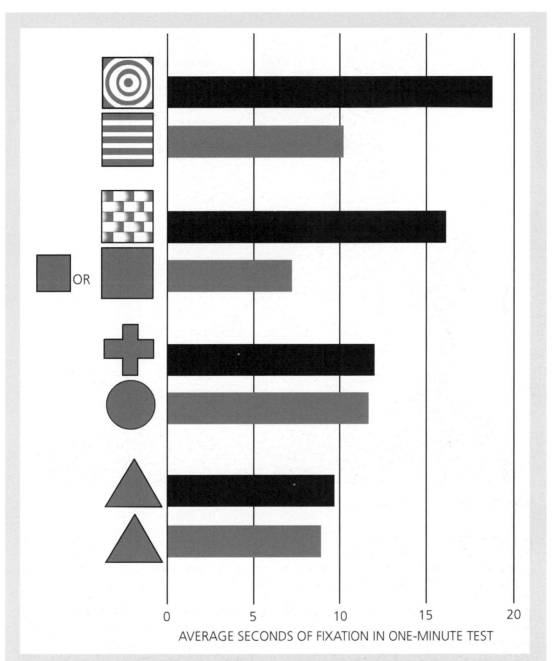

Box Figure 10.1.1 Average of infants' looking times for pairs of patterns. The data are from 22 infants tested each week for 10 weeks.

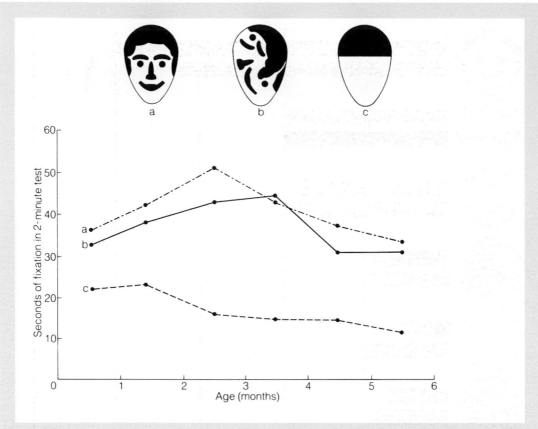

Box Figure 10.1.2   Average time infants spent looking at each of the three stimuli (from Fantz, 1961).

(see box figure 10.1.2). Fantz (1961) concluded that the consistent preference for the 'real' face implied an unlearned ability to perceive different forms.

In a third experiment Fantz compared looking times for other patterns and colours. These were six flat disks, each 15 cm in diameter. Three disks were patterned, with a face, a bull's-eye and part of a printed page, and three disks were plain colours (red, white or yellow). These were presented one at a time against a blue background. The infants attended most to the face, and then to the bull's-eye and the printed patterns. There was much less interest shown in the three coloured disks (see box figure 10.1.3).

Fantz's series of studies were important for starting to identify the sort of patterns that very young infants preferred to look at. He concluded that form perception was an unlearned ability and that the ability to

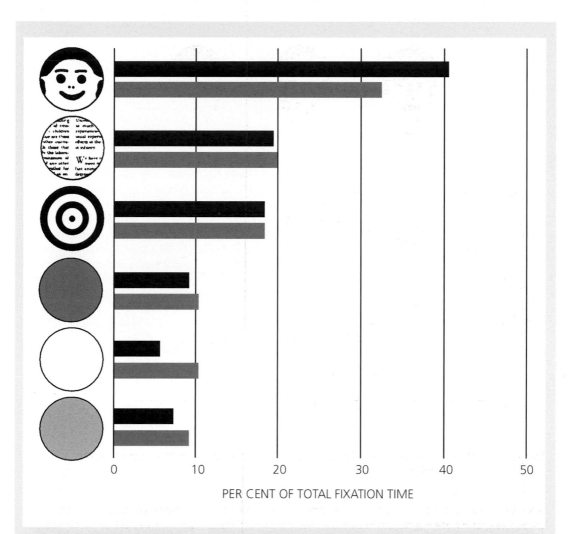

Box Figure 10.1.3   Time spent looking at each pattern. The bars of the graph show the time that infants looked at each pattern as a percentage of the total time they looked at all the patterns. Black bars represent the results from infants who were two- to three-months of age and grey bars represent the results from infants who were more than three months of age (from Fantz, 1961).

distinguish between different shapes and patterns was the foundation on which infants later learnt to recognize objects and people. More recent studies of pattern and face recognition are discussed in the chapter (pp. 323–8).

Based on material from Fantz, R. L. 1961: The origin of form perception. *Scientific American*, 204 (May), 66–72.

Box 10.2
Effects of prior experience on 4.5-month-old infants' object segregation

When adults look at a scene they do not see a confused mixtures of lines, shapes, and surfaces. Instead adults see distinct objects in the scene. We know, for example, that a cup standing on a saucer is a separate object and not fixed to the saucer. Do young infants also understand that features that may touch or occlude each other are still distinct objects? Several researchers have shown that infants have difficulty distinguishing separate objects in a three-dimensional scene and Needham and Baillargeon confirmed these findings in their first experiment.

Needham and Baillargeon tested 32 infants aged 4.5 months. The infants could see through the front wall of a wooden cubicle (1.8 m high, 1 m wide, and 0.45 m deep). The floor of the cubicle was coloured blue and the walls were white. The cubicle contained a blue and white rectangular box and a yellow zigzag-edged cylinder (see box figure 10.2.1). In other words, the two objects had different sizes, shapes, textures and colours. The two objects were placed in the cubicle so that they were touching each other. The right end of the cylinder was covered with a metallic end and inside the

Test Events

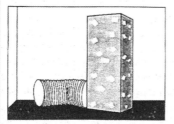

Move-apart Event

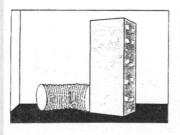
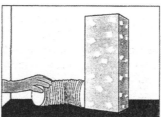
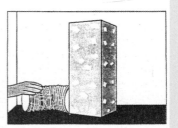

Move-together Event

Box Figure 10.2.1   The apparatus used by Needham and Baillargeon (1998).

box (but not visible to the infants) there was a magnet so that the box and the cylinder could be moved together. When the box and cylinder were moved separately the magnet was covered and a weight placed in the box.

Half the infants took part in one of two conditions. In the move-apart condition infants saw a gloved hand reached into the apparatus through a curtained opening on the left. The hand slowly pulled the cylinder to the left so that it was separate from the box. After a pause the hand pushed the cylinder back to its starting position. This procedure was repeated several times, and at the end of these movements a curtain was lowered across the front of the apparatus. Exactly the same procedure was used for the move-together condition except that the hand pulled the cylinder and the box together.

Infants sat on their parent's lap about 0.65 m from the apparatus. Two observers viewed the infant through peepholes in the apparatus. Each observer had a button box connected to a computer and they pressed the button each time the infant attended to the events. There was high agreement between the two observers' recording of the infants' gaze. Each trial was finished when infants had looked away from the event for at least two seconds, or when they had looked at the event for 60 continuous seconds. Each infant had six trials.

Needham and Baillargeon argued that infants would look more at events that were surprising. On the one hand, if infants saw the items as two separate objects, they would be surprised if the objects moved together and should spend more time looking at such an event. On the other hand, if infants saw the two items as a unit, they would be surprised if they saw the objects moving individually, and should attend more to this event. Needham and Baillargeon used analysis of variance to compare infants' performance in the two conditions (move-apart and move-together). There was no difference in how long the infants looked at either of the events. Needham and Baillargeon concluded that the infants 'were uncertain

whether the cylinder and box constituted one or two units and thus tended to look equally at the move-together and move-apart test events' (1998, p. 7).

Having shown that 4.5-month-old infants were unsure whether objects that touched each other were a single item or two individual objects, Needham and Baillargeon went on to investigate whether infants could learn from the experience of seeing the objects as separate items. If infants have had experience of an object as a single entity will they then distinguish this object when they see it as part of a scene? Needham and Baillargeon tested 16 infants aged 3.5 months in a second experiment with nearly the same procedure as their first study. The only difference was that before the trials when the infants saw the cylinder and the box together they were given experience of one object on its own. Prior to the test trials the infants saw just the box in the apparatus and they saw the hand lift and tilt the box for a period of five seconds. Then they had the test trails as in the first study. Half the infants took part in the move-apart condition and half took part in the move-together condition.

In the second experiment Needham and Baillargeon found that infants looked significantly longer at the objects in the move-together condition and they interpreted this result to mean that the infants were more surprised when the objects moved together than when they moved separately. This implies that as infants gain experience of individual objects they become better at separating them in complex scenes. In other words, infants may need experience of individual objects so that they can segregate information from scenes that include those objects and Needham and Baillargeon's experiments demonstrated the importance of such experience in contributing to perceptual understanding.

Based on material in Needham, A. and Baillargeon, R. 1998: Effects of prior experience on 4.5-month-old infants' object segregation. *Infant Behavior and Development*, 21, 1–24.

11 Language

Barrett (1999, p. 1) defines spoken language as 'a code in which spoken sound is used in order to encode meaning'. The way in which children acquire the complex system of language in the early years of life is not yet fully understood. It is likely that children are in some way programmed to learn language (canalized development, see chapter 2) but psychologists also emphasize the role of dialogue between child and significant others in the achievement of meaning. A number of questions have intrigued developmental psychologists. Do children go through identical stages as they learn to talk? Is there any connection between the non-verbal sounds and gestures that a baby produces and later speech? What part do adults play in creating a context in which a child's language will flourish? How important is it to examine the child's growing competence in a socially meaningful context? These and other issues will be explored in the following sections as we examine the sequences of language development through which children progress and the contexts where this happens. We will look at some research findings in the field and major theoretical explanations of the processes involved in learning language.

■ Main Areas of Language Development

There are four main areas of language competence that the child must acquire. These are the rules of sounds (phonology), meaning (semantics), grammar (syntax) and knowledge of social context (pragmatics).

Phonology is the study of the system that governs the particular sounds (or phonemes) used in the language of a child's community in order to convey meaning. For example, an English speaker treats the sounds 'l' and 'r' as two separate phonemes; to a Japanese speaker they are one. Scottish people use the speech sound 'ch' (as in 'loch'), which many English people cannot pronounce properly. Phonology investigates the ways in which these phonemes can be combined into syllables, morphemes and words.

Semantics refers to the meanings encoded in language. Phonemes, which are by themselves meaningless, are combined to form morphemes, the smallest meaningful units of language. These may be whole words ('dog' in English, 'chien' in French) or grammatical markers, such as '-ed' at the end of a verb to make the past tense. The child learns that morphemes, words and longer utterances refer to events, people, objects, relationships, in short, that they convey meaning.

Syntax refers to the form in which words are combined to make grammatical sentences. The child progresses, for example, from saying 'Anna cup' to saying 'Anna please pass me that cup over there.' The words themselves are not the only things that convey meaning as we see in the following sentences:

> Yasmin hit Jane
> Jane hit Yasmin

Each phrase has the same words but the sentences express different meanings. The difference comes from the sequencing of the words. The rules that govern such sequences are known as *syntax*. The term *grammar* refers to the study of the rules that determine sequences of morphemes and words in any language. These grammatical rules determine how words and morphemes in a language can be combined and sequenced to produce meaningful sentences.

Pragmatics is knowledge about how language is used in different contexts. The young child must learn to adapt her language to the situation in which she finds herself. A toddler may shout out loudly in the restaurant, 'That man's greedy!': the sentence shows understanding of phonology, syntax and semantics, but lacks sensitivity to others.

Sequences in Language Development

There seem to be great similarities in all human societies in the sequence of language development, as children progressively master the rules of sounds (phonology), of meaning (semantics) and of grammar (syntax), and learn to combine words in ways which are acceptable and understandable (pragmatics) within their linguistic community. For example, whether the child speaks pidgin, dialect, patois, Japanese, French or English, he constructs a grammar with rules and strategies. Let us start with the newborn baby to see how this complex process of acquiring language begins.

Shared rhythms

In chapter 3 we saw how babies can pass on vital information about their needs to their parents through different patterns of crying. From around 1 month babies produce the vowel 'ooo', a sound which seems to grow out of pleasurable social interactions, especially out of the dialogues that occur spontaneously during normal caregiving activities like nappy-changing and bathing. This is the period of 'shared rhythms and regulations' (Kaye, 1984, p. 66) where the parent builds on the biological rhythms of the baby to develop a mutual 'dialogue' that will form the basis for the communication patterns that characterize the adult world.

Stern (1990) has collected detailed observational data on the interactions between caregiver and baby in the early months of the baby's life. These observations indicate that the interaction is distinctively different from typical adult–adult interaction. When adults interact with infants there is close proximity, an emphasis on exaggerated facial expressions, much repetition and more eye contact – the sort of interaction which might sometimes occur between adults when acting playfully towards one another or at points in the course of a very intimate relationship. Stern plots 'phrases of interaction' organized into 'runs' – sequences that have a common characteristic. Stern explains the rationale for this characteristic form of interaction as being one that ensures optimal attention on the part of the infant. The adult tries to make sure that the baby is neither bored nor over-aroused by engaging in a sort of 'dance' with the infant in which each trades similar responses back and forth. These exchanges are rhythmic and both partners contribute to the rhythm.

Stern (1990) has attempted to recreate the world of a baby, Joey, from the age of 6 weeks. He does this in an original way, by describing events both from the adult's perspective, and also from the infant's point of view. You can see in table 11.1 that Stern has used images, metaphors, space and movement to capture the essence of Joey's non-verbal experience. Stern's key point is that exchanges between the parent and Joey involve a communication of affect. During the pre-linguistic stage, mother and child show a very sensitive attunement to each other's emotional state. The 'gaze coupling', in which caregiver and baby appear to take different roles in their 'dialogue', may anticipate later turn-taking, or alternative speaker-listener roles, that are at the heart of conversation.

Babbling and echolalia

From 6 to 9 months, the baby produces more vowels and some consonants. She no longer confines herself to cries and cooing sounds. Echolalia is the frequent repetition of sounds – like 'dadadadad' or 'mummummummum'. The baby can also shout for attention or scream with rage; she spends time making noises when alone. During this stage infants begin to develop a whole range of behaviours some of which are directed only at familiar people. For example, certain gestures, facial expressions and sounds seem to be reserved only for the mother or primary caregiver (see chapter 4).

Table 11.1   Joey at four and one-half months: a face duet

Adult perspective	Joey's perspective
Joey is sitting in his mother's lap, facing her. She looks at him intently but with no expression on her face, as if she were preoccupied and absorbed in thought elsewhere. At first, he glances at the different parts of her face but finally looks into her eyes.	I enter the world of her face. Her face and its features are the sky, the clouds and the water. Her vitality and spirit are the air and the light. It is usually a riot of light and air at play. But this time when I enter, the world is still and dull. Neither the curving lines of her face nor its rounded volumes are moving. Where is she? Where has she gone? I am scared. I feel that dullness creeping into me. I search around for a point of life to escape to.
He and she remain locked in silent mutual gaze for a long moment. She finally breaks it by easing into a slight smile. Joey quickly leans forward and returns her smile. They smile together, or rather, they trade smiles back and forth several times.	I find it. All her life is concentrated into the softest and hardest points in the world – her eyes. They draw me in deep and deeper. They draw me into a distant world. Adrift in this world, I am rocked from side to side by the passing thoughts that ripple the surface of her eyes. I stare down into their depths. And there I feel running strong the invisible currents of her excitement. They churn up from those depths and tug at me. I call after them. I want to see her face again, alive. Gradually life flows back into her face. The sea and sky are transformed. The surface now shimmers with light. New spaces open out. Arcs rise and float. Volumes and planes begin their slower dance. Her face becomes a light breeze that reaches across to touch me. It caresses me. I quicken. My sails fill with her. The dance within me is set free.

Source: Adapted from Stern, 1990, pp. 57–9

There is still disagreement among researchers about the extent to which babbling and later speech are related to one another. It would seem, however, that babies' vocalizations at this stage have some of the phonetic characteristics of speech and that there is a process of continuity in the ways in which vocal abilities develop. (For a useful discussion on the origins and significance of babbling see Messer, 1994, pp. 84–7.)

In any event, parents tend to believe that their babies' babbling is an attempt to communicate meaningfully and seem to spend a lot of time guessing at the intentions which underlie the baby's actions and sounds. The fact that they often

Plate 11.1   A mother and her 9-month-old baby engage in 'turn-taking' during their 'conversation'; although he cannot talk, he responds to her with speech-like rhythms, gestures and facial expressions.

go beyond the actual meaning of the baby's actions (as far as we can determine) plays a crucial part in the parents' integration of the young child into their social system, and provides an early example of scaffolding (see chapters 4 and 15). It is certainly clear that long before the first words appear the baby shows signs of understanding some of what is said to him. This capacity to share the adult's intentions has been called 'a shared memory' (Kaye, 1984, p. 67) based on the attributions of intentionality on the part of adults to the baby's utterances. Fogel (1993) identifies complex micro interactions or 'co-regulation of intentions' during the communication process between adult and child. This process of co-regulation, he claims, is a form of ongoing elaboration of actions and intentions in response to the other's actions. Fogel uses the metaphor of the jazz band to demonstrate how the communication between adult and child is a shared achievement not an individual one. Just as members of a jazz group respond to one another's rhythms and sounds to create their music, so parents and babies engage in a process of improvisation as they communicate with each other in mutually enjoyable ways.

First words and sentences

Ingram (1999) argues that children begin to use properties of phonological organization that are part of those that underlie the adult language, though in a less complex form. On the basis of his detailed phonological case study of the developing syllables, vowels and consonants of one child, Alice, from the age of 16 months, Ingram claims that children's phonological systems develop in ways that are parallel to adult languages. It is easy to miss the first words a baby utters since they are often sounds not to be found in the dictionary! However, they can be considered as words if the child uses them consistently in the presence of a particular object or situation. One 12-month-old baby, for example, said 'da' every time he pointed at something that he wanted, and 'oof' whenever he saw animals.

These first words have the function of naming or labelling the people and objects in the child's environment. But they also condense meaning. 'Milk' can mean 'I want milk' or 'My milk is spilt'. Even though the child can only say one word at a time, variations in context, intonation and gesture can convey a richer meaning. Single words used in this way are known as holophrases since the one word can be interpreted as expressing a whole idea.

It can take 3 or 4 months after the emergence of the first words before vocabulary increases very much, but after that the acquisition of new words is extraordinarily rapid. Vocabulary typically grows from around 20 words at 18 months to around 200 words at 21 months. New words are mainly object names ('daddy', 'car', 'cat') but also include action names ('look', 'gone'), state names ('red', 'lovely', 'sore') and some 'function' words referring to types of events ('there', 'more', 'bye-bye'). The vast majority of object names refer to objects that the child is able to manipulate (e.g., shoes, toys, foodstuffs) or which are spontaneously dynamic (e.g., people, animals, vehicles) (Dromi, 1999; Nelson, 1981).

At around 18 months the child starts to combine single words into two-word sentences. Of course single-word utterances continue to be used for some time, but they gradually give way to more complex word combinations. The child's first sentences are often described as telegraphic speech, i.e. speech in which the highly condensed meaning is transmitted from the child to another person. 'Ben shoe' means 'That is Ben's shoe' or 'Put on my shoe'. The child may also have a characteristic way of asking for more information – 'Who dat?' or of making observations – 'Mummy gone'; 'Sammy here', often repeated. However, as Fogel's research indicates, the metaphor of the jazz band seems to provide a more accurate representation of the process than the metaphor of the telegraph. Typically, when the child produces a holophrase the adult will expand it to clarify meaning:

Child: More.
Adult: You want more milk?

By 24 to 27 months the child is regularly producing three- and four-word utterances. There are many sentences which are in a strict sense 'ungrammatical' but which reveal that the child is in fact using grammatical rules of syntax. These errors are 'logical errors'. The child will produce sentences like 'Mouses gone away' in which the normal rule for plurals is extended to exceptions like 'mouse'. These 'errors' are made because the child is applying a basic set of rules (in this case, adding 's' to make a noun plural). Idiosyncratic words are also common. For example, one child called a chocolate biscuit a 'choskit', a word which he had invented himself. Grammatical rules are applied to such words; for example the plural is formed by adding 's' – choskits.

After the three- and four-word linking stage, there is a rapid increase in use of grammatical rules. Prepositions and irregular verb endings appear. Now the child can begin to re-order the words of a sentence, for example to make questions or negative statements. Thus, 'John is swimming?' becomes 'Is John swimming?' 'Wh-' questions are formed, though often at first in an unorthodox form – 'Where my glove?' or 'Why John is eating?' in which the 'wh-' form is just tacked on to the beginning of the sentence. The negative is used more, though also in unusual forms, such as 'Not my daddy work'; 'I no want it'; 'Not shut door, no!' In these sentences, 'no' or 'not' is put in to express negation. Later, the child will re-order the sentence in a more 'adult' way, e.g. 'My daddy not working'.

Children at this age show a great interest in rhymes and will sing songs they have learned, though sometimes in a distorted form. Imaginative play reflects developing language (see chapter 7). Conversations acted out in play or commentaries that accompany actions contribute greatly to the expression of ideas and experience. Pre-sleep monologues (table 11.2) may also be important for the processing of interpersonal experiences and their subsequent organization in memory. Schank (1982) and Nelson (1989) argued that autobiographical memories are processed, reprocessed and cross-indexed into a system of interlinked schema categories that retain aspects of the structure of the experienced event in terms of time, space, movement and causality. These become 'scripts' (for example, the script of putting a doll to bed or the script of a mealtime routine). A study by Bruner and Lucariello (1989) of the monologues of Emmy as she talked herself to sleep between the ages of 21 months and 3 years gives insight into the process of organizing information into such meaningful units. Emmy would often repeat the stories and add her own predictions and inferences. As the analysis of the tapes suggests, Emmy was actively constructing experience, not simply reflecting it.

As we have seen, the role of adult discourse is important throughout this period in facilitating the child's learning about how to highlight events in a particular scene in order to communicate intentions and meaning effectively. However, there is considerable disagreement among theorists about the extent to which children's early meanings and the words they use to express them arise directly from the input of adults. Intrinsic factors related to the child's cognitive functioning have also been shown to play a significant part. Findings in the literature are actually quite diverse about the initial mapping of new words, the child's growing ability to decontextualize words and the refinement of meaning relationships among the different words in the child's *lexicon* (or vocabulary). Here we present two models of word acquisition that present contrasting interpretations: the *syntactic bootstrapping hypothesis* (Gleitman, 1990) and the *multi-route model* (Barrett, 1986).

Table 11.2   Pre-sleep monologues

Weir (1962) studied her child Anthony as he talked himself to sleep each night between the ages of 28 and 30 months (see also chapter 7). The monologues which she recorded took the form of social exchanges even though he was alone. Anthony asked questions, responded to an imaginary companion, invented words and created rhythmical songs. It seems that his language served three purposes. First he seemed to be practising new words and grammar forms which he had recently learned. Second, he was playing with sounds for their own sake and creating poetic rhythms. Third, he seemed to be trying to make sense of his world by ordering events in a systematic way. Here is an example of one of Anthony's monologues; another is given on p. 214.

That's for he
Mamamama with Daddy
Milk for Daddy
OK
Daddy dance
Daddy dance
Hi Daddy
Only Anthony
Daddy dance
Daddy dance
Daddy give it
Daddy not for Anthony
   (Weir, 1962, pp. 138–9)

Weir argues that Anthony is practising language as well as trying to make sense of the non-linguistic world of which he is a part – the sharing of his attachment between Mama and Daddy is one theme, his offer of milk 'for Daddy' another. The second example shows sound play with no clear meaning at all.

Bink
Let Bobo bink
Bink ben bink

Blue kink.

You will notice the use of rhyming and alliteration, a skill which will have implications for the future process of learning to read (Weir, 1962, p. 105).

Gleitman's syntactic bootstrapping hypothesis

Gleitman (1990) called children's ability to infer the meanings of words from cues *syntactic bootstrapping*. By this she means that young children use grammatical information from the *structure* of sentences to infer meanings of unfamiliar target words – as if they are pulling themselves up by their own bootstraps. Gleitman and her colleagues (Hirsh-Pasek, Gleitman, Gleitman, Golinkoff and Naigles, 1988) argue that from an early age children are sensitive to syntactic and semantic correspondences that exist in the language and she designed ingenious experiments using invented words to prove that young children can extract the meanings of verbs from syntactic cues. For example, in one study of 27-month-old children, she showed two different videos. In one, Big Bird and Cookie Monster rotated next to each other; in the other, Big Bird rotated Cookie Monster. As the children watched the videos, they heard sentences each using a novel verb. The first sentence was: 'Big Bird is gorping with Monster Cookie'; the second was 'Big Bird is gorping Monster Cookie'. Note that the first verb is intransitive, that is has a subject but no object, while the second verb is transitive, Big Bird is the subject while Monster Cookie is the object of the verb. When hearing the intransitive verb form, the children were more likely to look at the video in which the two puppets performed the same action. When hearing the transitive verb form, they tended to look at the video that showed Big Bird performing an action on Monster Cookie. Gleitman's conclusion is that young children bring the verb's meaning into alignment with the syntax and not the other way round. Gleitman's model is grounded in linguistic theory.

Barrett's multi-route model

By contrast, Barrett's multi-route model of early lexical development takes account of the interactions he observed among the timing of acquisition, the child's linguistic experience, and the cognitive representational abilities. Barrett (1986), Harris et al. (1988) and Barrett et al. (1991) distinguished two classes of early words:

1 *context-bound* words that are only used in a specific behavioural context. For example, Emmy says 'duck' when she hits a toy duck off the edge of the bath; duck is only used in this context;
2 *referential* words that are used in a variety of different behavioural contexts. As examples, James initially uses 'teddy' to refer to one large teddy bear; later 'teddy' is extended to apply to a little teddy; James also initially uses 'more' to request or comment on recurrence of an object; later he uses 'more' to request repetition of a set of actions.

Barrett proposed that these two classes of words follow different routes in order to reach adult conventional meaning. Context-bound words are mapped on to holistic *event* representations while referential words are mapped on to *mental* representations of either specific *objects* (object names) or *actions* (action names). Barrett's approach was strongly influenced by Nelson's argument (see box 11.2) that during late infancy children build up holistic mental representations of the events that occur in everyday life. These representations of events underlying context-bound words are gradually analysed into their constituent components: people, objects, actions and relations, and so can also become categorical eventually. Barrett agrees that maternal input has a critical role in helping the child establish the initial uses for words but argues that children also rely on their own cognitive processing to establish subsequent use of words. In other words, while the initial focus is on external stimuli, later children focus more on their own inner representations in order to form theories about the linguistic system.

From 3 to 5 years

The 3-year-old's speech is largely understandable to adults, even outside the family. Her vocabulary is now around 1,000 words, length and complexity of utterances has increased, and she can carry on reasonable conversations, though these still tend to be rooted in the immediate present. Despite these skills, however, the child is still perfecting various linguistic systems, such as pronouns and auxiliary, passive and irregular verbs.

By 3 years children begin to use complex sentences containing relative clauses. Sentences like 'See the car that I got' appear before 'The car that I got is a red one'. The second sentence is more difficult for children since the relative clause 'that I got' is embedded. By the time a child enters school at around 5 years, she can understand and express complex sentences and her use of language is very similar to that of an adult. She can also adjust her speech in a number of ways to suit listeners of different ages with whom she is communicating.

She may still produce logical errors like 'That one's the bestest'. Some specific aspects of syntax continue to pose difficulties. In general, however, by the time children enter school their language use is correct, and their basic sentence types are similar to those used by adults.

The Development of Discourse and Narrative Skills

Pan and Snow (1999) argue that the ability to engage in extended discourse – a pragmatic skill, when the child needs to combine his own perspective with those of others and with outside events into a coherent account – emerges over time out of regular participation in conversation with peers and adults. This is not easy for children. The activity of participating in conversation, arguing, providing definitions or telling anecdotes and jokes involves a complex interplay of skills and processes, both linguistic and cognitive.

Taking account of one's own and others' perspective

Children need to learn to make appropriate use of linguistic indicators to show that they are aware of the listener's perspective, for example by manipulating words like 'this' and 'that' or 'I' and 'you' to differentiate the speaker's from the listener's stance. They also need to be able to distinguish between what they know as speakers and what the listener may not know, for example by contextualizing information or putting the listener into picture ('Isabel – she's a girl in my class' or 'That programme I saw yesterday on TV'). More subtly, children need to adjust their language to different contexts, for example saying 'please' and 'thank you' when in the company of older relatives, or adjusting their language to the social conventions of the community outside the family.

Children also extend their discourse skills by engaging in accounts of every-day events where they have the chance to express their own stance through appropriate repetition, emphasis, exclamations and other indicators of the capacity to make the shift between their own and others' perspectives. This ability usually emerges by the age of 4–5 years when children describe personal experiences. But in re-telling events from a book or a drama, it is not until much later – usually around 9 years – that children begin to move clearly among the perspectives of the author of the storyline, the characters, the events and their own views on the narrative.

By encouraging children to tell and write stories, parents and teachers can give them the opportunity to encompass both subjective and objective ways of knowing the inner world of experience as well as external reality. Narrative seems to help the child to shape ideas, to explore lines of thought in a playful or tentative way and to develop in the capacity to take the perspective of other people. There are wide individual differences in children's capacity to create and respond to stories, and research studies of adult–child interaction indicate that these processes may be nurtured or inhibited by the responses of other people, especially those who are significant to the child. The literature about children's personal narratives indicates that narratives are central for several developmental processes including

- autobiographical memory;
- integration into a particular social-cultural context;
- the capacity for self-awareness and emotional organization;
- the capacity to view interpersonal situations from multiple perspectives; and
- the capacity to see the self as having multiple sides or 'narrative voices'.

Oppenheim et al. (1997) found that there were clear associations between children's co-constructed narratives with their mothers and two aspects of their development: their ability to construct emotionally well-organized and regulated narratives independently; and their behavioural and emotional regulation in everyday life. Children who were rated higher on emotional coherence during co-constructed narrative-making had higher ratings on their independently created stories in terms of emotional coherence, the presence of prosocial themes, and the absence of aggressive themes. They were rated by their mothers as having fewer behavioural and emotional problems at the time of the study and also when re-tested one year later.

The role of fantasy and make-believe

Children also change over time in their capacity to indicate to the listener whether the discourse is to be taken literally or as fantasy. For example, the child can signal that the story is imaginary by saying 'Let's pretend' or 'Once upon a time', or can use a different tone of voice to signal a make-believe character (for example, Corrie, aged 3 years, announced 'My name is Mrs Dotty' in a high-pitched voice before launching into a role-play, so indicating that she was to be the teacher and her grandmother was to be a child at nursery school). By the age of 3 or 4 years, children are expert at moving easily between reality and fantasy through appropriate use of gaze, gesture, tone of voice, position and posture (see chapter 7). At around the same age, they can also speculate hypothetically, using words like 'would', 'might' and 'if', about events that have not yet taken place in their experience.

The narrative form, as demonstrated in the playful interchange between Corrie and her grandmother, plays a key part in the development of children's capacity to make sense of events in their lives and to evoke meanings. Their narratives may be elusive and fragmentary in nature but are still a rich source of insight into the child's mind. One opportunity, common in the preschool years, to practise the skills of story-telling comes through sociodramatic play (chapter 7). Scarlett and Wolf (1979) and Wolf et al. (1994) showed that, whereas children under the age of 3 demonstrate play that is mainly carried out by actions, by the time the children are ready to enter first school at 5, the meaning of their stories is much more likely to be expressed in linguistic ways – through the recounting of a narrative, through the dialogue of the characters in the story, and through communications that reveal a growing sense of audience.

Scarlett and Wolf (see table 11.3) concluded that the emergence of the different types of story language and the resolution of problems within the story itself are major advances which preschool children make as they gradually free themselves from concrete props and actions and rely more on the language itself. In addition, the children are becoming aware of the pragmatics of language – the rules which govern the most effective ways of communicating with others. Many contemporary researchers into reading argue that we need to build on this spontaneous creation of narrative if we are to sustain children's interest in actually reading stories for themselves (Engel, 1994; Root, 1986). The experience of being read to by adults and taking part in mutual story-telling during the preschool years creates conditions that facilitate the transition to independent reading by the child (plate 11.2).

Mastering the convention of different genres

Genre refers to the distinctive language of scripts, whether in the form of accounts of personal experience or in the form of fictitious stories. Scripts can be analysed in terms of content, organization and linguistic features. In the early years, children need a great deal of help from adults in forming scripts or accounts of events that have happened to them. As they grow older, they become more accomplished and learn to use linguistic features that are specific to the genre, for example the appropriate use of present or past tense. By the age of 3, children can usually produce fairly coherent personal stories in conversation with a beginning, some form of contextualization, a high point and an ending. Again, by 3 years, children are developing in their skills as narrators of fictitious stories, using beginnings ('Once upon a time') and endings ('They all lived happily ever after'). These stories are based on real-life experiences or on stories that they have heard from

Table 11.3 Stories told by one child at different ages

Age (yr. mth)	Story	Commentary
2.10	C. picks up the dragon prop and makes a hissing noise while having the dragon's mouth touch the king's crown. The dragon touches the queen and goes on to the forest where he touches, while hissing, the prince and all the animals. The story ends when the dragon knocks over the trees and the castle, all the while saying 'Bang!'	The meaning of the story depends almost entirely on the actions. The hissing sounds and bangs only embellish what is being enacted
3.3	C. uses a toy lion, man and house. While putting the man outside the house facing a window, she says, 'Him looks in window'. Next, putting the lion in the house, she says, 'This one's in'. Finally, putting the lion on its side, C. says 'Him lay down'	Language is emerging as an important aspect of the story presentation. The language outlines the basic structure of events in the story. Notice that the action is all in the present
3.8	C. takes the dragon and says, 'He's gonna killed them'. She then has the dragon fly up to the king and queen and knock them off the turret. She then says, 'And the dragon killed them'. C. then has the dragon knock over all the other props	The narrative refers to past enactments and forecasts future events. This time-split gives the story some independence from the immediate actions
3.11	C. moves the dragon towards the king and queen. C. says, 'He huffed and puffed and he blew, then the king and queen runned [C. moves king and queen to the forest]. Then he goes to the forest [C. moves the dragon to the forest] and scares the prince so he [the prince] goes home' [C. moves the prince to the castle]	Story language goes beyond the action. This is shown when C. conveys information which is not obvious from the enactment. This gives C. freedom to express feelings and intentions on the part of her characters. Without her narrative, we could not understand why the royal family move between castle and forest
4.00	C. makes a purple elephant walk up to and stand outside a toy house containing a girl prop. Without moving the props, C. says, 'And he [the elephant] says there's no one there. And he says, 'Knock, knock, knock! Who's there?' Then C. says for the girl prop, 'No-one', 'no one who?' [speaking for the elephant] 'There's not a little girl who lives here' [speaking for the little girl]	C. begins to speak for the characters so the language tells far more than the action. The dramatic speech and the voice intonations (deep for the elephant, squeaky for the girl) carry the meaning of the story event. Without changes in the props, the story moves on

Source: Adapted from Scarlett and Wolf, 1979

Plate 11.2   A mother shares her enjoyment of a book with her two daughters.

books and the media. Bruner (1990) suggests that we learn about the physical world by devising paradigms or models that are logical and rule-bound, whereas we come to understand the cultural world in a more personal, dynamic way – by, for example, telling stories. He argues that not only do children devise narratives as a way of understanding their own experiences but they also use narrative as a medium for communicating to others what these experiences mean.

Re-telling stories can enable children to become familiar with the convention of written stories, thus providing motivation and a framework for help with reading. Parents have a crucial part to play in the period before the child begins to read by making stories an enjoyable, shared experience through turn-taking, sharing and empathizing. The discourse processes that began in the preschool years can be fostered by sensitive parents and teachers and harnessed to the emerging skills of reading and writing (see plate 11.3).

Pre-reading and Pre-writing Skills

By 6 or 7 years of age most children have begun the process of learning to read and write. Obviously some perceptual skills are needed, but other aspects of language development in the preschool years may also be important or necessary if a child is to become a proficient reader and writer a few years later. These are called 'pre-reading skills' and 'pre-writing skills'. As well as the usual skills of perception and discrimination, these include the understanding of reading conventions and the concept of story, and the awareness of rhyming and alliteration. From an early age the child can be helped to develop these skills.

Plate 11.3 The child's interest in books develops throughout the preschool years; a nursery teacher facilitates pre-reading skills.

When a child begins to read and write he needs to consider visual information as well as the sound and sense of words, for an example, see 5-year-old Javier's writing in figure 11.1. During the preschool years, the child's perceptual skills can be sharpened by encouraging him to observe specific aspects of his environment. Training in visual discrimination can be done in an enjoyable way through games; for example, jigsaws, picture-matching games, exercises in grading shapes and objects by size or by colour, or the experience of noticing differences and similarities between objects can give the child useful preparation for discriminating among words and letters. It is also useful if the child understands concepts of 'up', 'down', 'forwards' and 'backwards'.

Bryant and Bradley (1985) and Bryant et al. (1990) argue that young children's awareness of rhyming and alliteration indicates a skill in analysing the constituent sounds of words, which is essential for learning to read. Young children usually respond with delight to nursery rhymes such as 'Ring a ring o' roses' which contain rhyming ('Roses' and 'posies') and alliteration (the recurrence of the letter 'r' in 'ring a ring o' roses' and 'p' in 'a pocket full of posies') and will often create their own rhymes, as we see in the rhyming couplets created by 3-year-olds

oiA

ᗡ AiOA i O Ai

Figure 11.1 Writing by Javier, aged 5 years 5 months. Top row, 'Gatito' (little cat); bottom row, 'Gatitos' (three little cats in the picture). He explains as he is writing: 'One little cat' (the first three letters); 'the little cats here' (six letters); 'another cat' (the three remaining letters). You can see that the plural is obtained by repeating the original word as many times as there are cats to be represented (adapted from Ferreiro, 1985).

(Chukovsky, 1963) and the alliteration in some of the presleep monologues produced by 2-year-old Anthony (Weir, 1962).

Bryant and Bradley (1985, pp. 47–8) quote (from Chukovsky) jingles by 3-year-olds which also demonstrate the children's ability to change words to suit the rules of rhyme:

> The red house
> Made of strouss
> The duckling and the big goose
> Sat on the broken sail-oose.

They argue that 'all these children know a great deal about how to spot the common sounds in different words. Children show this every time that they produce rhyme.' In the process of becoming familiar with rhymes and alliteration they are also developing an awareness of speech sounds (*phonological awareness*) that will have an influence on their later ability to read and spell. Bryant and Bradley hypothesize a direct link between sensitivity to sounds (as shown in responses to rhyming and alliteration games) and competence in learning to read. The backward reader is likely to be a child who has not developed this skill in detecting speech sounds during the preschool years. In a longitudinal study of 65 3- and 4-year-olds, Bryant et al. (1990) provided further evidence for the strong link between children's sensitivity to rhyme and alliteration and their success in reading. The awareness of rhyme, argue these authors, helps children to form spelling categories. For example, if the child knows how to read 'beak' it gives him a strategy to read and pronounce the new word 'peak'. Some support for these ideas is found in the study reported in box 11.1.

However, while acknowledging the great value of phonological awareness in forming a strong foundation for reading, Snowling and her colleagues argue that semantic skills are also extremely important (for detailed reviews see Snowling, 1996, 2002). Snowling recommends reading methods – such as the widely acclaimed New Zealand Reading Recovery method (Clay, 1985) – that integrate a structured phonological programme with meaningful use of context and content to help children develop effective reading strategies.

Dyslexia

Developmental dyslexia is an important topic, because it is the most common of the developmental disorders, with an estimated incidence rate of 5 per cent in the Western world (Badian, 1984). Children with dyslexia are identified in school when they fail to learn to read. The traditional definition of dyslexia is that provided by the World Federation of Neurology (1968): 'a disorder in children who, despite conventional classroom experience, fail to attain the language skills of reading, writing and spelling commensurate with their intellectual abilities'. These children seem to be as intelligent as the other children in their class, and therefore it is a surprise to both their teachers and their parents when they show these unexpected difficulties. However, any more careful analysis of the development of a dyslexic child typically shows a range of differences in their language development. Many, for example, will have had some form of speech therapy in the preschool period. Others may show subtle impairments in their speech, ranging from mislabelling to mispronunciation to word-finding difficulties. The most consistently reported phonological difficulties for dyslexic children are limitations of verbal short-term memory and problems with phonological awareness. They have difficulties with long-term verbal learning, for example in memorizing the days of the week or the months of the year, and with learning a foreign language. They also find it hard to retrieve phonological information from long-term memory (Snowling, 2002). In a particularly sensitive analysis of the dyslexic syndrome, Miles (1982, 1993) describes problems in repetition of polysyllabic words, in acquiring familiar sequences, such as the months of the year, in correctly labelling left and right, and learning tables, as well as the characteristic problems in reading and spelling. The problems of dyslexia interest a wide range of researchers, because it seems that whichever area of research you are interested in, dyslexics show intriguing deficits in just that area.

Explanations of dyslexia

The phonological deficit hypothesis suggests that dyslexic children for some reason have particular difficulty with the sounds of words, so that when they try to link the phoneme (the sound 'sss') to the grapheme (the letter squiggle 's') they make mistakes. Children who are going to have difficulties of this type can be identified preschool by their problems in rhyming and alliteration (see box 11.1). These children seem to have missed the stage of playing with words, which seems to come naturally to most children. Later on, they may have problems in segmenting a word – i.e., breaking it down into sounds. By the late 1980s, the phonological deficit hypothesis had become the dominant explanation for the difficulties dyslexic children suffer in reading and spelling, largely based on the work of researchers such as Bradley and Bryant (1985).

Plate 11.4   Testing for dyslexia. Difficulties in balancing can predict reading problems, according to Nicolson and Fawcett.

More recently, Nicolson and Fawcett (1990, 1996) suggest that the key to the dyslexic deficit seems to be early problems in articulation, which has been found to be significantly slower and more error prone in dyslexia (Snowling et al., 1986). Snowling (2002) suggests that dyslexic children may be able to compensate for their difficulties by relying on contextual cues to support decoding processes.

It may be that in the early stages of speech, dyslexic children are simply less efficient at repeating words correctly. These articulation difficulties lead to problems in basic phonological skills such as segmentation, which impacts on the development of grapheme-phoneme conversion skills, leading to reading difficulties. Reading and spelling are the most severely impaired skills in dyslexia, because not only does a dyslexic child have problems in acquiring the basic building blocks, such as the grapheme/phoneme correspondence, they also have problems in becoming expert in these skills. This leads to problems in identifying whole words, or noting the sequences of letters that traditionally occur together (these are known as orthographic regularities). The result is that at each stage dyslexics are investing too many resources in just coping with the basics, which leaves them less spare capacity for acquiring new information. Nicolson and Fawcett suggest that early screening tests (Fawcett and Nicolson, 1996; plate 11.4) allows many dyslexic children and those with more generalized difficulties to receive the help they need before they fail. Early identification and appropriate support should allow children with dyslexia to progress through the education system at a normal rate, thus limiting the impact of dyslexia on children's development. It should then be possible for dyslexic children to express their strengths, without being hampered by their weaknesses. Specially designed computer programs help teachers with component reading skills.

Theories of Language Development

Our review of sequences in language development has outlined the remarkable achievements that can be made during the preschool years. The child masters the phonology of her language. She has acquired grammatical morphemes (e.g., pluralizing nouns or adding modifiers such as '-ed' to verbs to indicate past tense) and learned how to produce declarative statements (e.g., 'I have a cup'), 'why-' questions (e.g., 'Where is my cup?' or 'Why is my cup on the floor?') and the negative ('I do not have a cup'). Sentences have become more complex and relative clauses appear ('The cup, which is on the table, is red'). Semantic development has progressed in that children can express quite subtle meanings in their language. Their skill as tellers of stories, jokes and riddles is increasing as they realize the layers of meaning embedded in language. The pragmatics of communication have improved and there is growing awareness that they need to adapt language to particular contexts and adjust speech to suit the requirements of different people.

How does the child achieve this? As yet, there is no one theory that successfully encompasses all aspects of language development. Explanations, as opposed to description, of the course of language development vary in emphasis. For a time, the principles of learning theory seemed to provide a logical explanation with an emphasis on reinforcement and imitation; while other theorists have suggested that there is a biological basis for language acquisition with innate mechanisms underlying it. Piagetians emphasize the importance of cognitive development. Still others take the interactionist approach and argue that the development of linguistic competence needs to be studied within its social context. We will consider each of these broad approaches in turn.

The role of reinforcement and imitation

Skinner (1957) argued that children acquire language because adults reinforce correct usage. The baby's random coos and babbling sounds are progressively shaped into words by adults rewarding those that are most 'word-like'. Later the adults reinforce word combinations into sentences. Successive approximations are rewarded or reinforced until finally the child's language is similar to the adult's. Other learning theorists suggested that imitation also plays an important part in language acquisition (Bandura, 1971).

At face value this explanation sounds plausible. The environment must be responsible for differences in learning one language or another, or one particular dialect. How else can we explain why one child speaks Russian and another Japanese, or why 'I were stood there while six' is said by one speaker and 'I was standing there until six o'clock' by another? But the empirical evidence suggests that the process is much more complicated. Brown et al. (1969), tape-recording mothers talking to their young children, found that as far as syntax was concerned there was very little evidence that mothers shaped their children's grammar. Statements like, 'Want milk' or 'Ben cup' were accepted. For the most part mothers corrected the content of what their children said rather than the grammatical structure. Thus they only corrected sentences which were untrue. For example, if the child said, 'That pig' (indicating a sheep), the mother would say, 'No, that's a sheep'. If the child said 'That sheep' the mother might then say, 'Yes'.

Findings like these gave no support for reinforcement or reward as an explanation for syntactic acquisition. What about the role of imitation? Clearly it must have some effect on language acquisition since children learn the same language and accent as members of their social group. They often learn new words by reproducing the words of other people. Furthermore, in terms of sheer quality of language, it has been found that children whose mothers talk a lot to them have larger vocabularies than those whose mothers do not (Clarke-Stewart, 1973).

Nelson et al. (1973), investigating the impact of different kinds of adult feedback on children's grammatical constructions, compared the effects of expanding children's incomplete sentences (that is, putting them in their complete form) and recasting them (that is, keeping the topic the same but giving the child a new way of talking about it). For example:

Child's incomplete sentence: Doggy eat
Adult expansion: Doggy is eating
Adult recasting: What is the doggy eating?

Children whose sentences were recast performed better in a sentence imitation task than children whose sentences were only expanded. Furthermore, the children whose utterances were recast used more complex grammatical forms in their spontaneous speech than those whose sentences were simply expanded. An even more specific effect was found when an experimenter recast children's utterances into questions or into complex verb constructions: each treatment group showed growth in the use of negative 'wh-' questions or complex verb constructions depending on the type of adult intervention. Box 11.2 gives the details of this study.

More recently, social learning theory has contributed to the debate. Moerke (1991) proposes a skill learning model based on an integration of learning theory (operant conditioning), social learning theory and aspects of Piaget's cognitive developmental theory. He uses the idea that language depends on continuous feedback cycles within which the 'trainer' – usually the parent – invites a response from the child and then provides feedback. Moerke provides many examples of this kind of learning interaction with the parent.

The innate basis of language: Chomsky's views

By contrast, other theorists focus on the universal properties of language, pointing out that the sequences of language acquisition are broadly similar in all societies; language occurs in all human cultures, and all languages have certain features in common (Chomsky, 1965; McNeill, 1970).

The essence of Chomsky's argument is that the relationship between speech sounds and meaning is not a simple one of association (as the behaviourist school of psychology and the learning theory approach suggested). Instead, we need to distinguish between the surface structure of the language and its deep structure, that is, between the arrangement of words in the utterance and the logical, grammatical relationships among the elements in that utterance. The connection between the two is specified by the transformational procedures or rules of grammar. Different languages use different transformational rules but the universal features are to be found in deep structure.

Chomsky proposed that humans have an innate 'language acquisition device' (LAD), without which language could not develop. The LAD is so constructed that it can 'perceive' regularities in the utterances that the child hears. The LAD generates hypotheses about these regularities (for example, that the plural is formed by adding -s to the noun). These are then tested against new utterances and so come to be rejected or accepted as appropriate. The LAD can acquire any language and faced with the utterances of a particular language, it develops a grammar. Brown and Bellugi (1964) analysed the early speech of two children, Adam and Eve, and noted the over-generalization of inflections described earlier. For example, the use of -s to form plurals was observed as 'deers', 'sheeps', 'knifes', 'tooths'. Use of -ed to form past tense was observed as 'comed', 'doed', 'growed', 'hurted', 'swimmed', 'caughted', 'drinked'. The child's innate propensity to use rules, argued Brown and Bellugi, led to 'errors' from which the linguist can infer the grammar being used. The incorrect grammatical constructions made by Adam and Eve did not come from adult models; it seemed that the children had produced them themselves on the basis of simple grammatical 'hypotheses'. This would be consistent with the LAD theory.

What are these universal characteristics of language? First they refer to phonological aspects of language, since every language has consonants, vowels and a syllabic structure. They also apply to syntax. All languages have sentences, noun phrases, verb phrases and a grammatical structure underlying them. Chomsky (1965) argued that there are deep structures and surface structures in all languages as well as rules of transformation that connect the two. The surface structure – that is the ordering of words in a sentence – can vary but still reflect the same deep structure, that is the underlying meaning. For example:

The dog bit the man.
The man was bitten by the dog.

These two sentences have the same deep structure in the sense that they are about the same occurrence, but the surface ordering of words is different. The relationship between deep and surface structures is achieved through the rules of transformation. These rules make the connection between sound and meaning in a language. Table 11.4 shows sentences that, by contrast, show differences in deep structure but a similar surface structure.

Table 11.4 Examples of sentences with similar surface structure but a different deep structure

Sentence	Paraphrase	Non-paraphrase
They are buying glasses	–	–
They are drinking glasses	They are glasses to use for drinking	They are glasses that drink
They are drinking companions	They are companions that drink	They are companions to use for drinking

Source: McNeill, 1970

We understand that, although the three sentences in table 11.4 have the same surface structures, different relationships among the words are implied and thus different meanings. Finally, some sentences can have two meanings: for example, 'The peasants are revolting'. It is the rules of transformation which enable us to understand whether the peasants 'are in revolt' or 'revolt us'. As McNeill (1970) writes: 'Every sentence, however simple, has some kind of underlying structure related to some kind of surface structure by means of certain transformations.'

Chomsky stresses the tacit knowledge that we all have of the structure of language even though we may not be able to describe the structures using the language of linguistics experts. Even young children have a tacit knowledge. By 5 years most children – whatever their background or culture – have a good grasp of the basic rules of their language. So who teaches them? Not the parents – most are not professional linguists. Chomsky proposes that it must be because of innate knowledge. This theory, then, encompasses not just specific languages but the general form of human language, and proposes that 'the theory of grammar and its universal constraints describes the internal structure of LAD, and, thus, of children' (McNeill, 1970, p. 151). The ability to infer such transformational rules from surface structure utterances was, Chomsky and McNeill both thought, embodied in the LAD.

Chomsky's theory of transformational, generative grammar provided the impetus for a great deal of research into child language. His own work investigated grammars in which deep structure or 'meaning' had transformational rules applied to it in order to change it to a surface or spoken utterance. This he called 'generative grammar' because the application of rules generates actual sentences. Chomsky argued that the child was involved in the creative process of generating language, as utterances like 'Two sheeps' or 'All done milk' seemed to show.

Brown and Fraser (1963), studying telegraphic speech in children, concluded that the utterances could all be classified as grammatical sentences from which certain words had been omitted. For example, 'Mummy hair' only omitted the possessive inflection ('Mummy's hair'); 'chair broken' was an acceptable sentence if 'is' was added. Similarly, McNeill (1966) noted other grammatical relationships in the telegraphic speech of young children. Ordering was important in the structure of children's speech even though it was not in direct imitation of the order

Table 11.5   Stages in the development of question forms

Ages for Adam	Questions	Commentary
28 months	Sit chair? Ball go? What that? Where mummy go? What mummy doing?	Expressed by intonation only The child has developed a routine form of the question
38 months	Will you help me? Does the kitty stand up? What I did yesterday? Why the Christmas tree going? How he can be a doctor?	The child has developed the use of *auxiliary verbs* For questions expecting the answer yes or no, there is inversion of the verb but not for 'what' and 'why' questions
42 months	Are you thirsty? Why can't we find it? I have two turn, huh? We're playing, huh? That's funny, isn't it? Why can't they put on their swimming suits?	Inversion of the verb in 'why' questions Development of 'tag' questions, e.g. tags on 'huh?' at the end of a sentence Later, inversion of auxiliary verbs appears too

Source: Adapted from Cazden, 1972

of adult language. The child might say 'Me want that coat', but phrases like 'Want that coat me' did not appear.

Linguistic research has also investigated transformational rules in child language. We will look at one kind of transformation, the question. Table 11.5 gives examples of a child using telegraphic speech and shows the gradual development of the correct form of question. This is one type of transformation; there are many others (e.g., use of the past tense, the negative, the use of plurals) which also seem to demonstrate that the child, from an early age, acts as though she expected language to be governed by a set of rules.

The analysis of children's utterances in terms of deep structure, surface structure and the transformational rules that relate the two (Brown, 1973; McNeill, 1970; Slobin, 1973), has greatly enriched our understanding of early language development. Children's language does seem to be governed by rules and does seem to develop in a systematic way. Children do seem to progress through similar stages in the acquisition of language. However, many contemporary psychologists question the notion of an inborn LAD. As we will see in following sections, many psycholinguists (for example, Tomasello and Brooks, 1999) challenge the whole concept of underlying structure.

Chomsky himself revised his views on transformational grammar. In a later version of his theory (Chomsky, 1986), he proposed Principles and Parameters Theory (PPT), in which he adds to his concept of deep and surface structures the idea of processes through which the child must pass in order to achieve grammatical utterances. He still holds to the assumption that humans have an innate capacity for language but puts more emphasis in the recent formulation of his theory, on the psychological processes of learning different kinds of grammatical structure. As with the earlier version, it is difficult to test PPT theory formally. (For a detailed exposition and critique of PPT, we recommend Messer, 1994, chapters 10 and 11.)

Pinker and the evidence from pidgins and creoles

Pinker (1994), in *The Language Instinct*, provides compelling evidence for the innate basis of language. He argues (p. 32) that 'complex language is universal because *children actually reinvent it*, generation after generation – not because they are taught, not because they are generally smart, not because it is useful to them, but because they just can't help it'. As one source of evidence for this view, Pinker indicates how pidgin languages have been transformed – by children learning and changing them – into full languages. He cites research (Bickerton, 1990) into the pidgin language developed by labourers who were imported into the sugar plantations in Hawaii around the turn of the twentieth century. These people came from China, Japan, Korea, Portugal, the Philippines and Puerto Rico, and developed a pidgin in order to communicate with one another. Typically, this pidgin did not have the usual grammatical structures; it had 'no consistent word order, no prefixes or suffixes, no tense or other temporal and logical markers, no structure more complex than a simple clause, and no consistent way to indicate who did what to whom' (Pinker, p. 34). He quotes examples from two speakers (p. 33):

Speaker 1:   Me cape buy, me check make.
Speaker 2:   Good dis one. Kaukau any-kin' dis one. Pilipine islan' no good. No mo money.

The meaning intended by these pidgin speakers is as follows:

Speaker 1:   He bought my coffee; he made me out a cheque.
Speaker 2:   It's better here than in the Philippines; here you can get all kinds of food, but over there there isn't any money to buy food with.

Pinker points out that, in each case, the meaning has to be filled in by the listener since pidgin does not have the grammatical resources to convey complex messages. But for the children who grew up in Hawaii it was a totally different matter. Their language – which is now called Hawaiian Creole – was grammatical, since it contained standardized word orders, markers for present, future and past tenses, and subordinate clauses, despite the fact that they had been exposed only to the pidgin of their parents. Here are some examples (Pinker, p. 34) each followed by a 'translation':

Speaker 3:   One time when we go home inna night dis ting stay fly up
Speaker 4:   One day had pleny of dis mountain fish come down.

The meaning of Speaker 3's sentence is: 'Once when we went home at night this thing was flying about'. Note that the event is contextualized by the use of 'one time'; there is a subordinate clause, 'when we go home' and the verb tense is indicated through the use of 'stay fly up'.

The meaning of Speaker 4's sentence is: 'One day there were a lot of these fish from the mountains that came down (the river).' Note the contextualization ('One day') and the use of past tense ('had')

Bickerton proposes that sentences like these are not haphazard but indicate a consistent use of the rules of Hawaiian Creole grammar. He concluded that creole languages that have been formed from unrelated language mixtures, have strong similarities that support the concept of a basic common grammar.

Similar insights come from research into sign language (Kegl et al., 1999; Morford and Kegl, 2000). In Nicaragua deaf children were not introduced to any form of sign language other than the basic signs that their families had separately devised to communicate with one another. After 1979, special schools for the deaf were founded in which the teachers tried to teach the children to lip-read, with small success. At the same time, and spontaneously, the children were devising their own sign language based on the signs that they had each individually developed within the family – a form of pidgin which linguists have named Lenguaje de Signos Nicaraguense (LSN). Over time, this has developed into a creole created by the younger children who had been exposed to the pidgin of the older children in the school (however unlike pidgin speakers who had a native language, these deaf children could *only* rely on visual and motor cues to convey meaning). This is now known as Idioma de Signos Nicaraguense (ISN) and has become a standardized language with grammatical devices absent in LSN. The new language is so sophisticated that a dictionary of its signs has been published. The children use ISN to tell one another stories, make jokes and plays on words, and share experiences in their linguistic community. These researchers suggest that this is clear evidence of the claim that language has universal rules. Kegl and colleagues point out that the older students, who had entered school in their teens, failed to achieve the level of fluency that was obtained by the younger children, who had gained exposure to one another and had signed to one another at an earlier age. (This supports the idea of a sensitive period in language development; see also pp. 37 and 558.)

Language and cognition: a Piagetian perspective

Chomsky and his colleagues suggested that the child has an innate knowledge of the basic rules and constraints of language, and of her community. But some psychologists have suggested that the rule-bound nature of children's speech arises not so much from an innate LAD as from the child's prelinguistic knowledge, since the child, it is argued, already has some ability to categorize her world even before she can communicate with others in language.

From this perspective, the investigator focuses on the *precursors* of early language, for example, gestures, facial expression, actions. This approach moves its emphasis away from grammatical competence to the study of understanding and communication. As we see in chapter 12, Piaget claims that during the first 2 years of life the child's intellectual skills do not rely on symbols, such as words and images, but are rooted in sensori-motor experiences, such as seeing, hearing and touching. Symbolic actions do not appear until the end of the sensori-motor period. Although interactionists would accept that children develop a system of rules, they would not accept that the rules grow out of an innate LAD but rather that they come from a much wider cognitive system. Children talk alike because they share many similar experiences and their language is facilitated by the sensori-motor schemas of early infancy. This hypothesis – called the 'cognition hypothesis' (Cromer, 1974) – states that:

1 we understand and use particular linguistic structures only when our cognitive abilities enable us to do so (for example, the child can gesture that he wants an apple before he uses the holophrase 'Apple');
2 even once our cognitive abilities allow us to grasp an idea, we may say it in a less complex way because we have not yet acquired the grammatical rule for expressing it freely. Thus the child may not be able to say 'Have you looked?' but he can express the same meaning in the less complex sentence 'Did you look yet?'

What Piagetians suggested was that children form schemas to explain events in their lives and only then talk about them. Language development reflects the stages of cognitive development through which the child is progressing. This is a reciprocal relationship, in which the child plays an active part. However, the child is not applying an innate LAD to the talk that he hears. Instead, his understanding arises out of his existing knowledge of the world.

Many observations support this interactionist approach. In chapter 12, we examine Piaget's work on the object concept, which shows that by the end of the first year the child understands that objects exist independently of herself, whether in her sight or not. In Piaget's view, the child needs to have this sense of object permanence before she can begin to understand that words can represent things. Observations of first words show that children usually focus on familiar actions or objects. In this way, they are using words to express aspects of their environment that they already understand non-verbally, and there seem to be regularities in the ways in which children combine their early one- and two-word utterances with gestures or with knowledge of the context in which the word occurs.

This cognitive approach to children's language development was very influential in the 1970s, until some psychologists began to suggest that it gave a rather narrow view of the child. It ignored, for example, the child's social skills and the effect of the social environment on a child's capacity to learn. It is this shift of emphasis towards the child as communicator in a social world that we will consider next.

Tomasello's construction grammar approach

As a complement to the constructivist views of Piagetians, Michael Tomasello adopts a *construction grammar* approach. He argues that children acquire language gradually, beginning with concrete linguistic structures based on words and mor-phemes, and building up to more abstract structures based on linguistic schemes and constructions. As we have seen, by the time children begin to produce holophrases they have already become quite skilled at communicating through gestures and vocalizations. Children's early one-word utterances have both semantic and pragmatic dimensions (e.g., 'Da!' meaning 'That is a dog!' and 'Milk!' meaning 'Give me that cup of milk because I am thirsty!') but at this stage they are only able to communicate in a condensed, 'telegraphic' way without detailing the scene or marking the various participant roles of the other people involved in the conversation. By 18 months, children begin to combine words, ini-tially to talk in more detail about the same kinds of scenes as they did through their holophrases.

Tomasello's model is grounded in children's cognitive understanding of the various 'scenes' that make up their lives, for example pushing and pulling, eating, seeing objects move up and down, people going in and out of rooms, objects being broken and mended. In his view, children move through specific steps in their language development: *holophrases, word combinations, verb island combinations* and *adult-like constructions*. At each step the child produces creative new utter-ances, suggesting, Tomasello argues, that they have constructed some kind of schema or category based on the specific utterances that they have heard from adult speakers (Tomasello and Olguin, 1993). But children are creative with their language in different ways at different developmental points. When given novel object labels ('Look! A wug!'), 18-month-old children were able to use the new label in combination with words they already knew (for example, 'Wug gone!' or 'More wug'). But at the same age, they had difficulty in being creative in their use of verbs.

Tomasello et al. (1997) tested children's capacity to make word combinations with new nouns and verbs. The researchers did this by teaching the children novel words – e.g., 'gop' and 'tam' – that they could never have encountered before. Ten children, aged between 18 and 23 months, were taught four new words – two nouns and two verbs – over many sessions. All four words were modelled by the experimenters in minimal syntactic contexts, for example 'That's a gop' in the noun condition and 'It is gopping' in the verb condition. The researchers then gave the children frequent opportunities to reproduce the words and to create mor-phological endings, such as plurals for nouns and past tense endings for verbs. What they found was that the children combined the novel nouns with already-known words 10 times more often than they did with the novel verbs. For example, several children produced plurals ('Some gops') but none formed a past tense with the verb ('It gopped').

Tomasello and his colleagues concluded that children of this age have some form of category of noun or noun phrase; they called it a *pivot grammar* on which the children can 'hang' new nouns as they are learned. Children in this age group appeared to have learned that a noun could be a subject ('the wug is kissing') and an object ('kissing the wug'). They had a construct of the order patterns char-acteristic of subject (the wug as kisser) going before object (the wug as one being kissed). They could also form plurals ('wugs'). But they could not do the same on the basis of the category of verb. In other words, Tomasello concluded, children between 18 and 24 months do not have a general schema of subject – verb – object.

After the age of around 24 months, the pattern changes. Tomasello developed the *verb-island hypothesis* to describe early sentences produced by his own daughter in the second year of her life. 'Each verb seemed like an island of organization in an otherwise unorganized language system' (Tomasello and Brooks, 1999, p. 170). His daughter did not appear to know how to partition events in a general way but rather appeared to develop her language in a 'verb-specific' way. Some verbs were only used in one type of simple sentence frame (e.g., 'Cut –') whereas others were used in more complex frames of several types (e.g., 'Draw –', 'Draw – on –' 'Draw – for –' or '– draw on –').

Tomasello concluded that she did not have a general semantic category of verb as instrument but rather something that was more verb-specific, for example 'thing to draw with' or 'thing to cut with'. His explanation is that the child is exposed to rich discourse involving multiple participants and a range of pragmatic functions for some activities (in his daughter's case for the verb 'draw') while in others the child is not exposed to complex talk involving multiple participants and functions (in his daughter's case with regard to the verb 'cut'). Clearly, these experiences would vary from child to child. As a result, each verb is developed on a verb by verb basis to apply to specific scenes in the child's everyday life. That is, the child of around two years produces new verbs only after she has heard them in specific adult discourse – for example 'a thing to draw with' or 'a person to kiss'.

> Early in their linguistic development, young children are not primarily creating a lexical category of verb for purposes of syntax, but rather they are creating different types of schemas or constructions, with particular verbs as their central organizing elements.
>
> (Tomasello et al., 1997, pp. 385–6)

As Tomasello and his colleagues have shown, once children have acquired an inventory of verb-islands, they use them in increasingly differentiated ways. During the preschool years, they move beyond verb-island construction and show their ability to make more abstract linguistic constructions. They use transitives ('Imtiaz broke the vase'), locatives ('Jason picked it up' or 'Put that down!'), datives ('Give it to me' or 'I sent it to Flora') and passives ('he was hurt').

Tomasello proposes that syntax develops *out of* the child's experience of learning specific verbs and nouns before they are able to partition events in a general way. In his view, children do not generalize across scenes to make syntactically similar participant roles in similar ways without first having heard them in adult discourse. From this perspective, it is adult discourse that plays a critical role in the child's production of syntax. As Barrett (1999, p. 20) summarizes this position, syntactic development depends on the child's ability to understand and partition scenes into events, states and participants and then to extract commonalities across linguistic constructions, using the same cognitive processes that are

Table 11.6 Tomasello's construction grammar: children's early syntactic development and the characteristics in which they are defined

	Lexical partitioning of scenes	Syntactic marking of participant roles	Categorization of specific scenes
Holophrases (12 months)	−	−	−
Word combinations (18 months)	+	+	−
Verb island construction (24 months)	+	+	−
Adult-like constructions (36 + months)	+	+	+

Source: adapted from Barrett, M. (ed.) 1999: *The Development of Language*. London: Academic Press, p. 164

used in other domains to construct schemas, categories and scripts. Table 11.6 summarizes Tomasello's types of early syntactic development and their characteristics from holophrases through to adult-like speech.

Language and social interaction

A third interactionist approach places a general emphasis on the child's early experiences of communicating and interacting socially with the people in her surroundings; the baby masters a social world on to which she later 'maps' language.

One powerful factor according to this theory is the adults' tendency to give meaning to the sounds and utterances of infants. Observations of parents interacting with very young babies indicate that burps, gurgles and grunts are interpreted as expressions of intention and feeling on the part of the baby: 'You really enjoyed that, didn't you?', or 'Will you please make up your mind?' Many infants experience extensive verbal exchanges with their mothers, during which the mother actively interprets, comments upon, extends, repeats and sometimes misinterprets what the child has said, in a 'conversational' format.

Another important development, according to this viewpoint, is the development of joint attention, and mutual understanding of gestures. As early as 6 months, infants will follow the mother's gaze to see what she is looking at (Butterworth, 1991); and by 9 or 10 months, they will start pointing at objects in a communicative way (see chapter 3). It is communicative because the infant clearly wants to direct the mother's attention to the object, and is not satisfied until this is achieved. Non-verbally, it is the equivalent of saying 'look at this!' A good response of the adult is to name the object or say something about it

By this age, too, reaching for objects changes and becomes more social. At 6 months, a baby reaching is really trying to get the object herself. By 9 months, she may make a more ritualized gesture of reaching, and look at the mother. This is the non-verbal equivalent of 'give me this!' At about this age infants will show or give objects to a parent or adult, as well.

The crucial development at this age, shortly before first words appear, is joint attention; both adult and infant are jointly giving their attention to a particular object, and are communicating about this by shared understanding of gestures such as looking, pointing, reaching and showing. The adult often names the object in these situations; and one can see that it is a relatively small step for the infant to start naming objects also. In this view, joint attention, together with the experience of turn-taking or 'conversational' formats of interaction, are crucial precursors of early language development.

The psycholinguist's emphasis on grammar obscures the function that these interactions have in preparing the infant for language. Infants and adults together create a range of formats, that is, habitual exchanges, which form the basis for interpreting what both parent and child mean. In the course of these dialogues or pre-speech 'conversations', the child is developing skills which are 'as essential to speaking and understanding language as the mastery of grammar is supposed to be'. Furthermore, the skills are extended by ritualized games such as peek-a-boo, and joint picture-book reading.

Bruner (1983) calls these interactive precursors and later supports for language the Language Acquisition Support System (LASS). These social formats or rituals, and experience of social reciprocity, are important parts of the environmental context that structures the child's understanding of the world and hence her early language utterances. The distinctions between subject and object, or between nouns and verbs, for example, may be facilitated in this way. In fact, Bruner argues, adult conversation would be impossible if this prior shared meaning and reciprocity between speakers had not been established.

This sociocognitive perspective traces the child's competence in language back to her experience as a communicator in the pre-verbal stage – a time when the responsiveness of adults is a key factor. It considers both social and cognitive functioning, with particular reference to the adult's sensitivity to the child's early capacity to perceive and understand experiences. Where infants do not experience this reciprocity and shared social interaction, or where the parents fail to give feedback to the baby's early vocalizations and gestures (as happens with children reared in restricted environments), then later linguistic development is likely to suffer (see chapter 17).

Adult–child speech

Research into Adult–Child (A–C) speech gives a fourth perspective on the interactionist stance. In the 1960s it was believed that A–C speech to children (motherese, as it was called then) was similar to that between adults. Chomsky (1965) took this position, indicating that language acquisition was very difficult – too difficult for the young child to do unless some innate capacity were present. But empirical research since that time has indicated that A–C speech is distinctively different from Adult–Adult (A–A) speech.

Table 11.7   A comparison of Adult–Child (A–C) speech with Adult–Adult (A–A) speech

Syntax	A–C speech	A–A speech
Mean length of utterance (MLU)	3.7 words	8.5 words
Verbs per utterance	0	81.5
Percentage of utterances with conjunctions (e.g., 'since', 'because', 'then')	20%	70%
Percentage of pauses at end of sentence	75%	51%
Speed, words per minute	70	132

Source: Adapted from Messer, 1994, p. 221

Mothers typically use the simplest speech with infants of 8–12 months (Stern et al., 1983). This could be because prior to this age children cannot understand the content of speech but after this age they are more able to deal with increasingly complex material. Adults also adjust their speech to the cognitive ability of the child, whether it is first or later born and whether siblings are present. Messer (1994) argues that adults do in fact modify their speech when talking to young children, as is evidenced in the work of Snow (1977) and Snow et al. (1996). The most commonly used measure of grammatical complexity has been the mean length of utterance (MLU). Messer shows that when you compare A–C speech with A–A speech there are very clear differences (see table 11.7). A–C speech has a higher pitch, a greater range of pitch and is simpler in meaning. The mean length of utterance is shorter; A–C speech is also simpler, for example, through number of verbs or conjunctions per utterance. It is also more likely to be in the present tense. It is easier to process; it is slower; it has more repetitions and an exaggerated form. It is more likely to concern events that are happening in the here and now, contains more concrete nouns, uses proper names rather than pronouns. It will also use special words like 'tummy', 'poo', 'dummy', 'doggy'.

Babies indicate soon after birth that they prefer A–C speech to the Adult–Adult speech they hear (see also chapters 3 and 10). Why is this? Before infants are able to speak or even to respond to words, they seem to be able to respond to the sound patterns – or 'prosodic' characteristics – of speech. This refers to the general pattern of sound, which is not related to individual words. Stern et al. (1983) identified a number of distinctive prosodic patterns in speech to infants. For example, when infants were inattentive, parents would typically raise the pitch of their voice; so a form of bell-shaped pitch contours – a pattern of rising and falling pitch – took place as a means of capturing and then maintaining the infant's attention.

Papousek et al. (1987) found that A–C speech has the following kinds of melodic units: level, rising, falling, U-shaped, bell-shaped or complex sinusoidal. These were found across three languages – English, Mandarin and German. They suggest that these melodic units may be universal patterns of pre-linguistic communication. They are used in consistent ways in a culture and, in addition, are attuned to the perceptual preferences and abilities of infants (see chapter 10). Papousek et al. (1991) found that Chinese mothers use similar melodic contours, suggesting that there are universal patterns across languages and cultures which parents use to communicate with their infants. They are also present in SES blacks in the USA, and in non-Western cultures, e.g., the Kaluli of New Guinea (Schieffelin and Ochs, 1983).

It would appear that the prosodic contours enable infants to understand the intent of speech before they can identify the meaning of individual words. In addition, they must identify individual words in the speech that they hear before they can produce words themselves. But how do they reach the point where, like adults, they can distinguish individual words in the speech that they hear? Gleitman (1990) suggested that infants are predisposed to attend to smaller segments of speech (such as stressed syllables) and that this is how they eventually identify words. First of all they identify whole utterances by 'silences before and after them, suprasegmental contour, the melody of the utterance and its rhythm' (Messer, 1994, p. 79). At the same time as the infants begin to segment or split an utterance into smaller units the mothers also stress words in their speech in ways which help the infants to locate them in speech – for example by stressing the ones which are especially important or by speaking loudly at particular points in the 'conversation'. (Gleitman calls this process 'syntactic bootstrapping'.)

Some support for this idea comes from a study by Messer (1981) of the amplitude of words in mothers' speech to 14-month-old infants. He found that labels for objects were more likely than any other word class to be the loudest in an utterance. This emphasis, on the part of the mothers, clearly helps infants to identify the words for everyday objects in the child's world. These labels also occurred more frequently in the last position in an utterance and therefore were more likely to be remembered.

Such findings have been confirmed by Fernald and Mazzie (1991). They found that mothers consistently gave new words prominence when reading a story to an infant of 14 months. Again these new words were more likely to be positioned at the end of the utterance and be spoken with more emphasis. This suggests that there are a number of strategies which infants use to identify certain words but also that the mother provides useful cues which help the infant to identify important words.

Research into children's developing language (see box 11.2) indicates that adults' and peers' feedback plays an important role in children's language learning, but that the principles of reinforcement and imitation are not in themselves sufficient to explain how the process occurs. The issue of the value and nature of the role of adult discourse in child language development remains controversial. Some researchers argue that the sentences which parents use to children are 'finely-tuned' to the child's needs as a learner (e.g., Furrow et al., 1979); others disagree (e.g., Gleitman, 1990). A number of questions remain unanswered. How short should the mother's MLU ideally be, for example? No-one has suggested that mothers should speak in one-word utterances! One theory might be that optimal MLU should be longer, but only a bit longer, than child MLU, through a process of scaffolding.

Researchers have also explored the ways in which social interaction between adults and children reflect cultural attitudes and beliefs about children.

Schieffelin (1990) reports on the Kaluli of Papua New Guinea who develop language despite the fact that mothers and babies do not appear to engage in mutual eye-contact as is customary in Western society. In this society conversation is given a high status. However, the Kaluli do not talk at any length about their feelings. Kaluli mothers usually put babies in such a position as to be seen by others and to see others, but they do not engage in mutual gaze. Although Kaluli mothers are very attentive to their infants, they do not seem to view them as conversational partners, so they are rarely addressed except to call them by name or in the use of expressive vocalizations. When the babies are 6–12 months old adults begin to speak to them using short utterances. Teaching is done by giving the child a model utterance and then instructing the child to repeat it. When an adult talks to an infant, the mothers reply on the part of their infants in a high-pitched child-like voice. Such exchanges seem to be designed to foster certain social relationships rather than to teach language.

Work with blind children, who also learn to speak without mutual eye-gaze and peek-a-boo games, indicates that joint attention seems to develop whatever the means of achieving it may be. Blind babies obviously do not 'look', but they learn how to direct their parents' attention and may even use the word 'look'. Transcripts of Kaluli children and parents talking indicate that they also develop mutual points of focus. It could be that interactions between adults and babies do not occur according to one particular biologically designed choreography (Schieffelin and Ochs, 1983, p. 127) but it does happen in all these different environments.

Summary

Themes in the study of child language development focused initially on the debate between nativists and developmentalists. More recent, alternative interactionist positions have been proposed that place much more emphasis on the social context in which children grow, on the child's intention to communicate meaningfully and on the child's construction of language through discourse with others. Still further debate concentrates on whether the child's language is domain-general (that is, reflects the child's changing representations of concepts, categories, events and scripts across cognitive domains) or domain-specific (that is, the child's linguistic processes are specialized and arise out of domain-specific information-processing systems).

As the painstaking analysis of real-life conversations between parents and their children has shown, children do not directly imitate adult language and adults do not normally use reinforcement techniques to teach their children to speak. The presence of involved adults and other children who use a form of discourse closely adapted to the child's level, and who recast sentences in a form to which the child has access, seems to provide an environment in which language will flourish. To date, however, there is still no agreement among theorists about the precise ways in which the child's phonological, syntactic, semantic and pragmatic language development takes place.

Further Reading

Stern, D. 1990: *Diary of a Baby*. Harmondsworth: Penguin, takes everyday interactions and describes them from the two perspectives of adult and child. This is a highly original attempt to enter the inner world of the baby.

For more advanced reading, Barrett, M. (ed.) (1999) *The Development of Language*. London: Psychology Press gives a thoughtful and wide-ranging overview of the main strands in language development. Messer, D. 1994: *The Development of Communication from Social Interaction to Language*. Chichester: Wiley, describes the development of communication and language from birth to 3 years. He discusses a number of research traditions in the field, notably those that emphasize language as an innate process and those that stress language as the outcome of learning.

For reference, Rosenblith, J. 1992: *In the Beginning: Development from Conception to Age Two*. London: Sage, gives an exhaustive review of research into the early years of the child and provides a scholarly synthesis of current thinking in the field. A clear introduction to Chomsky's ideas is provided by Lyons, J. 1985: *Chomsky*. London: Fontana.

On the subject of story development, Engel, S. 1994: *The Stories Children Tell*. New York: W. H. Freeman, argues that through hearing and telling stories children are enabled to understand more deeply the people and events in their lives. She examines language use, the development of the concept of story and the ways in which parents and teachers can nurture the child's narrative voice.

Wood, D. (1998) *How Children Think and Learn*. 2nd edn. Oxford: Blackwell describes competing views on the relationship between language, learning and educational achievement.

Pinker, S. 1994: *The Language Instinct*. London: Allen Lane, Penguin Press, argues persuasively that language has a biological, modular basis. The book is scholarly but also immensely readable and draws on research from a wide range of sources.

Discussion Points

1 What is the developmental importance of pre-linguistic communication between adult and baby?
2 Discuss how research findings on A–C speech can help parents to talk more effectively with their young children.
3 How important is it to take semantic (or meaning) aspects into account when examining the language of young children?
4 Does the study of child grammar in the preschool years help us to understand the process through which children acquire language?
5 Evaluate the belief that language development is an innately guided process.

Box 11.1
Categorizing sounds and learning to read:
a causal connection

The investigators in this study wished to test the hypothesis that the child's experience of categorizing sounds, as in rhyming and alliteration, has a considerable effect on later success in learning to read and spell. To do this, they used two methods – a large-scale correlational study, and a small-scale experimental study.

The correlational study started with 118 4-year-olds and 285 5-year-olds. None could yet read. The children were tested on their ability to categorize sounds, by detecting the odd word out, i.e. the one that did not share a common sound, in a series of words. This common sound could be at the end of the word (e.g. bun, hut, gun, sun), the middle (e.g. hug, pig, dig, wig) or the beginning (bud, bun, bus, rug). Where it came at the end or the middle of the word, the task was to spot words which rhymed. Where it came at the beginning of the word, the children's awareness of alliteration was tested.

In addition, each child was given a test of verbal intelligence (the English Picture Vocabulary Test, or EPVT), and a memory test. Four years later, when the children were 8 or 9 years old, Bradley and Bryant gave them standardized tests of reading and spelling. They also tested their IQ, using the WISC-R, and their mathematical ability on a standardized test. (By this time, 368 of the original 403 children remained in the project sample.)

There were high correlations between the initial sound categorization scores (at ages 4–5 years) and the children's reading and spelling scores 4 years later (box table 11.1.1). This in itself does not prove the hypothesis that the ability to categorize sounds has a causal connection with reading success. Some third factor might lie behind both abilities. For example, general intelligence, or perhaps memory for words, might help in both. However, as can be seen in box table 11.1.1, the correlations of reading and spelling scores with sound categorization are a bit higher than with the EPVT or memory scores. This means that while intelligence and memory may explain some of the association between sound categorization and reading and spelling, it is unlikely that they can explain all of it.

To provide more definite evidence for the causal relationship that this suggested, the

Box Table 11.1.1 Correlations between initial sound categorization, EVPT and memory scores, and final reading and spelling levels

| | | Initial scores | | | | | |
| | | Sound categorization | | EPVT | | Memory | |
	Age (yr)	4	5	4	5	4	5
Final reading score (Schonell test)		0.57	0.44	0.52	0.39	0.40	0.22
Final spelling score (Schonell test)		0.48	0.44	0.33	0.31	0.33	0.22

Source: Bradley and Bryant, 1983

Box Plate 11.1.1   Children receiving training in sound categorization skills: (a) selecting pictures with names which have common sounds (e.g. bat, mat, hat); (b) identifying sounds with the aid of plastic letters.

investigators carried out a training study with an experimental design (a field experiment, see chapter 1), using 65 children from the larger sample. They were selected from those whose original scores on sound categorization were at least two standard deviations below the mean.

Two experimental groups received training in sound categorization skills for 40 individual sessions over 2 years. In Group 1

Box Table 11.1.2 Mean final reading, spelling and mathematics levels, and intelligence test scores, in groups from the training study (adapted from Bradley and Bryant, 1983)

	Experimental groups		Control groups		Significance of group differences
	1	2	3	4	
Reading age in months (Schonell test)	92.2	97.0	88.5	84.5	$p < 0.01$
Spelling age in months (Schonell test)	86.0	98.8	81.8	75.2	$p < 0.001$
Mathematics score	91.3	91.1	88.0	84.1	n.s.
Final IQ (WISC-R)	97.2	101.2	103.0	100.2	n.s.

Source: Adapted from Bradley and Bryant, 1983

($n = 13$) coloured pictures of familiar objects were used to teach the children that the same word could share common beginning (hen, hat), common middle (hen, pet) and common end (hen, man) sounds with other words. This training experience was purely concerned with increasing awareness of rhyming and alliteration. For Group 2 ($n = 13$), in addition to the rhyming and alliteration training, the children were shown plastic letters and taught how to identify the sounds which the names of the pictures had in common with particular letters ('c' for 'cat' and 'cup'). The relationship between common sounds and letters of the alphabet which represented them was made clear (box plate 11.1.1).

Two control groups were also used. Group 3 ($n = 26$) were taught over the same period of time to categorize the same pictures in a conceptual way (e.g. hen and bat are animals: hen and pig are farm animals) but received no tuition in sound categorization. Group 4 ($n = 13$) received no training at all. All four groups were matched for age, initial EPVT scores and initial scores on sound categorization. The results are shown in box table 11.1.2. Group 1, the experimental group which had been trained on sound categorization only, was ahead of Group 3 (the group trained to categorize conceptually) by 3–4 months in reading and spelling levels. The second experimental group, Group 2, which had been trained on sound categorization and alphabetic letters as well, performed best of all in reading and spelling. The authors conclude that not only does training in sound categorization have an influence on reading and spelling, but that if it is combined with alphabetic teaching, it will be even more effective. They also argue that the effect is specific to reading and spelling since the differences among the four groups in scores in the mathematics test were considerably smaller and not statistically significant.

The drawbacks of this training study are that the numbers in the experimental groups are small, and some differences are not statistically significant (for example, the scores for Group 1 in themselves do not differ significantly from those in Group 3). Also, as the investigators point out, we do not know how well such experimental results would generalize to a wider spectrum of children in real-life teaching conditions.

This is where the strength of combining two methods comes in. The original correlational study strongly suggests that the relationship between sound categorization skills and later reading and spelling abilities is an ecologically valid one. Taken together, these results provide strong evidence for a moderate degree of causal influence along the lines the investigators hypothesized.

The educational implications are considered further in Bryant, P. and Bradley, L. 1985: *Children's Reading Problems*. Oxford: Blackwell, and in Bryant, P., MacLean, M. and Bradley, L. 1990: Rhyme, language and children's reading. *Applied Psycholinguistics*, 11, 237–52. In view of the large number of children who do experience reading diffi-culties, this study offers practical guidelines for identifying specific problem areas and intervening to overcome them.

Based on material in Bradley, L. and Bryant, P. E. 1983: Categorizing sounds and learning to read: a causal connection. *Nature*, 301, 419–21.

Box 11.2
Facilitating children's syntax development

Nelson had already shown (Nelson et al., 1973) that the recasting of children's incomplete sentences by adults had a positive effect on both performance on a sentence-imitation task, and complexity of grammar use in spontaneous speech. In this experiment he aimed to discover whether these effects were specific. Would children whose utterances were recast into complex questions show improvement in the use of question forms? Would children whose utterances were recast into sentences that contained complex verbs show greater use of verbs? To answer these questions he devised an experimental intervention study.

His sample was 12 children (six boys and six girls), aged 28–29 months, who all lacked two categories of syntactic structures in their spontaneous speech. These were complex questions and complex verbs of the type shown below.

Complex questions:

1 Tag questions: for example 'I changed them round, didn't I?' where 'didn't I?' is tagged on to the end of a statement.
2 'Wh-' negative questions: negative questions beginning with 'what', 'why', 'where' 'who', etc., e.g. 'Why can't I go?'
3 Other negative questions: for example, 'Doesn't it hurt?' or 'It won't fit?'

Complex verbs:
1 Single verbs in future or conditional tense: for example, 'He will help me' or 'He would help me'.
2 Sentences in which two verbs were used: For example, 'He will run and jump.' or 'The bear ate the girls who visited.'

Two one-hour sessions with each child were taped to determine initial language levels. Assignment of children to groups was based on mean length of utterance (MLU) in words. Three boys and three girls were assigned to an intervention schedule focused on complex questions; the remaining six children were assigned to receive an intervention designed to facilitate the use of complex verbs. Each group had an average MLU of 3.69 words per utterance (range 3.09–4.29). Both groups were closely comparable in terms of the presence or absence of complex verbs and complex questions in their spontaneous speech during these two sessions.

Five 1-hour sessions of intervention were scheduled for each child. Three women were the experimenters, each one working with four children (two assigned to question intervention and two to verb intervention).

Box Table 11.2.1 Type of sentence structure used by each participant (numbered) after intervention but not prior to intervention

Sentence type	Question intervention						Verb intervention					
	1	2	3	4	5	6	1	2	3	4	5	6
Tag questions	+			+	+	+						+
'Wh-' negative questions			+									
Other negative questions		+										
Future tense (one verb)						+			+			
Conditional tense (one verb)						+	+	+				+
Future tense (two verbs)							+	+			+	
Conditional tense (two verbs)							+					
Past tense (two verbs)						+		+	+			+

Sign tests show the results to be significant ($p < 0.01$) for both question and verb intervention. MLU for both groups was not affected. Examples of sentences with complex questions or verb structures which appeared after intervention are given in the text

In question intervention sessions the experimenter frequently recast the child's sentences in the form of tag or negative questions. For example, when one child said, 'You can't get in', the researcher replied, 'No, I can't get in, can I?' If recastings did not come readily, the experimenter constructed new examples. When one child said, 'And you're a girl', the experimenter replied, 'Right! And aren't you a little girl?'

Similarly in verb intervention sessions both recastings and new constructions were used. If the child said, 'Where it go?', the adult replied, 'It will go there'. When one child said, 'I got it, I reached it', the adult said, 'You got under the bed and reached it'.

The children's utterances during the fourth and fifth sessions (the last two intervention sessions) were recorded. Each child's transcript was scored for presence or absence of sentences containing complex questions or complex verbs, using the measures shown in box table 11.2.1. Analysis of the data revealed clear-cut effects of the interventions. Complex questions, which had been lacking before intervention, were used by all six children in the question intervention group; only one of the children in this group (subject 6) also showed use of complex verbs. The opposite pattern held for the acquisition of new verb forms. All the children in the verb intervention group used complex verbs which they had not expressed before intervention; only one (subject 6) also used new complex questions. Sign tests showed the results to be significant for both question and verb intervention. MLU was not affected for either group.

Nelson concluded that this experiment increases our understanding of how children get information from adults about syntax. In comparing the experimenters' recasting with normal parental responses, he noted that in real life adults do use negative and tag questions, and complex verbs when they talk to their children, but they do not use them frequently. So why did recastings of children's sentences have the effect shown by this experiment?

Nelson suggested that the experimental recasting probably drew the child's attention to the new forms. The experience of hearing complex questions and verbs was not a wholly new one to the child but the researchers, by reworking the child's own sentences, pointed attention to a more complex form which was close to the child's existing language use and which made immediate sense to the child. The experimenter's response to 'Donkey ran' of 'The donkey did run didn't he?' was more complex but also entirely appropriate in a playful, conversational content. The child was thus able to make a direct comparison between her own utterances and the sentence structure of the adult's reply. The introduction of new grammatical forms that are still closely tied to the child's language use thus seems to be one way of extending language development.

Based on material in Nelson, K. 1977: Facilitating children's syntax development. *Developmental Psychology*, 13, 101–7.

12 Cognition: Piaget's Theory

Jean Piaget (1896–1980) was born in Neuchâtel, Switzerland. At an early age he showed a keen interest in observing animals in their natural environment. At the age of 10 years he published his first article, a description of an albino sparrow which he had observed in the park, and before he was 18 years old journals had accepted several of his papers about molluscs. During his adolescent years he developed an interest in philosophy, in particular the branch of philosophy concerned with knowledge – 'epistemology'. His undergraduate studies, however, were in the field of biology and his doctoral dissertation was on molluscs.

Piaget then worked for a period at Bleuler's psychiatric clinic in Zurich where he became interested in psychoanalysis. As a result, he went to the Sorbonne University in Paris in 1919 to study clinical psychology. There he pursued his interest in philosophy. While in Paris, he worked at the Binet Laboratory with Theodore Simon on the standardization of intelligence tests (see chapter 16). Piaget's role was to examine children's correct responses to test items, but he became much more interested in the mistakes the children made, and came to believe that a study of children's errors could provide an insight into their cognitive processes.

Piaget saw that through the discipline of psychology he had an opportunity to forge links between epistemology and biology. By integrating the disciplines of psychology, biology and epistemology, Piaget aimed to develop a scientific approach to the understanding of knowledge – the nature of knowledge and the ways in which an individual acquires knowledge. Although the quantitative methods of the French intelligence testers did not appeal to Piaget, he was strongly influenced by the developmental work of Binet. Binet was a French psychologist who had pioneered studies of children's thinking, and his method of observing children in their natural settings was one that Piaget followed himself when he left the Binet Laboratory.

Plate 12.1   Jean Piaget in 1936. Courtesy Archives Jean Piaget, Université de Genève.

Piaget integrated his experiences of psychiatric work in Bleuler's clinic with the questioning and observational strategies that he had learned from Binet. Out of this fusion emerged the 'clinical interview' – an open-ended, conversational technique for eliciting children's thinking processes. His interest was in the child's own judgements and explanations. He was not testing a particular hypothesis, but rather looking for an explanation of how the child comes to understand his or her world. The method is not easy, and Piaget's researchers were trained for a year before they actually collected data. They learned the art of asking the right questions and testing the truth of what the children said.

Piaget's life was devoted to the search for the mechanisms of biological adaptation on the one hand, and the analysis of logical thought on the other (Boden, 1979). He wrote more than 50 books and hundreds of articles, revising many of his early ideas in later life. In essence Piaget's theory is concerned with the human need to discover and to acquire deeper knowledge and understanding. Piaget's prolific output of ideas suggests that he was constantly constructing and reconstructing his theoretical system, but this, as we shall see, was quite consistent with his philosophy of knowledge.

In this chapter we will describe the model of cognitive structure developed by Piaget. We will also take notice of modifications and re-interpretations that subsequent researchers have made to Piaget's ideas. Although many aspects of Piaget's theory are now questioned, no one denies the valuable contribution he made to our understanding of the thinking processes of both children and adults.

Piaget argued that to understand how children think we have to look at the qualitative development of their ability to solve problems. Let us look at two examples of children's thinking. These examples show how children develop more sophisticated ways to solve problems.

The first example is taken from one of Piaget's dialogues with a seven-year-old:

Adult: Does the moon move or not?
Child: When we go, it goes.
Adult: What makes it move?
Child: We do.
Adult: How?
Child: When we walk. It goes by itself.

(Piaget, 1929, pp. 146–7)

From this, and other similar observations, Piaget described a period during childhood that was characterized by egocentrism. Because the moon appears to move with the child, she concludes that it does indeed do so. But later, with the growth of logic, she makes a shift from her own egocentric perspective and learns to distinguish what she sees from what she knows. Gruber and Vonèche (1977) give a nice example of how an older child used logic to consider the movement of the moon. This child sent his little brother to walk down the garden while he himself stood still. The younger child reported that the moon moved with him, but the older boy could disprove this from his own observation that the moon did not move with his brother.

The second example is adapted from Piaget's research into children's understanding of quantity. Suppose John, aged four years, and Mary, aged seven years, are given a problem. Two glasses, A and B, are of equal capacity but glass A is short and wide and glass B is tall and narrow (see figure 12.1). Glass A is filled to a certain height and the children are each asked, separately, to pour liquid into glass B so that it contains the same amount as glass A. In spite of the striking difference in the proportions of the two containers, John cannot grasp that the smaller diameter of glass B requires a higher level of liquid. To Mary, John's response is

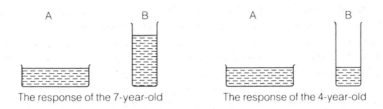

The response of the 7-year-old   The response of the 4-year-old

Figure 12.1   Estimating a quantity of liquid.

incredibly stupid: of course you have to add more to glass B. From Piaget's per-spective both responses are revealing. John cannot 'see' that the liquid in A and the liquid in B are not equal, since he is using a qualitatively different kind of reasoning not yet having the mental operations that will enable him to solve the problem. Mary finds it difficult to understand why John cannot see his mistake. We will discuss this aspect of children's problem solving in more detail later.

Piaget proposed that the essence of knowledge is activity. This may refer to the infant directly manipulating objects and so learning about their properties. It may refer to a child pouring liquid from one glass to another to find out which has more in it. Or it may refer to the adolescent forming hypotheses to solve a scientific problem. In all these examples, the child is learning through action, whether phys-ical (e.g., exploring a wooden brick) or mental (e.g, thinking of different outcomes and what they mean). Piaget's emphasis on activity was important in stimulating the child-centred approach to education, because he believed that to learn, children not only need to manipulate objects they also need to manipulate ideas. We discuss the educational implications of Piaget's theory later in this chapter.

Underlying Assumptions: Structure and Organization

Using observations, dialogues and small-scale experiments, Piaget suggested that children progress through a series of stages in their thinking, each of which corresponds to broad changes in the structure or logic of their intelligence (see table 12.1). Piaget called the main stages of development the sensori-motor, pre-operational, concrete operational and formal operational stages and empha-sized that they occur in that order.

Piaget's structures are sets of mental operations, which can be applied to objects, beliefs, ideas or anything in the child's world. Such a mental operation is called a *schema*. The schemas are seen as evolving structures, in other words, struc-tures that grow and change from one stage to the next. We will look at each stage in detail in the next section, but first we need to look at Piaget's concepts of the unchanging (or 'invariant', to use his term) aspects of thought, that is the broad characteristics of intelligent activity that remain the same at all ages. These are the *organization* of schemas and their *adaptation* through *assimilation* and *accommodation*.

Table 12.1 The stages of intellectual development according to Piaget

Stage	Approximate age (years)	Characteristics
Sensori-motor	0–2	The infant knows about the world through actions and sensory information. Infants learn to differentiate themselves from the environment; begin to understand causality in time and space; and develop the capacity to form internal mental representations.
Pre-operational	2–7	Through the symbolic use of language and intuitive problem-solving the child begins to understand about the classification of objects. But thinking is characterized by egocentrism, children focus just one aspect of a task and lack operations like compensation and reversibility. By the end of this stage children can take another's perspective and can understand the conservation of number.
Concrete operational	7–12	Children understand conservation of mass, length, weight and volume, and can more easily take the perspective of others; can classify and order, as well as organize objects into series. The child is still tied to the immediate experience, but within these limitations can perform logical mental operations.
Formal operational	12	Abstract reasoning begins. Children can now manipulate ideas; can speculate about the possible; can reason deductively, and formulate and test hypotheses.

Organization: Piaget used this term to refer to the inborn capacity to coordinate existing cognitive structures, or schemas, and combine them into more complex systems. For example, the baby of three months has learned to combine looking and grasping with the earlier reflex of sucking. She can do all three together when feeding, an ability which the newborn baby did not have. Or, to give another example, at the age of two Ben has learned to climb downstairs, to carry objects without dropping them and to open doors. He can combine all three operations to deliver a newspaper to his grandmother in the basement flat. In other words, each separate operation combines into a new action that is more complex than the sum of the parts.

Organization also grows in complexity as the schemas become more elaborate. Piaget described the development of a particular action schema in his son Laurent as he attempted to strike a hanging object. At first Laurent only made random movements towards the object, but by the age of six months the movements had become deliberate and well directed. As Piaget described it, by six months Laurent possessed the mental structure that guided the action involved in hitting a toy. He had also learned to accommodate his actions to the weight, size and shape of the toy and its distance from him.

This leads us to the other invariant function identified by Piaget – *adaptation*. By adaptation he meant the striving of the organism for balance (or equilibrium) with the environment which is achieved through the complementary processes of assimilation and accommodation. Through assimilation the child 'takes in' a new experience and fits it into an existing schema. For example, a child may have learnt the words 'dog' and 'car'. For a while all animals are called 'dogs' (i.e., different animals taken into a schema related to the child's understanding of dog), or all four-wheeled vehicles might be considered 'cars'. This process is balanced by accommodation, in which the child adjusts an existing schema to fit in with the nature of the environment. From experience, the child begins to perceive that cats can be distinguished from dogs (and may develop different schema for these two types of animals) and that cars can be discriminated from other vehicles.

Through the twin processes of assimilation and accommodation the child achieves a new state of equilibrium. This equilibrium, however, is not permanent. The balance will soon be upset as the child assimilates further new experiences or accommodates her existing schemas to another new idea. In a sense, equilibrium only prepares the child for disequilibrium, that is further learning and adaptation; the two cannot be thought of separately. Assimilation helps the child to consolidate mental structures; accommodation results in growth and change. All adaptation contains components of both processes and striving for balance between assimilation and accommodation results in the child's intrinsic motivation to learn. When new experiences are close to the child's capacity to respond, then conditions are at their best for change and growth to occur.

The Stages of Cognitive Development

Piaget considered intellectual development to be a continuous process of assimilation and accommodation. Although we go on here to describe the four stages he identified, there is no sharp dividing line between each. The order of stages is the same for all children, but the ages at which they are achieved may vary from one child to another.

The Sensori-motor Stage

During the sensori-motor stage the child changes from a newborn, who focuses almost entirely on immediate sensory and motor experiences, to a toddler who possesses a rudimentary capacity for thinking. Piaget described in detail the process by which this occurs, by carefully documenting his own children's behaviour. On this basis of such observations, carried out over the first two years of life, Piaget divided the sensori-motor period into six substages (see table 12.2).

The first stage, *reflex activity*, included the reflexive behaviours and spontaneous rhythmic activity with which the infant was born. Piaget called the second substage *primary circular reactions*. His use of the term 'circular' was to emphasize

Table 12.2 Substages of the sensori-motor period according to Piaget

Substage	Age (months)	Characteristics
Reflex activity	0–1	Infants practice innate reflexes, e.g., sucking, looking. Behaviour is largely, but not entirely, assimilative.
Primary circular reactions	1–4	Behaviour is primary in the sense that it is basically made up of reflexes or motor responses; it is circular in the sense that the child repeats it. Primary circular reactions centre on the infant's own body. There appears to be no differentiation between self and outside world.
Secondary circular reactions	4–10	Infants now focus on objects rather than on her own body. They begin to make interesting things happen, e.g., moving a hanging toy by hitting it. They have begun to change their surroundings intentionally.
Coordination of secondary circular reactions	10–12	Infants begin to combine schemas to achieve goals, and to solve problems in new situations. E.g., they will use the hitting schema to knock down a barrier between themselves and a toy.
Tertiary circular reactions	12–18	Infants actively uses trial and error methods to learn about objects. Increased mobility enables them to experiment and explore. They learn new ways of solving problems and discover more about the properties of the environment.
Internal representation	18–24	The beginning of mental action, and insightful solutions to problems. Objects and people can be represented symbolically; behaviour can be imitated from previous observations.

the way that children will repeat an activity, especially one that is pleasing or satisfying (e.g., thumb sucking). The term 'primary' refers to simple behaviours that are derived from the reflexes of the first period (e.g., thumb sucking develops as the thumb is assimilated into a schema based on the innate suckling reflex).

Secondary circular reactions refer to the child's willingness to repeat actions, but the word 'secondary' points to behaviours that are the child's own. In other words, she is not limited to just repeating actions based on early reflexes, but having initiated new actions can repeat these if they are satisfying. At the same time, such actions tend to be directed outside the child (unlike simple actions like thumb sucking) and are aimed at influencing the environment around her.

This is Piaget's description of his daughter Jacqueline at five months of age kicking her legs (in itself a primary circular reaction) in what becomes a secondary circular reaction as the leg movement is repeated not just for itself, but is initiated in the presence of a doll:

> Jacqueline looks at a doll attached to a string which is stretched from the hood to the handle of the cradle. The doll is at approximately the same level as the child's feet. Jacqueline moves her feet and finally strikes the doll, whose movement she immediately notices ... The activity of the feet grows increasingly regular whereas Jacqueline's eyes are fixed on the doll. Moreover, when I remove the doll Jacqueline occupies herself quite differently; when I replace it, after a moment, she immediately starts to move her legs again.
>
> (Piaget, 1936, p. 182)

In behaving as she did Jacqueline seemed to have established a general relation between her movement and the doll's and was engaged in a secondary circular reaction.

Coordination of secondary circular reactions. As the word coordination implies it is in this substage that children start to combine different behavioural schema. In the following extract Piaget described how his daughter (aged eight months) combined several schemas, such as 'sucking an object' and 'grasping an object' in a series of coordinated actions when playing with a new object:

> Jacqueline grasps an unfamiliar cigarette case which I present to her. At first she examines it very attentively, turns it over, then holds it in both hands while making the sound apff (a kind of hiss which she usually makes in the presence of people). After that she rubs it against the wicker of her cradle then draws herself up while looking at it, then swings it above her and finally puts it into her mouth.
>
> (Piaget, 1936, p. 284)

Jacqueline's behaviour illustrates how a new object is assimilated to various existing schema in the fourth substage. In the following stage, that of *tertiary circular reactions* children's behaviours become more flexible and when they repeat actions they may do so with variations, which can lead to new results. By repeating actions with variations children are, in effect, accommodating established schema to new contexts and needs.

The last substage of the sensori-motor period is called the substage of *internal representation*. Internal representation refers to the child's achievement of mental representation. In previous substages the child has interacted with the world via her physical motor schema, in other words she has acted directly on the world. But by the final substage she can act indirectly on the world because she has a mental representation of the world. This means that instead of just manipulating the world around her directly she can also manipulate her mental representation of the world – that is, she can think and plan.

What evidence did Piaget put forward to demonstrate that children have achieved mental representations by the end of the sensori-motor period? He pointed out that by this substage children have a full concept of *object permanence*. Piaget noticed that very young infants ignored even attractive objects once they were out of sight. For example, if an infant was reaching for a toy, but then the toy was covered with a cloth the infant would immediately lose interest in it, she would not attempt to search for it and might just look away. According to Piaget it was only in the later substages that children demonstrated an awareness (by searching and trying to retrieve the object) that the object was permanently present even if it was temporarily out of sight. Searching for an object that cannot be seen directly implies that the child has a memory of the object, i.e., a mental representation of it.

Piaget suggested that it was only towards the end of the sensori-motor period that children demonstrated novel patterns of behaviour in response to a problem. For example, if children want to reach for a toy, but there is another object between them and the toy, younger children might just try to reach the toy directly. It may be that in the course of trying to reach the toy they happen to knock the object out of the way and succeed in reaching the toy itself, but this is best described as 'trial-and-error' performance. A child in the later substages of the sensori-motor period might solve the problem by not reaching for the toy immediately, but first removing the object and then getting the toy easily. If a child carries out such structured behaviour it implies that she was able to plan ahead and to plan ahead indicates that she had a mental representation of what she was going to do.

Piaget gave an example of planned behaviour by Jacqueline at 20 months. She was trying to solve the problem of opening a door while carrying two blades of grass at the same time:

> She stretches out her right hand towards the knob but sees that she cannot turn it without letting go of the grass. She puts the grass on the floor, opens the door, picks up the grass again and enters. But when she wants to leave the room things become complicated. She put the grass on the floor and grasps the door knob. But then she perceives that in pulling the door towards her she will simultaneously chase away the grass which she placed between the door and the threshold. She therefore picks it up in order to put it outside the door's zone of movement.
>
> (Piaget, 1936, pp. 376–7)

Jacqueline solved the problem of the grass and the door before she opened the door. In other words, she must have had a mental representation of the problem, which permitted her to work out the solution, before she acted.

A third line of evidence for mental representations comes from Piaget's observations of *deferred imitation*. This is when children carry out a behaviour that is copying other behaviour that they have seen some time before. Piaget provides a good example of this:

> At 16 months Jacqueline had a visit from a little boy of 18 months who she used to see from time to time, and who, in the course of the afternoon got into a terrible temper. He screamed as he tried to get out of a playpen and pushed it backward, stamping his feet. Jacqueline stood watching him in amazement, never having witnessed such a scene before. The next day, she herself screamed in her playpen and tried to move it, stamping her foot lightly several times in succession.
>
> (Piaget, 1951, p. 63)

If Jacqueline was able to imitate the little boy's behaviour a day later she must have retained an image of his behaviour, in other words she had a mental representation of what she had seen from the day before, and that representation provided the basis for her own copy of the temper tantrum.

In summary, during the sensori-motor period the child progresses from very simple and limited reflex behaviours at birth, to complex behaviours at the end of the period. The more complex behaviours depend on the progressive combination and elaboration of schema, but are, at first, limited to direct interaction with the world – hence the name Piaget gave to this whole period because he thought of the child developing through her sensori-motor interaction with the environment. It is only towards the end of the period that the child is freed from immediate interaction by developing the ability to mentally represent her world. With this ability the child can then manipulate her mental images (or symbols) of her world, in other words she can act on her thoughts about the world as well as on the world itself.

Re-interpretations of Piaget: the Sensori-motor Stage

Piaget's observations of babies during this first stage have been largely confirmed by subsequent researchers, but he may have underestimated children's mental capacity to organize the sensory and motor information they take in. Several investigators have shown that children have abilities and concepts earlier than Piaget thought.

Bower (1982) examined Piaget's hypothesis that young children did not have an appreciation of objects if they were out of sight. Children a few months old were shown an object, then a screen was moved across in front of the object, and finally, the screen was moved back to its original position. There were two conditions in the experiment, in one condition when the screen was moved back the object was still in place, but in the second condition the object had been removed and there was only an empty space. The children's heart rate was monitored to measure changes, which reflected surprise. According to Piaget young children do not retain information about objects which are no longer present, and if this is the case there would be no reason for them to expect an object behind the screen when it was moved back. In other words, children should not show any reaction in the second condition. However, Bower found that children showed more surprise in the second condition than in the first condition. Bower inferred that the children's reaction was because they *had* expected the object to re-appear. If so, this would be evidence that young children retained an image or representation of the object in their head, and this could be interpreted as children having a concept of object permanence at an earlier age than Piaget suggested.

In another experiment, Baillargeon and DeVos (1991) showed three-month-old children objects that moved behind a screen and then re-appeared from the other side of the screen. The upper half of the screen had a window in it. In one condition children saw a short object move behind the screen. The object was below the level of the window in the screen and therefore it was not visible again until it had passed all the way behind the screen. In a second condition a tall object was moved behind the screen. This object was large enough to be seen through the window as it passed behind the screen. However, Baillargeon and DeVos created an 'impossible event' by passing the tall object all the way behind the screen but without it appearing through the window. Infants showed more interest by looking longer at the event when it included the tall object than when it included the short object. Baillargeon and DeVos argued that this was because the children had expected the tall object to appear in the window. If so, this would be further evidence that young children are aware of the continued existence of objects even when they have been out of view. The results from Bower (1982) and from Baillargeon and DeVos (1991) indicate that children have some understanding of object permanence earlier than Piaget suggested.

Other researchers have considered Piaget's conclusion that it is only towards the end of the sensori-motor period that children demonstrate planned actions that reflect their ability to form a mental representation of the event. Willatts (1989) placed an attractive toy out of reach of nine-month-old children. The toy was placed on a cloth (and therefore children could pull the cloth to move the toy closer). But the children could not reach the cloth directly because Willatts placed a light barrier between the child and the cloth (and therefore they had to move the barrier to reach the cloth). Willatts found that children were able to get the toy by carrying out the appropriate series of actions – first moving the barrier, and then pulling the cloth to bring the toy within reach. Most importantly, many of the children carried out these actions on the first occasion they were faced with the problem, and did not need to go through a period of 'trial and error' learning to work out how to get the toy. If children at this age can demonstrate novel, planned actions, it can be inferred from such behaviour that they are operating on a mental representation of the world which they can use to organize their behaviour before carrying it out. This is earlier than Piaget suggested.

Piaget pointed out that deferred imitation was evidence that children must have a memory representation of what they had seen at an earlier time. From soon after birth babies can imitate an adult's facial expression or head movement (Meltzoff and Moore, 1983, 1989; and see p. 81), but this type of imitation is performed while the stimulus being imitated is present (in other words, there is no need to store a memory of the stimulus). According to Piaget, imitation based on stored representations only develops towards the end of the sensori-motor period. However, Meltzoff and Moore (1994) showed that six-week-old infants could imitate a behaviour a day after they had seen the original behaviour. In Meltzoff and Moore's study some children saw an adult make a facial gesture (for example, stick out her tongue) and others just saw the adult's face while she maintained a neutral expression. The following day all the children saw the same adult again, but on this occasion she maintained a passive face. Compared to children who had not seen any gesture, the children who had seen the tongue protrusion gesture the day before were more likely to make tongue protrusions to the adult the second time they saw her. Meltzoff and Moore argued that to do this the infants must have had a memory representation of the gesture. If so, this is evidence of mental representations at a much earlier age than Piaget proposed.

■ The Pre-operational Stage

Piaget divided this stage into the pre-conceptual period (2–4 years) and the intuitive period (4–7 years).

The pre-conceptual period

The pre-conceptual period builds on the capacity for internal, or symbolic, thought that has developed in the sensori-motor period. In the pre-conceptual period there is a rapid increase in children's language which, in Piaget's view, results from the development of symbolic thought. Piaget differs from other theorists who argue that thought grows out of linguistic competence. However, as we saw in chapter 11 Piaget maintained that thought arises out of action and this idea is supported by research into the cognitive abilities of deaf children who, despite limitations in language, are able to reason and solve problems. Piaget argued that thought shapes language far more than language shapes thought, at least during the pre-conceptual period. Symbolic thought is also expressed in imaginative play (see chapter 7).

Despite the rapid development of children's thinking and language in the pre-conceptual period Piaget identified limitations in the child's abilities in this stage. For example, Piaget pointed out that the pre-operational child is still centred in her own perspective and finds it difficult to understand that other people can look at things differently. Piaget called this 'self-centred' view of the world *egocentrism*.

Egocentric thinking occurs because of the child's view that the universe is centred on herself. She finds it hard to 'decentre', that is, to take the perspective of another person. The following dialogue illustrates a three-year-old's difficulty in taking the perspective of another person:

Adult: Have you any brothers or sister?
John: Yes, a brother.
Adult: What is his name?
John: Sammy.
Adult: Does Sammy have a brother?
John: No.

John's inability to decentre makes it hard for him to realize that from Sammy's perspective, he himself is a brother.

Children's egocentrism is also apparent in their performance in perspective taking tasks. One of Piaget's most famous studies is the three mountains experiment (see figure 12.2). Piaget and Inhelder (1956) asked children between the ages of four and 12 years to say how a doll, placed in various positions, would view an array of three mountains from different perspectives. For example, in figure 12.2, a child might be asked to sit at position A, and a doll would be placed at one of the other positions (B, C, or D). Then the child would be asked to choose, from a set of different views of the model, the view that the doll could see. When

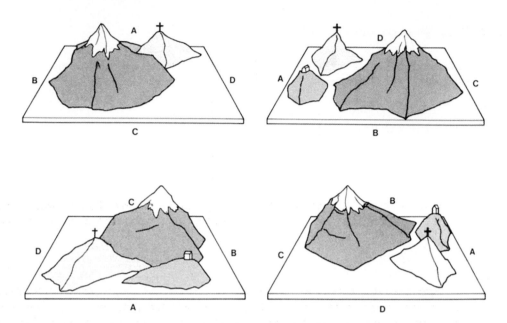

Figure 12.2   The model of the mountain range used by Piaget and Inhelder viewed from four different sides.

four- and five-year-old children were asked to do this task they often chose the view that they themselves could see (rather than the doll's view) and it was not until eight or nine years of age that children could confidently work out the doll's view. Piaget interpreted this result as an example of young children's egocentricity – that they could not decentre from their own view to work out the doll's view.

Several criticisms have been made of the three mountains task. Some researchers (e.g., Donaldson, 1978) have pointed out that it is a particularly unusual task to use with young children who might not have much familiarity with model mountains or be used to working out other people's views of landscapes. Borke (1975) carried out a similar task to Piaget's, but rather than model mountains she used layouts of toys that young children typically play with themselves. She also altered the way that children were asked to respond to the question about what another person looking at the layout might see. Borke found that children as young as three or four years of age had some understanding of how another person would view the layouts from a different position. This was much earlier than suggested by Piaget and shows that the type of procedures and materials that are used in a task can have a marked effect on how well children perform the tasks. By using a model of mountains, Piaget may have selected a particularly difficult context for children to demonstrate their perspective taking skills. Borke's experiment is described in box 12.1. Other researchers have used other visual perspective taking tasks and also shown that four-year-olds can appreciate another's viewpoint (Masangkay et al., 1974) and these studies are discussed in chapter 14.

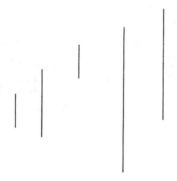

Figure 12.3   The pre-operational child's ordering of different-sized sticks. An arrangement in which the child has solved the problem of seriation by ignoring the length of the sticks.

Piaget used the three mountains task to investigate visual perspective taking and it was on the basis of this task that he concluded that young children were egocentric. There are also other kinds of perspective taking and these include the ability to empathize with others people's emotions, and the ability to know what other people are thinking. Researchers have found that by four or five years of age children do understand that different people can interpret the world in different ways (Wimmer and Perner, 1983). In other words, young children are less egocentric than Piaget assumed. The research concerned with children's insights into other people's minds is discussed in chapter 14.

The intuitive period

Piaget suggested that there was a further shift in thinking about the age of four years, and that it is about this time that a child begins to develop the mental operations of ordering, classifying and quantifying in a more systematic way. Piaget applied the term *intuitive* to this period because even though a child can carry out such operations she is largely unaware of the principles that underlie the operations and cannot explain why she has done them, nor can she carry them out in a fully satisfactory way.

If a pre-operational child is asked to arrange sticks in a certain order, this poses difficulties. Piaget gave children ten sticks of different sizes from A (the shortest) to J (the longest), arranged randomly on a table. The child was asked to seriate them, that is to put them in order of length. Some pre-operational children could not do the task at all. Some children arranged a few sticks correctly, but could not sustain the complete ordering. And some put all the small ones in a group and all the larger ones in another. A more advanced response was to arrange the sticks so that the tops of the sticks were in the correct order even though the bottoms were not (see figure 12.3). In short, the child at this stage is not capable of ordering more than a very few objects.

Piaget found that pre-operational children also have difficulty with class inclusion tasks. These are tasks that involve part–whole relations. Suppose a child is given a box that contains 18 brown beads and two white beads; all the beads are wooden. When asked 'Are there more brown beads than wooden beads?', the pre-operational child will typically reply that there are more brown beads. According to Piaget the child finds it hard to consider the class of 'all beads' at the same time as considering the subset of beads, the class of 'brown beads'.

Such findings tend to be true of all children in the pre-operational stage, irrespective of their cultural background. Investigators found that Thai and Malaysian children gave responses very similar to Swiss children and in the same sequence of development. Here a Thai boy, shown a bunch of seven roses and two lotus, states that there are more roses than flowers when prompted by the standard Piagetian questions:

Child:	More roses.
Experimenter:	More than what?
Child:	More than flowers.
Experimenter:	What are the flowers?
Child:	Roses.
Experimenter:	Are there any others?
Child:	There are.
Experimenter:	What?
Child:	Lotus.
Experimenter:	So in this bunch which is more roses or flowers?
Child:	More roses.

(Ginsburg and Opper, 1979, pp. 130–1)

One aspect of the pre-operational child's thinking processes that has been extensively investigated is what Piaget called *conservation*. Conservation refers to a person's understanding that superficial changes in the appearance of a quantity do not mean that there has been any fundamental change in that quantity. For example, if you have ten dolls standing in a line, and then you re-arrange them so that they are standing in a circle, this does not mean that there has been any alteration in the number of dolls. If nothing is added or subtracted from a quantity then it remains the same (i.e., it is conserved).

Piaget discovered that a pre-operational child finds it hard to understand that if an object is changed in shape or appearance its qualities remain the same. There is a series of conservation tests; examples are given in figure 12.4 and plate 12.2. If a child is given two identical balls of clay and asked if they each have the same amount of clay in them, the child will agree that they are. But if one of the two balls is rolled into a sausage shape (see figure 12.4b), and the child is asked again whether they have the same amount of clay she is likely to say that one is larger than the other. When asked why, she will not be able to give an explanation, but will just say something like 'because it is larger'.

Piaget suggested that a child has difficulty in a task like this because she can only focus on one attribute at a time. For example, if she focuses on length she

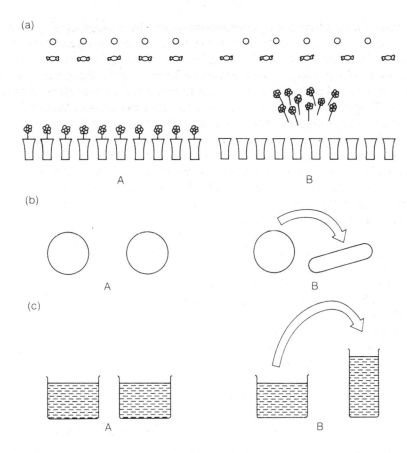

Figure 12.4 Some tests of conservation: (a) two tests of conservation of number (rows of sweets and coins; and flowers in vases); (b) conservation of mass (two balls of clay); (c) conservation of quantity (liquid in glasses). In each case illustration A shows the material when the child is first asked if the two items or sets of items are the same, and illustration B shows the way that one item or set of items is transformed before the child is asked a second time if they are still the same.

may think that the sausage shape, being longer, has more clay in it. According to Piaget, for a child to appreciate that the sausage of clay has the same amount of clay as the ball means understanding that the greater length of the sausage is *compensated* for by the smaller cross section of the sausage. Piaget said that pre-operational children cannot apply principles like compensation.

Let's look at another example of a conservation task. A child is shown two rows of sweets with the same number of sweets in each, and presented in a one-to-one layout (as in figure 12.4a). She is asked if there are the same number of sweets in each row and will usually agree that there are. Then one row of sweets is made

Plate 12.2   A 4-year-old puzzles over Piaget's conservation of number experiments; he says that the rows are equal in number in arrangement (a), but not in arrangement (b) 'because they're all bunched together here'.

longer by spreading them out, and the child is asked again whether there are the same number of sweets in each row. The pre-operational child often says that there are now more sweets in one of the rows. She may, for example, think that a longer row means that there are more objects in that row. She does not realize that the greater length of the row of sweets is compensated for by the greater distance between the sweets.

According to Piaget compensation is only one of several processes that can help children overcome changes in appearance. Another process is *reversibility*. This means that children could think of 'reversing' the change they have seen. For example, if children imagine the sausage of clay being rolled back into a ball, or the row of sweets being pushed back together, they may realize that once the change has been reversed the quantity of an object or the number of items in the row is the same as it was before. According to Piaget, pre-operational children lack the thought processes needed to apply principles like compensation and reversibility, and therefore they have difficulty in conservation tasks.

In the next stage of development, the concrete operational stage, children have achieved the necessary logical thought processes that give them the ability to use appropriate principles and deal with conservation and other problem-solving tasks easily.

Re-interpretations of Piaget: the Pre-operational Stage

We have seen how Piaget claims that the pre-operational child cannot cope with tasks like part–whole relations or conservation, because they lack the logical thought processes to apply principles like compensation. However, other researchers have pointed out that children's lack of success in some tasks may be due to factors other than ones associated with logical processes.

The pre-operational child seems unable to understand the relationship between the whole and the part in class inclusion tasks, and will happily state that there are more brown beads than wooden beads in a box of brown and white wooden beads 'because there are only two white ones'. However, some researchers have pointed out that the questions that children are asked in such studies are unusual, for example it is not often in everyday conversation that we ask questions like: 'Are there more brown beads or more wooden beads?'

Even slight variations in the wording of the questions that help to clarify the meaning of the question can have positive effects on the child's performance. McGarrigle (quoted in Donaldson, 1978) showed children four toy cows, three black and one white, all lying asleep on their sides. If the children were asked 'Are there more black cows or more cows?' (as in a standard Piagetian experiment) they tended not to answer correctly. If the question was re-phrased 'Are there more black cows or more sleeping cows?', pre-operational children were more likely to respond correctly. McGarrigle found that in a group of children aged six years 25 per cent answered the standard Piagetian question correctly. When it was re-phrased, 48 per cent of the children were correct, a significant increase. In other words, some of the difficulty was in the wording of the question rather than just an inability to understand part–whole relations.

Donaldson (1978) put forward a different reason from Piaget for why young children performed poorly in conservation tasks. Donaldson argued that children build up a model of the world by formulating hypotheses that help them anticipate future events on the basis of past experience. The child, therefore, has expectations about any situation, and the child's interpretation of the words she hears will be influenced by the expectations she brings to the situation. In a conservation experiment, for example, an experimenter asks a child if there are the same numbers of sweets in two rows (figure 12.4a). Then the experimenter changes one of the rows while emphasizing that it is being altered. Donaldson suggested that it is quite reasonable for a child to think that there must be a link between that action (changing the display) and the following question (about the number of sweets in each row). Why should an adult ask the child such a question if there hasn't really been a change? If the child thinks that adults don't usually carry out actions unless they want to alter something, then the child may assume that there really has been a change in the material.

McGarrigle and Donaldson (1974) explored this idea in an experiment that included a character called 'Naughty Teddy'. It was Naughty Teddy, rather than the experimenter who muddled up the display and the change was explained to the children as an 'accident'. In this context the child might have less expectation that a deliberate action had been applied to the material, and that there was no reason to believe that a real change had taken place. This was the case because McGarrigle and Donaldson found that children were more likely to give the correct answer (that the material remained the same after being messed up by Naughty Teddy) in this context than in the classical Piagetian context (see box 12.2).

Piaget was right to point out difficulties that pre-operational children have with conservation and other reasoning tasks. But researchers since Piaget have found that, given appropriate wording and context, young children seem capable of demonstrating at least some of the abilities that Piaget thought only developed later. In the right social context, the child emerges as a more competent being than Piaget's work would suggest (see chapter 15).

Piaget also found that pre-operational children had difficulty with *transitive inferences*. He showed children two rods A and B. Rod A was longer than rod B. Then he put rod A away and showed the children rods B and C. Rod B was longer than rod C. Then he asked children which rod was longer A or C? Young children find such questions difficult and Piaget suggested that they cannot make logical inferences such as: if A is longer than B and B is longer than C, then A must be longer than C.

Bryant and Trabasso (1971) also considered transitive inference tasks. They wondered if children's difficulties were less to do with making an inference and more to do with remembering all the information in the task. For children to make a correct response they not only have to make the inference they also have to remember the lengths of all the rods they have seen. Bryant and Trabasso thought it was possible that young children, who have limited working memory capacity (see chapter 13), were unable to retain in memory all the information they needed for the task. They investigated transitive inferences using a task similar to Piaget's original task, but before asking the children to carry out the task itself, they trained them to remember the lengths of the rods. Of course they did not train them using rods A and C together, but the children were trained on the other comparisons they needed to remember (i.e., that A was longer than B and that B was longer than C). Only when Bryant and Trabasso were satisfied that the children could remember all the relevant information were they asked the test question. Bryant and Trabasso found that the children could now answer correctly. In other words, the difficulty that Piaget noted in such tasks was to do more with forgetting some of the information needed to make the necessary comparisons, rather than a failure in making logical inferences.

The Concrete Operational Stage

From about the age of seven years children's thinking processes change again as they develop a new set of strategies that Piaget calls *concrete operations*. These strategies are called 'concrete' because children can only apply them to immediately present objects. Nonetheless thinking becomes much more flexible in the concrete operational period because children no longer have a tendency just to focus on one aspect of problem, rather they are able to consider different aspects of a task at the same time. They have processes like compensation, and other processes like reversibility. For these reasons children succeed on conservation tasks. For example, when a round ball of clay is transformed into a sausage shape, children in the concrete operational stage will say, 'It's longer but it's thinner' or 'If you change it back, it will be the same'. Conservation of number is achieved first (about five or six years), then conservation of weight (around seven or eight years), and conservation of volume is fully understood about ten or 11 years. Operations like addition and subtraction, multiplication and division become easier. Another major shift comes with the concrete operational child's ability to classify and order, and to understand the principle of class inclusion. The ability to consider different aspects of a situation at the same time enables a child to perform successfully in perspective taking tasks. For example, in the three mountains task a child can consider that she has one view of the model and that someone else may have a different view.

There are still some limitations on thinking, because children are reliant on the immediate environment and have difficulty with abstract ideas. Take the following question: 'Edith is fairer than Susan. Edith is darker than Lily. Who is the darkest?' This is a difficult problem for concrete operational children who may not be able to answer it correctly. However, if children are given a set of dolls representing Susan, Edith and Lily they are able to answer the question quickly. In other words, when the task is made a 'concrete' one, in this case with physical representations, children can deal with the problem, but when it is presented verbally, as an abstract task, children have difficulty. According to Piaget abstract reasoning is not found until the child has reached the stage of formal operations.

Re-interpretations of Piaget: the Concrete Operational Stage

Many of Piaget's observations about the concrete operational stage have been broadly confirmed by subsequent research. For example, Tomlinson-Keasey (1978) found that conservation of number, weight and volume are acquired in the order stated by Piaget.

As in the previous stage, children's performance in the concrete operational period may be influenced by the context of the task. In some contexts children in the concrete operational stage may demonstrate more advanced reasoning than would typically be expected of children in that stage. Jahoda (1983) showed that nine-year-olds in Harare, Zimbabwe, had more advanced understanding of economic principles than British nine-year-olds. The Harare children, who were involved in their parents' small businesses, had a strong motivation to understand the principles of profit and loss. Jahoda set up a mock shop and played a shopping game with the children. The British nine-year-olds could not explain about the functioning of a shop, did not understand that a shopkeeper buys for less than he sells, and did not know that some of the profit has to be set aside for purchase of new goods. The Harare children, by contrast, had mastered the concept of profit and understood about trading strategies. These principles had been grasped by the children as a direct outcome of their own active participation in running a business. Jahoda's experiment, like Donaldson's studies (1978), indicated the important function of context in the cognitive development of children, and we discuss this issue more in chapter 15.

◼ The Formal Operational Stage

We have seen that during the period of concrete operations the child is able to reason in terms of objects (e.g., classes of objects, relations between objects) when the objects are present. Piaget argued that it is only during the period of formal operations that young people are able to reason hypothetically. Young people no longer depend on the 'concrete' existence of things in the real world. Instead, they can reason in terms of verbally stated hypotheses to consider the logical relations among several possibilities or to deduce conclusions from abstract statements. For example, consider the syllogism 'all green birds have two heads'; 'I have a green bird at home called Charlie'; 'How many heads does Charlie have?'. The young person who has reached formal operational thinking will give the answer that is correct by abstract logic: 'two heads'. Children in the previous, concrete operational stage, will usually not get beyond protesting about the absurdity of the premise.

Young people are also better at solving problems by considering all possible answers in a systematic manner. If asked to make up all the possible words from the letters A, S, E, T, M, a person at the formal operational level can do this in a logically ordered way. She can first consider all combinations of two letters AS, AE, AT, etc., checking whether such combinations are words, and then going on to consider all three letter combinations, and so on. In earlier stages children attempt tasks like this in an unsystematic and disorganized way.

Inhelder and Piaget (1958) described the process of logical reasoning used by young people when presented with a number of natural science experiments. An example of one of their tasks – the pendulum task – is shown in figure 12.5. The person is given a string, that can be shortened or lengthened, and a set of weights,

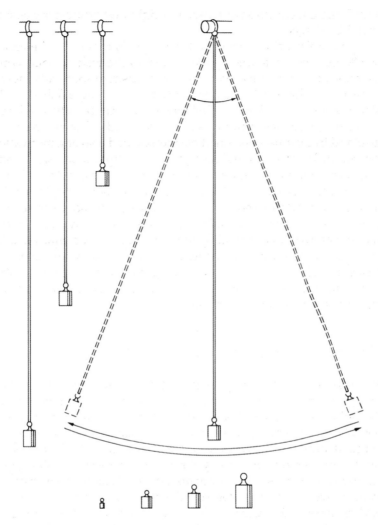

Figure 12.5 The pendulum problem. The child is given a pendulum, different lengths of string, and different weights. She is asked to use these to work out what determines the speed of the swing of the pendulum (from Inhelder and Piaget, 1958).

and is asked to find out what determines the speed of swing of the pendulum. Possible factors are the length of the string, the weight at the end of the string, the height of the release point and the force of the push. In this problem the materials are concretely in front of the person, but the reasoning, to be successful, involves formal operations. These operations would include a systematic consideration of the various possibilities, the formulation of hypotheses (e.g., 'what would happen if I tried a heavier weight?') and logical deductions from the results of trials with different combinations of materials.

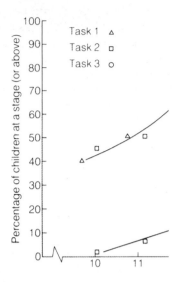

Figure 12.6 Proportion of boys at different Piagetian stages as assessed by three tasks (from Shayer and Wylam, 1978).

Other tasks considered by Inhelder and Piaget (1958) included determining the flexibility of metal rods, balancing different weights around a fulcrum, and predicting chemical reactions. These tasks mimic the processes of scientific inquiry, and Piaget argued that formal scientific reasoning is one of the most important characteristics of formal operational thinking. From his original work, carried out in schools in Geneva, Piaget claimed that formal operational thinking was a characteristic stage which children or young people reached between the ages of 11 and 15 years, having previously gone through the earlier stages of development.

Re-interpretations of Piaget: the Formal Operational Stage

Piaget's claim has been modified by more recent research. More recent researchers have found that the achievement of formal operational thinking is more gradual and haphazard than Piaget assumed. It may be dependent on the nature of the task and is often limited to certain domains.

Shayer et al. (1976; Shayer and Wylam 1978) gave problems such as the pendulum task (see figure 12.5) to schoolchildren in the UK. Their results (see figure 12.6) showed that by 16 years of age only about 30 per cent of young people had achieved 'early formal operations'. Martorano (1977) gave ten of Piaget's formal operational tasks to girls and young women aged 12–18 years in the USA. At 18

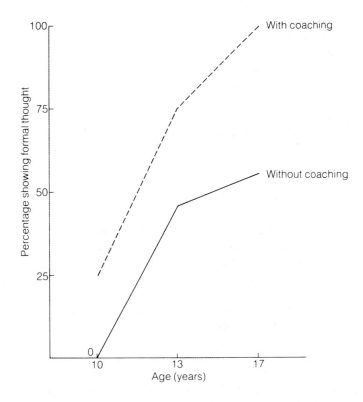

Figure 12.7 Levels of availability of formal thought. Percentage of adolescents showing formal thought, with and without coaching (from Danner and Day, 1977).

years of age success on the different tasks varied from 15 per cent to 95 per cent; but only two children out of 20 succeeded on all ten tasks. Young people's success on one or two tasks might indicate some formal operational reasoning, but their failure on other tasks demonstrated that such reasoning might be limited to certain tasks or contexts. It may only be much later that young people can apply formal reasoning across a range of problem tasks.

Some researchers have shown that formal thinking can be trained. Figure 12.7 shows the results of a study by Danner and Day (1977). They coached students aged ten years, 13 years and 17 years in three formal operational tasks. As would be expected, training only had a limited effect at ten years, but it had marked effects at 17 years. In summary, it seems that the period from 11–15 years signals the start of the potential for formal operational thought, rather than its achievement. Formal operational thought may only be used some of the time, in certain domains we are familiar with, are trained in, or which are important to us. Often formal thinking is not used. After all, we all know of areas of life where we should have thought things out logically, but in retrospect realize we did not do so!

Piaget's Theory: an Overview

Piaget's theory was elaborated over many decades throughout his long life. At first, it was slow to make an impact in the UK and the USA, but from the 1950s its ambitious, embracing framework for understanding cognitive growth was becoming the accepted and dominant paradigm in cognitive development. Since the 1970s Piaget's theory has received extensive evaluation, so that many aspects of the theory, and indeed its whole basis, have been subject to major criticisms.

No one denies the stature of Piaget's achievement, beginning his work as he did in the 1920s, when scientific psychology was in its infancy. However, several objections have been raised as to his methods. He seldom reported quantitative information on the number of children tested, or the percentage who passed a certain test (although researchers who replicated his findings in the 1950s and 1960s did support their findings with statistical analyses). He used a flexible method of interviewing children, the 'clinical method', which meant that he adapted his procedure to suit the child rather than following a standardized approach. This has advantages, but it puts a heavy premium on the interviewer's skill and makes replication of his experiments difficult. Piaget also relied on cross-sectional data (with the exception of the observations of his own children, during the sensori-motor period) rather than longitudinal data that would have given a better insight into stage progressions. Piaget has also been criticized for putting too much emphasis on the child's failures rather than successes.

As we have seen, more recent researchers have found that children can perform tasks either earlier than Piaget predicted (for concrete operations), or later than he predicted (for formal operations). His stage model has clearly been 'stretched' well away from its original periods. So is the stage model still useful? It may only be appropriate if certain abilities go hand-in-hand, linked by similar processes of thinking. For example, concrete operational thought might occur earlier and still be a stage, but only if the various aspects (conservation, classification, seriation, decline of egocentrism) remain linked together. Unfortunately, the evidence for this kind of linkage is not strong, either for concrete or formal operations. For example, different measures of egocentrism do not correlate together strongly (Ford, 1979). Also, Piaget himself admitted that formal operational thought is achieved in a limited, patchy way. However, some researchers (called 'neo-Piagetians') have taken the framework proposed by Piaget, and rather than describing different stages in terms of different reasoning abilities they have tried to explain the stages with reference to the development of children's information processing abilities and limitations. The latter approach will be described in chapter 13.

Educational Implications

Whatever its shortcomings, Piaget's approach provided the most comprehensive account of cognitive growth ever put forward. It has had considerable implications for education, most notably for child-centred learning methods in nursery and infant schools, for mathematics curricula in the primary school, and for science curricula at the secondary school level.

Piaget argued that young children think quite differently from the adult and view the world from a qualitatively different perspective. It follows that a teacher must make a strong effort to adapt to the child and not assume that what is appropriate for adult learning is necessarily right for the child. At the heart of this child-centred approach to education lies the idea of active learning. From the Piagetian standpoint, children learn from actions rather than from passive observations; for example, telling a child about the properties of materials is less effective than creating an environment in which the child is free to explore, touch, manipulate and experiment with different materials. A teacher must recognize that each child needs to construct knowledge for him or herself, and that active learning results in deeper understanding.

How can the teacher promote active learning on the part of the pupil? First, it is the child rather than the teacher who initiates the activity. This does not mean that the children are free to do anything they want, but rather that a teacher should set tasks which are finely adjusted to the needs of their pupils and which, as a result, are intrinsically motivating to young learners. For example, nursery school classrooms can provide children with play materials that encourage their learning; sets of toys that encourage the practice of sorting, grading and counting; play areas, like the Wendy House, where children can develop role-taking skills through imaginative play; and materials like water, sand, bricks and crayons that help children make their own constructions and create symbolic representations of the objects and people in their lives. From these varied experiences the child constructs knowledge and understanding for herself. A teacher's role is to create the conditions in which learning may best take place, since the aim of education is to encourage the child to ask questions, try out experiments and speculate, rather than accept information unthinkingly.

Second, a teacher should be concerned with process rather than end-product. From this it follows that a teacher should be interested in the reasoning behind the answer that a child gives to a question rather than just in the correct answer. Conversely, mistakes should not be penalized, but treated as responses that can give a teacher insights into the child's thinking processes at that time.

The idea of active learning resulted in changed attitudes towards education. A teacher's role is not to impart information, because in Piaget's view, knowledge is not something to be transmitted from an expert teacher to an inexpert pupil. It is the child, according to Piaget, who sets the pace. A teacher's part in the educational process is to create situations that challenge the child to ask questions, to form hypotheses and to discover new concepts. A teacher is the guide in the child's process of discovery, and the curriculum should be adapted to each child's individual needs and intellectual level.

In mathematics and science lessons at primary school, children are helped to make the transition from pre-operational thinking to concrete operations through carefully arranged sequences of experiences which develop an understanding, for example, of class inclusion, conservation, and perspective taking. At a later period a teacher can encourage practical and experimental work before moving on to abstract deductive reasoning. In this way, a teacher can provide the conditions that are appropriate for the transition from concrete operational thinking to the stage of formal operations. The post-Piagetian research into formal operational thought (see above) also has strong implications for teaching, especially science teaching, in secondary schools. Tasks used in teaching can be analysed for the logical abilities that are required to fulfil them, and the tasks can then be adjusted to the age and expected abilities of the children who will attempt them.

Ideally, in view of the wide range of activities and interests that appear in any class of children, learning should be individualized, so that tasks are appropriate to individual children's level of understanding. However, Piaget did not ignore the importance of social interaction in the learning process. He recognized the social value of interaction and viewed it as an important factor in cognitive growth. Piaget pointed out that through interaction with peers, a child can move out of an egocentric viewpoint (see also chapter 14). This occurs through cooperation with others, arguments and discussions. By listening to other children's opinions, having one's own view challenged and experiencing through others' reactions the illogicality of certain concepts, a child can learn about perspectives other than her own. Communication of ideas to others also helps a child to sharpen concepts by finding the appropriate words.

◾ Further Reading

Donaldson, M. 1978: *Children's Minds*, London: Fontana is a very readable book that is critical of Piaget's research and argues forcefully that he underestimated the logical powers of young children. Donaldson also summarizes many of the studies that have demonstrated young children's abilities. The first few chapters of Wood, D. 1998: *How Children Think and Learn*. 2nd edn. Oxford: Blackwell include a good commentary on Piaget's work and influence in the context of other developmental theories. Wood also discusses some of the educational implications of Piaget's work.

Bremner, J. G. 1994: *Infancy*. 2nd edn. Oxford: Blackwell focuses on infancy, but it has a good chapter on the sensori-motor period, and includes a summary of some of the post-Piagetian research with infants.

◾ Discussion Points

1 Piaget said that by the end of the sensori-motor stage children have achieved 'internal representations'. What evidence led him to this conclusion?
2 What does Piaget mean by egocentrism? How have his ideas on egocentrism been challenged?
3 Did Piaget underestimate children's abilities in the pre-operational stage of development?
4 Discuss ways in which Piaget seems to have misjudged the age at which formal operations are acquired. Illustrate with examples from your own experience.
5 What are the implications of Piaget's theory for education? Discuss in relation to your own educational experiences.

Box 12.1
Piaget's mountains revisited: changes in the egocentric landscape

Borke questioned the appropriateness for young children of Piaget's three mountains task (described on p. 400). Borke thought it possible that aspects of the task not related to perspective-taking might have adversely affected the children's performance. These aspects included the following possibilities. First, viewing a mountain scene from different angles may not have been an interesting or motivating problem for young children. Second, Piaget had asked children to select pictures of the doll's views and young children might have had difficulty with such response. Third, because the task was so unusual children may have performed poorly because they were unfamiliar with the nature of the task. Borke considered whether some initial practice and familiarity with the task might improve performance. With those points in mind, Borke repeated the basic design of Piaget and Inhelder's experiment but changed the content of the task, avoided the use of pictures and gave children some initial practice. She used four three-dimensional displays: these were a practice display and three experimental displays (box figure 12.1.1).

Borke's participants were eight three-year-old children and 14 four-year-old children attending a day nursery. Grover, a character from the popular children's television programme 'Sesame Street', was used instead of Piaget's doll. There were two identical versions of each Display (A and B). Display A was for Grover and the child to look at, and Display B was on a turntable next to the child.

The children were tested individually and were first shown a practice display. The practice display was a large toy fire engine. Borke placed Grover at one of the sides of practice Display A so that Grover was looking at the fire engine from a point of view that was different from the child's own view of this display.

An exact duplicate of the fire engine (practice Display B) appeared on the revolving turntable, and Borke explained that the table could be turned so that the child could look at the fire engine from any side. Children were asked to turn the table until they were looking at Display B in the same way that Grover was looking at Display A. If necessary, Borke helped the children to move the turntable to the correct position or walked the children round Display A to show them how Grover saw it.

After this practice period the child was ready to move on to the experiment itself. Here the procedure was the same, except that the experimenter provided no help. Each child was shown three experimental displays, one at a time (see box figure 12.1.1). Display 1 included a toy house, lake and animals. Display 2 was based on Piaget's model of three mountains. Display 3 included several scenes with figures and animals. There were two identical copies of each display. Grover was placed at different places round one copy of each display, and children then rotated the other copy on the turntables to demonstrate Grover's point of view.

Most of the children were able to work out Grover's perspective for Display 1 (three- and four-year-olds were correct in 80 per cent of trials) and for Display 3 (three-year-olds were correct in 79 per cent of trials and four-year-olds, in 93 per cent of trials). For Display 2, however, the three-year-olds were correct in only 42 per cent of trials and four-year-olds in 67 per cent of trials. Borke used analysis of variance, and found that the difference between the Displays 1 and 3 and Display 2 was significant at $p < 0.001$.

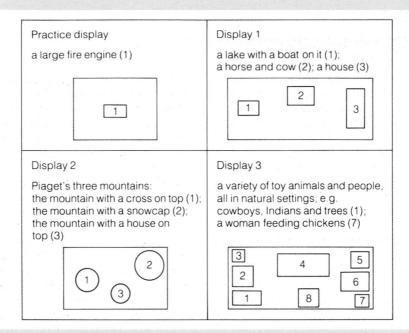

Box Figure 12.1.1 A schematic view of Borke's four three-dimensional displays viewed from above.

As for errors, there were no significant differences in the children's responses for any of the three positions – 31 per cent of errors were egocentric (i.e., the child rotated Display B to show their own view of Display A, rather than Grover's view).

Borke demonstrated clearly that the task itself had a crucial influence on the perspective-taking performance of young children. When the display included recognizable toys and the response involved moving a turntable the children could work out Grover's perspective even when the display was a comparatively complex one like Display 3. This demonstrated that the poor performance of young children in Piaget's original three mountains task was due in part to the unfamiliar nature of the materials that the children were shown.

Borke's conclusion was that the potential for understanding another's viewpoint is already present in children as young as three and four years of age – a strong challenge to Piaget's assertions that children of this age are egocentric and incapable of taking the viewpoint of others. It would seem that young children make egocentric responses when they misunderstood the task, but given the right conditions show that they are capable of working out another's viewpoint.

However, Borke's finding that children as young as three years can perform correctly in a perspective taking task stands in contrast to other researchers who have found that three-year-olds have difficulty realizing another person's perspective when the child and the other person are both looking at the same picture from different points of view (e.g., Masangkay et al, 1974). Children's perspective taking will be discussed again in chapter 14.

Based on material in Borke, H. 1975: Piaget's mountains revisited: changes in the egocentric landscape. *Developmental Psychology*, 11, 240–3.

Box 12.2
Conservation accidents

McGarrigle and Donaldson set out to discover whether young children could succeed at conservation tasks if a different procedure from Piaget's was used. McGarrigle and Donaldson tested 80 children, aged between 4 years 2 months and 6 years 3 months in two situations involving conservation of number (with equal or unequal numbers) and two involving conservation of length (with equal or unequal lengths of string). Each child performed each conservation task under two conditions:

1 an 'accidental' transformation when the materials were disarranged 'accidentally' by a mischievous teddy bear; and
2 an 'intentional' transformation when the transformation of materials was clearly intended by the experimenter. This corresponded to the traditional Piagetian procedure.

The children were divided into two groups of 40, each balanced for age and gender. Group 1 had the accidental condition before the intentional condition. Group 2 had the intentional condition before the accidental one. Within each of the two groups, half of the children were given the number conservation task first and half were given the length conservation first (thus counterbalancing for the order of the tasks).

In the number equal situation, four red and four white counters were arranged in a one-to-one correspondence in two rows of equal length (see box figure 12.2.1). Transformation occurred when the counters of one row were moved until they touched one another. In the intentional condition, the experimenter did this deliberately. In the accidental condition, a 'Naughty Teddy' appeared and swooped over the counters and pushed them together. The child, who had already been warned that Teddy might 'mess up the toys', helped to put Teddy back in its place. Before and after the transformation the child was asked: 'Is there more here or more here, or are they both the same number?'

In the number unequal situation, rows of four and five counters were used and the child was asked: 'Which is the one with more – this one, or this one?' (box figure 12.2.2). A similar procedure was carried out for the conservation of length, using lengths of black and red string. As can be seen in box table 12.2.1, the largest effect was between the accidental and the intentional conditions. Correct responses were more frequent when the transformation was accidental: 72 per cent of the responses were correct when the display was moved accidentally, but only 34 per cent were correct in the intentional transformation condition (i.e., the usual Piagetian procedure). There was little difference between the equal and unequal conditions.

However, the order in which the displays were presented did affect children's responses. When McGarrigle and Donaldson compared performance by Group 1 and 2, the difference was significant ($p < 0.05$), because children who were given the accidental condition before the intentional condition performed better than the children who did the tasks in the reverse order (see box table 12.2.1). This might mean that experiencing Naughty Teddy first could have helped the children realize in the later intentional condition, that the change to the materials was superficial rather than a real alteration.

McGarrigle and Donaldson concluded that the experimenter's behaviour towards the task materials can influence the interpretation a child makes of the situation

Box Table 12.2.1   Number of correct responses given by Groups 1 and 2 under accidental (A) and intentional (I) conditions

	A	then	I	I	then	A
Number equal	32		19	14		22
Number unequal	36		18	13		22
Length equal	34		15	8		24
Length unequal	37		12	9		23
	139		64	44		91

Group 1 $n = 40$
Group 2 $n = 40$

Before transformation   After transformation

Box Figure 12.2.1   Transformation of counters in the number equal situation, either accidentally or intentionally.

Before transformation   After transformation

Box Figure 12.2.2   Transformation of counters in the numbers unequal situation, either accidentally or intentionally.

because the child will be trying to make sense of the situation, and understand what the experimenter wants. Unless the setting is considered, the child's ability to conserve may be greatly underestimated. The original experiments in number conservation might have made the child think that a real change in the materials has taken place – why else would an adult alter something? However, if the change was of no obvious importance (because something was simply messed up by a 'Naughty Teddy' who was only playing about) the child's ability to con-serve improved markedly. This result indicated that how children interpret the social context of the conservation experiments may be an important factor in whether or not they demonstrate the ability to conserve. As McGarrigle and Donaldson (p. 349) concluded:

It is possible that the achievements of the concrete operational stage are as much a reflection of the child's increasing independence from features of the interactional setting as they are evidence of the development of a logical competence.

It should be noted that although this experiment has been widely cited to support the view that Piaget underestimated the abilities of pre-operational children subsequent investigators have not always replicated McGarrigle and Donaldson's main findings (see Eames et al., 1990).

Based on material in McGarrigle, J. and Donaldson, M. 1974: Conservation accidents. *Cognition*, 3, 341–50.

Cognition: The
13 Information
Processing
Approach

In the previous chapter we described the theory put forward by Piaget to describe the development of children's thinking. Some of Piaget's work was re-evaluated by researchers like Donaldson (1978) and her colleagues who found that children can be successful in problem solving tasks (based on Piaget's original tasks) at an earlier age than Piaget suggested. As Donaldson and others have argued there may be many factors associated with a task that can influence performance on that task, including the language used in the instructions, the context of the information which is used in the experiment, and the familiarity of the materials (see chapter 12).

Other researchers have pointed out how a number of factors in experiments could influence children's success. As Bryant and Trabasso (1971) found in their study of transitive inferences (see chapter 12) children may have difficulty with the task, not because they are incapable of making the appropriate inferences to solve the problem (as Piaget had suggested), but because they do not always remember the information required to make the inferences. Once the experimental procedure was changed and children were given the opportunity to learn all the information they needed before making an inference they were much more successful. Many factors associated with the presentation of a task will influence the way that children perform the task.

The discovery that apparently minor changes in experimental materials and procedures can affect children's performance is important for several reasons. First, it has made researchers very aware that what might be thought of as quite superficial changes (e.g., in the way that a question is phrased) may have a significant impact on the way that children interpret a task. Second, knowing that factors associated with the presentation of a task influence children's success can highlight some important aspects of cognitive development – it tells us that compared to older children, young children may be more dependent on the context

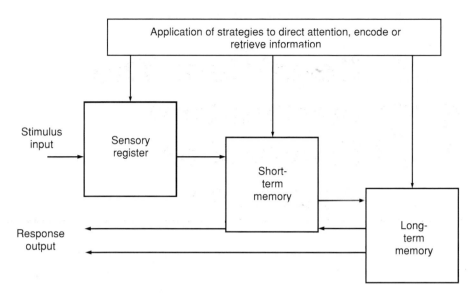

Figure 13.1   Model of information processing (from Atkinson and Shiffrin, 1968).

of the task, or more dependent on the clarity of the instructions if they are to succeed in solving a problem. Third, if children can succeed on some tasks earlier than Piaget predicted it influences how we interpret his theory.

However, as Piaget himself emphasized, describing development means more than just describing task factors, it means understanding the *cognitive* factors that influence the way that children approach problem-solving tasks. As we saw in chapter 12 Piaget described children's intellectual development in terms of their ability to apply processes (like 'compensation' and 'reversibility') in progressively more effective ways. Other researchers have also investigated the mental processes associated with cognitive development, but rather than following Piaget's description of mental operations, they have used the *information process-ing approach* to describe the development of cognitive abilities.

One of the first models of information processing was put forward by Atkinson and Shiffrin (1968) who described cognitive processing in terms of three memory stores and the control processes that operate on those stores (see figure 13.1). This model emphasized the flow of information through or between the different components. Any information in the environment that is attended to will be encoded via *the sensory register*. This will encode what is seen, heard, or otherwise sensed, in full, but only for a very brief period of time before the information decays or is overwritten by new information coming into the sensory register. Some of the information from the sensory store may be selected for processing in *short-term memory*.

Atkinson and Shiffrin's (1968) model of short-term memory was of a store that could only retain a limited number of 'units' of information. However, more recent theorists have placed less emphasis on the 'capacity' of short-term memory and more emphasis on short-term memory as the conscious part of information processing, which is constrained by the number and the processes being carried out at the same time (Baddeley, 1992). Processes will vary, depending on how well practised they are. For example, a novice car driver may need all her attention just to drive the car, but for an experienced driver many aspects of driving are automatic and require little active thought – this will leave the experienced driver with available cognitive resources (perhaps to listen to the car radio and carry out a conversation at the same time as driving). In other words, some processes (if they are relatively unpractised) may require a lot of capacity, but others (which are well learnt and automatic) may make little demand on capacity. This emphasis on processing capacity has led to the original term short-term memory being replaced by the term *working memory* (Andrade, 2001; Cowan, 1997a).

How information is processed in working memory will determine whether it is transferred into long-term memory. Long-term memory is unlimited and retains information indefinitely, and information from that store can be retrieved and re-entered into working memory. Information can be processed by various control mechanisms as it flows through the system, and such mechanisms include strategies for retaining information in working memory – these are called *encoding strategies*. We will discuss how children develop effective encoding strategies later in this chapter.

To provide an example of the flow of information through the different components think about glancing at the front page of a newspaper for a moment and then closing your eyes. You might, very briefly in the sensory register, retain an image of the whole page, but only that part of the page that is specifically attended to (e.g., the headline) will be transferred to working memory. The headline will only be kept in working memory if it is actively processed – for instance, you may need to keep repeating the headline to retain it in working memory; or you may link the words in the headline with some information you already know in long-term memory. Such strategies increase the likelihood that the headline will be transferred to long-term memory. If some time later you want to recall the headline you may be able to retrieve the words directly from long-term memory, or you may find that you cannot immediately remember them and you need to find some way of recalling them. You might, for example, try to think what the headline was about, or what you associated it with when you first encoded it. The latter processes are referred to as *retrieval strategies* and we will describe some of these later in the chapter.

▪ Information Processing Limitations

The flow of information is subject to many limitations. As well as attentional limitations there are also processing limitations. For example, few adults could calculate a mathematical problem like $(123 \times 456)/78$ in their working memory. That is not because adults do not know the appropriate rules for multiplication and division, it is simply because the complexity of the calculation will exceed the processing space available in working memory. However, most adults can solve $(12 \times 34)/5$ without using a calculator, because the figures in the problem and the calculation itself can be held in working memory. But children have more limited processing abilities than adults and therefore, even if they understand multiplication and division, they may not find it possible to solve $(12 \times 34)/5$ by mental arithmetic.

Models such as Atkinson and Shiffrin's provided the basis for describing cognitive development with reference to the components described in information processing models. For example, Brainerd (1983) considered how limitations in different components might affect children's performance in problem-solving tasks. Brainerd discussed five aspects of information processing limitations in working memory:

1   *Encoding limitations*: Children may not encode the appropriate information about a problem. In a problem like $(12 \times 34)/5$, a child might not encode the multiplication symbol correctly, and add the figures in the bracket rather than multiply them. Brainerd pointed out that failure in some Piagetian problem solving tasks (e.g., those that involve part–whole relationships – see chapter 12) may be because when children listen to the question in that task they fail to encode the crucial information about the required comparison.

2   *Computational limitations*: Children may encode all the relevant information about a problem and retain it in working memory, but they may not have appropriate strategies in long-term memory that they can apply to the encoded information. For example, they may not be able to solve the mathematical problem because they do not know a procedure for multiplying two digit numbers.

3   *Retrieval limitations*: Children may have the necessary strategies in long-term memory but when they try to retrieve the strategy from their long-term store they retrieve an inappropriate strategy. For example instead of retrieving the procedures for multiplication they retrieve, in error, the procedures for division.

4   *Storage limitations*: Children may have encoded all the information, and have retrieved the appropriate strategies from long-term memory, but they may not be able to retain all the relevant information in working memory while they carry out the calculation. For example, while children are calculating (12×34) they may forget the information relating to the rest of the original equation (the need to divide by 5) and be unable to complete the problem.

5   *Work-space limitations*: As working memory is limited, children will only be able to retain a few items of information at the same time. For example, if a mathematical problem only involves two digits and one calculation $(4 + 5)$ this may all be held in working memory (as the two digits, the addition, and the sum of the two digits). But if the problem is $(4 + 5)/(6 + 7)$ the need to retain information about several digits, addition and division, might mean there is no storage space left to hold information about the sub-totals that are needed to achieve the final answer.

After a consideration of these limitations Brainerd (1983) investigated Piaget and Inhelder's (1951) 'probability judgement' task. In one version of this problem four- and five-year-old children were shown ten tokens – seven of the tokens had a picture of a rabbit on them and three had a picture of a horse. All the tokens were placed in an opaque bag, which was shaken, and then the experimenter pulled out one of the tokens and held it in his hand so that the child could not see it. Children were asked to predict the picture on the token in the experimenter's hand. After one trial the token was replaced in the bag (without the child seeing it) and then the procedure was repeated for another four trials.

The best way to be correct in this task is always to predict that the token that will be pulled out is the one that occurs most frequently in the bag (i.e., rabbit). But Piaget and Inhelder (1951) found that young children were poor at this task – children did not consistently predict the picture with the higher frequency. Brainerd carried out a series of studies to find out why children had difficulty. He found that on the first trial the majority of children predicted that the token taken out of the bag would have a rabbit on it. This meant that most of the children realized the need to choose the more frequent picture (and if they knew this they did not have an encoding problem). However on the remaining four trials the children did not go on predicting the rabbit tokens (e.g., after the first trial they might just predict the horse and rabbit tokens alternatively).

Brainerd's first hypothesis was that the children had *storage limitations* so that by the second and later trials the children had forgotten the frequency of the pictures in the bag and were simply guessing. Therefore, in a further experiment Brainerd placed a second set of seven tokens with rabbits and three tokens with horses on the table in front of the child throughout the experiment, to help children retain the relative frequency of the tokens. However, children's performance did not change (they still did poorly after the first trial). As there was no need to store information about the frequency of the tokens (because that information was always in front of them) Brainerd assumed that it was something other than storage limitations that was the cause of the children's difficulty.

Brainerd therefore considered what was different between the first (often successful) trial and the later (unsuccessful trials). He thought that *after* the first trial the most recent information in children's working memory was their own response to the previous trial, and that this might have been influencing their predictions – for example on the second trial children remembered that they had said rabbit (or horse) on the first trial and in recalling that response some children went on to repeat that response, and some decided to say the alternate response. In other words, they based their later predictions on the recall of their previous response, and this strategy was not related to the crucial information about the relative frequency of the tokens. Brainerd called this a *retrieval problem* because the children were retrieving the wrong information (their own previous response) as the basis for their predictions and ignoring the frequency information. When Brainerd changed the experimental procedure so that the most recent item in working memory (before the children made a prediction) was information about token frequency the children were successful on all the trials.

We have described Brainerd's (1983) studies in some detail because they illustrate how a model of information processing can provide the stimulus for a series of studies that identify not just whether children succeed or fail a task at a certain age, but can explain why children have difficulty with a task. In the case of the probability task, Brainerd's first studies supported Piaget and Inhelder's (1951)

A   B

Figure 13.2 An example of the juice problem. Children are shown each set of glasses and told that each set will be poured into a different jug. The children are asked which jug will taste more strongly of juice (based on Noelting, 1980).

conclusion that young children were poor at the task, but by generating a series of hypotheses based on a theoretical model Brainerd was able to go beyond the initial findings, identify children's retrieval difficulties and then demonstrate that when these difficulties were overcome children could perform successfully. This latter finding leads to a very different conclusion about children's ability and illustrates the need to have a specific model of the processes that may be involved in a task.

Neo-Piagetians and Information Processing

The information processing approach implies that children's cognitive abilities develop in three possible ways. First, the 'size' of components like working memory may increase – with increasing age children may develop more 'slots' in memory which means that more items of information can be stored at the same time (Kail, 1990). Second, as children get older they may become more efficient at processing items of information, and increased efficiency will mean that there are less demands on working memory and therefore the free capacity can be used for processing more information at the same time (Case, 1985). Third, it is possible that both size and processing efficiency develop during childhood.

Case (1978, 1985), like Piaget, thought that cognitive development could be interpreted as a series of stages. But unlike Piaget (who described stages in the development of children's logical thinking and reasoning – see chapter 12), Case described children's stage-like performance on particular problem-solving tasks in information processing terms (and for this reason Case is sometimes referred to as a 'Neo-Piagetian'). This can be exemplified by Case's analysis of Noelting's (1980) orange juice problem (see figure 13.2).

In Noelting's problem children were shown two sets of glasses. In each set some of the glasses contained orange juice and some contained water. Children were also shown two empty jugs and told that the contents of one of the sets of glasses would be poured into one jug, and the other set would be poured into the second jug. The children were then asked which of the two jugs would taste more strongly of juice. For example, in figure 13.2 one set of glasses includes a glass of orange juice and a glass of water, and the second set includes two glasses of orange juice and three of water. Children have to compare the proportion of orange juice in each set and (if they do this correctly) say that the first jug will taste more strongly of orange. Noelting described children's performance in terms of four age-related strategies:

- 3- to 4-year-olds only considered whether orange was present or absent in each set. They could only succeed if one set of glasses had some orange in it and the other did not. If both sets included glasses of orange they would say that both jugs would taste more strongly of orange juice.
- 5- to 6-year-olds chose the set that had more glasses of orange (so, in the example in figure 13.2 they would make an incorrect prediction).
- 7- to 8-year-olds compared the number of glasses of water and orange in each set, and if one set had more glasses of orange than glasses of water they said that the jug receiving that set would taste more strongly of juice. If both or neither sets had more glasses of orange, the children just guessed.
- 9- to 10-year-olds were able to use more appropriate strategies to select the correct set of glasses (e.g., by subtracting the number of glasses with water from the number with orange and choosing the set with the larger remainder – this works for many but not all problems).

Each of the strategies described above takes into account an additional aspect of the task, and therefore the later strategies can be applied successfully to a larger number of different problems. Case (1978) suggested that information-processing limitations restricted younger children to the less effective strategies. For example, the strategy used by the 3- and 4-year-olds can be described in the following terms:

> Look for orange juice in one set of glasses. If there is orange juice say that set will taste more strongly of juice. If there is no orange juice say that it won't taste of juice.

This strategy only requires a minimum of information in working memory (the colour of the glasses in the set). Then children can turn to the other set of glasses and repeat the strategy:

> Look for orange juice in the other set of glasses. If there is orange juice say that set will taste more strongly of juice. If there is no orange juice say that it won't taste of juice.

Again this only requires one item of information (the colour of the glasses) in working memory. Of course, this is not a very effective strategy because, as we have pointed out, it sometimes leads children to make apparently contradictory responses such as both jugs will taste more strongly of orange juice.

The strategy used by 5- and 6-year-olds requires the children to count the number of glasses of juice in one set (and retain this number in working memory); then count the number of glasses of orange in the other set (and retain this number in working memory); then compare the two numbers and predict the set with the greater number will taste more strongly of orange. In other words, to complete this strategy children need to hold two items (the numbers) in working memory, as well as having the processing space to carry out the comparison of these items. The other two strategies, used by older children, each require increasing amounts of working memory capacity for completion.

Case (1985) analysed the strategies required for a number of Piagetian and other problem-solving tasks and concluded that one of the main constraints on children's performance was their information processing capacity. Other factors will also influence children's cognitive development, which we will discuss later, but if a particular problem-solving strategy requires more processing capacity than a child has available it will be difficult for the child to apply that strategy.

Noelting's (1980) analysis of the orange juice problem focused on the strategies that children used in attempting to solve the problem. Many such analyses are carried out after an experimenter has collected data, because then the experimenter can look for patterns in the children's performance (when they were correct, when they were incorrect, the type of errors they made, and so on). Having analysed the performance, an experimenter can often suggest the likely strategies that children brought to the problem.

Problem-solving strategies

An alternative way of investigating children's strategies was used by Siegler (1976, 1978). He examined the way that children of different ages attempted a balance scale task. In this task the children were shown a balance scale that already had several weights placed on either side of the fulcrum. The scale was fixed by a wedge and the children were asked which way the scale would tip if the wedge was removed. In contrast to most researchers who specify the possible task strategies that children use after testing them, Siegler considered the possible strategies prior to testing the children. He outlined four progressively more sophisticated strategies that could be used and then predicted how a child using one of those strategies would perform across a set of different balance scale problems (see Box 13.1). This meant that if a child's pattern of performance matched one that he had predicted, he could infer that the child was using a specific strategy. Older children used progressively more effective strategies to solve the balance scale problems and Siegler described children's development on this problem as a series of steps (or stages) as the children adopted more successful strategies to solve the problems.

Researchers like Noelting (1980) and Siegler (1976) have described cognitive development in terms of steps or stages. As explained above, this is in the tradition of Piaget's approach to describing children's development. However, Siegler (1996) has suggested that this approach has limitations. First, he pointed out that although children's performance on tasks like the balance scale can be described in terms of distinct and progressively more complex cognitive strategies, other tasks cannot be analysed in the same way. Second, he argued that the most important aspect of development is how children progress from one stage to another, but most researchers have focused on describing the stages and few have investigated the way that children progress from one stage to the next. We will discuss these two points in turn.

Many researchers have used tasks that have well-defined dimensions. For example, in the juice problem (see above) children need to consider the number of glasses of juice and water in each jug, and in the balance scale task (see box 13.1) children need to work out the weight and distance of the weight from the fulcrum. The tasks are also ones with which children are unfamiliar. Young children are unlikely to have been asked to work out the strength of a jug of juice or estimate which way a balance scale will tip. Siegler (1996) suggested that the salience of particular dimensions in these sorts of tasks might lead children to attempt just one or two particular strategies. He also pointed out that when children have had little experience of a task they will not have had time to develop diverse strategies. On other, less-novel tasks, children might not show such clearly defined strategies and Siegler and Robinson (1982) showed that this was the case when they analysed children's strategies for adding numbers.

Siegler and Robinson (1982) gave 4- and 5-year-olds addition problems like 'How much is 1 + 2?'. Each child was given several problems and took part in six sessions. Some of the problems were repeated in different sessions. Siegler and Robinson found that children used four strategies. These were (1) counting fingers (for instance to work out 1 + 2 children would put up one finger and then two fingers and count them out loud). (2) The same strategy but without counting out loud. (3) Counting out loud without using fingers. (4) When children showed no audible or visible behaviour Siegler and Robinson classed this as 'retrieval' and assumed that children were retrieving the answers from memory. They found that only 20 per cent of the children used one of the four strategies for all the addition problems. Rather, 23 per cent used two strategies, 30 per cent used three, and 27 per cent used four strategies. Siegler and Robinson also found that when children were given the same problem in different sessions a third of them used different strategies each time. This was not necessarily because children used a less sophisticated strategy the first time (e.g., counting fingers) and a more sophisticated strategy the second time (e.g., retrieval), because in fact many used a less advanced strategy the second time.

Siegler and Robinson's (1982) results demonstrated that children used different rules at the same time and even for the same problems. This stands in contrast to the more distinct and age-related strategies that can be identified on tasks like the balance scale, and led Siegler (1996) to suggest that the use of multiple strategies is most likely when children have a moderate amount of experience at a task. When tasks (like the balance scale) are unfamiliar children may attempt to solve them using just one strategy for all examples of the task. When tasks are very familiar (e.g., adults solving addition problems) people will have established the best strategy they can, and will use that strategy consistently for all similar problems. However, when children are still learning (as in Siegler and Robinson's addition problems) they may use a range of different strategies and be willing to use several different ones at the same time. This is in contrast to the neat stage-like progression described for very unfamiliar or very familiar tasks, and led Siegler to describe the use of multiple strategies as 'overlapping waves'. He used

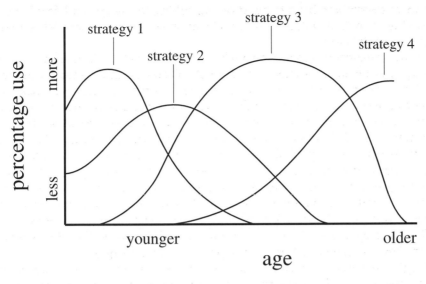

Figure 13.3 A graphical representation of the overlapping waves metaphor used by Siegler to describe children's strategy use over time, At any specific age children might be using two or more strategies (adapted from Siegler, 1996).

this metaphor to capture the idea that children's progression on tasks they are still learning might involve the increase and decrease in the use of several strategies at the same time, and this metaphor is best expressed graphically – see figure 13.3. This metaphor is in contrast to the traditional view of strategy development as a series of distinct steps or stages (see figure 13.4).

Siegler (1996) argued that the period when children are learning a new task is a period of rapid change as children identify and experiment with different problem-solving strategies. However, traditional methodologies for studying children's development tend to ignore these periods. As we explained in chapter 1, the most commonly used methodologies for developmental research are cross-sectional (when several different age groups are tested) and longitudinal (when the same children are tested at intervals over a period of time). Most longitudinal studies test children at intervals of weeks or months. Such methods will identify major differences in performance, but they may not be appropriate for examining periods of rapid learning. Siegler suggested that changes in children's strategy use are best investigated by taking a *microgenetic* approach. This means studying change in children's performance as it is occurring, and this implies intensive and repeated testing of the same children over very short periods of time.

Siegler and Jenkins (1989) used the microgenetic approach to investigate the development of one particular addition strategy. This strategy is called the 'min' strategy which can be illustrated with an addition problem like 'What is 3 + 4?'. A child using the min strategy will identify the larger number and then count up by the value of the smaller number. In this case counting '5, 6, 7' to achieve the answer. Siegler and Jenkins identified eight children aged 4 to 5 years who could do addition problems but did not use the min strategy. The children were given

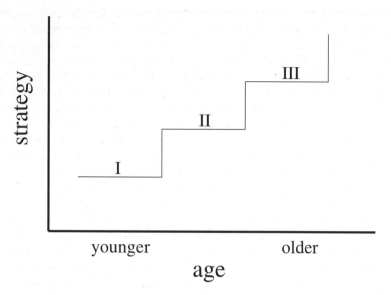

Figure 13.4 A graphical representation of children's strategy development as distinct steps or stages. This example represents the distinct stages implied in the development of better strategies in tasks like the balance scale task (based on Siegler 1996).

problems (that required the addition of two numbers) three times a week for 11 weeks, and their performance was assessed from videotape records and by interviewing the children about their strategies. Siegler and Jenkins found (like Siegler and Robinson, 1982) that children's strategies varied both within and between sessions. During the course of the study all but one of the children discovered the min strategy and Siegler and Jenkins then examined the context in which it occurred for each child.

Previous researchers had suggested that the min strategy developed from children realizing that they could count from either of the numbers in the problem. For instance, in the example above (3 + 4), children might realize that they could count from 3 to 4, 5, 6, 7. Earlier researchers had assumed that children would first notice that counting from either number would be successful before realizing that counting from the larger number (the min strategy) was the most effective way to solve the problem. However, Siegler and Jenkins found that only one child in the study went from counting from either number before adopting the min strategy, and this finding contradicted earlier assumptions. Nearly all the children who discovered the min strategy did so after using a strategy that researchers had not noted before. Given a problem like 3 + 4 the children started counting at 1 to 2, 3, 4, 5, 6, 7. Soon after using this strategy children would move to the min strategy and count from the higher number. This was a new finding and provided some insight into the way that children progress to the min strategy.

Siegler and Jenkins's study demonstrated how the detailed investigation and analysis of children's performance over a short period of time can elicit information about strategy change. Those studies that have used the cross-sectional methodology to examine children in different age group have been important for finding out what children can do at different ages, but say little about how children progress from one strategy to another, because changes may be subtle and short-lived. Siegler and Jenkins found that most children used the 'counting from 1' strategy only once or twice before adopting the min strategy.

However, discovering exactly how children progress to more effective strategies does not explain *why* children realize the importance of a new strategy. Siegler and Jenkins found that even after children had started to use the min strategy they used it for only 12 per cent of the addition problems. But half way through the testing sessions Siegler and Jenkins moved from just giving children sums like 3 + 4 and included ones with larger numbers like 3 + 20. For the latter additions the min strategy is by far the most effective way to solve the problem. When faced with these additions children used the min strategy for two-thirds of such problems, and then quickly went on to use the min strategy for all addition problems irrespective of the size of the numbers. This pattern of development suggested that children may discover new strategies and use those strategies alongside other older strategies, as implied by Siegler's (1996) wave metaphor. But as the context changes (in the above example the context changed as the difficulty of the addition problem increases) children will focus on the most effective of the several strategies they use. Once children have used their most effective strategy more frequently that strategy is then applied to all problems. As children get older they will develop other new strategies alongside the min strategy, and eventually will drop the min strategy and adopt further and more effective addition strategies.

The above provides a neat example of how strategy change might apply to many tasks. First children may use a variety of strategies, some of which will be more or less effective, and then as the context alters children realize the importance of using one particular strategy. This process indicates the dual role of children's increasing cognitive sophistication (developing new strategies) and the environment that creates a context in which children realize the usefulness of one particular strategy. The interaction between the child's developing cognition and the environment is a key factor in learning. We can also see the implications for education. Vygotsky stressed the importance of helping children progress with their 'zone of proximal development' (see chapter 15). Siegler's idea of overlapping waves is complementary to the zone of proximal development. If a child is already on the point of using a new strategy (or using a new strategy but only rarely) then just a little support from a teacher can encourage the child to focus more on that strategy and help to channel the child's learning. Piaget emphasized the importance of giving children the opportunity to explore and experiment for themselves (see chapter 12). As exemplified by Siegler and Jenkins's (1989) addition study, as children attempt more difficult problems they come to select the most effective strategy they have. In other words, the more children explore new problems and new contexts the more likely they are to identify and refine their problem-solving strategies.

Attention

It is a truism that for any information to be processed at all, it must be attended to in the first instance. One difference between young children and older children is in the ability to identify the most crucial aspects of a task and pay attention to those aspects. Vurpillot (1968) demonstrated differences in the attentional strategies of children between three and nine years of age. Vurpillot showed the children drawings of two houses and each house had six windows (see figure 13.5). Some pairs of houses were identical, but other pairs of houses had different windows (e.g., in one house a specific window might have a blind, but the corresponding window in the other house might have curtains). Children were asked to look at the drawings and say whether the two houses were the same or different.

The most appropriate strategy in this task is to look at a window in one house and then check that the corresponding window in the other house is the same, and to continue this until either a difference is found, or all six windows in each house have been examined. Then you can conclude that there are no differences. While the children were looking at the houses Vurpillot recorded their eye movements, and found that all the children aged five years or below, only examined a few windows, and made few comparisons between corresponding windows. As a result the younger children often concluded incorrectly that the houses were the same because they had not detected differences in unchecked windows. Children from the age of six years were more likely to examine pairs of windows, and between six and nine years of age the children used this strategy more effectively, by considering all the windows exhaustively.

■ Memory Development

The word 'strategy' is used in two ways, either to refer to the strategies used in specific problem-solving tasks (like Noelting's juice problem, or Siegler's balance scale problem) or to refer to general strategies that can be applied across a range of different tasks. Such general strategies include memory strategies like *encoding* and *retrieval* strategies (Bjorklund and Douglas, 1997).

Encoding strategies

Rehearsal: This refers to the mental repetition of information. For example, if you want to remember a telephone number you can repeat it to yourself until you have a chance to write it down. To investigate children's use of rehearsal, Flavell et al. (1966) showed groups of 20 five-, seven-, and ten-year-olds a set of seven pictures. The experimenters pointed to some of the pictures and told the children that they should try to remember those specific pictures. Then 15 seconds later the children were asked to say, aloud, all the pictures they could recall. During the 15-second interval the children were observed by a lip reader to assess what they might be

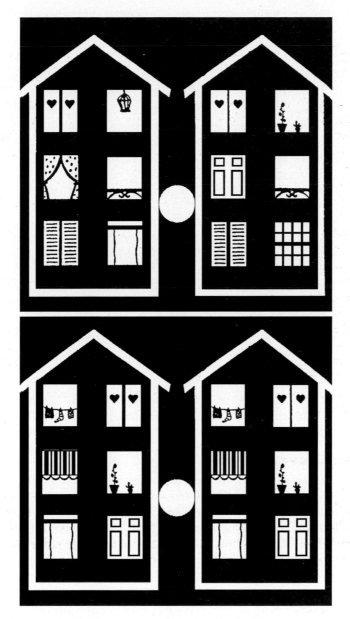

Figure 13.5 Pairs of houses used by Vurpillot (1968). Children were asked whether the houses were the same or different.

saying to themselves while waiting to recall the pictures. Only two of the five-year-olds repeated the pictures to themselves, but more than half the seven-year-olds and nearly all the ten-year-olds could be seen repeating the pictures. Flavell et al. found that children who rehearsed recalled more pictures than children who did not use recall, and therefore they concluded that some age-related differences in memory might be the result of developmental differences in the use of strategies like rehearsal.

Flavell et al. were among the first researchers to investigate rehearsal and this experiment stimulated many other studies into the development. However, Flavell et al.'s methodology was limited because some children might have been rehearsing without making any observable behaviours like lip movements. McGilly and Siegler (1990) carried out an experiment like Flavell et al.'s study with similar age groups, but as well as assessing children's observable behaviour they also asked the children, after the test, to report how they had tried to remember the material. On the basis of observable behaviour McGilly and Siegler found that children appeared to use rehearsal on 39 per cent of the trials, but when the evidence from children's self-reports was included they found that rehearsal was used on 74 per cent of the trials.

If children do use rehearsal (McGilly and Siegler, 1990) then why are age differences in recall found in the studies of rehearsal (Flavell et al., 1966)? One reason might be that younger children do not use rehearsal as effectively as older children. Ornstein et al. (1975) asked seven-year-olds and adults to remember a list of words, which were presented at the rate of one every five seconds. During this task participants were asked to say what they were thinking while they tried to remember the words. Ornstein et al. found a difference in the way that the children and adults rehearsed the words. The children's rehearsal was sometimes limited to repeating a word when it was presented, and then repeating the next word and so on. The adults grouped a number of words and rehearsed these as a group. For example, imagine a list made up of the words 'cat . . . dog . . . house . . . car . . .'. Children might try to remember this list by saying 'cat, cat, cat' and then 'dog, dog, dog' as each word is presented. In contrast adults might begin by saying 'cat, cat, cat,' and then after the presentation of the second word say 'cat, dog, cat, dog' and then 'cat, dog, house' and so on. The latter procedure is a more effective way of encoding the list, but it depends not only on the use of rehearsal but also on an awareness of the benefits of organizing (or 'chunking') information together to increase the likelihood of remembering it (see below).

The results from studies like Ornstein et al. (1975) suggest that developmental changes are less to do with using or not using rehearsal, and more to do with how effectively children apply the strategy. As children get older they use rehearsal in more sophisticated ways. The importance of using rehearsal effectively was demonstrated by Naus et al. (1977) who trained eight-year-olds to rehearse by grouping items in sets of three. In a later memory test the eight-year-olds recalled as much information as 12-year-olds. But Naus et al.'s results beg a further question – if young children can learn and use an effective rehearsal strategy why do they not use that strategy spontaneously? We will discuss this below, in the section on the development of memory strategies.

Organization: Grouping information together is another aspect of encoding. If information is linked together it may be encoded more effectively than unlinked information, and this effect will be greater when the information can be linked in a meaningful way. Moely et al. (1969) showed children a set of pictures that were laid out in front of them in no particular order. Within the set of pictures there were several showing animals, several showing pieces of furniture, etc. The children were asked to learn the names of all the pictures and were told that they could re-arrange the pictures if they thought that would help them to remember the pictures. Moely et al. found that it was only after the age of ten years that children realized the usefulness of re-arranging the pictures into categories so that they could learn all the animals as a group, and then all the furniture as a group and so on.

Children younger than 10 years do show evidence of organizing material, but often they do so in only a partially effective way. Organizing a set of items is achieved best if the items are grouped into a small number of categories containing several items each, but young children may use a large number of categories with only a couple of items in each (Frankel and Rollins, 1982). Like the development of rehearsal the development of organization as a strategy may depend on children learning more sophisticated ways to use it.

Elaboration: Elaboration means making associations between items to help recall them better. For example, to remember that two words like 'fish' and 'hat' occur together in a list of items, they could be linked together in several ways. One way would be to include them in a sentence like 'the fish put her hat on', and another way would be to form a mental image of a fish wearing a hat. In general, the more unusual the image that is generated the more likely the information will be remembered. Foley et al. (1993) suggested images to six and nine-year-olds to help them remember pairs of words like 'ant' and 'comb'. At both ages the children recalled the words better if they thought of images like 'the large black ant was using a comb to fix its hair' than if they thought of images like 'the black ant crawled in and out of the teeth of the comb'.

Pressley and Levin (1980) found that seven-year-olds did not use elaboration spontaneously to learn pairs of English and Spanish words, but could use elaboration if they were provided with an effective mnemonic at the time of learning the pairs. For example, if children had to learn that the word 'carta' in Spanish means letter in English, they were shown a picture of a giant envelope in a cart. Given this support the six-year-olds learnt the pairs of words nearly as well as eleven-year-olds. If children do have the potential to use elaboration with support then developmental differences may be because, like other encoding strategies, children's use of elaboration becomes progressively more sophisticated. For example, Buckhalt et al. (1976) found that when children started to use elaboration spontaneously they tended to use less effective elaborations than older children. Buckhalt et al. asked children to think of ways to remember pairs of words like 'broom' and 'lady'. They found that younger children used what might be called 'static' elaborations like 'the lady had a broom', but older children were more likely to use 'active' elaborations like 'the lady flew on the broom on Hallowe'en'. The latter are often more effective because they generate a more memorable and distinctive image.

Retrieval strategies

Adults are familiar with the feeling of knowing something but not being able to recall it immediately, and most adults have learnt ways to retrieve information from long-term memory. For instance, when trying to recall the name of a person, it is useful to go through the letters of the alphabet and sometimes the initial letter of the name will trigger the rest of the person's name. As with encoding strategies the use of retrieval strategies is an ability that develops gradually. In one study of retrieval strategies Kreutzer et al. (1975) told five- and ten-year-old children a story about a boy who wanted to remember which Christmas he was given a puppy, and then they were asked what the boy could do to remember the correct Christmas. Possible ways to do this include working out the age of the dog, thinking about other presents received at the same time as the puppy, or going back from the most recent Christmas to each previous Christmas in turn until the one when the puppy was received. All the ten-year-olds were able to suggest at least one appropriate retrieval strategy, but only about half the five-year-olds were able to do so.

In another study of retrieval strategies Kobasigawa (1974) showed six-, eight- and 11-year-olds a set of 24 pictures. The pictures showed items from eight different categories (for example, toys, musical instruments, vehicles or playground equipment). Children were shown all 24 pictures and asked to learn them, and at the same time they were shown eight cue cards that reflected the categories (for example the cue cards showed a play pen, music book, street, and park). Later the children were shown (just) the cue cards and asked to recall as many of the original pictures as they could. Only one-third of the six-year-olds spontaneously used the cue cards as an aid, but the majority of the older groups did so, and what was of particular interest was how the children used the cues. The six- and eight-year-olds who used the cues did so by looking at a cue card and recalling one of its associated small pictures, and then they moved on to the next cue card. In contrast, 11-year-olds looked at a cue card and tried to recall as many associated pictures as possible before moving on to the next cue. In this way the oldest children were able to recall the majority of the small pictures effectively.

How do Memory Strategies Develop?

As shown by the research into different strategies, children do not simply change from not using a strategy to using it, rather there is a gradual progression in how effectively children apply them (e.g., Buckhalt et al., 1976; Frankel and Rollins, 1982; Ornstein et al., 1975).

As we have described above there are many studies showing that young children can sometimes be taught more effective strategies (e.g., Naus et al., 1977; Pressley and Levin, 1980). However, although such experiments show that children are capable of more effective strategies a typical finding is that young children do not apply the strategy they have learnt in one task to other similar tasks. For example, Keeney et al. (1967) identified six-year-olds who did not use rehearsal, and then prompted them to use this strategy – they were told to keep whispering the names of several items to themselves until they needed to recall them. After this instruction the majority of the children were able to use rehearsal effectively. But they only used rehearsal in tasks when they were explicitly prompted to do so by the experimenters, they did not spontaneously apply the new strategy to other tasks.

Bjorklund and Harnishfeger (1987) have suggested that young children might not use a strategy that they have been taught because they will find the strategy requires cognitive effort to use. If the strategy itself takes up young children's limited processing capacity then they may not have enough capacity left to encode the material that they are trying to remember. Bjorklund and Harnishfeger examined eight- and twelve-year-olds' ability to use organization. Children were given a list of items that could be recalled in categories. Children were trained in the use of an organizational strategy that emphasized the usefulness of considering which items could be grouped together at encoding. When Bjorklund and Harnishfeger tested the children's recall they found that when the older children used the strategy their recall improved significantly, but using the strategy did not improve the younger children's recall. Bjorklund and Harnishfeger suggested that the lack of improvement in the younger children's recall was because the cognitive processing they needed to apply the strategy left the children too little processing capacity in working memory to encode additional items. Such an interpretation would explain why young children are capable of learning a strategy in experimental contexts (e.g., Kecney et al., 1967) but do not use the same strategy outside those contexts. If children attempt to use a strategy that does not result in improved recall they will have little incentive to use it. As children's processing capacity improves with age they will have the capacity to use strategies without detriment to the material they are encoding.

As well as increased processing capacity older children also have other abilities that contribute to strategy use and successful recall. For example, to employ a strategy like elaboration children need to make memorable connections between diverse words or items. Compared to younger children, older children have more general knowledge and may therefore be better at inventing useful mnemonics for elaboration. Similarly, older children may use their greater knowledge to group items in better and more effective ways when using strategies like organization. The importance of knowledge will be discussed below. In addition, older children usually know more about their own abilities and they are therefore better able to assess when a strategy will be effective. Knowing about one's own abilities is called *metacognition*.

Metacognition

Metacognition refers to a person's awareness of his or her own cognitive abilities and limitations. For example, most adults know that their memory span is six or seven items and that they may be able to hold that many items in working memory. Adults also know that to retain information for more than a short time it is necessary to process that information in such a way that it is retained in long-term memory. An awareness of one's own memory capacity and processes is an understanding that develops gradually (Joyner and Kurtz-Costes, 1997).

Awareness of capacity: Flavell et al. (1970) showed children cards with up to ten pictures on them, and asked them how many pictures they thought they could remember. The children were later given a test to find out how many pictures they could actually remember. Young children were unrealistic in the number they said that they would remember. Four- and five-year-olds actually recalled only three or four pictures, but thought they would be able to recall at least eight pictures. It was only after about the age of nine years that the majority of children made accurate predictions about the number of items they were likely to remember.

How do children develop a better understanding of their own memory capacity? They may learn from experience. Kail (1990) cited a study by Markman who showed five-year-olds a set of items, asked the children how many they thought they could remember, and then tested their actual recall. Markman repeated this procedure several times with the same children and found that with repeated testing they became more realistic about how many items they could remember. Children may also learn about memory by considering how well other people can recall information. For example, Yussen and Levy (1975) asked four- and eight-year-olds to estimate how many items they could remember (from a large number of items that they were shown). The children were also told what an average child of their own age would be able to recall, and this information helped the eight-year-olds to make realistic estimates about their own ability. The information had little effect on the four-year-olds, who may not have realized that knowing how other four-year-olds performed had implications for their own performance.

Awareness of strategies: Children must also become aware of the usefulness of memory strategies and which ones are the most appropriate for a particular task. Kreutzer et al. (1975) asked five-, six-, eight- and ten-year-olds how they would remember to take their skates to school. The suggested strategies could be divided into several categories. For example, using the skates as a direct reminder (e.g., putting them with other things to be taken to school); using an external aid (e.g., writing a note and putting it where it would be seen); relying on someone else's memory (e.g., asking parents to remind them) or just relying on their own memories. The older children were able to suggest more different types of strategy, and were more likely to suggest the most reliable ones.

■ Knowledge and Memory Development

An important aspect of memory development is the knowledge that children can bring to bear on a memory task – knowledge here does not just mean a knowledge of memory strategies, but children's general knowledge and experience. As children learn more, they can build up a rich information base and newly learnt information can be linked to the known information in a more meaningful and effective way. As children know more they become better at processing and encoding novel information that can be related to pre-existing knowledge.

The importance of knowledge was demonstrated in a study by Chi (1978) who compared the memory of children who were experienced chess players with the memory of adults who knew how to play chess but were not particularly proficient. Both groups were asked to carry out two memory tasks; in one they were asked to learn lists of ten digits, and in the other they were asked to memorize chess board positions with an average of 22 pieces. The adults were better at remembering the digits, but the children were much better at learning the chess positions. It is unusual for children to perform better than adults in a memory task, and Chi argued that the children's greater knowledge of chess contributed to their performance. As they were familiar with chess positions it may have been easier for them to 'chunk' groups of pieces into meaningful patterns and encode them more effectively than the less experienced adult chess players. This advantage only applied to learning chess positions and indicated the importance of having an established knowledge base that was directly relevant to the task.

Other researchers have also demonstrated that if children have established information in a particular domain of knowledge it is easier for them to encode new information related to that domain. For example, Schneider and Bjorklund (1992) divided a number of seven- to nine-year-olds into a group who knew a lot about soccer and a group who only knew a little. The children were asked to learn two sets of drawings. One set included drawings of unrelated items and the other set included drawings that were related to soccer. There was no difference between the two groups in their recall of unrelated items, but the group who knew more about soccer were better at remembering the related items. Such studies have demonstrated how relevant knowledge can increase the likelihood of information being learnt successfully.

Bjorklund et al. (1990) suggested that having good knowledge of a subject can contribute to recall of information about that subject, because it allows a child to recognize and understand the information more readily so that more capacity remains in working memory. Having more capacity leads to more effective or more extensive encoding. In other words, as children get older they have more information and they can make more links and connections between that information. Over time these connections will become comparatively automatic and require little explicit processing. Therefore strategies like grouping and elaboration become easier to apply, and as they become easier more information can be encoded successfully.

Constructive Memory and Knowledge Structures

Constructive memory refers to a person's ability to infer, extrapolate, or invent information that might never have been directly experienced. Suppose a person hears sentences like 'the box is to the right of the tree' and 'the chair is on top of the box'. If that person is later given several similar sentences and asked to say which ones they heard previously, they may be convinced that a sentence like 'the chair is to the right of the tree' is one they heard before. From the original information people may infer the scene being described and then come to believe that a sentence which includes information corresponding to the inferred scene must be one that they had heard previously. In this example constructive memory leads to an incorrect inference.

Brown et al. (1978) showed that children can make false inferences. They told seven and 12-year-olds a story about an invented group of people called the Targa. All the children heard the same story but half were told that the Targa were Eskimos and half were told that the Targa lived in the desert. Later, the children were asked to re-tell the story from memory. Brown et al. examined the recalled stories for any intrusions that were related to assumptions about where the Targa lived. For example, the original story included a reference to bad weather, and some of the children who thought that the Targa were Eskimos recalled this reference as a mention of cold conditions. But the children who had been told that the Targa lived in the desert recalled it as a reference to hot weather. The older children made many more of this type of error than the younger children. Brown et al. suggested that the intrusions were due to the children introducing information from knowledge they already had about Eskimos or desert people, and the larger number of intrusions by the older children reflected their greater knowledge of such cultures.

Constructive memory is related to 'scripts' and 'schema'. The term script was used by Schank and Abelson (1977) to describe a sequence of actions that are appropriate within a particular context and lead to a specific goal. For example, you might have a script for going to a restaurant and this would include an expected sequence of actions involving specific aspects of the restaurant. The script would include sequences for entering (locating a table, sitting down, etc.); ordering (reading menu, speaking to the waiter, etc.); eating (being served, eating courses in expected sequence, etc.) and leaving (paying bill, leaving a tip, etc.). Each part of the script can be thought of as a 'slot' that needs to be filled, with both obligatory and optional actions. For example, it would be obligatory to order before eating, but leaving a tip might depend on how much you liked the service. Adults may have any number of scripts relating to different events. They are important because without generalized script knowledge it would be difficult to function in new contexts. When we go into almost any new restaurant most of what happens can be predicted from a script derived from previous visits to other restaurants.

Do children structure their knowledge of the world as scripts? Nelson and Gruendel (1981) investigated eight preschool children's scripts by asking them what happened in different eating contexts (at lunch in their day care centre, eating dinner at home, and going to McDonald's). Most of the children mentioned the same actions for each event, and focused on main actions. For example, children typically said they ate food, but did not usually specify what they ate – in other words they reported the events as if they had an 'open slot' that could be filled with more specific information if that was required. All the children reported, without error, the sequence of actions involved in eating a meal, with the significant exception that children reported paying for food at McDonald's after eating it. This error suggests that children were referring to script based knowledge about what it means to go out for food – at nearly all restaurants, payment is made at the end of a meal, but the procedure at McDonald's is an exception. On the one hand, children's ability to develop scripts is important in structuring their experience in such a way that they can use and adapt their knowledge of previous events to make sense of similar, but novel events. On the other hand, a dependence on script-based knowledge can lead to inaccurate assumptions when recalling information, if specific events do not correspond to the script (as in the McDonald's example). With age and experience children's scripts become more elaborate, and they become better at distinguishing specific events from generalized script knowledge (Fivush, 1997).

A schema is similar to a script because it refers to an organized grouping of knowledge, but unlike a script, the term schema denotes what is known (for example) about a scene, or a place or an object. A schema can generate expectations about what a scene should include. For instance, a schema for a kitchen might include 'slots' for sink, cooker, refrigerator, table and so on. Even young children can have established schema for objects or places that are well known. Blades and Banham (1990) asked children to learn a realistic model of a kitchen. The model included ten items of typical kitchen furniture, but it did not include a cooker. When the children had learnt the model layout all the items were removed and placed in a box with an additional ten items of toy furniture (for example, a bed, an armchair, book shelves). These additional items included a cooker. The children were asked to use the box of toy furniture to reconstruct the model kitchen from memory as accurately as possible. The reconstruction was generally accurate, and very few of the children included non-kitchen items in their models. However, nearly two-thirds of the children included the cooker in their reconstructions. Blades and Banham suggested that the inclusion of the cooker indicated that children's reconstructions were based not only on recall of the model they had learnt, but also on their knowledge, or schema, about kitchens in general.

Generating schemas and scripts is an important way to represent knowledge and to use that knowledge effectively to make inferences and predictions about the world. However, in using schema-based knowledge it is also important to retain flexibility because there may sometimes be exceptions to the schema (e.g., paying for food before eating it at McDonald's, or kitchens without cookers) and this flexibility may only develop with age and experience (Nelson, 1986). As Kail (1990, p. 95) said:

> Knowledge is a double-edged sword. On the one hand, knowledge allows us to understand novel versions of familiar experiences (e.g., going to a restaurant) that would be completely uninterpretable if knowledge consisted only of specific previous experiences. On the other hand, knowledge does so at the cost of introducing some distortions into our perception of experiences and our later recall of those experiences.

Summary

In the previous sections we described some examples of the information processing approach to the study of children's cognitive development. The emphasis of this approach is on the mechanisms that children bring to bear in any task, coupled with an appreciation of the limitations that might effect children's performance. The information processing approach includes detailed studies of children's performance in specific tasks (see box 13.1) as well as investigating the more general processes (such as memory strategies) that might be applied across a range of different tasks. Researchers in the information processing tradition attempt to explain developmental change with reference to a number of interrelated and inseparable factors – these include, for example, the changing capacity of the child's processing abilities as they mature; changes in children's ability to focus attention; the development of memory strategies; the ability to apply progressively more sophisticated strategies in specific tasks; the growth of children's structured knowledge; and children's increasing awareness of their own abilities.

Children's Eyewitness Research

Much of the research into children's memory has focused on the development of memory capacity and strategies. Such research can be carried out successfully using well-established and appropriate paradigms – for example, asking children to learn lists of words, remember the names of pictures, or recall stories they have heard. However, in the past few years researchers have investigated memory development in the context of children's ability to give accurate testimony about events that they have witnessed. (For a description about how the focus of memory research has changed see Schneider and Pressley, 1997.) These investigations have been driven by the fact that more, and younger, children are taking part in court proceedings. One of the reasons for children's greater involvement in courts has been the growing realization about the frequency of child abuse and the need to bring abusers to court (see pp. 125–7). The nature of child abuse often means that the child himself or herself may be the only witness that the prosecution can call on for evidence (Perry and Wrightsman, 1991).

In the past, children were rarely called as witnesses, because there was a general belief that children would be unreliable when giving testimony. Several different and influential arguments contributed to this belief. Freud reported that, during therapy, a number of his adult patients claimed to have been abused when they were children. Although Freud at first accepted such accounts as accurate descriptions of what had happened during childhood, he later concluded that such claims were fantasies invented by his patients. Freud's belief that adults invented fantasies about early sexual experience became a key part of his psychoanalytic theory (see Masson, 1992) and his belief that people invent traumatic events was frequently cited as evidence that adults or children's reports of abuse could not be accepted as reliable.

Other researchers argued that children were too suggestible to be accurate witnesses. In a series of classic studies Varendonck (1911) investigated children's suggestibility after the murder of a young girl in Belgium in 1910. The police had arrested a man on the basis of testimony provided by a nine-year-old friend of the girl. The friend described the man in detail and claimed that she saw him take the murdered girl into a wood. However, this testimony was given the day after the murder; when the friend had been questioned on the day the girl disappeared the friend had not mentioned seeing a man at all. Varendonck was concerned that the friend's statement might have been suggested to her.

Varendonck therefore carried out several experiments with children of a similar age. In one experiment he tested 58 children aged between seven and nine years. He went into their classrooms and referring to a teacher (Monsieur Th.) who was not present, but with whom the children were familiar, simply wrote a question on the blackboard: 'What colour is Monsieur Th.'s moustache?'. Fifty-one of the children gave a colour,. Only seven either gave no answer or realized that the teacher did not have a moustache at all!

In other studies Varendonck asked eight-year-olds to name a man who had visited the school earlier in the day. A few of the children named the man without further prompting, and when Varendonck asked the others, who had made no response 'Wasn't it Monsieur M. who came to me?' nearly all agreed. After further questioning some children went on to describe what Monsieur M. had said and did. However, no-one had visited the school earlier in the day.

On the basis of these findings Varendonck argued that young children were too suggestible to be regarded as credible witnesses, and when his findings were presented at the trial of the man accused of murder, the man was acquitted. Varendonck concluded his argument about the unreliability of children with the words 'When are we going to give up, in all civilised countries, listening to children in courts of law?' (1911, p. 136). These studies and several similar ones meant that courts of law did give up listening to children for many years (see Ceci and Bruck, 1993).

In the context of memory research it is only comparatively recently that researchers have investigated how well children recall real-life events. Marin et al. (1979) tested the recall of six-, nine-, 13-year-olds and adults for a brief staged incident (an argument between two people). A few minutes after seeing the event participants were given an unexpected recall test. They were asked to recall as much as they could about the incident, answer 20 objective questions about it, and then pick out a photograph (from a set of six) of one of the people who took part in the argument.

In free recall the youngest children gave little information about the event (only one or two items), but there was an age-related increase in the number of items of information recalled (the adults mentioned seven or eight items). However, the youngest participants made virtually no errors in free recall, but on average the adults gave approximately one incorrect item of information in free recall. In other words, the children said little but what they did say was usually accurate. This latter finding has been replicated in most studies of children's memory for events – in free recall young children say very little but their reports are generally accurate if they have not been given deliberately misleading information by interviewers (see below).

The most surprising result from Marin et al. (1979) was that there was no difference between the groups for the objective questions – all groups answered three-quarters of the questions correctly. Nor were there any age differences for the photograph recognition task. The results from Marin et al. demonstrated that children could be as accurate as adults in reporting information about an event, at least when answering specific objective questions about it. This finding contradicted the earlier assumptions that children would be poor eye-witnesses.

However, Marin et al.'s experiment was limited in two ways. First, the participants were only exposed to a brief incident lasting a few seconds, and the task may have been so difficult that all age groups did poorly and this might have masked developmental differences. Second, Marin et al. only asked a single misleading question (and found that about half of each age group answered it correctly). Nonetheless, Marin et al.'s study was an important stimulus for later experiments, most of which did confirm Marin et al.'s original findings.

One such experiment was by Goodman and Reed (1986) who used a more elaborate event, and then asked six-year-olds and adults objective and leading questions about it. The participants were told that they were taking part in an experiment about motor skills (i.e., physical movement) and were introduced to a confederate of the experimenters who asked them to copy a series of arm movements. Four days later the participants were given a surprise recall test. They were asked for free recall and to say everything they could about the event, and they were shown five pictures and asked to pick out the confederate. They were also asked 17 objective questions (e.g., 'What colour was the man's hair?' or 'Did the man have a ring on?') and four leading questions (e.g., 'The man was wearing a sweater wasn't he?' or 'Was the man wearing a watch on his right or left hand?').

Goodman and Read found that in free recall the adults reported three times as much information as the six-year-olds. But, as Marin et al. (1979) found, although the adults said more in free recall they also reported more inaccurate information than the children. On the identification task 95 per cent of the six-year-olds picked out the confederate's picture correctly, which was better than the adults (74 per cent). There was no difference in the accuracy of six-year-olds and adults on the objective questions. This replicated Marin et al.'s (1979) finding for six-year-olds and confirmed that children of this age could answer questions accurately. In other words, when children were asked objective questions that, in this experiment, required brief one word answers or yes/no responses they could report information as well as adults could. (Later we will say more about the effects that the exact form of objective questioning can have on children's responses.) However, Goodman and Reed found that the children were more likely than the adults to give incorrect answers to the misleading questions. This result replicates the earlier work by researchers like Varendonck (1911) and is a common finding, because many researchers have found that children can be misled by suggestive interviewing.

Children's Suggestibility

Children are easily misled. Leichtman and Ceci (1995) demonstrated this in an elaborate study in which they interviewed three- to six-year-olds repetitively about an event. The event was a visit by 'Sam Stone' to their classroom. This visit involved little more than Sam Stone walking round the classroom and saying a few words. When children were later interviewed in a neutral and objective way about what had happened during the visit they were nearly always correct in reporting details. But if the children were given misleading questions that implied that Sam Stone had damaged a book and a toy, they began to report that such events had actually happened. Leichtman and Ceci also introduced a condition in which children were told (in advance of the event) that Sam Stone was a careless and clumsy man. Some of the children who had been given this 'stereotypical' information also came to believe, incorrectly, that they had seen Sam Stone damage the items. In other words, even though Sam Stone had done nothing but walk around the classroom, interviewers who used suggestive questions and information led the children into saying that they had seen things happen that had never been part of the event. This study is summarized in box 13.2.

In another study Ceci et al. (1994) gave preschool children repeated interviews for several weeks. The researchers asked the children's parents for details of distinctive events that had actually happened (e.g., a particular accident or injury). The researchers also included events that had never happened (e.g., getting a finger caught in a mousetrap and having to go to hospital for treatment). During each interview the interviewer read out brief details of actual or invented events and asked the children to think hard about the events and prompted them to think about any details associated with it (e.g., who else might have been around at the time). The children were asked to consider the same events in interviews each week for 10 weeks. Then, in the eleventh week the children were questioned by a new interviewer. The new interviewer went through each event and asked the children if the event had really happened. Ceci et al. found that more than half the children claimed that at least one of the invented events had actually taken place. Some children even provided elaborate 'details' of the fictitious events, for example they explained how they got their fingers caught in the mousetrap, who took them to the hospital and what sort of treatment they had had. Ceci et al. (1994) demonstrated that just getting young children to think about invented events during repeated interviews led many of the children to believe that the invented event had really happened. These results added to the evidence about the suggestibility of young children.

There are several reasons why children might be suggestible (Ceci and Bruck, 1995). Children may encode less information about an event than adults, for example, if they have less effective strategies for attention (Vurpillot, 1968, see above). Or children may attend to information, but because of working memory constraints encode that information less completely than adults. Such limitations may mean that children have more 'gaps' in memory that can be filled with information implied by suggestive questioning. Even if children encode information it may be encoded only weakly, for example, because they have fewer schema and less existing knowledge to which they can link new information (see above). Some researchers (e.g., Warren et al., 1991) have found that if some aspects of an event are only weakly encoded it is those aspects that are most open to suggestive questioning.

Children may also have more difficulty than adults at distinguishing between information that they have actually experienced during an event and different information that was mentioned during a later interview. For example, suppose a child saw a man with a brown shirt during an event. Perhaps during a first interview about the event the child is asked 'Did the man have a red shirt?' The child may well reply quite accurately that the man had a brown shirt. However, at a second interview the child might be asked again, 'What colour was the man's shirt?' At this point, the child has to realize that she actually saw a brown shirt, but only heard that the man might have had a red shirt during the first interview. The ability to recall the origin of memories is called *source monitoring* (Roberts, 2000). Young children sometimes have difficulty recalling the sources of their memories and this means that they may confuse something that actually happened with something that they had only thought about. For example, Foley and Johnson (1985) compared the source monitoring of six-year-olds and adults. The participants were asked to either carry out several brief actions (e.g., wave goodbye) or just to imagine performing such actions. A few minutes later the participants were given a surprise memory test and asked which actions they had really carried out. Foley and Johnson found that the adults were more accurate than the children at recalling which actions they had actually performed. Sometimes the six-year-olds thought that they had actually done something that they had only imagined doing (and vice versa). Source confusions may be one of the reasons why some children in Ceci et al. (1994) believed that events that they had only thought about during the course of the interviews had actually happened.

As well as cognitive factors there will be other factors associated with the conduct of an interview that may influence children's suggestibility. These include factors like the perceived authority of the interviewer. If a parent, teacher or police officer makes a suggestion a child may feel under greater pressure to go along with the suggestion than if it comes from a less authoritative person (Ceci and Bruck, 1995). The repetition of a question during an interview may lead children to change their answer. For example, Moston (1987) asked six-year-olds the same question twice. The first time the children were asked the question about an event two-thirds of the children's answers were correct, but when the question was repeated only about one-third of the responses were correct. Children may have assumed that being asked a question more than once implied that their first answer was wrong. After all, teachers and parents do not usually ask a question a second time if they receive an adequate answer the first time.

Children may think that if an adult asks a question there should be an answer, and they will try to give a response rather than say that they don't understand the question or don't know the answer. Hughes and Grieve (1980) asked five- and seven-year-olds questions like 'Is red heavier than yellow?' and found that most of the children answered yes or no. None of the children said that the question was impossible to answer. Questions asked by police officers and lawyers may be hard for children to understand because they include difficult vocabulary or phrasing (Carter et al., 1996). But Hughes and Grieve's finding implies that children will still attempt to answer a question that does not make sense to them, and in answering the question they may give a misleading answer to the interviewer.

Hughes and Grieve (1980) asked only nonsensical questions that could be answered with yes or no. In another study, Waterman et al. (2000) asked five- to eight-year-olds such yes/no questions and also 'open' questions that required an answer (e.g., 'What do bricks eat?') and 'scrambled' questions like 'Many does how person legs have a?' Waterman et al. found, like Hughes and Grieve, that children answered most of the yes/no questions, but in contrast, children hardly ever tried to answer the nonsensical open questions or the scrambled questions.

In a similar study, Waterman et al. (2001) read five- to nine-year-olds a brief story about a picnic and then asked the children questions about what had happened in the story. Some of the questions were impossible to answer because the relevant information had not been included in the story. If the unanswerable questions required an answer (e.g., 'What flavour ice-cream did Mary have?') children usually said they didn't know. But if the unanswerable questions implied a yes/no response (e.g., Did they drink lemonade?) children often gave an answer. These studies demonstrated the importance of the exact form of questioning in eliciting correct answers from children. Some types of questions (like yes/no ones) may tempt children to give inappropriate responses to questions they do not understand, or to speculate about information that they do not know.

The cognitive interview

Most researchers have found that children are unlikely to offer much information in free recall, even when they know a lot about an event (Goodman and Reed, 1986; Marin et al., 1979) and for this reason researchers have considered ways to maximize the amount of information given by a witness. One technique is called the *cognitive interview* (Fisher and Geiselman, 1992).

The cognitive interview relies on established cognitive principles to maximize what witnesses recall. These include asking a witness to reconstruct the original context of the event by describing the scene (e.g., by closing their eyes and trying to visualize the scene) and how they felt at the time. Encouraging the witness to report as much as possible, even if some details are only partially remembered or thought not to be important. Re-telling the event in different orders (e.g., from the last thing that happened to the first). Asking the witness to report the events from different perspectives (e.g., by describing what someone else who was involved would have seen and heard). And encouraging the use-specific retrieval techniques. For example, associating memories (e.g., 'Did the man's face remind you of anyone you knew?') or, if trying to recall an overheard name or word, thinking of similar words or going through the alphabet to trigger recall of the name when the initial letter of the name is reached.

Compared to a standard interview (in which witnesses are just asked to recall as much as they can) the cognitive interview can elicit twice as much information from adults without increasing the amount of inaccurate information reported (Fisher et al., 1987). Researchers have also found that the cognitive interview can be effective with children. McCauley and Fisher (1995) asked seven-year-olds to play a game with an unfamiliar adult, and a few hours later the children were interviewed about the game using either a standard interview or a cognitive interview. The children who were given the cognitive interview reported about fifty per cent more information than children who received the standard interview. Although the cognitive interview is effective with children the improvement in their recall is often less than the improvement found with adults. This may not be surprising, because as discussed earlier in this chapter, children may have less well-developed memory strategies than adults, and some of the techniques employed in the cognitive interview may be less applicable for children. Nonetheless, the research into the cognitive interview provides a good example of how an understanding of cognitive processes can be used to develop better ways to question eyewitnesses.

The effects of stress on children's recall

If children are witnesses they may have to report events that were stressful and stress may influence memory in either a negative or a positive way (Baddeley, 1993). It is possible that an event that is stressful or frightening will be recalled more vividly than more mundane events, or alternatively, as Freud suggested, an unpleasant experience might be repressed or lost because it is too stressful to hold in conscious memory.

Researchers are limited in how much they can investigate this issue, because it is clearly inappropriate to place experimental participants under stress just to find out how stress might effect their recall. Nonetheless, some researchers have taken advantage of 'naturally' occurring stressful experiences to find out how well children remember unpleasant or traumatic events. Goodman et al. (1986) compared two groups of children, aged between three and seven years. Both groups visited a clinic, the 'high stress' group were taken to the clinic to have a blood sample taken, and the 'low stress' group went through the same procedure but instead of a blood sample they had a washable transfer placed on their arm. A few days later the children were questioned about the visit. Both groups had good recall of the events that had happened at the clinic, and there was no difference between the groups – the children in the high stress group recalled as much as the other children.

In a similar experiment, Saywitz et al. (1991) investigated how well five- and seven-year-olds recalled a visit to a clinic, which involved them being examined by a doctor who asked them to undress for a physical examination. Half the children (in the low stress group) were given an examination of their spine by a doctor who only touched them on their back. The other half (in the high stress group) were given a physical examination that involved touching genital areas. A week later the children were interviewed about what had happened. In free recall there was no difference between the five-year-olds in the low and high stress groups, both groups recalled a similar amount of correct information. However, in free recall the seven-year-olds in the high stress group offered less information about the event than the seven-year-olds in the low stress group. Nonetheless, when these children were asked specific questions about what had happened they correctly answered questions about where they had been touched. The older children may have been more hesitant in spontaneously revealing what had happened, but this was not due to forgetting the stressful information (because they were able to report the event accurately when specifically asked about it). Rather, and not surprisingly, children may sometimes be less willing to report information that is distressing. But this only points to the need for sensitive interviewing techniques.

Children may not only experience stress at the time of witnessing an event, but also at the time of re-telling it, especially if they have to appear in an open court. Saywitz and Nathanson (1993) showed eight- to ten-year-old children a staged event. Then half the children were interviewed on their own by an interviewer in a classroom at their school, and the other half were interviewed in a full mock courtroom (in a university law school) with actors representing all the key court figures as well as jurors and spectators. The children in the court condition found the experience more stressful than the ones interviewed in the classroom. Most importantly, the children in school recalled more correct information about the event than did the children in court, and the children in school were less likely to make errors in response to misleading questions. In this experiment it was clear that stress at the time of recall had a negative effect on children's performance as witnesses.

Summary

Research into children's ability as witnesses is important for what it can reveal about memory in everyday contexts. Such research has implications for interviewing children who have been involved in events that might become the focus of legal proceedings (Bull, 2001) and the results from the research have made a significant contribution to the treatment of children in courts. For example, in the UK there are now carefully constructed guidelines about the initial interviewing of children who may later have to appear in court (Home Office and Dept of Health, 1992). The frequent publication of psychological research in legal and other journals has meant that all those involved in the interviewing of children are more aware of the issues relating to the development of children's memory abilities.

Further Reading

Memory and information processing: Cowan, N. (ed.) 1997: *The Development of Memory in Childhood*. Hove, East Sussex: Psychology Press, includes a good collection of chapters about different aspects of memory development. Each chapter is well written by an expert in the area, and provides a very good set of reviews about current issues and debates. One of the most comprehensive surveys of the literature on memory development is in Schneider, W. and Pressley, M. 1997: *Memory Development Between Two and Twenty*, 2nd edn. Mahwah, NJ: Erlbaum.

A well written book that is a good introduction to most aspects of cognitive development is Siegler, R. S. 1998: *Children's Thinking*, 2nd edn. Englewood Cliffs, NJ: Prentice Hall. For a more detailed discussion of cognitive development see Flavell, J. H., Miller, P. H. and Miller, S. A. 2002: *Cognitive Development*, 4th edn. Englewood Cliffs: NJ, Prentice Hall, but this is a specialized book, and research results are often referred to briefly and the authors assume that the reader will already have some knowledge of the field.

Children's eyewitness memory: Ceci, S. J. and Bruck, M. 1995: *Jeopardy in the Courtroom. A Scientific Analysis of Children's Testimony*, Washington, DC: American Psychological Association, provides a good review of the research into children's suggestibility which integrates the empirical findings from psychological studies with examples of courtroom practice. For a good collection of papers covering many contemporary issues including reviews of the empirical research with children see Westcott, H. L., Davies, G. M. and Bull, R. H. C. (eds) 2002: *Children's Testimony. A Handbook of Psychological Research and Forensic Practice*, Chichester: Wiley.

Poole, D. A. and Lamb, M. E. 1998: *Investigative Interviews of Children. A Guide for Helping Professionals*. Washington, DC: American Psychological Association provides a comprehensive review of the research into interviewing children, and guidelines about conducting interviews. Bull, R. (ed.) 2001: *Children and the Law. The Essential Readings*, Oxford: Blackwell, has a good selection of reprinted papers reporting research into many aspects of children and the law, including children's recall and testimony, children and abuse, and children in the legal system.

■ Discussion Points

1 Contrast Piaget's approach to studying cognitive development with the information processing approach.
2 Does children's problem solving and strategy use develop gradually or in distinct stages?
3 What factors contribute to children's memory development?
4 How does research into children's eyewitness memory differ from earlier research into memory development?
5 What advice would you give to an interviewer who needed to interview young children about events that they had witnessed?

Box 13.1
The origins of scientific reasoning

Siegler (1976) investigated the strategies that children used in Inhelder and Piaget's balance scale problem. In this task children were shown a balance scale with four equally spaced pegs on either side of the fulcrum (see box figure 13.1.1). A number of weights (each of the same value) were placed on some of the pegs. While the weights were placed the balance was held in place by a wedge. Then the child was asked to predict which side of the balance would go down, or whether it would remain in balance if the wedge was removed.

Rather than test children with the balance scale and then interpret their performance in terms of the strategies which they might have used, Siegler first considered what strategies were possible, and only then did he test children. Siegler's (1976) methodology involved four steps. First, he considered the dimensions of the balance scale problem and the potential strategies that

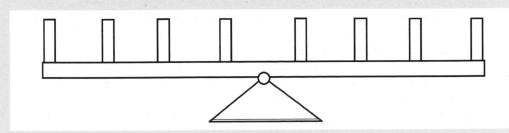

Box Figure 13.1.1   Balance scale – redrawn and based on R. S. Siegler (1976), Three aspects of cognitive development, *Cognitive Psychology*, 8, 481–520.

could be used to solve it. Second, he designed a set of tasks. Third, he predicted how a child who used a specific strategy would perform on the set of tasks. Fourth, he used the set of tasks to test a large number of children at different ages to establish developmental differences in the way they approached the task.

Strategies

According to Siegler there were four strategies that children might use (and there was also the possibility that they would have no strategy at all and just guess the answer):

- No strategy (i.e., just guess)
- Strategy I: If there are a different number, then say the side with more weights will go down. If the number of weights is the same on both sides, then say the scale will balance. (This strategy considers only the number of weights on either side of the fulcrum and ignores the distance of the weights.)
- Strategy II: If there are a different number, then say the side with more weights will go down. If the number of weights is the same on both sides, then say the side with the weights furthest from the fulcrum will go down.
- Strategy III: If the number of weights and the distance of the weights from the fulcrum on both sides are equal, then predict that the scale will balance. If both sides have the same number of weights

then consider the distance of the weights and say that the side with weights furthest from the fulcrum will go down. If both sides have weights at equal distance from the fulcrum, then say the side with the greater number of weights will go down. If one side has more weights and the other side has weights at greater distance from the fulcrum, then guess.
- Strategy IV: Follow Strategy III, unless one side has more weights and one has weights at greater distance. In this case, calculate torques by multiplying weights times distance. Then predict that the side with the greater torque will go down.

These strategies are shown diagrammatically in box figure 13.1.2. As can be seen particularly well from these diagrams, each strategy incorporates the preceding strategy. In other words, each strategy is like the preceding one, but with additional components, which contribute to progressively more accurate solutions to the balance problem.

Designing the tasks

Having described the possible strategies, Siegler then generated a set of different balance weight problems (these problems are shown in box figure 13.1.3):

1   Balance problems: have the same configuration of weights on either side of the fulcrum.

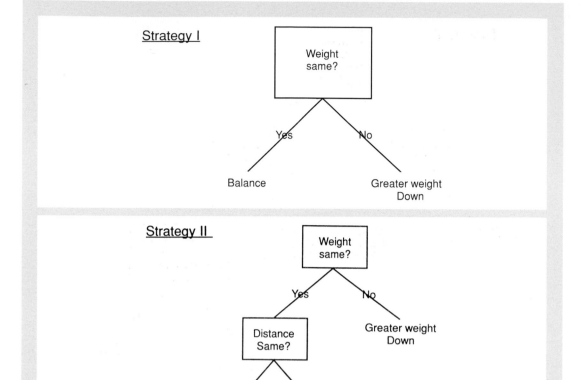

Box Figure 13.1.2   Diagrammatic representation of the strategies used for the balance scale task – redrawn and based on R. S. Siegler (1976), Three aspects of cognitive development, *Cognitive Psychology*, 8, 481–520.

2   Weight problems: have unequal number of weights, but at the same distance on either side of the fulcrum.

3   Distance problems: have equal number of weights on both sides, but at different distances.

4   Conflict-weight problems: one side has more weights, and the other side has weights further from the fulcrum. The side with the greater number of weights goes down.

5   Conflict-distance problems: one side has more weights, and the other side has weights further from the fulcrum. The side with the greater distance goes down.

6   Conflict-balance problems: one side has more weights, and the other side has weights further from the fulcrum. The two sides balance.

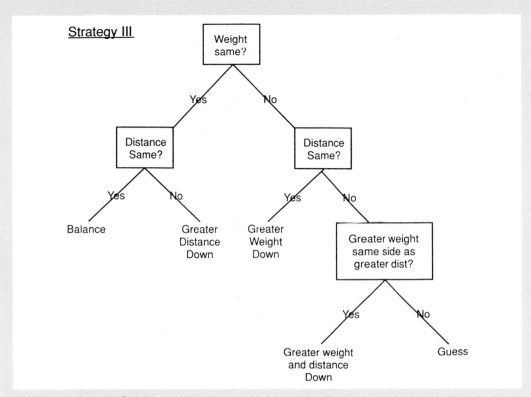

Box Figure 13.1.2 *Continued*

Predicting performance

Box figure 13.1.3 also describes the answer that you would expect a child to give to that problem if she was using one of the four strategies. For example, if a child is applying Strategy I to the balance, weight and conflict-weight problems she will give correct answers each time. However, if she uses Strategy I with distance problems, conflict-distance, and conflict balance problems, not only will she be wrong but it is possible to predict her incorrect answer. With the set of tasks designed by Siegler, the use of each strategy will generate a different pattern of responses. In other words, if children are given a set of tasks, it is then possible to iden-tify the strategy that they are using from the pattern of their answers.

An intriguing aspect of box figure 13.1.3 is that on conflict-weight problems children who use Strategy III will perform worse than children who use the less sophisticated Strategy I. It is not often in developmental psychology that children using a less advanced problem solving strategy are pre-dicted to perform better than children using a more complete strategy.

Testing children

Siegler asked five- to 17-year-olds to carry out balance scale problems (like the ones described above) and he found that most of them consistently used one of the expected strategies. Five-year-olds usually used Strat-egy I; nine-year-olds used Strategy II or III,

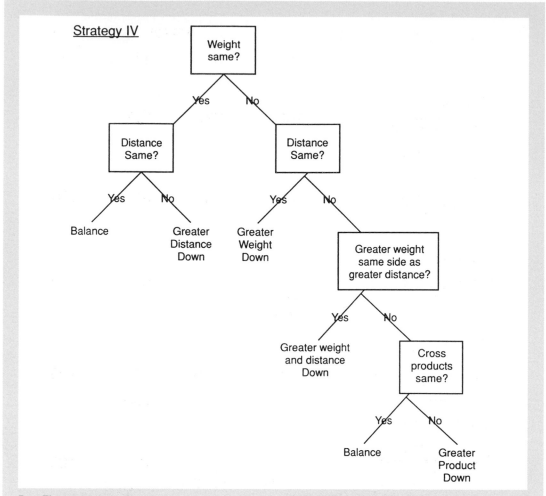

Box Figure 13.1.2 *Continued*

and older children used Strategy III. Very few children used Strategy IV. Siegler also found that five-year-olds (who nearly always used Strategy I) were correct on 89 per cent of the conflict-weight problems, but the 17-year-olds (who generally used Strategy III) were correct on only 51 per cent of these problems. These findings support Siegler's predictions about the use of the strategies.

Siegler's approach provides a good example of how cognitive development can be investigated by generating hypothetical models (in this case the description of possible strategies prior to the data collection) and making specific predictions (in this example, the expected performance of children) which can then be empirically tested.

Based on material in Siegler, R. S. 1976: Three aspects of cognitive development. *Cognitive Psychology*, 8, 481–520.

	Strategy			
	I	II	III	IV
Balance	100	100	100	100
Weight	100	100	100	100
Distance	0 say balance	100	100	100
Conflict (weight)	100	100	33 Chance	100
Conflict (distance)	0 say right down	0 say right down	33 Chance	100
Conflict (balance)	0 say right down	0 say right down	33 Chance	100

Box Figure 13.1.3 Examples of balance scale problems. The table shows percentages of correct answers if a child uses a particular strategy with a particular problem. In some cases a strategy will always result in a correct prediction (100%), sometimes it will always leads to an incorrect prediction (0%) and sometimes the child has to guess and (as there are three possible responses) will be correct, by chance, on 33% of that type of problem – redrawn and based on R. S. Siegler (1976), Three aspects of cognitive development, *Cognitive Psychology*, 8, 481–520.

Box 13.2
The effects of stereotypes and suggestions on preschoolers' reports

Leichtman and Ceci (1995) were interested in the suggestibility of young children. They pointed out that many researchers had found that, compared to older children and adults, young children are much more susceptible to misleading and suggestive questions. However, Leichtman and Ceci noted that these findings were derived mainly from small laboratory-based experiments in which children were interviewed just once. They argued that it was difficult to extrapolate from these studies to the sort of interviews that children experience in forensic and other contexts when they may undergo many repeated interviews over several weeks or months. Leichtman and Ceci also discussed court cases in which children's testimony had been influenced because adults had earlier told the children that the accused was a 'bad man'. For these reasons Leichtman and Ceci investigated the effects of multiple interviews and stereotypical information on children's recall and suggestibility.

Ninety 'early preschoolers' (three- and four-year-olds) and 86 'older preschoolers' (five- and six-year-olds) took part in the study. Roughly equal numbers of each age group took part in four conditions.

All the children experienced the same event. A stranger visited their classrooms during a story telling session, and was introduced as Sam Stone. He said hello to the teacher and commented on a story that was being read by saying 'I know that story; it's one of my favourites!'). He walked round the sides of the classroom, and then left the room, waving goodbye. Sam Stone's visit lasted for two minutes.

There were four conditions in the experiment:

1   *Control condition*: Children were not given any information about Sam Stone prior to his visit. These children were interviewed once a week for four weeks after the visit. They were asked what Sam Stone had done during the visit, but they were not given any suggestions about Sam Stone or his visit.

2   *Stereotype condition*: Each week for four weeks *before* Sam Stone visited the classroom, the children were given information about him. He was described as a well-meaning, but clumsy person. For example, the children were told: 'You'll never guess who visited me last night. That's right, Sam Stone! And guess what he did this time? He asked to borrow my Barbie [doll] and when he was carrying her down the stairs, he accidentally tripped and fell and broke her arm. That Sam Stone is always getting into accidents and breaking things! But it's okay, because Sam Stone is very nice and he is getting my Barbie doll fixed for me.' After Sam Stone's visit the children in the stereotype condition were treated in exactly the same way as children in the control condition – i.e., they received the four neutral interviews each week following the visit.

3   *Suggestion condition*: Children in this condition did not receive any information about Sam Stone before his visit, but during the four interviews *after* his visit they were given erroneous suggestions. In the first of the four interviews, they were shown a book with a torn page and asked who they thought might have ripped it. Then they were shown a dirty teddy bear and asked who they thought had made it dirty. In the second interview they were shown the torn book again and given leading questions like 'Remember when Sam Stone ripped the book? Did he rip it on purpose or by accident?' Then they were shown the dirty

Box Table 13.2.1 Percentage of responses from each condition and age group. The row labelled 'made errors' shows the percentage of incorrect responses children made to the questions about what Sam Stone did (rip the book or dirty the teddy bear). The row labelled 'said seen' shows the percentage of incorrect responses when children were asked if they had actually seen Sam Stone do either of the actions. The row labelled 'maintained' shows the percentage of responses in which children continued to say that they had seen something even after being asked 'You didn't really see him do this, did you?' (n.b. Leichtman and Ceci did not provide a data table and therefore some of the percentages are taken from the graphs they included in their paper. For this reason some figures are approximate)

| | (a) control | | (b) stereotype | | (c) suggestions | | (d) stereotype plus suggestions | |
	3–4yrs (%)	5–6yrs (%)	3–4yrs (%)	5–6yrs (%)	3–4yrs (%)	5–6yrs (%)	3–4yrs (%)	5–6yrs (%)
Made errors	10	4	37	18	50	38	72	37
Said seen	5	0	18	10	38	11	44	12
Maintained	2.5	0	10	2.5	12	9	21	6

Source: Leichtman and Ceci, 1995

teddy bear again and asked questions like 'When Sam Stone got the bear dirty was he in the classroom, the hallway, or the bathroom?' Children heard three leading questions about the book and three about the teddy bear. In the third and fourth interview the children were also asked similar questions.

4 *Stereotype plus suggestion condition*: This group received both the stereotype information before Sam Stone's visit (like condition 2) and the suggestive questions in the four interviews after the visit (like condition 3).

All the children were give a further interview ten weeks after Sam Stone's visit. This interview was carried out by a new interviewer. The children were asked what had happened when Sam Stone had visited the classroom; if they had 'heard something' about the book or the teddy bear; and whether they had seen Sam Stone do anything to those items. If children did say they had seen Sam do something to the book or the bear, they were asked a further question to find out how sure they were, 'You didn't

really see him do this, did you?' The percentage of children in each condition who gave incorrect answers are shown in box table 13.2.1. The children in the control condition (especially the older ones) rarely gave incorrect answers. They described what happened when Sam Stone visited their classroom without inventing events that did not happen. In all the other conditions children gave more incorrect answers than in the control condition.

Leichtman and Ceci used 2 (age) × 4 (group) multivariate analyses of variance (MANOVA) to analyse any differences in the children's answers about what happened during Sam Stone's visit (the row labelled 'made errors' in box table 13.2.1). There were effects for age and for group. Taking all the conditions together the five- to six-year-olds were less likely than the three- to four-year-olds to say that events had happened when they had not. The control group were less likely to invent events, than the stereotype group, who were less likely to invent events than the suggestion group, who in turn were less likely to invent events than the stereotype plus suggestion group.

In other words, the more strongly that children had been given suggestions about Sam Stone's behaviour the more likely they were to believe that they had seen him do damage to the book or the teddy bear. Leichtman and Ceci concluded that repeated suggestions and stereotypical information could result in young children inventing events that had not actually occurred. In particular, a combination of both suggestion and stereotypical information had the greatest effect, especially on the younger age group.

As Leichtman and Ceci showed, some of the children said that they had actually seen the invented events, and a few maintained that an invented event had taken place even after being asked a question like, 'You didn't really see him do this, did you?' Some of the children did not just answer 'yes' or 'no' to a suggestive question about what Sam Stone had done, but elaborated details. For example, one claimed that Sam Stone had taken the teddy bear into a bathroom and soaked it in hot water before marking it with crayon. Such invented detail might lead an interviewer to believe that the child really had witnessed the event.

Leichtman and Ceci also investigated whether adults could discriminate between children who were reporting events correctly or incorrectly. They showed videotapes of three interviews to 119 researchers and clinicians. The videotapes showed three children during their final interview in the stereotype plus suggestion condition. Child 1 was shown saying that Sam Stone had tossed things in the air, ripped a book, made the teddy bear dirty, and had visited the classroom with a 'another Sam Stone'. Child 2 said only that Sam Stone had visited the classroom, said hello, and walked round the classroom (all of which was accurate). Child 3 initially said only that Sam Stone had walked around the classroom, but when asked the suggestive questions the child agreed that Sam Stone had ripped the book and put ice-cream on the teddy with a paint brush while in the school yard.

The adults were told that all the children had witnessed the same visit by Sam Stone, and were then asked to decide what had happened during the visit from the children's reports. The adults were asked to rate (on a seven-point scale) the events described by the children as ones that had definitely occurred or ones that had definitely not. The adults rated Child 1 as the most credible, Child 3 as the next most credible and Child 2 as the least credible. In other words, the two children who included inaccurate details were rated as more credible than the child who gave the perfectly accurate account. The adults were unable to identify which of the specific events reported by children were accurate or not. The adults usually believed the reports of items being tossed in the air and the book being ripped. They could not decide about the teddy bear, but were unlikely to think that there had been two visitors both named Sam Stone.

Leichtman and Ceci suggested that Child 1 and Child 3 were seen as more credible because they provided more detail about the event. As Leichtman and Ceci (1995, p. 575) conclude 'the accuracy of children's reports is extremely difficult to discern when children have been subjected to repeated erroneous suggestions over long retention intervals, especially when coupled with the induction of stereotypes.'

This study has implications for the way that children are interviewed. Children who have witnessed a crime or have been the victims of a crime, may be interviewed many times about the events that have happened (e.g., by parents, teachers, social workers, police officers, lawyers and so on). Leichtman and Ceci demonstrated that over repeated interviews children can be misled, and misled in such a way that adults cannot distinguish between children's accurate and inaccurate statements. However, a positive aspect of the findings was the performance of the children in the control group. The children in this group received no suggestions about Sam Stone or about the event, and in general, they were accurate in reporting what happened. In other words, if inter-viewers avoid suggestions and misleading questions even young children who have been questioned several times may report events accurately.

Based on material in Leichtman, M. D. and Ceci, S. J. 1995: The effects of stereo-types and suggestions on preschoolers' reports. *Developmental Psychology*, 31, 568–78.

14 Children's Understanding of Mind

In chapter 2 we have discussed the possible evolution of 'mind reading' in primates. As Byrne and Whiten (1987) argued there are some observations of chimpanzees which are most easily interpreted as examples of deliberately deceptive behaviour. The presence of deceptive behaviour in other primates is the best evidence we have that some animals may be able to take into account the beliefs of others. Deception means altering the beliefs of others. In the example given on p. 43 one chimpanzee did not immediately go to some food which was available, but rather acted as if the food was not there at all. This was because a second chimpanzee was nearby and would have made an attempt to grab the food for himself. The first chimpanzee was, in effect, generating a false belief in the mind of the second chimpanzee, and this implies that the first chimpanzee had some understanding that the beliefs of the other chimpanzee could be manipulated. Put simply, the first chimpanzee understood that the other chimpanzee had a mind.

This chapter will concentrate on children's understanding of the mind. With a few exceptions (discussed later in the chapter) we assume that all adults have an awareness that other people have minds. It is basic to our everyday human understanding that both ourselves and others have beliefs. We know this in many ways: we know that we ourselves have beliefs about the world, that our beliefs change, that they might be wrong, and that what we say and what we do are based on our beliefs. We also assume that other people have beliefs; they can tell us those beliefs directly or that we can work out their beliefs indirectly from the way they behave.

Understanding that most individual behaviour is based on individuals' beliefs about the world is not just a useful facet of human knowledge, it is vital if we are to make sense of what others say and how they act. If, for example, we know that there is some chocolate in the kitchen cupboard (and nowhere else in the house) but a friend goes to look for the chocolate on the dining room table, our friend's behaviour would make no sense to us at all if we could not interpret it in terms of what our friend believed about the world. We would assume that she thought that the chocolate was on the table, because we know that she has a mind, which includes beliefs, which, as in this case, are incorrect. If we did not take into account her beliefs it would be very difficult to explain why she went to the dining room (except as some form of random behaviour).

Having an understanding of other people as people who have desires, beliefs and their own interpretations of the world is often referred to as having a 'theory of mind' – calling it a 'theory' stresses two aspects of understanding about the mental world. First, we cannot directly see or touch the mind, and therefore we have to infer (or theorize) about others' mental states from what they say or the way they behave. Second, a theory is usually a complex interconnected set of ideas, and an adult's understanding of the mental world, taking into account emotions, desires, pretence, deception, beliefs, and different perspectives of the world is certainly a rich and complementary set of concepts, which it might be appropriate to call a 'theory'. However, the phrase 'theory of mind' is also troublesome, because it cannot be defined with precision (how much knowledge about the mind do you have to have for a theory of mind?). Some researchers have argued explicitly that the development of understanding the mind is similar to the development of theories in science, but others are against drawing too close an analogy between the development of understanding minds and the development of scientific theories (Russell, 1992).

What does it mean to have an understanding of the mind? The mind can be considered in different ways. We understand that we have emotions and feelings (e.g., we can feel happy or sad) and that we have desires (I want some chocolate) and that desires and feelings are related (I will be happy if I find some chocolate). We realize that the mind includes knowledge (I know what chocolate is, I know where it is); that we can think about information (I am thinking about chocolate); that there is a difference between thoughts and real things (I can only touch or eat real chocolate); and that we have beliefs about the state of the world (I believe that the chocolate is in the cupboard). Adults also have an appreciation of some aspects of how the mind can be used – for example in learning new information, or using mnemonics (see discussion of metacognition in chapter 13) and we know that knowledge is derived from particular sources, for example, if I see the chocolate in the cupboard then I know where it is and that my knowledge is derived from looking.

One of the most important aspects of understanding the mind is the realization that just as I have a mind so do other people. They too have feelings, desires and beliefs and that just as I behave on the basis of my beliefs about the world, so do they. One of the most crucial points about understanding other people's minds is the realization that they may have beliefs that differ from our own. To put this another way – a person's set of beliefs about the world can be referred to as their (mental) representation of the world. Different people may represent the world in different ways; I believe the chocolate is in the cupboard, but my friend believes it is on the table. It is possible that we are both wrong about these beliefs (perhaps unknown to either of us someone has come along and eaten all the chocolate), but we cannot both be right about the same block of chocolate. If I'm right and the chocolate still is in the cupboard, then my friend's belief is incorrect and she has a false belief about the world.

The False-Belief Task

Do children, like adults, appreciate that other people can have false beliefs? In an influential experiment Wimmer and Perner (1983) investigated this question (see box 14.1). They used models to act out a story about a little boy called Maxi who put some chocolate in a blue cupboard. Then Maxi left the room, and while he was out of the room the children saw Maxi's mother transfer the chocolate to a green cupboard. The children were asked to predict where Maxi would look for the chocolate when he came back into the room. Four-year-olds usually said that he would look in the green cupboard. From an adult point of view this is a very surprising response, because of course, Maxi could not possibly know that the chocolate had been moved. We can infer from such a result that young children do not understand that Maxi's beliefs about the world are different from how the world really is, and they do not understand that he will act on the basis of his beliefs and not on the actual state of the world.

This was a very important result because it indicated that young children's reasoning about other people's behaviour may be quite different from the assumptions that adults make about other people's behaviour. The discovery of such a major developmental difference has generated a wealth of research into how children think about the mind and the relationship between mind and behaviour.

Wimmer and Perner's (1983) task is referred to as a 'false-belief' task because Maxi's belief that the chocolate is in the blue cupboard is an incorrect belief after the chocolate is moved. Some researchers questioned the length of Wimmer and Perner's (1983) story, and suggested that children may have had difficulty with the amount of information they needed to consider to fully understand the story. Therefore, other researchers (Baron-Cohen et al., 1985) reduced the complexity of the story, with a version called the Sally-Anne task (see figure 14.1). In this version, children are shown two dolls, Sally (who has a basket) and Anne (who has a box). Sally puts a marble in her basket and then leaves. While she is absent Anne takes the marble from the basket and puts it in the box. Sally returns and children are asked 'Where will Sally look for her marble?'. The typical result from this task is that four-year-olds realize that Sally will look in the basket, three-year-olds say that she will look in the box. In other words, with this briefer version of the false-belief task children perform correctly at a slightly earlier age, but three-year-olds seem unable to understand how Sally will act. Indeed Wimmer and Perner (1983) found that by altering the story about Maxi and the chocolate, so that some features of the story were more salient four-year-olds could succeed, but three year olds remained unable to work out what Maxi would do (see box 14.1).

Other false-belief tasks, such as the 'Smarties task', have produced the same result (Perner et al., 1987). In the Smarties task children are shown a closed box of Smarties and asked to say what is in the box. Children nearly always say 'Smarties' or 'sweets'. Then the lid is taken off and the children are shown that

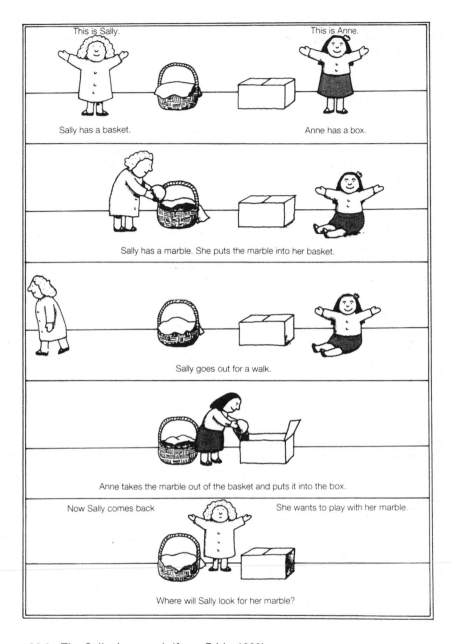

Figure 14.1   The Sally-Anne task (from Frith, 1989).

the box actually contains pencils. After this the lid is replaced and children are asked what one of their friends will think is in the box: 'When X [friend's name] comes in I'm going to show her this box. What will X think is in the box?' The correct answer is Smarties, and although this is the most common answer given by four-year-olds, younger children answer that their friend will say there are pencils in the box. Children can also be asked what they thought was in the box before it was opened. Four-year-olds give the correct answer ('Smarties'), but three-year-olds say (incorrectly) that they thought there were pencils in it. In other words, three-year-olds seem to lack insight into their own mind – they do not acknowledge that at an earlier time they believed there were Smarties in the box.

It is clear from experiments like these that children before the age of about four years have difficulty understanding that another person can have a false belief about the world. They respond as if Sally (in the Sally-Anne task) or their friend (in the Smarties task) will know what the actual state of the world is, even though they could not possibly know this. However, even if three-year-olds fail the false-belief task it does not mean that they nothing at all about the mind, and in the next section we will give examples of the research into very young children's understanding of the mind.

Children's Knowledge of Mind before about Four Years of Age

Distinguishing mental states in language

From about two years of age children start to use words which refer to internal states of perception or emotion – words like 'want', 'see', 'look', 'taste' (see chapter 6) and by the age of three years children also use cognitive terms like 'know', 'think' and 'remember'. When children use such words spontaneously it may be difficult to work out whether they use them to refer to mental states or whether they are being used in a more casual manner (for example, adults say 'you know' or 'know what' without any implication that the word 'know' refers to a mental state).

Shatz et al. (1983) examined three-year-old children's spontaneous use of mental terms and to avoid instances of casual use they focused on utterances that included a contrasting use of terms. The statements collected by Shatz et al. included ones like:

> 'I thought it was an alligator. Now I know it's a crocodile.'
>
> 'I was teasing you. I was pretending 'cept you didn't know that.'
>
> 'I thought there wasn't any socks [in the drawer], 'cept when I looked I saw them. I didn't know you got them.'

In these examples children spontaneously contrasted reality and a belief – for instance, in the first example, the belief was that an animal was an alligator, the reality was that it was a crocodile. Shatz et al. inferred from such examples that these three-year-olds could distinguish between mental states and external reality.

In another study, Wellman and Estes (1986) showed three-year-olds two story characters and the children were told that character A had a biscuit, and that character B was, for example, thinking about a biscuit. The children were then asked which of the two biscuits (the physical one or the mental one) could be touched, be seen by the character, or be seen by another character. Different stories were used so that several contrasts could be made between the physical object (with character A) and the same object that character B was thinking about, or dreaming about, or remembering, or pretending about. Wellman and Estes found three-quarters of the children's judgements accurately reflected the distinction between physical and mental entities.

Understanding the relationship between seeing and knowing

Children from the age of two years have some understanding of the relationship between seeing and knowing. Lempers et al. (1977) asked two-year-olds to show another person a picture that was glued to the inside bottom of a box. The children realized the need to angle the box so that the other person could see into it. Children of the same age also appreciated that if a person had their hands over their eyes it was necessary to move their hands if they were to see a picture. By the age of three years children understood that if they hid something from another person that person would not be able to see it. In other words, by three years of age children realize something of the relationship between seeing an object and knowing about that object.

Three-year-olds also understand that different people may have a different view of the same object. For example, Masangkay et al. (1974) used a card with a cat drawn on one side and a dog drawn on the other. The card was placed with one side facing the child and the other facing the experimenter, and children were asked what each person could see. Three-year-olds realized that the experimenter saw a different picture from the one they were looking at. More than this, children of this age are aware that if people see something they will know about it, if they do not see something they will be unaware of. For example if an object is hidden in a box, three-year-olds understand that if person A has looked into the box she will know what is in it and if person B has not looked in the box she will not know its contents (Hogrefe et al., 1986). The results of these experiments show that young children appreciate that different people can have different knowledge about the world, and that some people may have less complete knowledge than others.

However, it is not until about four years of age that children realize that people may have different views of an object which is equally and completely visible to both. Masangkay et al. (1974) had a child (aged three to five years) sit opposite an experimenter, and between the two of them was a picture showing the side view of a turtle. The experimenter explained when that the turtle appeared as if it was standing on its feet, it was the right way up and when it appeared as if it was on its back it was 'upside down'. The picture was placed flat on the table and children were asked which of the two views they saw and which the experimenter saw. All the children were correct in describing their own view of the turtle, but only a third of the three-year-olds could describe the experimenter's view, and it was not until four years of age that children understood that their view and the experimenter's were different. This is an important realization, because it means that, at least in perspective-taking tasks, children by the age of four can recognize that the same object can be thought about in different ways.

Understanding the appearance-reality distinction

Most adults know that a realistic looking apple which is made of wax is not a real apple, and they can distinguish what it looks like – an apple (its appearance), from what it is – wax (the reality). In other words, they realize that the *same* person can think about an object in different ways – they can represent the same object as fruit and as wax. However, young children have difficulty in tasks that involve distinguishing appearance and reality – for example, Flavell et al. (1986) showed children a sponge, which looked like a rock. The children were shown it from a distance (when it could be interpreted as a rock) and then they had an opportunity to feel it, and discovered that it was a sponge. After this they were asked two questions: 'What does it look like?' (correct answer was, of course, a rock) and 'What is it really and truly?' (a sponge). Three-year-olds had difficulty in this task, once they had found out that it was a sponge they tended to answer 'sponge' to both questions.

The three-year-olds had difficulty considering two (contradictory) representations of the object at the same time. As Flavell (1988 p. 246) said: 'they do not clearly understand that even though something may be only one way out there in the world, it can be more than one way up here in our heads, in our mental representations of it.' In other words, at the age of three years children do not realize that the appearance of an object is only a representation (that can be changed), instead they only consider one interpretation of the object – what they know it to be. It is only after about the age of four years that children begin to appreciate that an object can be represented as both what it looks like and what it is. Such an appreciation includes an awareness that at least one of the representations is false (as when the sponge is represented as a rock). Children may also realize that it is possible for one person to have a true belief about an object (in this case know that the object is a sponge), but another person might have a false belief about the same object (and think it is a rock).

Predicting behaviour

Two-year-olds understand that people have desires, and that these can influence the way they behave. Wellman (1990) told children a story about a character called Sam who wanted to find his rabbit so he could take it to school. The children were told that the rabbit could be hiding in one of two locations, and they saw Sam going to one of the two locations. At that location Sam either found his rabbit (the desired object) or he found a dog. After Sam had looked in one location, the children were asked 'Will he look in the other location, or will he go to school?' Two-year-olds answered correctly (if Sam found the rabbit) that he would then go to school, and (if he found the dog) that he would go on searching. In other words, they predicted what Sam would do from what they knew about his desires.

By the age of three years children understand that people not only have desires, they also have beliefs about the world. Wellman (1990) showed three-year-olds two locations (for example, a shelf and a toy box), and the children were shown that there were books on the shelf and in the box. Then a character was introduced: 'This is Amy. Amy thinks there are books only on the shelf; she doesn't think there are books in the toy box. Amy wants some books. Where will Amy look for books?' (The children could have answered 'shelf, or 'toy box', or both places). Two-thirds of the responses made by the children were correct – they realized that Amy's beliefs would lead to her looking for the books on the shelf.

In this last experiment Amy had a true belief about the world – she thought that there were books on the shelf and there were books in that place, and three-year-olds appreciated the relationship between a true belief and behaviour. However, as we saw in the previous section, three year-olds cannot predict someone else's behaviour when that person has a false belief (as in the Sally-Anne or Smarties tasks). In other words, three-year-olds realize that other people's behaviour is based on their beliefs about the world, and that those beliefs may be incomplete (as in the case of Amy). But three-year-olds do not yet realize that people can act on the basis of a belief that is inaccurate (as in the case of Sally).

When is Theory of Mind Achieved?

Most children succeed on a typical false-belief task such as the Smarties task (Perner et al., 1987, described above) between four and five years of age. However, some researchers have suggested that younger children can succeed on false-belief tasks if the questions in the task are made more specific. For example, Lewis and Osborne (1990) suggested that children may have difficulty in the Smarties task if they think they are being questioned about what another person will think is in the Smarties box after that person has been shown the actual contents (pencils) in the box. Lewis and Osborne changed the wording of the question and asked children what their friend would think was in the box before *she opens the lid*. This made it explicit that the friend could only make a judgement about the contents from seeing the outside of the box. Lewis and Osborne found that, with the change in the format of the question some three-year-olds could succeed on the Smarties task. Some researchers have also found that young children are more likely to succeed on the Maxi task if the wording of the Maxi task is made more explicit (Siegal and Beattie, 1991). Other changes in the procedure of false-belief tasks can also contribute to younger children's success (e.g., Freeman et al., 1991; Mitchell, 1996; Mitchell and Lacohee, 1991).

Although nearly all children achieve success on false-belief tasks at approximately the same age there are individual differences in that achievement, with some children succeeding at a slightly younger age than other children. DeVilliers and deVilliers (2000) have emphasized that performance on false-belief tasks depends on understanding complex language and that individual differences may reflect differences in language ability. Several researchers have found that children with better language skills perform better on false-belief tasks (e.g., Jenkins and Astington, 1996). Children who have delayed language abilities may also show a delay in their ability to perform false-belief tasks – for example, some children with hearing impairments have difficulty on false-belief tasks (Woolfe et al., 2002).

Some researchers have pointed out that family background may also account for some differences. For example, Lewis et al. (1996) carried out a study with children who lived in extended families in the Greek communities on Crete and Cyprus. Lewis et al. gave the children several false-belief tasks and gathered details about the number of people with whom the children interacted on a daily basis. They found that children who were the most successful on false-belief tasks were the children who interacted most with adults and had more older friends and more older siblings. Lewis et al. suggested that those young children who have a greater opportunity to talk to and interact with older children and adults will have a better chance of developing their theory of mind skills at an earlier age. Brown et al. (1996) investigated the way that children who were nearly four years of age talked with mothers, friends and siblings. They collected samples of conversations and found that the children were more likely to talk about thoughts and beliefs when interacting with their siblings and friends than when they were interacting with their mothers. Brown et al. also found a correlation between children's talk of thoughts and beliefs with their siblings and friends and their performance on false-belief tasks.

These findings have led Dunn (1999) to speculate that conversation with other children may be particularly important for the development of theory of mind. Dunn pointed out that there is a rapid increase in the amount of child–child interaction between two and four years of age, and suggested that during this period children may learn more from interacting with other children than with adults. Dunn gave two reasons for this suggestion. First, other children may be more likely than adults to take part in shared make-believe and pretend activities. Planning, discussing and acting out such activities necessitate children discussing their thoughts and ideas with each other. Second, when adults and a young child communicate the adult will usually take into account the child's lack of conversational experience and make allowances for the child when structuring the interaction. However, when children talk to other young children they are less likely to make such allowances and therefore successful communication may be more challenging and force the children into explicit consideration of each others' knowledge and beliefs.

Knowledge of the Mind after about Four Years of Age

The results from experiments with false-belief tasks that we described earlier showed that after about four years for age children realize that another person can have inaccurate belief about the world. Put another way, they realize that people's representation of the world does not necessarily coincide with the state of the world. Understanding the distinction between a mental representation and reality is a very important realization, but it is not the end point of children's insights into the mind.

The false-belief task involves a 'first order' belief (i.e., I think that Sally thinks that the marble is in the basket). A 'second order belief' is one that involves understanding that someone else can have beliefs about a third person (for example, I think that Jack thinks that Jill thinks that the marble is in the basket). Children's understanding of second order false belief was investigated by Perner and Wimmer (1985) who told children a story about John and Mary, who are playing in a park. They see an ice-cream man at the park. Mary wants to buy an ice-cream, but has no money, so she goes home to get some money. John goes home for his lunch. The ice-cream man leaves the park, and goes to the school. Mary is on her way back to the park with some money when she sees the ice-cream man going to the school. She asks him where he is going and says she will follow him to buy an ice-cream at the school. John finishes his lunch and goes to Mary's house. When he gets there Mary's mother says that Mary has gone to buy an ice-cream. John leaves Mary's house to look for her. At the end of the story children were asked 'Where does John think that Mary went to buy an ice-cream?' Wimmer and Perner found that children only succeeded on this type of task after about the age of six years (in other words, about two years later than they succeeded on first order belief tasks like the Sally-Anne task).

Some researchers have stressed that theory of mind is not an ability that is achieved fully and finally by the age of four or five years. Chandler and Sokol (1999) have argued that children's understanding of others' minds is a skill that develops for several years after children are successful on a typical false-belief task. To demonstrate this Carpendale and Chandler (1996) gave five- to eight-year-olds a false-belief task based on Wimmer and Perner's (1983) Maxi task (see above). The children were then given a second task involving an ambiguous drawing that could be interpreted as either a duck or a rabbit (see figure 14.2).

Carpendale and Chandler checked that children could recognize both interpretations and then introduced a puppet called Ann. The children were asked, 'now we will show this picture to Ann, do you think Ann will think it's a duck or a rabbit, or wouldn't you know what she would say?' If children said that Ann would say it was (for example) a rabbit they were asked, 'How can you tell what she will think?' If children said they did not know what Ann would think, they were asked, 'Why is it hard to tell what Ann will think?' All the children succeeded on the false-belief task, but most of the five-year-olds were unable to answer the questions about Ann appropriately. They either made a clear and specific prediction about how Ann would interpret the picture, or if they said they did not know what Ann would say they could not explain why it is impossible to predict another person's response to the picture. In other words, five-year-olds did not appreciate that another person has to interpret the picture and that such an interpretation cannot be predicted. Children's ability to answer the questions appropriately improved with age, but even some of the eight-year-olds had difficulty answering them. From these results Carpendale and Chandler argued that even after children have achieved success on a false belief task there is still much

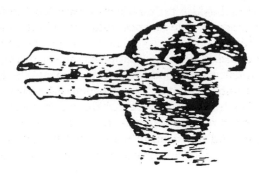

Figure 14.2 An ambiguous drawing that can be interpreted as a duck or a rabbit (Jastrow, 1900).

that they must learn about others' minds. It may be some years later before children are fully aware that, in all contexts, the mind is always an interpreter of reality.

False belief in other contexts

Even though children understand about false beliefs in tasks like the Sally-Anne and Smarties tasks, it may be slightly later that they apply similar understanding in other contexts. In chapter 6 (p. 184) we discussed a study by Harris (1989) in which children were told about Ellie the elephant who only liked to drink Coke. Ellie was given a can of Coke which, unknown to her, had been filled with milk (which she did not like). Children were asked how Ellie would feel when she received the can (and before she had drunk from it). Although the four-year-olds realized that Ellie did not know what was in the can, when the children were asked how she would feel, most of them said that she would feel sad. It was only after five years of age that children realized that Ellie would feel happy when she was given the can of Coke. In other words, understanding the relationship between false belief and emotion (as in Harris's experiment) may be a slightly later development than understanding the relationship between false belief and behaviour (as in the Sally-Anne task).

Once children realize that people can have false beliefs, they can also become aware of the possibility of deceptive behaviour. Deception involves planting a false belief in another person's mind (see the examples of chimpanzee deception in chapter 2), and obviously this is only possible if you realize that other people can have false beliefs! Peskin (1992) investigated young children's ability to deceive another person. Three-, four- and five-year-olds were shown four stickers and each child was told that she could have the one she liked best. But the children were also told that two puppet characters would each be allowed to choose a sticker before the child could take the one she wanted. Children were told that one puppet was friendly, and would never take a sticker that the child wanted, but the other puppet was mean and always wanted the same sticker that the child wanted.

After the child had said which sticker she wanted the friendly puppet came, and before choosing the friendly puppet asked the child which sticker she wanted. Nearly all the children, truthfully, pointed out the one they preferred and the friendly puppet chose a different one. Then the mean puppet arrived and also asked the child which she wanted. Nearly all the three- and four-year-olds pointed out the one they wanted and the mean puppet took it. Most of the five-year-olds pointed to a sticker they did not want. This result could be taken as evidence that the younger children did not have any understanding of how to deceive the mean puppet. They did not seem to realize that by telling the puppet a lie they could instill a false belief in the puppet so that he would not take the sticker they wanted.

What is particularly interesting about Peskin's experiment is that after the first trial (that we have just described) Peskin gave the children a further four trials using the same procedure. Not surprisingly the five-year-olds were as good in the later trials as they were in the first trial. The four-year-olds showed a rapid improvement in performance and by their second trial half of them realized the need, when the mean puppet was around, to point to a sticker that was not their preferred one. Presumably these children's rapid learning was based on an awareness that others can have a false belief. However, the three-year-olds never improved; even by the fifth trial nearly all of them continued to point to the sticker they wanted and every time the mean puppet took it from them. Despite the children's dismay and frustration and despite the repeated trials, it appeared that the three-year-olds had no way of deceiving the mean puppet – they did not realize that they could generate a false belief in the mean puppet by pointing to a sticker they did not want.

Some researchers have argued that there are examples of deception by three-year-olds that show that children of this age do attempt to manipulate the beliefs of another. For example, in chapter 6 (pp. 182–3) we described an experiment by Lewis et al. (1989) in which children peeked at a toy they were not supposed to look at. Most of the children who peeked later told an adult they had not done so, and some of the children who lied did so with positive facial expressions. As we suggested in chapter 6 the results from Lewis et al.'s study might indicate that at three years of age children realize the need to encourage a false belief in the mind of someone else. However, such an interpretation is at odds with the poor performance of the three-year-olds in Peskin's experiment.

Theories about the Development of Understanding the Mind

Several theories have been put forward to explain how children develop an understanding of their own and other people's minds. We will only mention these briefly to give an indication of the different approaches that researchers have taken. We described a couple of Wellman's (1990) experiments earlier, and on the basis of such studies he suggested that children's understanding develops in three phases. Two-year-olds have a 'theory' based on 'desire psychology' – they assume that people's desires influence their behaviour. For example, in the experiment with Sam looking for his rabbit, Sam's behaviour (searching) is determined by his desire (to take the rabbit to school).

By the age of three, children have a 'theory' based on 'belief-desire psychology' – they not only take into account a person's desires, but also their beliefs about the world. For example, in the experiment with Amy looking for some books, three-year-olds realize that, although there are books in two places, if Amy only knows that they are in one place she will go there. This means that three-year-olds are able to take Amy's beliefs into account – they can predict her behaviour on the basis of Amy's representation of the world. However, Amy had a true (if incomplete) belief about the world – her representation reflected the actual state of the world. Wellman (1990) originally suggested that three-year-olds may think of beliefs as a 'copy' of the world and they do not realize that a belief is not a copy but an interpretation of the world. As Bartsch and Wellman (1995, p. 203) said, 'three-year-olds can conceive that people either have a belief about the world or they don't; if they have one, however, it reflects the world veridically, like a good photograph would.' Such a view of three-year-olds excludes the possibility that children of this age can understand false belief. However, Bartsch and Wellman examined the conversation of ten children as they developed from infants into young children. Bartsch and Wellman found that at the age of three years children occasionally showed a realization that a person's beliefs and reality could be different, and as mentioned above some researchers have also found that three-year-olds can sometimes succeed on false-belief tasks (Freeman et al., 1991). For these reasons, Bartsch and Wellman concluded that three-year-olds' have some awareness that other people can have false representations of the world, but for the most part their theory of mind is still very much based on desire psychology (as in the case of younger children). It is only after about four years of age that children consistently adopt a theory that includes the crucial realization that beliefs are interpretations, and like all interpretations they may be inaccurate (like Sally's belief in the Sally-Anne task).

Wellman (1990) referred to children's understanding as progressively more sophisticated 'theories' about the mind. Put another way, they are developing a 'theory of mind'. By describing development in this way Wellman made an explicit comparison between children's developing understanding and the way that scientific theories develop. A scientist tries to understand a large number of facts or events by proposing a theory that explains the relationships between those facts, and then on the basis of that theory the scientist can predict the existence of other facts or relationships. Wellman suggested that in the same way that a scientist uses a theory to explain the world around her, so a child (who sees and experiences a constant stream of information about others' actions and behaviours) also tries to make sense of all this information by establishing a 'theory'. At first this may be quite a simple theory (e.g., one based on 'desire psychology'). Such a theory may explain some behaviours but as the child comes across examples of behaviour that cannot be explained simply from knowing a person's desires, she will be forced to consider a more elaborate theory (e.g., one based on belief-desire psychology). This shift in theories is rather like a scientist considering new facts that do not fit into an already established scientific theory – at a point when the old theory no longer helps understand the new facts, the scientist has to develop a new theory.

Wellman (1990) suggested that children's understanding of the mind progresses through several theory changes between the ages of two and four years. Support for the theory view of children's development comes from research that has shown that children achieve success on several different tasks at roughly the same age (Astington, 1994). For example, children's perspective taking ability (that two people can have different, and contrary, views of the same picture); children's appreciation of the distinction between appearance and reality (that the same person can have different, contradictory, representations of an object); and children's awareness of false belief (that different people can have contrary representations of the world) are all achieved about the same time. That children start to succeed on a variety of tasks at the same age can be taken as evidence that there has been a significant underlying change in their thought, which is influencing their understanding of a number of related mental concepts. Such a change might well be described as a shift in their 'theory' about the mind.

Rather than postulating several phases, Perner (1991) put great emphasis on the major change that occurs about four years when children can understand false belief. He argued that the most important aspect of understanding the mind occurs when a child has acquired the concept of 'metarepresentation'. This means an understanding of the distinction between what is being referred to (the referent) and what it is represented as. For example, consider a photograph (i.e., a representation) of a pyramid. If the photograph is taken from the ground the pyramid will be represented by a triangular shape, if taken from a plane flying directly above the pyramid it will be represented as a rectangular shape, if taken from a satellite it will be represented as a dot. These are all representations of the pyramid, but they are not copies of the pyramid. To think of representations simply as copies of reality is to misunderstand the nature of representations. It is only when you understand that representations are not copies of reality that you have the concept of metarepresentation. So that when a four-year-old succeeds on a false-belief task like the Maxi task she can make the distinction between *what* is represented (chocolate in location A) and *how* it is represented (by Maxi, as chocolate in location B).

As Perner (1991) pointed out, having the concept of metarepresentation, about the age of four years of age, is a major achievement. Perner said that younger children can, of course, understand a lot about minds (see the examples we gave in the previous section) but he argued that they can do so without an understanding the nature of mental representations (see Perner, 1991). In other words, Perner put most emphasis on a major change in children's representational thinking at the age of four years.

Leslie (1987) also used the word 'metarepresentation' but in a different way from Perner (1991). Leslie used the word in relation to young children's pretend play. Leslie pointed out that children start to demonstrate pretend play from about 18 months of age (see chapter 7) and he also noted that pretend play should actually be very confusing for a child who is still learning to categorize objects. For example, suppose a child has learnt that yellow curved fruits are called bananas and that mechanical instruments you put to your ear are called telephones. Children do not usually mistake bananas for telephones or vice versa. However, in pretend play the child herself or someone else (e.g., her mother) might pick up a banana, put it against her ear and pretend to be using it as a telephone. It might be expected that re-labelling the banana as a telephone has every potential to disrupt a child's categorization of objects. But this does not happen, young children are quite happy to pretend that a banana is a telephone, or a block of wood with wheels is a car, and they do not then get so confused that they start calling all bananas 'telephones' or all blocks of wood 'cars'.

In considering why children can indulge in pretend play without getting confused, Leslie (1987) suggested that children must have two types of representations when they indulge in pretend play. One is a primary representation (thinking about the banana as a banana) and the other is a secondary representation. The latter is the child's re-representation of the primary representation (so that the banana is also thought of as a telephone). Leslie called these secondary representations 'metarepresentations'. He also pointed out that in pretend play with others, young children interact with what other children are pretending (and not what they are actually doing). Children's ability to coordinate pretend play implies that they understand what is in the mind of the children they are playing with.

If young children can represent representations, and have some insight into other's minds, this might be thought of as a good basis for developing a fuller understanding of other minds. But it is at least two years between the beginning of pretend play and succeeding on a false-belief task. This is a surprisingly long time if the representational abilities proposed by Leslie (1987) really are the foundation for later understanding of minds. For this reason, several researchers have argued that pretend play is not dependent on representational abilities at all, and suggested that children can pretend by acting out behaviours. They can act out picking up a banana or talking into it, because that is what they would do with a telephone. In other words, the pretence is based on applying well known actions to an object, and to do this children do not necessarily need to have a representation of the banana as a telephone, all they need to do is think about all the actions they would use with a telephone and apply those to the banana (Lillard, 1993; Perner, 1991; and see p. 232).

Counterfactual reasoning

Wellman (1990), Perner (1991) and Leslie (1987) all suggested that children's understanding of mind is based the development of their representational abilities. In contrast, Harris (1989) suggested that children can understand others' minds without necessarily understanding that others have mental representations, instead children could use a process that Harris called 'simulation'. In chapter 6 we discussed Harris's description of how children might develop an understanding of emotions. He pointed out that young children know about their own emotions and that they have the ability to pretend. With this knowledge and ability they can project emotions on to others (e.g., if they have felt upset when they have fallen down, then in doll play they can pretend that the doll feels upset when it has fallen down). In the same way, children can project emotions and explanations for those emotions onto other people (see chapter 6).

Harris (1991, 1992) argued that by simulation children can work out, not only other people's emotions, but also their desires and beliefs. It is worth noting that adults probably use simulation all the time to imagine other people's feelings and behaviour. For example, if you hear that a friend has just passed an important examination, you may be able to imagine your friend's emotions and how she felt immediately before and after she received the result. You could also imagine her behaviour – what she will do and what plans she can make now that she knows that she has passed. This simulation can be achieved by considering how you felt and behaved in a similar situation and applying that information to your friend. In the same way, a child faced with the Sally-Anne task could imagine what she herself would think and do if she was Sally, and then work out what actions and consequences would follow.

Harris suggested that children at the age of three years can work out what someone else is thinking even if the other person is focusing on an aim or object different from the child's own. For example, if child A wants chocolate and her friend B wants ice-cream, child A can still work B's thoughts and beliefs. She can predict B's behaviour from simulating how the she herself might feel and act towards the chocolate, and applying that simulation to work out B's likely responses with regard to the ice-cream. By the age of four years children realize that different people may have different attitudes towards the same object, and can take into account alternative views of the same situation. This involves reasoning about situations that are counter to reality. So that in the Sally-Anne task, the child knows that the marble is in the box, but to work out how Sally construes the same situation the child has to imagine a hypothetical situation in which the marble is in the basket (and can then simulate Sally's likely behaviour). Generating a hypothetical situation like this involves the child thinking about situations that do not exist, and to do this requires 'counterfactual' reasoning (Harris, 2000).

Other researchers have also emphasized the importance of counterfactual reasoning in false-belief tasks. Riggs et al. (1998) pointed out that in the Maxi task (see box 14.1) the child has to imagine how something might be (chocolate in the blue cupboard) had some event not occurred (mother moved it to the green cupboard). This involves imagining a non-existent state of the world, and then working out where Maxi will look.

To consider the relationship between false-belief tasks and counterfactual reasoning Riggs et al. (1998) tested three- and four-year-old children. The children were told the following story: Maxi and his mother put chocolate in the cupboard, Maxi goes to school, mother uses some of the chocolate to make a cake, and puts the remaining chocolate in the fridge, then Maxi comes home. Children were asked two questions about the story. One was the typical question in false-belief tasks: 'Where does Maxi think the chocolate is?' – in such tasks it has been assumed that a correct answer to this question depends on children understanding Maxi's mental representation (i.e., his false belief). The other question was a reasoning question: 'If mum had not made a cake, where would the chocolate be?' – the answer to this question depends on the hypothesized reasoning that is needed in the false-belief task, but does not involve any understanding of false belief or mental representations.

Nearly all the children who answered the false-belief question correctly answered the reasoning question correctly, and nearly all the children who failed the false-belief question also failed the reasoning question. All the children who failed the false-belief question said that Maxi would think the chocolate was in the fridge, and all the children who failed the reasoning question said that the chocolate would be in the fridge. In other words, irrespective of the whether the question involved understanding a mental representation or not, the children performed in the same way. From this result Riggs et al. (1998) concluded that children's failure in false-belief tasks was due, not to their lack of understanding of mental representation, but to their inability to reason about the task. Riggs and Peterson (2000) argued that other false-belief tasks (such as the Smarties task) also involve elements of counterfactual reasoning, and that young children's difficulties with all such tasks may be due to limitations in their reasoning rather than limitations in their understanding of mental representation.

Despite the argument put forward by Riggs and Peterson (2000) there is evidence that children can engage in counterfactual reasoning before the age of four years. For example, Harris et al. (1996) told three- and four-year-olds a story about a girl who chose to go outside in a cardigan rather than in a coat. As a result the girl got cold. After hearing the story the children were asked questions like 'What should she have done instead so that she wouldn't get cold?' In answering this question the majority of the three- and four-year-olds suggested that the girl could have taken the coat. This answer refers to an action that the girl did not carry out – in other words, to a counterfactual situation. If children can use counterfactual reasoning before the age when they usually pass false-belief tasks, this weakens Riggs and Peterson's argument that successful performance on false-belief tasks is only possible after the development of counterfactual reasoning. Put another way, if three-year-olds are able to use counterfactual reasoning why don't they employ such reasoning to pass false-belief tasks like Riggs et al.'s (1998) Maxi task?

Harris and Leevers (2000) suggested that young children may be able to use counterfactual reasoning in some tasks, but not in others. They pointed out that in Harris et al. (1996) the story had a negative outcome (the girl got cold) and that most researchers who have shown that very young children use counterfactual reasoning have also used stories or events with negative outcomes. Harris and Leevers suggested that the focus on a negative outcome may prompt young children to consider explicitly a preferred alternative (such as staying warm) and this may then prompt successful counterfactual reasoning (when the children say the girl could have taken the coat).

In contrast to such studies the Maxi false-belief task involves an object being moved (the chocolate is put in a new location) and this is just a neutral change, rather than a negative or unfortunate outcome. Harris and Leevers proposed that without a negative outcome to prompt the appropriate reasoning young children may not engage in spontaneous counterfactual thinking in tasks like the ones used by Riggs et al. (1998). Such proposals will no doubt generate further research into the reasoning used by children when they are faced with a false-belief task. An improved understanding of the reasoning necessary for successful performance will be important in identifying how much false-belief tasks reflect children's developing appreciation of others' minds and how much they reflect the development of abilities like counterfactual reasoning.

Do Children with Autism Lack an Understanding of Other's Minds?

Autism was first described by Kanner (1943) and Asperger (1944) who both (independently) used the term 'autism' to label a disorder that they described in children who usually, but not always had a low IQ. Kanner described two main features in the children he saw. One is 'autistic aloneness' which referred to children's inability to relate to others – for example, they make little physical contact with parents, make little eye contact, prefer to be alone, and prefer playing with objects to playing with people. The second feature is a 'desire for sameness', because children often become very upset by changes in their surroundings or routine (for example, they may insist on always having the same furniture arrangement in a room, or want the same food at every meal).

Kanner also discussed several secondary features in the children he examined. These include difficulties with language; children with autism might have a good vocabulary, but may use language without meaning, may use correct language but in inappropriate contexts, and may demonstrate 'echolalia' (repeating what another speaker has just said). Children with autism also lack spontaneous activities, they have repetitious behaviours, restricted interests, and sometimes have an obsessive interest in what most people might think are obscure activities. They may also be oversensitive to particular stimuli, reacting excessively to noises or to particular objects.

Contemporary diagnosis of people with autism is based on the criteria described in DSM-IV (the *Diagnostic and Statistical Manual of Mental Disorders, fourth edition*, of the American Psychiatric Association, 1994). For a discussion of the DSM criteria and other terms and definitions used in the literature on autism see Baron-Cohen et al. (2000). The DSM criteria include three fundamental impairments:

1   qualitative impairments in social interaction (e.g., impairment of nonverbal behaviours such as a lack of eye-to-eye contact, or a failure to develop peer relations);
2   qualitative impairments in communication (e.g., delay in the development of language, or a lack of varied, spontaneous make-believe play); and
3   restricted repetitive and stereotyped patterns of behaviour, interests and activities (e.g., an inflexible adherence to specific routines and rituals that have no practical function).

One other feature of autism is that people often show 'islets of ability', this means that in contrast with their generally poor performance in most areas, they may be as good if not better than typically developing people on specific tasks. For example, people with autism often have good rote memory and good perform-ance on some spatial tasks (like finding a hidden shape in a complex pattern).

Autism affects about four or five people in 10,000, and although all people who are diagnosed as having autism will have the impairments we described above, they may have them to a greater or lesser degree. Some people with autism may have very severe learning difficulties, but others, who may have average levels of intelligence might be able to function with some independence.

The challenge for any researcher investigating autism, is to explain how one syndrome can lead to the specific combination of impairments which typify a person with autism (lack of socialization, communication and imagination); how different people with autism can be affected in markedly different ways, and how it is that people with autism can sometimes have better than average abilities in one or two areas (the 'islets of ability').

Several theories have been put forward to explain autism (see Frith, 1989; Happé, 1994) but most of these theories have only explained a small part of the pattern of impairments that are seen in people with autism. Then researchers began to consider whether people with autism had an understanding of minds, using the same types of experiment that had been used to investigate typically developing children's understanding. Baron-Cohen et al. (1985) were the first to do this using the Sally-Anne false-belief task. They tested children with autism who had a mental age of over four years – because it is about this age that typi-cally developing children succeed on false-belief tasks. They also tested a group of typically developing children aged four years and a group of children with Down's syndrome with a mental age of four years or more. (For an explanation of the need for matched groups in experiments that include children with autism, see box 14.2.)

Baron-Cohen et al. (1985) found that more than 80 per cent of the typically developing children and the children with Down's syndrome succeeded on the Sally-Anne task, but only 20 per cent of the children with autism were successful. Failure on the task was unlikely to be due to learning difficulties in general (otherwise the children with Down's syndrome would have failed as well), but it seemed to be specific to the group with autism. Perner et al. (1989) also tested chil-dren with autism using the Smarties false-belief task with similar results – most of the children failed the task.

Children with autism also have difficulty in other tasks that require an appre-ciation of another's false belief. Baron-Cohen et al. (1986) showed children with autism sets of four pictures each of which made a story (see figure 14.3). One type of story was called a 'mechanical' story because the action in the story did not involve any people:

- Picture 1: shows a balloon leaving a person's hand;
- Picture 2: the balloon in the air;
- Picture 3: the balloon near a tree;
- Picture 4: the balloon bursts on the tree.

Another type was called 'behavioural' stories because they included people but did not require any understanding of what the people were thinking:

A mechanical story

A behavioural story

A mentalistic story

Figure 14.3   Examples of pictures from Baron-Cohen et al. (1986) experiment.

- Picture 1: shows a girl walking in a street;
- Picture 2: the girl goes into a sweet shop;
- Picture 3: the girl buys sweets at the counter;
- Picture 4: the girl leaves the shop with the bag of sweets.

The third type of story required an understanding of the beliefs about the characters in the pictures:

- Picture 1: shows a boy putting a sweet into a box;
- Picture 2: the boy leaves the room, to play soccer outside;
- Picture 3: mother takes the sweet out of the box and eats it;
- Picture 4: the boy comes back to the box and looks surprised.

The children were given the pictures in a mixed up order, and were asked to put them in an appropriate sequence, and they were asked to explain what was happening in the story. The children with autism were able to order and describe the events in both the mechanical and the behavioural stories, but they were poor at understanding the mentalistic stories – they put the pictures in a jumbled order and only reported what they could see in them. They did not refer to the 'mentalistic' aspect of the story (for example in the story about the boy and the chocolate, they could not explain why the boy was surprised when he found that the box was empty).

We said earlier that having an understanding of another person's mind is essential if you want to deceive them by giving them a false belief. If children with autism have difficulty understanding other people's minds how well can they deceive others? This was examined by Sodian and Frith (1992) who showed children a closed box that contained a sweet, and the children were told about a robber puppet (who would take the sweet). They were also told that the robber was lazy and would not try to open the box if it was locked. In the 'sabotage' condition of the experiment children had a key and could decide whether to leave the box unlocked or to lock it when they were told that the robber was coming. In the 'deception' condition children did not have a key and therefore could not lock the box, but before the robber reached the box he asked the child whether the box was open or locked (and therefore the children could deceive him by saying that the box was locked).

In the sabotage condition the children were, in effect, manipulating the robber's *behaviour* (by locking the box so that he could not look in it). In the deception condition they were manipulating the robber's *beliefs* (by telling him that the box was locked). Children with autism were successful in the sabotage condition, but failed to think of ways to deceive the robber in the other condition. Even though they understood the task and were motivated to stop the robber getting the sweet (as demonstrated by their success in the sabotage condition) they were unable to manipulate the robber's belief in the deception condition. This again demonstrated the difficulty children with autism have in a task that depends on understanding the mind of someone else.

These studies have shown that children with autism have difficulty in tasks that involve mental representations. But is this difficulty specific to understanding mental representations or do children with autism have a difficulty understanding all types of representations? There are several 'non-mental' representations of the world: maps represent the landscape; drawings and photographs represent scenes in the world. As we pointed out before, all these represent the world in a (single) specific way, and they may often no longer portray the world in its current state. For example, a map of a city might have been an accurate representation of that city when it was drawn, but if several buildings are pulled down the map is then a 'false' representation of the world. If children with autism have a general difficulty with representations then it might be predicted that they would have difficulty understanding the nature of pictures, photographs and other such representations.

Leslie and Thaiss (1992) investigated this issue. They tested typically developing children and children with autism using a false-belief task (a test of understanding a mental representation) and a 'false' photograph task (a test of understanding a non-mental representation). Leslie and Thaiss's procedure and findings are described in box 14.2, and it was clear that although the children with autism performed poorly in the false-belief task, they performed very well in the 'false' photograph task. This suggests that children with autism have a specific deficit in understanding *mental* representations.

How Far can a Deficit in Understanding Mental Representations Contribute to an Explanation of Autism?

One problem for any explanation of autism based on children's lack of understanding of mental representations, is the fact that in most studies a proportion of children with autism succeed on false-belief tasks (e.g., in Baron-Cohen et al., 1985; in Leslie and Thaiss, 1992 – see box 14.2). As Charman (2000) has emphasized, if a failure to understand minds is not a universal deficit in autism any explanation based on understanding minds is very much weakened.

However, even though some people with autism can pass a first order false-belief task like the Sally-Anne task, when the same people are given a second order false-belief task, like John and Mary in the park (see p. 469) they rarely succeed (Baron-Cohen, 1989). It seems that some people with autism may be able to pass first order tasks but the fact that they fail second order tasks, suggests that they do not have a secure understanding of other's minds. It could be that people with autism may succeed on first order tasks using strategies that do not necessarily include an understanding of mental representation (see Happé, 1994).

If people with autism do not have an understanding of minds, does this explain the impairments seen in autism? Major social impairments might be expected in anyone who does not realize that other people have thoughts and beliefs about the world, and that their behaviour is based on those beliefs. A failure to understand that people have independent beliefs, and a failure to appreciate that people's beliefs may not coincide with reality must make it very difficult to interpret why other people act as they do, and this will limit effective social understanding. It will also make it difficult to communicate, because people with autism will not realize that what a speaker says is a statement based on the speaker's thoughts, and requires interpretation. Being unable to interpret what people do and what they say, may lead to a world in which many things appear to be, at best puzzling and confusing, and at worst, arbitrary and disturbing. In such a world it would not be surprising if people with autism insist on sameness and routine, because at least in this way, some sense of consistency and predictability might be maintained.

The finding that people with autism have a deficit in understanding of minds has been a major discovery. It has led to the recognition of many, previously unrecognized, aspects of the autistic syndrome, it has stimulated much new and original research into autism, and it goes part of the way to explaining some of the impairments, especially social ones, that typify autism. However, a deficit in understanding minds does not help us to understand all the impairments associated with autism. For example, it is not obvious how specific language problems (e.g., echolalia), obsessive behaviours, or 'islets of ability' could be linked to a lack of understanding minds.

Other hypotheses have also been put forward to explain the difficulty that people with autism have in tasks like the false-belief task. Hughes and Russell (1993) suggested that people with autism are unable to 'disengage from an object'. They argued that when children with autism fail false-belief tasks like the Sally-Anne task and say that Sally will look for her marble in the box (where the marble actually is, even though Sally does not know that) the children do so because they are unable to overcome the salience of knowing that the marble *is* in the box. The salience of the fact that the marble is in the box overwhelms children's ability to ignore the marble's actual position and consider where it was before (in Sally's basket). If this interpretation is correct then children with autism do not fail the Sally-Anne task because they do not understand Sally's mind, rather they fail because they cannot ignore the information they have about the marble's position. To demonstrate this possibility Hughes and Russell used what they called a 'windows task'.

In the windows task children were shown two boxes, and each box had a window in one side so that the children could see inside. One box had a sweet in it and the other box was empty. Children were told that if they pointed to the *empty* box they would win the sweet. They were then given twenty trials. Children with autism were poor at this task, and half the children persisted in pointing to the box with the sweet on every trial (and therefore they never received a sweet at all). Hughes and Russell (1993) argued that the children were unable to ignore the presence of the sweet and could not inhibit themselves pointing to it, even though they 'lost' the sweet every time.

Hughes and Russell's (1993) results support the hypothesis that children with autism are unable to disengage from an object. However, this is not the case in all tasks. For example, in the photograph task used by Leslie and Thaiss (1992) – see box 14.2, children watched as a photograph was taken of Polly the horse sitting on a box. Then Polly was moved and a toy mouse was placed on the box. The children were asked who was sitting on the box in the photograph. Even though the children with autism could see the mouse on the box in front of them, they all correctly realized that the photograph showed Polly. In other words, they were capable of ignoring the scene they could see – they did not say that the photograph showed the mouse on the box, and this result does not support the hypothesis that children are 'unable to disengage from the object' as Hughes and Russell suggested.

Unlike Hughes and Russell (1993) other researchers accept that the poor performance of children with autism on false-belief tasks does reflect a deficit in their understanding of mind, but do not accept that this is a core impairment in autism. Baron-Cohen (1995) has suggested a more fundamental deficit. He described a 'shared attention mechanism', which combines information about your own direction of gaze and another person's direction of gaze. This includes information like: I see that X sees the object; X sees that I see the object. For example: I see that Mummy sees a toy; Mummy sees that I see the toy. Baron-Cohen suggested that the shared attention mechanism allows a child to work out whether she and someone else are both looking at the same thing. Such a mechanism would also mean that a child could understand the perceptual mental state of another person (i.e., that Mummy sees the toy). More than this, a child may also be able to interpret another's look in terms of desire – for example, young typically developing children know that if someone is looking at one of four blocks of chocolate that she wants that particular block (Baron-Cohen et al., 1995). Baron-Cohen argued that from an early understanding about gaze a young typically developing child can gain insights into another's mental state, and that these insights are the foundation for children's later understanding of mind. Baron-Cohen et al. (1995) found that in contrast to typically developing children, when children with autism saw someone looking at one of four blocks of chocolate they did not realize that it was that block that the person wanted.

In an extensive study, Baron-Cohen et al. (1996) screened 16,000 infants at the age of 18 months using five tests, including a test of shared attention. Only 12 children failed all five tests. When these children were followed up at 42 months of age, nearly all of them had been diagnosed with autism. This implies that lack of shared attention is one of the early deficits in autism and Baron-Cohen (1995) argued that the lack of a shared attention mechanism in children with autism could explain the later deficit in their understanding of mind.

The research into how children develop an understanding of another person's mind has became a large and important area of developmental research. The discovery that typically developing three-year-olds have difficulty understanding the concept of mind has stimulated many new studies, and has led to the generation of radical new theories about early cognitive development. The equally important discovery that many children with autism lack insight into others' minds has provoked many new directions of research into autism and stimulated a new look at the causes and development of autism (Charman, 2000).

Further Reading

For a very good description of the empirical research into children's understanding of mind, see Mitchell, P. 1997: *Introduction to Theory of Mind*. London: Arnold. This book covers the research with non-human species and has sections on autism, and on deceptive behaviour. Despite the title, it goes beyond just an introduction, and is a very clearly written summary of the empirical research. A more advanced book that goes into more detail about the different theoretical approaches in this area is Mitchell, P. 1996: *Acquiring a Conception of Mind. A Review of Psychological Research and Theory*. Hove: Erlbaum.

Bartsch, K. and Wellman, H. M. 1995: *Children Talk About the Mind*. Oxford: Oxford University Press. Focuses on evidence drawn from an analysis of children's early talk and conversation, and the implications of this evidence for understanding the development of theory of mind. The book includes references to and a good discussion of other theories and approaches to the study of theory of mind. Mitchell, P. and Riggs, K. (eds) 2000: *Children's Reasoning and the Mind*. Hove, East Sussex: Psychology Press is quite an advanced book, but one that includes chapters by many of the most influential researchers in the field of theory of mind. The book therefore provides an insight into many of the contemporary controversies about the development of theory of mind.

Frith, U. 1989: *Autism. Explaining the Enigma*. Oxford: Blackwell is a good readable introduction to autism, which provides a vivid description of the impairment, but some parts of the book are slightly dated. For a more recent discussion of autism, Happé, F. 1994: *Autism. An Introduction to Psychological Theory*. London: University College London Press gives a good assessment of the contribution that theory of mind research has made in the understanding of autism, with summaries of other theories as well.

■ Discussion Points

1 Why are false belief tasks important?
2 Are false belief tasks a valid way to measure children's understanding of other people's minds?
3 Is children's achievement of theory of mind a major cognitive change, which occurs during a brief period of time, or is it a gradual development over several years?
4 How much has the research into children's theory of mind contributed to an understanding of autism?
5 Compare the way that understanding the mind has been investigated in children with the way that it has been investigated in non-human primates (see chapter 2).

Box 14.1
Beliefs about beliefs: representations and constraining function of wrong beliefs in young children's understanding of deception

Wimmer and Perner carried out the first investigation of children's understanding of false belief. In their study children heard a story about a boy (Maxi) who was looking for some chocolate. The children knew where the chocolate actually was, but they were told that Maxi thought the chocolate was in another place. The children were asked to predict where Maxi would look for the chocolate, and the key aspect of the experiment was whether children would predict that Maxi would look for the chocolate where they knew it was or where he thought it was. Of course, this is not a difficult task for most adults who reason that

Maxi can only look for the chocolate in the place where he believes it to be (i.e., that people's behaviour is based on what they believe about the world rather than how the world really is). Wimmer and Perner wanted to find out if children would also reason in the same way. They tested three groups of 12 children, aged four, six and eight years, in Austria.

The children were told a story that was also acted out in front of them with three differently coloured matchboxes that were glued high up on a model wall, and paper cut outs for the characters. The story was given in two versions. One was called the cooperative story (because one character offers to help Maxi find the chocolate) and one was called the competitive version, because another character may take the chocolate from Maxi.

The story was as follows (taken from Wimmer and Perner, 1983, where it was translated into English):

Mother returns from her shopping trip. She brought chocolate for a cake. Maxi may help her put away the things. He asks her: 'Where should I put the chocolate?' 'In the blue cupboard' says the mother.

'Wait I'll lift you up there, because you are too small.'

Mother lifts him up. Maxi puts the chocolate into the blue cupboard. [A toy chocolate is put into the blue matchbox]. Maxi remembers exactly where he put the chocolate so that he could come back and get some later. He loves chocolate. Then he leaves for the playground. [The boy doll is removed.] Mother starts to prepare the cake and takes the chocolate out of the blue cupboard. She grates a bit into the dough and then she does *not* put it back into the *blue but* into the *green* cupboard. [Toy chocolate is thereby transferred from the blue to the green matchbox.] Now she realizes that she forgot to buy eggs. So she goes to her neighbour for some eggs. There comes Maxi back from the playground, hungry, and he wants to get some chocolate. [Boy doll reappears.] He still remembers where he had put the chocolate.

Children were then asked the 'belief' question: 'Where will Maxi look for the chocolate?' and had to indicate one of the three matchboxes. Then in the cooperative story children were told: 'OK, there he'll look, but he is too small to reach up there. There comes Grandpa and Maxi says: dear

Grandpa, please could you help me get the chocolate from the cupboard?' Grandpa asks 'Which cupboard?'

The children were then asked the 'utterance' question: 'Where will Maxi say the chocolate is?' and had to indicate one of the matchboxes.

In the competitive story children were told: 'However, before Maxi gets a chance to get at the chocolate his big brother comes into the kitchen. He, too, is looking for the chocolate. He asks Maxi where the chocolate is. 'Good grief', thinks Maxi, 'now big brother wants to eat up all the chocolate. I will tell him something completely wrong so that he won't find it, for sure'.

As with the cooperative story the children were then asked an 'utterance' question: 'Where will Maxi say the chocolate is?' and had to indicate one of the matchboxes.

Then, to make sure that the children had paid attention to the story, the children were asked two questions. First, to check that they had not forgotten where the chocolate actually was, they were asked the 'reality' question: 'Where is the chocolate really?' Second, to check that they also remembered where the chocolate had been put, they were asked the 'memory' question: 'Do you remember where Maxi put the chocolate in the beginning?'

There was also a second story, with the same structure as this one, but it was set in a nursery school room where a little girl hid her favourite book. While she was out of the room the caretaker moved it to a different place. In the cooperative version, when the girl came back into the room, she offered to show the book to her friend. In the other version another child was competing for the book and the girl tried to mislead him. The questions paralleled the ones in the Maxi story.

Each child heard both stories and box table 14.1.1 shows the number of children giving correct answers to the belief question 'Where will Maxi look for the chocolate?' (or 'Where will the little girl look for the book?').

Box Table 14.1.1 Number of children giving correct answers to the belief questions in Wimmer and Perner's first experiment

	Number of correct answers		
Age	2	1	0
4 years	4	2	6
6 years	11	0	1
8 years	11	1	0

The children could have been correct for both stories, for one, or for neither.

As shown in the table, the two older age groups were successful, but the four-year-olds did comparatively poorly. It was important to be sure that the younger children's poor performance was not just due to them forgetting information from the story. When Wimmer and Perner examined the children who gave incorrect answers to the belief question they found that 100 per cent gave correct responses to the reality question and 80 per cent gave correct responses to the memory question. In other words, all the children had paid attention to the stories and remembered the details. Therefore, the four-year-olds' poor performance was not likely to be due to task factors, it was more likely that they only had a limited understanding that Maxi might hold an incorrect belief about the location of the chocolate.

Of the children who were correct on the belief question (predicting where Maxi would look for the chocolate, or where the girl would look for the book) in the cooperative versions, 85 per cent gave appropriate answers to the utterance question (e.g., they said that Maxi would tell Grandpa that the chocolate was in the blue cupboard). Similarly, of the children who were correct on the belief question in the competitive versions, 82 per cent gave an appropriate answer to the utterance question (e.g., they said that Maxi would tell his brother that the chocolate was not in the blue cupboard, but in one of the others).

Children who were incorrect on the belief question (and said that Maxi would look for the chocolate in the green cupboard) tended to indicate the green cupboard in response to the utterance questions. For example, in the cooperative version they said that Maxi would tell Grandpa that the chocolate was where it actually was; and in the competitive version they also said that Maxi would tell his brother where the chocolate really was. These responses were inappropriate given Maxi's false belief, and even if these children thought that Maxi would know that the chocolate was in the green cupboard, it was rather ineffective for him to tell his brother where he thought the chocolate was if he wanted to stop his brother getting it. In other words, these children did not seem to understand how to deceive the brother.

Wimmer and Perner went on to rule out some of the possible reasons why the youngest children gave inappropriate replies to the belief question. They thought that because the children had seen the toy chocolate put in the green box and it was still there when they were asked the questions, the knowledge of where the chocolate was may have encouraged inappropriate responses from the four-year-olds. One possibility was that the four-year-olds were responding without much reflection and simply pointing to where they knew the chocolate was. Wimmer and Perner also suggested another possibility – that Maxi's belief, 'the chocolate is in the blue cupboard' might have been overridden by the child's own, similar, knowledge that 'the chocolate is in the green cupboard', and that this effect was less likely to apply to the

Box Table 14.1.2 Number of children in each condition answering the belief questions correctly in Wimmer and Perner's second experiment

			Number correct		
Age	Condition	No. of children	2	1	0
3 years	2. Stop and think displaced	10	0	0	10
	3. Disappear	10	0	3	7
4 years	1. Displaced	14	6	1	7
	2. Stop and think displaced	14	4	2	8
	3. Disappear	14	11	0	3
5 years	1. Displaced	10	5	0	5
	2. Stop and think displaced	10	10	0	0
	3. Disappear	10	10	0	0

older children. (For similar arguments about the dominance of knowledge in false belief tasks, see Hughes and Russell (1993), discussed in this chapter.)

Therefore, in a second experiment, Wimmer and Perner introduced two new conditions (as well as the one they had used in the first experiment). Hence there were three conditions:

1 Displaced condition – this was the same as in the first experiment – children saw the chocolate moved from the blue to the green cupboard.
2 Stop and think displaced condition – to reduce the possibility of unconsidered responses the children were told, before the belief question, to pause and think carefully before they answered.
3 Disappear condition – the children were told that the chocolate was all used up in the baking (in other words, it no longer existed in any cupboard).

Both the chocolate story and the book story were modified as necessary. Wimmer and Perner tested 20 three-year-olds, 42 four-year-olds and 30 five-year-olds. Box table 14.1.2 shows the number of children in each condition answering the belief question correctly (as there were two stories children could have been right on both, one or neither). Wimmer and Perner did not report any results for three-year olds in the dis-

placed condition and presumably they did not test such young children in this condition on the assumption that they were unlikely to succeed if most of the four-year-olds in the first experiment had failed in this condition.

As can be seen in the table, five-year-olds were always correct in conditions two and three, though they were poorer in the original task. Four-year-olds also did well in condition three. In other words, the older children in this experiment performed best in the disappear condition, and this was support for Wimmer and Perner's suggestion that some of the four-year-olds in the first experiment may have had difficulty because of the continuing presence of the chocolate. However, the three-year-olds performed poorly irrespective of condition and there was no evidence that this age group could appreciate Maxi's false belief. Most of these children gave no response at all to the belief question (or because they had seen the experimenter remove the toy chocolate in the course of telling the story, they suggested that Maxi would look behind the model for it!).

Taken together these experiments demonstrated that young children had difficulty ascribing a false belief to another person. In particular, three-year-olds were unable to appreciate Maxi's false belief even in the 'Disappear' condition of the second experiment, when there was little direct conflict between Maxi's belief (chocolate in cupboard) and their own knowledge (chocolate disappeared).

Wimmer and Perner's experiment has been criticized because of the length of the story, and the amount of information children had to remember to understand it. Although four-year-olds performed poorly in Wimmer and Perner's first experiment other researchers have shown that when the task is presented in the context of a briefer story (as in the Sally-Anne task described on p. 462) four year olds can give appropriate answers to belief questions.

Based on material in Wimmer, H. and Perner, J. 1983: Beliefs about beliefs: representations and constraining function of wrong beliefs in young children's understanding of deception. *Cognition*, 13, 103–28.

Box 14.2
Domain specificity in conceptual development: neuropsychological evidence from autism

Several experiments had shown that people with autism often have difficulty appreciating that other people behave on the basis of their beliefs about the world (Baron-Cohen et al., 1985; Perner et al., 1989). A belief about the world is usually referred to as a representation, and we all have a mental representation of the world derived from our knowledge and experience of the world. Most adults also realize that other people may have different representations from our own, and that both ourselves and other people may have a representation of the world which is inaccurate, but this realization often seems to be lacking in people with autism.

Leslie and Thaiss pointed out that as well as mental representations there are other types of representations (pictures, photographs, maps and so on). If children with autism are impaired in their understanding of mental representations are they also impaired in understanding other forms of representation?

In any experiment with people with learning difficulties it is very important to find an appropriate control group. If, for example, children with autism aged 12 years were compared with typically developing children aged 12 years, it is likely that on almost any cognitive measure the typically developing children would perform better than the children with autism, because the typically developing children would have a mental age which was approximately the same as their chronological age, but the children with autism would have a much lower mental age. Discovering that a group of children with a typically developing mental age performed better than a group of children with a comparatively low mental age would not be very surprising or informative.

Therefore, to measure the abilities of children with autism, it is usual to compare them to other children who have the same mental age (but who do not have the diagnosis of autism). For example, if a group of children with autism who have a mental age of six years are compared to a group of typically developing children who also have a mental age of six years, and the children with autism perform less well than the typically developing children on a task, it can be assumed that their poorer performance is due to their autism.

Box Table 14.2.1   Mean ages and age ranges of children in Leslie and Thaiss's (1992) experiment

	Chronological age	Mental age
children with autism	Mean 12:0 Range 7:10–18:7	Mean 6:3 Range 4:4–14:5
typically developing children	Mean 4:0 Range 3:8–4:5	Mean 4:5 Range 2:6–7:3

However, in such an experiment it would be likely that the chronological age of the typically developing children would be about six years of age, but the children with autism might (say) have a chronological age of twelve years. In other words, there may be a large difference in the actual age, and therefore the experience of the two groups. To overcome this, some researchers have compared children with autism with children with other learning difficulties. For example, researchers might find a group of children with autism with an average chronological age of 12 years and an average mental age of six years, and a group of children with learning difficulties who also have an average chronological age of 12 years and an average mental age of six years. If both groups carried out the same test, and the children with autism perform less well then the children with learning difficulties it can be inferred that the deficit in the performance of the children with autism was due to some factor associated with autism, because other factors like chronological and mental age were the same for both groups.

Leslie and Frith compared 15 children with autism with 20 typically developing children who had a similar average mental age. The details of the children are given in box table 14.2.1.

All the children were given two tasks. In one task the children's understanding of mental representations was tested by asking them about a false belief. In the other task the children's understanding of a non-mental representation (a photograph) was

tested by asking them about the content of the photograph.

The false-belief task was based on the Smarties task (see pp. 462–4). The children were shown a Smarties box and asked what it contained. All the children said 'Smarties'. The top was then removed and the child was shown that the box actually contained a pencil. The pencil was then replaced in the box and the top put back. The child was then asked 'Now [name of child's friend] has not seen this box before. When I show this box to [name of friend] before I take the top off – what will [name of friend] say is in here?

The children were also asked a 'reality' question: 'What is really in here?' to check that they remembered what was actually in the box.

The photograph task involved a story about three puppets and a toy box. A cat puppet took a photograph of Polly the horse puppet while Polly was sitting on the toy-box. After the photograph was taken it was placed face down (without the child seeing it). Then Polly was moved from the toy box and a mouse puppet was put in Polly's place. The child was then asked the photograph question: 'In the photograph who is sitting on the toy-box?'

The child was also asked a 'memory' question; 'Who was sitting on the toy-box when the cat took the photograph?' and a 'reality' question: 'Who is sitting on the toy-box now?' to check that they had remembered all the story details.

Four of the children with autism and three of the typically developing children failed

Box Table 14.2.2   Percentage of children in each age group who were correct in the false belief and photograph tasks (from Leslie and Thaiss, 1992)

	False belief task (%)	Photograph task (%)
Children with autism	33	100
Typically developing children	75	66

one or both of the memory and reality questions and they were excluded from the analysis.

Box table 14.2.2 shows the percentage of children in each group who gave a correct answer to the belief question in the Smarties task, and the percentage who gave a correct answer to the photograph question.

There was a significant interaction in the performance of the children (p < 0.001). As can be seen in the table, the typically developing children performed similarly on both the false-belief and the photograph task. In contrast, the children with autism performed poorly in the false-belief task and were all correct in the photograph task. Their poor performance in the false-belief task (a task that required an appreciation of someone else's mental representation) is typical of the findings from other researchers (see this chapter).

However, the children with autism had no difficulty in the photograph task. This means that any impairment that children with autism have in understanding representations does not extend to non-mental representations like photographs. In a second experiment Leslie and Thaiss carried out a similar study, but instead of showing children a photograph they showed them a map of a model room (and a sticker on the map marked the position of a puppet character who later moved). The children were then asked where the character was sitting 'in the map' to test whether they realized that the map did not change even though the character had moved. As in the photograph task, the children with autism were much better in the map task than in a false-belief task.

This experiment by Leslie and Thaiss (and similar studies with photographs by Leekam and Perner, 1991, and with drawings by Charman and Baron-Cohen, 1992), demonstrated that although children with autism have an impaired understanding of mental representations, they are not impaired in understanding non-mental representations, such as photographs and maps.

Based on material in Leslie, A. M. and Thaiss, L. 1992: Domain specificity in conceptual development: neuropsychological evidence from autism. *Cognition*, 43, 225–51.

15 Learning in a Social Context

We saw in chapter 12 Piaget's account of how children develop as thinkers and learners. Essentially the Piagetian model shows us children as individual 'scientists' who formulate and test increasingly complex hypotheses about their world and about their own experiences and interactions. By and large, it is the inanimate world of objects to which Piagetian psychologists have paid most attention. But developmental psychologists have also explored the idea of the child as someone who negotiates meaning and understanding in a *social* context. Margaret Donaldson and her colleagues, for example, have demonstrated young children's competence at taking the perspective of another person in tasks that are socially meaningful to them (chapter 12). Developmental psychologists are also increasingly interested in the critical role that language plays in enabling children to enter into their culture (chapter 11). The child develops repertoires of shared meanings even before the emergence of language, starting with such phenomena as 'joint attention' (p. 376). But with language the child gains a much more powerful entry point into the images, metaphors and ways of interpreting events which are distinctive in her own culture. The point is that these are social representations that give to the child a framework for constructing knowledge.

The Challenge of Vygotsky

A major challenge to Piaget's theory comes from this more recent emphasis, within the field of developmental psychology, on the intricate and reciprocal relationship between the individual person and the social context. One influential strand in this shift of perspective comes from Russian psychologists; in particular from the writings of Vygotsky (1896–1934), whose work was unknown in the West until it began to be translated in the 1960s and 1970s. By the end of the twentieth century,

Plate 15.1 L. S. Vygotsky.

he was increasingly cited in the literature; there were several new translations of his work and biographies written of his life. In the twenty-first century, his ideas continue to influence a growing number of empirical and theoretical studies, and are currently viewed as highly relevant to applied fields such as education.

Vygotsky (plate 15.1) created an ambitious model of cognition with a sociohistoric approach at its centre. He came from a Jewish family; his father was a bank official; and he was a brilliant student of law, literature and cultural studies at the University of Moscow, and at Shaniavskii People's University (an unofficial university that appeared in Moscow when the authorities expelled staff and students from Moscow University on suspicion of being involved in anti-tsarist activities).

Like Piaget, he saw the child as an active constructor of knowledge and understanding. But he differed from Piaget in his emphasis on the role of direct intervention by more knowledgeable others in this learning process. Vygotsky argued that it is as a result of the social interactions between the growing child and other members of that child's community that the child acquires the 'tools' of thinking and learning. In fact, it is out of this cooperative process of engaging in mutual activities with more expert others that the child becomes more knowledgeable. Instruction, according to Vygotsky, is at the heart of learning.

During his short life, despite poor health, he worked intensely and productively. Yet much of his work was censored or simply hidden by his colleagues out of fear. *The Psychology of Art*, which led to the award of his Ph.D. in 1925, was not published even in Russian until 1965; *Thought and Language*, his best-known work, was first published in 1934 but was suppressed by the Stalinist authorities in 1936 and did not reappear until 1956.

Vygotsky's colleagues have been unforthcoming about his path through the stormy years of the Russian Revolution, but we have to remember how dangerous it was for social scientists during the Stalinist era to express views that did not conform to party doctrine. In the 1930s many eminent scholars and intellectuals were arrested, imprisoned or deported for their ideas. The very fact that Vygotsky had visited several European countries during the 1920s was sufficient grounds for suspicion, and we do know that for a period Vygotsky was disgraced for his part in Luria's research into the changing mentality of peasant farmers as they experienced collectivization. He and his colleagues worked constantly under this threat.

During this period, a reductionist model of mind predominated in Russia, as it did in the USA, and was derived from a distorted interpretation of the physiologist Pavlov's work (which Pavlov himself never endorsed). This was that higher mental processes, such as reasoning, and even consciousness itself, could be accounted for within the conditioned reflex approach. Vygotsky distanced himself from this dominant view:

> A human being is not at all a skin sack filled with reflexes, and the brain is not a hotel for a series of conditioned reflexes accidentally stopping in. (Vygotsky, quoted in Joravsky, 1989, p. 260)

By contrast, he argued that consciousness is central to the science of mind and that human beings are subject to 'dialectical interplay' between biological and cultural factors.

Vygotsky's psychology was consistent with Marxism, but it was far more sophisticated than the psychology favoured by Stalinist party ideologists. He had to tread a minefield and, for the most part, managed to avoid head-on conflict with the authorities while stating his own views with integrity:

> Our science will become Marxist to the degree that it will become true, scientific; and we will work precisely on that, its transformation into a true science, not on its agreement with Marx's theory. (Vygotsky, quoted in Joravsky, 1989, p. 264)

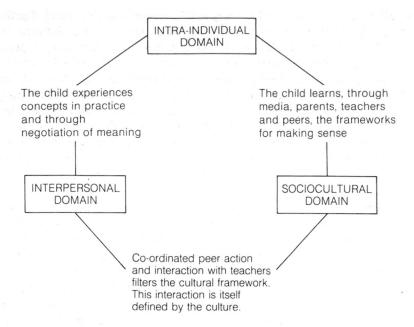

Figure 15.1   A model for the relationship between the intra-individual, interpersonal and social domains (adapted from Haste, 1987).

It says a great deal for him that he was able to separate himself from the Stalinist pressure to reject 'bourgeois' aspects of science and to address himself to the study of the self-directed, conscious mind.

Individual Mental Functioning: its Sociocultural Origins

From Vygotsky's perspective, we can only understand mental functioning in the individual if we take account of the social processes on which it is based:

> Children solve practical tasks with the help of their speech, as well as with their eyes and hands. This unity of perception, speech and action . . . constitutes the central subject matter for any analysis of the origins of uniquely human forms of behaviour. (Vygotsky, 1978, p. 26)

Vygotsky placed a greater emphasis on language than Piaget, but in addition he stressed that this process must also be seen in the context of the person's culture, and the tools and aids that exist in that culture.

The interactions between the individual child, the significant people in her immediate environment, and her culture can be represented diagrammatically (figure 15.1). From this diagram we can see that Vygotsky saw mental functioning as action, and argued that before this conscious, self-directed control develops, action is the way in which the child responds to the world. Furthermore, it is the action of turning round and reflecting on one's own thoughts, using language, that enables one to see things in a new way. Learning is achieved first through cooperation with others in a whole variety of social settings – with peers, teachers, parents and other people who are significant to the child, and second through the 'symbolic representatives' of the child's culture – through its art and language, through play and songs, through metaphors and models. In this two-way process, the child's development as a learner reflects her cultural experience; in turn, significant cultural experiences become internalized into the structure of the child's intellect. Vygotsky's theory stresses the role of interpersonal processes and the role of society in providing a framework within which the child's construction of meaning develops.

Vygotsky (1981, p. 163) stated that 'social relations or relations among people genetically underlie all higher functions and their relationships.' Wertsch and Tulviste (1996, p. 55), in their commentary on this statement, highlight the originality of Vygotsky's perspective by indicating that, in contemporary Western psychology, the terms 'cognition', 'memory' and 'attention' are automatically assumed to be individual characteristics. We only place them in the social plane by adding markers such as 'socially shared' or 'socially distributed'. Vygotsky was especially interested in the cognitive processes that are directly influenced by the specific culture in which the person happens to exist.

The kinds of changes in activity that could have an impact on higher cognitive processes were documented in an early study by Vygotsky's colleague, A. R. Luria, who investigated the effect of Marxist reforms and the introduction of schooling on the cognitive processes of the peasants of Uzbekistan (Luria, 1979). Luria compared traditional, nonliterate peasants with similar villagers who had experienced a literacy course and who had participated in the new collective farms. One of his experiments was to test his participants' capacity for reasoning by presenting them with problems in logic. He found differences between those who had experienced formal schooling and those who had not. For example, uneducated peasants would respond to logical syllogisms on the basis of their everyday knowledge and not in terms of the logical nature of the problem. When presented with the following syllogism: 'In Siberia all the bears are white; my friend Ivan was in Siberia and saw a bear; what colour was it?' an uneducated peasant would typically reply: 'I have never been to Siberia, so I can't say what colour the bear was; Ivan is your friend, ask him.' Luria concluded that the extensive changes brought about by economic reconstruction of traditional peasant farming methods and formal schooling were paralleled by changes in the ways in which the peasants formed concepts and drew logical conclusions. The implication appeared to be that schooling develops a particular kind of theoretical thinking.

Cole's work with the Kpelle

Influenced by this work, Cole and his colleagues (Cole et al., 1971; Scribner and Cole, 1978) carried out a similar intensive study of the Kpelle of Liberia, a tribal group whose culture is very different from that of Western societies, at a point in their history where economic and educational changes were taking place. However, these researchers came to a more complicated conclusion than Luria. They found that in some domains the adult Kpelle performed less well than Americans, but that in others they were greatly superior. For example, the Kpelle were very good at estimating various amounts of rice; by contrast, they performed less well than Westerners when asked to estimate length. This difference could be explained by the fact that, for the Kpelle, rice farming is central to their culture and so involves a whole network of related activities. They have an elaborate system for measuring rice in its harvested and processed form. As Cole et al. (1971, pp. 36–7) write:

> The rice . . . is measured by the cup, bucket, tin and bag. Rice is normally sold for ten cents a cup, which is the size of two English measuring cups or one pint dry measure. However, the price varies according to the season and the availability of rice. The largest measure for harvested rice is the bag. There are nearly 100 cups of rice in the typical bag in which rice is imported or sold from one part of Liberia to another. This fact is known to the Kpelle, who value a bag of rice at 100 times the going rate per cup.'

Consequently, their ability to estimate quantity is very highly developed. When it comes to measuring length, however, this activity is specific to the task and depends on the object being measured. The Kpelle are not nearly as accurate in doing length measurement, as are Westerners.

Cole gives another example of cultural differences in cognitive ability. The Kpelle had quite complex reasons for preferring to plant their rice on the upland hillsides rather than on more convenient, low-lying swampland, including the taste of the rice, the social cohesion that arises from communal planting activity, the lesser yield from swamps, and their custom of growing other crops (not suited to swamps) within the rice plantations. But when Western agriculturalists for reasons of apparent efficiency tried to persuade them to plant instead in swamplands, the Kpelle did not articulate their objections and often gave the casual observer the impression of being stupid and irrationally recalcitrant.

On the basis of extensive ethnographic observations such as these, Cole and his colleagues concluded that, in order to understand a people, the researcher must consider their social life as a central arena within which much thinking is manifested. Cole drew comparisons with the under-performance of minority groups on standard psychological tests, which, he argued, was the result of situational factors and not the result of deficits. He also suggested that the observations made among the Kpelle could be applied to the problem of subcultural differences in Western societies, in that cultural differences in cognition resided more in the situation to which cognitive processes are applied than in the existence of a process in one cultural group and its absence in another. But he recognized that members of minority cultures were not always able to make appropriate connections between the knowledge of their own culture and the knowledge that is required in a Western classroom. In other words, Cole and his colleagues concluded that cultural variations in logical thinking are the result of differences in the cognitive content brought to the task rather than differences in generalized thinking skills.

Cole's research in the Vygotskian tradition pioneered psychological research into the relationship between culture and learning, and it challenged the widespread view at the time that nonliterate peoples in developing countries were less intelligent than Western people, or that some cultures did not push young people far enough (as, for example, schooling does) so that their cognitive structures operated at a lower level. In particular, this research undermined the view that a psychologist could administer cognitive tests that had been developed in one culture in order to measure the abilities of people in another culture. Within Western societies, this principle has frequently been applied to 'culturally disadvantaged children' (see chapter 17) to explain their relative underachievement in comparison with more privileged groups.

The zone of proximal development (ZPD)

A central concept of Vygotsky's is the zone of proximal development, or ZPD, which provides an explanation for how the child learns with the help of others. The ZPD is the distance between the child's actual developmental level and his or her potential level of development under the guidance of more expert adults or in collaboration with more competent peers. To Vygotsky the child is initiated into the intellectual life of the community and learns by jointly constructing his or her understanding of issues and events in the world. Unlike Piaget, Vygotsky did not wait for the child to be 'ready'. Instead, he argued, children learn from other people who are more knowledgeable (figure 15.2).

How does this 'expert intervention' enable the child to learn? It should be at a level beyond the child's existing developmental level so that it provides some challenge; but not too far ahead, so that it is still comprehensible. This is then within the ZPD and the child can accomplish something he or she could not do alone, and learn from the experience. When the child's level of understanding is deliberately challenged (but not challenged too much), then he or she is more likely to learn new things effectively without experiencing failure. Instruction itself should be geared to the ZPD of the person receiving the instruction (Wertsch and Tulviste, 1996). The intervention is at its most effective when it is contingent upon the child's existing repertoire of skills and knowledge, that is, when it is within the ZPD. However, as we see in the section 'Implications for education' (p. 509), some social contexts are not conducive to learning and may even inhibit it, for example, where the teacher asks too many closed questions or where the child is in a group of domineering or intimidating peers.

The process of collaborating with another person who is more knowledgeable not only gives the child new information about a topic but also confirms those aspects of the issue which the child does understand. This cooperation between the child and more expert others helps the child to move on intellectually (Vygotsky, 1978; Wood, 1998). Child-initiated encounters upon which the teacher can be immediately contingent are difficult to establish and sustain in the classroom. There is less opportunity for exploratory activity in which the teacher can

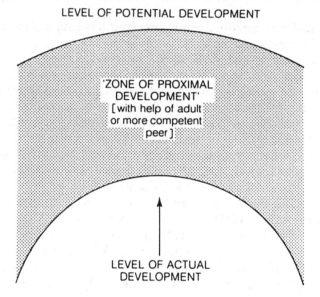

Figure 15.2   Vygotsky's concept of the zone of proximal development (ZPD).

find out the individual child's ZPD. Ideally what the adult seeks to 'show and tell' children should be contingent on what they know already. In sharp contrast to the home, however, teachers are much more likely to control the learners and to ask questions that require a specific answer. Wood (1998) argues that this kind of questioning strategy is counter-productive and all too frequently only serves to highlight children's *lack* of knowledge. So how can the teacher, managing a class of 30 pupils, create conditions in which to become more aware of each child's existing thoughts and tentative ideas on a topic and then respond to them contingently?

Hedegaard's teaching experiment

Hedegaard (1996) describes a teaching experiment based on the methodology developed by Leontiev (1981) and other followers of Vygotsky. From this perspective, the children's understanding grows out of the process of making the shift from *actions*, through *symbolization*, to *formulation*. Action involves direct exploration of the subject through research based on, for example, observation in the field, at the museum or through film. Symbolization is achieved once the children are able to find ways of representing relationships among things that they have observed; this may be done by means of charts, drawings or models of their research findings. Formulation of broader principles comes when the children can clearly state principles that go beyond the specific subjects of their research. At each stage, the concept of the ZPD provides an essential framework for evaluating children's development as thinkers.

Hedegaard's longitudinal study involved teaching a class of Danish children, from third through to fifth grade in elementary school, a method for integrating three distinct but related areas of the curriculum – evolution of species, origin of humans and historical change in societies. In order to achieve this aim, she and the teachers in the project designed carefully structured learning experiences to give the children the 'tools' to tackle questions like: 'How can an animal population adapt to changes in its habitat while many individual animals do not succeed in managing this adaptation and so die?' As an abstract question this would be difficult for elementary-school children to answer. But, claimed Hedegaard, if the problem is presented through the direct study of, say, the polar bear and how it adapts to its Arctic surroundings, children can use this information first to symbolize adaptations of the polar bear and later, on the basis of other similarly concrete studies, to formulate broader laws about survival and change in a whole species. Hedegaard proposed that theoretical knowledge has a 'tool character'; the initial models proposed by the children may become the tools that guide the next stage of the inquiry. By the direct experience of finding contradictions in their active modelling of the problem area under study, pupils' concepts become richer and clearer.

The teachers' method of deliberately working within the ZPD built on shared, concrete activities using whole-class dialogue, cooperative group work and collective problem-solving tasks. At the heart of the method was the tool of research activity, which in turn led to a critical appraisal on the part of the children of the models that they themselves had constructed. These intellectual tools were then applied to other learning situations that the children encountered.

Hedegaard's results demonstrated that teachers could successfully work with the ZPD in a whole-class context. The children developed a qualitative change in their interest in the subject matter and in the methods used to discover new things. They showed loss of interest in specific animals when they became too familiar and shifted instead to an interest in general formulation of models applicable in a more general way to the issue of animals' adaptation to living conditions. They also developed a critical interest in the teaching methods as they related to problem identification and solution. Overall, the children demonstrated a shift in interest from the concrete to an interest in general principles that might, in turn, be applied to new concrete situations. Significantly, she found that fast learners were stimulated by the approach but that the less able children, too, maintained interest and motivation.

Language and Thought

As we have seen, Vygotsky's model proposed not only the idea of an individual functioning in his own immediate social context (for example, in the family or social group) but also the idea that the human mind itself 'extends beyond the skin' (Wertsch and Tulviste, 1996, p. 60) and is inherently social. This view suggests that all human functioning is by its nature sociocultural in the sense that it incorporates socially evolved and socially organized cultural tools, such as language, systems for counting, works of art, diagrams, maps, signs and models.

These systems become part of the shared knowledge of a culture. For example, theoretical knowledge which has become part of everyday knowledge can be seen among young people who know enough about electronics to build themselves a sound system, or who have the mechanical knowledge to repair their motorbikes (Hedegaard, 1996).

This view has strong implications for education and differs quite sharply both from the child-centred model of education, which sprang from Piaget's theory, and from traditional, didactic models of education. From the Vygotskian standpoint children do not operate in isolation but make knowledge their own in a community of others who share a common culture. Language plays a key part in this process. Vygotsky suggested that it was through speech – which had been formed through the processes of social interaction as outlined above – that the child developed as a thinker and learner.

Vygotsky argued that language reflects our culture and its forms, whether in academic texts, professional practice, the arts, folklore or customs. The person as a conscious thoughtful being could accomplish very little without the aids and tools that are provided by his or her history and culture. Piaget had not stressed the importance of language as the principal source of cognitive development. As discussed in chapter 12, he maintained that language was strongly influenced by the underlying cognitive structures in the child. We have already examined one of his major theoretical constructs – egocentrism. Piaget made extensive observations of children at the Rousseau Institute in Geneva and, on that basis, concluded that up to half of the utterances made by children under the age of 7 years are examples of egocentric speech; in other words, they show no sign that the children have attempted to communicate with another person or adapted their speech so that another might understand it. Piaget observed further that young children often did not seem to care whether anyone else could understand them or not. He noticed that young children would often talk at length to themselves while engaged in solitary activity; these monologues were like commentaries on the children's own actions rather than forms of communication. They might also carry out collective monologues where children were close to one another and spoke in pairs or a group, but where the utterances were not made in response to other children's speech.

Piaget interpreted this behaviour as a sign of the child's inability to take account of the perspective of another, and argued that, with maturity, the child comes to decentre and also becomes more logical. She is then able to take the perspective of others and engage in socially meaningful verbal exchanges. This process of decentration, according to Piaget, unfolds between the ages of 4 and 7 (see also chapter 12). By 7 the child's speech would become more fully socialized.

Vygotsky's view was quite different. He did not accept that the young child's language is largely egocentric and that monologues have no part to play in cognitive development. The monologues of younger children were to Vygotsky highly social and represented the transition from language as a tool for regulating action and communicating needs, to language as a tool for thought (see also chapter 11). In fact, he argued that the monologues show children's development in their capacity – already socially formed – to regulate their own activities. The monologues, as a form of communication with the self, help children to plan and

Table 15.1   The contrasting views of Piaget and Vygotsky on preschoolers' private speech

Piaget's model	Vygotsky's model
Repetition: the child merely repeats sounds	*Social dialogue* between adult and child: children and adults engage in joint activities, e.g., peek-a-boo play
Monologue: the child alone speaks to herself as if she were thinking aloud	*Monologues or overt inner speech*: these are internalized to regulate a child's activity, and originate from social dialogues
Collective monologue: the child uses monologue in social settings but does not take the listeners' viewpoint into consideration. True dialogue does not emerge until around age 7	*Inner speech*: utterances internalized in private speech to guide behaviour. Inner speech is internalized by the end of the preschool period

organize their behaviour. Three-year-old Ben, for example, talks to himself as he cuts out a paper figure: 'Now I'm going to make a man. Cut round here. This is his magic wand. He's a wizard now. Oops! Too far. Oh! Start again'.

Vygotsky suggested that monologues become internalized at around 7 years to become inner speech – the dialogue with ourselves in which we all engage – which becomes thought. You may even still experience a tendency to revert to *externalized* monologues when tasks are too challenging, for example, talking yourself through a difficult problem ('Now how do I open this door now that the high-tech new lock has been installed?') or commenting on your lack of expertise ('Stupid! Try turning the key the other way!' or 'I'd better ring the locksmith.')! Vygotsky's and Piaget's contrasting views are summarized in table 15.1.

In Vygotsky's words, language reflects 'the organizing consciousness of the whole culture' (see figure 15.1). He argued that the child's development as a thinker arises both from the dialogue with parents and other adult carers, and in relation to the wider society of which the parents are a part. His perspective encompasses the use of language as a framework for thought and the use of language as a representation of the culture. The two are inextricably intertwined. This is a fundamental point of disagreement between Vygotskian and Piagetian thinking and many developmental psychologists have become increasingly critical of the lack of emphasis on social and cultural context in Piaget's model, with its concentration on the child as an individual progressing through developmental stages. The debate continues in the field of academic developmental psychology but it is of more than academic significance. There are important practical implications for the ways in which we educate and socialize our children.

The Impact of Bruner

Vygotsky's ideas were extensively developed and applied in educational settings by the American psychologist Jerome Bruner (plate 15.2). Vygotsky's *Thought and*

Plate 15.2 Jerome Bruner.

Language was not translated into English until 1962. Bruner (1986, p. 72) describes how he welcomed the invitation to write an introduction to the book and how he read the ongoing translation with 'astonishment'. Vygotsky's ideas on thought and speech as instruments for planning out action were in tune with Bruner's views. He was intrigued by Vygotsky's suggestion that society provides the tools that enable the child to become more advanced as a thinker. Bruner was especially interested in the concept of the ZPD and the role that other people play in helping the child to learn and reflect on things. Bruner called this help 'the loan of consciousness'. However, Vygotsky had not actually spelt out in any detail how the more expert adult might 'lend' consciousness to the child who did not already have it. Bruner and his colleagues proposed the concept of 'scaffolding' (Wood et al., 1976) to refer to the wide range of activities through which the adult, or the more expert peer, assists the learner to achieve goals which would otherwise be beyond them, for example by modelling an action, by suggesting a strategy for solving a problem or by structuring the learning into manageable parts. The metaphor of scaffolding is illuminative. Imagine the tutor has erected scaffolding that could help the child to climb to a higher level of understanding. To be more effective, scaffolding has to be constructed so that the child is not asked to climb too much at once. It has to take account not only of the child's existing level, but of how far she can progress with help; essentially the idea of Vygotsky's ZPD.

Scaffolding in practice

Bruner and his colleagues initiated a number of research studies to investigate the role of scaffolding in learning. For example, Wood et al. (1976) decided to look at what happens when a tutor tries to pass on her knowledge to a child. Scaffolding, they concluded, has distinctive aspects:

- *Recruitment*: The tutor's first task is to engage the interest of the child and encourage the child to tackle the requirements of the task.
- *Reduction of degrees of freedom*: The tutor has to simplify the task by reducing the number of acts needed to arrive at a solution. The learner needs to be able to see whether he has achieved a fit with task requirements or not.
- *Direction maintenance*: The tutor needs to keep the child's motivation up. Initially the child will be looking to the tutor for encouragement; eventually the solution of the problem should become interesting in its own right.
- *Marking critical features*: A tutor highlights features of the task that are relevant. This gives information about any discrepancies between what the child has produced and what he would recognize as a correct production.
- *Demonstration*: Modelling solutions to the task involves completion of a task or explanation of a solution already partly done by the young learner. The aim is that the learner will imitate this back in a better form.

As you can see, scaffolding does not imply a rigid structure or a didactic teaching method but rather a flexible and child-centred strategy, which supports the child in learning new things and which enables the child to have a sounding board for action. As the child becomes more independent in the mastery of a new skill, the adult is able gradually to remove the scaffolding until the child no longer needs it. The idea of scaffolding is, of course, a metaphor, since the more expert adult or peer does not literally build a structure of scaffolding to support the child. Although it evokes a powerful visual image, it is no more than a metaphor and does not in itself explain the processes through which the child internalizes new learning (Daniels, 1996, p. 270). However, the concept of scaffolding has been extremely useful to educators in giving a theoretical justification for methods which structure learning without being unnecessarily didactic, and in exploring the area which covers the distance between learning with adult support and performing without help, that is the ZPD.

Scaffolding appears in a whole variety of forms. It may appear when the parent responds to the child's first attempts at speech (see the section on Adult–Child speech in chapter 11). We might see it when the adult, closely in tune with the child's ongoing monologues, helps to solve a problem. We might see it when the child, frustrated by its inability to convey the excitement of a new experience, is guided by the adult to use appropriate words and images.

Plate 15.3   A child shows her knowledge of the Sun as a sphere; but she still thinks that the Earth is a flat disc beneath it.

Dunn (1984) describes the scaffolding process in operation when mothers structured the feeling states of 2-year-olds, so giving the child a framework for interpreting emotions (see chapter 4). Butterworth's (1987) studies highlight the scaffolding processes at work when the mother builds on the infant's capacity to adjust his or her own line of gaze to that of the mother, by commenting on the object of joint attention; and through the enjoyable experience of turn-taking in ritual language games and rhymes (see chapters 4 and 11).

Vosniadou et al. (2001) indicate that teachers very rarely initiate a discussion of gravity as it relates to children's understanding of the shape of the Earth (plate 15.3). One key problem for children is to understand why people do not fall off the Earth. Instruction based only on the presentation of scientific facts cannot by itself lead to conceptual change if it does not give children all the information they need to counteract their naïve theories. If this is not acknowledged, children will retain inconsistencies in their thinking. Vosniadou et al. (2001) suggest that instead of focusing on misconceptions educators might be better advised to focus on naïve presuppositions through finely tuned scaffolding (see box 15.1).

Greenfield and Lave (1982) observed how Zinacanteco Mexican women scaffolded the weaving skills of young girls who were 'apprenticed' to them to learn their traditional craft. Initially the girls spent up to 50 per cent of their time watching the skilled weavers; the next step was to work cooperatively with the women, under their close guidance; finally, they were able to take responsibility for their own work. At each stage of the process, however, the teachers adjusted the level of difficulty and structured the amount of help they gave so that the girls learned an increasing repertoire of weaving skills.

These examples, commonplace in family and community life, show the collaborative nature of the learning process and suggest that language, foremost among the social representations, provides a framework within which the growing child comes to interpret and understand experience.

Guided participation in sociocultural activity

Bruner's interpretation of Vygotskian ideas has generated a great deal of current research on the nature of scaffolding and its role in promoting learning in various social settings, including experimental settings, schools, home environments and informal apprenticeship situations, as well as through the mediation of computers. A huge literature describes how learning processes are shaped by the particular contexts in which they take place. A useful concept that has grown out of the metaphor of scaffolding is that of *guided participation*, a form of apprenticeship in which children actively engage in cultural practices where adults model, guide and regulate performance while creating temporary scaffolds that offer a form of bridge between old patterns and new. Guided participation allows novices to increase their familiarity and control over the diverse activities involved in a particular culture. As they become more accomplished, these novices reconstruct the knowledge and appropriate it for themselves. Progress towards competence arises through a complex interplay among social factors. Despite the diversity of the contexts studied, a common feature in the research is the role of scaffolding within guided participation.

Rogoff and her colleagues (Rogoff et al., 1995) further developed the Vygotskian idea that individual cognitive development is inseparable from interpersonal and community processes. They used the concept of guided participation to study a particular social practice – not, in this instance, the study of a remote culture but a reflective investigation into cultural practices in her own community – the practice of Girl Scout cookie sales. Rogoff analysed a number of interlocking practices at different levels, including active contributions from individuals involved (the Girl Scouts), their social partners (mothers and other mentors) and the historical traditions of their community (the cultural history of the Girl Scout movement).

Rogoff developed a research method for investigating guided participation at three levels of analysis: community, interpersonal and individual planes of analysis, each integrated one with the other. She defined the different planes of analysis as follows:

- *Community plane of analysis*: focuses on people participating with others in a culturally organized activity that is guided by cultural values and goals.

506 Children's Developing Minds

This could refer to formal systems, such as education, or informal ones such as voluntary activities.

- *Interpersonal plane of analysis*: focuses on how people communicate and coordinate efforts in face-to-face interaction. This also refers to choices about who may be involved and who should be excluded from the activity. Parents and more experienced peers played a key role here.
- *Personal plane of analysis:* focuses on how individuals change through their involvement in the activity, a process that prepares them for further, related activities in the future. For example, we can study the process of children's growing responsibility through participation in an activity under the guidance of adults or more experienced peers. This included their increased confidence in the role of door-to-door salesperson, their accomplishment in managing accounts, the efficiency in arranging deliveries of cookies. All of these social and conceptual skills could also be built on for future activity.

A detailed account of the study with Girl Scouts is given in box 2.2 where you can see in practice how Rogoff provides empirical evidence for her assertion that development (whether in the personal, interpersonal or community plane) is a process of transformation through people's participation in shared activities.

Rojas-Drummond (2000) has also evaluated the impact of guided participation in classroom settings. She compared Mexican preschool children following a High Scope curriculum (see chapter 17) with matched preschoolers who followed the official state curriculum. By the end of one year, the High/Scope children's performance in problem solving was significantly higher. Further qualitative analysis of the children's performance indicated that by the end of the year the High/Scope children could solve virtually all the problems unaided while the control children still required help and prompting from the experimenter.

Rojas-Drummond argues that, given the homogeneity of the two populations, the nature of the guided participation and daily discourse between pupil and teacher facilitated this change in the problem-solving competence of the children. Table 15.2 indicates the action, categorized here under five dimensions, that expressed the guided participation offered to the children. High/Scope teachers engaged in these actions significantly more frequently than control teachers.

Collective argumentation

A related pedagogical strategy that has also been systematically researched is *collective argumentation*, another sociocultural approach to classroom learning. Central to this approach is the emphasis on the process whereby cultural tools, such as language, are transformed into internal tools of thinking. This process from the social to the internal plane of functioning requires active engagement on the part of children as they interact with adults and peers in a socially situated way. Key aspects to collective argumentation are:

Table 15.2 Dimensions for describing how teachers and students enact the process of teaching and learning

I.   Learning is a social-communicative process
For example, pupils are used as a resource for the social-cognitive support of fellow-pupils; group work is organized so that there are interchanges of viewpoints between pupils and sharing of responsibility in solving problems

II.   Knowledge can be jointly constructed
For example, there is frequent use of reformulations, elaborations and recaps; teachers regularly ask questions which explore pupils' levels of understanding; they also negotiate meanings with pupils

III.   Becoming educated includes learning ways to solve problems
For example, teachers make frequent use of 'why?' questions to get pupils to justify answers; they elicit problem-solving strategies from the pupils; they create opportunities for constructing knowledge jointly with pupils

IV.   Emphasis placed on the process of learning
For example, teachers take time to recap or review learning with pupils; they emphasize the meaning or purpose of tasks

V. Learning can be nurtured by a teacher
For example, teachers encourage the active participation of pupils; they provide elaborated feedback on a pupil's response to a problem; they gradually withdraw expert support when pupil demonstrates competence

Source: Adapted from Rojas-Drummond, 2000

- *individual representations* of the issue;
- *comparisons* of these representations with those of others in the class;
- *explanations* and *justifications* of a position;
- *co-construction* of a perspective by the group;
- *presentation* of the group co-construction to the whole class;
- leading to *validation* or *testing for acceptance* in the wider community of the class.

The teacher's role in the groups is highly proactive as he or she observes, challenges and listens critically to the quality of argumentation at each stage of the process. The final validation stage is especially important as the teacher rephrases and re-represents the views from the various groups. The teacher also makes connections back to previous argumentations in order to maintain a sense of continuity in the process of inquiry.

Brown and Renshaw's (2000) research with Australian 10- to 11-year-olds provides an exciting example of sociocultural theory in practice. Students in classes that practiced Collective Argumentation produced significantly higher levels of verbal interaction than students in control classes that engaged in unstructured open discussion of the same topics. Collective Argumentation groups produced more requests for clarification, justification and elaboration of ideas. In these classes there was a substantially higher percentage of student-talk than in control classes. The larger number of restatements, rephrasings, evaluations and explanations by students indicated that they were working more with one another's ideas rather than with those of the teacher only.

An interesting outcome in one class was that the students developed their own Charter of Values that incorporated such qualities as: sharing, persistence, patience in waiting turns, respect for others, peer support, honesty, humility. As a result, in this particular school, aspects of Collective Argumentation were incorporated into school policy documents for both English and mathematics, indicating that the method had in turn become recognized as an important part of the school culture by senior management and administrators. The researchers consider that studies of this form of social construction of knowledge show how exploratory discourse can be used in ordinary classrooms to enhance children's learning. In their words (Brown and Renshaw, 2000, p. 66): 'Collective Argumentation is only one of many possible ways – one of many different types of social scaffolds – that promote the occurrence of such discourse.'

The community of inquiry

Just as Cole and his co-researchers carried out intensive observations of the Kpelle in order to make deductions about their thinking processes, so some current researchers treat classrooms as miniature cultures from the observation of which it is possible to make wider generalizations about how young people reflect on their own learning processes. The metaphor of the community of inquiry has been devised by Elbers and Streefland (2000) as a guideline for structuring lessons as a communal rather than individual activity. In a community of inquiry, children are given the opportunity to take responsibility for their own learning and that of others, and to become aware of a relationship with their teachers that is different from that normally allowed in a formal classroom. The idea of the community of inquiry is strongly influenced by Rogoff's (1994) research into communities of learners where pupils play a far more active role in guiding their own learning than they do in traditional, teacher-centred classrooms.

The study by Elbers and Streefland of 11- to 13-year-olds in the Netherlands was at a point where a new mathematics curriculum was being introduced into state schools. The teacher began by announcing to the class that both he and the students would work under new, discursive rules as the experimental curriculum was introduced. Specifically, the children were given a new role, that of 'researcher' with their teachers (the usual class teacher and a researcher) as 'senior researchers'. This announcement immediately created a 'zone of uncertainty' as teachers and children redefined their roles and negotiated new patterns of interaction in the classroom. The teacher began each of the weekly 90-minute lessons with the reminder: 'We are researchers. Let us do research.' The children were then given a mathematical problem as the subject for their research. They worked in small groups or as a whole class, but never as individuals.

The children responded very positively to their new roles as researchers and even, on occasion, when the 'senior researchers' slipped back into traditional roles, had to remind them that 'we are all researchers now.' They quickly adapted to the active inquiry that was expected of them and worked productively in collaborative groups to solve real mathematical problems. The teachers too had to reflect carefully on their roles as senior researchers and to keep a balance between imposing their knowledge (for example, of correct solutions to a maths problem) on the children and facilitating inquiry even when, at times, the pupils were making inadequate deductions. The teachers addressed this issue by paraphrasing what the children said and re-casting it in a more acceptable form, by eliminating incorrect terminology and errors, and by reminding the young researchers of earlier deductions. This approach follows very closely the idea of apprenticeship as developed by Rogoff and her colleagues.

The metaphor of 'community of inquirers' was an effective framework within which to guide activities and identify new social roles within that community. Critically, the concept of learning changed from one of reproducing knowledge to one of learning to listen, learning to use evidence constructively, and learning to critique another person's statement. Their identities as researchers gave the children a critical stance so that the teachers in turn had to give good arguments and justifications for what they said. Elbers and Streefland give insight into how young people view themselves as learners and how they learn and work together.

Implications for Education

The teacher in the Piagetian tradition is a facilitator who provides the right materials for the child's level of development and helps the child to 'discover' by herself, through the conflict between her existing schemas and the evidence facing her. The teacher does not confront the child with these discrepancies but stands back and allows the child to find out for herself. The view of Vygotsky and of Bruner is that the adult and child can work together to construct new schemas, and that the intervention by the more expert adult is positively helpful in moving the child's thinking on. The adult's expertise should be actively harnessed to the child's level of competence and to the ZPD. Concepts are jointly constructed through interaction with those who already embody them, together with the ways of doing and thinking that are cultural practices, recreated with children through processes of formal and informal teaching (Wood, 1998). It is important, from this standpoint, to give help to the child that is contingent on her failure to give a correct response. If the child succeeds, it is important to give less help. The more the teacher's behaviour is contingent on the child's behaviour in these sorts of ways the more able the child becomes to work independently.

Bruner argued forcefully that educators need to be concerned with the role of structure in learning. Teachers must address the issue of enabling students to grasp the structure of a discipline rather than simply mastering facts. The structure of a body of knowledge is as important as its mode of representation. By structure he means the principles and concepts of a discipline – relative and related to the needs of the learner. The mastery of structure gives the learner purpose and direction; it is a process that enables the child to go beyond the information given in order to generate ideas of her own. Bruner also stressed the need to encourage students to make links and to understand relationships between and across subjects. Curriculum planning should be concerned to enhance learning as an active and problem-solving process.

Even if children do not properly understand something, they may know enough for the adult to be able to direct them to a relevant activity. If this activity is within the ZPD, then, as we have seen, the scaffolding function supports the young learners. 'Contingent control helps to ensure that the demands placed on the child are likely neither to be too complex, producing defeat, nor too simple, generating boredom or distraction' (Wood, 1988, p. 201). In fact, the commentary from more expert people helps the child integrate existing knowledge into a wider framework. Thus it supports existing understanding while giving the opportunity to branch out into new regions.

Children may also need help in having their attention directed towards significant features of a task or a situation, when, left alone, they might not make the right connections. The interventions by the knowledgeable adult give the child a structure within which to formulate meaning. By helping the young learner to use language as an instrument of thought, the adult frees the child from the world of immediate perceptions and enables her to 'go beyond the information given'.

Bruner pointed out that the invention of 'schooling' itself has had a great impact on the nature of thinking since schooling creates particular ways of looking at problems and of acting on the world. Teachers are not, he argues, simply handing on knowledge but actively recreating distinctive ways of thinking. This can be enabling or inhibiting. Donaldson's research has shown how children's will to learn may be unwittingly crushed by the educational experience. Competence, where not recognized or fostered, can wither. Failure to scaffold on the part of teachers, failure to build on the knowledge that the child brings to the classroom, may well lead the child to learn to fail in school settings. In box 15.2, for example, we see that Brazilian street children are more expert at mathematical calculation in the marketplace than in the classroom.

There are some similarities here with Piaget's theory (chapter 12). Both Bruner and Piaget view action as important in cognitive development. There are also similarities in the ways in which the two psychologists consider that abstract thinking grows out of action and perception. Both would agree that competence in any area of knowledge must be rooted in active experience and concrete mental operations. Where the two theorists differ, and where Bruner has been greatly influenced by the work of Vygotsky, is first in the part in which language and interpersonal communication play a role in the process; and second in the need for active intervention by expert adults (or more knowledgeable peers) at a suitable level, so enabling the child to develop as a thinker and problem solver. Like Vygotsky, Bruner argues that instruction is an essential part of learning.

The role of peers as tutors

We have seen how teachers can use Vygotskian principles in whole-class settings. Are there ways in which peers might also play a part in scaffolding one another's learning? Slavin, a proponent of cooperative learning, asserts (1987, p. 1166) that:

> Under the right motivational conditions, peers can and, more important, will provide explanations in one another's proximal zones of development and will engage in the kind of cognitive conflict needed for disequilibration and cognitive growth.

Group learning environments, if properly structured, encourage questioning, evaluating, and constructive criticism, leading to restructuring of knowledge. For example, in these learning settings a child may need to explain something to another, defend his or her own viewpoint, engage in debate or analyse a disagreement. This can result in learning with understanding, and, many proponents claim, in fundamental cognitive restructuring.

Peer tutoring provides a good example of interaction as a necessary condition for cognitive growth since it is through the processes that are involved in this interaction between tutor and tutee that the less expert child masters a new skill (Shamir 2000; Topping and Ehly, 1998). Here the expert tutor is a fellow pupil. Foot et al. (1990) stress the appropriateness of Vygotsky's model in explaining how peer-tutoring works. One child (the tutor) is more knowledgeable than the other (the tutee) and each is aware of the distinctiveness of their roles as expert and novice; it is clear to each child that the aim is for the expert to impart his or her knowledge to the novice. However, the 'expert' is not likely to be that much ahead of the 'novice', and so more readily appreciates the latter's difficulties and thus can scaffold effectively within the latter's ZPD. Note that it is not simply the encounter between child and child that brings about the change but the impact of communication and instruction from the more capable peer. As Shamir (2000) found, the enhancement of mediation skills was demonstrated not only by the trained peer tutors who participated in a peer mediation intervention, but was also transferred to the children who were taught by their qualified peers. In other words, the tutees benefited from the mediating style used by peer tutors and were more likely to adopt this style of interaction themselves in other contexts. Studies like these demonstrate how such joint intellectual activity becomes internalized. The instruction is effective when it is slightly ahead of the tutee's actual level and when the assistance from the peer tutor lies within the ZPD.

Cooperative group work (CGW) in the classroom (Cowie et al., 1994) can offer one effective method for enabling children in the role of experts to act contingently upon one another, so guiding their peers through the ZPD. For example, the Jigsaw method (Aronson, 1978) is designed in such a way that children work interdependently by splitting a task into four or five sections. Each pupil has access to only part of the material to be mastered and must work with others to fit together all the pieces of the 'Jigsaw'. The pupils work in groups where they become expert in one section; the expert pupils then return to their home groups where they tutor other members of their team in the material that they have mastered.

Bennett and Dunne (1992) investigated the effect of three types of grouping arrangement (one of which was Jigsaw) on primary-school children's talk. They noted an increase in the quality of children's language and thinking when they were given the opportunity to work in small, interactive cooperative groups. The children who participated in cooperative group work showed less concern for status, less competitiveness and were significantly more likely to express evidence of logical thinking. This was particularly so when the children were encouraged to engage in an exchange of views, often conflicting, and to explore a range of possible perspectives. Even the most stilted discussions were characterized by talk in abstract modes rarely found in individualized work.

Computer-Assisted Learning (CAL)

Advances in technology also offer support to the model of instruction outlined in this chapter. The recent development of computer-assisted learning (CAL) enables teachers to harness the educational potentialities of computers to the specific needs of the child. The computer can present a series of information and tasks to the child. In intelligent tutoring systems, the student does not just go through a rigid linear sequence of tasks, but (depending on his or her prior responses) is taken down a branching route suited to the student's ability; for example being given more detailed help or prompts when required. Additionally, computers can increase opportunities for socially interactive learning. Pupils, knowledgeable in this area, often become a valued resource in the classroom, thus increasing the opportunities for genuine peer tutoring.

Wood and Wood (1996) demonstrated how computer instruction could use scaffolding effectively to help children solve problems. The child's encounters with the computer can be extremely collaborative with a high degree of participation by the child and contingent responses by the computer program. When children work together in CAL there is a great deal of collaboration and jointly coordinated problem solving in which the novice (or less expert child) witnesses and takes part in more advanced strategies for achieving goals. This learning takes place on an intra-individual plane (see figure 15.1) and is an example of socially shared cognition.

At one level, the computer is like a useful partner in the learning process that provides feedback, structured guidance and access to factual knowledge. But we should not forget, as Crook (1994) points out, that the pupil's experience takes place in a socially organized context. Computers are configured by programmers and designed for a schedule determined by teachers and administrators – features that are socially constituted! At a deeper level, the computer is a medium that 'reorganises interaction among people' (Cole and Griffin, 1987) and actually creates new educational environments such as the domains of the World Wide Web. There are enormous implications that go far beyond the classroom since children now have access to a huge range of communities, some educational, some social and recreational, that were unthinkable a generation ago. Furthermore, in the realm of computer use, it is common to find that children know more than their teachers, leading to the phenomenon of the 'expert' child and the 'novice' teacher. Saljö (1998) describes a study that documented dangers in this reversal of traditional roles in that the expert children became gatekeepers of knowledge and did not always use this power in ways that were most conducive to learning!

Crawford (1998) describes how the mathematics curriculum can highlight cultural and historical tensions between schools and information technology. The computer-based problem-solving intervention that she introduced to a girls' school was perceived initially as being so far from the 'real' purposes of the curriculum that it could only be implemented as an optional activity in the computer club. The more playful activities involved in modelling with Lego bricks were experienced as personally meaningful by the girls, and their confidence grew in terms of playing and experimenting collaboratively with the new artefacts. However, when it came to programming, there was considerably less evidence of ownership as the teachers intervened with what were perceived as 'incomprehensible' solutions. In this context, programming activities had not become part of their consciousness. The solution, argues Crawford, might come through a radical realignment of traditional roles and power relationships within schools. These findings indicate the need for more research into the actual processes through which the computer as medium has transformed the ways in which human cognitive activity is organized and the ways in which people collaborate (or fail to collaborate) to learn. The research of Elbers and Streefland (2000), as we saw in the section on learning communities, indicated positive outcomes when pupils developed a culture of inquiry in their classrooms and where they became 'expert' researchers.

Research studies like these affirm the importance of understanding more clearly the nature of the teacher's role in the scaffolding process, and caution about the danger of relegating responsibility to the software, no matter how sophisticated. The nature of the educational experience is far more than a straightforward interaction between a pupil and a computer, though it is common for teachers to define CAL almost entirely in terms of the software. Rather, learning is embedded in a complex system that is in turn inseparable from the way in which education is defined in the particular situation of the classroom and the wider context of the culture. As Saljö suggests (1998, p. 63), 'thinking is part of a situated activity system' so we also need to look at the roles and responsibilities that people adopt in the course of collective activities such as CAL. As the situation changes, as it frequently does in IT, so does the way in which problems are framed and perceived.

Is a Synthesis Possible between Piagetian and Vygotskian Theory?

As we have seen, there are a number of ways in which Piaget's and Vygotsky's theories differ. They have contrasting views on language and thought. Piaget argues that thinking develops out of action rather than out of language. Language does not create thought but enables it to emerge. Before the age of around seven, that is before the onset of concrete operations, the child, in Piaget's view, is unable to think or discuss things rationally. Preschoolers' language and thought is primarily egocentric since the child is unable to enter into the perspective of another person. Children do not enter into discussions with one another since there is no real reciprocity or attempt at mutual understanding.

Vygotsky, by contrast, did not view children's speech as egocentric but as highly social. Vygotsky saw the collective monologues in which preschoolers typically engage as representing a transition between the communicative function of language and its function as a tool of thought, that is between the social and the intellectual. The child who talks to herself, then, is involved in a process of regulating and planning ongoing activity. This overt commentary will later be internalized as inner speech or thought. Vygotsky proposed that language arises out of social interaction.

With regard to learning and thinking, Piaget claimed that children pass through a series of stages of intellectual development before they are able to reason and think logically. Teaching, from this standpoint, is only effective if the child is 'ready' to assimilate the new idea or experience. Conflicting viewpoints can lead to cognitive change through the twin processes of assimilation and accommodation. Piaget emphasized the key part of action for the child's learning. Vygotsky agreed that action underlined thinking and learning but placed much more emphasis on the role of language, and of direct intervention and help by others more skilled in a task. However, it is sometimes overlooked that Piaget too valued peer interactions as playing a significant part in facilitating children's intellectual development.

Contemporary psychologists have begun to examine ways in which the insights from both Piaget's and Vygotsky's perspectives might be synthesized (for a review, see Smith et al., 1997). Piagetian researchers such as Doise and Mugny (1984) have documented the types of cooperative context in which children progress in their understanding. Conflict of views and perspectives can encourage children to rethink. Doise and Mugny have shown that children working in pairs or in small groups come to solve problems more effectively than when they work alone. The reason seems to be that it is through social interaction that they come to see the solution. When the child encounters conflicting views this stimulates internal disequilibrium that the child is motivated to resolve. The social process of negotiating with peers erects a 'scaffold' that helps each child to reconstruct his or her ideas. This interpretation by Doise and Mugny starts from a Piagetian standpoint but takes account of the social context of peer interaction within which the child operates.

Others have identified problems inherent in collaborative learning. For example, Foot et al. (1990), despite their sympathy with the Vygotskian perspective, found that friendship groupings were not always the most productive and that in those settings there were more opportunities for being 'off-task'. Other researchers into cooperative learning (Slavin, 1987) have also identified 'free-riders' who allow fellow group members to do all their work for them! Cowie et al. (1994) found wide differences in the capacity that children in three multi-ethnic classrooms had to work cooperatively with one another, and suggested that children worked best in groups where there was a positive climate of mutual regard.

However, they also noted the huge difficulties facing teachers in trying to achieve this goal. It would appear that the dynamics of the group or of the whole class must be taken into account. Studies in both the Piagetian and the Vygotskian traditions have given us great insights into cognitive development, but there is still a great deal to be discovered about the interface between social perceptions, personal emotions and cultural constructions, on the one hand, and the nature of the learning context on the other. We have much to learn about the most productive ways to engage in collaborative work and about working with conflicts as well as cooperation. These issues challenge both Piagetians and Vygotskians, indicating a case for a much fuller integration of developmental and social theories.

Grossen (2000) identifies two problems that have yet to be addressed, despite the enormous number of studies that have been carried out in the field. The first, she argues, is to think that social organizations are homogeneous and to forget that an activity may be situated in various, sometimes oppositional, institutions. The second is to consider that institutions are static and that the rules, routines and habits are unchanging. Grossen's research indicates that participants and institutions are actively engaged in the process of framing both the adult's and the child's representations of the body of knowledge which is to be taught in school. In this way they influence both the construction of knowledge and the negotiation of social identities. Grossen's critical perspective is useful when we consider ways in which Western-style educational systems have been imposed on developing cultures by powerful political forces without due respect for the traditions that have worked well for these cultures in the past. Cole (1998) warns about social disruption, human misery and other negative outcomes that occur in the name of 'progress' when too little thought is given to local values.

Nearly one hundred years on, the issues are still being debated fiercely in contemporary psychology precisely because they continue to be of such importance for our personal and social development as individuals in society and for our understanding of wider social processes. We benefit from the huge intellectual advances made by Piaget and Vygotsky, but we cannot simply rest on the shoulders of these giants of the past. We have to continue to play an active part in the dialogues and debates if we are to progress further in our discipline and in our social world. As Kuhn (1997, p. 258) commented in her post-face to the Piaget-Vygotsky Centenary Conference held in 1996:

> The desire to share knowing with another human being is a fundamental one. It is at heart a desire to make your thoughts known to the other and to learn whether they are understood, even shared – always with the chance that I will mean more than I meant before because of the way the other has understood what I have said. The process is one that truly works from both the inside out and the outside in, as we each become different persons through our interaction with one another. I propose this collaborative process as one worthy focus of attention in our efforts to build on the substantial foundations laid by Piaget and Vygotsky.'

■ Further Reading

van der Veer, R. and Valsiner, J. 1991: *Understanding Vygotsky: A Quest for Synthesis*, Oxford: Blackwell, give a comprehensive and critical account of Vygotsky's life and work with an analysis of the social context in which he developed his ideas. An accessible introduction to Vygotsky's ideas with topical research studies and recommendations for further reading is Daniels, H. (ed.) 1996: *An Introduction to Vygotsky*. London: Routledge. Daniels's book also contains a useful review (chapter 2) on the implications of Vygotsky's ideas for current thinking in psychology and education: J. Wertsch and P. Tulviste 'L. S. Vygotsky and contemporary developmental psychology'. For a scholarly and insightful psychological analysis of Vygotsky's cultural-historical approach to human development read Wertsch, J. 1991: *Voices of the Mind*. London: Harvester Wheatsheaf. For another overview see Kozulin, A. 1990: *Vygotsky's Psychology: A Biography of Ideas*. New York and London: Harvester Wheatsheaf.

Piaget, J. 1959: *The Language and Thought of the Child*. London: Routledge & Kegan Paul, was originally written in 1923. It contains his ideas on children's egocentric speech, which Vygotsky disagreed with in Vygotsky, L. 1962: *Thought and Language*. Cambridge, MA: MIT Press. This actually dates from 1934, and was the first of Vygotsky's writings to be widely available in English (though in truncated form).

Smith, L., Dockrell, J. and Tomlinson, P. 1997: *Piaget, Vygotsky and Beyond*. London: Routledge give a useful collection of chapters deriving from the Piaget-Vygotsky Centenary Conference held in 1996.

For an original discussion of the interface between cultural and developmental psychology, read Valsiner, J. 2000: *Culture and Human Development*. London: Sage. Rogoff, B. 2002: *The Cultural Nature of Human Development*. Oxford: Oxford University Press presents an account of human development that looks at both the differences and the similarities between cultures, including the influence of culture on cognition.

■ Discussion Points

1 Vygotsky argued that instruction is at the heart of developing and internalizing new ideas. How can the adult most effectively help children to do this?

2 Think of the strategies that teachers might use to scaffold children's learning in the classroom. Can you think of examples from your own experience as a student?

3 Bruner claimed that 'any subject can be taught in some intellectually honest form to any child at any stage of development' (Bruner, 1963, p. 33). Do you agree? For example, how could you teach a 10-year-old about developmental psychology?

4 How do the views of Piaget and Vygotsky differ? In what ways might they be reconciled?

5 Does language structure our thinking, or thinking structure our language?

Box 15.1
Capturing and modelling the process of conceptual change

This is a study of the ways in which young children acquire knowledge about the physical world. Stella Vosniadou argues that children have a naïve framework theory of physics from early on in infancy. The presuppositions of this framework theory act as constraints on the ways in which children interpret both their own observations and the information they receive from their culture. As we saw in chapter 10, there are basic principles that seem to guide the infant's process of learning about the properties of the physical world. Children generate specific theories derived from observations of the objects in their physical world and from information that is presented to them by their culture.

The theories that children form through this process are continuously *enriched* and *revised*. Some kinds of conceptual change require the simple addition of new information to an existing conceptual construct (*enrichment*). For example, primary school children find it easy to add to their existing concept of the moon the information that the moon has craters.

Other theories are accomplished only when existing beliefs and presuppositions are modified (*revision*). Such conceptual change is difficult to achieve, argues Vosniadou. In an earlier study of 8-year-olds' understanding of the day–night cycle, she found that they could learn in class that the sun does not move, as stated in their textbook, but that later, when asked to describe the day/night cycle, many continued to explain that 'the sun goes down behind the mountains'. Clearly the children were more confused after reading the text than they had been before since their framework theory had been challenged.

Vosniadou was particularly interested to investigate the nature of children's misconceptions when they were asked to assimilate new information into existing conceptual structures that contain information that is contradictory to the scientific view. Learning failures can happen at any time during the knowledge acquisition process, but especially when the process requires the revision of deeply entrenched presuppositions that belong to the framework theory. Inconsistencies are produced when children attempt to reconcile conflicting pieces of information.

She developed a methodology that consisted of a series of questions about the concept in question. Some required a verbal response, some elicited drawings and other required the construction of physical models. There are two aspects of this method: the *types of question* used and the *test of internal consistency*. Here we focus on her study of children's developing mental models of the Earth. Young children find it difficult to believe that the Earth is a sphere because this information contradicts their naïve framework theory that space is organized in terms of 'up' and 'down' and that the earth appears to be flat.

Types of question

If children are asked factual questions like 'What is the shape of the Earth?' or 'Does the Earth move?' they can often repeat information that they have been exposed to during instruction. The fact that their answers are scientifically correct does not necessarily mean that they fully understand the concept. Generative questions, by contrast, are those that confront children with phenomena about which they have not yet received any instruction. For example, when asked 'Does the Earth have an edge?' or 'Would you ever reach the end of the Earth?' children retrieve the answers from their own mental model of the Earth and use this model to answer the question. Generative questions, argues Vosniadou, have greater potential than factual questions to unravel the underlying mental models of the Earth that children use.

Test of internal consistency

This aspect of the method is concerned to determine for each child whether the pattern of his/her responses can be explained by a single, underlying mental model. A first example comes from Kirsti, aged 6 years:

E: What is the shape of the Earth?
Kirsti: Round.
E: Can you make a drawing which shows the real shape of the Earth?
Kirsti: (Child draws a circle.)
E: If you walked and walked for many days in a straight line, where would you end up?
Kirsti: You would end up in a different town.
E: Well, what if you kept on walking and walking?
Kirsti: In a bunch of different towns, states, and then, if you were here and you kept on walking here (child points with her finger to the 'edge' of the circle which she had drawn to depict the Earth) you walk right out of the Earth.
E: You'd walk right out of the Earth?
Kirsti: Yes, because you just go that way and you reach the edge and you gotta be kinda careful.
E: Could you fall off the edge of the Earth?
Kirsti: Yes, if you were playing on the edge of it.
E: Where would you fall?

Kirsti: You'd fall on this edge if you were playing here. And you fall down on other planets.

Here Kirsti demonstrated that she can answer a factual question about the shape of the Earth correctly but that her overall responses are not consistent with the model of a spherical Earth. Rather, Kirsti's model appears to be that the Earth is a suspended disc or a truncated sphere. A second example comes from Venica, aged 8 years, who, in answer to previous questions, has inconsistently stated that 'the Earth is round' but that 'it has an edge':

E: Can people fall off the end or edge of the Earth?
Venica: No.
E: Why wouldn't they fall off?
Venica: Because they are inside the Earth.
E: What do you mean inside?
Venica: They don't fall, they have side-walks, things down like on the bottom.
E: Is the Earth round like a ball or round like a pancake?
Venica: Round like a ball.
E: When you say that they live inside the Earth do you mean they live inside the ball?
Venica: Inside the ball. In the middle of it.

Venica appears to have constructed a mental model of the Earth as a hollow sphere with people living on flat ground inside it.

On the basis of their responses to all the questions designed to investigate a given concept, Vosniadou placed children in a 'mental model' category. Her study of the concept of the Earth showed that 80 per cent of children used one out of a small number of well-defined mental models of the Earth in a consistent fashion (see box figure 15.1.1 for a graphical representation of these mental models). Younger children view the

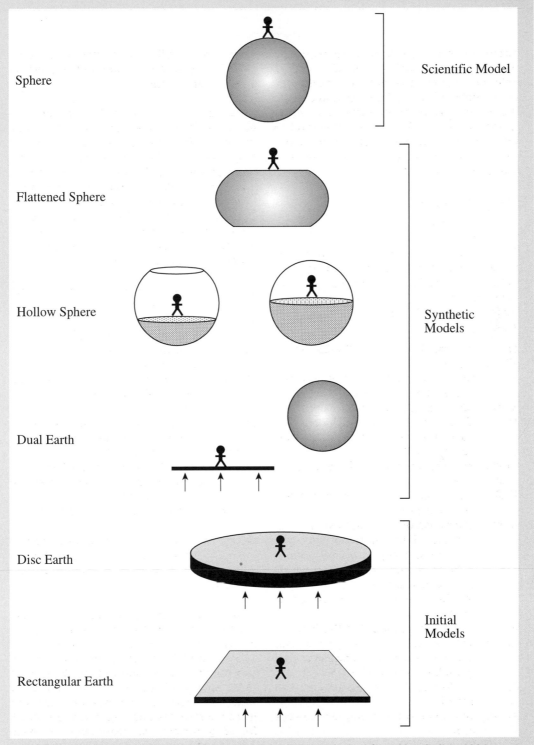

Sphere

Flattened Sphere

Hollow Sphere

Dual Earth

Disc Earth

Rectangular Earth

Scientific Model

Synthetic Models

Initial Models

Box Figure 15.1.1 Children's mental models of the Earth. Adapted from Vosniadou, 1994.

Box Table 15.1.1   Frequency of Earth shape models as a function of age

Earth shape models		6 yrs	8 yrs	10 yrs	Total
Culturally accepted	Sphere	3	8	12	23
Synthetic	Flattened sphere	1	3	0	4
	Hollow sphere	2	4	6	12
	Dual earth	6	2	0	8
Initial	Disc Earth	0	1	0	1
	Rectangular Earth	1	0	0	1
Mixed		7	2	2	11
Total		20	20	20	60

Source: Vosniadou, 1994

Earth as a rectangle or a disc supported by ground underneath and surrounded by sky and solar objects above its flat top. Vosniadou calls these *initial* models since they are based on everyday experience and show no influence from the scientific model of the Earth. Older children tend to form models that combine aspects of the initial model with aspects of the culturally accepted spherical model. She calls these *synthetic* models, which included the following:

- *dual earth*: consisting of two Earths, one flat on which people live and the other spherical which is a planet up in the sky;
- *hollow sphere*: in which people live on flat ground deep inside the sphere; and
- *flattened sphere*: in which the Earth is a sphere flattened at the top and bottom parts where people live.

The distribution of these models by age is shown in box table 15.1.1. Only 23 of the 60 children had formed the culturally accepted spherical model of the earth. The others had either a synthetic or initial model or were mixed up.

   Having identified the mental models children used to answer her questions, Vosniadou was able to unravel some of the underlying theoretical structures and begin to understand the process of conceptual change. She concluded that children find it

hard to construct a mental model of the Earth because it violates certain entrenched presuppositions of the naïve framework theory of physics within which their concept of the Earth is embedded.

Initial model

Children seem to begin by categorizing the Earth as a physical object rather than as an astronomical object and apply it to fit the properties of other physical objects in their environment – that is with reference to solidity, stability, 'up/down' organization and 'up/down' gravity. From this presupposition, the children conclude that the earth is flat, supported and stable, and that solar objects and the sky are located above it.

Synthetic models

Later, the children have to reconcile their initial model with the culturally accepted model of a spherical Earth, and they do so by a number of modifications. For example, by adopting the misconception of the dual Earth, they resolve the conflict between their initial concept of the flat Earth and the culturally accepted view of the spherical Earth, and so they are able to retain their initial framework theory through a modification but do not change their underlying beliefs. Partial changes in underlying beliefs are achieved through the models of the hollow sphere and the flattened sphere. These children have given up the idea that the Earth needs to be supported and have abandoned the 'up/down' gravity presupposition so far as it applies to the Earth itself. This is the first step that children take in the differentiation of the concept of the Earth from the concept of the physical object to which it initially seemed to belong. These children accept the notion that the Earth is a sphere surrounded by space but continue to operate under the constraints of the 'up/down' gravity presupposition when they consider the physical objects located on the Earth. So they cannot understand how it is possible for people and objects on Earth to stand outside it without falling down. In order to resolve this conflict, they create a model to which the spherical earth is hollow and people live on flat ground inside it. In the model of the flattened sphere, children have revised their 'up/down' gravity presupposition but still believe that the ground on which people walk is flat.

Vosniadou concludes that the process of conceptual change is slow and it proceeds through the gradual suspension and revision of the presuppositions of the naive framework theory and their replacement with a different explanatory framework. By the end of the primary school years, most children seem to have constructed the concept of a spherical Earth, as an astro-nomical object, suspended in the sky and surrounded by space and solar objects. There are implications for education at school. It is important for teachers to take account of children's deeply held naïve pre-suppositions and beliefs when they design science lessons. For example, telling a child who believes that people live on flat ground inside a hollow sphere that the Earth is *not* hollow, will not resolve this child's misconception. A lesson on gravity and a lesson on how round things can sometimes appear flat might allay some of this child's confusion.

Vosniadou et al. (2001) argue, on the basis of this study and others in the domain of children's understanding of scientific concepts, that knowledge is acquired in specific domains and that learning is a process that requires the substantial *reorganization* of existing knowledge structures and not just their *enrichment*. Vosniadou's conceptual change approach to learning proposes that, for children to learn about science, they must create new, qualitatively different representations of the physical world. Children need to be helped to become aware of their existing beliefs and presuppositions in ways that are more consistent with scientifically accepted views.

Based on material in Vosniadou, S. 1994: Capturing and modelling the process of conceptual change. *Learning and Instruction*, 4, 45–69.

Box 15.2
Mathematics in the streets and in schools

Mathematical problem solving in the street market is significantly superior to that carried out with paper and pencil. This was the conclusion of Nunes Carraher and her colleagues, using a research method combining participant observation and the Piagetian clinical method, in their study, which demonstrated that youngsters who work on the streets have developed computational strategies that are different from those taught in schools. These young people performed better in problems that were embedded in real-life contexts than they did when asked to solve context-free problems involving the same numbers and mathematical operations.

Nunes Carraher and her colleagues carried out this research in Recife, Brazil, among the children of street vendors who often helped out their parents from the age of 8 years onwards. Young people may also develop their own small businesses selling peanuts, popcorn or coconut milk. As part of this work, the children have to be able to carry out mathematical problem solving, usually mentally, involving addition (4 coconuts and 12 lemons cost x + y), multiplication (one coconut costs x; 4 coconuts cost 4x), subtraction (500 cruzeiros minus the purchase price = the amount of change to be given) and, less frequently, division (where a customer wants a fraction of a unit, such as 0.5 kilo of oranges).

In the study there were four boys and one girl, age range 9–15, with a mean age of 11.2. All were from poor backgrounds. They were recruited to the study from street-corner stalls where they were working with their parents or alone. The researchers acting as customers in the course of a normal transaction posed test items. The children were asked to take part in a formal test a week later administered by the same researcher. There were 99 questions in the formal test and 63 questions in the informal test. The order of testing was the same for all participants.

The informal test

This was carried out in Portuguese in the naturalistic setting of the street-corner market. A researcher, posing as a customer, asked the children successive questions about potential purchases. Another researcher wrote down the responses. After receiving the answer, the researcher asked the child how they had solved the problem. Here is an example of an informal test taken by M., a 12-year-old vendor:

Researcher: How much is one coconut?
M.: 35.
Researcher: I'd like ten. How much is that?
M. (pause): Three will be 105; with three more, that will be 210. (Pause) I need four more. That is . . . (pause) . . . 315 . . . I think it is 350.

M. has solved the problem in the following way:

a) 35 × 10
b) 35 × 3 (a sum which he probably already knew)
c) 105 + 105
d) 210 + 105
e) 315 + 35
f) 3 + 3 + 3 + 1

Even though he had been taught in school that to multiply any number by 10 you simply add a zero to the right of that number, M. used a different problem-solving routine.

The formal test

After the test in a naturalistic setting, participants were invited to take part in the second part of the study. This took place on the street corner or at the child's home. The items for the formal test were devised on the basis of the problems that the child had successfully solved in the naturalistic context. These test items were presented as 38 mathematical problems dictated to the child (e.g., 105 + 105) and 61 word problems (e.g., Mary bought x bananas; each banana cost y; how much did she pay altogether?). In either case, the child solved problems involving the same numbers as those that

Box Table 15.2.1   Test results in three conditions: each participant's score is the percentage of correct items divided by 10

Child	Informal test Score	Formal test Score
M	10	2.5
P	8.9	3.7
Pi	10	5.0
MD	10	1.0
S	10	8.3

Adapted from Nunes Carraher et al., 1985

were used in the informal test. The children were given paper and pencil, and were encouraged to use them if they wished. When the problems were solved mentally, the child was still asked to write down the answer. Only one of the children refused to do this on the grounds that he did not know how to write.

As you can see in box table 15.2.1, problems that were embedded in the context of the street market were much more easily solved than those that were context-free. In the informal test, 98.2 per cent of the 63 problems presented were correctly solved. By contrast, in the formal test, word problems (which provided some context) were correctly answered in 73.7 per cent of cases; mathematical problems with no context were solved in only 36.8 per cent of cases. The frequency of correct answers for each child was converted into scores from 1 to 10 reflecting the percentage of correct answers. A two-way analysis of variance of score ranks compared the scores of each participant in the three types of testing situation. The scores differ significantly across conditions ($\chi^2 = 6.4$, $p = 0.039$). Mann-Whitney U's were calculated. The children performed better on the informal test than on the formal test ($U = 0$, $p < 0.05$).

How can we interpret these results? One possible explanation is that errors in the formal test were related to the transforma-tions that had been performed on the informal test problems in order to construct the formal test. But when the researchers tested this hypothesis by separating items which had been changed by inverting the operation or changing the decimal point from those which remained identical to their informal test equivalents they found no significant difference between the rates of correct response in each of these conditions.

A second explanation is that the children were still 'concrete' thinkers. This meant that in their natural setting they could solve problems about coconuts and lemons because these items were physically present in front of them. But the researchers rejected this interpretation on the grounds that the presence of the food items in itself does not make a mathematical calculation any easier. In any case, the children carried out the calculations mentally, without external memory aids in the form of coconuts!

A third interpretation was confirmed by a qualitative analysis of the interview protocols. This analysis suggested that the children were using different routines in each of the two situations. In the context of the street market, they were using 'convenient groups'; in the formal context, they were using school-based routines. Let's look again at how 12-year-old M. solved the same problem in informal and formal contexts:

Informal test

Researcher: I'm going to take four coconuts. How much is that?

M.: Three will be 105, plus 30, that's 135 ... one coconut is 35 ... that is ... 150!

Formal test

M. (asked to solve 35 × 4): 4 times 5 is 20, carry the 2; 2 plus 3 is 5, times 4 is 20.

Written answer: 200.

Here are two examples from MD, aged 9 years:

Informal test

Researcher: OK, I'll take three coconuts (at the price of Cr$40.00 each). How much is that?

MD (without gestures calculates out loud): 40, 80, 120.

Formal test

MD solves the problem 40 × 3 and obtains 70. She says: 'Lower the zero; 4 and 3 is 7.'

Informal test

Researcher: I'll take 12 lemons (1 lemon is Cr$5.00).

MD: 10, 20, 30, 40, 50, 60 (while separating out two lemons at a time).

Formal test

In solving 12 × 5 she proceeds by lowering first the 2, then the 5 and the 1, obtaining 152. She explains this to the researcher when she is finished.

When solving the informal test items, the children relied on mental calculations closely linked to the quantities that they were dealing with. The strategy for dealing with multiplication was a form of successive additions. When the addition became too difficult, the child would 'decompose' a quantity into 10s and units. But in the formal tests, the children would try, unsuccessfully, to use school-based routines in which mistakes were frequent. They did not show any sign of checking the final answer in order to assess whether it was a reasonable answer.

The researchers conclude that thinking which is sustained by daily 'common sense' can be at a higher level than thinking out of context. They are, therefore, critical of teaching mathematical operations in a disembedded form before they are applied to real world problems. In many of the cases that they observed, the school-based routines actually seemed to interfere with the successful solution of the problem. Even when the answers were absurd, children would not notice.

They do not conclude that teachers should allow children to develop their own strategies independently of conventional systems devised in our culture! However, they point out that the mathematics taught in school has the potential to serve 'as an "amplifier" of thought processes' (Bruner, 1971). They recommend that schools should develop methods in which mathematical systems are introduced to children in ways that allow them to be sustained by common sense, rooted in everyday contexts. This study has demonstrated that children have the potential for devising their own efficient routines that have little to do with the formal procedures of school.

Based on material in Nunes Carraher, T., Carraher, D. W. and Schliemann, A. D. 1985: Mathematics in the streets and in schools. *British Journal of Developmental Psychology*, 3, 21–9.

16 Intelligence and Attainment

As we have seen in previous chapters, psychologists studying cognitive development have been interested in the processes of intellectual growth, but the 'psychometric' approach is a rather different way of looking at intelligence. In the psychometric tradition psychologists have devised tests to measure a person's ability with an emphasis on comparing individuals' performance in a way that can be quantified – usually people are given a 'score' to indicate their performance on a test. The best known tests of ability are 'intelligence' tests.

■ The Development of Intelligence Tests

The first tests

Galton, in England, in the 1880s was the first to attempt the scientific measurement of intelligence with a series of tests (Gregory, 1992). These tests included both physical measures like the strength of hand squeeze or the capacity of the lungs and behavioural measures like reaction time tests (e.g., how quickly a person could make a response after they heard a sound). Galton believed that intelligence was an underlying trait that would influence a person's performance on all tasks. In other words, if someone had more intelligence than someone else they would generally be better on all tests whatever the type of test. Galton also believed that there would be a relationship between a person's status (i.e., their rank in society) and their performance on his tests. But he failed to find such a relationship, and when other researchers compared how well college students performed on Galton's tests and how well they performed academically they too found little relationship between the tests and academic achievement (e.g., Wissler, 1901).

Early in the twentieth century, two French psychologists, Binet and Simon (1905), published tests which, they claimed, could identify children who were failing to make progress within the normal school system. Their aim was to identify such children so that they could be removed from the overcrowded French schools and be given special education. The battery of tests which Binet and Simon devised represented the kinds of abilities which, in their view, children typically used during the school years. The tests included word definitions, comprehension tests, tests of reasoning and knowledge of numbers. Binet and Simon spent a long time in schools using different tests with students who had a range of ability to find out which tests distinguished between younger and older children and between good and poor learners. The latter were defined by teachers – in other words Binet and Simon selected tests on which children who were rated as bright by their teachers did well, and on which children who were considered less able did poorly. Therefore the selection of the original tests by Binet and Simon was based on purely practical considerations – the tests which most effectively differentiated between good and poor students.

Once Binet and Simon (1905) had identified the 30 most effective tests they listed them in order of difficulty (see table 16.1). For example, a younger child might be able to repeat three numbers; an older child would not only be able to do this but could also repeat a sentence with fifteen words in it. Any particular child would then attempt test items of increasing difficulty until he or she consistently failed them, at which point the tester could calculate the child's mental level. The average 5-year-old, for example, would complete test items at the 5-year-old level; a less able 5-year-old might fail to solve test problems beyond the 4-year-old level, and would be said to have a mental level of four.

The use of Binet and Simon's ordered series of tests (or 'scale') was an effective way of measuring children's abilities: it was simple to administer, it could be used by teachers, it made it easy to compare different children, and it was successful. Not surprisingly, given the reasons behind the choice of tests, if a child did well on Binet–Simon scale she was likely to be successful academically, if a child did poorly on the scale she was likely to have difficulties in school. In other words, the test was an effective way of identifying those children who might be in need of extra help.

Revisions of the Binet–Simon scale

After Binet and Simon had produced their scale of items for measuring mental age, it was adapted by Terman at Stanford University in California, for use in the USA. Terman increased the number of tests to 90, and the new version, called the Stanford–Binet Intelligence Scale, was introduced in 1916.

In this new scale were two main types of test item – verbal and non-verbal. Verbal tests relied on language abilities, e.g., general knowledge, comprehension, vocabulary and understanding similarities between concepts. Non-verbal or performance tests measured perceptual skills and non-verbal reasoning, such as the ability to arrange pictures in a logical sequence to make a coherent story, to copy

Table 16.1 Items used in the 1905 Binet–Simon scale

1 Follows a moving object with the eyes
2 Grasps a small object that is touched
3 Grasps a small object that is seen
4 Recognizes the difference between a square of chocolate and a square of wood
5 Finds and eats a square of chocolate wrapped in paper
6 Executes simple commands and imitates simple gestures
7 Points to familiar objects (e.g., 'show me the cup')
8 Points to objects represented in pictures (e.g., 'put your finger on the window')
9 Names objects in pictures
10 Compares two lines of markedly unequal length
11 Repeats three spoken digits
12 Compares two weights
13 Shows susceptibility to suggestion
14 Defines common words by function
15 Repeats a sentence of fifteen words
16 Tells how two common objects are different (e.g., paper and cardboard)
17 Names from memory as many as possible of 13 objects displayed on a board
18 Reproduces from memory two designs shown for ten seconds
19 Repeats a series of more than three digits
20 Tells how two common objects are alike (e.g., butterfly and flea)
21 Compares two lines of slightly unequal length
22 Compares five blocks to put them in order of weight
23 Indicates which of the previous five weights the examiner has removed
24 Produces rhymes for given words
25 Word completion test
26 Puts three nouns in a sentence (e.g., Paris, river, fortune)
27 Given set of 25 comprehension questions
28 Reverses the hands of a clock
29 After paper folding and cutting, draws the form of the resulting holes
30 Distinguishes abstract words (e.g., boredom and weariness)

designs using a set of coloured blocks, or assemble pieces of a jigsaw-type puzzle into the right arrangement as quickly as possible.

One of the limitations of the original Binet–Simon scale was the way it led to a comparison between a child's mental level as tested on the scale and her chronological age. For example, if a child aged seven years performed at the level of a four-year-old it could be said that the seven-year-old had a developmental delay of three years. However, if a child aged 12 years performed at the level of a nine-year-old then she also would be classified as delayed by three years. However, a three-year delay at the age of seven years might have very different implications than the same length of delay at 12 years. A better measure of the ability of a child can be calculated by taking a ratio of mental level to chronological age. This gives the child's mental age as a fraction, and Terman suggested multiplying the fraction by 100 and describing the result as the 'Intelligence Quotient' (or IQ):

$$\frac{\text{Mental age}}{\text{Chronological age}} \times 100 = \text{IQ}$$

This change was introduced with the first Stanford–Binet scale. The average child's IQ by this calculation is 100 and the IQs of children above or below the average can be calculated accordingly. The numerical scores of the IQ were less cumbersome than the original age scores and made it possible to make direct comparisons between the intellectual capability of individuals, even at different ages. The IQ assessment also made it easier to calculate correlations between intelligence and other variables. Nonetheless, the idea of labelling people with an 'IQ' has always been controversial. Binet had died before the use of IQ was introduced, but Simon described the concept of IQ as a betrayal of his and Binet's original objectives in assessing children (Gregory, 1992). From a scale that had been intended to identify children who needed special education, the scale had become a way of to make comparisons between all people and rank them according to 'IQ'.

The Stanford–Binet scale has undergone many revisions, and its most recent form, the fourth edition, is still used today (Thorndike et al., 1985). The scale now consists of 15 sub-tests, though not all are used with younger children because some would be too difficult for them. The sub-tests can be scored individually, or they can be grouped to give measures of different abilities (e.g., verbal reasoning), or they can be combined in total to give an overall measure of intelligence. See table 16.2 – the examples in this table are similar but not identical to the actual test items. One of the differences between the Stanford–Binet and other tests of general intelligence is the emphasis placed on short-term memory as an important component of intelligence.

Each time a scale is revised it is important to 'standardize' the new version. For example, the fourth edition of the Stanford–Binet was tested on over 5000 people from two to 24 years of age. Before choosing these people, the United States Census was used to make sure that the individuals in the sample were representative of the age, sex, ethnic background, community size, and geographic region of the whole country. In this way the results from the sample could be considered as representative of all the people who might be tested on the scale. Scales designed for use in particular countries or with particular age groups also have to be standardized on appropriate samples from those countries or age groups.

It is important that intelligence scales are tested on large samples, because IQ is no longer calculated by the MA/CA formula. Instead a person's performance on an intelligence scale is compared to the distribution of the performance of everyone else of the same age on the same scale. Intelligence scales are designed so that that at each age the average performance of all people of that age will be a score of 100. For example, if several thousand ten-year-olds were assessed using the Stanford–Binet scale, their average score would be 100, and the scores of all the children would be normally distributed. This means that there will be a large number scoring 100, and only a slightly smaller number scoring 99 (or 101) with slightly fewer scoring 98 (or 102), slightly fewer again with a score of 97 (or 103) and so on with only very small numbers of children having particularly low or high scores.

Intelligence scales are also designed so that the distribution of scores at each age follows the same pattern. If the mean score is 100 then 34 per cent of scores

Table 16.2 Items similar to those used in the Stanford–Binet Intelligence Scale

---

Verbal reasoning

Vocabulary:	the child is asked to name pictures of objects and give the meaning of words which increase in difficulty – 'What is an apple?'; 'What is harmony?'
Comprehension:	the child is asked questions that test practical and social judgment; 'What is the thing to do if you are lost in a strange city?' 'What should you do if a child younger than you hits you?'
Absurdities:	the child is asked to say what is silly about a picture in which the characters are doing something odd like sunbathing in the rain
Verbal relations:	the child is asked to say why one of four items is different from the rest 'how are a horse, a cow and a sheep different from a dog?'

Abstract and visual reasoning

Pattern analysis:	the child has to place pre-cut forms into a form board or copy patterns by putting together blocks
Copying:	copying a design with paper and pencil
Matrices:	the child is asked to select an item (a design or an object) which completes a given set of items
Paper folding:	the child is shown a folded piece of paper and shown several possible examples of what it would look like if it was unfolded. The child has to choose the correct one.

Quantitative reasoning

Arithmetic:	the child is given a series of arithmetical problems to solve
Number series:	the child is given a sequence and asked to say which number should come next: '1, 2, 4, 7, 11, 16, 22, . . .'
Equations:	the child is asked to re-arrange an equation which has been mixed up: $2\ 3\ 4\ 10 - x =$

Tests of short-term memory

Memory for beads:	the child is shown a photograph of several beads (in different shapes and colours) for five seconds. She must then reproduce the order of beads, from memory, with real beads
Memory for sentences:	the child must repeat, exactly, a sentence they have heard
Memory for digits:	the child is asked to repeat a series of numbers, either forwards or backwards, e.g., 4-7-3-8-5-9
Memory for objects:	the child is shown several pictures of objects (at the rate of one every second). Then she is shown a larger set of pictures and asked to point to just the pictures she saw presented (and in the same order)

Other items

Missing parts:	the child is asked to say what is missing in a picture: e.g., a drawing of a table showing the table without a leg
Spatial:	the child traces a path through a maze

---

will fall between 85 and 100 and 34 per cent will be between 100 and 115. Four-teen per cent will fall between 70 and 85, and 14 per cent between 115 and 130. Two per cent will fall between 55 and 70, and 2 per cent between 130 and 145. In this way a child's score can be compared easily with the expected scores for the whole of his or her age group.

Other intelligence scales

The Stanford–Binet test is still in use, but one of the tests most commonly used nowadays was designed by Wechsler. His first test, for adults in 1939, was based on other tests that existed at the time (including the Stanford–Binet). Since then it has been revised many times and a children's version of the scale was first produced in 1949. The most recent versions of the scales are:

- for adults (16–89 years): Wechsler Adult Intelligence Scale – Revised UK Edition (WAIS-R-III[UK]) (Wechsler, 1997).
- for children (6–16 years): Wechsler Intelligence Scale for Children – Third UK Edition (WISC-III[UK]) (Wechsler, 1992).
- for young children (3–7 years): Wechsler Pre-school and Primary Scale of Intelligence – Revised UK Edition (WPPSI-R[UK]) (Wechsler, 1990).

Examples of the type of items in the WISC are given in table 16.3. As well as the Stanford–Binet and the Wechsler scales there are other tests that include similar batteries of tests. For example, the British Ability Scales II (Elliot et al., 1996) is a battery of tests designed to assess information processing speed, reasoning, spatial imagery, perceptual matching, short-term memory, and knowledge retrieval (e.g., giving word definitions).

Intelligence scales like the Stanford–Binet and the Wechsler scales are to some extent dependent on verbal abilities. Not only are there specific items that test children's performance in various verbal tests (like 'vocabulary' or 'similarities') but the instructions and many of the children's responses also depend on verbal abilities. Tests with a large verbal component may underestimate the intellectual capacity of children who speak a different dialect, or for whom the language of the test is not their mother tongue. In other words, children who have language difficulties or who come from another cultural background may be at a disad-vantage when taking the test.

Tests, like the Stanford–Binet and the Wechsler scales have to be administered individually (see plate 16.1), usually in clinical or educational settings to help in the diagnosis of learning difficulties. Psychologists have also devised tests that can be given to groups of people, and these are often used for personnel selection. Correlations between performance on individually administered tests and on group tests are fairly high and therefore it is assumed that they are each measur-ing the same abilities. However, group testing has some disadvantages. For example, the tester may not notice signs of anxiety in those being tested which

Table 16.3 Items similar to those used in the Wechsler Intelligence Scale for Children

Information:	the child is asked a series of general knowledge questions
Comprehension:	the child explains why certain courses of action are appropriate: 'What should you do if you break a friend's toy by mistake?'
Similarities:	the child is asked to say in what way two things are alike, e.g., a pear and a plum
Vocabulary:	the child is asked to define words of increasing difficulty
Picture arrangement:	the child is shown a series of cartoon pictures which are out of order and asked to arrange them correctly
Picture completion:	the child is asked to say which part is missing in a picture; a dog with one ear, a cup with no handle
Block design:	the child is shown blocks which have some sides all white, some all red and some half white and half red; the child is asked to reproduce a series of designs using first four blocks and later nine blocks
Object assembly:	the child has to assemble a jigsaw of parts into a whole shape; e.g., six pieces into the shape of a dog
Digit span:	the child is asked to repeat a series of numbers which increase in length, either in the same order or backwards
Arithmetic:	the child answers a series of arithmetical problems
Coding:	the child matches symbols with numbers according to a given key. For example, on the key, number 1 may be symbolized by †; number 2 by ¶, and so on. The child is given a random list of numbers and against each number has to write down its corresponding symbol
Mazes:	the child traces routes in a series of mazes
Symbol search:	the child is shown rows of abstract shapes. In some rows all the shapes are different, in some the same shape occurs more than once, and the child has to distinguish between the two types of rows

would be more obvious in a one-to-one context, and people with language diffi-culties may be at a disadvantage if they find it hard to read the instructions for each item.

One example of a test that can be administered to a group is Raven's Progres-sive Matrices. This test also has the advantage that it requires little specific verbal ability – the way that a person completes the test can, if necessary, be demon-strated with examples which avoid verbal instructions, and the tests do not depend on people giving verbal responses. Raven's Progressive Matrices are avail-able in three different versions for different levels of ability, but the principle behind each test is the same (Raven, 1994, 1995, 1996). A person is shown a 'matrix' of nine patterns, with one of the patterns missing (see figure 16.1). Below the

Plate 16.1   A preschool child is tested on one of the subscales of the WPPSI.

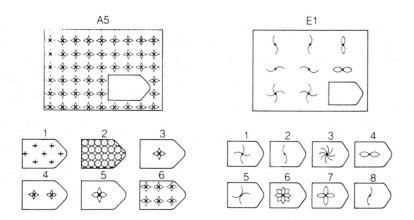

Figure 16.1   Sample items from the Raven Progressive Matrices (from Raven, 1958).

matrix there is a selection of different patterns and the person is asked to choose the one that they think best fits the missing piece in the matrix. The test is called 'progressive' because a person completes a number of different matrices, which are presented one at a time, in a booklet, in order of increasing difficulty. A person's performance on Raven's Progressive Matrices correlates with their performance on other intelligence tests.

Reliability and Validity

All tests of intelligence should meet several criteria if they are to be effective ways of measuring a person's ability.

Reliability

A test must be 'reliable'. This means that each time a person takes a test they should achieve the same result. For example, if someone is given an intelligence scale one day and then the same scale on the next day, it is essential the person's level of performance is the same both times. Of course, there is a difficulty in checking reliability in this way because if someone has done a test once it is likely that practice and familiarity will lead to better performance the second time. One way round this problem is to give a person half the test (perhaps alternate questions from it) on one occasion and the other half of the test on a second occasion. The person should have the same level of performance on both halves of the test. The most frequently used intelligence scales like the Stanford–Binet and the Wechsler scales have very high levels of reliability.

Validity

Concurrent validity, means assessing a scale against either another scale or an independent measure of performance. For example, if a child performed well on the Stanford–Binet scale it would be expected that the same child would also perform well on the WISC. Similarly, if a teacher thought that a child was at the top of the class it would be expected that the child would have one of the highest levels of performance in the class when tested with an intelligence scale.

Predictive validity means that performance on a test should predict future performance. For example if a child scores highly on an intelligence test, it would be expected that the child will do well academically. Similarly, the level a student achieves in a college entrance exam should predict the grade they achieve at the end of college.

Content validity (which is also called face validity) refers to how appropriate a test is. For example, if you wanted to test a person's driving ability it would be appropriate to test how well she actually drove a car on the road and how well she answered questions about driving. It would not be appropriate to test that person's short-term memory or vocabulary. This example makes content validity appear rather obvious, and for many practical abilities (like driving) it is not difficult to see the relationship between the test and what it is measuring. However, as we will explain later, intelligence is not easy to define, and the content validity of a test depends on what the test designers believe intelligence to be. If you believe that intelligence is mainly about how accurately people process and remember information you might include several measures of short-term memory, comprehension and general knowledge. If the you think that intelligence is about how well a person adapts to the world around her you might want to include tests of social and practical skills.

Content validity is difficult to define if there is no common agreement on the meaning of a construct. Although many researchers have considered that tests of memory, reasoning, and knowledge are appropriate ways to measure intelligence, other researchers have developed concepts of intelligence that include skills and abilities that are not directly tested by the more established intelligence scales. We will discuss the different concepts of intelligence in a later section.

The Early Uses of Intelligence Tests

The Binet–Simon scale was initially used simply to differentiate between average children and children with learning difficulties who might be in need of special education. However, during World War I (1914–18) when large numbers of people were being categorized to meet the requirements of different work roles, there was a proliferation of intelligence testing (Gregory, 1992). After the war, large industrial companies also demanded batteries of tests, which could measure specific aptitudes in skills such as engineering, typing, dressmaking. This type of selection procedure, it was claimed, provided an effective means of assigning individuals to occupations appropriate to their abilities. In the UK, Cyril Burt was one of the first psychologists in the National Institute of Industrial Psychology. Burt was committed to the idea that intelligence was innate, static throughout a person's lifetime, and measurable using intelligence tests.

Burt proposed that intelligence tests also be used in schools with the aim of providing all children with an education appropriate to their level of mental ability. He argued that in any group of children, the variations in mental ability would be large and he therefore recommended that the organization of school classes should be on the basis of mental ability rather than chronological age. It was this view that the individual should be assigned a place in society according to his or her intellectual ability which was to have far-reaching effects on the educational system in Britain (Broadfoot, 1996). In his day Burt was highly respected as an educational psychologist, although he is now largely discredited because of his fraudulent research into the heritability of intelligence (Hearnshaw, 1979).

In the early days of intelligence testing it was believed that intelligence tests were objective and accurate means of assessing mental ability. The tests appeared to offer a fairer measure of the potential ability of children from differing backgrounds than did conventional examinations and school reports, and they were thought to be less susceptible to social biases that might affect teachers' evaluations. Unfortunately, because of Burt's strong assumption that intelligence tests measures 'innate ability', insufficient consideration was given to the way that a child's environment might also influence her test performance.

What then were the implications of the psychometric approach for educational practice? If, as Burt and many psychometrists believed, intelligence is an innate, stable factor, it would follow logically that once suitable measures had been devised, children could be grouped according to ability levels for educational purposes. This belief had a strong influence on educational policy in the UK in the years following World War I, and the Hadow Report (1926) recommended several types of school for children after the age of 11 years. These were 'modern' schools, 'technical' schools and traditional grammar schools. To assign each child to an appropriate school, some form of assessment had to take place, and by the late 1930s it was standard practice to select children on the basis of an 11-plus examination which assessed children's English and mathematical abilities, and their performance on an intelligence test.

Towards the end of World War II (1939–45) attitudes changed again. A Labour government came to power in the UK with a large majority and popular support for an attack on inequality in society. There was a growing awareness of the detrimental effects that selection and streaming could have on children, and the way in which the selective system discriminated against children from underprivileged backgrounds. The 1944 Education Act aimed to provide equality of opportunity for all children 'according to age, aptitude and ability'. But the government left the implementation of this policy to local education authorities, and the selective system was so firmly entrenched that the change to a comprehensive system of secondary education was only achieved very gradually (Broadfoot, 1996).

The original intelligence scales were designed primarily to meet educational needs (e.g., to distinguish children who had learning difficulties) and therefore they focused on tasks that related to knowledge, reasoning and memory. However, more recent researchers have argued that such tasks may only reflect a rather narrow concept of intelligence, and that many other aspects of a person's abilities should be taken into account when assessing intelligence. We will discuss different concepts of intelligence in the following section.

Concepts of Intelligence

As we pointed out earlier, Galton who was the first to invent intelligence tests believed that intelligence was a general ability that would be reflected in any test or task undertaken by an individual. The implication of Galton's view is that any test that produces differences in individual performance could be used as an intelligence test. Some tests (e.g., stating your name) are unlikely to produce many individual differences but many others (like vocabulary tests) result in a range of performance and might therefore be used to compare people. Other researchers also came to the conclusion that intelligence was an underlying trait which affected performance across all the tasks used in typical intelligence scales. For example, Spearman (1904) found that there were correlations between children's performance on different academic tests. Spearman (1927) found the same when he gave adults a range of different mental tests i.e., those who did better than others on one test also tended to do better on other tests. From this Spearman concluded that there was probably a single factor, which he labelled 'g' (for 'general' intelligence) which influenced a person's performance on all tests.

Galton and Spearman can be seen as part of the tradition of researchers who put most emphasis on a single general intelligence permeating an individual's performance. In contrast, other psychologists have emphasized the independence of the different factors that might make up a person's intelligence. Thurstone (1931) suggested that there were seven factors that accounted for performance on the type of tests found in traditional intelligence scales. Thurstone called these 'primary mental abilities' and labelled them 'verbal meaning' (e.g., vocabulary and comprehension) 'word fluency' (e.g., speed of naming all the words in a category, like all the animal names beginning with C), 'numerical reasoning' (e.g., mental arithmetic), 'spatial' (e.g., imagining what objects looked like after they are rotated), 'perceptual speed' (e.g., being able to quickly check through lists of items for a specific target item), 'memory' (e.g., recall of words or sentences), and 'inductive reasoning' (e.g., completing number series). This 'group factor' approach has the implication that a child might perform differently on different sets of items, for example, a child might have very good memory and verbal meaning; but average numerical reasoning, and poor spatial ability. This means that children cannot easily be assessed in terms of general intelligence, rather, they may perform differently across a range of tasks.

Although Spearman argued for a single underlying factor that affected performance across all measures of intelligence and Thurstone argued for a set of separate abilities the difference between these two viewpoints is somewhat artificial. More recent researchers have pointed out that Thurstone's factors are not independent, but some of them may be closely related (Gustafsson, 1981). For example, a child who does well on a test involving inductive reasoning will often do well on a test of memory, and a child who does well on tests of verbal ability will tend to do well on tests of numerical ability. Therefore reasoning and memory can be combined into a higher order factor, and verbal and numerical ability can also be combined into a higher order factor. These higher order factors can also be combined together to produce a single factor (in Spearman's term's, the 'g' factor). In summary, some researchers have preferred to emphasize the differences between the abilities that make up intelligence (Thurstone) and others have preferred to focus on the close relationships between those abilities (Spearman). But most contemporary researchers would agree that intelligence is best thought of as a hierarchy of inter-related factors (Cooper, 1999).

Gardner (1983) proposed a more radical view of intelligence. He proposed a theory of 'multiple intelligences' and suggested that there were six distinct kinds of intelligence – linguistic, logical-mathematical, spatial, musical, body-kinesthetic and personal. The first three are already familiar from our discussion of intelligence scales, but the last three constitute a marked departure in thinking about intelligence. Musical intelligence refers to the abilities to comprehend and play or compose music. Bodily-kinesthetic intelligence refers to bodily control and grace of movement as shown, for example, in athletics, dance or skating. Personal intelligence refers to an awareness of one's own behaviour and that of others; and this is related to social and interpersonal skills and to role-taking ability (see chapters 6 and 11). By putting forward the theory of multiple intelligences, Gardner was effectively criticizing the use of conventional intelligence scales that do not measure abilities like musical, athletic or social skill.

Sternberg's theory of intelligence

Other researchers have also pointed out that conceptions of intelligence based only on academic abilities are too narrow and that other aspects of human performance must be taken into account to provide a full picture of intelligent behaviour. Sternberg et al. (1981) asked a number of people to give examples of what they thought of as intelligent, or unintelligent behaviour (see box 16.1). Sternberg et al. collected 250 different types of intelligent behaviour, and classified these under different headings. What was notable about the behaviours that Sternberg et al. collected is that people included many aspects of practical and social behaviour in their examples of intelligent behaviours. Although researchers like Gardner (1983) pointed out the importance of social intelligence, other theorists had not included such behaviours under the heading of intelligence. Sternberg (1985) proposed a triarchic theory of intelligence, which recognized the importance of social and practical skills as well as purely academic ones.

Sternberg's (1985) triarchic theory was so called because it consisted of three subtheories. One was called the 'experiential subtheory', and this emphasized how effectively a person learns new skills. For instance, many skills (e.g., driving a car) become automatic, that it is they do not require much conscious attention, and an experienced driver can not only drive, but also hold a conversation at the same time. Sternberg pointed out that how quickly someone achieves task automaticity could be a reflection of their intelligence. For instance, a person might be able to achieve automaticity in a task after so many hours of experience. Another person might also achieve automaticity on the same task, but only after twice as much experience. Such differences are not examined by conventional intelligence scales but may be important. Vygotsky (see chapter 15) made a similar point when he criticized testing children's intelligence. He argued that finding out that one child scored the same as another on an intelligence scale might not mean very much unless there also were other measures of the children's potential to learn – one child might progress faster than another if she was able to gain more from her environment and the support she received from others. However, assessing how quickly and how well a person achieves automaticity on a task, or assessing a child's potential to learn are both very difficult to measure. In practice it is unlikely that a convenient and realistic test of such abilities could be devised. As it is, most intelligence scales include novel tasks and measure a child's reasoning and knowledge at one point in time – they do not measure a child's ability to learn from practice or experience.

Sternberg's (1985) called another subtheory the 'contextual subtheory' which referred to the way that people interact with their environment (e.g., in school, at home, with their families, with friends and so on). Sternberg pointed out that people can adapt themselves to the environment they find themselves in at the time, or they can try to change their environment, or they can select an alternative environment. Much of what Sternberg says applies more to adults than children, nonetheless the idea of adapting to an environment is important at all ages (for example children who adapt most successfully to school may do better academically).

The contextual subtheory has important implications for measuring intelligence, because Sternberg (1985) suggested that this aspect of intelligence is best measured with tests of practical and social skills. Practical measures might include sets of tests that, for example, include filling in forms, reading street maps, understanding bus and railway timetables, following technical instructions and so on. Measures of social skills might include tests of how well a person interprets nonverbal information. For example, Sternberg took photographs, in the street, of couples standing together. Sometimes the couples were genuine couples, but at other times they were two strangers who had been asked to stand together just for the purpose of the photograph. Sternberg then used the photographs as a test to find out if people could work out, from just looking at the photographs, which couples were 'genuine' and which couples were 'fake'. Such tests of practical and social intelligence have been designed primarily for adults, but they are mentioned here because they highlight how the concept of intelligence has been broadened and extended by researchers like Sternberg. As yet, little emphasis is placed on the measurement of children's abilities in social and practical contexts.

The other subtheory was called the componential subtheory and was concerned with the information processing aspects of tasks typically used in tests of intelligence. For example, Sternberg and Rifkin (1979) analysed the components required for the picture analogy task shown in figure 16.2. They suggested that one way to solve the task involved six components:

1 *encoding* (e.g., considering the type of hat, footwear, clothing, etc. of all five figures);
2 *inference* (this involves working out the changes needed to make A into B, e.g., changing A's hat to match B's hat);
3 *mapping* (means comparing A and C, e.g., in this example noting that they have the same hat but all their other features are different);
4 *application* (means applying the changes worked out by the inference component to C, e.g. changing C's hat, to produce an 'ideal' answer for the analogy, and then the ideal answer can be compared to the two alternatives and the appropriate figure selected);
5 *justification* (if neither of the given figures matches, choosing the better one and justifying this choice);
6 *respond* (giving the answer).

The analysis we have described is not the only way to solve the problem in figure 16.2 – in this example one of the given figures is the correct match and, therefore, there is no need for the justification component. Sternberg (1985) made the point that if such a task was included in an intelligence scale, a person's answer would be scored as correct or incorrect without any reference to how they reached their answer. But Sternberg and Rifkin (1979) found that adults and children approached the picture analogy in different ways. At the encoding stage adults attended to all the information in the picture (i.e., all the features of the figures) before applying the other components, and at this stage they were actually slower than 10-year-olds. The children, probably because of limited working memory capacity (see chapter 13) may only have encoded one or two features before

Figure 16.2   Picture analogy used by Sternberg and Rifkin.

moving on to the other components. The latter would either result in more errors, or mean that sometimes the children had to return to the encoding process again to consider other features. Analysing such tasks provides a greater insight into children's approach to the problem then simply scoring them as right or wrong on the basis of their final response.

Sternberg's (1985) triarchic theory is an ambitious theory of intelligence, however, the three sub-theories are not very well integrated into the whole and this weakens the attempt to bring all the different aspects of intelligence together. Nonetheless, Sternberg demonstrated how extensive a description of intelligence needs to be if it is to include all the contemporary ideas about intelligence.

■ Savants

Savants are individuals who usually have a low intelligence score as measured on traditional scales, but may have one (or sometimes more) exceptional abilities. For this reason, such people used to be referred to as 'idiots savants'. Howe and Smith (1988) described the case of 'Dave' who, despite having a low IQ, had an exceptional ability to calculate calendar dates. When Dave was asked what day of the week a certain date would be he was able to answer almost perfectly for any date between 1900 and 2060. Howe and Smith tried to work out how Dave was able to calculate such dates so accurately (for a summary of their study, see box 16.2).

Savants are also known with other outstanding skills including ones with exceptional memories, mathematical abilities, musical abilities, or drawing skills (Hermelin et al., 1999; Howe, 1989) (see figure 16.3). For instance, Smith and Tsimpli (1995) described Christopher, an English boy, who had a much lower than average IQ, but despite this he had an outstanding linguistic ability. Smith and Tsimpli found that Christopher knew elements of at least 16 foreign languages and was fluent in some. In addition, he could read and write several different scripts, for example, he was fluent in reading and writing modern Greek. Most of these languages he had learnt himself from text books and grammars. Christopher's remarkable language abilities stand in contrast to his lack of other abilities, for example, he was unable to play noughts and crosses (tic-tac-toe) or

Figure 16.3 Panorama of Edinburgh by Stephen Wiltshire, a young person with autism who has an exceptional (and untrained) talent for drawing. Reproduced by permission of John Johnson Ltd.

even draw the simple grid needed for this game. It is difficult to explain how the same person can learn fluent Greek, among many other languages, but remain unable to play a simple game of noughts and crosses.

The performance of savants like Dave or Christopher has implications for the different theories of intelligence that we discussed earlier. Savants are people with generally low intelligence with one exceptional skill, and this pattern of performance may be easiest to consider in the context of theories that emphasize that 'intelligence' is made of a number of different abilities. As discussed above, Gardner (1983) suggested that different 'intelligences' may be independent abilities. A person can be poor in one area of skill, but excellent in another domain, and if this is the case it would not be surprising to find a person with a low IQ who does have an outstanding ability.

An alternative explanation for the skills shown by savants has been put forward by Howe (1999) who emphasized the role of extensive practice in the development of many of the skills shown by savants. As Howe argued, many savants are solitary and withdrawn individuals who show little interest in the world around them, but may spend many hours practising one particular skill, whether it is calculating dates or learning a language. Anyone, irrespective of their IQ, who focuses their attention and effort on one particular task is likely to become an expert at that task. For example, Ericsson and Charness (1994) estimated that a 20-year-old first class violinist will have already spent over 10,000 hours practising the instrument, and will know many long and complex pieces of music. Howe would argue that we are not surprised when we learn that an expert musician has devoted many thousands of hours to rehearsing music. We should therefore not be surprised when savants, who may well have spent very long periods of time practising a skill like calendar calculating, also demonstrate remarkable abilities (Howe et al., 1999).

Intelligence in a Social-cultural Context

Several early researchers have pointed to the importance of considering intelligence in the context of the real world. Binet and Simon (1916) described intelligence in the following terms:

> It seems to us that in intelligence there is a fundamental faculty, the impairment or the lack of which is of the utmost importance for practical life. This faculty is judgment, otherwise called good sense, practical sense, initiative, the faculty of adapting oneself to circumstances. To judge well, to reason well, these are the essential activities of intelligence.

and Wechsler (1944) said:

> Intelligence is the aggregate or global capacity of the individual to act purposefully, to think rationally, and to deal effectively with his environment.

However, despite these descriptions of intelligence, it is only comparatively recently, in the work of psychologists like Sternberg (1985) described above, that specific emphasis has been placed on the context of intelligent behaviour. Children's performance can differ markedly depending on context. Nunes Carraher et al. (1985) asked children to solve mathematical problems in the context of their everyday activities (helping their parents at a street market) by asking them, for example, to calculate the cost of several items of fruit which the experimenters purchased at the market. At a different time the children were given the same problems as a paper and pencil test in their own homes. Even though the problems were the same the children performed much better in the market context than in the more 'formal' test at home (see box 15.2). Nunes Carraher et al.'s results showed how children's performance cannot be divorced from the context of that performance.

Contextualists take the view that intelligence should be defined within a particular cultural context and that comparisons across cultures can only be made with caution (Miller, 1997; Sternberg, 1999). For example, Berry (1984) argued that it is important to define intelligence in terms of the 'cognitive competence' that is needed in a particular culture, and that psychologists should take local conceptions of intelligence into account when they design tests (figure 16.4). For example, the ability to construct and use a bow and arrow is irrelevant for most people in our society, but such skills may well be of prime importance among hunter-gatherers. Intelligence scales that have been validated in a technologically advanced society would not assess skills like using a bow and arrow, but it cannot be concluded that the hunter-gatherers are less intelligent.

The constructs of intelligence will vary across cultures. Some cultures (e.g., Western industrial societies) place most emphasis on the intelligence 'within' an

'YOU CAN'T BUILD A HUT, YOU DON'T KNOW HOW TO FIND EDIBLE ROOTS AND YOU KNOW NOTHING ABOUT PREDICTING THE WEATHER. IN OTHER WORDS, YOU DO TERRIBLY ON OUR I.Q. TEST."

Figure 16.4   Intelligence needs to be seen in its cultural context (from *Current Contents* 1981). Reproduced by permission of Sidney Harris.

individual, but other cultures have conceptualized intelligence more in terms of the relationship between the individual and society. Wober (1974), in Uganda, found that 'intelligence' referred to shared knowledge and wisdom, and in particular the way an individual acted to the benefit of his or her community. Serpell (1977), in Zambia, asked adults to explain why particular children could be labelled intelligent. The adults not only referred to the children being clever (i.e., having good mental abilities) but also said that intelligent children were ones who were obedient, who could be trusted to follow instructions, and who had respect for their elders. Similarly, Harkness and Super (1992) found that in Kenya the concept of children's intelligence included reference to the children's competence in carrying out family duties effectively and obediently. In another study in Kenya, Grigorenko et al. (2001) found that people put most emphasis on practical skills and on social qualities like respect, obedience, consideration, caring for others and willingness to share. In general, the descriptions of intelligence from other cultures place far more importance on social behaviour and responsibility than do the traditional Western descriptions of intelligence.

Sternberg (1985) argued that it is much more useful to see intelligence as being embedded in a particular context than as a static quality possessed by an individual; what is important is the relative emphasis that different cultures place upon certain skills at different historical times. For example, skills needed for reading are present in individuals from pre-literate societies but are not developed and are thus not important until literacy becomes widespread. As a second example, consider the children in contemporary Western society, who have gained familiarity with computers for both academic work and for recreation. Interacting with a computer may depend more on visual, auditory and manual aspects of intelligence that are skills that are not so readily measured by traditional intelligence tests. In other words, the contextualist view emphasizes a malleable concept of intelligence that can accommodate different ideas about intelligence over space and time.

The Use of Intelligence Tests

Despite concerns about the content validity of traditional intelligence scales, they are still used frequently, because they are one way to find out about a child's strengths and weaknesses. Over and above just measuring a child's performance, many educational psychologists treat intelligence tests like a clinical interview in which they can gain insights into the child's personality, self-image, attention-span and motivation as well as level of intelligence. Thus, in the hands of an experienced clinician, a test can be of important diagnostic value. From this point of view, intelligence scales can be useful. They can be used to identify children with particularly low levels of ability who may need special help and schooling (which was Binet's original intention in designing tests); they can be used to identify gifted children who may also need special educational provision; and they can also be used to identify distinctive patterns of performance. For example adults with dyslexia (see chapter 11) often have a pattern of performance on the WAIS that is called the 'ACID' profile – this means that they have below average scores on four tests on this scale – i.e. Arithmetic, Coding, Information and Digit span tests (these are similar but more advanced versions of the tests described in table 16.3), but they may have average or above average scores on the other tests. This particular profile is typical of adults who have dyslexia.

Children with learning difficulties

In assessing children who perform poorly in school educational psychologists may rely only partly on the results from an intelligence test. They would also try to assess children in the context of their home background, medical history of life events and in relation to the problems that the children might be experiencing. For example, if a child has had prolonged periods of illness or a traumatic event such as the loss of a parent, then these circumstances would need to be taken into account when assessing the child's level of attainment.

Some learning difficulties have been ascribed to general intellectual impairment. Others, however, may be due to an unstimulating or stressful home background, to emotional disturbance, to a physical condition, to poor diet, or to a combination of factors and therefore psychologists may use methods of assessment that best identify such potential problems. In addition to intelligence scales, many other measures can be used; for example, naturalistic observation of the child's behaviour as recorded by parents and teachers can lead to a greater understanding of the child's difficulties. Social assessment can also be helpful to indicate a child's communicative abilities, social skills and emotional adjustment. Psychologists can also use attainment tests to measure performance in specific areas, such as mathematics and reading, and diagnostic tests can help to unravel the reasons for a child's poor performance. We will say more about attainment tests later in this chapter.

Gifted children

A child may be described as 'gifted' who is outstanding in either a general domain such as exceptional performance on an intelligence test, or a more specific area of ability, like music or sport (Howe, 1999; Radford, 1990). The borderline between gifted children and others is not clearly defined, and different researchers have used different levels of performance on intelligence scales to define a gifted child as one with an IQ of more than 120, more than 130, or more than 140. Children with such high scores are rare: only 1 in 10 children have scores over 120; 1 in 40 have scores over 130; 1 in 200 have scores over 140; and 1 in 1000 have a score over 150.

The most famous investigation of giftedness is Terman's (1925) 35-year study (at Stanford University in California) that began in 1921 with children aged about ten years. Terman used gifted to refer to children with IQ scores about or above 140 (on the Stanford–Binet scale) and all the children in his sample had scores of between 130 and 190. The children were followed up for most of their lives and Terman published regular reports about their achievements. Physical health and growth were superior from birth on, they walked and talked early, and the children excelled in reading, language and general knowledge.

A follow-up in 1947 when the average age was 35 indicated that the initial level of intelligence had been maintained (Terman and Oden, 1947). Sixty-eight per cent had graduated from college, and many had been outstanding in their professions; for example, they had produced a large number of publications and patents. In 1959 another follow-up found that they had continued to maintain their high achievements in occupational level. Seventy-one per cent were in professional, semi-professional or managerial positions (compared with 14 per cent of the

Californian population as a whole) and their average income was higher than that of the average college graduate (Terman and Oden, 1959).

Terman's study showed that gifted children are, perhaps not surprisingly, very likely to become successful adults. However, one limitation of his study should be noted. The children in his sample were selected partly on the basis of teachers' ratings and in this way home background factors may have been confounded with his criterion of high intelligence; for instance, working class and ethnic minority children may have been under-represented from the start of the study. In other words, the children in the sample may have come from advantageous social environments, and some of their success may have been due as much to this factor as to their high IQ.

Most of the participants in Terman's sample appeared to be well-integrated, healthy and well-adjusted individuals. However some researchers have pointed out the problems and difficulties that gifted children can face. Gross (1993) described the case of Ian who, at the age of five years, hated school, was uncontrollable in class, was aggressive towards other children, and was to be referred to a special school for children with behavioural problems. As part of the referral process, Ian was assessed by an educational psychologist who tested him on the Stanford–Binet scale, and found that he had an IQ of over 170; he also had the reading age of a 12-year-old. The psychologist suggested that any behavioural problems were most likely to be the result of frustration. When measured at the age of nine, Ian's IQ was about 200 (put another way, he had the mental age of an 18-year-old), and yet his school insisted that he undertook the curriculum designed for nine-year-olds. Clearly, this was inappropriate, and Gross argued that such exceptional children should be given special consideration and support.

However, other researchers who have investigated gifted children have come to different conclusions about the causes of their behavioural difficulties. Freeman (1980) investigated two groups of children aged 5–16 years. Group 1 were gifted children (with an average IQ of 147 on the Stanford–Binet scale) who were labelled as such and were in a national association for gifted children. Group 2 children had a similarly high IQ but were not in the national association. Freeman carried out interviews with the children's parents and found that the children in Group 1 were rated as more 'difficult', more 'sensitive', more 'emotional', and having 'few friends'. Freeman argued that such difficulties were unlikely to be due directly to the children's giftedness because Group 2 also had high IQs but the children in Group 2 had far fewer problems. Freeman pointed out that the difference between the two groups was how much emphasis the parents placed on being gifted (e.g., by joining an association) and suggested that it was parental pressures and expectations that contributed to the difficulties of the children in Group 1.

In a follow-up study Freeman (2001) interviewed the participants in the original study. The participants were now young adults, but there were still differences between the two groups. The children in Group 1 were more likely than the ones in Group 2 to say that they were unhappy or unfulfilled, and some had found it hard to form friendships and relationships. As the participants in Group 1 were the ones who had been labelled gifted from being young, Freeman (2000) argued that the emotional problems found in Group 1 were more the result of that labelling than the result of being gifted.

◼ Attainment Tests

Measures of intelligence usually include tests that are unfamiliar to the person taking the test – in other words the test designers are attempting to measure the performance of a person on tests which are novel and that have not been practised. In contrast, tests of attainment measure what a person has achieved after specific training (Black, 1998). Examples of attainment tests include school examinations; driving tests; examinations for music, tests of sporting achievement, and so on. Such measures have a variety of purposes and we will give examples of the different ways that educational tests can be used.

Certification and selection: Passing an examination is an indication that a person has achieved a specified level of competence. Examinations were first introduced in the UK in 1815 for doctors, and were later also used by other professions (e.g., solicitors and accountants) to determine entry into the profession. They were also used from the mid-nineteenth century to assess candidates for the Civil Service, and for university entrance. These examinations were meant to be a way of giving more (middle class) people access to the professions or university, because previously such opportunities had been based on family background or payment. The early professional examinations were all written ones and established the tradition of written examinations throughout school and university. The use of tests for selection at all ages and levels is one of the main perceived uses of examinations, and earlier we discussed the use of the 11 plus examination for selection to secondary school. In the present UK educational system, performance in GCSE examinations at 16 years of age determines the opportunity to study for AS-level and A-level examinations, and they in turn determine access to higher education.

Motivation: Assessment is a way to motivate children to be successful. At a minimum, examinations focus attention on hard work and channel behaviour into what is educationally and socially desirable. But more than this, assessment may be seen as both intrinsically rewarding (because children learn as they prepare for tests) and externally rewarding (if success in an examination gives access to the next step on the educational ladder). At all stages children can be given feedback which should contribute to both their learning and their motivation to improve.

Record keeping All assessment (e.g., examinations or teachers' judgements) can contribute to a record of a child's performance. This can be used to check on a child's progress, and is particularly important if a child is having difficulties, as the course and extent of those difficulties can be identified.

Screening and diagnostic assessment: Screening means that all the children at a certain age or level are given the same test, or set of tests, to identify any who might be in need of special help. Once a child who needs special help has been identified he or she can be given diagnostic tests to find out about their particular weaknesses. For example, if a child is poor at reading, diagnostic tests of reading can be used to discover the specific reading disabilities that she may have. Measures used for screening are usually standardized tests

Standardized tests: There are a wide range of tests designed to measure attainment in reading, verbal reasoning, English, numeracy and comprehension and so on. Standardized tests (like intelligence scales) have been pre-tested on large numbers of children to eliminate badly worded questions or items that fail to discriminate between different children. The instructions for administering the tests are also standard so that all children take the test under the same conditions. Such tests have been used on large numbers of children, so that the test designers can state how an average child at any given age should perform on the test. This allows a teacher to make a meaningful assessment of an individual child's abilities by comparing her performance to other children of the same age. Performance on many attainment tests correlates quite highly with IQ, but the primary function of an attainment test is to measure achievement within a particular subject area rather than general intelligence.

Criterion-referenced tests: These are tests that measure whether a child can achieve a specified level of performance on a task. For example, a teacher might want to know whether a child understands how to do long division, and might set the criterion of understanding as successfully solving 20 long division problems. A criterion-referenced test is different from a standardized test (which is based on comparisons between children of the same age) because set criteria are given. For example, a driving test is a criterion-referenced test because a person either meets the requirements of the test and passes, or does not meet them and fails. In other words, you either pass or fail; the test is the same whatever your age. If all driving test candidates met the required criteria then 100 per cent could pass the test. In contrast, on a standardized test 50 per cent of children at any age will be below the average score and fifty per cent will be above that score.

Curriculum control and school evaluation: One use of assessment is to determine what is taught in schools. If children are to take a particular examination, the school syllabus must include the appropriate teaching needed for that examination. More explicitly, following the 1988 Education Reform Act in the UK, a National Curriculum was introduced that included specific attainment targets. Pupils are assessed at the ages of seven, 11, 14 and 16 years of age using tests that are the same nationally. These are criterion-referenced tests because, ideally, all children, at each age, should have achieved the knowledge and ability to succeed on them. The use of common tests for all pupils can provide important information about the progress of individual children, and at the same time both teachers and schools can be assessed in terms of their pupils' performance. However, a major concern in the use of national assessment tests is whether they might be biased against particular groups of pupils – for example that one or other gender, or that children from minority ethnic groups, might be disadvantaged by the tests (see Gipps and Murphy, 1994).

Conclusions

Intelligence and attainment tests are useful for assessing an individual child. This can often be of great importance for identifying children who are exceptional (in terms of either learning difficulties or giftedness), or in identifying a particular child's strengths and weaknesses. However, the results from all tests should be treated with caution, because both intelligence scales and attainment tests are designed for specific educational purposes. They may often be effective for the very specific purposes for which they were designed, but a child's performance on a single test should not lead to any more extensive assumptions about that child's ability. For example, a child's performance on an intelligence test may be helpful to an educational psychologist who needs to assess that child. But as we pointed out in the section on concepts of intelligence, the 'intelligence' measured by a traditional intelligence scale may not reflect the whole range of behaviours and abilities that go together to make up an intelligent individual. While there is so little agreement about the nature of intelligence, any measures of it have to be considered carefully.

Further Reading

A very good, brief, introduction to all aspects of intelligence research can be found in Cooper, C. 1999: *Intelligence and Abilities*. London: Routledge, and there is a good introduction to the theories and concepts underlying intelligence testing in Richardson, K. 1991: *Understanding Intelligence*. Buckingham: Open University Press. A more advanced text with an excellent and critical review of all the issues relating to intelligence is Mackintosh, N. J. 1998: *IQ and Human Intelligence*. Oxford: Oxford University Press. For a critical review of educational assessment in the UK, including a discussion of ethnic and gender bias in tests see Gipps, C. and Murphy, P. 1994: *A Fair Test? Assessment, Achievement and Equity*. Buckingham: Open University Press.

A note about intelligence and attainment tests. Many intelligence and attainment tests can be purchased. However, the publishers of tests only sell them to registered users. Before registering a user the publishers require evidence of the user's qualifications, and in addition, for specific tests they may require evidence that a user has been on an appropriate course for training in the use of that test. These procedures are followed to ensure that tests are used responsibly and correctly, and that both test material and test results are always kept confidential. For these reasons it is not possible to borrow tests from libraries or other sources, nonetheless, most publishers maintain extensive websites and therefore it is possible to find information about specific tests by searching those sites.

Discussion Points

1   What does 'intelligence' mean?
2   Is an individual's 'intelligence' a single trait or is it made up of many different abilities?
3   Do different concepts of intelligence have different implications for the way we measure people's intelligence?
4   Do school and college examinations measure intelligence?
5   What purposes do attainment tests serve?

Box 16.1
People's conceptions of intelligence

Sternberg et al. asked 186 people to list behaviours that they thought were characteristic of 'intelligence', 'academic intelligence', 'everyday intelligence', and 'unintelligence'. The people included 61 studying in a Yale college library, 63 waiting for trains, and 62 shoppers at a supermarket. In total they collected 250 different behaviours which included 170 examples of intelligent behaviour and 80 examples of unintelligent behaviour.

Sternberg et al. then found two further groups of people. One group were 'laypersons' recruited through newspaper advertisements, and the other group were 'experts' all of whom had higher degrees in psychology and were carrying out research in universities. These groups were given questionnaires which included the list of 250 behaviours and they were asked to rate each behaviour, on a 1 (low) to 9 (high) scale, according to how important they thought that behaviour was in defining the concept of (a) an intelligent person, (b) an academically intelligent person, and (c) an everyday intelligent person.

The experts' view of an ideally intelligent person could be divided into three factors that Sternberg et al. labelled as verbal intelligence, problem-solving ability, and practical intelligence. The first factor included behaviours like: 'displays a good vocabulary', 'reads with high comprehension', 'displays curiosity', and 'is intellectually curious'. The second factor included behaviours such as 'able to apply knowledge to problems at hand', 'makes good decisions', 'poses problems in an optimal way', and 'displays common sense'. The third factor included behaviours like 'sizes up situations well', 'determines how to achieve goals', 'displays awareness of world around him or herself', and 'displays interest in the world at large'.

Laypersons' views of an ideally intelligent person could also be divided onto three main factors that were labelled practical problem-solving ability, verbal ability and social competence. Although there was an overlap with the experts' views, there was also an important difference because laypersons put more emphasis on social competence, a category that included behaviours such as 'accepts others for what they are', 'admits mistakes', and 'is on time for appointments'.

Experts' views of academic intelligence were divided into three factors: problem-solving ability, verbal ability and motivation. Clearly there was an overlap between their views of ideal intelligence and ideal academic intelligence, but with the difference that experts also stressed motivation in the context of academic intelligence. This was a factor that included behaviours like, 'displays dedication and motivation in chosen pursuits', 'gets involved in what he or she is doing', 'studies hard', and 'is persistent'. The layperson's view of academic intelligence was slightly different because they included behaviours linked to verbal ability, problem-solving ability and social competence, rather than motivation.

For everyday intelligence the experts' views could be divided into three factors: practical problem solving ability, practical adaptive behaviour, and social competence. The layperson's description of everyday intelligence included four factors. The first two were the same as the first two factors proposed by the experts, but laypersons also thought that character and an interest in learning and culture were important.

As all the participants were asked to describe types of intelligence it is not sur-

prising that that there were many similarities in the patterns that Sternberg et al. identified. Nonetheless, there were also differences, both in the way that the same groups described different types of intelligence, and between the groups. These differences reflect the difficulty of describing intelligence with any brief or single definition of the term. What is most noticeable about Sternberg et al.'s data is the very large number of behaviours that people were willing to include as examples of intelligent behaviour. As Sternberg et al. say in summing up their results, no one theory of intelligence is likely 'to do justice to the full scope of intelligence' (1981, p. 55).

Based on material in Sternberg, R. J., Conway, B. E., Ketron, J. L. and Bernstein, M. 1981: People's conceptions of intelligence. *Journal of Personality and Social Psychology*, 41, 37–55.

Box 16.2
Calendar calculating in 'idiots savants'. How do they do it?

Howe and Smith carried out a case study with a 14-year-old boy called 'Dave' (not his real name) who had a low IQ but a remarkable ability to work out dates. Dave attended a non-residential school for children who were developmentally delayed. Howe and Smith used a series of tests to establish Dave's IQ and found that he scored 50 on the Stanford–Binet test, and 54 on the Wechsler Intelligence Scale for Children. As typically developing children have an average score of 100 on such intelligence scales, Dave's scores were very low. Howe and Smith also used a reading test to establish Dave's reading age and found it was

about six years (i.e., eight years behind his chronological age).

Dave was withdrawn and said very little, and when he did spoke what he said was often irrelevant to the situation. He showed little interest in other people and resented interference from others. Dave's solitariness meant that it was difficult for Howe and Smith to ask him questions because he often chose not to answer. Nonetheless, Howe and Smith were able to get Dave to answer a number of questions that involved calculating dates. They asked him questions like 'What day of the week was it/will it be on the . . . th of . . . , in the year of . . . ?' The range of dates included ones between 1900 and 2060 and Dave gave the correct day of the week for 94 per cent of the questions. It goes without saying that this was a remarkable achievement from a child who was otherwise so developmentally delayed.

Earlier researchers who have investigated other individuals with calendar calculating skills have suggested several ways that savants might be able to work out dates. First, the day of the week for a particular date can be calculated using published mathematical formulae, and these can be learnt and practiced (see Howe, 1989, for examples of these formulae). Second, some calendar calculators have memorized a large number of specific dates (e.g., the days and dates of the birthdays of everyone they have ever met) and they might use these as reference points for other dates by working forwards or backwards from the ones that they have already memorized. Third, some calendar calculators may use a form of visual imagery to imagine a calendar. For example, Roberts (1945) reported one savant who could recall dates and the colour of those dates as they appeared on a printed calendar. Of course, none of the approaches are mutually exclusive and a calendar calculator could use a combination of them. Nonetheless, Howe and Smith tried to find out if they could exclude any of these methods in the case of Dave.

It did not seem likely that Dave was using any published formula, because his reading ability was poor and there was no reason to believe he had access to such formulae. But Howe and Smith asked Dave to answer questions like. 'In what years will the 9th October be on a Wednesday?' because this type of question cannot be answered by using any available formula. Dave was able to answer all the questions in this form quickly and without difficulty. This showed that Dave was quite capable of calendar calculating in contexts where no formula was possible.

Howe and Smith had asked Dave to name the day of the week for particular dates between 1900 and 2060. Dave was thought to know the days and dates of the birthdays of all the pupils and staff at his school, and he might have been able to use these as reference points for dates in the past. But it would not have been possible to use this technique for working out dates that occurred in the future. When Smith and Howe asked Dave to give the day of the week for future periods they found that he remained very accurate. This suggested that Dave had some way of calculating dates without relying on reference ones.

Howe and Smith came to the conclusion that Dave was probably using some form of visual imagery. He often drew calendars, and included in his drawings the additional details sometimes included on printed calendars (e.g., representations of the moon). When recalling dates he sometimes made comments like 'Thursdays are always black' or 'it's on the top line' as if he was recalling an image of a page of a calendar. Howe and Smith asked Dave to say which month of each year began with a Friday. They reasoned that this would be a very difficult task if Dave had to calculate the day of the week for the first of every month for every year, but would be possible if Dave had an image of a calendar that he could work through. In fact, Dave was able to name correctly and quickly all the months beginning with a Friday between 1970 and 1990. Howe and Smith suggested that Dave's speed and accuracy indicated that he was able to access some image of each month as a whole.

Given the difficulty of eliciting information from anyone like Dave who had limited language abilities and was generally withdrawn, any findings from this study must be speculative. Nonetheless, Howe and Smith showed that it was possible to hypothesize several ways that dates could be calculated, and then, by carefully designing the questions they asked, to eliminate some of these ways in the case of Dave. By using this method they concluded that Dave's calendar calculating was based on a mental image, perhaps derived from printed calendars he had seen. This does not necessarily mean that all savants with calendar calculating skills use the same method, because there is evidence that other savants do have some appreciation of calendar regularities (O'Connor and Hermelin, 1992) or may have memorized so many individual dates they can recall them easily (Kahr and Niesser, 1982, cited by Howe and Smith, 1988).

As yet we know little about how savant skills develop, but studies of savants like Dave will undoubtedly continue. They will continue partly because of the fascination of observing such exceptional skills, and partly because the fact that some people with generally low IQ can have one or more outstanding abilities has many implications for theories of intelligence (see p. 540 above).

Based on material in Howe, M. J. A. and Smith, J. 1988: Calendar calculating in 'idiots savants'. How do they do it? *British Journal of Psychology*, 79, 371–86.

17 Deprivation and Enrichment: Risk and Resilience

In this final chapter we look at disadvantage, deprivation and enrichment and the part played by families, by schools and by society itself in the cognitive and emotional development of children, with particular emphasis on those from less advantaged environments. We will consider the role of risk and protective factors in the psychological development of the child. There are ethical considerations to take into account when undertaking the study of deprivation since children cannot, of course, be deliberately deprived of essential experiences. So, as you will see, many of the research studies tend to be carried out in naturalistic settings in circumstances that were occurring anyway. This makes for particular problems in research design (see chapter 1). By contrast, it is ethically permissible to provide enrichment for children in conditions of adversity, and we will review studies, both experimental and in naturalistic settings, which attempt to evaluate the effect on children of ameliorating the conditions of their lives.

Disadvantage

Disadvantage usually means a relatively enduring condition that results in lower academic achievement at school and reduced opportunities in the wider society. This tends to refer to social or cultural characteristics, for example being a member of an ethnic minority group, living in an inner city area or having a low income. Wedge and Essen (1982, p. 11) defined the disadvantaged as 'that group of children who failed to thrive, who failed to mature as much or as quickly physically, or who have failed to achieve as well in school as other . . . children'.

Why are some children at a disadvantage in society? How significant a factor is social class or membership of an ethnic minority? What effects does poverty have on a child's emotional and intellectual development? Can schools compen-

Plate 17.1   Children make the most of a dismal inner city environment, using available materials for play.

sate for deprivation in the home? How does the wider culture shape the direction of a child's aspirations and achievements? None of the answers is simple since these questions concern the complex interaction of many factors, from the parent–child relationship to the social context within which the child develops. In Britain in the 1970s, Wedge and Essen found that important social and economic factors included family composition (a large number of children in the family, or only one parent figure), low income and poor housing. Each of these factors was related to poor physical and academic development and less acceptable behaviour.

It may help to consider Baltes' emphasis on historical factors and Bronfenbrenner's ecological model of human development, summarized in chapter 1. Both Baltes and Bronfenbrenner warn of the dangers of focusing on the individual without taking into account the context within which he or she exists or the processes of interaction through which the behaviour of individuals in a particular system or historical period develops. It is useful to bear their ideas in mind as you consider the issues raised in this chapter. But first, let us look at the effects of extreme deprivation and neglect.

◼ Extreme Deprivation and Neglect

Feral children

We look first at studies of the effects of extreme deprivation and neglect on young children. There have, for example, been anecdotal accounts of 'feral' children, that is children discovered in the wild with apparently no form of human contact. When rescued, these children tended to display behaviour more characteristic of animals, such as running on all fours, and this led some to believe that the children had survived through being reared by and among animals. Such cases are often inadequately documented. Whatever the circumstances of their rearing, the prognosis for feral children has been poor. Their linguistic and cognitive attainment has tended to remain low, and their social behaviour strange. However, we cannot be sure that such children were developing 'normally' when their parents abandoned them, and some investigators have suggested that feral children may have been psychotic or developmentally delayed in the first instance. We do have a few more reliable case studies of children who have been reared in conditions of extreme deprivation in their own homes and who have subsequently been rescued. These accounts can help answer the question of how far an enriched environment can compensate for the effects of very severe neglect in the early years.

The Koluchova twins

Koluchova's (1972; 1991) case study of Czechoslovakian twins, Paul and John, born in 1960 gives evidence to support the argument that the effects of severe neglect need not be irreversible. The twins' mother died when they were born and they spent the next 11 months in an institution where they were said to be making normal progress. The father then took them back into his home but, on his remarriage, they were again put into care until the new household was formed. From around the age of 18 months until 7 years the twins lived with their father and his new wife. However, the stepmother kept them in conditions of extreme deprivation. She forbade her own children to talk to the twins and denied them any affection herself. They spent their time either in a bare, unheated room apart from the rest of the family or, as a punishment, were locked in the cellar. They never went out, and lacked proper food, exercise and any kind of intellectual or social stimulation apart from what they could provide for themselves. Neighbours did not know of their existence but from time to time heard strange, animal-like sounds coming from the cellar. By the age of 7, when the authorities became aware of the twins' existence, they had the appearance of 3-year-olds; they could hardly walk because of rickets, they could not play, their speech was very poor and they relied mainly on gestures to communicate. On their discovery, they were removed from the family and placed in a home for preschool children.

They had experienced such severe emotional, intellectual and social deprivation that the prognosis seemed very poor, but once placed in a supportive environment, they began to make remarkable gains. After a year they were ready to be placed in a school for children with special educational needs. There they made such progress that they were transferred the next year to the second class of a mainstream infant school. At the same time, they were placed in the care of an unmarried middle-aged woman, with a long experience of rearing children in her extended family. At the time, she lived with her sister who had already adopted an 11-year-old girl. The two sisters gave the twins the emotional security and intellectual stimulation that had been so lacking in their own family environment.

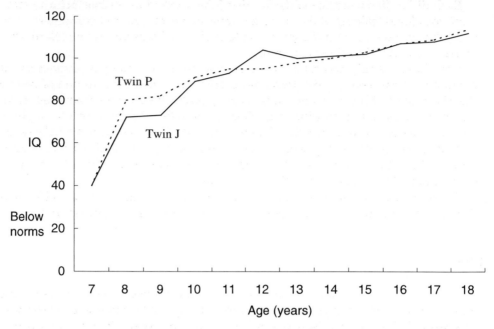

Figure 17.1   Changes in the IQ score of the Koluchova twins, measured by the WISC, after intervention began.

Age 7: placed in institutional care
Age 8–9: attend school for children with special needs
Age 10: attend second class of mainstream infant school
Age 11–13: progress through mainstream primary school
Age 14–16: progress to secondary school class of pupils 18 months younger than twins
Age 17: complete schooling; attain school leaving certificate
Age 18: attend college for vocational training

As a result, in the next 15 months, the twins' mental age increased by 3 years, showing clearly how the environmental change had compensated for early neglect. Prior to that, Koluchova had estimated their intelligence to be around an IQ of 40, although no formal assessment was possible because of their unfamiliarity with any of the tasks that appear in intelligence tests. A follow-up at the age of 14 found complete 'catch-up' in the twins' language development; school performance was good and motivation high. They were now functioning at an average academic level in a class of children who were only 18 months younger than they. They were socially adjusted and had realistic aspirations to go on to take a vocational training. They finished schooling at the age of 17 when their educational standard corresponded broadly to that of their peers. After leaving school, they went to college to train as typewriter mechanics where they were among the best in their class. They lived in a students' residence while maintaining strong relationships with their adoptive family. Figure 17.1 indicates the intellectual progress made by the twins from 3 months after intervention began.

Each did military service and after that John worked as an instructor in technical vocational training and Paul as a technician specializing in computers. Paul and John are now in their 40s with a wide circle of friends and family. Both have married and each has three children.

Koluchova's study indicates how removal from an extremely impoverished environment can reverse the effects of deprivation. It could be argued of course that the success of the intervention was only possible because the twins had experienced some normal nurturing in the first few months of their lives; second, they were not totally isolated since they had the support of one another; third, the twins were discovered when they were still relatively young. But their case illustrates the extent to which children can be rehabilitated despite being exposed to extreme emotional and physical deprivation in early life.

A less favourable outcome was found in another case study, that of a girl called 'Genie', where two of these ameliorative factors were absent (Curtiss, 1977).

Genie

Genie's isolation was even more extreme than that of the Czechoslovakian twins and lasted for a longer period of time. From the age of 20 months until she was 13 years old she was imprisoned alone in a darkened room. By day she was tied to an infant potty chair in such a way that she could only move her hands and feet; at night, she was put in a sleeping bag and further restrained by a wire straitjacket. Her father beat her if she made any sound and he forbade other members of the family to speak to her. She lived in an almost silent world deprived of warmth, proper nourishment and normal human contact. She was kept in these conditions until her mother, who was partially blind and dominated by Genie's father, finally escaped with her. At this point, Genie could not walk, she was emaciated, weighing only 59 pounds, she spent much of her time spitting and salivating, and was virtually silent apart from the occasional whimper. When tested soon after admission to hospital, she was functioning at the level of a 1-year-old.

Curtiss (1977), a graduate student of linguistics at the time, has given a moving and detailed account of Genie's development after she was taken into care. Despite the terrible conditions she had endured, Genie did respond to treatment. She soon learned to walk. Her level of intellectual functioning (measured by a non-verbal intelligence test developed for use with deaf children) increased (see figure 17.2) and in some perceptual tasks, such as the Mooney Faces Test, which required subjects to distinguish between real and distorted faces, she performed well above average. She also became able to form relationships with other people.

In the area of language, however, Genie's development proved puzzling. During the first 7 months in care she learned to recognize a number of words and then began to speak. At first she produced one-word utterances like 'pillow'; later, like any normal toddler, she produced two-word utterances, first nouns and adjectives (e.g., 'big teeth') and later verbs ('want milk') (chapter 11). She was even able to use words to describe her experience of isolation and neglect (Curtiss records Genie as saying, 'Father hit arm. Big wood. Genie cry'). However, there were unusual aspects to her language development. She never asked questions, she

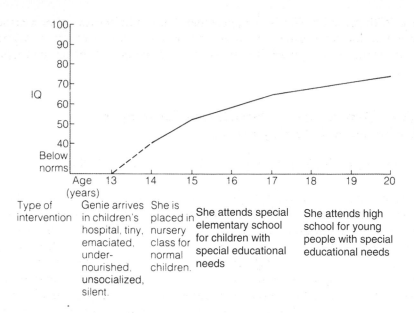

Figure 17.2 Changes in Genie's IQ scores, measured by the Leiter International Performance Scale (a non-verbal test), after intervention began.

never learned to use pronouns and the telegraphic speech did not develop into more complex sentences. In fact, she was more inclined to use gestures in order to convey meaning.

Thus, although Genie showed great interest in language and developed some competence, she did not catch up with other children of her own age. Curtiss speculated that Genie was using the right hemisphere of the brain for language not the left as is usual. Since the right hemisphere is not predisposed to language, this could explain some of the strange aspects of Genie's speech. Such an interpretation is confirmed by Genie's competence at discriminating faces, which is a right hemisphere task. Curtiss's explanation of Genie's unusual language development is that when language is not acquired at the right time, the cortical tissue normally committed for language and related abilities may functionally atrophy. If Curtiss is right, Genie provides support for the idea that there is indeed a critical or sensitive period for the development of some left hemisphere functioning.

Some of the questions remain unanswered since all research into Genie's development abruptly stopped in 1978 when a court allowed her mother to become her legal guardian. At this point Genie's mother filed a lawsuit claiming that Curtiss and others had used Genie for their own personal gain (see Rymer, 1994). Intervention did have a considerable impact on Genie's development, but apparently without such dramatic success as was obtained with the twins in Koluchova's study.

Skuse (1984, p. 567), in a review of studies of extreme deprivation (including the Koluchova twins and Genie), concluded that 'in the absence of genetic or congenital anomalies or a history of gross malnourishment, victims of such deprivation have an excellent prognosis. Some subtle deficits in social adjustment may persist.' Having a secure attachment to a good caregiver is a key factor in recovery. With regard to Genie, it is possible that the help came after a critical or sensitive period for normal language development; however, Skuse argues that we cannot rule out the possibility of organic dysfunction in the left hemisphere in her case.

The Effects of Institutional Rearing on Children's Development

Early studies during and after World War II (1939–45)

Another area of research that provides information about the impacts of deprivation on children's development focuses on the experience of children reared in orphanages or children's homes. Studies in this field began in the years before and soon after World War II. Spitz (1946) noted that infants in institutions fared very badly in comparison with infants reared at home. They were under-weight, reached developmental milestones later, and were more vulnerable to illness. As we saw in chapter 4, at that time children's institutions provided little stimulation of any kind. The children had few toys or playthings, little conversation with staff, and experienced extreme multiple caregiving. As a result, institutionally reared children scored very poorly on tests of cognitive or linguistic development, as well as showing problems in later social adjustment. It was the work of Bowlby and other psychologists that drew attention to these consequences of institutional rearing, and hence led to great improvements in the quality of the institutional environment. The success of these efforts was one factor contributing to the enthusiasm for compensatory education and enrichment programmes discussed later on in this chapter.

Two early studies showed the effects that could be achieved by enriching the environment for institutionally reared children. Skeels and Dye (1939) chanced to notice the effect of environmental change on two developmentally delayed children who had been transferred at 18 months from an orphanage to the women's ward in an institution for adults with severe learning difficulties, which had an associated school. Their new environment was in fact an enriched one in comparison with the orphanage. Both staff and patients lavished attention and affection on them, played with them and took them on outings, and the children were given a much more stimulating experience than they had had previously. The gains were dramatic and after 15 months of this experience the children were considered to be within the normal range of intelligence. By contrast, children who had remained in the stultifying environment of the orphanage did not make progress in the same way.

Skodak and Skeels (1945) then carried out a more systematic longitudinal study in which 13 developmentally delayed infants from the orphanage were transferred in the same way as the earlier two. The infants were aged 11–21 months, and had a mean IQ of 64. Again the children made dramatic gains; after an average of 19 months' stay their mean IQ was 92. By the age of 3 or 4 most were adopted by families and went on to attend mainstream school. A similar, control group of 12 children who stayed in the orphanage, however, actually decreased in IQ from a mean of 87 to 61 over this period. More than 20 years later, a follow-up study (Skeels, 1966) indicated that the gains made by the experimental group of children were lasting. They had obtained significantly more grades at school than the control group, four had attended college, and one had graduated and then gone on to achieve a Ph.D.; they had formed stable partnerships, and had a varied range of occupations (e.g., teacher, beautician, flight attendant, sales manager). In the control group, all but one were in unskilled occupations, were unemployed or still living in the institution. These dramatic findings suggested that intervention at an early age had crucial effects on later educational and vocational success.

However, Kirk (1958) advised caution in interpreting the findings of Skeels and Skodak. Was it the intervention in the women's ward that had the effect, or was it the continuing long-term stimulation and care from the adopted families? Kirk followed groups of developmentally delayed children during the preschool and first school years and found that much of the intervention effect 'wore off' or 'washed out' after the experimental period was over. The reason for this could have been acceleration on the part of the control children once they experienced the stimulation of school, or deceleration on the part of the experimental children once their enriched experience was over. The Kirk experiment suggested that early intervention could have immediate effects, but needed to be reinforced by a continuing experience of enrichment, warmth and stimulation (like that of the adopted children in Skeels and Skodak's study) if the gains were to be permanent.

Later studies in other cultures

Although these studies have been criticized for their small number of participants, possible lack of random assignment to experimental and control groups, and the diversity of the sample, the striking results provide a strong indication that environmental stimulation can undo at least some of the negative effects of deprivation. Later studies in different cultures tell a very similar story. Dennis (1973) carried out a series of studies in the Crèche, a Lebanese orphanage run by French nuns. The children were fed and kept clean, but were given very little intellectual stimulation; the ratio of caregivers to children was 1–10; the babies were kept in cribs with white sheets round them; if they cried, no-one came; the caregivers rarely talked to them. As you would expect, the children were very delayed in terms of locomotor, intellectual and linguistic development. The children stayed in the Crèche until the age of 6 when boys and girls were transferred to separate institutions. The girls went to another orphanage where the emphasis was on domestic work and where again the environment was extremely unstimulating; many of them were destined to work as caregivers in the Crèche. By the age of 16, the girls had an average IQ of 50. By contrast, the boys went to a different orphanage where the emphasis was on giving them a much wider range of skills to equip them for work in the outside world; they were also taken on outings. By the age of 15, their average IQ was 80.

Dennis also investigated the intellectual development of those children from the Crèche who were adopted, following a change in legislation in the Lebanon in the 1950s. He found that children who were adopted by the age of 2 years regained normal IQs, even though their average IQ at the time of adoption was 50. However, Crèche children who were adopted at a later age were less likely to 'catch up' intellectually. Dennis concluded that deprivation up to the first 2 years of life can be overcome if the later environment is normal, and that if there was a critical period (see chapter 2) for intellectual development it would be later – between 2 and 8 years. Alternatively, the difficulties older children experience might be because they suffer more deficit. For example, a 4-year-old with an IQ of 50 has a mental age of 2 years; an 8-year-old with an IQ of 50 has a mental age of 4 years. By 12 years of age, the 4-year-old had 8 years of normal growth; but the 8-year-old had only 4 additional years of normal growth.

Kagan (1976) confirmed Dennis's conclusion that deprivation in infancy does not necessarily have permanent effects. He studied children in an isolated Guatemalan community where the custom was to keep babies in what would be by Western standards an extremely unstimulating environment until they could walk, at around 13–16 months. There seemed to be very little verbal stimulation; the babies slept a lot; there were no toys or other objects to play with; the babies lived in a state of near darkness for most of the time. Kagan found that, at the age of 1 year, these babies were 3–4 months delayed in comparison with American babies of the same age. They were passive, uncommunicative, did not appear to be alert, and rarely smiled. However, when they were followed up in late childhood and early adolescence, the children were found to be normal on a range of cognitive and social tasks. However, these children had formed a close one-to-one relationship with their mothers and so were not emotionally deprived as the orphanage children at the Crèche were; in fact, their situation could be considered as culturally appropriate despite the difference from Western norms.

Romanian adoptees

Ongoing rigorous longitudinal research by Rutter and his colleagues (O'Connor et al., 2000; Rutter et al., 1998) has investigated the deficit and developmental 'catch-up' following adoption to the UK of Romanian children who had spent the first years of their lives in orphanages where they suffered neglect and deprivation. This was at a time when Romania was going through a period of acute political upheaval; the previous Ceaucescu regime had encouraged policies that resulted in many children being placed in orphanages in conditions ranging from poor to appalling. The Romanian children in this study, who were severely developmentally delayed on their entry to the UK, were compared to a sample of UK children placed for adoption before the age of 6 months.

Initial measurements at 4 years (Rutter et al., 1998) indicated considerable resilience with regard to cognitive and physical development on the part of the Romanian adoptees. The strongest predictor was the children's age on entry to the UK. For those who were adopted before 6 months, there appeared to be almost complete cognitive and physical catch-up by 4 years; for those adopted after 6 months, the mean was one standard deviation below that of adopted UK children. Rutter and his colleagues also considered the impact of emotional deprivation on

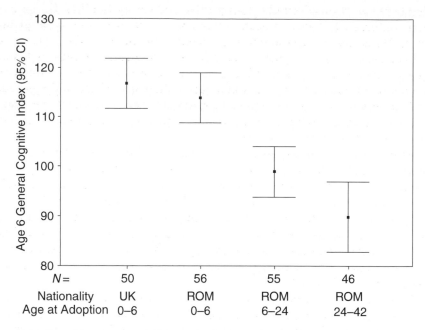

Figure 17.3 Cognitive scores of UK and Romanian adoptees at 6 years of age as a function of age at adoption in months. Adapted from O'Connor et al., 2000.

these children since there had been malnutrition and possibly abuse in some cases. However, despite this, there was a high degree of emotional resilience.

A later study of the same children in comparison with UK-born adoptees included the separate analysis of the scores of a sub-sample of 48 Romanian children who were adopted after more than 2 years of severe global deprivation (O'Connor et al., 2000). One finding was that cognitive catch-up for the Romanian children was virtually complete provided adoption was before 6 months (as in the earlier study). The second finding was that those who had been adopted between 6 months and 24 months scored significantly higher on cognitive tests than those who had been adopted between 24 and 42 months. The third finding, focused on the late-placed adoptees, was that in comparison with earlier-placed groups there was general developmental impairment.

Figure 17.3 illustrates cognitive differences at age 6 according to age of adoption. The analysis of the cognitive scores indicated that the UK and Romanian 0–6 month-old adoptee groups did not differ from one another. In other words, in comparison with UK adoptees, the early placed Romanian children had achieved and maintained the cognitive catch-up that was indicated at age 4. Both groups (UK and Romanian early placed adoptees) scored significantly higher, on average, than the 6–24 month-old and the 24–42 month-old groups. In turn, the 6–24 month and 24–42 month groups were significantly different from one another ($p < 0.001$).

The latest-placed adoptees (in the 24–42 month group) exhibited low-average cognitive scores as a group. These children had long-term difficulties. As a group they showed lower cognitive scores and a general developmental impairment in comparison with those children who had been adopted earlier. Despite the fact

that they had been adopted by supportive and caring families, the early deprivation continued to have a negative influence on their emotional adjustment at 6
years. While there was some improvement, unfortunately there was no differential catch-up for these later-placed adoptees between the ages of 4 and 6 even
though the length of time with their adoptive families was by now longer than
the period of time spent in the Romanian orphanages. These findings suggest that
early deprivation rather than the time spent in the adoptive home beyond a period
of 2 years seemed to be the key factor in explaining the extent of their cognitive
and physical developmental catch-up.

Rutter and his colleagues conclude that if children are rescued from extreme
deprivation at earlier than 2 years of age there is evidence that they will demonstrate considerable resilience and catch-up. Additionally the catch-up of the immediate adoption period is maintained and not 'washed out' (as Kirk suggested)
provided that the adoptive family is caring and supportive. At the same time, deprivation is associated with impairment and there are long-term difficulties for
those children who experience severe deprivation for more than the first two years
of their lives (so confirming the findings of the earlier research by Skeels and
Skodak and by Dennis).

This 'natural experiment' arose out of a humanitarian response to a social
problem. The study enabled researchers to examine basic questions about risk and
resilience in development and the causal role of early experience on later outcomes. As we saw, there was strong evidence of resilience but also long-term difficulties for some children depending on their age at adoption.

Socially Disadvantaged Children

Another key line of research examines the impact of severe social disadvantage,
continuing through childhood and adolescence, on young people's development.

Social disadvantage in the UK

Historically, concern about the impact of social disadvantage on children coin-
cides with the philosophy of 'equality of opportunity' that emerged in most
Western societies, including Britain and the USA, in the years following World
War II. As the Newsom Report (1963) put it, 'all children should have an equal
opportunity of acquiring intelligence, and developing their talents and abilities to
the full'. It was assumed by many that this would also result in an equality of
achievement among different social class and racial groups. Yet, despite decades
of research, policy-making and intervention, huge inequalities remain in our
society to this day. Surveys consistently show that children from working class
groups and ethnic minorities, and those experiencing adverse social conditions
have, on average, achieved poorly in the school system. A large body of international research indicates strong links between poverty and negative outcomes for
children at all ages (McGurk and Soriano, 1998). Adverse outcomes include behaviour problems and difficulties with peer relationships; adjustment difficulties and

Table 17.1 Evidence of academic underachievement by young black students (Rampton Report, 1981)

	Asians	Afro-Caribbeans	All other leavers	All school leavers in England
Five or more passes at 'O' level or CSE Grade 1	18%	3%	16%	21%
One or more 'A' level passes	13%	2%	12%	13%
Went to university	3%	1%	3%	5%
n =	527	799	4,852	693,840

Source: Rampton Report, 1981

delinquency; lesser likelihood of going on to further or higher education; greater likelihood of becoming unemployed as an adult. It is not simply poverty itself but the stresses associated with poverty that make it hard for parents and children to function as well as they might.

The impact of racial prejudice and discrimination

In the past 20 years, many countries in the European Community have been experiencing large influxes of asylum seekers and economic migrants from a variety of countries. Among the refugee communities in the UK, at least 40 per cent are aged under 18 years (Hodes, 2000), so communities have a key part to play in ensuring that these young people are supported during critical periods in their lives. Refugee families will have left their country of origin for reasons that include persecution, war, violence and widespread social disruption. In addition, they are likely to be exposed to socioeconomic adversity, such as difficulties in finding work, frequent moves and insecurity about asylum applications.

Research has very often indicated underachievement on the part of young people from ethnic minority backgrounds. A series of reports in the UK (Commission for Racial Equality, 1988; Eggleston et al., 1986; Rampton Report, 1981; Swann Report, 1985) provided large-scale statistical evidence about the educational underachievement of ethnic minority groups in the UK (see table 17.1). The reports looked at examination results, and destinations, of school leavers from schools with high concentrations of ethnic minority children. All the reports recommended that it is the responsibility of schools to give their pupils, regardless of gender, class or ethnic background, the confidence and the ability to have an equal opportunity in society.

One area of particular concern is the excessively high rate of school exclusions, especially for boys of African Caribbean heritage who are between 4 and 15 times more likely to be officially excluded from school than their white counterparts, depending on where they live (DfEE, 2000; Wright et al., 2000). In addition, pupils seen as 'different' may be symbolically excluded through the marginalization of their histories, beliefs and cultures, so leading to disaffection and underachievement (Gillborn and Gipps, 1996). School exclusions have also been shown to have negative consequences for young people's sense of identity, ambition and potential for successful transfer to adulthood (Hayden and Dunne, 2001; Schools Exclusion Unit, 1998).

A study by Troyna and Hatcher (1992) found that black children were subject to frequent experiences of racism in their daily lives. The children in their study reported that teachers tended not to notice or challenge racist name-calling or pejorative references to skin colour. Furthermore, these children viewed their experiences of racism as part of a wider discrimination endemic in the community. As a result, they felt disillusioned with the power of authorities to do anything about the problem and believed that if you appeal to authority figures you end up getting the blame yourself. Kelly's (1988) investigation into the relationship between race and friendship among school students in Manchester found that 24 per cent of boys and 21 per cent of girls indicated that they had never been friends with someone of a different racial group. (See also Wright et al., 2000.)

Mixed-race children can experience particular difficulties, since they might not be readily accepted by either white or black communities. Banks (1996) interviewed young white single mothers aged between 17 and 23 years who had mixed-race children of a black father and who were in therapy. The most common theme was the experience of isolation from both black and white communities; this was demonstrated by the community at large, by the women's own families and by the former partners. Banks argued that the extent of the prejudice and discrimination experienced by children and their families must not be underestimated if we are to devise effective strategies for helping such families to challenge racism when they encounter it and for helping professionals and community leaders to consider ways of enabling a change in attitude to take place.

Katz (1996) studied eleven sets of parents of varying ethnic origins using a narrative, biographical methodology. The children in these families ranged in age from 4 months to 4 years of age. Katz came to the following conclusions:

- The most striking similarity between all the parents was that they were all in a process of negotiating difference, both between the couple and their families and between themselves and their own societies before they had met a partner from a different ethnic group.
- Where colour as well as race was an issue, hostility was experienced from both the black and the white extended families, but the parents seemed to find the experience of white hostility the most threatening.
- In all of the families the birth of the children heralded some form of reconciliation and re-established a sense of continuity.

Issues concerning race, culture and ethnicity had affected all of the families and they had all involved their children in discussing these issues from an early age. But the outcomes reported by this study were not as negative as the Banks study described above. One common feature in the families was an elaborate, thoughtful process through which questions around 'sameness' and 'difference' were negotiated and combined with other differences such as age, gender and class.

The clear message from this study was that the experiences of mixed-race families can be considerably more rewarding than the polemic of some discussions might suggest.

However, we should not underestimate the complexity of relationships between politics, culture, gender and race.

Street children

In some countries, considerable numbers of children live on the streets, apparently without family or social support. The research of Huggins et al. (1996) arose from their work in shelters and on street programmes for impoverished youth in São Paulo, Rio de Janeiro and Recife, Brazil; their statistical data were gathered from morgue and police records, newspaper archives and work with children's rights groups. They discovered that the official statistics greatly underestimated (in fact, by nearly 50 per cent) the actual number of youth homicides in Brazil. In fact, between 1988 and 1991, alone, more than 7000 poor children and adolescents were murdered in Brazil, mostly by strangers, who were on- and off-duty police, citizen 'justice-makers', death-squad exterminators and private security police; most of the murderers received a fee for their services and the vast majority were never identified or prosecuted. In July 1991, the going rate for killing a street youth was half-a-month's adult minimum wage. The authors estimated that, in 1993 in Brazil's four biggest cities, up to five youths were murdered each day; 80 per cent of these victims were aged between 15 and 17.

Ethnicity structures the probability of being among Brazil's poorest and of having to live on the streets, and influences who among poor youth are bearers of multiple social stigmas, since they are both poor and black. And where goods, services and justice are allocated and awarded according to a group's relative class and colour, the blackest poor youth are in a highly disadvantaged position – excluded economically, socially and civilly (Huggins et al., 1996, p. 95). At this age, the more privileged young people are usually given opportunities to engage in studies and to prepare for life in their society. By contrast, hard-core street youths devote most of their time trying to survive harsh conditions by day and by night, with a constant requirement to maintain vigilance against danger. This study identifies particular conditions that transform certain types of Brazilian young people into 'social problems' or even 'non-persons'. These young people are often labelled as seriously delinquent or deviant. Their behaviour is often violent and anti-social (see also chapters 5 and 9).

Growing up with political violence

The Brazilian street children are marginalized even in their own society. Some children grow up in societies experiencing chronic political instability and often violence. Children see violence, death and destruction as part of their daily lives. In box 17.1 we explore the impact on children and also document the complexity of the factors involved, and the difficulties of doing research in these extreme circumstances.

Explanatory Models

The 'deficit' and 'difference' models

In the 1960s and early 1970s many psychologists and educational researchers thought that the reasons for the relative failure in school of children from working class groups, and ethnic minorities, must lie in psychological factors such as the quality of parent–child language in the home, or parental attitudes to school. It was felt that parents of these children did not provide the intellectual stimulation that children needed. In the UK the Newsom Report (1963) identified linguistic disadvantage in some home backgrounds; the abilities of boys and girls, it stated, were often unrealized because of their 'inadequate powers of speech'. These ideas came to be known as the 'deficit' model, which places blame on the home for failing to give an adequate socialization experience for the children; as a result children have poor language skills, and/or inadequate intellectual skills to cope at school.

Advocates of an alternative approach, known as the 'difference' model, argued that schools are essentially white, middle-class institutions in terms of their values, the language used by teachers and the content of courses. Hence, children from different backgrounds achieve less well. Difference theorists advocated greater tolerance of the values, attitudes and behaviour that children bring to school from their home background or even separate kinds of schooling for ethnic minorities. For example, Labov (1969) demonstrated the verbal skills that American ghetto children can display in the right context, but also argued that educators seldom valued or encouraged the non-standard English of inner city children. Both the deficit and the difference positions indicate the 'social disadvantage' of some social class and ethnic minority groups, for example through lower income, poor housing and more difficult family circumstances, though difference theorists argued more strongly that so-called 'deficits' produced by the culture were exaggerated by actual discrimination against working class or ethnic minority children in schools.

Since the 1950s, there have been great improvements in the living conditions of most people in the economically developed countries. However, while physical health is considerably better in these countries, social and psychological health may actually have deteriorated, for example with regard to the incidence of depression and the effects of drug and alcohol abuse. Services for children in need have grown in volume and extent of provision but there is still no firm agreement among professionals about when and how to respond to the needs of children and their families (Little and Mount, 1999). While prevention in the field of physical health has been effective (for example, in the near elimination of some illnesses, including tuberculosis and childbed fever, that were widespread in previous centuries), it has been far more difficult to reduce social and psychological problems.

It has been found useful to identify different types of intervention, as follows:

- *Prevention*: this implies activity to stop a social or psychological problem happening in the first place.

- *Early intervention*: this aims to stop those at highest risk of developing social or psychological problems, or those who show the first signs of difficulty.
- *Intervention or treatment*: this seeks to stabilize or achieve realistic outcomes among those who develop the most serious manifestation of a social or psychological problem.
- *Social prevention*: this seeks to reduce the damage that those who have developed a disorder can inflict on others in a community and on themselves.

(Little and Mount, 1999, p. 49)

The potential impact of these kinds of intervention can be better assessed by consideration of *risk* factors and *protective* factors.

Risk and protective factors

Rutter and Smith (1995) and Rutter (2000) have identified the more general social context within which young people develop and have taken account of the changes over time that are associated with changed risks of individual vulnerability to disorders. At the turn of the twenty-first century, there have been huge changes in the social, economic, educational and family structures within which children and young people develop. These changes have led to increased risk factors on the one hand and the potential for resilience on the other.

There is growing recognition of individual differences in children's responses to stress and adversity. Even family-wide experiences impact differently on each child in the family. The effect of these research findings has been to shift the emphasis to children's coping strategies and to their processing of their experiences. There are protective mechanisms both in the child and in the interplay between the child and the environment. Changes for the better can occur even in adult life provided that the right 'turning point' experiences occur. Research evidence shows the importance of influences outside the parent–child relationship, including peers, siblings, the community and school. There are great opportunities for prevention and treatment that are only just beginning to be taken up.

Risk factors are those factors that render an individual more likely to develop problems, such as delinquency or poor mental health, in the face of adversity; they do not in themselves necessarily *cause* these problems. Risk factors (many considered in earlier chapters) can include:

- family factors: violence, abuse, neglect, discordant family relationships, being a young person who is looked-after outside the family;
- psychosocial factors: poverty, economic crises, deprivation;
- individual factors: low intelligence, brain damage, chronic physical illness;
- rejection by parents or peers; and
- being a member of a deviant peer group

Webster-Stratton (1999) points out that young people who have two or more of these risk factors are four times more likely to develop a mental health problem than other young people; those with four risk factors are ten times more likely to have a mental health problem.

Protective factors   are those factors that act to protect an individual from developing a problem even in the face of adversity and risk factors such as those described above. Although the presence of risk factors, such as a poor environment or unsupportive relationships with primary caregivers, or being looked after outside the family, increases the likelihood of a negative outcome for the individual, studies of competence and resilience have shown that, regardless of background, children are generally resourceful. Competence has been shown to be a mediating variable that predicts positive or negative outcomes (Garmezy and Masten, 1991); so too is the belief that others are available to offer support when it is needed (Wetherington and Kessler, 1991). Protective factors include:

- supportive relationships with adults;
- access to good educational facilities;
- a sense of mastery;
- participation in activities, sports and outside interests;
- being a member of a non-deviant peer group;
- small family size;
- personal attributes, such as good health, even temperament, positive self-esteem, intelligence or good social skills;
- material resources, such as adequate family income; and
- religious affiliation.

Emmy Werner (1989) reported on a 30-year longitudinal study on the Hawaiian island of Kauai that demonstrates how some individuals can triumph over physical disadvantages and deprived childhood. Werner and her colleagues Bierman, French and Smith, aimed to assess the long-term consequences of prenatal and perinatal stress, and to document the effects of adverse early rearing conditions on children's physical, cognitive and psychosocial development. The women of Kauai reported 2203 pregnancies in 1954, 1955 and 1956; there were 1963 live births and 240 fetal deaths. The researchers chose to focus on the cohort of 698 infants born in 1955 and followed the development of these individuals at one, two, 10, 18 and 31 years of age. The majority – 422 – were born without complications and grew up in supportive environments. Some, however, grew up in families where they experienced disadvantage and neglect. But the researchers observed a subset of these 'high risk' children who, despite exposure to reproductive stress, discordant and impoverished homes and uneducated, alcoholic or mentally disturbed parents, grew into competent young adults, worked well and related positively to others. Take the examples of Michael and Mary:

> Michael was born prematurely to teenage parents, weighing four pound five ounces. He spent the first three weeks of life in hospital, separated from his mother. Immediately after his birth, his father was sent with the US army to Southeast Asia where he remained for two years. By the time Michael was 8 years old he had three siblings and his parents were divorced. His mother had deserted the family and had no

further contact with her children. His father raised Michael and his siblings with the help of their grandparents.

Mary's mother experienced several miscarriages before that pregnancy and the birth was difficult. Her father was an unskilled labourer with four years of formal education. Between Mary's fifth and tenth birthdays her mother became severely mentally ill and was hospitalized several times. She had also subjected Mary to frequent physical and emotional abuse.

Despite having been exposed to these risk factors in their childhood, by the age of 18 both Mary and Michael were individuals with high self-esteem and sound values who cared about others and were well-liked by their peers. They were successful at school and looked forward to their future careers and relationships.

What contributed to the resilience of these children? The researchers identified a number of protective factors in the families, outside the family circle and within the children themselves. Children such as Mary and Michael tended to have temperamental characteristics that included being active and sociable and having a low degree of excitability and distress. They were often described as 'easygoing', 'even-tempered' and 'affectionate'. Their teachers noted that they concentrated well in class and were alert and responsive; they were physically active and excelled at sports like fishing, swimming, riding and hula dancing. These children also tended to have formed a close bond with at least one caregiver from whom they received positive attention during their early years. The nurturing came from grandparents, older siblings, aunts and uncles, or from regular babysitters. As these resilient children grew older, they seemed to be adept at seeking out surrogate parents when a biological parent was unavailable or incapacitated. Resilient girls seemed to gain a sense of responsibility from looking after younger siblings; resilient boys, by contrast, tended to be firstborns who did not have to share attention with younger siblings, but they, like girls, had a structured routine of household chores and duties; they usually had a male in the family who served as a role model. Resilient children also seemed to find a great deal of support outside the family from classmates, neighbours and elders in the community. School became a refuge from a disordered home and many retrospectively recalled a favourite teacher who had supported them in times of crisis. With the help of the support networks, these resilient children developed a sense of meaning in their lives and a belief that they had control over their future.

Clearly, not all of the deprived children in this community fared so well. The resilient children's competence and hopefulness contrasted starkly with feelings of futility and helplessness expressed by troubled peers within the same cohort. Resilience does not happen in a vacuum. A key feature was that each of the resilient children had at least one person in their lives that accepted them unconditionally. They also had temperamental characteristics that enabled them to take advantage of the support networks available to them in the community even when their biological parents were unable to look after them well. As a result of this study, several community-action and educational programmes were established on Kauai to provide opportunities and caring people that could compensate for the difficulties being experienced by high-risk children and offer them an escape from adversity.

Risk-focused intervention

Research by Farrington and colleagues (Farrington, 1995; Farrington and Welsh, 1999; Loeber and Farrington, 1998) documents successful interventions to reduce aggressive and violent behaviour in the young. These studies provide essential information about the impact that prevention programmes can have on disruptive behaviour in young people. Four types of programme have been especially effective in the community: parent education, parent management training, child skills training and pre-school intellectual enrichment programmes. Generally, these programmes focus on the risk factors of poor parental monitoring, lack of discipline, high impulsivity, low empathy and self-centredness, and low intelligence and attainment (Farrington and Welsh, 1999). Some of these programmes have had significant effects over time, so confirming the value to society of investing in risk-focused prevention to improve the mental health and emotional well-being of young people. In the next sections, we examine evaluations of the role that families themselves play in responding with resilience to adversity. We also look at large-scale government initiatives to combat inequalities in opportunities provided for certain groups of children in society.

■ Interventions: The Role of families

One American study gives evidence of the vital part that can be played by families themselves in ensuring that their children achieve well in the educational system. Caplan et al. (1992) reviewed key factors that, in their view, contributed to the outstanding academic achievement of refugee children in their study. During the 1970s and 1980s many Vietnamese and Lao people sought a new life in the USA. The children of these families had lost months or years of formal schooling, they lived in relocation camps and had suffered trauma and disruption as they escaped from SE Asia. They had little knowledge of English and had experienced extreme poverty and material hardship. The researchers surveyed 6750 members of refugee families and, from this larger group, selected a random sample of 200 nuclear families and their 536 children of school age; 27 per cent of the families had 4 or more children, a factor not usually associated with high academic achievement. At the time of the study, the children had been in the USA for an average of three and a half years. All attended schools in low-income, inner city areas, not known for their scholastic success.

The children did outstandingly well in their academic grades, since their mean grade point average was B; (27 per cent had an A; 52 per cent had a B; 17 per cent had a C; and only 4 per cent were below C). As expected, their grades in English and liberal arts were unexceptional. But in mathematics and science almost half had A scores; another third earned Bs. These grades were matched by test scores on the California Achievement Test, which indicated that they out-performed 54 per cent of all students taking the test, placing them just above the national average. These achievements held for the majority of the children, not just a few gifted individuals.

The researchers explored aspects of the family context that might be encouraging the high academic achievement of these children. They found through interviews conducted in the language of the families that in the evenings the whole family would typically collaborate on the children's homework. The children spent an average of 3 hours and 10 minutes each evening on their homework. (American students spend on average only 1 hour and 30 minutes each day.) The parents were usually unable to engage in the content of the homework, but they set standards and goals for each evening and took responsibility for the household chores so that the children could get on with their studies. In addition, the parents read regularly to their children, either in English or in their own language, and it seemed to be the experience of reading which strengthened emotional ties between parent and child, strengthened cultural understanding of traditions, and transmitted the wisdom of the culture through stories. Not only that, the experience was enjoyable and shared with all members of the family.

Caplan et al. concluded that the parents had carried their cultural heritage with them to the USA and handed it down to their children. This meant that the families were securely linked to their own past as well as to the realities of the present and the possibilities of the future in a new environment. This study explored the role of the family in the academic performance of Indochinese children from refugee families, and the results firmly confirm the need for close integration between home and school, the importance of familial commitment to education, and the need for the creation of an environment that is conducive to learning. Yet we cannot expect the families to do all this by themselves; nor do the authors of this paper suggest this. Families need acknowledgement of what they are doing and some sense that their own experiences are valued within the school system. Studies like these can help us identify some of the cultural components which contribute to the academic success or failure of children in order to give educators insights into the processes at work and the ways in which they can encourage these processes.

Compensatory Education Programmes in the UK

The Plowden Report of 1967 (HMSO, 1967) advocated a policy of positive discrimination in favour of children from poor areas throughout Britain, through the provision of more resources, more teachers and better school buildings. These areas were to be designated 'Educational Priority Areas' (EPAs). In response to the recommendations of the Plowden Report, Halsey (1972) mounted a large project, the Educational Priority Area Project, to initiate and evaluate compensatory education programmes in exceptionally deprived communities in London, Birmingham, Liverpool, Yorkshire and Dundee. Each area formulated its own programme within the wider framework of the Project in order to take account of the particular needs of the region. Halsey's overall conclusion was a positive one. He argued that the concept of Educational Priority Areas was a useful one that enabled positive discrimination to be made in favour of underprivileged children. He advocated the use of structured programmes that were flexible enough to accommodate to local needs and he recommended the development of community schools as one means of bridging the gap between home and school. Although he did not claim that programmes like this could fully compensate for deprived social conditions, he argued that education could play an important role in extending young children's cognitive and linguistic abilities.

Recent government attention, policy and guidance in the UK has also focused on action to tackle the cycle of disadvantage that can trap too many families in breakdown and consequent emotional difficulties for the young people involved. The poorest families in the UK today face a lack of employment and training opportunities and bad housing; they are also more likely to fall ill and to experience mental health problems. The report of the UK Policy Action Team on Young People (Social Exclusion Unit, 2000) looked at ways in which the Government could improve the coordination of policies and services for children and young people. The report showed that a great deal is known about how 'at risk' children and families can be identified early and that effective intervention can often improve their prospects. The report proposes that there should be more emphasis on the identification of the developmental needs of young people and a corresponding shift of resources into preventive action, both to help parents and children deal with problems before they become acute, and to promote effective interventions for children and young people most at risk. In 2000, the government established a Children and Young People's Unit (CYPU) (DfES, 2001) with the brief to support cross-government work on child poverty and youth disadvantage, and to implement The Children's Fund, an initiative that supports services to identify children and young people who are showing early signs of emotional and behavioural disturbance and provide them and their families with the support they need to get them back on track (DfES, 2001).

Compensatory Education Programmes in the USA

As we have seen, in the later 1960s, a deficit or cultural deprivation model became the most accepted hypothesis to explain the educational disadvantage and underachievement of working class and ethnic minority children. This led to a large number of programmes of compensatory education for preschool children in the USA (and also in the UK). Following the apparent success of these kinds of compensatory education programmes, a massive policy of intervention occurred in the USA with 'Project Head Start'. This started in the summer of 1965 and built up over the next few years until millions of preschool children across the USA had participated in some form of Head Start programme. The general goal was to give 'deprived' children a head start in schools by some form of early intervention to stimulate cognitive and linguistic development. Up to the 1960s, nursery schools had tended to be more orientated towards the needs of the middle-class child. Much of the emphasis was on social and emotional development through free play and unstructured imaginative activities. Preschool programmes of compensatory education, by contrast, aimed directly to prepare children for entry into infant school and to give them skills that, it was felt, their homes had failed to provide. Programmes were often based on the assumption that the children's language was deficient, that they lacked cognitive strategies appropriate for school learning, and that their parents used ineffective modes of control. However, no detailed syllabus was laid down and the exact nature and length of programmes varied widely.

Compensatory Programmes Evaluated

Some of the early evaluation studies showed disappointing results for the compensatory programmes. The Westinghouse Learning Corporation carried out the first national evaluation of Project Head Start in Ohio University in 1969. This research study showed that the intervention programmes had very little, if any, effect on the children who had taken part. Also, any benefits seemed to be very transient, disappearing after a year or so at school. Some psychologists, such as Arthur Jensen (1969), took this to confirm their view that children from poor families had inherited low academic ability that no amount of compensatory education could make up for. Others thought there should be more intervention. This might mean more intensive intervention, involving parent as well as child education; or starting intervention earlier; or following intervention through into the early school years. At an extreme, this might virtually involve removing a young child from a 'deficient' home environment. Yet others – the difference theorists – argued that the whole premise of intervention was biased or racist. As Baratz and Baratz (1970, p. 43) put it, 'Head Start has failed because its goal is to correct a deficit that simply does not exist'. By now the ignorance and insensitivity that many white researchers had shown to black culture and to the thoughts and feelings of black mothers and children had become more obvious. Baratz and Baratz claimed that the 'Head Start programs may inadvertently advocate the annihilation of a cultural system which is barely considered or understood by most social scientists'.

However, the Ohio–Westinghouse study took place only 5 years after Project Head Start began. By 1976, researchers who were following the long-term effects of intervention programmes began to report more encouraging results. One major research project (Lazar and Darlington, 1982) was a collaborative study in which 11 preschool research teams came together to pool their results for a group named the Consortium for Longitudinal Studies. Each researcher had independently designed and carried out preschool programmes in the 1960s; the children who had participated, mainly black children from low-income families, were followed up in 1976 when their ages ranged from 9 to 19.

For example, the High/Scope Perry Preschool Project, organized by Weikart et al. (1970) in Ypsilanti, Michigan, involved 123 children from low-waged black families. Half of them, selected at random, experienced an intervention programme; the other half, the control group, had no preschool educational provision. The programme children spent 12.5 hours per week for 2 years in a special preschool intervention programme which stressed active learning and a

Table 17.2 Changes in IQ with age, for programme and control group children, in Weikart's preschool programme

	Pretest	3	4	5	6	7	8	9	10	14
Programme group	79.6	79.9	92.7	94.1	91.3	91.7	88.1	87.7	85.0	81.0
Control group	78.5	79.6	81.7	83.2	86.3	87.1	86.9	86.8	84.6	80.7

Source: Lazar and Darlington, 1982

great deal of communication between child and adults and between child and child. There were also home visits by the teachers.

The results for IQ scores from the project and later follow-ups are shown in table 17.2. The programme group children showed an initial increase (more than the control group) in the year or so immediately following the intervention, but through the middle school years this showed a familiar falling-off or wash-out effect. However, some long-term effects of the intervention were found in other areas. By the age of 15, the programme group scored on average 8 per cent higher on reading, arithmetic and language tests than the control group. By the end of high school, only 19 per cent of the programme children had been placed in remedial classes compared with 39 per cent in the control group. Socially too there were effects. The programme youngsters were less likely to be delinquent (36 per cent as compared with 42 per cent of the control group). Ten per cent of the programme group went on to college but none of the control group did. These findings were fairly typical of the other ten projects in the survey.

The most recent follow-up of the children, who are now in their late twenties, has shown some dramatic results (Weikart, 1996). The researchers managed to interview 95 per cent of the original study participants when they were 27, and additional data were gathered from their school, social services and arrest records. There were significant differences between programme and control groups. One-third more programme than control members had graduated from high school; they were also significantly more likely to be literate and to score more highly on achievement tests. By the age of 27, only one-fifth as many programme members as control members had been arrested five or more times (7 per cent versus 35 per cent) and only one-third as many were arrested for drug dealing. Those who had experienced the programme were four times as likely to earn $2000 per month as controls; they were three times as likely to own their own homes and to own a second car.

Weikart (1996, p. 120) concludes that the evidence gives very strong support for the effectiveness of preschool interventions and argues that the benefits are long-term because they:

- empower children by enabling them to initiate and carry out their own learning activities and to make independent decisions;

- empower parents, by involving them in ongoing relationships as full partners with teachers in supporting their children's development; and
- empower teachers by providing them with systematic in-service training, supportive curriculum supervision, and observational tools to assess children's development.

As discussed in box 17.2, the Consortium for Longitudinal Studies concluded that early intervention programmes could have significant, long-term effects (Lazar and Darlington, 1982). The interpretation of achievement test scores was difficult because of variability in the tests themselves. However, the authors reported some evidence that children who had experienced early intervention performed better on school attainment tests than controls. But perhaps more important were the non-cognitive differences – the changes in attitudes towards themselves as learners, in aspirations and beliefs in their own competence (box 17.2).

A Continuing Debate

The apparent failure of Project Head Start around 1970 led many educationalists to reject the idea of compensatory education and to replace the deficit model with the difference model. The deficit theorists had certainly been naïve in their assumptions. Nevertheless, the difference model too may be naïve if taken to the extreme of supposing that all kinds of rearing conditions are equally valid. Poor material conditions, inadequate housing, and poverty will affect the quality of a child's development. Working class groups, and many ethnic minorities, tend to suffer from these material and social disadvantages, as well as possible prejudice or bias within and outside the educational system.

The best schemes of compensatory education appear to be those that involve the families, since those that focus on the child alone tend to have only short-term effects (Little and Mount, 1999). If parents are involved throughout, they can sustain the effects after the programme is over. Bronfenbrenner recommends child-care education for young people before they become parents, and support for them once the children are born, as well as a network of community support services among parents and other members of the community. However, he concluded that programmes of compensatory education are not effective for the most deprived groups if they concentrate only on the parent–child relationship. He calls also for intervention at other levels (see figure 1.3) to alleviate the desperate conditions in which some families are forced to live. Removal of educational disadvantage requires that the families themselves have adequate health care, reasonable housing, enough food and a sufficient income. Programmes of compensatory education cannot by themselves undo the inequalities that continue to exist in our society, and should not replace efforts to tackle poverty and racial prejudice.

More recent research shows that material disadvantage and discrimination in the educational system remain convincing explanations of much educational underachievement. There is plenty of evidence to show that poor children perform less well at school than children from better-off families, are less healthy and have

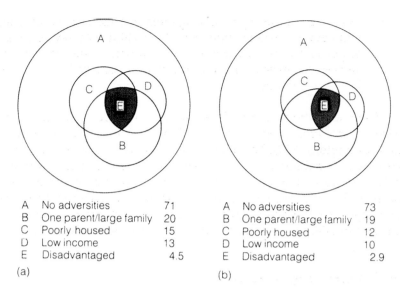

	(a)			(b)	
A	No adversities	71	A	No adversities	73
B	One parent/large family	20	B	One parent/large family	19
C	Poorly housed	15	C	Poorly housed	12
D	Low income	13	D	Low income	10
E	Disadvantaged	4.5	E	Disadvantaged	2.9

Figure 17.4 An analysis of social adversities among British children at (a) age 11 and (b) age 16 in percentages (from Wedge and Essen, 1982).

a narrower range of opportunities in later life. As we saw earlier, reports from the National Child Development Study (Wedge and Essen, 1982) defined social disadvantage in terms of adverse family composition, poor housing and low income. Children experiencing all three of these were defined as 'disadvantaged' in their analyses (see figures 17.4 and 17.5).

These children had more difficulties than ordinary children; besides their poor housing and income, the fathers were more likely to be unemployed, and both parents were more likely to be chronically sick. In school these children were less motivated; at 16 only 41 per cent hoped to continue their education as compared with 71 per cent of their peers. Teachers were asked to say whether the 16-year-olds in the survey were able to do all the calculations normally required of an everyday shopper, and whether they were able to read well enough to cope with everyday needs. Again, the largest proportion of those unable to do these tasks were pupils from disadvantaged homes.

A dilemma facing educators is that if the curriculum is changed to accommodate issues arising in the home and in the community, there is no guarantee that what is taught will still be valued by wider society, e.g., by employers or examining boards. However, we know that there is a danger that a *laissez-faire* attitude may block the avenues that help children from disadvantaged backgrounds gain access to mainstream culture. By failing to take action, educators help to perpetuate injustice in our society. Clearly this is a topic in which the values of society and the political possibilities of the times must be considered together with our psychological knowledge of the processes of children's development.

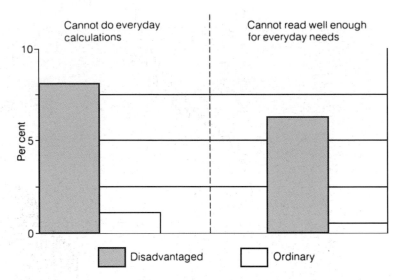

Figure 17.5 Percentage of 16-year-olds assessed by their teacher to be without basic arithmetic and reading skills (from Wedge and Essen, 1982).

Reason to hope?

Deprivation and disadvantage arise out of a complex interaction among biological, ecological, cultural, historical, demographic and psychological risk factors. Given that there are so many varied factors and given the different theories and explanations offered for disadvantage, it may be thought to be unrealistic to expect an easy solution to such a complex problem. Rutter (2000) argues that the main benefits come from circumstances in which it is possible to bring about a long-lasting change in the environment. Much less is achieved by inputs – however effective at the time – when overall deprivation and disadvantage continue. He proposes the need for rigorous research that puts environmental mediation mechanisms under scrutiny so that we understand more clearly what are specific risk and protective factors. We need multi-method, cross-disciplinary research methods that integrate perspectives on the individual children in their social contexts.

So is there any reason to hope that as a society we can create better conditions for the children of the future? As we saw in the study by Caplan et al. (1992), one line of inquiry might be through the study of those children and families who, against all the odds, overcome incredible hardships and achieve intellectual and social goals that could not have been predicted. We know, for example, that children who have experienced bad parenting do not necessarily mature into adults who lack parenting skills. Street children do not necessarily stay on the street. Asylum seekers can integrate into their new communities. Children born into poor families can make good. History does not need to repeat itself.

As we have seen, psychologists have recently begun to address the concept of resilience. Rutter (1990; 2000) points out that resilience is most usefully thought

Plate 17.2   Street market in Brick Lane, London: What does the future hold for this child?

of as a process that is part of a complex social system at a particular point in time.

One key factor in all of this may be the capacity on the part of children and their parents to develop a reflective stance on themselves and their circumstances (Fonagy et al., 1994; see also p. 103). A second may be the development of political awareness (see box 17.1). Children who live in impoverished conditions are strongly affected by them, even if they have the qualities of resilience and the opportunities to rise above them. But rescuing them is not enough. The environmental conditions need to be changed in order to offer to all children the opportunity to realize their potential. This surely is a fundamental human right. We should not wait until their presence on the streets and in the inner city slums occurs in such numbers that they are a threat. We know enough from the literature to understand that there are ways in which we can give respect, initiative, autonomy and opportunity to disadvantaged children and families.

Further Reading

A good general resource is Rutter, M. and Smith, D. J. 1995: *Psychosocial Disorders in Young People*. Chichester: John Wiley. A very readable account of risk and protective factors and interventions in the fight against adversity is Little, M. and Mount, K. 1999: *Prevention and Early Intervention with Children in Need*. Cambridge: Cambridge University Press. This monograph examines success and failure in responding to children's needs, drawing on carefully evaluated programmes and refers to overviews of research and recent policy driven initiatives both in Europe and the USA.

An earlier collection of useful articles can be found in Clarke, A. M. and Clarke, A. D. B. 1976: *Early Experience: Myth and Evidence*. London: Open Books. The authors challenge the belief that the early years have an irreversible effect on later development. The book includes chapters on the effects of parent–child separation, the effects of institutionalization on children's cognitive development, and the case study of severe deprivation of the Czech twins. Their more recent book – Clarke, A. M. and Clarke, A. D. B. (2000) *Early Experience and the Life Path*. London: Jessica Kingsley – also challenges the assumption that early experience has a 'disproportionate' effect on later development. Here they present recent evidence in support of the idea of resilience in children in the face of adversity. For a detailed account of the Genie case, see Pines, M. 1981: The civilizing of Genie. *Psychology Today*, 15 (September), 28–34. This describes the effects that an intensive programme of intervention had on the social, intellectual and linguistic development of Genie. A number of important theoretical and practical issues are raised about deprivation and the extent to which its effects can be reversed. See also Rymer, R. 1994: *Genie: A Scientific Tragedy*, Harmondsworth: Penguin, where you can read about the professional rivalries among the scientists who studied Genie's progress.

Discussion Points

1 Discuss the meaning of the terms 'disadvantage', 'deficit' and 'difference' in explaining educational underachievement.
2 How useful are the concepts of 'risk' and 'protective' factors?
3 Consider the problems involved in evaluating the effects of a programme of compensatory education. How would you attempt to do this?
4 Boys with African Caribbean heritage are between 4 and 15 times more likely to be officially excluded from school than their white peers. Discuss how educators might change this state of affairs.
5 What effects do family composition, poor housing and low income have on a child's school performance, and why?

Box 17.1
Children and political violence: an overview

Do children suffer psychological changes as a result of growing up in regions where there is ongoing violent conflict? In a special section of the *International Journal of Behavioural Development* devoted to the impact of political violence on children's psychological development, Ed Cairns reviews four empirical studies, which represent the geographical areas most researched – the Middle East, Northern Ireland and South Africa. Should researchers focus on the stresses which children face as a result of political violence or should the emphasis be on the resilience which children so often demonstrate? Cairns explores the view that the impact of political violence may not be as dramatic as some outside observers might predict but also considers the need to look at individual reactions to danger and violence both in the wider social context and with regard to longer-term political and historical perspectives.

Kostelny and Garbarino documented the dangers faced by Palestinian children for whom experiences with violence were a part of everyday life. They found that the younger children (aged 6–9) appeared to be more negatively affected with regard to personality and behavioural changes than older children and youths (aged 12–15). They noted the impact on young people of the community's ideology, which made them articulate about social and political issues in their country and which also acted as a protection against the stresses of experiencing violence. They concluded that political conflict is a collective phenomenon and that it may not be enough to research the impact on individuals while ignoring the wider context in which the conflict takes place. Furthermore, the group aspect of political conflict often establishes close feelings of solidarity which act as strong buffers against stress. So researchers in this field are challenged to find innovative ways of observing individuals in a particular social setting with a particular ideological belief system.

Liddell and her colleagues observed levels of aggressiveness among 5-year-old children from four communities in South Africa before apartheid ended. Contrary to expectation, they found that, while children from violent communities were involved in aggressive behaviour, the context and nature of the aggression was broadly similar to that observed in less violent communities. But there was an interaction effect. Children's rates of involvement with aggression were influenced by their contact with older boys and men, which seemed to take place indirectly through modelling and imitation rather than through direct involvement in fights. The researchers conclude that it is the combination of community- and child-related variables that explains the children's involvement in aggression. Young children's tendency to be involved in aggressive episodes was related to their contact with older males and this relationship was more marked the more violent the community. The researchers raise the question of direct versus indirect effects and suggest that children may become more aggressive in violent circumstances through the impact of ongoing violence on their families or on other significant people in their community.

Reick's study highlighted the fact that there may be more value for researchers to examine the long-term, subtle effects on children rather than the short-term effects, which are more obvious because of their dramatic nature. She investigated the frequency of emotional problems among a sample of 5–16-year-old children of survivors of the Holocaust and found that they did not demonstrate any more difficulties than did controls. She found no evidence of excessive psychopathology in this sample of young people, contrary to the predictions of some earlier clinical work. She explored the idea that there may be a form of adaptation or resilience in the children of survivors, which suggests some impact of stress on later facility for coping.

Toner's study in Northern Ireland, where conflict between Catholics and Protestants has continued for centuries, pointed to the changing aspects of a politically violent situation which need to be taken account of by researchers, and he contrasted 'inside' and 'outside' perspectives. His study of reconciliation programmes indicated that, while individual children might be helped, such interventions did little to change intergroup attitudes. He argued that there is an urgent need for researchers from a range of disciplines to develop valid methods that allow comparisons to be made among different regions around the world so that we can know more precisely what are the best ways of overcoming intergroup conflict.

Cairns overviews the main issues that seem to have emerged from this work:

1   He suggests that social scientists need a more flexible theory to guide their understanding of the interface between shared group identities and political ideologies on the one hand, and individual behaviour and beliefs on the other. In this way he asks researchers to cross traditional divisions among disciplines (for example, sociology, history, political science) and within the discipline of psychology itself (for example, between social and developmental psychology) in order to take account of political, economic and ethnic factors in the communities which they investigate.

2   He indicates that researchers in this field often face danger to themselves and pressures from various groups to report 'the truth' in particular ways. This means that research designs are not always as rigorous as they might otherwise be. As a result, researchers in the area of political violence may be less likely to secure funding or to be published in international journals. The outcome is that research in this area is often small-scale and consequently limited in time and place. If it is only published in local journals, the findings may not be disseminated to fellow researchers in other parts of the world, and so valuable insights and observations are lost.

3   He concludes that there is great need for longitudinal studies with a cross-cultural dimension if we are to do more than document atrocities and actually work towards well-evaluated interventions that may have an impact on the cycle of political violence. This research also offers a unique opportunity to observe resilience and coping strategies among young people exposed to unacceptably high levels of societal violence.

Based on material in E. Cairns 1994: Children and political violence: an overview. *International Journal of Behavioral Development*, 17 (4), 669–74.

Box 17.2
Lasting effects of early education: a report from the Consortium of Longitudinal Studies

Lazar and Darlington attempted an impartial evaluation of the longer-term effectiveness of 11 compensatory education programmes. The individual projects differed; six had used preschool centres, two were home-based and three combined the two methods. The programmes also varied in the content of their curriculum. But what they had in common was that all were concerned with the acquisition of basic cognitive concepts and many stressed language development. All were well-designed studies that had compared the programme children with a control group, and that tested the children before, during and after the intervention began. As many as possible of the children (about three-quarters of the original samples) were traced, assessed

Box Table 17.2.1   Percentage of students retained in grade, in programme versus control groups from eight early intervention programmes

Location of programme	Programme group	Control group	Significance level
North Central Florida	27.6	28.6	n.s.
Tennessee	52.9	68.8	n.s.
New York	24.1	44.7	$p < 0.01$
Ypsilanti, Michigan	4.0	14.9	n.s.
Philadelphia	42.9	51.6	n.s.
Long Island, NY	12.9	18.8	n.s.
Louisville, Kentucky	7.8	0.0	n.s.
New Haven, Connecticut	26.6	32.3	n.s.
Median all projects	25.4	30.5	$p < 0.05$

Source: Lazar and Darlington, 1982

Box Table 17.2.2   Percentage of students giving achievement-related reasons for being proud of themselves, in programme versus control groups from six early intervention programmes

Location of programme	Programme group	Control group	Significance level
North Central Florida	88.2	76.5	n.s.
Tennessee	75.8	52.9	n.s.
Ypsilanti, Michigan	86.2	77.1	n.s.
Philadelphia	65.7	60.0	n.s.
Louisville, Kentucky	78.9	71.9	n.s.
Harlem, NY	77.8	52.4	$p < 0.05$
Median all projects	78.4	66.0	$p < 0.01$

Source: Lazar and Darlington, 1982

on a range of educational and psychological tests, and both they and their families were interviewed.

Four main sets of dependent variables were examined:

1 School competence: e.g., whether the child had ever been assigned to a remedial class, or retained in grade (held back to repeat a year in school).
2 Developed abilities: performance in IQ tests and standardized tests of achievement in reading and mathematics.
3 The children's attitudes and values: their self-concept, achievement orientation, and aspirations and attitudes towards education and a career.

4 Impact on family: the effect which participation in an intervention programme had had on the families, how the parents thought about children and what their aspirations were for their children.

Two samples of results are shown in box tables 17.2.1 and 17.2.2. (The number of projects varies, as not all the original projects had data on all the dependent variables.) Box table 17.2.1 shows that in seven out of eight projects fewer programme children were ever held back a year in school compared with control children. Box table 17.2.2 shows that in six out of six projects more programme children gave achievement-related reasons for being proud of themselves in interview.

These tables show the strength of combining the results of independent studies. Most of the comparisons for individual studies are not statistically significant, but the pooled data are significant and the consistency of individual studies is convincing.

The overall conclusion was that these intervention programmes did have an effect in the long-term on the capacity of low-income children to meet school requirements. Other significant findings were that those who had experienced a programme of compensatory education were significantly less likely to be assigned to special education. Scores on intelligence tests did improve among the programme groups but the differences between the programme and control groups became insignificant over time (see table 17.2).

However, the authors reported some evidence that programme children performed better at mathematics than at reading in relation to controls. More striking were the differences in attitudes towards education. In all groups, children's aspirations far exceeded those of their parents; but the programme children were significantly more likely than controls to give reasons related to school success when asked to describe ways in which they felt proud of themselves. The parents too seemed to have changed as a result of the programmes. Mothers of the programme group children were more likely to report higher educational aspirations for their children than control mothers, and they also reported more satisfaction with their children's performance at school. Interestingly, the authors did not find any significant differences in the long-term effects of early intervention programmes among sub-groups of their samples. There was no difference reported between boys and girls, between single-parent families and two-parent families, nor did family size appear to be a significant factor.

The long-term effects of intervention programmes were found to be not so much on developed abilities (academic test achievement) as on school competence, attitudes and values. The authors conclude that there may be 'mutual reinforcement processes' in that children who take part in early intervention programmes may raise their mothers' expectations of them. The mothers' encouragement may in turn spur them on and furthermore, positive attitudes towards school are rewarded by teachers. Thus, they argue, high quality programmes can be effective for a number of different types of low-income families. The benefits are measurable; some of the qualitative changes are harder to assess objectively but can be inferred from interview material and from self-evaluation reports.

The quality of the Consortium report rests on the quality of data from the individual projects. The main reservation here is that not all the investigators were truly able to assign children randomly to programme or control groups. Thus (to varying degrees) some of the projects are best described as quasi-experiments rather than true experiments (chapter 1). Nevertheless, the findings rank among the most important and substantial in the area of compensatory education and early intervention.

Based on material in Lazar, I. and Darlington, R. 1982: Lasting effects of early education: a report from the Consortium of Longitudinal Studies. *Monographs of the Society for Research in Child Development*, 47 (2–3).

Appendix A
Ethical Principles
for Conducting
Research with
Human Participants

1 Introduction

1.1   The principles given below are intended to apply to research with human partici-
      pants. Principles of conduct in professional practice are to be found in the Society's
      Code of Conduct and in the advisory documents prepared by the Divisions, Sections
      and Special Groups of the Society.

1.2   Participants in psychological research should have confidence in the investigators.
      Good psychological research is possible only if there is mutual respect and con-
      fidence between investigators and participants. Psychological investigators are po-
      tentially interested in all aspects of human behaviour and conscious experience.
      However, for ethical reasons, some areas of human experience and behaviour may
      be beyond the reach of experiment, observation or other form of psychological in-
      vestigation. Ethical guidelines are necessary to clarify the conditions under which
      psychological research is acceptable.

1.3   The principles given below supplement for researchers with human participants
      the general ethical principles of members of the Society as stated in the British Psy-
      chological Society's Code of Conduct (1993). Members of the British Psychological
      Society are expected to abide by both the Code of Conduct and the fuller principles
      expressed here. Members should also draw the principles to the attention of research
      colleagues who are not members of the Society. Members should encourage col-
      leagues to adopt them and ensure that they are followed by all researchers whom
      they supervise (e.g., research assistants, postgraduate, undergraduate, A-level and
      GCSE students).

1.4   In recent years, there has been an increase in legal actions by members of the general
      public against professionals for alleged misconduct. Researchers must recognize the
      possibility of such legal action if they infringe the rights and dignity of participants
      in their research.

2   General

2.1   In all circumstances, investigators must consider the ethical implications and psychological consequences for the participants in their research. The essential principle is that the investigation should be considered from the standpoint of all participants; foreseeable threats to their psychological well-being, health, values or dignity should be eliminated. Investigators should recognize that, in our multi-cultural and multi-ethnic society and where investigations involve individuals of different ages, gender and social background, the investigators may not have sufficient knowledge of the implications of an investigation for the participants. It should be borne in mind that the best judges of whether an investigation will cause offence may be members of the population from which the participants in the research are to be drawn.

3   Consent

3.1   Whenever possible, the investigator should inform all participants of the objectives of the investigation. The investigator should inform the participants of all aspects of the research or intervention that might reasonably be expected to influence willingness to participate. The investigator should, normally, explain all other aspects of the research or intervention about which the participants enquire. Failure to make full disclosure prior to obtaining informed consent requires additional safeguards to protect the welfare and dignity of the participants (see section 4).

3.2   Research with children or with participants who have impairments that will limit understanding and/or communication such that they are unable to give their real consent requires special safeguarding procedures.

3.3   Where possible, the real consent of children and of adults with impairments in understanding or communication should be obtained. In addition, where research involves any persons under sixteen years of age, consent should be obtained from parents or from those *in loco parentis*. If the nature of the research precludes consent being obtained from parents or permission being obtained from teachers, before proceeding with the research, the investigator must obtain approval from an Ethics Committee.

3.4   Where real consent cannot be obtained from adults with impairments in understanding or communication, wherever possible the investigator should consult a person well-placed to appreciate the participant's reaction, such as a member of the person's family, and must obtain the disinterested approval of the research from independent advisors.

3.5   When research is being conducted with detained persons, particular care should be taken over informed consent, paying attention to the special circumstances which may affect the person's ability to give free informed consent.

3.6   Investigators should realize that they are often in a position of authority or influence over participants who may be their students, employees or clients. This relationship must not be allowed to pressurize the participants to take part in, or remain in, an investigation.

3.7   The payment of participants must not be used to induce them to risk harm beyond that which they risk without payment in their normal lifestyle.

3.8   If harm, unusual discomfort, or other negative consequences for the individual's future life might occur, the investigator must obtain the disinterested approval of independent advisors, inform the participants, and obtain informed, real consent from each of them.

3.9   In longitudinal research, consent may need to be obtained on more than one occasion.

4   Deception

4.1   The withholding of information or the misleading of participants is unacceptable if the participants are typically likely to object or show unease once debriefed. Where this is in any doubt, appropriate consultation must precede the investigation. Consultation is best carried out with individuals who share the social and cultural background of the participants in the research, but the advice of ethics committees or experienced and disinterested colleagues may be sufficient.

4.2   Intentional deception of the participants over the purpose and general nature of the investigation should be avoided whenever possible. Participants should never be deliberately misled without extremely strong scientific or medical justification. Even then there should be strict controls and the disinterested approval of independent advisors.

4.3   It may be impossible to study some psychological processes without withholding information about the true object of the study or deliberately misleading the participants. Before conducing such a study, the investigator has a special responsibility to (a) determine that alternative procedures avoiding concealment or deception are not available; (b) ensure that the participants are provided with sufficient information at the earliest stage; and (c) consult appropriately upon the way that the withholding of information or deliberate deception will be received.

5   Debriefing

5.1   In studies where the participants are aware that they have taken part in an investigation, when the data have been collected, the investigator should provide the participants with any necessary information to complete their understanding of the nature of the research. The investigator should discuss with the participants their experience of the research in order to monitor any unforeseen negative effects or misconceptions.

5.2   Debriefing does not provide a justification for unethical aspects of an investigation.

5.3   Some effects which may be produced by an experiment will not be negated by a verbal description following the research. Investigators have a responsibility to ensure that participants receive any necessary debriefing in the form of active intervention before they leave the research setting.

6   Withdrawal from the investigation

6.1   At the onset of the investigation investigators should make plain to participants their right to withdraw from the research at any time, irrespective of whether or not payment or other inducement has been offered. It is recognized that this may be difficult in certain observational or organizational settings, but nevertheless the investigator must attempt to ensure that participants (including children) know of their right to withdraw. When testing children, avoidance of the testing situation may be taken as evidence of failure to consent to the procedure and should be acknowledged.

6.2   In the light of experience of the investigation, or as a result of debriefing, the participant has the right to withdraw retrospectively any consent given, and to require that their own data, including recordings, be destroyed.

7 Confidentiality

7.1   Subject to the requirements of legislation, including the Data Protection Act, information obtained about a participant during an investigation is confidential unless otherwise agreed in advance. Investigators who are put under pressure to disclose confidential information should draw this point to the attention of those exerting such pressure. Participants in psychological research have a right to expect that information they provide will be treated confidentially and, if published, will not be identifiable as theirs. In the event that confidentiality and/or anonymity cannot be guaranteed, the participant must be warned of this in advance of agreeing to participate.

8 Protection of participants

8.1   Investigators have a primary responsibility to protect participants from physical and mental harm during the investigation. Normally, the risk of harm must be no greater than in ordinary life, i.e., participants should not be exposed to risks greater than or additional to those encountered in their normal lifestyles. Where the risk of harm is greater than in ordinary life the provisions of 3.8 should apply. Participants must be asked about any factors in the procedure that might create a risk, such as pre-existing medical conditions, and must be advised of any special action they should take to avoid risk.

8.2   Participants should be informed of procedures for contacting the investigator within a reasonable time period following participation should stress, potential harm, or related questions or concern arise despite the precautions required by these Principles. Where research procedures might result in undesirable consequences for participants, the investigator has the responsibility to detect and remove or correct these consequences.

8.3   Where research may involve behaviour or experiences that participants may regard as personal and private the participants must be protected from stress by all appropriate measures, including the assurance that answers to personal questions need not be given. There should be no concealment or deception when seeking information that might encroach on privacy.

8.4   In research involving children, great caution should be exercised when discussing the results with parents, teachers or others *in loco parentis*, since evaluative statements may carry unintended weight.

9 Observational research

9.1   Studies based upon observation must respect the privacy and psychological well-being of the individuals studied. Unless those observed give their consent to being observed, observational research is only acceptable in situations where those observed would expect to be observed by strangers. Additionally, particular account should be taken of local cultural values and of the possibility of intruding upon the privacy of individuals who, even while in a normally public space, may believe they are unobserved.

10   Giving advice

10.1   During research, an investigator may obtain evidence of psychological or physical problems of which a participant is, apparently, unaware. In such a case, the investigator has a responsibility to inform the participant if the investigator believes that by not doing so the participant's future well-being may be endangered.

10.2   If, in the normal course of psychological research, or as a result of problems detected as in 10.1, a participant solicits advice concerning educational, personality, behavioural or health issues, caution should be exercised. If the issue is serious and the investigator is not qualified to offer assistance, the appropriate source of professional advice should be recommended. Further details on the giving of advice will be found in the Society's Code of Conduct.

10.3   In some kinds of investigation the giving of advice is appropriate if this forms an intrinsic part of the research and has been agreed in advance.

11   Colleagues

11.1   Investigators share responsibility for the ethical treatment of research participants with their collaborators, assistants, students and employees. A psychologist who believes that another psychologist or investigator may be conducting research that is not in accordance with the principles above should encourage that investigator to re-evaluate the research.

This statement was approved by the Council of the British Psychological Society in January 2000. It forms part of the Code of Conduct, Ethical Principles & Guidelines, in a booklet that may be obtained from the British Psychological Society, St Andrews House, 48 Princess Road East, Leicester LE1 7DR. The British Psychological Society website is at http://www.bps.org.uk

Appendix B
Careers in Psychology

Psychology can be studied for intrinsic interest or as part of the general educational process, especially at GSCE or AS and A level. It is also a component of training in many people-orientated professions such as teaching, social work, nursing and occupational therapy, speech therapy and management studies. There are a number of careers, however, for which further training in psychology is required, at degree level and sometimes beyond. The following careers all require a first degree in Psychology. In many cases a taught Master's course or practitioner Doctorate, or in some cases a research postgraduate qualification (MPhil or PhD), is required or is very helpful.

Educational psychologists work with children of school age and their parents and teachers in cases where there are behavioural or emotional problems manifest at school. A postgraduate qualification in educational psychology is needed, as well as a teaching qualification and experience.

Clinical psychologists work in hospitals, clinics, or in the community, usually with mentally ill persons, or persons experiencing difficulties of a psychological nature. A postgraduate qualification in clinical psychology is required. *Health psychologists* carry out more general work concerned with psychological health and well-being of individuals in the community.

Occupational psychologists work in industry or government, dealing with issues such as personnel selection, job design and the quality of the working environment. A postgraduate qualification in occupational psychology is an asset.

Counselling psychologists work in hospitals, clinics, or in the community, usually with people experiencing psychological difficulties; it can be viewed as the application of psychological principles to the practice of counselling. A postgraduate qualification in counselling psychology is required.

Prison psychologists work in prisons and detention centres. They are concerned with aspects of counselling and training of prison staff, and training and rehabilitation of offenders. *Forensic psychologists* help the police in investigations or may work for the Home Office.

Sports psychologists advise on facilities and training of athletes and their preparation for competitive and sporting events.

Neuropsychologists may work in hospitals or research centres, on aspects of brain functioning and performance.

Teaching in psychology is carried out at universities, institutes of higher education, further education colleges, schools and other educational centres. In higher education a postgraduate qualification is useful and often required.

Research psychologists work in universities, government departments, or other organizations, on diverse aspects of psychological inquiry. Often a postgraduate research qualification such as a PhD is required.

Information on all of these careers can be obtained from the website of the British Psychological Society, at http://www.bps.org.uk; booklets on Studying Psychology and on Careers in Psychology can be ordered by post, or downloaded.

Altogether there are over 10,000 chartered psychologists currently registered in the UK. Only a small proportion of psychology graduates become professional psychologists, but many (more than a third) go into careers closely related to psychology, such as social work, teaching, nursing, market research, personnel management or counselling/psychotherapy.

References

Aboud, F. 1988: *Children and Prejudice*. Oxford: Basil Blackwell.

Aboud, F. and Doyle, A. B. 1996: Parental and peer influences on children's racial attitudes. *International Journal of Intercultural Relations*, 20, 371–83.

Adams, R. J., Courage, M. L. and Mercer, M. E. 1994: Systematic measurement of human neonatal colour vision. *Vision Research*, 34, 1691–1701.

Ainsworth, M. D. S. 1967: *Infancy in Uganda: Infant Care and the Growth of Love*. Baltimore, MD: Johns Hopkins University Press.

Ainsworth, M. D. S. 1973: The development of mother–infant attachment. In B. M. Caldwell and H. N. Ricciutti (eds), *Review of Child Development Research*, vol. 3. Chicago: University of Chicago Press.

Ainsworth, M. D. S. and Bowlby, J. 1991: An ethological approach to personality development. *American Psychologist*, 46, 333–41.

Ainsworth, M. D. S., Blehar, M. C., Waters, E. and Wall, S. 1978: *Patterns of Attachment*. Hillsdale, NJ: Erlbaum.

Alsaker, F. 1996: Annotation: the impact of puberty. *Journal of Child Psychology and Psychiatry*, 37, 249–58.

American Psychiatric Association 1994: *Diagnostic and Statistical Manual of Mental Disorders*, 4th edn. Washington, DC: American Psychiatric Association.

Ananiadou, K. and Smith, P. K. 2002: Legal requirements and nationally circulated materials against school bullying in European countries. *Criminal Justice*, 2, 471–91.

Anderson, D. R., Huston, A. C., Schmitt, K. L., Linebarger, D. L. and Wright, J. C. 2001: Early childhood television viewing and adolescent social behavior. *Monographs of the Society for Research in Child Development*, 66, serial no 264.

Anderson, J. W. 1972: Attachment behaviour out of doors. In N. Blurton Jones (ed.), *Ethological Studies of Child Behaviour*. Cambridge: Cambridge University Press.

Andrade, J. 2001: An introduction to working memory. In J. Andrade (ed.), *Working Memory in Perspective*. Hove, East Sussex: Psychology Press.

Apgar, V. 1953: A proposal for a new method of evaluation of the newborn infant. *Anesthesiology and Analgesia*, 32, 260–7.

Appel, M. H. 1942: Aggressive behaviour of nursery school children and adult procedures in dealing with such behaviour. *Journal of Experimental Education*, 11, 185–99.

Archer, J. 1989: Childhood gender roles: structure and development. *The Psychologist*, 12, 367–70.

Archer, J. and Lloyd, B. 1986: *Sex and Gender*, 2nd edn. Harmondsworth: Penguin.

Archer, S. L. 1982: The lower age boundaries of identity development. *Child Development*, 53, 155–66.

Aries, P. 1962: *Centuries of Childhood: A Social History of the Family*. New York: Vintage Books.

Arnett, J. 1992: Reckless behavior in adolescence: a developmental perspective. *Developmental Review*, 12, 339–73.

Arnett, J. 1995: Broad and narrow socialization: the family in the context of a cultural theory. *Journal of Marriage and the Family*, 57, 617–28.

Arnett, J. 1999: Adolescent storm and stress, reconsidered. *American Psychologist*, 54, 317–26.

Aronson, E. 1978: *The Jigsaw Classroom*. Beverly Hills: Sage.

Asher, S. R. and Coie, J. D. 1990: *Peer Rejection in Childhood*. Cambridge: Cambridge University Press.

Asher, S. R., Parkhurst, J. T., Hymel, S. and Williams, G. A. 1990: Peer rejection and loneliness in childhood. In S. R. Asher and J. D. Coie (eds), *Peer Rejection in Childhood*, pp. 253–73. Cambridge: Cambridge University Press.

Asher, S. R. and Wheeler, V. A. 1985: Children's loneliness: a comparison of rejected and neglected peer status. *Journal of Consulting and Clinical Psychology*, 53, 500–5.

Aslin, R. N. 1981: Development of smooth pursuit in human infants. In D. F. Fisher, R. A. Monty and J. W. Senders (eds), *Eye-Movements: Cognition and Visual Perception*. Hillsdale, NJ: Erlbaum.

Asperger, H. 1944: Die 'Autistischen Psychopathen' in Kindesalter. *Archiv für Psychiatrie und Nervenkrankheiten*, 117, 76–136.

Asquith, S. 1996: When children kill children. *Childhood*, 3, 99–116.

Astington, J. W. 1994: *The Child's Discovery of the Mind*. London: Fontana.

Atkinson, J. and Braddick, O. J. 1981: Acuity, contrast sensitivity and accommodation in infancy. In R. N. Aslin, J. R. Roberts and M. R. Petersen (eds), *The Development of Perception: Psychobiological Perspectives, Vol. 2: The Visual System*. New York: Academic Press.

Atkinson, R. C. and Shiffrin, R. M. 1968: Human memory: a proposed system and its control processes. In K. W. Spence and J. T. Spence (eds), *Advances in the Psychology of Learning and Motivation*, vol. 2. New York: Academic Press.

Atkinson, R. L., Atkinson, R. C. and Hilgard, E. R. 1981: *Introduction to Psychology*, 8th edn. New York: Harcourt, Brace, Jovanovich.

Auerbach, J. G., Faroy, M., Ebstein, R., Kahana, M. and Levine, J. 2001: The association of the dopamine D4 receptor gene (DRD4) and the serotonin transporter promoter gene (5-HTTLPR) with temperament in 12-month-old infants. *Journal of Child Psychology and Psychiatry*, 42, 777–83.

Aviezer, O., Van IJzendoorn, M. H., Sagi, A. and Schuengel, C. 1994: 'Children of the Dream' revisited: 70 years of collective early child care in Israeli Kibbutzim. *Psychological Bulletin*, 116, 99–116.

Azmitia, M. and Montgomery, R. 1993: Friendship, transactive dialogues, and the development of scientific reasoning. *Social Development*, 2, 202–21.

Baddeley, A. 1992: Working memory. *Science*, 255, 556–9.

Baddeley, A. 1993: *Your Memory: A User's Guide*, 2nd edn. Harmondsworth: Penguin.

Badian, N. A. 1984: Reading disability in an epidemiological context: Incidence and environmental correlates. *Journal of Learning Disabilities*, 17, 129–36.

Bagwell, C. L., Newcomb, A. F. and Bukowski, W. M. 1998: Preadolescent friendship and peer rejection as predictors of adult adjustment. *Child Development* 69, 140–53.

Bahrick, L. E. 1992: Infants' perceptual differentiation of amodal and modality-specific audio-visual relations. *Journal of Experimental Child Psychology*, 53, 180–99.

Bahrick, L. E. 2000: Increasing specificity in the development of intermodal perception. In D. Muir and A. Slater (eds), *Infant Development. The Essential Readings*. Oxford: Blackwell.

Baillargeon, R. and DeVos, J. 1991: Object permanence in young infants: further evidence. *Child Development*, 62, 1227–46.

Baldwin, D. A. and Moses, L. J. 1996: The ontogeny of social information gathering. *Child Development*, 67, 1915–39.

Baltes, P. B., Reese, H. W. and Lipsitt, L. P. 1980: Life-span developmental psychology. *Annual Review of Psychology*, 31, 65–110.

Bandura, A. 1969: Social learning theory of identificatory processes. In D. A. Goslin (ed.), *Handbook of Socialization Theory and Research*. Chicago: Rand McNally.

Bandura, A. 1971: An analysis of modeling processes. In A. Bandura (ed.), *Psychological Modeling*. New York: Lieber-Atherton.

Banks, M. and Ginsberg, A. P. 1985: Infant visual preferences. A review and new theoretical treatment. *Advances in Child Development and Behaviour*, 19, 207–46.

Banks, M. H. and Ullah, P. 1986: *Youth Unemployment in the 1980s: A Psychological Analysis*. London: Croom Helm.

Banks, N. 1996: Young single mothers with black children in therapy. *Clinical Child Psychology and Psychiatry*, 1, 19–28.

Baratz, S. S. and Baratz, J. C. 1970: Early childhood intervention: the social science base of institutional racism. *Harvard Educational Review*, 40, 29–50.

Barkow, J. 1989: *Darwin, Sex and Status*. Toronto: University of Toronto Press.

Baron-Cohen, S. 1989: The autistic child's theory of mind: a case of specific developmental delay. *Journal of Child Psychology and Psychiatry*, 30, 285–97.

Baron-Cohen, S. 1995: *Mindblindness: An Essay on Autism and Theory of Mind*. Cambridge, MA: MIT Press.

Baron-Cohen, S., Campbell, R., Karmiloff-Smith, A., Grant, J. and Walker, J. 1995: Are children with autism blind to the mentalistic significance of the eyes? *British Journal of Developmental Psychology*, 13, 379–98.

Baron-Cohen, S., Cox, A., Baird, G., Swettenham, J., Nightingale, N., Morgan, K., Drew, A. and Charman, T. 1996: Psychological markers of autism at 18 months of age in a large population. *British Journal of Psychiatry*, 168, 158–63.

Baron-Cohen, S., Leslie, A. M. and Frith, U. 1985: Does the autistic child have a 'theory of mind'? *Cognition*, 21, 37–46.

Baron-Cohen, S., Leslie, A. and Frith, U. 1986: Mechanical, behavioral and intentional understanding of picture stories in autistic children. *British Journal of Developmental Psychology*, 4, 113–25.

Baron-Cohen, S., Tager-Flusberg, H. and Cohen, D. J. 2000: A note on nosology. In S. Baron-Cohen, H. Tager-Flusberg and D. J. Cohen (eds), *Understanding Other Minds. Perspectives from Developmental Cognitive Neuroscience*. Oxford: Oxford University Press.

Barrett, M. D. 1986: Early semantic representations and early word usage. In S. A. Kuczaj and M. D. Barrett (eds), *The Development of Word Meaning*, pp 39–67. New York: Springer.

Barrett, M. D. (ed.) 1999: *The Development of Language*. London: Psychology Press.

Barrett, M. and Buchanan-Barrow, E. 2002: Children's understanding of society. In P. K. Smith and C. H. Hart (eds), *Blackwell Handbook of Childhood Social Development*. Oxford: Blackwell.

Barrett, M. D., Harris, M. and Chasan, J. 1991: Early lexical development and maternal speech: a comparison of children's initial and subsequent uses of words. *Journal of Child Language*, 18, 21–40.

Barry, H., Bacon, M. K. and Child, I. L. 1957: A cross-cultural survey of some sex differences in socialization. *Journal of Abnormal and Social Psychology*, 55, 327–32.

Barry, H. I., Child, I. L. and Bacon, M. K. 1959: Relations of child training to subsistence economy. *American Anthropologist*, 61, 51–63.

Bartsch, K. and Wellman, H. M. 1995: *Children Talk about the Mind*. Oxford: Oxford University Press.

Bar-Heim, Y., Sutton, D. B., Fox, N. A. and Marvin, R. S. 2000: Stability and change of attachment at 14, 24, and 58 months of age: behavior, representation, and life events. *Journal of Child Psychology and Psychiatry*, 41, 381–8.

Bar-On, D., Eland, J., Kleber, R. J., Krell, R., Moore, Y., Sagi, A., Soriano, E., Suedfeld, P., van der Velden, P. G. and van IJzendoorn, M. H. 1998: Multigenerational perspectives on coping with the Holocaust experience: an attachment perspective for understanding the developmental sequelae of trauma across generations. *International Journal of Behavioral Development*, 22, 315–38.

Bar-Tal, D., Raviv, A. and Goldberg, M. 1982: Helping behavior among preschool children: an observational study. *Child Development*, 53, 396–402.

Bates, E., Bretherton, I. and Snyder, L. 1988: *From First Words to Grammar: Individual Differences and Dissociable Mechanisms*. Cambridge: Cambridge University Press.

Bateson, P. P. G. 1982: Preference for cousins in Japanese quail. *Nature*, 295, 236–7.

Baumeister, R. F., Smart, L. and Boden, J. M. 1996: Relation of threatened egotism to violence and aggression: the dark side of self-esteem. *Psychological Review*, 103, 5–33.

Baumrind, D. 1967: Child care practices anteceding three patterns of preschool behavior. *Genetic Psychology Monographs*, 75, 43–88.

Baumrind, D. 1980: New directions in socialization research. *American Psychologist*, 35, 639–52.

Baumrind, D. 1993: The average expectable environment is not good enough: a response to Scarr. *Child Development*, 64, 1299–317.

Baydar, N. and Brooks-Gunn, J. 1991: Effects of maternal employment and child-care arrangements on preschoolers' cognitive and behavioral outcomes. *Developmental Psychology*, 27, 932–45.

Belsky, J. 1984: The determinants of parenting: a process model. *Child Development*, 55, 83–96.

Belsky, J. 1988: Infant day care and socioemotional development: the United States. *Journal of Child Psychology and Psychiatry*, 29, 397–406.

Belsky, J. 2001: Developmental risks (still) associated with early child care. *Journal of Child Psychology and Psychiatry*, 42, 845–59.

Belsky, J. and Steinberg, L. D. 1978: The effects of day care: a critical review. *Child Development*, 49, 929–49.

Belsky, J., Steinberg, L. and Draper, P. 1991: Childhood experience, interpersonal development, and reproductive strategy: an evolutionary theory of socialization. *Child Development*, 62, 647–70.

Bem, S. L. 1975: Sex role adaptability: one consequence of psychological androgyny. *Journal of Personality and Social Psychology*, 31, 634–43.

Bem, S. L. 1981: Gender schema theory: A cognitive account of sex typing. *Psychological Review*, 88, 354–64.

Bem, S. L. 1989: Genital knowledge and gender constancy in preschool children. *Child Development*, 60, 649–62.

Ben Shaul, D. M. 1962: The composition of the milk of wild animals. *International Zoo Yearbook*, 4, 333–42.

Benedict, R. 1934: *Patterns of Culture*. Boston: Houghton Mifflin.

Bennett, N. and Dunne, E. 1992: *Managing Classroom Groups*. Hemel Hempstead: Simon and Schuster.

Bereiter, C. and Engelmann, S. 1966: *Teaching Disadvantaged Children in the Preschool*. New York: Prentice-Hall.

Bergen, D. 1990: Young children's humour at home and school. Paper given at Eighth International Conference on Humour, Sheffield.

Berndt, T. J. 1982: The features and effects of friendship in early adolescence. *Child Development*, 53, 1447–60.

Berndt, T. J. and Keefe, K. 1995: Friends' influence on adolescents' adjustment to school. *Child Development*, 66, 1312–29.

Bernstein, B. 1962: Social class, linguistic codes and grammatical elements. *Language and Speech*, 5, 31–46.

Bernstein, B. 1971: A sociolinguistic approach to socialization: with some reference to educability. In D. Hymes and J. J. Gumperz (eds), *Directions in Sociolinguistics*. New York: Holt, Rinehart and Winston.

Berry, J. W. 1984: Towards a universal psychology of competence. *International Journal of Psychology*, 19, 335–61.

Best, D. L., Williams, J. E., Cloud, L. M., Davis, S. W., Robertson, L. S., Edwards, J. R., Giles, H. and Fowles, J. 1977: Development of sex-trait stereotypes among young children in the United States, England and Ireland. *Child Development*, 48, 1375–84.

Bickerton, D. 1990: *Language and Species*. Chicago: University of Chicago Press.

Bigelow, B. J. and La Gaipa, J. J. 1980: The development of friendship values and choice. In H. C. Foot, A. J. Chapman and J. R. Smith (eds), *Friendship and Social Relations in Children*. Chichester: Wiley.

Binet, A. and Simon, T. 1905: New methods for diagnosis of the intellectual level of subnormals. *L'Année Psychologique*, 14, 1–90.

Binet, A. and Simon, T. 1916: *The Development of Intelligence in Children*. Baltimore, MD: Williams and Wilkins.

Bischof-Kohler, D. 1988: Uber der Zusammenhang von Empathie und der Fahigkeit, sich im Spiegel zu erkennen. *Schweizerische Zeitschrift für Psychologie*, 47, 147–59.

Bjorklund, D. F. and Douglas, R. N. 1997: The development of memory strategies. In N. Cowan (ed.), *The Development of Memory in Childhood*. Hove, East Sussex: Psychology Press.

Bjorklund, D. and Green, B. 1992: The adaptive nature of cognitive immaturity. *American Psychologist*, 47, 46–54.

Bjorklund, D. F. and Harnishfeger, K. K. 1987: Developmental differences in the mental effort requirements for the use of an organizational strategy in free recall. *Journal of Experimental Child Psychology*, 44, 109–25.

Bjorklund, D. F., Muir-Broaddus, J. E. and Schneider, W. 1990: The role of knowledge in the development of strategies. In D. F. Bjorklund (ed.), *Children's Strategies: Contemporary Views of Cognitive Development*. Hillsdale, New Jersey: Erlbaum.

Bjorklund, D. F. and Pellegrini, A. D. 2000: Child development and evolutionary psychology. *Child Development*, 71, 1687–708.

Björkqvist, K., Lagerspetz, K. M. J. and Kaukainen, A. 1992: Do girls manipulate and boys fight? Developmental trends in regard to direct and indirect aggression. *Aggressive Behavior*, 18, 117–27.

Björkvist, K., Österman, K. and Kaukiainen, A. 2000: Social intelligence – empathy = aggression? *Aggression and Violent Behavior*, 5, 191–200.

Black, P. 1998: *Testing: Friend or Foe? Theory and Practice of Assessment and Testing*. London: Falmer.

Blades, M. and Banham. J. 1990: Children's memory in an environmental learning task. *Journal of Environmental Education and Information*, 9, 119–31.

Blakemore, C. and Cooper, C. R. 1970: Development of the brain depends on the visual environment. *Nature*, 228, 477–8.

Blank, M. and Solomon, F. 1969: How shall the disadvantaged child be taught? *Child Development*, 40, 47–61.

Blass, E. M., Ganschrow, J. R. and Steiner, J. E. 1994: Classical conditioning in newborn humans 2–48 hours of age. *Infant Behavior and Development*, 7, 223–35.

Blos, P. 1962: *On Adolescence*. London: Collier-Macmillan.

Blurton Jones, N. 1967: An ethological study of some aspects of social behaviour of children in nursery school. In D. Morris (ed.), *Primate Ethology*. London: Weidenfeld & Nicolson.

Blurton Jones, N. G. and Konner, M. J. 1973: Sex differences in behaviour of London and Bushmen children. In R. P. Michael and J. H. Crook (eds), *Comparative Ecology and Behaviour of Primates*. London and New York: Academic Press.

Blurton Jones, N. G. and Konner, M. J. 1976: Bushmen knowledge of animal behavior. In R. B. Lee and I. De Vore (eds), *Kalahari Hunter-Gatherers*. Cambridge, MA: Harvard University Press.

Boden, M. A. 1979: *Piaget*. London: Fontana.

Borke, H. 1975: Piaget's mountains revisited: Changes in the egocentric landscape. *Developmental Psychology*, 11, 240–3.

Bornstein, M. H., Gaughran, J. M. and Segui, I. 1991: Multimethod assessment of infant temperament: mother questionnaire and mother and observer reports evaluated and compared at five months using the Infant Temperament Measure. *International Journal of Behavioral Development*, 14, 131–51.

Boulton, M. J. 1992: Rough physical play in adolescents: does it serve a dominance function? *Early Education and Development*, 3, 312–33.

Boulton, M. J. and Smith, P. K. 1991: Ethnic and gender partner and activity preferences in mixed-race schools in the UK; playground observations. In C. H. Hart (ed.), *Children in Playgrounds*. New York: SUNY Press.

Boulton, M. J. and Smith, P. K. 1996: Liking and peer perceptions among Asian and White British children. *Journal of Social and Personal Relationships*, 13, 163–77.

Boulton, M., Trueman, M., Chau, C., Whiteland, C. and Amatya, K. 1999: Concurrent and longitudinal links between friendship and peer victimization: implications for befriending interventions. *Journal of Adolescence*, 22, 461–6.

Bower, T. G. R. 1965: Stimulus variables determining space perception in infants. *Science*, 149, 88–9.

Bower, T. G. R. 1966: The visual world of infants. *Scientific American*, 215, 80–92.

Bower, T. G. R. 1982: *Development in Infancy*, 2nd edn. San Francisco: W. H. Freeman.

Bowlby, J. 1953: *Child Care and the Growth of Love*. Harmondsworth: Penguin.

Bowlby, J. 1969: *Attachment and Loss, Vol. 1, Attachment*. London: Hogarth Press.

Bowlby, J. 1988: *A Secure Base: Clinical Applications of Attachment Theory*. London: Routledge.

Bradley, L. and Bryant, P. E. 1985: *Rhyme and Reason in Reading and Spelling*. International Academy for Research in Learning Disabilities series. Michigan: University of Michigan Press.

Brainerd, C. J. 1983: Working memory systems and cognitive development. In C. J. Brainerd (ed.), *Recent Advances in Cognitive Developmental Theory*. New York: Springer-Verlag.

Breakwell, G. M. and Fife-Schaw, C. 1992: Sexual activities and preferences in a United Kingdom sample of 16 to 20 year olds. *Archives of Sexual Behavior*, 21, 271–93.

Bremner, J. G. 1994: *Infancy*. 2nd edn. Oxford: Blackwell.

Bretherton, I. 1992: The origins of attachment theory: John Bowlby and Mary Ainsworth. *Developmental Psychology*, 28, 759–75.

Bretherton, I. and Waters, E. (eds) 1985: Growing points of attachment theory and research. *Monographs of the Society for Research in Child Development*, 50, nos 1–2.

Bretherton, I., Fritz, J., Zahn-Waxler, C. and Ridgeway, D. 1986: Learning to talk about emotions; a functionalist perspective. *Child Development*, 57, 529–48.

Brindle, D. 1996: Blacks and Asians at a social disadvantage. *Guardian*, 8 August, p. 9.

British Psychological Society 1990: Psychologists and child sexual abuse. *The Psychologist*, 3, 344–8.

Broadfoot, P. M. 1996: *Education, Assessment and Society*. Buckingham: Open University Press.

Brody, G. H., Ge, X., Conger, R., Gibbons, F. X., Murry, V. M., Gerrard, M. and Simons, R. L. 2001: The influence of neighbourhood disadvantage, collective socialization, and parenting on African American children's affiliation with deviant peers. *Child Development*, 72, 1231–46.

Bronfenbrenner, U. 1979: *The Ecology of Human Development*. Cambridge, MA: Harvard University Press.

Bronfenbrenner, U. and Ceci, S. J. 1994: Nature-nurture reconceptualized in developmental perspective: a bioecological model. *Psychological Review*, 101, 568–86.

Brooks-Gunn, J. and Lewis, M. 1981: Infant social perception: responses to pictures of parents and strangers. *Developmental Psychology*, 17, 647–9.

Brown, A. L. and Palenscar, A. S. 1989: Guided, cooperative learning and individual knowledge acquisition. In L. B. Resnick (ed.), *Knowing, Learning and Instruction*. Hillsdale, NJ: Lawrence Erlbaum.

Brown, A. L., Smiley, S. S. and Lawton, S. Q. C. 1978: Intrusion of a thematic idea in children's comprehension and retention of stories. *Child Development*, 48, 1454–66.

Brown, G. W. and Harris, T. 1978: *Social Origins of Depression: A Study of Psychiatric Disorders in Women*. London: Tavistock.

Brown, J. R., Donelan-McCall, N. and Dunn, J. 1996: Why talk about mental states? The significance of children's conversations with friends, siblings, and mothers. *Child Development*, 67, 836–49.

Brown, R. 1973: *A First Language*. Cambridge, MA: Harvard University Press.

Brown, R. and Bellugi, U. 1964: Three processes in the child's acquisition of syntax. In E. H. Lennenberg (ed.), *New Directions in the Study of Language*. Cambridge, MA: MIT Press.

Brown, R., Cazden, C. and Bellugi, U. 1969: The child's grammar from I–III. In J. P. Hill (ed.), *Minnesota Symposia on Child Psychology*, vol. 2. Minneapolis: University of Minnesota Press.

Brown, R. and Fraser, C. 1963: The acquisition of syntax. In C. N. Cofer and B. Musgrave (eds), *Verbal Behavior and Learning: Problems and Processes*, pp. 158–201. New York: McGraw-Hill.

Brown, R. A. J. and Renshaw, P. 2000: Collective argumentation: a sociocultural approach to reframing classroom teaching and learning. In H. Cowie and G. van der Aalsvoort (eds), *Social Interaction in Learning and Instruction*. (pp. 52–66) Amsterdam: Pergamon, Elsevier Science.

Browne, K. 1989: The naturalistic context of family violence and child abuse. In J. Archer and K. Browne (eds), *Human Aggression: Naturalistic Approaches*. London: Routledge.

Bruner, J. S. 1963: *The Process of Education*. New York: Vintage Books.

Bruner, J. S. 1966: On cognitive growth. In J. S. Bruner, R. R. Oliver and P. M. Greenheld (eds), *Studies in Cognitive Growth*. New York: Wiley.

Bruner, J. S. 1971: *The Relevance of Education*. New York: Norton.

Bruner, J. S. 1972: The nature and uses of immaturity. *American Psychologist*, 27, 687–708.

Bruner, J. S. 1983: *Child's Talk*. New York: Norton.

Bruner, J. S. 1986: *Actual Minds: Possible Worlds*. Cambridge, MA: Harvard University Press.

Bruner, J. S. 1990: *Acts of Meaning*. Cambridge, MA: Harvard University Press.

Bruner, J. S. and Lucariello, J. 1989: Monologue as narrative recreation of the world. In K. Nelson (ed.), *Narratives from the Crib*. Cambridge, MA: Harvard University Press.

Bruner, J. S. and Sherwood, V. 1976: Peekaboo and the learning of rule structures. In J. S. Bruner, A. Jolly and K. Sylva (eds), *Play: its Role in Development and Evolution*. Harmondsworth: Penguin.

Bryant, B., Harris, M. and Newton, D. 1980: *Children and Minders*. London: Grant McIntyre.

Bryant, P. and Bradley, L. 1985: *Children's Reading Problems*. Oxford: Basil Blackwell.

Bryant, P. E., MacLean, M. and Bradley, L. 1990: Rhyme, language and children's reading. *Applied Psycholinguistics*, 11, 3, 237–52.

Bryant, P. E. and Trabasso, T. 1971: Transitive inferences and memory in young children. *Nature*, 232, 456–8.

Buchanan, C. M., Eccles, J. S. and Becker, J. B. 1992: Are adolescents the victims of raging hormones?: evidence for activational effects of hormones on moods and behavior at adolescence. *Psychological Bulletin*, 111, 62–107.

Buckhalt, J. A., Mahoney, G. J. and Paris, S. G. 1976: Efficiency of self-generated elaborations by EMR and nonretarded children. *American Journal of Mental Deficiency*, 81, 93–96.

Buis, J. M. and Thompson, D. N. 1989: Imaginary audience and personal fable: a brief review. *Adolescence*, 24, 773–81.

Bukowski, W. M., Hoza, B. and Boivin, M. 1994: Measuring friendship quality during pre- and early adolescence: the development and psychometric properties of the Friendship Qualities Scale. *Journal of Social and Personal Relationships*, 11, 471–84.

Bull, R. (Ed.) 2001: *Children and the Law. The Essential Readings*. Oxford: Blackwell.

Bullough, V. L. 1981: Age at menarche: a misunderstanding. *Science*, 213, 365–6.

Burman, E. 1994. *Deconstructing Developmental Psychology*, London: Routledge.

Burman, E. 1996: International Children's Rights Legislation. *Childhood*, 3, 45–66.

Buss, D. M. and Schmitt, D. P. 1993: Sexual strategies theory: an evolutionary perspective on human mating. *Psychological Review*, 100, 204–32.

Bussey, K. and Bandura, A. 1999: Social cognitive theory of gender development and differentiation. *Developmental Review*, 106, 676–713.

Butterworth, G. 1987: Some benefits of egocentrism. In J. S. Bruner and H. Haste (eds), *Making Sense*. London: Methuen.

Butterworth, G. 1991: The ontogeny and phylogeny of joint visual attention. In A. Whiten (ed.) *Natural Theories of Mind*. Oxford: Blackwell.

Byers, J. A., and Walker, C. 1995: Refining the motor training hypothesis for the evolution of play. *American Naturalist*, 146, 25–40.

Byrne, R. and Whiten, A. 1987: The thinking primate's guide to deception. *New Scientist*, 116, 54–6.

Byrne, R. W. and Whiten, A. (eds) 1988: *Machiavellian Intelligence: Social Expertise and the Evolution of Intellect in Monkeys, Apes, and Humans*. Oxford: Clarendon Press.

Cabrera, N. J., Tamis-LeMonda, C. S., Bradley, R. H., Hofferth, S. and Lamb, M. E. 2000: Fatherhood in the twenty-first century. *Child Development*, 71, 127–36.

Cairns, R. B., Cairns, B. D., Neckerman, H. J., Gest, S. D. and Gariepy, J. L. 1988: Social networks and aggressive behavior. Peer acceptance or peer rejection? *Developmental Psychology*, 24, 815–23.

Cairns, R. B., Leung, M-C., Buchanan, L. and Cairns, B. D. 1995: Friendships and social networks in childhood and adolescence: fluidity, reliability, and interrelations. *Child Development*, 66, 1330–45.

Call, J. and Tomasello, M. 1999: A nonverbal false belief task: the performance of children and great apes. *Child Development*, 70, 381–95.

Cameron, J. A., Alvarez, J. M., Ruble, D. N. and Fulgini, A. J. 2001: Children's lay theories about ingroups and outgroups: reconceptualizing research on prejudice. *Personality and Social Psychology Review*, 5, 118–28.

Campos, J., Bertenthal, B. I. and Kermoian, R. 1992: Early experience and emotional development: the emergence of wariness of heights. *Psychological Science*, 3, 61–4.

Campos, J. J., Caplovitz, K. B., Lamb, M. E., Goldsmith, H. H. and Stenberg, C. 1983: Socioemotional development. In M. M. Haith and J. J. Campos (eds), *Handbook of Child Psychology: Vol. 2, Infancy and Developmental Psychobiology*. New York: Wiley.

Caplan, N., Choy, M. and Whitmore, J. 1992: Indochinese refugee families and academic achievement. *Scientific American*, 266, February, 18–24.

Carlson, E. A. 1998: A prospective longitudinal study of attachment disorganization/disorientation. *Child Development*, 69, 1107–28.

Carlsson-Paige, N. and Levin, D. E. 1987: *The War Play Dilemma: Balancing Needs and Values in the Early Childhood Classroom*. New York: Teachers College, Columbia University.

Carlsson-Paige, N. and Levin, D. E. 1990: *Who's Calling the Shots?: How to Respond Effectively to Children's Fascination with War Play and War Toys*. Philadelphia, PA: New Society Publishers.

Caron, A. J., Caron, R. F. and Carlson, V. R. 1979: Infant perception of the invariant shape of objects varying in slant. *Child Development*, 50, 716–21.

Carpendale, J. I. M. and Chandler, M. J. 1996: On the distinction between false belief understanding and subscribing to an interpretive theory of mind. *Child Development*, 67, 1686–706.

Carr, R. 1994: Peer helping in Canada. *Peer Counselling Journal*, 11, 6–9.

Carr, W. 1991: Education for citizenship. *British Journal of Educational Studies*, 39, 373–85.

Carroll, A., Houghton, S., Hattie, J. and Durkin, D. 1999: Adolescent reputation enhancement: differentiating delinquent, nondelinquent and at-risk youths. *Journal of Child Psychology & Psychiatry*, 40, 593–606.

Carter, C. A., Bottoms, B. L. and Levine, M. 1996: Linguistic and socioemotional influences on the accuracy of children's reports. *Law and Human Behavior*, 20, 335–58.

Case, R. 1978: Intellectual development from birth to adulthood: a neo-Piagetian interpretation. In R. S. Siegler (ed.), *Children's Thinking: What Develops?* Hillsdale, NJ: Erlbaum.

Case, R. 1985: *Intellectual Development: Birth to Adulthood*. New York: Academic Press.

Caspi, A. 2000: The child is father to the man: personality continuities from childhood to adulthood. *Journal of Personality and Social Psychology*, 78, 158–71.

Caspi, A., Henry, B., McGee, R. O., Moffitt, T. E. and Silva, P. A. 1995: Temperamental origins of child and adolescent behavior problems: from age three to age fifteen. *Child Development*, 66, 55–68.

Ceci, S. J. and Bruck, M. 1993: The suggestibility of the child witness: a historical review and synthesis. *Psychological Bulletin*, 113, 403–39.

Ceci, S. J. and Bruck, M. 1995: *Jeopardy in the Courtroom. A Scientific Analysis of Children's Testimony*, Washington, DC: American Psychological Association.

Ceci, S. J., Crotteau-Huffman, M., Smith, E. and Loftus, E. W. 1994: Repeatedly thinking about non-events. *Consciousness and Cognition*, 3, 388–407.

Chalmers, J. B. and Townsend, M. A. R. 1990: The effect of training in social perspective taking on socially maladjusted girls. *Child Development*, 61, 178–90.

Chan, R. W., Raboy, B. and Patterson, C. J. 1998: Psychosocial adjustment among children conceived via donor insemination by lesbian and heterosexual mothers. *Child Development*, 69, 443–57.

Chandler, M. J. and Sokol, B. W. 1999: Representation once removed: children's developing conceptions of representational life. In I. E. Sigel (ed.), *Development of Mental Representation*. Mahwah, NJ: Erlbaum.

Charman, T. 2000: Theory of mind and the early diagnosis of autism. In S. Baron-Cohen, H. Tager-Flusberg and D. J. Cohen (eds.), *Understanding Other Minds. Perspectives from Developmental Cognitive Neuroscience*. Oxford: Oxford University Press.

Charman, T. and Baron-Cohen, S. 1992: Understanding drawings and beliefs: a further test of the metarepresentation theory of autism. *Journal of Child Psychology and Psychiatry*, 33, 1105–12.

Chen, X., Dong, Q. and Zhou, H. 1997: Authoritative and authoritarian parenting practices and social and school performance in Chinese children. *International Journal of Behavioral Development*, 21, 855–73.

Chen, X., Hastings, P. D., Rubin, K. H., Chen, H., Cen, G. and Stewart, S. L. 1998: Child-rearing attitudes and behavioral inhibition in Chinese and Canadian toddlers: a cross-cultural study. *Developmental Psychology*, 34, 677–86.

Cherlin, A. J., Furstenberg, F. F. Jr., Chase-Lonsdale, P. L., Kiernan, K. E., Robins, P. K., Morrison, D. R. and Teitler, J. O. 1991: Longitudinal studies of effects of divorce on children in Great Britain and the United States. *Science*, 252, 1386–9.

Chi, M. T. H. 1978: Knowledge structures and memory development. In R. Siegler (ed.), *Children's Thinking: What Develops?* Hillsdale, NJ: Erlbaum.

Chomsky, C. S. 1969: *The Acquisition of Syntax in Children from 5 to 10*. Cambridge, MA: MIT Press.

Chomsky, N. 1959: Review of Skinner's Verbal Behaviour, *Language*, 35, 26–58.

Chomsky, N. 1965: *Aspects of a Theory of Syntax*. Cambridge, MA: MIT Press.

Chomsky, N. 1986: *Knowledge of Language*. New York: Praeger.

Chukovsky, K. 1963: *From Two to Five*. Berkeley and Los Angeles: University of California Press.

Cillessen, A. H. N., Van IJzendoorn, H. W., Van Lieshout, C. F. M. and Hartup, W. W. 1992: Heterogeneity among peer-rejected boys: subtypes and stabilities. *Child Development*, 63, 893–905.

Clark, A. H., Wyon, S. M. and Richards, M. P. M. 1969: Free-play in nursery school children. *Journal of Child Psychology and Psychiatry*, 10, 205–16.

Clarke, A. M. and Clarke, A. D. B. 1976: *Early Experience: Myth and Evidence*. London: Open Books.

Clarke, A. and Clarke, A. 1998: *Early Experience and the Life Path*. London: Jessica Kingsley.

Clarke, L. 1992: Children's family circumstances: recent trends in Great Britain. *European Journal of Population*, 8, 309–40.

Clarke-Stewart, A. 1973: Interactions between mothers and their young children: characteristics and consequences. *Monographs of the Society for Research in Child Development*, 38 (serial no. 153).

Clarke-Stewart, A. 1982: *Day Care*. Glasgow: Fontana.

Clarke-Stewart, A. 1989: Infant day care: maligned or malignant? *American Psychologist*, 44, 266–73.

Clarke-Stewart, K. A. 1991: A home is not a school. *Journal of Social Issues*, 47, 105–23.

Clay, M. 1985: *The Early Detection of Reading Difficulties* (3rd edn). Tadworth, Surrey: Heinemann.

Clifford, B. R., Gunter, B. and McAleer, J. 1995: *Program Evaluation, Comprehension and Impact*. Hillsdale, NJ: Erlbaum.

Cohen, L. J. and Campos, J. J. 1974: Father, mother and stranger as elicitors of attachment behaviour in infancy. *Developmental Psychology*, 10, 146–54.

Coie, J. D. and Dodge, K. A. 1983: Continuities and changes in children's social status: a five-year longitudinal study. *Merrill-Palmer Quarterly*, 29, 261–82.

Coie, J. D., Dodge, K. A. and Coppotelli, H. 1982: Dimensions and types of social status: a cross-age perspective. *Developmental Psychology*, 18, 557–70.

Coie, J. D. and Krehbiel, G. 1984: Effects of academic tutoring on the social status of low-achieving, socially rejected children. *Child Development*, 55, 1465–78.

Colby, A., Kohlberg, L., Gibbs, J. and Lieberman, M. 1983: A longitudinal study of moral judgement. *Monographs of the Society for Research in Child Development*, 48, nos 1–2.

Cole, M. 1992: *Developmental Psychology: An Advanced Textbook*. Hillsdale, NJ: Lawrence Erlbaum Associates.

Cole, M. 1998: Culture in development. In M. Woodhead, D. Faulkner and K. Littleton (eds), *Cultural Worlds of Early Childhood*. London: Routledge, pp 11–33.

Cole, M. and Griffin, P. 1987: Cultural amplifiers reconsidered. In D. Olson (ed.), *The Social Foumdations of Language and Thought*. New York: Norton.

Cole, M. and Scribner, S. 1978: Introduction. In *L. S. Vygotsky, Mind and Society: The Development of Higher Psychological Processes*. Cambridge, MA: Harvard University Press.

Cole, M., Gay, J. A. and Sharp, D. W. 1971: *The Cultural Context of Learning and Thinking*. New York: Basic Books.

Cole, P. M. 1986: Children's spontaneous control of facial expression. *Child Development*, 57, 1309–21.

Coleman, J. C. 1980: *The Nature of Adolescence*. London: Methuen.

Coleman, J. S., Campbell, E. Q., Hobson, C. J., McPortland, J., Wood, A. M., Weinfield, F. D. and York, R. L. 1966: *Equality of Educational Opportunity*. Washington, DC: Government Printing Office.

Collaer, M. L. and Hines, M. 1995: Human behavioral sex differences: a role for gonadal hormones during early development? *Psychological Bulletin*, 118, 55–107.

Commission for Racial Equality. 1988: *Learning in Terror: A Survey of Racial Harassment in Schools and Colleges*. London: CRE.

Conduct Problems Prevention Research Group 1999: Initial impact of the Fast Track prevention trial for conduct problems: I. The high-risk sample. *Journal of Consulting and Clinical Psychology*, 67, 631–47.

Connolly, J. A. and Doyle, A. B. 1984: Relation of social fantasy play to social competence in preschoolers. *Developmental Psychology*, 20, 797–806.

Cook, T. D. and Campbell, D. T. 1979: *Quasi-experimentation*. Chicago: Rand McNally.

Cooper, C. 1999: *Intelligence and Abilities*. London: Routledge.

Costabile, A., Genta, M. L., Zucchini, E., Smith, P. K. and Harker, R. 1992: Attitudes of parents towards war play in young children. *Early Education and Development*, 3, 356–69.

Costabile, A., Smith, P. K., Matheson, L., Aston, J., Hunter, T. and Boulton, M. 1991: Cross-national comparison of how children distinguish serious and playful fighting. *Developmental Psychology*, 27, 881–7.

Cote, J. E. and Levine, C. 1988: A critical examination of the ego identity status paradigm. *Developmental Review*, 8, 147–84.

Council of Europe 1993: *Vienna Declaration*, 9 October, Strasbourg, Council of Europe.

Cowan, F. M. and Johnson, A. M. 1993: HIV, AIDS and adolescents. *ACPP Review & Newsletter*, 15, 49–54.

Cowan, N. 1997a: The development of working memory. In N. Cowan (ed.), *The Development of Memory in Childhood*. Hove, East Sussex: Psychology Press.

Cowan, N. (ed.) 1997b: *The Development of Memory in Childhood*. Hove, East Sussex: Psychology Press.

Cowen, E. L., Pederson, A., Babigian, H., Izzo, L. D. and Trost, M. A. 1973: Long-term follow-up of early detected vulnerable children. *Journal of Consulting and Clinical Psychology*, 41, 438–46.

Cowie, H. 2000: Bystanding or standing by: gender issues in coping with bullying in English schools. *Aggressive Behavior*, 2, 85–97.

Cowie, H., Naylor, P., Talamelli, L., Chauhan, P. and Smith, P. K. 2002: Knowledge of and attitudes towards peer support: a two-year follow-up to the Prince's Trust. *Journal of Adolescence*, 25, 453–67.

Cowie, H. and Rudduck, J. 1988: *Cooperative Group Work: School and Classroom Studies*. London: British Petroleum Educational Services.

Cowie, H. and Sharp, S. 1996: *Peer Counselling in Schools: a Time to Listen*. London: David Fulton.

Cowie, H., Smith, P. K., Boulton, M. and Laver, R. 1994: *Cooperation in the Multi-ethnic Classroom*. London: David Fulton.

Cowie, H. and Wallace, P. 1999: *Peer Support in Action*. London: Sage.

Craig, W. and Pepler, D. 1995: Peer processes in bullying and victimisation: an observational study. *Exceptionality Education Canada*, 5, 81–95.

Crawford, K. 1998: Learning and teaching mathematics in the information era. In D. Faulkner, K. Littleton and M. Woodhead (eds), *Learning Relationships in the Classroom*. pp 293–309, London: Routledge/Open University.

Creighton, S. J. and Noyes, P. 1989: *Child Abuse Trends in England and Wales 1983–1987*. London: NSPCC.

Crick, N. R. and Dodge, K. 1994: A review and reformulation of social-information-processing mechanisms in children's social adjustment. *Psychological Bulletin*, 115, 74–101.

Crick, N. and Dodge, K. 1996: Social information processing mechanisms in reactive and proactive aggression. *Child Development* 67, 993–1002.

Crick, N. R. and Grotpeter, J. K. 1995: Relational aggression, gender, and social-psychological adjustment. *Child Development*, 66, 710–22.

Crittenden, P. M. 1988: Distorted patterns of relationship in maltreating families: the role of internal representation models. *Journal of Reproductive and Infant Psychology*, 6, 183–99.

Crittenden, P. M. 2000: A dynamic-maturational model of the function, development and organization of human relationships. In R. S. L. Mills and S. Duck (eds), *The Developmental Psychology of Personal Relationships*. Chichester: John Wiley.

Crook, C. 1994: *Computers and the Collaborative Experience of Learning*. London: Routledge.

Cullingford, C. 1984: *Children and Television*. Aldershot: Gower.

Cummings, E. M. and Davies, P. T. 2002: Effects of marital conflict on children: recent advances and emerging themes in process-oriented research. *Journal of Child Psychology & Psychiatry*, 43, 31–63.

Cummings, E. M., Iannotti, R. J. and Zahn-Waxler, C. 1985: Influence of conflict between adults on the emotions and aggression of young children. *Developmental Psychology*, 21, 495–507.

Cummings, E. M., Iannotti, R. J. and Zahn-Waxler, C. 1989: Aggression between peers in early childhood: individual continuity and developmental change. *Child Development*, 60, 887–95.

Cunningham, C. E., Cunningham, L. J., Martorelli, V., Tran, A., Young, J. and Zacharias, R. 1998: The effects of primary division, student-mediated conflict resolution programmes on playground aggression. *Journal of Child Psychology & Psychiatry*, 39, 653–68.

Curtiss, S. 1977: *Genie: A Psycholinguistic Study of a Modern-day 'Wild Child'*. New York: Academic Press.

Daly, M. and Wilson, M. I. 1982: Whom are newborn babies said to resemble? *Ethology and Sociobiology*, 3, 69–78.

Daly, M. and Wilson, M. 1996: Violence against stepchildren. *Current Directions in Psychological Science*, 5, 77–81.

Damon, W. 1977: *The Social World of the Child*. San Francisco: Jossey-Bass.

Damon, W. (ed.) 1998: *The Handbook of Child Psychology. Volume 2 (Cognition, perception and language)*, 5th edn. New York: Wiley.

Daniels, H. (ed.) 1996: *An Introduction to Vygotsky*. London: Routledge.

Danner, F. W. and Day, M. C. 1977: Eliciting formal operations. *Child Development*, 48, 1600–6.

Darling, N. and Steinberg, L. 1993: Parenting style as context: an integrative model. *Psychological Bulletin*, 113, 487–96.

Darwin, C. 1877: A biographical sketch of an infant. *Mind*, 2, 285–94.

D'Augelli, A. R. 1994: Identity development and sexual orientation: Towards a model of lesbian, gay, and bisexual development. In E. J. Trickett (ed.), *Human Diversity: Perspectives on People in Context*. pp. 312–33, San Francisco: Jossey-Bass.

D'Augelli, A. R., Hershberger, S. L. and Pilkington, N. W. 1998: Lesbian, gay, and bisexual youths and their families: disclosure of sexual orientation and its consequences. *American Journal of Orthopsychiatry*, 68, 361–73.

Davey, A. 1983: *Learning to be Prejudiced; Growing Up in Multi-ethnic Britain*. London: Edward Arnold.

Davie, R. 1973: Eleven years of childhood. *Statistical News*, 22, 14–18.

Davie, R., Butler, N. and Goldstein, H. 1972: *From Birth to Seven* (Second Report of the National Child Development Study). London: Longman and National Children's Bureau.

Davies, G. 1988: Use of video in child abuse trials. *The Psychologist*, 10, 20–2.

Davis, L. S. 1984: Alarm calling in Richardson's group squirrels (Spermophilus Richardsonii). *Zeitschrift für Tierpsychologie*, 66, 152–64.

Davis-Kean, P. E. and Sandler, H. M. 2001: A meta-analysis of measures of self-esteem for young children: a framework for future measures. *Child Development*, 72, 887–906.

DeCasper, A. J. and Fifer, W. P. 1980: Of human bonding: newborns prefer their mothers' voices. *Science*, 208, 1174–6.

Deater-Deckard, K. 2001: Recent research examining the role of peer relationships in the development of psychopathology. *Journal of Child Psychology and Psychiatry*, 42, 565–79.

DeCasper, A. J. and Prescott, P. A. 1984: Human newborns' perception of male voices: preference, discrimination, and reinforcing value. *Developmental Psychobiology*, 17, 481–91.

DeCasper, A. J. and Spence, M. J. 1986: Prenatal maternal speech influences newborn's perception of speech sounds. *Infant Behavior and Development*, 9, 133–50.

de Haan and Nelson 1998: Discrimination and categorization of facial expressions of emotion during infancy. In A. Slater (ed.), *Perceptual Development. Visual, Auditory and Speech Perception in Infancy*. Hove, East Sussex: Psychology Press.

Dekovic, M. and Janssens, J. M. A. M. 1992: Parents' child-rearing style and child's sociometric status. *Developmental Psychology*, 28, 925–32.

Dennis, W. 1973: *Children of the Crèche*. New York: Appleton-Century-Crofts.

Department for Education and Employment 2000: *Statistics of Education: Permanent Exclusions from Maintained Schools in England (10/00)*. London: DfES website.

Department for Education and Skills 2001: *Promoting Children's Mental Health within Early Years and School Settings*. London: DfES.

Department of the Environment. 1973: Children at Play. *Design Bulletin*, 27. London: HMSO.

Descartes, R. 1965: La Diotrique. In R. J. Herrnstein and E. G. Boring (eds), *A Sourcebook in the History of Psychology*. Cambridge, MA: Harvard University Press, (first published 1938).

deVilliers, J. G. and deVilliers, P. A. 2000: Linguistic determinism and the understanding of false belief. In P. Mitchell and K. Riggs (eds), *Children's Reasoning and the Mind*. Hove, East Sussex: Psychology Press.

De Wolff, M. S. and van IJzendoorn, M. H. 1997: Sensitivity and attachment: a meta-analysis on parental antecedents of infant attachment. *Child Development*, 68, 571–91.

Dias, M. G. and Harris, P. 1988: The effect of make-believe play on deductive reasoning. *British Journal of Developmental Psychology*, 6, 207–21.

Dias, M. G. and Harris, P. 1990: The influence of the imagination on reasoning by young children. *British Journal of Developmental Psychology*, 8, 305–18.

DiPietro, J. A., Hodgson, D. M. and Costigan, K. A. 1996: Fetal antecedents of infant temperament. *Child Development*, 67, 2568–83.

Dishion, T., Andrews, D. W. and Crosby, L. 1995: Antisocial boys and their friends in early adolescence: relationship characteristics, quality, and interactional process. *Child Development*, 88, 139–51.

Dixon, P. 1986: *The Silver Toilet Roll*. Winchester: Cheriton Books.

Dockett, S. 1998: Constructing understandings through play in the early years. *International Journal of Early Years Education*, 6, 105–16.

Dodge, K. A., Pettit, G. S., McClaskey, C. L. and Brown, M. M. 1986: Social competence in children. *Monographs of the Society for Research in Child Development*, 51, 2.

Dodge, K. A., Schlundt, D. C., Shocken, I. and Delugach, J. D. 1983: Social competence and children's sociometric status: the role of peer group entry strategies. *Merrill-Palmer Quarterly*, 29, 309–36.

Doise, W. 1990: The development of individual competencies through social interaction. In H. Foot, M. Morgan and R. Shute (eds), *Children Helping Children*. Chichester: John Wiley.

Doise, W. and Mugny, G. 1984: *The Social Development of the Intellect*. Oxford: Pergamon.

Donaldson, M. 1978: *Children's Minds*. London: Fontana.

Douglas, J. W. B. and Ross, J. M. 1964: Age of puberty related to educational ability, attainment and school leaving age. *Journal of Child Psychology and Psychiatry*, 5, 185–96.

Dozier, M., Stovall, K. C., Albus, K. E. and Bates, B. 2001: Attachment for infants in foster care: The role of caregiver state of mind. *Child Development*, 72, 1467–77.

Drew, L. M. and Smith, P. K. 1999: The impact of parental separation/divorce on grandparent–grandchild relationships. *International Journal of Aging and Human Development*, 48, 191–215.

Dromi, E. 1999: Early lexical development. In M. Barrett (ed.) *The Development of Language*, (pp 99–131). London: Psychology Press.

Drumm, P., Gardner, B. T. and Gardner, R. A. 1986: Vocal and gestural responses to announcements and events by cross-fostered chimpanzees. *American Journal of Psychology*, 99, 1–30.

Dunn, J. 1984: *Sisters and Brothers*. London: Fontana.

Dunn, J. 1988: *The Beginnings of Social Understanding*. Oxford: Basil Blackwell.

Dunn, J. 1992: Siblings and development. *Current Directions in Psychological Science*, 1, 6–9.

Dunn, J. 1995: Studying relationships and social understanding. In P. Barnes (ed.), *Personal, Social and Emotional Development of Children*. Oxford: Basil Blackwell, in association with the Open University.

Dunn, J. 1999: Mindreading and social relationships. In M. Bennett (ed.), *Developmental Psychology. Achievements and Prospects*. Philadelphia: Psychology Press.

Dunn, J., Brown, J. R. and Beardsall, L. 1991: Family talk about emotions, and children's later understanding of others' emotions. *Developmental Psychology*, 27, 448–55.

Dunn, J. and Hughes, C. 2001: 'I got some swords and you're dead!': Violent fantasy, antisocial behavior, friendship, and moral sensibility in young children. *Child Development*, 72, 491–505.

Dunn, J. and Kendrick, C. 1982: *Siblings: Love, Envy and Understanding*. Oxford: Basil Blackwell.

Dunphy, D. C. 1963: The social structure of urban adolescent peer groups. *Sociometry*, 26, 230–46.

Durkin, K. 1985: *Television, Sex Roles and Children*. Milton Keynes: Open University Press.

Durkin, K. 1995: *Developmental Social Psychology*. Oxford: Blackwell Publishers.

Dyson-Hudson, N. 1963: Karimojong age system. *Ethnology*, 3, 353–401.

Eals, M. and Silverman, I. 1994: The hunter-gatherer theory of spatial sex differences: Proximate factors mediating the female advantage in recall of object arrays. *Ethology and Sociobiology*, 15, 95–105.

Eames, D., Shorrocks, D. and Tomlinson, P. 1990: Naughty animals or naughty experimenters? Conservation accidents revisited with video-simulated commentary. *British Journal of Developmental Psychology*, 8, 25–37.

Edwards, C. P. and Lewis, M. 1979: Young children's concepts of social relations: social functions and social objects. In M. Lewis and L. A. Rosenblum (eds), *The Child and its Family*. New York: Plenum Press.

Eggleston, J., Dunn, D. and Anjali, M. 1986: *Education for Some: The Educational and Vocational Experiences of 15–18-year-old Members of Minority Ethnic Groups*. Stoke-on-Trent: Trentham Books.

Eibl-Eibesfeldt, I. 1971: *Love and Hate*. London: Methuen.

Eibl-Eibesfeldt, I. 1989: *Human Ethology*. New York: Aldine de Gruyter.

Eifermann, R. 1970: Level of children's play as expressed in group size. *British Journal of Educational Psychology*, 40, 161–70.

Eimas, P. D., Siqueland, E. R., Jusczyk, P. W. and Vigorito, J. 1971: Speech perception in infants. *Science*, 171, 303–6.

Eisenberg, N. 1983: Children's differentiations among potential recipients of aid. *Child Development*, 54, 594–602.

Eisenberg-Berg, N. and Hand, M. 1979: The relationship of preschoolers' reasoning about prosocial moral conflict to prosocial behaviour. *Child Development*, 50, 356–63.

Eisenberg, N. and Mussen, P. 1989: *The Roots of Pro-social Behaviour in Children*. Cambridge: Cambridge University Press.

Eisenberg, N., Wentzel, M. and Harris, J. D. 1998: The role of emotionality and regulation in empathy-related responding. *School Psychology Review*, 27, 506–21.

Elbers, E. and Streefland, L. 2000: 'Shall we be researchers again?' Identity and social interaction in a community of inquiry. In H. Cowie and G. van der Aalsvoort (eds), *Social Interaction in Learning and Instruction*, pp 35–51. Amsterdam: Pergamon, Elsevier Science.

Elkind, D. 1967: Egocentrism in adolescence. *Child Development*, 38, 1025–34.

Elliot, C. D., Murray, D. J. and Pearson, L. S. 1996: *British Ability Scales II*. Windsor: NFER-Nelson.

Ellis, B. J. and Garber, J. 2000: Psychosocial antecedents of variation in girls' pubertal timing: Maternal depression, stepfather presence, and marital and family stress. *Child Development*, 71, 485–501.

Emler, N., Reicher, S. and Ross, A. 1987: The social context of delinquent conduct. *Journal of Child Psychology & Psychiatry*, 28, 99–109.

Emmerich W., Goldman, K. S., Kirsh, B. and Sharabany, R. 1976: Development of gender constancy in disadvantaged children. Unpublished report, Educational Testing Service, Princeton, NJ.

Engel, S. 1994: *The Stories Children Tell*. New York: Freeman.

Engestrom, Y. 1996: Non scolae sed vitae discimus. In H. Daniels (ed.), *An Introduction to Vygotsky*. London: Routledge.

Ericsson, K. A. and Charness, N. 1994: Expert performance: its structure and acquisition. *American Psychologist*, 49, 725–47.

Erikson, E. 1968: *Identity: Youth and Crisis*. London: Faber.

Eron, L. D. 1987: The development of aggressive behavior from the perspective of a developing behaviorism. *American Psychologist*, 42, 435–42.

Espin, O. M., Stewart, A. J. and Gomez, C. A. 1990: Letters from V: adolescent personality development in sociohistorical context. *Journal of Personality*, 58, 347–64.

Fagan, R. M. 1974: Selective and evolutionary aspects of animal play. *American Naturalist*, 108, 850–8.

Fagot, B. I. 1978: The influence of sex of child on parental reactions to toddler children. *Child Development*, 49, 459–65.

Fagot, B. I. 1985: Beyond the reinforcement principle: another step toward understanding sex role development. *Developmental Psychology*, 21, 1097–104.

Falbo, T. 1991: The impact of grandparents on children's outcomes in China. *Marriage and Family Review*, 16, 369–76.

Falbo, T. and Polit, D. F. 1986: Quantitative review of the only child literature: research evidence and theory development. *Psychological Bulletin*, 100, 176–89.

Fantz, R. L. 1961: The origin of form perception. *Scientific American*, 204 (May), 66–72.

Fantz, R. L. and Fagan, J. F. 1975: Visual attention to size and number of pattern details by term and pre-term infants during the first six months. *Child Development*, 46, 3–18.

Fantz, R. L. and Miranda, S. B. 1975: Newborn infant attention to form of contour. *Child Development*, 46, 224–8.

Farrell, C. 1978: *My Mother Said*. London: Routledge & Kegan Paul.

Farrington, D. P. 1992: Explaining the beginning, progress and ending of anti-social behaviour problems: stability and factors accounting for change. *Journal of Child Psychology & Psychiatry*, 31, 891–909.

Farrington, D. P. 1995: The development of offending and anti-social behaviour from childhood: Key findings from the Cambridge Study in Delinquent Development. *Journal of Child Psychology & Psychiatry*, 36, 929–64.

Farrington, D. P. and Welsh, B. C. 1999: Delinquency prevention using family-based interventions. *Children and Society*, 13, 287–303.

Fawcett, A. J. and Nicolson, R. I. 1996: Impaired performance of children with dyslexia on a range of cerebellar tasks. *Annals of Dyslexia*, 46, 259–83.

Fein, G. G. 1975: A transformational analysis of pretending. *Developmental Psychology*, 77, 291–6.

Feinberg, M. E. and Hetherington, E. M. 2000: Sibling differentiation in adolescence: implications for behavioral genetic theory. *Child Development*, 71, 1512–24.

Feinberg, M. E., Neiderhiser, J. M., Simmens, S., Reiss, D. and Hetherington, E. M. 2000: Sibling comparison of differential parental treatment in adolescence: gender, self-esteem, and emotionality as mediators of the parenting-adjustment association. *Child Development*, 17, 1611–28.

Feinman, S. 1982: Social referencing in infancy. *Merrill-Palmer Quarterly*, 28, 445–70.

Feiring, C., Lewis, M. and Starr, M. D. 1984: Indirect effects and infants' reaction to strangers. *Developmental Psychology*, 20, 485–91.

Fernald, A. and Mazzie, C. 1991: Prosody and focus in speech to infants and adults. *Developmental Psychology*, 27, 209–21.

Ferreiro, E. 1985: Literacy development: a psychogenic perspective. In D. Olson, N. Torrance and A. Hildyard (eds), *Literacy, Language and Learning*. Cambridge: Cambridge University Press.

Ferri, E. 1984: *Stepchildren: a National Study*. London: NFER-Nelson.

Field, T. 1984: Separation stress of young children transferring to new school. *Developmental Psychology*, 20, 786–92.

Field, T. M., Woodson, R. W., Greenberg, R. and Cohen, C. 1982: Discrimination and imitation of facial expression by neonates. *Science*, 218, 179–81.

Fifer, W. P. and Moon, C. 1989: Psychobiology of newborn auditory preferences. *Seminars in Perinatology*, 13, 430–3.

Finkelstein, N. W. and Haskins, R. 1983: Kindergarten children prefer same-color peers. *Child Development*, 54, 502–8.

Fishbein, H. D. 1976: *Education, Development, and Children's Learning*. Pacific Palisades, CA: Goodyear Publishing Company.

Fisher, R. P. and Geiselman, R. E. 1992: Memory-enhancing techniques for investigative interviewing. *The Cognitive Interview*. Springfield, IL: Charles Thomas.

Fisher, R. P., Geiselman, R. E., Raymond, D. S., Jurkevich, L. M. and Warhaftig, M. L. 1987: Enhancing enhanced eyewitness memory: refining the cognitive interview. *Journal of Police Science and Administration*, 15, 291–7.

Fivush, R. 1997: Event memory in early childhood. In N. Cowan (ed.), *The Development of Memory in Childhood*. Hove, East Sussex: Psychology Press.

Flavell, J. H. 1988: The development of children's knowledge about the mind: from cognitive correlations to mental representation. In J. W. Astington, P. L. Harris and D. R. Olson (eds), *Developing Theories of Mind*. Cambridge: Cambridge University Press.

Flavell, J. H., Beach, D. R. and Chinsky, J. M. 1966: Spontaneous verbal rehearsal in a memory task as a function of age. *Child Development*, 37, 283–99.

Flavell, J. H., Friedrichs, A. G. and Hoyt, J. D. 1970: Developmental changes in memorization processes. *Cognitive Psychology*, 1, 324–40.

Flavell, J. H., Green, F. L. and Flavell, E. R. 1986: Development of knowledge about the appearance–reality distinction. *Monographs of the Society for Research in Child Development*, 51, no. 212.

Flavell, J. H., Miller, P. H. and Miller, S. A. 2002: *Cognitive Development*, 4th edn. Englewood Cliffs, New Jersey: Prentice-Hall.

Fogel, A. 1993: Two principles of communication: co-regulation and framing. In J. Nadel and L. Camaioni (eds), *New Perspectives in Early Communicative Development*. (pp 9–22). London: Routledge.

Foley, M. A. and Johnson, M. K. 1985: Confusions between memories for performed and imagined actions: a developmental comparison. *Child Development*, 56, 1145–55.

Foley, M. A., Wilder, A., McCall, R. and Van Vorst, R. 1993: The consequences for recall of children's ability to generate interactive imagery in the absence of external supports. *Journal of Experimental Psychology*, 56, 173–200.

Fonagy, P., Steele, M., Steele, H., Higgitt, A. and Target, M. 1994: The theory and practice of resilience. *Journal of Child Psychology and Psychiatry*, 35, no. 2, 231–57.

Fonzi, A., Schneider, B. H., Tani, F. and Tomada, G. 1997: Predicting children's friendship status from their dyadic interaction in structured situations of potential conflict. *Child Development* 68, 496–506.

Foot, H., Morgan, M. and Shute, R. (eds) 1990: *Children Helping Children*. Chichester: John Wiley.

Ford, M. E. 1979: The construct validity of egocentrism. *Psychological Bulletin*, 86, 1169–88.

Foster, S. L., Martinez, C. R., Jr. and Kulberg, A. M. 1996: Race, ethnicity, and children's peer relations. *Advances in Clinical Child Psychology*, 18, 133–71.

Fox, N. 1977: Attachment of Kibbutz infants to mother and metapelet. *Child Development*, 48, 1228–39.

Fox, N., Kimmerly, N. L. and Schafer, W. D. 1991: Attachment to mother/attachment to father: a meta-analysis. *Child Development*, 62, 210–25.

France, A. 2000: *Youth Researching Youth: The Triumph and Success Peer Research Project*. Leicester: National Youth Agency.

Frankel, M. T. and Rollins, H. A. 1982: Age-related differences in clustering: a new approach. *Journal of Experimental Psychology*, 34, 113–22.

Freeman, D. 1996: *Franz Boas and the Flower of Heaven: Coming of Age in Samoa and the Fateful Hoaxing of Margaret Mead*. Harmondsworth: Penguin.

Freeman, D. 2000: Was Margaret Mead misled or did she mislead on Samoa? (plus commentaries, and reply). *Current Anthropology*, 41, 609–22.

Freeman, J. 1980: Giftedness in a social context. In R. Povey (ed.), *Educating the Gifted Child*. London: Harper and Row.

Freeman, J. 2000: Gifted children: the evidence. *The Psychology of Education Review*, 24, 35–40.

Freeman, J. 2001: *Gifted Children Grown Up*. London: David Fulton.

Freeman, N. H., Lewis, C. and Doherty, M. J. 1991: Preschoolers grasp of a desire for knowledge in false-belief prediction: practical intelligence and verbal report. *British Journal of Developmental Psychology*, 9, 139–57.

Freedman, J. L. 1984: Effect of television violence on aggressiveness. *Psychological Bulletin*, 96, 227–46.

Friedrich, L. K. and Stein, A. H. 1973: Aggressive and prosocial television programs and the natural behavior of preschool children. *Monographs of the Society for Research in Child Development*, 38, no. 4.

Frisch, R. E. 1988: Fatness and fertility. *Scientific American*, March, 71–8.

Frith, U. 1989: *Autism: Explaining the Enigma*. Oxford: Basil Blackwell.

Froebel, F. 1906: *The Education of Man*. New York: Appleton.

Fry, D. P. and Fry, C. P. 1997: Culture and conflict resolution models: exploring alternatives to violence. In D. P. Fry and K. Björkvist (eds) *Cultural Variations in Conflict Resolution*, pp 9–24. Mahwah, NJ: Lawrence Erlbaum.

Fundudis, T. 1989: Children's memory and the assessment of possible child sex abuse. *Journal of Child Psychology and Psychiatry*, 30, 337–46.

Furman, W., Rahe, D. F. and Hartup, W. W. 1979: Rehabilitation of socially withdrawn preschool children through mixed-age and same-age socialization. *Child Development*, 50, 915–22.

Furrow, D., Nelson, K. and Benedict, H. 1979: Mothers' speech to children and syntactic development: some simple relationships. *Journal of Child Language*, 6, 423–42.

Galambos, N. L. and Almeida, D. M. 1992: Does parent–adolescent conflict decrease in early adolescence? *Journal of Marriage and the Family*, 54, 737–47.

Galen, B. R. and Underwood, M. K. 1997: A developmental investigation of social aggression among children. *Developmental Psychology*, 33, 589–600.

Gallup, G. G. Jr. 1982: Self-awareness and the emergence of mind in primates. *American Journal of Primatology*, 2, 237–48.

Ganchrow, J. R., Steiner, J. E., and Daher, M. 1983: Neonatal facial expressions in response to different qualities and intensities of gustatory stimuli. *Infant Behavior and Development*, 6, 473–84.

Garcia, J., Ervin, F. R. and Koelling, R. A. 1966: Learning with prolonged delay of reinforcement. *Psychonomic Science*, 5, 121–2.

Gardner, H. 1983: *Frames of Mind: the Theory of Multiple Intelligence*. New York: Basic Books.

Gardner, R. A. and Gardner, B. T. 1969: Teaching sign language to a chimpanzee. *Science*, 165, 664–72.

Garmezy, N. and Masten, A. 1991: The protective role of competence indicators in children at risk. In E. M. Cummings, A. L. Greene and K. H. Karraker (eds), *Life Span Developmental Psychology: Perspectives of Stress and Coping*. Hillsdale, NJ: Lawrence Erlbaum Associates.

Garvey, C. 1977: *Play*. London: Fontana/Open Books.

Gauthier, I. and Nelson, C. 2001: The development of face expertise. *Current Opinion in Neurobiology*, 11, 219–24.

Ge, X., Conger, R. D. and Elder, G. H. Jr. 1996: Coming of age too early: pubertal influences on girls' vulnerability to psychological distress. *Child Development*, 67, 3386–400.

Geary, D. C. and Bjorklund, D. F. 2000: Evolutionary developmental psychology. *Child Development*, 71, 57–65.

Gelfand, D. M., Hartmann, D. P., Cromer, C. C., Smith, C. L. and Page, B. C. 1975: The effects of instructional prompts and praise on children's donation rates. *Child Development*, 46, 980–3.

Gibson, E. J. and Walk, R. D. 1960: The 'visual cliff'. *Scientific American*, 202 (April), 64–71.

Gil, D. 1970: *Violence against Children*. Cambridge, MA: Harvard University Press.

Gillborn, D. and Gipps, C. 1996: *Recent Research on the Achievement of Ethnic Minority Pupils*. London: HMSO.

Gilligan, C. 1982: *In a Different Voice: Psychological Theory and Women's Development*. Cambridge, MA: Harvard University Press.

Ginsburg, H. and Opper, S. 1979: *Piaget's Theory of Intellectual Development: An Introduction*. Englewood Cliffs, NJ: Prentice-Hall.

Gipps, C. and Murphy, P. 1994: *A Fair Test? Assessment, Achievement and Equity*. Buckingham: Open University Press.

Gipps, C. and Stobart, G. 1993: *Assessment. A Teacher's Guide to the Issues*, 2nd edn. London: Hodder & Stoughton.

Glaser, D. and Collins, C. 1989: The response of young, non-sexually abused children to anatomically correct dolls. *Journal of Child Psychology and Psychiatry*, 30, 547–60.

Gleitman, L. R. 1990: The structural sources of verb meaning, *Language Acquisition*, 1, 3–55.

Gleitman, L. R. and Wanner, E. 1982: Language acquisition: The state of the state of the art. In E. Wanner and L. R. Gleitman (eds), *Language Acquisition: The State of the Art*. Cambridge: Cambridge University Press.

Gleitman, L. R., Newport, E. and Gleitman, H. 1984: The current status of the motherese hypothesis. *Journal of Child Language*, 11, 43–79.

Golbeck, S. L. and Harlan, S. 1997: Family child care. In S. K. Thurman, J. R. Cornwell and S. R. Gottwald (eds), *Contexts of Early Intervention: Systems and Settings*, (pp. 165–89). Baltimore, MD: Paul. H. Brookes Pub. Co.

Goldberg, S. 1983: Parent–infant bonding: another look. *Child Development*, 54, 1355–82.

Goldfarb, W. 1947: Variations in adolescent adjustment of institutionally reared children. *American Journal of Orthopsychiatry*, 17, 449–57.

Goldman, R. and Goldman, J. 1982: *Children's Sexual Thinking*. London: Routledge & Kegan Paul.

Goldstein, J. H. 1994: Sex differences in toy play and use of video games. In J. H. Goldstein (ed.), *Toys, Play and Child Development*. Cambridge: Cambridge University Press.

Goldstein, J. H. 1995: Aggressive toy play. In A. D. Pellegrini (ed.), *The Future of Play Theory*. Albany, NY: SUNY Press.

Goleman, E. 1996: *Emotional Intelligence*. London: Bloomsbury.

Golombok, S. and Fivush, R. 1994: *Gender Development*. Cambridge: Cambridge University Press.

Golombok, S. and Hines, M. 2002: Sex differences in social behaviour. In P. K. Smith and C. H. Hart (eds), *Blackwell Handbook of Childhood Social Development*. Oxford: Blackwell.

Golombok, S., Tasker, F. and Murray, C. 1997: Children raised in fatherless families from infancy: family relationships and the socioemotional development of children of lesbian and single heterosexual mothers. *Journal of Child Psychology & Psychiatry*, 38, 783–91.

Goncu, A., Patt, M. B. and Kouba, E. 2002: Understanding young children's pretend play in context. In P. K. Smith and C. H. Hart (eds), *Blackwell Handbook of Childhood Social Development*. Oxford: Blackwell.

Goodman, G. S. and Bottoms, B. L. (eds) 1993: *Child Victims, Child Witnesses. Understanding and Improving Testimony*. New York: Guilford Press.

Goodman, G. S. and Reed, R. S. 1986: Age differences in eyewitness testimony. *Law and Human Behavior*, 10, 317–32.

Goodman, G. S., Hepps, D. and Reed, R. S. 1986: The child victim's testimony. In A. Haralambie (ed.), *New Issues for Child Advocates*. Phoenix, AZ: Arizona Association for Children.

Gordon, I. and Slater, A. 1998: Nativism and empiricism: the history of two ideas. In A. Slater (ed.), *Perceptual Development. Visual, Auditory and Speech Perception in Infancy*. Hove, East Sussex: Psychology Press.

Goren, C., Sarty, M. and Wu, P. 1975: Visual following and pattern discrimination of face-like stimuli by new born infants. *Pediatrics*, 56, 544–9.

Gottman, J. M. and Katz, L. F. 1989: Effects of marital discord on young children's peer interaction and health. *Developmental Psychology*, 25, 373–81.

Gould, S. J. 1996: *The Mismeasure of Man*, 2nd edn. New York: Norton.

Greenberg, M. T., Kusche, C. A., Cooke, E. T. and Quamma, J. P. 1995: Promoting emotional competence in school aged children: the effects of the PATHS curriculum. *Development and Psychopathology*, 7, 7–16.

Greenfield, P. M. 1984: *Mind and Media: the Effects of Television, Video Games and Computers*. Aylesbury: Fontana.

Greenfield, P. M. and Lave, J. 1982: Cognitive aspects of informal education. In D. A. Wagner and H. W. Stevenson (eds), *Cultural Perspectives on Child Development*. San Francisco: W. H. Freeman.

Gregory, R. J. 1992: *Psychological Testing. History, Principles and Applications*. Boston: Allyn and Bacon.

Greif, E. B. and Ulman, K. J. 1982: The psychological impact of menarche on early adolescent females: a review of the literature. *Child Development*, 53, 1413–30.

Grigorenko, E. L., Geissler, P. W., Prince, R., Okatcha, F., Nokes, C., Kenny, D. A., Bundy, D. A. and Sternberg, R. J. 2001: The organisation of Luo conceptions of intelligence: a study of implicit theories in a Kenyan village. *International Journal of Behavioral Development*, 25, 367–78.

Groos, K. 1898: *The Play of Animals*. New York: Appleton.

Groos, K. 1901: *The Play of Man*. London: William Heinemann.

Gross, M. U. M. 1993: *Exceptionally Gifted Children*. London: Routledge.

Grossen M. 2000: Insititutional framings in thinking, learning and teaching. In H. Cowie and G. van der Aalsvoort (eds), *Social Interaction in Learning and Instruction*. London: Elsevier.

Grossman, K. E., Grossman, K., Huber, F. and Wartner, U. 1981: German children's behavior towards their mothers at 12 months and their fathers at 18 months in Ainsworth's 'strange situation'. *International Journal of Behavioral Development*, 4, 157–81.

Gruber, H. and Vonèche, J. J. 1977: *The Essential Piaget*. London: Routledge & Kegan Paul.

Grusec, J. E. 1982: The socialization of altruism. In N. Eisenberg (ed.), *The Development of Prosocial Behavior*. New York: Academic Press.

Grusec, J. E. and Goodnow, J. J. 1994: Impact of parental discipline methods on the child's internalization of values: A reconceptualization of current points of view. *Developmental Psychology*, 30, 4–19.

Grusec, J. E., Davidov, M. and Lundell, L. 2002: Prosocial and helping behaviour. In P. K. Smith and C. Hart (eds), *Handbook of Childhood Social Development*. Malden, MA: Blackwell.

Grusec, J. E., Saas-Kortsaak, P. and Simutis, Z. M. 1978: The role of example and moral exhortation in the training of altruism. *Child Development*, 49, 920–3.

Gunter, B. and McAlean, J. 1997: *Children and Television*, 2nd edn. London: Routledge.

Gustafsson, J. E. 1981: A unifying model for the structure of intellectual abilities. *Intelligence*, 8, 179–203.

Hadow Report 1926: *The Education of the Adolescent*. London: HMSO.

Hadow Report 1931: *Primary Education*. London: HMSO.

Haight, W. L. and Miller, P. J. 1993: *Pretending at Home: Early Development in a Sociocultural Context*. Albany: SUNY Press.

Hainline, L. 1998: The development of basic visual abilities. In A. Slater (ed.), *Perceptual Development. Visual, Auditory and Speech Perception in Infancy*. Hove, East Sussex: Psychology Press.

Hall, G. S. 1908: *Adolescence*. New York: Appleton.

Halsey, A. H. 1972: *Educational Priority, Vol. I: E. P. A. Problems and Policies*. London: HMSO.

Hamilton, W. D. 1964: The genetical evolution of social behaviour. *Journal of Theoretical Biology*, 7, 1–52.

Hanawalt, B. A. 1992: Historical descriptions and prescriptions for adolescence. *Journal of Family History*, 17, 341–51.

Happé, F. 1994: *Autism. An Introduction to Psychological Theory*. London: University College London Press.

Harkness, S. 2002: Culture and social development: explanations and evidence. In P. K. Smith and C. H. Hart (eds), *Blackwell Handbook of Childhood Social Development*. Oxford: Blackwell.

Harkness, S. and Super, C. 1992: Parental ethnotheories in action. In I. E. Sigel (ed.), *Parental Belief Systems: The Psychological Consequences for Children*. Hillsdale, NJ: Erlbaum.

Harlow, H. F. 1958: The nature of love. *American Psychologist*, 13, 673–85.

Harlow, H. F. and Harlow, M. 1969: Effects of various mother–infant relationships on rhesus monkey behaviours. In B. M. Foss (ed.), *Determinants of Infant Behaviour*, vol. 4. London: Methuen.

Harris, H., Barrett, M. D., Jones, D. and Brookes, S. 1988: Linguistic input and early word meaning. *Journal of Child Language*, 15, 77–94.

Harris, J. 2001: *The effects of computer games on young children – a review of the research*. RDS Occasional Paper No 72. London: Home Office. [www.homeoffice.gov.uk/rds/index.html]

Harris, J. R. 1995: Where is the child's environment? A group socialization theory of development. *Psychological Review*, 102, 458–89.

Harris, J. R. 1998: *The Nurture Assumption*. London: Bloomsbury.

Harris, J. R. 2000: Socialization, personality, and the child's environments: comment on Vandell, *Developmental Psychology*, 36, 711–23.

Harris, M. 1968: *The Rise of Anthropological Theory*. London: Routledge and Kegan Paul.

Harris, P. L. 1989: *Children and Emotion*. Oxford: Basil Blackwell.

Harris, P. L. 1991: The work of the imagination. In A. Whiten (ed.), *Natural Theories of Mind: Evolution, Development and Stimulation of Everyday Mindreading*. Oxford: Blackwell.

Harris, P. L. 1992: From simulation to folk psychology: the case for development. *Mind and Language*, 7, 120–44.

Harris, P. L. 2000: *The Work of the Imagination*. Oxford: Blackwell.

Harris, P. L. and Leevers, H. J. 2000: Reasoning from false premises. In P. Mitchell and K. Riggs (eds), *Children's Reasoning and the Mind*. Hove, East Sussex: Psychology Press.

Harris, P. L., German, T. and Mills, M. 1996: Children's use of counterfactual reasoning in causal reasoning. *Cognition*, 61, 233–59.

Harter, S. 1985: *Manual for the Self-perception Profile for Children*. Denver, CO: University of Denver.

Hartup, W. W. 1996: The company they keep: friendships and their developmental significance. *Child Development*, 67, 1–13.

Hartup, W. W. and Abecassis, M. 2002: Friends and enemies. In P. K. Smith and C. H. Hart (eds), *Blackwell Handbook of Childhood Social Development*. Oxford: Blackwell.

Haviland, J. M. and Lelwica, M. 1987: The induced affect response: 10-week-old infants' responses to three emotional expressions. *Developmental Psychology*, 23, 97–104.

Hawker, D. S. J. and Boulton, M. J. 2000: Twenty years' research on peer victimization and psychosocial maladjustment: A meta-analytic review of cross-sectional studies. *Journal of Child Psychiatry and Psychiatry*, 41, 441–55.

Hayden, C. and Dunne, S. 2001: *Outside, Looking in: Children and Families' Experience of School Exclusion*. London: The Children's Society.

Hayes, C. 1952: *The Ape in our House*. London: Gollancz.

Hearnshaw, L. 1979: *Cyril Burt: Psychologist*. London: Hodder & Stoughton.

Hedegaard, M. 1996: The zone of proximal development as basis for instruction. In H. Daniels (ed.), *An Introduction to Vygotsky*. London: Routledge.

Held, R. 1965: Plasticity in sensory-motor systems. *Scientific American*, 213 (Nov.), 84–94.

Helwig, C. C. and Turiel, E. 2002: Children's social and moral reasoning. In P. K. Smith and C. Hart (eds), *Handbook of Childhood Social Development*. Malden, MA: Blackwell.

Hermann-Giddens, M., Slora, E. and Wasserman, R. 1997: Secondary sexual characteristics and menses in young girls. *Paediatrics*, 99, 505–12.

Hermelin, B., Pring, L., Buhler, M., Wolff, S. and Heaton, P. 1999: A visually impaired savant artist: interacting perceptual and memory representations. *Journal of Child Psychology and Psychiatry*, 40, 1129–39.

Hertz-Lazarowitz, R. and Miller, N. 1992: *Interaction in Cooperative Groups*. Cambridge: Cambridge University Press.

Hertz-Lazarowitz, R., Feitelson, D., Zahavi, S. and Hartup, W. W. 1981: Social interaction and social organisation of Israeli five-to-seven-year olds. *International Journal of Behavioral Development*, 4, 143–55.

Hess, R. D. and Shipman, V. C. 1965: Early experience and the socialization of cognitive modes in children. *Child Development*, 36, 869–86.

Hetherington, E. M. 1989: Coping with family transitions: winners, losers, and survivors. *Child Development*, 60, 1–14.

Hetherington, E. M. and Stanley-Hagan, M. 1999: The adjustment of children with divorced parents: A risk and resiliency perspective. *Journal of Child Psychology & Psychiatry*, 40, 129–40.

Hetherington, E. M., Cox, M. and Cox, R. 1982: Effects of divorce on parents and children. In M. Lamb (ed.), *Nontraditional Families*. Hillsdale, NJ: Erlbaum.

Hewlett, B. S. 1987: Intimate fathers: patterns of paternal holding among Aka pygmies. In M. Lamb (ed.), *The Father's Role: Cross-cultural Perspectives*. Hillsdale, NJ: Lawrence Erlbaum.

Himmelweit, H. T., Oppenheim, A. N. and Vince, P. 1958: *Television and the Child: An Empirical Study of the Effect of Television on the Young*. Oxford: Oxford University Press.

Hinde, R. A. and Stevenson-Hinde, J. (eds) 1973: *Constraints on Learning: Limitations and Predispositions*. London and New York: Academic Press.

Hirsh-Pasek, K., Gleitman, H., Gleitman, L. R., Golinkoff, R. M. and Naigles, L. G. 1988: Syntactic bootstrapping: evidence from comprehension. Paper presented at Boston Language Conference, Boston.

HMSO 1967: *Children and their Primary Schools*. London: HMSO.

HMSO 1992: *Memorandum of Good Practice. On Video Recorded Interviews with Child Witnesses for Criminal Proceedings*. London: HMSO.

HMSO 1996: *Social Focus on Ethnic Minorities*. London: HMSO.

Hodes, M. 2000: Psychologically distressed refugee children in the UK. *Child Psychology and Psychiatry Review*, 5, 57–68.

Hodges, E. Boivin, M., Vitaro, F. and Bukowski, W. M. 1999: The power of friendship: Protection against an escalating cycle of peer victimisation. *Developmental Psychology*, 35, 94–101.

Hodges, J. and Tizard, B. 1989: IQ and behavioural adjustment of ex-institutional adolescents; and, Social and family relationships of ex-institutional adolescents. *Journal of Child Psychology and Psychiatry*, 30, 53–76; 77–98.

Hoffman, M. L. 1970: Moral development. In P. H. Mussen (ed.), *Carmichael's Manual of Child Psychology*, vol. 2. New York: Wiley.

Hogrefe, G., Wimmer, H. and Perner, J. 1986: Ignorance versus false belief: a developmental lag in attribution of epistemic states. *Child Development*, 57, 567–82.

Holden, C. 2000: Ready for citizenship? A case study of approaches to social and moral education in two contrasting primary schools in the UK. *The School Field*, XI, 1/2, 117–30.

Home Office and Department of Health 1992: *Memorandum of Good Practice on Video Recorded Interviews with Child Witnesses for Criminal Proceedings*. London: Her Majesty's Stationery Office.

Hooff, J. A. R. A. M. van 1972: A comparative approach to the phylogeny of laughter and smiling. In R. A. Hinde (ed.), *Non-Verbal Communication*. Cambridge: Cambridge University Press.

Hopkins, J. R. 1983: *Adolescence: The Transitional Years*. New York and London: Academic Press.

Howe, M. J. A. 1989: *Fragments of Genius. The Strange Feats of Idiot Savants*. London: Routledge.

Howe, M. J. A. 1999: *The Psychology of High Abilities*. London: Macmillan.

Howe, M. J. A., Davidson, J. W. and Sloboda, J. A. 1999: Innate talents: reality or myth? In S. J. Ceci and W. M. Williams (eds), *The Nature-Nurture Debate. The Essential Readings*. Oxford: Blackwell.

Howe, M. J. A. and Smith, J. 1988: Calendar calculating in 'idiots savants': how do they do it? *British Journal of Developmental Psychology*, 79, 371–86.

Howes, C. and Matheson, C. C. 1992: Sequences in the development of competent play with peers: social and pretend play. *Developmental Psychology*, 28, 961–74.

Howes, C., Droege, K. and Matheson, C. C. 1994: Play and communicative processes within long- and short-term friendship dyads. *Journal of Social and Personal Relationships*, 11, 401–10.

Huggins, M., Mesquita, M. P. and de Castro, M. 1996: Exclusion, civic invisibility and impunity as explanations for youth murders in Brazil. *Childhood*, 3, 1, 77–98.

Hughes, C. H. and Russell, J. 1993: Autistic children's difficulty with mental disengagement from an object: its implications for theories of autism. *Developmental Psychology*, 29, 498–510.

Hughes, M. and Grieve, R. 1980: On asking children bizarre questions. *First Language*, 1, 149–60.

Hughes, P., Turton, P., Hopper, E., McGauley, G. A. and Fonagy, P. 2001: Disorganised attachment behaviour among infants born subsequent to stillbirth. *Journal of Child Psychology and Psychiatry*, 42, 791–801.

Humphrey, N. 1984: *Consciousness Regained*. Oxford: Oxford University Press.

Hunter, F. T. 1984: Socializing procedures in parent–child and friendship relations during adolescence. *Developmental Psychology*, 20, 1092–9.

Hutt, C. 1966: Exploration and play in children. *Symposia of the Zoological Society of London*, 18, 61–81.

Hutt, C. 1970: Curiosity in young children. *Science Journal*, 6, 68–72.

Hutt, C. and Bhavnani, R. 1972: Predictions from play. *Nature*, 237, 171–2.

Hwang, H. J. and St James-Roberts, I. 1998: Emotional and behavioural problems in primary school children from nuclear and extended families in Korea. *Journal of Child Psychology and Psychiatry*, 39, 973–9.

Hwang, P. 1987: The changing role of Swedish fathers. In M. Lamb (ed.), *The Father's Role: Cross-Cultural Perspectives*. Hillsdale, NJ: Lawrence Erlbaum.

Hwang, P., Broberg, A. and Lamb, B. 1990: Swedish childcare research. In E. Melhuish and P. Moss (eds), *Daycare for Young Children: International Perspectives*. London: Routledge.

Hymel, S., Vaillancourt, T., McDougall, P. and Renshaw, P. D. 2002: Peer acceptance and rejection in childhood. In P. K. Smith and C. H. Hart (eds), *Blackwell Handbook of Childhood Social Development*. Oxford: Blackwell.

Ingram, D. 1999: Phonological acquisition. In M. Barrett (ed.) 1999: *The Development of Language*, pp 73–97. London: Psychology Press.

Inhelder, B. and Piaget, J. 1958: *The Growth of Logical Thinking from Childhood to Adolescence*. London: Routledge & Kegan Paul.

Isaacs, S. 1929: *The Nursery Years*. London: Routledge & Kegan Paul.

Izard, C. E., Hembree, E. A., and Huebner, R. R. 1987: Infants' emotion expressions to acute pain. *Developmental Psychology*, 23, 105–13.

Jackson, B. and Jackson, S. 1979: *Childminder: A Study in Action Research*. London: Routledge and Kegan Paul.

Jacobsen, T., Hibbs, E. and Ziegenhain, U. 2000: Maternal expressed emotion related to attachment disorganization in early childhood: a preliminary report. *Journal of Child Psychology and Psychiatry*, 41, 899–906.

Jacobson, J. L. 1980: Cognitive determinants of wariness toward unfamiliar peers. *Developmental Psychology*, 16, 347–54.

Jaffee, S. R., Caspi, A., Moffitt, T. E., Taylor, A. and Dickson, N. 2001: Predicting early fatherhood and whether young fathers live with their children: prospective findings and policy reconsiderations. *Journal of Child Psychology and Psychiatry*, 42, 803–15.

Jahoda, G. 1983: European 'lag' in the development of an economic concept: a study in Zimbabwe. *British Journal of Developmental Psychology*, 1, 113–20.

James, A. and Prout, A. 1990: *Constructing and Reconstructing Childhood*. Basingstoke: Falmer.

James, J., Charlton, T., Leo, E. and Indoe, D. 1991: A peer to listen. *Support for Learning*, 6, 165–9.

James, W. 1890: *Principles of Psychology*. New York: Holt.

Janelli, L. M. 1988: Depictions of grandparents in children's literature. *Educational Gerontology*, 14, 193–202.

Jarrold, C., Carruthers, P., Smith, P. K. and Boucher, J. 1994: Pretend play: is it metarepresentational? *Mind and Language*, 9, 445–68.

Jastrow, J. 1900: *Fact and fable in psychology*. Boston: Houghton Mifflin.

Jenkins, J. and Astington, J. 1996: Cognitive factors and family structure associated with theory of mind development in young children. *Developmental Psychology*, 32, 70–8.

Jensen, A. R. 1969: How much can we boost IQ and scholastic achievement? *Harvard Educational Review*, 39, 449–83.

Jersild, A. T. and Markey, F. V. 1935: Conflicts between preschool children. *Child Development Monographs*, 21. Teachers College, Columbia University.

Johanson, D. C. and Edey, M. A. 1981: *Lucy: the Beginnings of Humankind*. London: Granada.

Johnson, C. L. 1983: A cultural analysis of the grandmother. *Research on Aging*, 5, 547–67.

Johnson, J. E., Ershler, J. and Lawton, J. T. 1982: Intellective correlates of preschoolers' spontaneous play. *Journal of Genetic Psychology*, 106, 115–22.

Johnson, M. H. 1998: The neural basis of cognitive development. In W. Damon (ed.), *The Handbook of Child Psychology. Volume 2 (Cognition, Perception and Language)*, 5th edn. New York: Wiley.

Johnson, M. H., Dziurawiec, S., Ellis, H. and Morton, J. 1991: The tracking of face-like stimuli by newborn infants and its subsequent decline. *Cognition*, 40, 1–21.

Johnson, M. H. and Morton, J. 1991: *Biology and Cognitive Development: The Case of Face Recognition*. Oxford: Blackwell.

Johnson, S. P. 1998: Object perception and object knowledge in young infants: a view from studies of visual development. In A. Slater (ed.), *Perceptual Development. Visual, Auditory and Speech Perception in Infancy*. Hove, East Sussex: Psychology Press.

Johnson, S. P. and Aslin, R. N. 1995: Perception of object unity in two-month-old infants. *Developmental Psychology*, 31, 739–45.

Joravsky, D. 1989: *Russian Psychology*. Oxford: Basil Blackwell.

Joyner, M. H. and Kurtz-Costes, B. 1997: Metamemory development. In N. Cowan (ed.), *The Development of Memory in Childhood*. Hove, East Sussex: Psychology Press.

Juang, L. P., Lerner, J. V., McKinney, J. P. and von Eye, A. 1999: The goodness of fit in autonomy timetable expectations between Asian-American late adolescents and their parents. *International Journal of Behavioral Development*, 23, 1023–48.

Jusczyk, P. W., Houston, D. and Goodman, M. 1998: Speech perception during the first year. In A. Slater (ed.), *Perceptual Development. Visual, Auditory and Speech Perception in Infancy*. Hove, East Sussex: Psychology Press.

Kagan, J. 1976: Resilience and continuity in psychological development. In A. M. Clarke and A. D. B. Clarke (eds), *Early Experience: Myth and Evidence*. New York: Free Press.

Kagan, J. 1997: Temperament and reactions to unfamiliarity. *Child Development*, 68, 139–43.

Kail, R. 1990: *The Development of Memory in Children*, 3rd edn. New York: Freeman.

Kanner, L. 1943: Autistic disturbances of affective content. *Nervous Child*, 2, 217–50.

Kant. I. 1958: *Critique of Pure Reason*. New York: Modern Library, (first published 1781).

Karmiloff-Smith, A. 1995: The extraordinary cognitive journey from foetus through infancy. *Journal of Child Psychology and Psychiatry*, 36, 1293–1313.

Karniol R. 1978: Children's use of intention cues in evaluating behavior. *Psychological Bulletin*, 85, 76–85.

Katchadourian, H. 1977: *The Biology of Adolescence*. San Francisco: W. H. Freeman.

Katz, I. 1996: *The Construction of Racial Identity in Children of Mixed Parentage: Mixed Metaphors*. London: Jessica Kingsley.

Katz, L. F. and Gottman, J. M. 1993: Patterns of marital conflict predict children's internalising and externalising behaviors. *Developmental Psychology*, 29, 940–50.

Kaye, K. 1984: *The Mental and Social Life of Babies*. London: Harvester Press.

Kaye, K. and Marcus, J. 1978: Imitation over a series of trials without feedback: age six months. *Infant Behavior and Development*, 1, 141–55.

Kaye, K. and Marcus, J. 1981: Infant imitation: the sensorimotor agenda. *Developmental Psychology*, 17, 258–65.

Keenan, E. O. and Klein, E. 1975: Coherency in children's discourse. *Journal of Psycholinguistic Research*, 4, 365–80.

Keeney, T. J., Cannizzo, S. R. and Flavell, J. H. 1967: Spontaneous and induced verbal rehearsal in a recall task. *Child Development*, 38, 953–66.

Kegl, J., Senghas, A. and Coppola, M. 1999: Creation through construct: Sign language emergence and sign language change in Nicaragua. In M. DeGrasf (ed.), *Language Creation and Language Change: Creolization, Diachrony and Development*. Cambridge, MA.: MIT Press.

Kellman, P. J. and Spelke, E. R. 1983: Perception of partly occluded objects in infancy. *Cognitive Psychology*, 15, 483–524.

Kelly, E. 1988: Pupils, racial groups and behaviour in schools. In E. Kelly and T. Cohn (eds), *Racism in Schools*. Stoke-on-Trent: Trentham Books.

Kempe, C. H. 1980: Incest and other forms of sexual abuse. In C. H. Kempe and R. E. Helfer (eds), *The Battered Child*. 3rd edn. Chicago: Chicago University Press.

Kim, K., Smith, P. K. and Palermiti, A-L. 1997: Conflict in childhood and reproductive development. *Evolution and Human Behavior*, 18, 109–42.

Kinsey, A. C., Pomeroy, W. B. and Martin, C. E. 1948: *Sexual Behavior in the Human Male*. Philadelphia: W. B. Saunders.

Kinsey, A. C., Pomeroy, W. B., Martin, C. E. and Gebherd, P. H. 1953: *Sexual Behavior in the Human Female*. Philadelphia: W. B. Saunders.

Kirby, P. 1999: *Involving Young Researchers*. York: York Publishing Services/Joseph Rowntree Foundation.

Kirk, S. A. 1958: *Early Education of the Mentally Retarded*. Urbana, IL: University of Illinois Press.

Klaus, M. H. and Kennell, J. H. 1976: *Maternal–Infant Bonding*. St Louis: Mosby.

Kline, S. 1995: The promotion and marketing of toys: time to rethink the paradox? In A. D. Pellegrini (ed.), *The Future of Play Theory*. Albany, NY: SUNY Press.

Klinnert, M. D. 1984: The regulation of infant behavior by maternal facial expression. *Infant Behavior and Development*, 7, 447–65.

Kobasigawa, A. 1974: Utilization of retrieval cues by children in recall. *Child Development*, 45, 127–34.

Kochanska, G. 2001: Emotional development in children with different attachment histories: the first three years. *Child Development*, 72, 474–90.

Kochenderfer, B. and Ladd, G. 1996: Peer victimisation: cause or consequence of school maladjustment? *Child Development*, 67, 1305–17.

Koeppen-Schomerus, G., Eley, T. C., Wolke, D., Gringras, P., and Plomin, R. 2000: The interaction of prematurity with genetic and environmental influences on cognititve development in twins. *Journal of Pediatrics*, 137, 527–33.

Kohlberg, L. 1966: A cognitive developmental analysis of children's sex role concepts and attitudes. In E. E. Maccoby (ed.), *The Development of Sex Differences*. Stanford, CA: Stanford University Press.

Kohlberg L. 1969: Stages and sequence: the cognitive-developmental approach to socialization. In D. A. Goslin (ed.), *Handbook of Socialization Theory and Research*. Chicago: Rand McNally.

Kohlberg, L. 1976: Moral stages and moralization: the cognitive-developmental approach. In T. Lickona (ed.), *Moral Development and Behavior*. New York: Holt, Rinehart and Winston.

Kojima, Y. 2000: Maternal regulation of sibling interactions in the preschool years: Observational study in Japanese families. *Child Development*, 71, 1640–47.

Koluchova, J. 1972: Severe deprivation in twins: a case study. In A. M. Clarke and A. D. B. Clarke (eds), *Early Experience: Myth and Evidence*. London: Open Books.

Koluchova, J. 1991: Severely deprived twins after 22 years of observation. *Studia Psychologica*, 33, 23–8.

Koluchova, J. 2000: Developmental and educational outcome for children in foster care in the Czech Republic. Lecture given to the Association for Child Psychology and Psychiatry, 18 May, Leicester.

Kramer, R. 1976: *Maria Montessori: A Biography*. Oxford: Basil Blackwell.

Krasnor, L. R. and Pepler, D. J. 1980: The study of children's play: some suggested future directions. In K. H. Rubin (ed.), *Children's Play*. San Francisco: Jossey-Bass.

Kreutzer, M. A., Leonard, C. and Flavell, J. H. 1975: An interview study of children's knowledge about memory. *Monographs of the Society for Research in Child Development*, 40, 1–58.

Krevans, J. and Gibbs, J. C. 1996: Parents' use of inductive discipline: relations to children's empathy and prosocial behavior. *Child Development*, 67, 3263–77.

Kruk, E. 1995: Grandparent-grandchild contact loss: findings from a study of 'Grandparents Rights' members. *Canadian Journal on Aging*, 14, 737–54.

Kuczaj II, S. A. 1986: Language play. In P. K. Smith (ed.), *Children's Play: Research Developments and Practical Applications*. London: Gordon and Breach.

Kuhl, P. K. 1979: Speech perception in early infancy: perceptual constancy for spectrally dissimilar vowel categories. *Journal of the Acoustical Society of America*, 66, 1168–79.

Kuhn, D. 1997: On giants' shoulders. In L. Smith, J. Dockrell and P. Tomlinson (eds), *Piaget, Vygotsky and Beyond: Future Issues for Developmental Psychology and Education*, pp. 246–59. London: Routledge.

Kuhn, D., Nash, S. C., and Bruken, L. 1978: Sex role concepts of two- and three-year-olds. *Child Development*, 49, 445–51.

Kurtines, W. and Greif, E. B. 1974: The development of moral thought: review and evaluation of Kohlberg's approach. *Psychological Bulletin*, 81, 453–70.

Kusche, C. A. and Greenberg, M. T. 2001: PATHS in your classroom: Promoting emotional literacy and alleviating emotional distress. In J. Cohen (ed.) *Social Emotional Learning and the Elementary School Child: A Guide for Educators*. New York: Teachers College Press.

Labov, W. 1969: The logic of non-standard English. Reprinted in 1972: *Language in Education: A Source Book*. London and Boston: Routledge & Kegan Paul/Open University Press.

Ladd, G. W. 1981: Effectiveness of a social learning method for enhancing children's social interaction and peer acceptance. *Child Development*, 52, 171–8.

Ladd, G. W. 1983: Social networks of popular, average and rejected children in school settings. *Merrill-Palmer Quarterly*, 29, 283–307.

Ladd, G. W., Buhs, E. S. and Troop, W. 2002: Children's interpersonal skills and relationships in school settings: Adaptive significance and implications for school-based prevention and intervention programs. In P. K. Smith and C. H. Hart (eds), *Blackwell Handbook of Childhood Social Development*. Oxford: Blackwell.

Ladd, G. W., Kochenderfer, B. J. and Coleman, C. C. 1996: Friendship quality as a predictor of young children's early school adjustment. *Child Development*, 67, 1103–18.

Lahey, B. B., Waldman, I. D. and McBurnett, K. 1999: Annotation: the development of antisocial behavior: an integrative causal model. *Journal of Child Psychology & Psychiatry*, 40, 669–82.

Lakatos, K., Nemoda, Z., Birkas, E., Ronai, Z., Kovacs, E., Ney, K., Toth, I., Sasvari-Szekely, M. and Gervai, J. 2003: Association of D4 dopamine D4 receptor gene and serotonin transporter polymorphisms with infants' response to novelty. *Molecular Psychiatry*, in press.

Lakatos, K., Toth, I., Nemoda, Z., Ney, K., Sasvari-Szekely, M. and Gervai, J. 2000: Dopamine D4 receptor (DRD4) gene polymorphism is associated with attachment disorganization in infants. *Molecular Psychiatry*, 5, 633–7.

Lamb, M. E. 1987: Introduction: the emergent American father. In M. E. Lamb (ed.), *The Father's Role: Cross-cultural Perspectives*. Hillsdale, NJ: Lawrence Erlbaum.

Lamb, M. E. (ed.) 1997: *The Role of the Father in Child Development*, 3rd edn. New York: Wiley.

Lamb, M. E., Thompson, R. A., Gardner, W. P., Charnov, E. L. and Estes, D. 1984: Security of infantile attachment as assessed in the 'strange situation': its study and biological interpretation. *Behavioural and Brain Sciences*, 7, 127–71.

Langlois, J. H. and Downs, A. C. 1980: Mothers, fathers, and peers as socialization agents of sex-typed play behaviors in young children. *Child Development*, 51, 1217–47.

Larson, R. W. 2000: Toward a psychology of positive youth development. *American Psychologist*, 55, 170–83.

Larson, R. W. 2001: Commentary: Children and adolescents in a changed media world. *Monographs of the Society for Research in Child Development*, 66, serial no 264.

Larson, R. and Ham, M. 1993: Stress and 'Storm and Stress' in early adolescence: the relationship of negative events with dysphoric affect. *Developmental Psychology*, 29, 130–40.

Larson, R. W. and Verma, S. 1999: How children and adolescents spend time across the world: work, play, and developmental opportunities. *Psychological Bulletin*, 125, 701–36.

Larzelere, R. E. 2000: Child outcomes of nonabusive and customary physical punishment by parents: an updated literature review. *Clinical Child and Family Psychology Review*, 3, 199–221.

Laucht, M., Esser, G. and Schmidt, M. H. 1997: Developmental outcome of infants born with biological and psychosocial risks. *Journal of Child Psychological and Psychiatry*, 38, 843–53.

Laursen, B., Cox, K. C. and Collins, W. A. 1998: Reconsidering changes in parent-child conflict across adolescence: a meta-analysis. *Child Development*, 69, 817–32.

Lawton, D. 1968: *Social Class, Language and Education*. London: Routledge & Kegan Paul.

Lazar, I. and Darlington, R. 1982: Lasting effects of early education. *Monographs of the Society for Research in Child Development*, 47, nos 2–3.

Leach, P. 2002: You can't beat psychological input. *The Psychologist*, 15 (January), 8–9.

Leakey, R. E. and Lewin, R. 1977: *Origins*. London: Macdonald and Janes.

Leaper, C. 2000: Gender, affiliation, assertion and the interactive context of parent-child play. *Developmental Psychology*, 36, 381–93.

Lecanuet, J-P. 1998: Foetal responses to auditory and speech stimuli. In A. Slater (ed.), *Perceptual Development. Visual, Auditory and Speech Perception in Infancy*. Hove, East Sussex: Psychology Press.

Lecanuet, J-P., Granier-Deferre, C., Jacquet, A. Y., Capponi, I. and Ledru, L. 1993: Prenatal discrimination of a male and female voice uttering the same sentence. *Early Development and Parenting*, 2, 217–28.

Leekam, S. and Perner, J. 1991: Does the autistic child have a metarepresentational deficit? *Cognition*, 40, 203–18.

Leevers, H. J. and Harris, P. L. 1999: Persisting effects of instruction on young children's syllogistic reasoning with incongruent and abstract premises. *Thinking and Reasoning*, 5, 145–73.

Lefkowitz, M. M., Eron, L. D., Walder, L. O. and Huesmann, L. R. 1977: *Growing Up to be Violent*. New York and Oxford: Pergamon.

Leichtman, M. D. and Ceci, S. J. 1995: The effects of stereotypes and suggestions on preschoolers' reports. *Developmental Psychology*, 31, 568–78.

Lemerise, E. A. and Arsenio, W. F. 2000: An integrated model of emotion processes and cognition in social information processing. *Child Development*, 71, 107–18.

Lempers, J. D., Flavell, E. R. and Flavell, J. H. 1977: The development in very young children of tacit knowledge concerning visual perception. *Genetic Psychology Monographs*, 95, 3–53.

Leontiev, A. N. 1981: The problem of activity in psychology. In J. V. Wertsch (ed.), *The Concept of Activity in Soviet Psychology*, pp. 37–71. Armonk, NY: Sharpe.

Leslie, A. M. 1987: Pretence and representation: the origins of 'theory of mind'. *Psychological Review*, 94, 412–26.

Leslie, A. M. and Thaiss, L. 1992: Domain specificity in conceptual development: neuropsychological evidence from autism. *Cognition*, 43, 225–51.

Leutenegger, W. 1981: Encephalization and obstetrics in primates with particular reference to human evolution. In E. Armstrong and D. Falk (eds), *Primate Brain Evolution: Methods and Concepts*. New York: Plenum.

Lever, J. 1978: Sex differences in the complexity of children's play and games. *American Sociological Review*, 43, 471–83.

Lewis, C. 1986: *Becoming a Father*. Milton Keynes: Open University Press.

Lewis, C. and Osborne, A. 1990: Three-year-olds' problems with false belief: conceptual deficit or linguistic artifact? *Child Development*, 61, 1514–19.

Lewis, C., Freeman, N. H., Kyriakidou, C., Maridaki-Kassotaki, K. and Berridge, D. M 1996: Social influences on false belief access: Specific sibling influences or general apprenticeship? *Child Development*, 67, 2930–47.

Lewis, M. and Brooks-Gunn, J. 1979: *Social Cognition and the Acquisition of Self*. New York: Plenum Press.

Lewis, M., Feiring, C., McGuffoy, C. and Jaskir, J. 1984: Predicting psychopathology in six-year-olds from early social relations. *Child Development*, 55, 123–36.

Lewis, M., Feiring, C. and Rosenthal, S. 2000: Attachment over time. *Child Development*, 71, 707–20.

Lewis, M., Stanger, C. and Sullivan, M. W. 1989: Deception in 3-year-olds. *Developmental Psychology*, 25, 439–43.

Lewis, M., Young, G., Brooks, J. and Michalson, L. 1975: The beginning of friendship. In M. Lewis and L. Rosenblum (eds), *Friendship and Peer Relations*. New York: Wiley.

Liddiard, M. 1928: *The Mothercraft Manual*. London: Churchill.

Lillard, A. S. 1993: Pretend play skills and the child's theory of mind. *Child Development*, 64, 348–71.

Linares, L. O., Heeren, T., Bronfman, E., Zuckerman, B., Augustyn, M. and Tronick, E. 2001: A mediational model for the impact of exposure to community violence on early child behavior problems. *Child Development*, 72, 639–52.

Linaza, J. 1984: Piaget's marbles: the study of children's games and their knowledge of rules. *Oxford Review of Education*, 10, 271–4.

Little, M. and Mount, K. 1999: *Prevention and Early Intervention with Children in Need*. Cambridge: Cambridge University Press.

Locke, J. 1939: An essay concerning human understanding. In E. A. Burtt (ed.), *The English Philosophers from Bacon to Mill*. New York: Modern Library (first published 1690).

Loeber, R. and Farrington, D. P. (eds) 1998: *Serious and Violent Juvenile Offenders: Risk Factors and Successful Interventions*. Thousand Oaks: Sage.

Lopatka, A. 1992: The rights of the child are universal: the perspective of the UN Convention on the Rights of the Child. In M. Freeman and P. Veerman (eds), *The Ideologies of Children's Rights*. Dordrecht: Martinus Nijhoff.

Lovejoy, C. O. 1981: The origin of man. *Science*, 211, 341–50.

Luepnitz, D. A. 1986: A comparison of maternal, paternal, and joint custody: understanding the varieties of post-divorce family life. *Journal of Divorce*, 9, 1–12.

Luria, A. R. 1979: *The Making of Mind*. Cambridge, MA: Harvard University Press.

Ma, L. 1989: Premarital sexual permissiveness of American and Chinese college students: a cross-cultural comparison. *Sociological Spectrum*, 9, 285–99.

Maccoby, E. E. 1998: *The Two Sexes: Growing up Apart, Coming Together*. Cambridge, MA: Belknap Press.

Maccoby, E. E. 2000: Perspectives on gender development. *International Journal of Behavioral Development*, 24, 398–406.

Maccoby, E. E., and Jacklin, C. N. 1974: *The Psychology of Sex Differences*. Stanford, CA: Stanford University Press.

Maccoby, E. E. and Martin, J. A. 1983: Socialization in the context of the family: parent–child interaction. In P. H. Mussen (ed.), *Handbook of Child Psychology*, Vol. 4: *Socialization, Personality, and Social Development*. New York: Wiley.

MacDonald, I. 1989: *Murder in the Playground*. London: Longsight Press.

MacDonald, K. 1992: Parent–child play: an evolutionary perspective. In K. MacDonald (ed.), *Parent–Child Play: Descriptions and Implications*. Albany, NY: SUNY Press.

Mackintosh, N. J. 1998: *IQ and Human Intelligence*. Oxford: Oxford University Press.

Magnusson, D., Stattin, H. and Allen, V. L. 1985: Biological maturation and social development: a longitudinal study of some adjustment processes from mid-adolescence to adulthood. *Journal of Youth and Adolescence*, 14, 267–83.

Mahoney, J. L., Stattin, H. and Magnusson, D. 2001: Youth recreation center participation and criminal offending: a 20-year longitudinal study of Swedish boys. *Journal of Child Psychology and Psychiatry*, 25, 509–20.

Main, M. and Cassidy, J. 1988: Categories of response to reunion with the parent at age 6: predictable from infant attachment classifications and stable over a 1-month period. *Developmental Psychology*, 24, 415–26.

Main, M., Kaplan, N. and Cassidy, J. 1985: Security in infancy, childhood, and adulthood: a move to the level of representation. In I. Bretherton and E. Waters (eds), *Growing Points of Attachment Theory and Research. Monographs of the Society for Research in Child Development*, 50, nos 1–2.

Malik, N. and Furman, W. 1993: Problems in children's peer relations: What can the clinician do? *Journal of Child Psychology and Psychiatry*, 34, 1303–26.

Malina, R. M. 1979: *Secular changes in size and maturity: causes and effects. Monographs of the Society for Research in Child Development*, 44, 59–102.

Malinosky-Rummell, R. and Hansen, D. J. 1993: Long-term consequences of childhood physical abuse. *Psychological Bulletin*, 114, 68–79.

Mannarino, A. P. 1980: The development of children's friendships. In H. C. Foot, A. J. Chapman and J. R. Smith (eds), *Friendship and Social Relations in Children*. Chichester: Wiley.

Marcia, J. E. 1966: Development and validation of ego-identity status. *Journal of Personality and Social Psychology*, 3, 551–58.

Marcia, J. 1980: Identity in adolescence. In J. Adelson (ed.), *Handbook of Adolescent Psychology*. New York: Wiley.

Marin, B. V., Holmes, D. L., Guth, M. and Kovac, P. 1979: The potential of children as eyewitnesses: a comparison of children and adults on eyewitness tasks. *Law and Human Behavior*, 3, 295–305.

Martin, C. L., Eisenbud, L. and Rose, H. 1995: Children's gender-based reasoning about toys. *Child Development*, 66, 1453–71.

Martin, C. L., Fabes, R. A., Evans, S. M. and Wyman, H. 1999: Social cognition on the playground: children's beliefs about playing with girls versus boys and their relations to sex segregated play. *Journal of Social and Personal Relationships*, 16, 751–71.

Martin, C. L. and Halverson, C. F. Jr. 1981: A schematic processing model of sex-typing and stereotyping in children. *Child Development*, 52, 1119–34.

Martin, P. and Bateson, P. 1991: *Measuring Behaviour: An Introductory Guide*, 2nd edn. Cambridge: Cambridge University Press.

Martorano, S. C. 1977: A developmental analysis of performance on Piaget's formal operations tasks. *Developmental Psychology*, 13, 666–72.

Masangkay, Z. S., McCluskey, K. A., McIntyre, C. W., Sims-Knight, J., Vaughn, B. E. and Flavell, J. H. 1974: The early development of inferences about the visual percepts of others. *Child Development*, 45, 237–46.

Mason, D. and Frick, P. 1994: The heritability of antisocial behaviour. *Journal of Psychopathology and Behavior Assessment*, 16, 301–23.

Masson, J. 1992: *The Assault on Truth. Freud and Child Sexual Abuse*. London: Fontana.

Maurer, D. and Barrera, M. 1981: Infants' perceptions of natural and distorted arrangements of a schematic face. *Child Development*, 52, 196–202.

Maurer, D. and Salapatek P. 1976: Developmental changes in the scanning of faces by young infants. *Child Development*, 47, 523–7.

Mayall, B. and Petrie, P. 1983: *Childminding and Day Nurseries: What Kind of Care?* London: Heinemann Educational Books.

McCauley, M. R. and Fisher, R. P. 1995: Facilitating children's eyewitness recall with the revised cognitive interview. *Journal of Applied Psychology,* 80, 510–16.

McGarrigle, J. and Donaldson, M. 1974: Conservation accidents. *Cognition,* 3, 341–50.

McGhee, P. E. 1979: *Humor: Its Origin and Development.* San Francisco: Freeman.

McGilly, K. and Siegler, R. S. 1989: How children choose among serial recall strategies. *Child Development,* 55, 172–82.

McGilly, K. and Siegler, R. S. 1990: The influence of encoding and strategic knowledge on children's choices among serial recall strategies. *Developmental Psychology,* 26, 931–41.

McGuire, A. 1994: Helping behaviors in the natural environment: dimensions and correlates of helping. *Personality and Social Psychology Bulletin,* 20, 1, 45–56.

McGurk, H. and Soriano, G. 1998: Families and social development: the 21st century. In A. Campbell and S. Muncer (eds), *The Social Child,* pp. 113–42. London: Psychology Press.

McLoyd, V. C. 1982: Social class differences in sociodramatic play: a critical review. *Developmental Review,* 2, 1–30.

McLoyd, V. C. and Ratner, H. H. 1983: The effects of sex and toy characteristics on exploration in preschool children. *Journal of Genetic Psychology,* 142, 213–24.

McNeill, D. 1966: Developmental psycholinguistics. In F. Smith and G. A. Miller (eds), *The Genesis of Language.* Cambridge, MA: MIT Press.

McNeill, D. 1970: *The Acquisition of Language.* New York: Harper and Row.

Mead, M. 1928: *Coming of Age in Samoa.* New York: Morrow.

Mead, M. 1935: *Sex and Temperament in Three Primitive Societies.* New York: Morrow.

Mead, M. 1949: *Male and Female.* New York: Morrow.

Mehler, J. and Dupoux, E. 1994: *What Infants Know. The New Cognitive Science of Early Development.* Oxford: Blackwell.

Meilman, P. W. 1979: Cross-sectional age changes in ego identity status during adolescence. *Developmental Psychology,* 15, 230–1.

Meins, E., Fernyhough, C., Fradley, E. and Tuckey, M. 2001: Rethinking maternal sensitivity: mothers' comments on infants' mental processes predict security of attachment at 12 months. *Journal of Child Psychology and Psychiatry,* 42, 637–48.

Melhuish, E. 1993: A measure of love? An overview of the assessment of attachment. *ACPP Review & Newsletter,* 15, 269–75.

Melhuish, E. C. 2001: The quest for quality in early day care and preschool experience continues. *International Journal of Behavioral Development,* 25, 1–6.

Melhuish, E. C. and Moss, P. 1992: Day care provision in Britain in historical perspective. In M. E. Lamb, K. J. Sternberg, P. Hwang and A. Broberg (eds), *Child Care in Context: Cross-cultural Perspectives.* New York: Erlbaum.

Melhuish, E. C., Lloyd, E., Martin, S. and Mooney, A. 1990a: Type of childcare at 18 months: II Relations with cognitive and language development. *Journal of Child Psychology and Psychiatry,* 31, 861–70.

Melhuish, E. C., Mooney, A., Martin, S. and Lloyd, E. 1990b: Type of childcare at 18 months: I Differences in children's experiences. *Journal of Child Psychology and Psychiatry,* 31, 849–60.

Meltzoff, A. and Borton, R. 1979: Intermodal matching by human neonates. *Nature,* 282, 403–4.

Meltzoff, A. and Moore, M. 1977: Imitation of facial and manual gestures by human neonates. *Science,* 198, 75–8.

Meltzoff, A. and Moore, M. 1983: Newborn infants imitate adult facial gestures. *Child Development*, 54, 702–9.

Meltzoff, A. N. and Moore, M. K. 1989: Imitation in newborn infants: exploring the range of gestures imitated and the underlying mechanisms. *Developmental Psychology*, 25, 954–62.

Messer, D. 1981: The identification of names in maternal speech to infants. *Journal of Psycholinguistic Research*, 10, 69–77.

Messer, D. 1994: *The Development of Communication from Social Interaction to Language*. Chichester: Wiley.

Meyrick, J. and Harris, R. 1994: Adolescent sexual behaviour, contraceptive use and pregnancy: a review. *ACPP Review & Newsletter*, 16, 245–51.

Miles, T. R. 1982: *The Bangor Dyslexia Test*. Cambridge: Learning Development Aids.

Miles, T. R. 1993: *Dyslexia: the Pattern of Difficulties*. London: Whurr.

Miller, J. G. 1997: A cultural-psychology perspective on intelligence. In R. J. Sternberg and E. Grigorenko (eds), *Intelligence, Heredity and Environment*. Cambridge: Cambridge University Press.

Miller, P. H. 1993: *Theories of Developmental Psychology*, 3rd edn. New York: Freeman.

Milner, D. 1983: *Children and Race: Ten Years On*. London: Ward Lock Educational.

Mischel, W. 1970: Sex-typing and socialization. In P. H. Mussen (ed.), *Carmichael's Manual of Child Psychology*, vol. 2, 3rd edn. New York: Wiley.

Mitchell, P. 1996: *Acquiring a Conception of Mind. A Review of Psychological Research and Theory*. Hove: Erlbaum.

Mitchell, P. 1997: *Introduction to Theory of Mind*. London: Arnold.

Mitchell, P. and Lacohee, H. 1991: Children's early understanding of false belief. *Cognition*, 39, 439–54.

Mitchell, P. and Riggs, K. (eds) 2000: *Children's Reasoning and the Mind*. Hove, East Sussex: Psychology Press.

Mitchell, R. W. 1986: A framework for discussing deception. In R. W. Mitchell and N. S. Thompson (eds), *Deception: Perspectives on Human and Nonhuman Deceit*. New York: SUNY Press.

Miyake, K., Chen, S. J. and Campos, J. J. 1985: Infant temperament, mother's mode of interaction and attachment in Japan: an interim report. In I. Bretherton and E. Waters (eds), Growing Points of Attachment Theory and Research. *Monographs of the Society for Research in Child Development*, 50, 276–97.

Moely, B. E., Olson, F. A., Halwes, T. G. and Flavell, J. H. 1969: Production deficiency in young children's clustered recall. *Developmental Psychology*, 1, 26–34.

Moerke, E. L. 1991: Positive evidence for negative evidence. *First Language*, 11, 219–51.

Møller, H. 1985: Voice change in human biological development. *Journal of Interdisciplinary History*, 16, 239–53.

Møller, H. 1987: The accelerated development of youth: beard growth as a biological marker. *Comparative Study of Society and History*, 29, 748–62.

Money, J. and Ehrhardt, A. A. 1972: *Man and Woman, Boy and Girl*. Baltimore, MD: Johns Hopkins University Press.

Montagu, A. 1961: Neonatal and infant immaturity in man. *Journal of the American Medical Association*, 178, 56–7.

Moon, C., Bever, T. G. and Fifer, W. P. 1992: Canonical and non-canonical syllable discrimination by two-day-old infants. *Journal of Child Language*, 19, 1–17.

Moon, C. and Fifer, W. P. 1990: Newborns prefer a prenatal version of mother's voice. *Infant Behavior and Development*, 13, 530.

Moon, C., Panneton-Cooper, R. P. and Fifer, W. P. 1993: Two-day-olds prefer their native language. *Infant Behavior and Development*, 16, 495–500.

Morford, J. P. and Kegl, J. 2000: Gestural precursors to linguistic constructs: how input shapes the form of language. In D. McNeill (ed.), *Language and Gesture*. Cambridge: Cambridge University Press.

Moses, L., Baldwin, D. A., Rosicky, J. G. and Tidball, G. 2001: Evidence for referential understanding in the emotions domain at twelve and eighteen months. *Child Development*, 72, 718–35.

Moss, P. 1987: *A Review of Childminding Research*. University of London: Thomas Coram Research Unit.

Moston, S. 1987: The suggestibility of children in interview studies. *First Language*, 7, 67–78.

Mueller, E. and Brenner, J. 1977: The origins of social skills and interaction among playgroup toddlers. *Child Development*, 48, 854–61.

Muir, D. and Field, J. 1979: Newborn infants orient to sounds. *Child Development*, 50, 431–6.

Muir, D. and Slater, A. (eds) 2000: *Infant Development. The Essential Readings*. Oxford: Blackwell.

Mumme, D. L., Fernald, A. and Herrera, C. 1996: Infants' responses to facial and vocal emotional signals in a social referencing paradigm. *Child Development*, 67, 3219–37.

Murray, L. and Trevarthen, C. 1985: Emotional regulation of interaction between two-month-olds and their mothers. In T. Field and N. Fox (eds), *Social Perception in Infants*, pp. 101–25. Norwood, NJ: Ablex.

Mussen, P. and Eisenberg-Berg, N. 1977: *Roots of Caring, Sharing and Helping*. San Francisco: W. H. Freeman.

Mussen, P. H. and Jones, M. C. 1957: Self-conceptions, motivations and interpersonal attitudes of late- and early-maturing boys. *Child Development*, 28, 243–56.

Myers, B. J. 1984: Mother–infant bonding: the status of this critical-period hypothesis. *Developmental Review*, 4, 240–74.

Nadel, J. and Butterworth, G. 1999: *Imitation in Infancy*. Cambridge: Cambridge University Press.

Nadel, J., Carchon, I., Kervella, C., Marcelli, D. and Reserbat-Plantey, D. 1999: Expectancies for social contingency in 2-month-olds. *Developmental Science*, 2, 164–73.

Nadel-Brulfert, J. and Baudonniere, P. M. 1982: The social function of reciprocal imitation in 2-year-old peers. *International Journal of Behavioural Development*, 5, 95–109.

Naus, M. J., Ornstein, P. A., and Aivano, S. 1977: Developmental changes in memory: The effects of processing time and rehearsal instructions. *Journal of Experimental Child Psychology*, 23, 237–51.

Naylor, P. and Cowie, H 1999: The effectiveness of peer support systems in challenging school bullying: the perspectives and experiences of teachers and pupils. *Journal of Adolescence*, 22, 467–79.

Needham, A. and Baillargeon, R. 1998: Effects of prior experience on 4.5-month-old infants' object segregation. *Infant Behavior and Development*, 21, 1–24.

Nelson, C. A. 2001: The development and neural bases of face recognition. *Infant and Child Development*, 10, 3–18.

Nelson, K. 1981: Individual differences in language development: implications for language and development. *Developmental Psychology*, 17, 170–87.

Nelson, K. (ed.) 1986: *Event Knowledge. Structure and Function in Development*. Hillsdale, NJ: Lawrence Erlbaum.

Nelson, K. (ed.) 1989: *Narratives from the Crib*. Cambridge, MA: Harvard University Press.

Nelson, K. and Gruendel, J. M. 1981: Generalised event representations. Basic building blocks of cognitive development. In M. E. Lamb and A. L. Brown (eds), *Advances in Developmental Psychology. Volume 1*. Hillsdale, NJ: Erlbaum.

Nelson, K., Carskaddon, G. and Bonvillian, J. D. 1973: Syntax acquisition: impact of experimental variation in adult verbal interaction with the child. *Child Development*, 44, 497–504.

Newcomb, A. F. and Bagwell, C. L. 1995: Children's friendship relations: a meta-analytic review. *Psychological Bulletin*, 117, 306–47.

Newcomb, A. F., Bukowski, W. M. and Pattee, L. 1993: Children's peer relations: a meta-analytic review of popular, rejected, neglected, controversial, and average sociometric status. *Psychological Bulletin*, 113, 99–128.

Newsom Report (Central Advisory Council for Education) 1963: *Half Our Future*. London: HMSO.

Newson, E. 1994: Video violence and the protection of children. *The Psychologist*, 7, 272–4.

NICHD Early Child Care Research Network 1997: The effects of infant child care on infant-mother attachment security: Results of the NICHD study of early child care. *Child Development*, 68, 860–79.

NICHD Early Child Care Research Network 2001: Child care and children's peer interaction at 24 and 36 months: The NICHD study of early child care. *Child Development*, 72, 1478–1500.

Nicholson, J. M., Fergusson, D. M. and Horwood, L. J. 1999: Effects on later adjustment of living in a stepfamily during childhood and adolescence. *Journal of Child Psychology & Psychiatry*, 40, 405–16.

Nicolson, R. I. and Fawcett, A. J. 1990: Automaticity: a new framework for dyslexia research? *Cognition*, 30, 159–82.

Nicolson, R. I. and Fawcett, A. J. 1996: *The Dyslexia Early Screening Test*. London: The Psychological Corporation.

Nishida, T. 1980: The leaf-clipping display: a newly-discovered expressive gesture in wild chimpanzees. *Journal of Human Evolution*, 9, 117–28.

Nobes, G., Smith, M., Upton, P. and Heverin, A. 1999: Physical punishment by mothers and fathers in British homes. *Journal of Interpersonal Violence*, 14, 887–902.

Noelting, G. 1980: The development of proportional reasoning and the ratio concept. *Educational Studies in Mathematics*, 11, 217–53.

Novak, M. A. 1979: Social recovery of monkeys isolated for the first year of life: II. Long term assessment. *Developmental Psychology*, 15, 50–61.

Nunes Carraher, T., Carraher, D. W. and Schliemann, A. D. 1985: Mathematics in the streets and in schools. *British Journal of Developmental Psychology*, 3, 21–9.

O'Connell, A. N. 1976: The relationship between life style and identity synthesis and resynthesis in traditional, neo-traditional and non-traditional women. *Journal of Personality*, 4, 675–88.

O'Connor, N. and Hermelin, B. 1992: Do young calendrical calculators improve with age? *Journal of Child Psychology and Psychiatry*, 33, 907–12.

O'Connor, R. D. 1972: Relative efficacy of modeling, shaping and the combined procedures for modification or social withdrawal. *Journal of Abnormal Psychology*, 79, 327–34.

O'Connor, T. G. and Croft, C. M. 2001: A twin study of attachment in preschool children. *Child Development*, 72, 1501–11.

O'Connor, T. G., Rutter, M., Beckett, C., Keaveney, L., Kreppner, J. M. and the Romanian Adoptees Study Team 2000: The effects of global severe privation on cognitive competence: extension and longitudinal follow-up. *Child Development*, 71, 376–90.

O'Connor, T. G., Thorpe, K., Dunn, J. and Golding, J. 1999: Parental divorce and adjustment in adulthood: findings from a community sample. *Journal of Child Psychology & Psychiatry*, 40, 777–89.

Oden, S. and Asher, S. R. 1977: Coaching children in social skills for friendship making. *Child Development*, 48, 495–506.

Olweus, D. 1991: Bully/victim problems among schoolchildren: basic facts and effects of a school based intervention program. In K. Rubin and D. Pepler (eds), *The Development and Treatment of Childhood Aggression*. Hillsdale, NJ: Erlbaum.

Olweus, D. and Endresen, I. M. 1998: The importance of sex-of-stimulus object: trends and sex differences in empathic responsiveness. *Social Development*, 3, 370–88.

Opie, I. and Opie, P. 1959: *The Lore and Language of School Children*. London: Oxford University Press.

Oppenheim, D., Nir, A., Warren, S. and Emde, R. 1997: Emotion regulation in other-child narrative co-construction: associations with children's narratives and adaptation. *Developmental Psychology*, 33, 284–94.

Oppenheim, D., Sagi, A. and Lamb, M. E. 1988: Infant–adult attachments on the kibbutz and their relation to socioemotional development four years later. *Developmental Psychology*, 24, 427–33.

Ornstein, P. A., Naus, M. J. and Liberty, C. 1975: Rehearsal and organizational processes in children's memory. *Child Development*, 46, 818–30.

Oser, F. K. 1996: Kohlberg's dormant ghosts: the case of education. *Journal of Moral Education*, 25, 253–75.

Österman, K., Björkvist, K., Lagerspetz, K., Landau, S., Fraczek, A. and Pastorelli, C. 1997: Sex differences in styles of conflict resolution: a developmental and cross-cultural study with data from Finland, Israel, Italy and Poland. In D. Fry and K. Björkqvist (eds), *Cultural Variations in Conflict Resolution*, pp. 185–97. Mahwah, NJ: Lawrence Erlbaum.

Ostersehlt, D. and Danker-Hopfe, H. 1991: Changes in age at menarche in Germany: evidence for a continuing decline. *American Journal of Human Biology*, 3, 647–54.

Overton, W. F. and Jackson, J. P. 1973: The representation of imagined objects in action sequences: a developmental study. *Child Development*, 44, 309–14.

Owens, L., Shute, R. and Slee, P. 2000: 'Guess what I just heard?': indirect aggression among teenage girls in Australia. *Aggressive Behavior*, 26, 67–83.

Packer, C. 1977: Reciprocal altruism in olive baboons. *Nature*, 265, 441–43.

Paikoff, R. L. and Brooks-Gunn, J. 1991: Do parent–child relationships change during puberty? *Psychological Bulletin*, 110, 47–66.

Pan, B. and Snow, C. 1999: The development of conversational and discourse skills. In M. Barrett (ed.), *The Development of Language*. London: Psychology Press, pp 229–50.

Papousek, M. 1989: Determinants of responsiveness to infant vocal expression of emotional state. *Infant Behavior and Development*, 12, 507–24.

Papousek, M. and Papousek, H. 1989: Forms and functions of vocal matching in interactions between mothers and their pre-canonical infants. *First Language*, 9, 137–58.

Papousek, M., Papousek, H. and Haekel, M. 1987: Didactic adjustments in fathers' and mothers' speech to their three-month-old infants. *Journal of Psycholinguistic Research*, 16, 491–516.

Papousek, M., Papousek, H. and Symmes, D. 1991: The meanings of melodies in mothers' in tone and stress languages. *Infant Behavior and Development*, 14, 415–40.

Parke, R. D. 1977: Some effects of punishment on children's behaviour – revisited. In E. M. Hetherington and R. D. Parke (eds), *Contemporary Readings in Child Psychology*. New York: McGraw-Hill.

Parke, R. D., Simpkins, S. D., McDowell, D. J., Kim, M., Killian, C., Dennis, J., Flyr, M. L., Wild, M. and Rah, Y. 2002: Relative contributions of families and peers to children's social development. In P. K. Smith and C. H. Hart (eds), *Blackwell Handbook of Childhood Social Development*. Oxford: Blackwell.

Parker, J. G. and Asher, S. R. 1987: Peer relations and later personal adjustment: are low-accepted children at risk? *Psychological Bulletin*, 102, 357–89.

Parker, S. T. and Gibson, K. R. 1979: A developmental model for the evolution of language and intelligence in early hominids. *Behavioral and Brain Sciences*, 2, 367–408.

Parten, M. B. 1932: Social participation among preschool children. *Journal of Abnormal and Social Psychology*, 27, 243–69.

Pascalis, O., de Schonen, S., Morton, J., Deruelle, C. and Fabre-Grenet, M. 1995: Mother's face recognition in neonates: A replication and an extension. *Infant Behavior and Development*, 18, 79–86.

Passow, A. H. 1970: *Deprivation and Disadvantage: Nature and Manifestations*. Hamburg: UNESCO Institute of Education.

Patrick, J. 1973: *A Glasgow Gang Observed*. London: Eyre Methuen.

Patterson, C. J. 1992: Children of lesbian and gay parents. *Child Development*, 63, 1025–42.

Patterson, C. J. 1995: Sexual orientation and human development: an overview. *Developmental Psychology*, 31, 3–11.

Patterson, F. G. 1978: The gestures of a gorilla: language acquisition in another pongid. *Brain and Language*, 5, 72–97.

Patterson, G. R., DeBaryshe, B. D. and Ramsey, E. 1989: A developmental perspective on antisocial behavior. *American Psychologist*, 44, 329–35.

Patterson, G. R., Reid, J. B. and Dishion, T. J. 1992: *Antisocial Boys*. Eugene, OR: Castalia.

Payne, J. 1995: Routes beyond compulsory schooling. *Youth Cohort Paper No. 31*. London: Department of Employment.

Pearson, G. 1983: *Hooligan: A History of Respectable Fears*. London: Macmillan Press.

Pellegrini, A. D. 1988: Elementary school children's rough-and-tumble play and social competence. *Developmental Psychology*, 24, 802–6.

Pellegrini, A. D. 1994: The rough play of adolescent boys of differing sociometric status. *International Journal of Behavioral Development*, 17, 525–40.

Pellegrini, A. D. 2002: Rough-and-tumble play from childhood through adolescence: development and possible functions. In P. K. Smith and C. H. Hart (eds), *Blackwell Handbook of Childhood Social Development*. Oxford: Blackwell.

Pellegrini, A. D. and Bartini, M. 2000: An empirical comparison of methods of sampling aggression and victimization in school settings. *Journal of Educational Psychology*, 92, 360–6.

Pellegrini, A. D. and Bartini, M. 2001: Dominance in early adolescent boys: Affiliative and aggressive dimensions and possible functions. *Merrill-Palmer Quarterly*, 47, 142–63.

Pellegrini, A. D. and Smith, P. K. 1998: Physical activity play: the nature and function of a neglected aspect of play. *Child Development*, 69, 577–98.

Pellegrini, A. D., Huberty, P. D., and Jones, I. 1995: The effects of recess timing on children's playground and classroom behaviours. *American Educational Research Journal*, 32, 845–64.

Peller, L. E. 1954: Libidinal phases, ego development and play. *Psychoanalytic Study of the Child*, 9, 178–98.

Pepler, D. J. and Craig, W. M. 1998: Assessing children's peer relationships. *Child Psychology and Psychiatry Review* 3, 176–82.

Perner, J. 1991: *Understanding the Representational Mind*. Cambridge, MA: MIT Press.

Perner, J. and Wimmer, H. 1985: 'John thinks that Mary thinks that . . .': attribution of second order beliefs by 5–10 year old children. *Journal of Experimental Child Psychology*, 39, 437–71.

Perner, J., Frith, U., Leslie, A. M. and Leekam, S. R. 1989: Exploration of the autistic child's theory of mind: knowledge, belief and communication. *Child Development*, 60, 689–700.

Perner, J., Leekam, S. R. and Wimmer, H. 1987: Three-year-olds' difficulty with false belief: the case for a conceptual deficit. *British Journal of Developmental Psychology*, 5, 125–37.

Perry, N. W. and Wrightsman, L. S. 1991: *The Child Witness. Legal Issues and Dilemmas*. Newbury Park, CA: Sage.

Peskin, J. 1992: Ruse and representations: on children's ability to conceal information. *Developmental Psychology*, 28, 84–9.

Pettit, G. S., Bates, J. E., Dodge, K. A. and Meece, D. W. 1999: The impact of after-school peer contact on early adolescent externalizing problems is moderated by parental monitoring, perceived neighbourhood safety, and prior adjustment. *Child Development*, 70, 768–78.

Pfungst, O. 1911: *Clever Hans: A Contribution to Experimental Animal and Human Psychology*. New York: Holt.

Phelps, J. L., Belsky, J. and Crnic, K. 1998: Earned security, daily stress, and parenting: a comparison of five alternative models. *Development and Psychopathology*, 10, 21–38.

Phoenix, A., Woollett, A. and Lloyd, E. 1991: *Motherhood: Meanings, Practices and Ideologies*. London: Sage.

Piaget, J. 1929: *The Child's Conception of the World*. New York: Harcourt Brace Jovanovich.

Piaget, J. 1932 (1977): *The Moral Judgement of the Child*. Harmondsworth: Penguin.

Piaget, J. 1936/1952: *The Origin of Intelligence in the Child*. London: Routledge & Kegan Paul.

Piaget, J. 1951: *Play, Dreams and Imitation in Childhood*. London: Routledge & Kegan Paul.

Piaget, J. 1966: Response to Brian Sutton-Smith. *Psychological Review*, 73, 111–12.

Piaget, J. 1972: Intellectual evolution from adolescence to adulthood. *Human Development*, 15, 1–12.

Piaget, J. and Inhelder, B. 1951: *La genèse de l'idée de hasard chez l'enfant*. Paris: Presses Universitaires de France.

Piaget, J. and Inhelder, B. 1956: *The Child's Conception of Space*. London: Routledge & Kegan Paul.

Pike, A. 2002: Behavioural genetics, shared and nonshared environment. In P. K. Smith and C. H. Hart (eds), *Blackwell Handbook of Childhood Social Development*. Oxford: Blackwell.

Pinker, S. 1994: *The Language Instinct*. London: Allen Lane.

Plomin, R. and Daniels, D. 1987: Why are children of the same family so different from each other? *Behavioural and Brain Sciences*, 10, 1–16.

Plomin, R. and Rutter, M. 1998: Child development, molecular genetics, and what to do with genes once they are found. *Child Development*, 69, 1223–42.

Plomin, R., DeFries, J. C., Rutter, M. and McClearn, G. E. 1997: *Behavioral Genetics: A Primer*, 3rd edn. New York: W. H. Freeman.

Poole, D. A. and Lamb, M. E. 1998: *Investigative Interviews of Children. A Guide for Helping Professionals*. Washington, DC: American Psychological Association.

Povinelli, D. J. and Eddy, T. J. 1996: What young chimpanzees know about seeing. *Monographs of the Society for Research in Child Development*, 61, 1–152.

Povinelli, D. J., Landau, K. R. and Perilloux, H. K. 1996: Self-recognition in young children using delayed versus live feedback: Evidence of a developmental asynchrony. *Child Development*, 67, 1540–54.

Powdermaker, H. 1933: *Life in Lesu*. New York: W. W. Norton.

Power, T. 2000: *Play and Exploration in Children and Animals*, Mahwah, NJ: Lawrence Erlbaum.

Premack, D. 1971: Language in chimpanzee? *Science*, 172, 808–22.

Pressley, M. and Levin, J. R. 1980: The development of mental imagery retrieval. *Child Development*, 61, 973–82.

Profet, M. 1992: Pregnancy sickness as adaptation: a deterrent to maternal ingestion of teratogens. In J. H. Barkow, L. Cosmides and J. Tooby (eds), *The Adapted Mind*, pp. 327–65. New York and Oxford: Oxford University Press.

QCA/DfEE 1999: *The National Curriculum Handbook for Primary Teachers in England*. London: DfEE.

Querleu, D., Lefebvre, C., Renard, X., Titran, M., Morillion, M. and Crepin, G. 1984: Réactivité du nouveau-né de moins de deux heures de vie à la voix maternelle. *Journal de Gynécologie, Obstrétrique et Biologie de la Réproduction*, 13, 125–34.

Radford, J. 1990: *Child Prodigies and Exceptional Early Achievers*. Hemel Hempstead: Harvester Wheatsheaf.

Radin, N., Oyserman, D. and Benn, R. 1991: Grandfathers, teen mothers, and children under two. In P. K. Smith (ed.), *The Psychology of Grandparenthood: An International Perspective*. London: Routledge.

Rampton Report 1981: *West Indian Children in our Schools*. London: HMSO, Cmnd 8273.

Rauh, H., Rudinger, G., Bowman, T. G., Berry, P., Gunn, P. V. and Hayes, A. 1991: The development of Down's syndrome children. In M. E. Lamb and H. Keller (eds), *Infant Development: Perspectives from German-speaking Countries*. Hillsdale, NJ: Erlbaum.

Raven, J. C. 1958: *Standard progressive matrices*. London: H. K. Lewis & Co. Ltd.

Raven, J. C. 1994: *Advanced progressive matrices*. Windsor: NFER-Nelson.

Raven, J. C. 1995: *Coloured progressive matrices*. Windsor: NFER-Nelson.

Raven, J. C. 1996: *Standard progressive matrices*. Windsor: NFER-Nelson.

Raven, M. 1981: Review: the effects of childminding: how much do we know? *Child: Care, Health and Development*, 7, 103–11.

Reinhold, R. 1979: Census finds unmarried couples have doubled from 1970 to 1978. *The New York Times*, 27 June, p. 1: B5.

Reiss, I. L. 1967: *The Social Context of Premarital Sexual Permissiveness*. New York: Holt, Rinehart and Winston.

Remafedi, G., Resnick, M., Blum, R. and Harris, L. 1992: Demography of sexual orientation in adolescents. *Pediatrics*, 89, 714–21.

Richards, M. P. M. 1995: The international year of the family: family research. *The Psychologist*, 8, 17–24.

Richardson, K. 1991: *Understanding Intelligence*. Buckingham: Open University Press.

Rigby, K. 1996: *Bullying in Schools and What to do About It*. Melbourne: Australian Council for Educational Research.

Riggs, K. J. and Peterson, D. M. 2000: Counterfactual thinking in pre-school children. In P. Mitchell and K. Riggs (eds), *Children's Reasoning and the Mind*. Hove, East Sussex: Psychology Press.

Riggs, K. J., Peterson, D. M., Robinson, E. J. and Mitchell, P. 1998: Are errors in false belief tasks symptomatic of a broader difficulty with counterfactuality? *Cognitive Development*, 13, 73–91.

Rivers, I. and Duncan, N. 2002: Understanding homophobic bullying in schools: building a safe learning environment for all pupils. *Youth and Policy* B, 75, 30–41.

Robarchek, C. A. and Robarchek, C. J. 1992: Cultures of war and peace: a comparative study of Waorani and Semai. In J. Silverberg and J. P. Gray (eds), *Aggression and Peacefulness in Humans and other Primates*. New York: Oxford University Press.

Roberts, A. D. 1945: Case history of a so-called idiot savant. *Journal of Genetic Psychology*, 66, 259–65.

Roberts, K. 2000: An overview of theory and research on children's source monitoring. In K. Roberts and M. Blades (eds), *Children's Source Monitoring*. Mahwah, NJ: Erlbaum.

Robson, C. 1993: *Real World Research*. Oxford: Blackwell.

Robson, C. 1999: *Experiment, Design and Statistics in Psychology*, 3rd edn. Harmondsworth: Penguin.

Roche, A. F. (ed.) 1979: Secular trends in human growth, maturation, and development. *Monographs of the Society for Research in Child Development*, 44 (3–4), Serial no. 179.

Rodkin, P. C., Farmer, T. W., Pearl, R. and van Acker, R. 2000: Heterogeneity of popular boys: antisocial and prosocial configurations. *Developmental Psychology*, 36, 14–24.

Rogers, M. J. and Tisak, M. 1996: Children's reasoning about responses to peer aggression. *Aggressive Behavior*, 22, 4, 259–69.

Rogoff, B., Baker-Sennett, J., Lacasa, P. and Goldsmith, D. 1995: Development through participation in sociocultural activity. In J. Goodnow, P. Miller and F. Kessel (eds), *Cultural Practices as Contexts for Development. New Directions for Child Development*, 67, 45–65. (series editor W. Damon).

Rojas-Drummond, S. 2000: Guided participation, discourse and the construction of knowledge in Mexican classrooms. In H. Cowie and G. van der Aalsvoort (eds), *Social Interaction in Learning and Instruction*, pp. 193–213. Amsterdam: Pergamon, Elsevier Science.

Roland, E. 1989: Bullying: the Scandinavian research tradition. In E. Roland and E. Munthe (eds), *Bullying: an International Perspective*. London: David Fulton.

Root, B. 1986: *Resources for Reading*. London: Macmillan.

Rose, S. R., Kamin L. J. and Lewontin, R. C. 1984: *Not in our Genes: Biology, Ideology and Human Nature*. Harmondsworth: Penguin.

Rosenblith, J. F. 1992: *In the Beginning: Development from Conception to Age Two*, 2nd edn. Newbury Park and London: Sage.

Rosenblum, G. D. and Lewis, M. 1999: The relations among body image, physical attractiveness, and body mass in adolescence. *Child Development*, 70, 50–64.

Rosser, R. 1994: *Cognitive Development. Psychological and Biological Perspectives*. Boston: Allyn and Bacon.

Rossi, A. H. and Rossi, P. H. 1991: *Of Human Bonding: Parent–Child Relations across the Life Course*. New York: de Gruyter.

Rothbaum, F., Weisz, J., Pott, M., Miyake, K. and Morelli, G. 2000: Attachment and culture: security in the United States and Japan. *American Psychologist*, 55, 1093–105.

Roy, P., Rutter, M. and Pickles, A. 2000: Institutional care: risk from family background or pattern of rearing? *Journal of Child Psychology and Psychiatry*, 41, 139–49.

Rubin, K. H. and Pepler, D. J. 1982: Children's play: Piaget's views reconsidered. *Contemporary Educational Psychology*, 7, 289–99.

Rubin, K. H., Burgess, K. B. and Coplan, R. J. 2002: Social withdrawal and shyness. In P. K. Smith and C. H. Hart (eds), *Blackwell Handbook of Childhood Social Development*. Oxford: Blackwell.

Ruble, D. N. and Brooks-Gunn, J. 1982: The experience of menarche. *Child Development*, 53, 1557–66.

Ruble, D. N., Balaban, T. and Cooper, J. 1981: Gender constancy and the effects of sex-typed televised toy commercials. *Child Development*, 52, 667–73.

Rushton, J. P. 1997: The Mismeasure of Gould. *The National Review*, 15 September.

Russell, A. and Saebel, J. 1997: Mother–son, mother–daughter, father–son, and father–daughter: are they distinct relationships? *Developmental Review*, 17, 111–47.

Russell, J. 1992: The 'theory-theory': so good they named it twice? *Cognitive Development*, 7, 485–519.

Rutter, M. 1981: *Maternal Deprivation Reassessed*, 2nd edn. Harmondsworth: Penguin.

Rutter, M. 1990: Psychological resilience and protective mechanisms. In J. Rolf, A. S. Masters, D. Cicchetti, K. H. Neuchterlein and S. Weintraub (eds), *Risks and Protective Factors in the Development of Psychopathology*. New York: Cambridge University Press.

Rutter, M. 1998: Practitioner review: routes from research to clinical practice in child psychiatry: retrospect and prospect. *Journal of Child Psychology & Psychiatry*, 39, 805–16.

Rutter, M. 1999: Blame it on their peers? *Times Higher Educational Supplement*, 22 January, 29.

Rutter, M. 2000: Psychosocial influences: critiques, findings, and research needs. *Development and Psychopathology*, 12, 375–405.

Rutter, M. and the English and Romanian Adoptees (ERA) team 1998: Developmental catch-up and deficit following adoption after severe global early privation. *Journal of Child Psychology & Psychiatry*, 39, 465–76.

Rutter, M. and Smith, D. J. 1995: *Psychosocial Disorders in Young People: Time Trends and their Causes.* Chichester: John Wiley.

Rutter, M., Graham, P., Chadwick, O. and Yule, W. 1976: Adolescent turmoil: fact or fiction? *Journal of Child Psychology and Psychiatry*, 17, 35–56.

Rymer, R. 1994: *Genie: A Scientific Tragedy.* Harmondsworth: Penguin.

Salapatek, P. 1975: *Infant Perception from Sensation to Cognition*, vol. 1. New York: Academic Press.

Saljö, R. 1998: Thinking with and through artifacts. In D. Faulkner, K. Littleton and M. Woodhead (eds), *Learning Relationships in the Classroom*, pp. 54–66. London: Routledge/Open University.

Salmivalli, C., Lagerspetz, K. M. J., Björkqvist, K., Österman, K. and Kaukiainen, A. 1996: Bullying as a group process: participant roles and their relations to social status within the group. *Aggressive Behavior*, 22, 1–15.

Sandstrom, M. J. and Coie, J. D. 1999: A developmental perspective on peer rejection: mechanisms of stability and change. *Child Development*, 70, 955–66.

Sanson, A., Hemphill, S. A. and Smart, D. 2002: Temperament and social development. In P. K. Smith and C. Hart (eds), *Blackwells Handbook of Social Development*. Oxford: Blackwell.

Savage-Rumbaugh, E. S. and Rumbaugh, D. M. 1978: Symbolization, language and chimpanzees: a theoretical re-evaluation based on initial language acquisition processes in four young *Pan troglodytes. Brain and Language*, 6, 265–300.

Savin-Williams, R. C. 1976: An ethological study of dominance formation and maintenance in a group of human adolescents. *Child Development*, 47, 972–9.

Savin-Williams, R. C. 1980: Social interactions of adolescent females in natural groups. In H. C. Foot, A. J. Chapman and I. R. Smith (eds), *Friendship and Social Relations in Children*. Chichester: Wiley.

Savin-Williams, R. C. and Demo, D. H. 1984: Developmental change and stability in adolescent self-concept. *Developmental Psychology*, 20, 1100–10.

Saywitz, K. J. and Nathanson, R. 1993: Children's testimony and their perceptions of stress in and out of the courtroom. *Child Abuse and Neglect*, 17, 613–22.

Saywitz, K. J., Goodman, G. S., Nicholas, E. and Moan, S. F. 1991: Children's memories of a physical examination involving genital touch: implications for reports of child sexual abuse. *Journal of Consulting and Clinical Psychology*, 59, 682–91.

Scaife, M. and Bruner, J. S. 1975: The capacity for joint visual attention in the infant. *Nature*, 253, 265–6.

Scarlett, G. and Wolf, D. 1979: When it's only make-believe: the construction of a boundary between fantasy and reality in story-telling. In E. Winner and H. Gardner (eds), *Fact, Fiction and Fantasy in Childhood*. San Francisco: Jossey-Bass.

Scarr, S. 1984: *Race, Social Class, and Individual Differences in I.Q.* London: Lawrence Erlbaum.

Scarr, S. 1992: Developmental theories for the 1990s: development and individual differences. *Child Development*, 63, 1–19.

Scarr, S. and Thompson, W. 1994: Effects of maternal employment and child-care arrangements on preschoolers' cognitive and behavioral outcomes. *Early Development & Parenting*, 3, 113–23.

Scarr, S. and Weinberg, R. A. 1976: IQ test performance of black children adopted by white families. *American Psychologist*, 31, 726–39.

Schafer, M. and Smith, P. K. 1996: Teachers' perceptions of play fighting and real fighting in primary school. *Educational Research*, 38, 173–81.

Schaffer, H. R. 1996: *Social Development*. Oxford: Blackwell Publishers.

Schaffer, H. R. and Emerson, P. E. 1964: The development of social attachments in infancy. *Monographs of the Society for Research in Child Development*, 28.

Schank, R. C. 1982: *Dynamic Memory: A Theory of Reminding and Learning in Computers and People*. Cambridge: Cambridge University Press.

Schank, R. C. and Abelson, R. P. 1977: *Scripts, Plans, Goals and Understanding*. Hillsdale, NJ: Lawrence Erlbaum.

Scharf, M. 2001: A 'natural experiment' in childrearing ecologies and adolescents' attachment and separation representations. *Child Development*, 72, 236–51.

Schieffelin, B. 1990: *The Give and Take of Everyday Life: Language Socialization of Kaluli Children*. Cambridge: Cambridge University Press.

Schieffelin, B. and Ochs, E. 1983: A cultural perspective on the transition from prelinguistic to linguistic communication. In R. M. Golinkoff (ed.), *The Transition from Prelinguistic to Linguistic Communication*, pp. 115–28. Hillsdale, NJ: Lawrence Erlbaum.

Schlegel, A. and Barry, H. III. 1991: *Adolescence: An Anthropological Inquiry*. New York: Free Press.

Schneider, W. and Bjorklund, D. E. 1992: Expertise, aptitude and strategic remembering. *Child Development*, 63, 461–73.

Schneider, W. and Pressley, M. 1997: *Memory Development between Two and Twenty*. 2nd edn. Mahwah, NJ: Erlbaum.

Schofield, J. W. and Francis, W. D. 1982: An observational study of peer interaction in racially mixed 'accelerated' classrooms. *Journal of Educational Psychology*, 74, 722–32.

Schofield, M. 1965: *The Sexual Behaviour of Young People*. London: Longmans.

Schools Exclusion Unit 1998: *Bringing Britain Together: A National Strategy for Neighbourhood Renewal*. London: Social Exclusion Unit, Cmd 4045.

Schwartz, A., Campos, J. and Baisel, E. 1973: The visual cliff: cardiac and behavioral correlates on the deep and shallow sides at five and nine months of age. *Journal of Experimental Child Psychology*, 15, 86–99.

Schwartz, D., Dodge, K. A., Pettit, G. S. and Bates, J. E. 1997: The early socialisation of aggressive victims of bullying. *Child Development*, 68, 665–75.

Scribner, S. and Cole, M. 1978: Literacy without schooling: testing for intellectual effects. *Harvard Educational Review*, 48, 448–61.

Segal, N. 2000: *Entwined Lives: Twins and What They Tell Us about Human Behavior*. New York: Plume.

Selman, R. L. and Jaquette, D. 1977: Stability and oscillation in interpersonal awareness: a clinical-developmental analysis. In C. B. Keasey (ed.), *The Nebraska Symposium on Motivation*, vol. 25. Lincoln: University of Nebraska Press.

Serbin, L. A., Powlishta, K. K. and Gulko, J. 1993: The development of sex-typing in middle childhood. *Monographs of Society for Research in Child Development*, 58, 1–74.

Serbin, L. A., Tonick, I. J. and Sternglanz, S. H. 1977: Shaping cooperative cross-sex play. *Child Development*, 48, 924–9.

Serpell, R. 1977: Estimates of intelligence in a rural community of Eastern Zambia. In F. Okatcha (ed.), *Modern Psychology and Cultural Adaptation*. Nairobi: Swahili Language Consultants and Publishers.

Seyfarth, R. M. and Cheney, D. L. 1984: The natural vocalisations of non-human primates. *Trends in Neurosciences*, 7, 66–73.

Shaffer, D. R. 1985: *Developmental Psychology: Theory, Research and Applications*. Monterey, CA: Brooks/Cole.

Shahidullah, S. and Hepper, P. G. 1993a: The developmental origins of fetal responsiveness to an acoustic stimulus. *Journal of Reproductive and Infant Psychology*, 11, 135–42.

Shahidullah, S. and Hepper, P. G. 1993b: Prenatal hearing tests? *Journal of Reproductive and Infant Psychology*, 11, 143–46.

Shamir, A. 2000: The effects of intervention for peer-mediation on mediational teaching style and cognitive modifiability. EARLI Symposium, wwwedu.oulu.fi/okl/earli/sympo4.htm

Shapiro, G. L. 1982: Sign acquisition in a home-reared/free-ranging orang-utan: comparisons with other signing apes. *American Journal of Primatology*, 3, 121–9.

Shatz, M., Wellman, H. M. and Silber, S. 1983: The acquisition of mental verbs: a systematic investigation of first references to mental state. *Cognition*, 14, 301–21.

Shayer, M., Kuchemann, D. E. and Wylam, H. 1976: The distribution of Piagetian stages of thinking in British middle and secondary school children. *British Journal of Educational Psychology*, 46, 164–73.

Shayer, M. and Wylam, H. 1978: The distribution of Piagetian stages of thinking in British middle and secondary school children: II. *British Journal of Educational Psychology*, 48, 62–70.

Shu, S. and Smith, P. K. 2001: Characteristics of three-generation Chinese families. In T. M. Gehring, M. Debry and P. K. Smith (eds), *The Family System Test (FAST): Theory and Application*, pp. 194–207. London: Brunner-Routledge.

Siegal, M. and Beattie, K. 1991: Where to look first for children's knowledge of false beliefs. *Cognition*, 38, 1–12.

Siegler, R. S. 1976: Three aspects of cognitive development. *Cognitive Psychology*, 8, 481–520.

Siegler, R. S. 1978: The origins of scientific reasoning. In R. S. Siegler (ed.), *Children's Thinking: What Develops?* Hillsdale, NJ: Erlbaum.

Siegler, R. S. 1996: *Emerging Minds: The Process of Change in Children's Thinking*. New York: Oxford University Press.

Siegler, R. S. 1998: *Children's thinking*. 3rd edn. Englewood Cliffs, NJ: Prentice-Hall.

Siegler, R. S. and Jenkins, E. 1989: *How Children Discover New Strategies*. Hillsdale, NJ: Erlbaum.

Siegler, R. S. and Robinson, M. 1982: The development of numerical understandings. In H. W. Reese and L. P. Lipsitt (eds), *Advances in Child Development and Behavior, Volume 16*. New York: Academic Press.

Simion, F., Cassia, V. M., Turati, C. and Valenza, E. 2001: The origins of face perception: specific versus non-specific mechanisms. *Infant and Child Development*, 10, 59–65.

Singer, D. G. and Singer, J. L. 1991: *The House of Make-Believe: Children's Play and the Developing Imagination*. Cambridge, MA: Harvard University Press.

Singer, E. 1992: *Childcare and the Psychology of Development*. London: Routledge.

Skeels, H. M. 1966: Adult status of children with contrasting early life experiences: a follow-up study. *Monographs of the Society for Research in Child Development*, 31, no. 3.

Skeels, H. and Dye, H. B. 1939: A study of the effects of differential stimulation on mentally retarded children. *Proceedings of the American Association of Mental Deficiency*, 44, 114–36.

Skinner, B. F. 1957: *Verbal Behavior*. New York: Appleton-Century-Crofts.

Skodak, M. and Skeels, H. M. 1945: A follow-up study of children in adoptive homes. *Journal of Genetic Psychology*, 66, 21–58.

Skuse, D. 1984: Extreme deprivation in early childhood – II. Theoretical issues and a comparative review. *Journal of Child Psychology and Psychiatry*, 25, 543–72.

Slater, A. (ed.) 1998: *Perceptual Development. Visual, Auditory and Speech Perception in Infancy*. Hove, East Sussex: Psychology Press.

Slater, A. 1998: The competent infant: Innate organization and early learning in infant visual perception. In A. Slater (ed.), *Perceptual Development. Visual, Auditory and Speech Perception in Infancy*. Hove, East Sussex: Psychology Press.

Slater, A., Brown, E. and Badenoch, M. 1997: Intermodal perception at birth: newborn infants' memory for arbitrary auditory-visual pairings. *Early Development and Parenting*, 6, 99–104.

Slater, A. M., Mattock, A. and Brown, E. 1990: Newborn infants' responses to retinal and real size. *Journal of Experimental Psychology*, 49, 314–22.

Slater, A. M. and Morison, V. 1985: Shape constancy and slant perception at birth. *Perception*, 14, 337–44.

Slater, A., Morison, V., Somers, M., Mattock, A., Brown, E., and Taylor, D. 1990: Newborn and older infants' perception of partly occluded objects. *Infant Behavior and Development*, 13, 33–49.

Slavin, R. E. 1987: Developmental and motivational perspectives on cooperative learning: a reconciliation. *Child Development*, 58, 1161–7.

Slobin, D. I. 1973: Cognitive prerequisites for the development of grammar. In C. A. Ferguson and D. I. Slobin (eds), *Studies in Child Language Development*. New York: Holt Rinehart.

Sluckin, A. 1981: *Growing Up in the Playground: the Social Development of Children*. London: Routledge & Kegan Paul.

Smetana, J. G. 1981: Preschool children's conceptions of moral and social rules. *Child Development*, 52, 1333–6.

Smetana, J. and Gaines, C. 1999: Adolescent-parent conflict in middle-class African American families. *Child Development*, 70, 1447–63.

Smilansky, S. 1968: *The Effects of Sociodramatic Play on Disadvantaged Preschool Children*. New York: Wiley.

Smilansky, S. and Shefatya, L. 1990: *Facilitating Play: A Medium for Promoting Cognitive, Socio-Emotional and Academic Development in Young Children*. Gaithersburg, MD: Psychosocial and Educational Publications.

Smith, L., Dockrell, J. and Tomlinson, T. 1997: *Piaget, Vygotsky and Beyond: Future Issues for Developmental Psychology and Education*. London: Routledge.

Smith, N. and Tsimpli, I. M. 1995: *The Mind of a Savant*. Oxford: Blackwell.

Smith, P. K. 1974: Ethological methods. In B. M. Foss (ed.), *New Perspectives in Child Development*. Harmondsworth: Penguin.

Smith, P. K. 1978: A longitudinal study of social participation in preschool children: solitary and parallel play re-examined. *Developmental Psychology*, 14, 517–23.

Smith, P. K. 1988: Children's play and its role in early development: a re-evaluation of the 'play ethos'. In A. D. Pellegrini (ed.), *Psychological Bases of Early Education*. Chichester: Wiley & Sons, pp. 207–26.

Smith, P. K. 1991: The silent nightmare: bullying and victimisation in school peer group. *The Psychologist*, 4, 243–8.

Smith, P. K. 1994: The war play debate. In J. H. Goldstein (ed.), *Toys, Play and Child Development*. Cambridge: Cambridge University Press.

Smith, P. K. 1996: Language and the evolution of mindreading. In P. Carruthers and P. K. Smith (eds), *Theories of Theories of Mind*, pp. 344–54. Cambridge: Cambridge University Press.

Smith, P. K. 1997: Play fighting and real fighting: Perspectives on their relationship. In A. Schmitt, K. Atswanger, K. Grammar and K. Schafer (eds), *New Aspects of Ethology*, pp. 47–64. New York: Plenum Press.

Smith, P. K., Morita, Y., Junger-Tas, J., Olweus, D., Catalano, R. and Slee, P. (eds) 1999: *The Nature of School Bullying: An International Perspective*. London: Routledge.

Smith, P. K. and Sharp, S. (eds) 1994: *School Bullying: Insights and Perspectives*. London: Routledge.

Smith, P. K. and Shu, S. 2000: What good schools can do about bullying: findings from a survey in English schools after a decade of research and action. *Childhood*, 7, 193–212.

Smith, P. K. and Simon, T. 1984: Object play, problem-solving and creativity in children. In P. K. Smith (ed.), *Play in Animals and Humans*. Oxford: Basil Blackwell.

Smith, P. K. and Sloboda, J. 1986: Individual consistency in infant–stranger encounters. *British Journal of Developmental Psychology*, 4, 83–91.

Smith, P. K. and Vollstedt, R. 1985: On defining play: an empirical study of the relationship between play and various play criteria. *Child Development*, 56, 1042–50.

Snarey, J. R. 1985: Cross-cultural universality of social-moral development: a critical review of Kohlbergian research. *Psychological Bulletin*, 97, 202–32.

Snow, C. 1977: The development of conversation between mothers and babies. *Journal of Child Language*, 4, 1–22.

Snow, C. E., Pan, B. A., Imbens-Bailey, A. and Herman, J. 1996: Learning how to say what one means: A longitudinal study of children's speech act use. *Social Development*, 5, 56–84.

Snowling, M. 1996: Annotation: contemporary approaches to the teaching of reading. *Journal of Child Psychology and Psychiatry*, 37, 139–48.

Snowling, M. 2002: *Individual Differences in Children's Reading Development: Sound and Meaning in Learning to Read*. The Twenty-first Vernon-Wall Lecture. London: British Psychological Society.

Snowling, M., Goulandris, N., Bowlby, M. and Howell, P. 1986: Segmentation and speech perception in relation to reading skill: a developmental analysis. *Journal of Experimental Child Psychology*, 41, 489–507.

Social Exclusion Unit 2000: *Report of the UK Policy Action Team on Young People*. London: HMSO.

Sodian, B. and Frith, U. 1992: Deception and sabotage in autistic, retarded and normal children. *Journal of Child Psychology and Psychiatry*, 33, 591–605.

Sommerville, J. 1982: *The Rise and Fall of Childhood*. Beverley Hills: Sage.

Sorce, J. F., Emde, R. N., Campos, J. J. and Klinnert, M. D. 1985: Maternal emotional signalling: its effects on the visual cliff behavior of 1-year-olds. *Developmental Psychology*, 21, 195–200.

Spaccerelli, S. 1994: Stress, appraisal, and coping in child sexual abuse: a theoretical and empirical review. *Psychological Bulletin*, 116, 340–62.

Spearman, C. 1904: 'General intelligence' objectively determined and measured. *American Journal of Psychology*, 15, 201–93.

Spearman, C. 1927: *The Abilities of Man: Their Nature and Measurement*. London: Macmillan.

Spelke, E. 1981: The infant's acquisition of knowledge of bimodally specified events. *Journal of Experimental Child Psychology*, 31, 279–99.

Spence, J. T. and Helmreich, R. L. 1978: *Masculinity and Femininity: Their Psychological Dimensions, Correlates and Antecedents*. Austin: University of Texas Press.

Spencer, H. 1878, 1898: *The Principles of Psychology*. New York: Appleton.

Spencer, M. B. 1983: Children's cultural values and parent's child-rearing strategies. *Developmental Review*, 3, 351–70.

Spitz, R. A. 1946: Hospitalism: a follow-up report. *Psychoanalytic Study of the Child*, 2, 113–18.

Spock, B. 1976: *Baby and Child Care*. New York: Pocket Books.

Sprinthall, N., Hall, J. and Gerber, E. 1992: Peer counselling for middle school students experiencing family divorce: a deliberate psychological education model. *Elementary School Guidance and Counselling*, 26, 279–94.

Sroufe, L. A. 1977: Wariness of strangers and the study of infant development. *Child Development*, 48, 731–46.

Steinberg, L. 1987: Impact of puberty on family relations: effects of pubertal status and pubertal timing. *Developmental Psychology*, 23, 451–60.

Steinberg, L. 1988: Reciprocal relation between parent–child distance and pubertal maturation. *Developmental Psychology*, 24, 122–8.

Steinberg, L., Lamborn, S. D., Dornbusch, S. M. and Darling, N. 1992: Impact of parenting practices on adolescent achievement: authoritative parenting, school involvement, and encouragement to succeed. *Child Development*, 63, 1266–81.

Stern, D. N. 1990: *Diary of a Baby*. Harmondsworth: Penguin.

Stern, D. N., Spieker, S., Barnett, R. K. and MacKain, K. 1983: The prosody of maternal speech: infant age and context related changes. *Journal of Child Language*, 10, 1–15.

Sternberg, R. J. 1985: *Beyond IQ. A Triarchic Theory of Human Intelligence*. Cambridge: Cambridge University Press.

Sternberg, R. J. 1999: Looking back and looking forward on intelligence: Toward a theory of successful intelligence. In M. Bennett (ed.), *Developmental Psychology. Achievements And Prospects*. Philadelphia: Psychology Press.

Sternberg, R. J., Conway, B. E., Ketron, J. L. and Bernstein, M. 1981: People's conceptions of intelligence. *Journal of Personality and Social Psychology*, 1, 37–55.

Sternberg, R. J. and Rifkin, B. 1979: The development of analogical reasoning processes. *Journal of Experimental Child Psychology*, 27, 195–232.

Sternglanz, S. H., Gray, J. L. and Murakami, M. 1977: Adult preference for infantile facial features: an ethological approach. *Animal Behaviour*, 25, 108–15.

Stevenson, J. 1999: The treatment of the long-term sequelae of child abuse. *Journal of Child Psychology & Psychiatry*, 40, 89–111.

Stevenson-Hinde, J. and Verschueren, K. 2002: Attachment in childhood. In P. K. Smith and C. H. Hart (eds), *Blackwell Handbook of Childhood Social Development*. Oxford: Blackwell.

Stewart, R. B. 1983: Sibling attachment relationships: child–infant interactions in the strange situation. *Developmental Psychology*, 19, 192–9.

St. James-Roberts, I. 1989: Persistent crying in infancy. *Journal of Child Psychology and Psychiatry*, 29, 21–42.

St. James-Roberts, I. and Wolke, D. 1984: Comparison of mothers' with trained observers' reports of neonatal behavioral style. *Infant Behavior and Development*, 7, 299–310.

Strayer, F. F. and Strayer, J. 1976: An ethological analysis of social agonism and dominance relations among preschool children. *Child Development*, 47, 980–9.

Suddendorf, T. and Whiten, A. 2001: Mental evolution and development: evidence for secondary representation in children, great apes, and other animals. *Psychological Bulletin*, 127, 629–50.

Sundet, J. M., Magnus, P., Kvalem, I. L., Samuelsen, S. O. and Bakketeig, L. S. 1992: Secular trends and sociodemographic regularities of coital debut age in Norway. *Archives of Sexual Behavior*, 21, 241–52.

Suomi, S. J. and Harlow, H. F. 1972: Social rehabilitation of isolate-reared monkeys. *Developmental Psychology*, 6, 487–96.

Super, C. N. and Harkness, S. 1997: The cultural structuring of child development. In J. W. Berry, P. Dasen and T. S. Saraswathi (eds), *Handbook of Cross-cultural Psychology: Volume 2, Basic Processes and Human Development*, pp. 1–39. Boston: Allyn & Bacon.

Sutton, J., Smith, P. K. and Swettenham, J. 1999: Bullying and theory of mind: a critique of the 'social skills deficit' view of anti-social behaviour. *Social Development*, 8, 117–27.

Sutton-Smith, B. 1966: Piaget on play: a critique. *Psychological Review*, 73, 104–10.

Sutton-Smith, B. 1967: The role of play in cognitive development. *Young Children*, 22, 361–70.

Sutton-Smith, B. 1986: *Toys as Culture*. New York: Gardner Press.

Sutton-Smith, B. 1988: War toys and childhood aggression. *Play and Culture*, 1, 57–69.

Swann Report 1985: *Education for All*. London: HMSO, Cmnd 9453.

Sylva, K. and Lunt, I. 1981: *Child Development: an Introductory Text*. Oxford: Basil Blackwell.

Sylva, K., Roy, C. and Painter, M. 1980: *Child Watching at Playgroup and Nursery School*. London: Grant McIntyre.

Symons, D. 1978: *Play and Aggression: A Study of Rhesus Monkeys*. New York: Columbia University Press.

Symons, D. 1979: *The Evolution of Human Sexuality*. New York and Oxford: Oxford University Press.

Takahashi, K. 1990: Are the key assumptions of the 'strange situation' procedure universal? A view from Japanese research. *Human Development*, 33, 23–30.

Takhvar, M. and Smith, P. K. 1990: A review and critique of Smilansky's classification scheme and the 'nested hierarchy' of play categories. *Journal of Research in Childhood Education*, 4, 112–22.

Takriti, R., Buchanan-Barrow, E. and Barrett, M. 2000: Children's perceptions of their own and one other religious group. Poster presented at XVIth Biennial Meeting of ISSBD, Beijing, China.

Tanner, J. M. 1962: *Growth at Adolescence*, 2nd edn. Oxford: Basil Blackwell.

Tanner, J. M. 1973: Growing Up. *Scientific American*, 229 (Sept.), 35–43.

Tattum, D. P. and Lane, D. A. 1989: *Bullying in Schools*. Stoke-on-Trent: Trentham Books.

Taylor, H. G., Klein, N., Minich, M. N. and Hack, M. 2000: Middle-school-age outcomes in children with very low birthweight. *Child Development*, 71, 1495–511.

Taylor, J., McGue, M. and Iacono, W. G. 2000: Sex differences, assortative mating, and cultural transmission effects on adolescent delinquency: a twin family study. *Journal of Child Psychology and Psychiatry*, 41, 433–40.

Taylor, M. and Carlson, S. M. 1997: The relation between individual differences in fantasy and theory of mind. *Child Development*, 68, 436–55.

Taylor M., Cartwright, B. S. and Carlson, S. M. 1993: A developmental investigation of children's imaginary companions. *Developmental Psychology*, 29, 276–85.

Teller, D. Y., Peeples, D. R. and Sekel, M. 1978: Discrimination of chromatic from white light by two-month-old human infants. *Vision Research*, 18, 41–8.

Terman, L. M. 1925: *Genetic Studies of Genius, Volume 1. Mental and Physical Traits of a Thousand Gifted Children*. Stanford, CA: Stanford University Press.

Terman, L. M. and Oden, M. H. 1947: *Genetic Studies of Genius, Volume 4. The Gifted Group Grows Up: Twenty-five Years' Follow-up of a Superior Group*. Stanford, CA: Stanford University Press.

Terman, L. M. and Oden, M. H. 1959: *Genetic Studies of Genius, Volume 5. The Gifted Group at Mid-life: Thirty-five Years' Follow-up of the Superior Child*. Stanford, CA: Stanford University Press.

Terrace, H. S., Pettito, L., Sanders, R. J. and Bever, T. G. 1979: Can an ape create a sentence? *Science*, 206, 891–902.

Tessier, R., Nadeau, L., Boivin, M. and Tremblay, R. E. 1997: The social behaviour of 11- to 12-year-old children born as low birthweight and/or premature infants. *International Journal of Behavioral Development*, 21, 795–811.

Thomas, A. and Chess, S. 1977: *Temperament and Development*. New York: Brunner/Mazel.

Thompson, S. K. 1975: Gender labels and early sex-role development. *Child Development*, 46, 339–47.

Thorndike, R., Hagen, E. and Sattler, J. 1985: *Stanford–Binet Intelligence Scale: Fourth Edition SB-FE*. Windsor: NFER-Nelson.

Thorpe, W. H. 1972: Vocal communication in birds. In R. A. Hinde (ed.), *Non-verbal Communication*. Cambridge: Cambridge University Press.

Thurstone, L. L. 1931: *Multiple Factor Analysis*. Chicago: University of Chicago Press.

Tinsley, B. J. and Parke, R. D. 1984: Grandparents as support and socialization agents. In M. Lewis (ed.), *Beyond the Dyad*. New York: Plenum.

Tizard, B. and Hodges, J. 1978: The effect of early institutional rearing on the development of eight-year-old children. *Journal of Child Psychology and Psychiatry*, 19, 99–118.

Tizard, B. and Phoenix, A. 1993: *Black, White or Mixed Race?* London: Routledge.

Tizard, B. and Rees, J. 1974: A comparison of the effects of adoption, restoration to the natural mother, and continued institutionalization on the cognitive development of 4-year-old children. *Child Development*, 45, 92–9.

Tomasello, M. 1996: Chimpanzee social cognition. *Monographs of the Society for Research in Child Development*, 61, no. 3, pp. 161–73.

Tomasello, M. 1999: The human adaptation for culture. *Annual Review of Anthropology*, 28, 509–29.

Tomasello, M., Akhtar, N., Dodson, K. and Rekau, L. 1997: Differential productivity in young children's use of nouns and verbs. *Journal of Child Language*, 24, 373–87.

Tomasello, M. and Brooks, P. J. 1999: Early syntactic development: a Construction Grammar approach. In M. Barrett (ed.), *The Development of Language*. London: Psychology Press, pp. 161–90.

Tomasello, M. and Olguin, R. 1993: Tewnty-three month-old children have a grammatical category of noun. *Cognitive Development*, 8, 451–64.

Tomlinson-Keasey, C. 1978: The structure of concrete operational thought. *Child Development*, 50, 1153–63.

Topping, K. and Ehly, S. (eds) 1998: *Peer-assisted Learning*. Mahwah, NJ: Lawrence Erlbaum.

Townsend, P. 1957: *The Family Life of Old People*. London: Routledge & Kegan Paul.

Tremblay-Leveau, H. and Nadel, J. 1996: Exclusion in triads: can it serve 'metacommunicative' knowledge in 11 and 24 months children? *British Journal of Developmental Psychology*, 14, 145–58.

Trevarthen, C. and Aitken, K. J. 2001: Infant intersubjectivity: Research, theory, and clinical applications. *Journal of Child Psychology and Psychiatry*, 42, 3–48.

Trevarthen, C. and Hubley, P. 1978: Secondary intersubjectivity: confidence, confiding and acts of meaning in the first year. In A. Lock (ed.), *Action Gesture and Symbol*, pp. 183–229. London: Academic Press.

Trevarthen, C. and Logotheti, K. 1989: Child in society, and society in children: the nature of basic trust. In S. Howell and R. Willis (eds), *Societies at Peace*. London: Routledge.

Trevathan, W. 1987: *Human Birth: An Evolutionary Perspective*. New York: Aldine de Gruyter.

Trivers, R. L. 1971: The evolution of reciprocal altruism. *Quarterly Review of Biology*, 46, 35–57.

Trivers, R. L. 1974: Parent–offspring conflict. *American Zoologist*, 14, 249–64.

Tronick, E., Als, H., Adamson, L., Wise, S. and Brazelton, T. 1978: The infant's response to entrapment between contradictory messages in face-to-face interaction. *Journal of the American Academy of Child Psychiatry*, 17, 1–13.

Troyna, B. and Hatcher, R. 1992: *Racism in Children's Lives*. London: Routledge.

True, M. M., Pisani, L. and Oumar, F. 2001: Infant–mother attachment among the Dogon of Mali. *Child Development*, 72, 1451–66.

Turiel, E. 1983: *The Development of Social Knowledge: Morality and Convention*. Cambridge: Cambridge University Press.

Turiel, E. 1998: The development of morality. In W. Damon and N. Eisenberg (eds), *Handbook of Child Psychology: vol 3 Social, Emotional and Personal*, 5th edn, pp. 863–92. New York: Wiley.

Underwood, B. and Moore, B. S. 1982: The generality of altruism in children. In N. Eisenberg (ed.), *The Development of Prosocial Behavior*. New York: Academic Press.

Updegraff, K. A., McHale, S. M. and Crouter, A. C. 2000: Adolescents' sex-typed friendship experiences: does having a sister versus a brother matter? *Child Development*, 71, 1597–610.

Valsiner, J. 2000: *Culture and Human Development*. London: Sage.

Valsiner, J. and van der Veer, R. 2000: *The Social Mind*. NewYork: Cambridge University Press.

Van Cantfort, T. E. and Rimpau, J. B. 1982: Sign language studies with children and chimpanzees. *Sign Language Studies*, 34, 15–72.

Vandell, D. 2000: Parents, peer groups, and other socializing influences. *Developmental Psychology*, 36, 699–710.

Van IJzendoorn, M. H. 1995: Adult attachment representations. *Psychological Bulletin*, 117, 387–403.

Van IJzendoorn, M. H. and Bakermans-Kranenburg, M. J. 1996: Attachment representations in mothers, fathers, adolescents and clinical groups: a meta-analytic search for normative data. *Journal of Consulting and Clinical Psychology*, 64, 8–21.

Van IJzendoorn, M. H. and De Wolff, M. S. 1997: In search of the absent father – meta-analyses of infant–father attachment: a rejoinder to our discussants. *Child Development*, 68, 604–9.

Van IJzendoorn, M. H. and Kroonenberg, P. M. 1988: Cross-cultural patterns of attachment: a meta-analysis of the Strange Situation. *Child Development*, 59, 147–56.

Van IJzendoorn, M. H., Juffer, F. and Duyvesteyn, M. G. C. 1995: Breaking the intergenerational cycle of insecure attachment: a review of the effects of attachment-based interventions on maternal sensitivity and infant security. *Journal of Child Psychology and Psychiatry*, 36, 225–48.

Van IJzendoorn, M. H., Moran, G., Belsky, J., Pederson, D., Bakermans-Kranenburg, M. J. and Kneppers, K. 2000: The similarity of siblings' attachments to their mother. *Child Development*, 71, 1086–98.

Van IJzendoorn, M. H., Sagi, A. and Grossman, K. I. 1999: Transmission of holocaust experiences across three generations. Symposium presentation at IXth European Conference on Developmental Psychology, Spetses, Greece, 3 September.

Van IJzendoorn, M. H., Schuengel, C. and Bakermans-Kranenburg, M. J. 1999: Disorganised attachment in early childhood: meta-analysis of precursors, concomitants, and sequelae. *Development and Psychopathology*, 11, 225–49.

Varendonck, J. 1911: Les témoignages d'enfants dans un procès retentissant. *Archives de Psychologie*, 11, 129–71.

Vaughn, B., Egeland, B., Sroufe, L. A. and Waters, E. 1979: Individual differences in infant–mother attachment at 12 and 18 months: stability and change in families under stress. *Child Development*, 50, 971–5.

Vaughn, B. E. and Langlois, J. H. 1983: Physical attractiveness as a correlate of peer status and social competence in preschool children. *Developmental Psychology*, 19, 561–7.

Vondra, J. I. and Barnett, D. 1999: Atypical attachment in infancy and early childhood among children at developmental risk. *Monographs of the Society for Research in Child Development*, 64(3), serial no. 258.

Vosniadou, S., Ioannides, C., Dimitrakopoulou, A. and Papademetriou, E. 2001: Designing learning environments to promote conceptual change in science. *Learning and Instruction*, 11, 381–419.

Vurpillot, E. 1968: The development of scanning strategies and their relation to visual differentiation. *Journal of Experimental Child Psychology*, 6, 632–50.

Vygotsky, L. 1962 (1934): *Thought and Language*. Cambridge, MA: MIT Press.

Vygotsky, L. S. 1966 (1933): Play and its role in the mental development of the child. *Voprosy Psikhologii*, 12, 62–76.

Vygotsky, L. S. 1978: *Mind in Society*. M. Cole, V. John-Steiner, S. Scribner and E. Souberman (eds), Cambridge, MA: Harvard University Press.

Vygotsky, L. S. 1981: The genesis of higher mental functions. In J. V. Wertsch (ed.), *The Concept of Activity in Soviet Psychology*. Armonk, NY: Sharpe.

Waddington, C. H. 1957: *The Strategy of the Genes*. London: Allen & Unwin.

Walk, R. D. 1981: *Perceptual Development*. Monterey, CA: Brooks/Cole.

Wallerstein, J. S. 1985: Children of divorce – emerging trends. *Psychiatric Clinics of North America*, 8, 837–55.

Wallerstein, J. S. 1987: Children of divorce: report of a ten-year follow-up of early latency-age children. *American Journal of Orthopsychiatry*, 57, 199–211.

Walton, G. E., Bower, N. J. A. and Bower, T. G. R. 1992: Recognition of familiar faces by newborns. *Infant Behaviour and Development*, 15, 265–9.

Warren, A. R., Hulse-Trotter, K. and Tubbs, E. 1991: Inducing resistance to suggestibility in children. *Law and Human Behavior*, 15, 273–85.

Waterman, A. H., Blades, M. and Spencer, C. 2000: Do children try to answer nonsensical questions? *British Journal of Developmental Psychology*, 18, 211–25.

Waterman, A., Blades, M. and Spencer, C. 2001: Interviewing children and adults: the effect of question format on the tendency to speculate. *Applied Cognitive Psychology*, 15, 521–31.

Waterman, A. S. 1982: Identity development from adolescence to adulthood: an extension of theory and a review of research. *Developmental Psychology*, 18, 341–58.

Waterman, A. S., Geary, P. S. and Waterman, C. K. 1974: Identity status of college students in occupational and ideological areas. *Developmental Psychology*, 10, 387–92.

Waterman, C. K. and Waterman, A. S. 1975: Fathers and sons: a study of ego identity across two generations. *Journal of Youth and Adolescence*, 4, 331–38.

Waters, E., Hamilton, C. E. and Weinfeld, N. S. 2000: The stability of attachment security from infancy to adolescence and early adulthood: general introduction. *Child Development*, 71, 678–83.

Waters, E., Vaughn, B. E., Posada, G. and Kondo-Ikemura, K. 1995: Caregiving, cultural, and cognitive perspectives on secure-base behavior and working models. *Monographs of the Society for Research in Child Development*, 60, nos 2–3.

Watson, J. S. and Ramey, C. T. 1972: Reactions to response-contingent stimulation in early infancy. *Merrill-Palmer Quarterly*, 18, 219–27.

Watson, M. W. and Peng, Y. 1992: The relation between toy gun play and children's aggressive behavior. *Early Education and Development*, 3, 370–89.

Webster-Stratton, C. 1999: *How to Promote Children's Social and Emotional Competence*. London: Paul Chapman.

Wechsler, D. 1944: *The Measurement of Adult Intelligence*, 3rd edn. Baltimore: Williams and Wilkins.

Wechsler, D. 1990: *Wechsler Pre-school and Primary Scale of Intelligence – Revised UK Edition* (*WPPSI-R^{UK}*). London: Psychological Corporation.

Wechsler, D. 1992: *Intelligence Scale for Children – Third UK Edition* (*WISC-III^{UK}*). London: Psychological Corporation.

Wechsler, D. 1997: Adult Intelligence Scale – Revised UK Edition (WAIS-R-III^{UK}). London: Psychological Corporation.

Wedge, P. and Essen, J. 1982: *Children in Adversity*. London: Pan.

Weikart, D., Deloria, D., Lawser, S. and Wiegerink, R. 1970: Longitudinal results of the Ypsilanti Perry preschool project. *Monographs of the High-Scope Educational Research Foundation*, No. 1.

Weikart, D. 1996: High quality pre-school programs found to improve adult status. *Childhood*, 3, 117–20.

Weinraub, M., Clemens, L. P., Sockloff, A., Ethridge, T., Gracely, E. and Myers, B. 1984: The development of sex role stereotypes in the third year: relationships to gender labeling, gender identity, sex-typed toy preference and family characteristics. *Child Development*, 55, 1493–503.

Weinraub, M. and Lewis, M. 1977: The determinants of children's responses to separation. *Monographs of the Society for Research in Child Development*, 42, 1–78.

Weir, R. 1962: *Language in the Crib*. The Hague: Mouton.

Weisel, T. N. and Hubel, D. H. 1963: Single-cell responses in striate cortex of kittens deprived of vision in one eye. *Journal of Neurophysiology*, 26, 1003–17.

Weisler, A. and McCall, R. B. 1976: Exploration and play. *American Psychologist*, 31, 492–508.

Weisner, T. S. and Gallimore, R. 1977: My brother's keeper: child and sibling caretaking. *Current Anthropology*, 18, 169–90.

Wellman, H. M. 1990: *The Child's Theory of Mind*. Cambridge, MA: MIT Press.

Wellman, H. M. and Estes, D. 1986: Early understanding of mental entities: a re-examination of childhood realism. *Child Development*, 57, 910–23.

Wells, C. G. 1983: Talking with children: the complementary roles of parents and teachers. In M. Donaldson (ed.), *Early Childhood Development and Education*. Oxford: Basil Blackwell.

Wells, C. G. 1985: *Language Development in the Preschool Years*. Cambridge: Cambridge University Press.

Wentzel, K. R. and Asher, S. R. 1995: The academic lives of neglected, rejected, popular, and controversial children. *Child Development*, 66, 754–63.

Werker, J. F. and Lalonde, C. E. 1988: Cross-language speech perception: Initial capabilities and developmental change. *Developmental Psychology*, 24, 672–83.

Werker, J. F. and Tees, R. C. 1985: Cross-language speech perceptions: evidence for perceptual reorganization during the first year of life. *Infant Behavior and Development*, 7, 49–63.

Werner, E. E. 1989: Children of the Garden Island. *Scientific American*, April, 106–11.

Werner, E. E. 1993: Risk, resilience and recovery: perspectives from the Kauai longitudinal study. *Development and Psychopathology*, 5, 503–75.

Werner, E. E. and Smith, R. S. 1982: *Vulnerable but Invincible: A Longitudinal Study of Resilient Children and Youth*. New York: McGraw-Hill.

Wertsch, J. V., McNamee, G. D., McLane, J. B. and Budwig, N. A. 1980: The adult–child dyad as a problem-solving system. *Child Development*, 51, 1215–21.

Wertsch, J. V. and Tulviste, P. 1996: L. S. Vygotsky and contemporary developmental psychology. In H. Daniels (ed.), *An Introduction to Vygotsky*. London: Routledge.

Westcott, H., Davies, G. and Clifford, B. 1989: The use of anatomical dolls in child witness interviews. *Adoption and Fostering*, 13, 6–14.

Westcott, H. L., Davies, G. M. and Bull, R. H. C. (eds) 2002: *Children's Testimony. A Handbook of Psychological Research and Forensic Practice*. Chichester: Wiley.

Westin-Lindgren, G. 1982: Achievement and mental ability of physically late and early maturing school children related to their social background. *Journal of Child Psychology and Psychiatry*, 23, 407–20.

Wetherton, E. and Kessler, R. C. 1991: Situations and processes of coping. In J. Eckenrode (ed.) *The Social Context of Coping*. New York: Plenum.

Whitbread, N. 1972: *The Evolution of the Nursery-Infant School*. London: Routledge & Kegan Paul.

Whiten, A. (ed.) 1991: *Natural Theories of Mind: Evolution, Development and Stimulation of Everyday Mindreading*. Oxford: Basil Blackwell.

Whiten, A. and Byrne, R. W. 1988: Tactical deception in primates. *Behavioral and Brain Sciences*, 11, 233–73.

Whiting, B. and Edwards, C. P. 1973: A cross-cultural analysis of sex differences in the behavior of children aged three through 11. *Journal of Social Psychology*, 91, 171–88.

Whiting, B. B. and Edwards, C. P. 1988: *Children of Different Worlds: The Formation of Social Behavior*. Cambridge, MA: Harvard University Press.

Whiting, B. B. and Whiting, J. W. M. 1975: *Children of Six Cultures: a Psycho-cultural Analysis*. Cambridge, MA and London: Harvard University Press.

Whiting, J. W. M., Kluckhohn, C. and Anthony, A. 1958: The functions of male initiation ceremonies at puberty. In E. Maccoby, T. Newcomb and E. Hartley (eds), *Readings in Social Psychology*. New York: Holt.

Whyte, W. 1943: *Street Corner Society*. Chicago: University of Chicago Press.

Willatts, P. 1989: Development of problem solving in infancy. In A. Slater and G. Bremner (eds), *Infant Development*. Hillsdale, NJ: Lawrence Erlbaum.

Williams, B. and Gilmour, J. 1994: Sociometry and peer relations. *Journal of Child Psychology and Psychiatry*, 35, 997–1013.

Wilson, E. O. 1978: *On Human Nature*. Cambridge, MA: Harvard University Press.

Wimmer, H. and Perner, J. 1983: Beliefs about beliefs: representations and constraining function of wrong beliefs in young children's understanding of deception. *Cognition*, 13, 103–28.

Winefield, A. 1997: The psychological effects of youth unemployment: international perspectives. *Journal of Adolescence*, 20, 237–353.

Wissler, C. 1901: The correlation of mental and physical tests. *The Psychological Review, Monograph Supplement*, 3(6).

Wober, M. 1974: Towards an understanding of the Kiganda concept of intelligence. In J. W. Berry and P. Dasen (eds), *Culture and Cognition: Readings in Cross-cultural Psychology*. London: Methuen.

Wohlwill, J. F. 1984: Relationships between exploration and play. In T. D. Yawkey and A. D. Pellegrini (eds), *Child's Play: Developmental and Applied*. Hillsdale, NJ: Lawrence Erlbaum.

Wolf, D., Moreton, J. and Camp, L. 1994: Children's acquisition of different kinds of narrative discourse: Genres and lines of talk. In J. Solokov and C. Snow (eds), *Handbook of Research in Language Development using CHILDES*, pp. 286–323. Hillsdale, NJ: Lawrence Erlbaum Associates Inc.

Wolff, S. and McCall Smith, A. 2000: Child homicide and the law: implications of the judgements of the European Court of Human Rights in the case of the children who killed James Bulger. *Child Psychology and Psychiatry Review*, 5, 133–8.

Wolfson, A. R. and Carskadon, M. A. 1998: Sleep schedules and daytime functioning in adolescents. *Child Development*, 69, 875–87.

Wolke, D. 1998: Psychological development of prematurely born children. *Archives of Disease in Childhood*, 78, 567–70.

Wolke, D., Woods, S., Bloomfield, L. and Karstadt, L. 2000: The association between direct and relational bullying and behaviour problems among primary school children. *Journal of Child Psychology and Psychiatry*, 41, 989–1002.

Wood, D. J. 1998: *How Children Think and Learn*, 2nd edn. Oxford: Basil Blackwell.

Wood, D. J., Bruner, J. S. and Ross, G. 1976: The role of tutoring in problem-solving. *Journal of Child Psychology and Psychiatry*, 17, 89–100.

Wood, D. J. and Wood, H. 1996: Vygotsky, tutoring and learning. *Oxford Review of Education*, 22, 5–15.

Wood, W., Wong, F. Y. and Chachere, J. G. 1991: Effects of media violence on viewers' aggression in unconstrained social interaction. *Psychological Bulletin*, 109, 371–83.

Woodhead, M., Faulkner, D. and Littleton, K. 1998: *Cultural Worlds of Early Childhood*. London: Routledge.

Woodward, L. J. and Fergusson, D. M. 2000: Childhood peer relationship problems and later risks of educational under-achievement and unemployment. *Journal of Child Psychology and Psychiatry*, 41, 191–201.

Woolfe, T., Want, S. C. and Siegal, M. 2002: Signposts to development: theory of mind in deaf children. *Child Development*, 73, 768–78.

Woollett, A. and Phoenix, A. 1991: Psychological views of mothering. In A. Phoenix, A. Woollett and E. Lloyd (eds), *Motherhoods: Meanings, Practices and Ideologies*. London: Sage.

World Federation of Neurology 1968: Available at: www.wfneurology.org/wfn/ or www.prentice.org/mission.html

Wright, C. 1985: The influences of school processes on the educational opportunities of children of West Indian origin. *Multicultural Teaching*, 4.1, Autumn.

Wright, C., Weekes, D. and McGlaughlin, A. 2000: *'Race', Class and Gender in Exclusion from School*. London: Falmer Press.

Wright, D. 1990: Towards an adequate coneption of early oral development. In P. Kutnick and C. Rogers (eds), *The Social Psychology of the Primary School*. London: Routledge.

Wright, J., Binney, V. and Smith, P. K. 1995: Security of attachment in 8–12-year-olds: a revised version of the Separation Anxiety Test, its psychometric properties and clinical interpretation. *Journal of Child Psychology and Psychiatry*, 36, 757–74.

Wright, L. 1999: *Twins: Genes, Environment and the Mystery of Identity*. London: Wiley.

Yau, J. and Smetana, J. 1996: Adolescent–parent conflict among Chinese adolescents in Hong Kong. *Child Development*, 67, 1262–75.

Young, F. W. 1965: *Initiation Ceremonies: A Cross Cultural Study of Status Dramatization*. Indianapolis: Bobbs-Merrill.

Youniss, J. 1980: *Parents and Peers in Social Development*. Chicago: University of Chicago Press.

Yussen, S. R. and Levy, V. M. 1975: Developmental changes in predicting one's own span of short-term memory. *Journal of Experimental Child Psychology*, 19, 502–8.

Zahn-Waxler, C. and Radke-Yarrow, M. 1982: The development of altruism: alternative research strategies. In N. Eisenberg (ed.), *The Development of Prosocial Behaviour*. New York: Academic Press.

Zahn-Waxler, C., Radke-Yarrow, M. and King, R. A. 1979: Child rearing and children's prosocial initiations toward victims of distress. *Child Development*, 50, 319–30.

Zarbatany, L., Hartmann, D. P. and Gelfand, D. M. 1985: Why does children's generosity increase with age: susceptibility to experimenter influence or altruism? *Child Development*, 56, 746–56.

Index